SHIPS OF THE ROYAL NAVY: AN HISTORICAL INDEX

Volume 2 Navy-built trawlers, drifters, tugs and requisitioned ships

SHIPS OF THE ROYAL NAVY
AN HISTORICAL INDEX

by

J. J. COLLEDGE

Volume 2 Navy-built trawlers, drifters, tugs and
requisitioned ships

DAVID & CHARLES : NEWTON ABBOT

7153 4396 3

© J J Colledge. 1970

Typesetting by The Western Litho Co (Plymouth) Ltd
Printed by Redwood Press Trowbridge
for David & Charles (Holdings) Ltd
South Devon House Newton Abbot Devon

CONTENTS

INTRODUCTION

The scope of the book:
Listed in this volume are the requisitioned vessels, hired or purchased
in two world wars, together with hired vessels of earlier periods. Also
included are navy-built trawlers, drifters, whalers, tugs, coastal forces
craft, landing craft and other types not listed in the first volume.
For requisitioned ships of the two world wars, only gross tonnage (for
yachts, Thames measurement)/year built is given for most, as builders
and other details can be obtained from Lloyd's Registers.
For a hired vessel, the final date given is the date of return to owners
after reconditioning.

Details of ship classes mentioned in the text:
Admiralty steel drifters, average 96gr, 199 tons, 86 x 18½ ft, 1–6pdr.
165 named vessels laid down 1917–18, of which 38 were cancelled.
Two were 'non-standard', being fishing vessels of similar dimensions
purchased on stocks. After December 1918, all unfinished boats were
completed by the Admiralty as fishing vessels with no armament.
Admiralty wood drifters, average 98gr, 175 tons, 86 x 19 ft, 1–6pdr.
111 named vessels laid down 1917–18 including 10 non-standard.
Nine were cancelled. 100 similar (CD.1–100) were built for the Royal
Navy in Canada.
'Basset' class M/S trawlers, 545 tons, 150 x 27½ ft, 1–12pdr, 1–20mm.
44 ordered in India for the RIN, of which 23 were cancelled in 1945.
Four ordered at Rangoon, two for the Burma government and two for
Ceylon; all four were lost on stocks by Japanese invasion.
'B.A.T' class rescue tugs, 783 tons, 135 x 33 ft, 1–3in, 2–20mm.
24 ships built in the USA on lend-lease 1942–43 including ten
transferred from the USN. One vessel, unnamed (contract No BAT.2)
was retained by the USN as MARICOPA.
'Castle' type trawlers, average 276gr, 547 tons (360 standard), 125 x
23½ ft, 1–12pdr. 217 vessels laid down 1917–18 including 18 non-
standard; 52 completed as unarmed fishing vessels 1919–20 and 20

cancelled. 60 built for the Royal Navy in Canada and nine ordered for the RIM in India. These nine were composite-built. A further 15 were ordered in 1940 in New Zealand for the RNZN, one being cancelled, and four ordered there for the Royal Navy, three being cancelled and the fourth completed for the RNZN.

'Isles' class M/S–A/S trawlers, average 545 tons, 150 x 27½ ft, 1–12 pdr, 3–20mm. 145 laid down 1940–44 including 16 ordered in Canada and on loan to the RCN until 1945. 14 vessels were completed as danlayers and four as minelayers.

'Mersey' type trawlers, average 324gr, 665 tons (438 standard), 138½ x 23½ ft, 1–12pdr. 148 vessels laid down 1917–18 including 7 non-standard; 35 completed as fishing vessels and 36 cancelled.

'Saint' class rescue tugs, 800 tons, 135 x 29 ft, 1–12pdr. 56 ordered in 1918 of which 18 were cancelled.

'Strath' type trawlers, average 203gr, 429 tons (311 standard), 115 x 22 ft, 1–12pdr. 173 vessels laid down 1917–18 including 21 non-standard; 46 completed as fishing vessels and 24 cancelled.

'Z' class Admiralty whalers, 336 tons, 125 x 25 ft, 1–12pdr. 15 (originally known as Z.1–15) built in 1915.

Abbreviations Used

A/A	anti-aircraft
ABS	armed boarding steamer
ABV	armed boarding vessel
A/C	aircraft
AMC	armed merchant cruiser
A/P	auxiliary patrol
BBV	barrage balloon vessel
BDV	boom defence vessel
BU	broken up; break up
carr.	carronades
compos.	composite
Cstr	coaster
Dr	drifter
DY	dockyard
HDPC	harbour defence patrol craft
MFV	motor fishing vessel
MG	machine gun
ML	motor launch
M/L	minelayer
mm	millimetre
MOT	Ministry of Transport
M/S	minesweeper
MWT	Ministry of War Transport
OBV	ocean boarding vessel
pdr	pounder
RAN	Royal Australian Navy
RCN	Royal Canadian Navy
RIM	Royal Indian Marine
RIN	Royal Indian Navy
RNZN	Royal New Zealand Navy
RPN	Royal Pakistan Navy
S	screw
SAN	South African Navy
S/M	submarine
Stmr	steamer
SY	shipyard
Tr	trawler
TRV	torpedo recovery vessel
TT	torpedo tubes
USN	United States Navy
Wh	whaler
YC	yard craft

AARLA Yt 471/03. Commissioned as A/S Yt 10.1939. Sold 8.7.45 at Freetown.

AARON HUBERT Tr 'Strath' type, 202gr. Fullerton, Paisley 1919. Sold 1919, renamed *Graffoe*.

ABADOL (ex-dummy battleship IRON DUKE renamed 7.7.1915, ex-*Montezuma*) Oiler (RFA), 7,345gr, 485 x 59 ft. Renamed OAK-LEAF 7.2.17. Lost 25.7.17.

ABBEYDALE Oiler (RFA), 17,210 tons, 464 x 62 ft. Swan Hunter 28.12.1936. Arrived 4.9.60 Ward, Barrow to BU.

ABEILLE 2 Tug 101/11. French, seized 7.1940. Free-French crew 8.40. Returned 1945.

ABEILLE 3 Tug 175/14. French, seized 7.1940. To MWT 1944.

ABEILLE 4 Tug 327/39. French, seized 3.7.1940. Rescue tug 9.40–46.

ABEILLE 5 Tug 199/10. French, seized 3.7.1940. Harbour service 1940–45.

ABEILLE 6 Tug 115/10. French, seized 7.1940. To MWT 1940.

ABEILLE 14 Tug 126/27. French, seized at Southampton 3.7.1940. Salvage vessel 1942 and to MWT.

ABEILLE 20 Tug 160/24. French, seized at Portsmouth 3.7.1940. To MWT 1940.

ABEILLE 21 Tug 232/25. French, seized at Swansea 3.7.1940. Rescue tug to 1944.

ABEILLE 22 Tug 433/19. French, seized at Plymouth 3.7.1940. To MWT 1940.

ABEILLE 109, 110, 145, 148, 150 and 152. Towing launches commissioned as M/S on the Suez canal 1941–46.

ABELARD Tr 187/09. Hired 1914. Wrecked 24.12.16 near Plymouth.

ABERDEEN Tr 163/96, 1–6pdr. Hired 1914–19.

ABERDONIAN 1,648/09, 2–12pdr. Hired as depot ship 2.1940–27.3.45.

ABERDOUR Dr 93/08, 1–3pdr. Hired 1915–19 and as M/S 4.40. BBV 11.40. Fate unknown.

ABERDOVEY Tender, 70gr, 75 x 18 ft. Pimblott, Northwich 11.12.1963.

ABERGELDIE Tr 200/15, 1–6pdr. Hired 1915–19.

ABIDING STAR Dr 117/17. Hired as M/S 1940. Degaussing vessel 3.41–8.46.

ABIGAIL A.ship, 309bm. Hired 1625 for the Cadiz expedition.

ABIGAIL (ex-*Hopper No 4*) 707/08. Hired as salvage vessel 1.1941–43.

ABINGER Tender, 70gr, 75 x 18 ft. Pimblott 25.3.1964.

ABLETTE 513/17. Hired as BBV 12.1939–25.7.45.

ABOYNE Tr 233/08, 1–6pdr. Hired as M/S 1914–19.

ABRONIA Tr 242/06. Hired 1915–19 and as M/S 11.39. Foundered 7.9.40 in the Thames. Raised 1941, BU 1947.

ACACIA Dr 70/83. Hired on harbour service 10.1914–23.4.15.

ACCEPTABLE Dr 82/11, 1–6pdr. Hired 12.1914–19.

ACCOLADE (ex-*Salvia)* MFV. Hired on harbour service 1941–12.45.

ACCORD Dr 100/18. Hired on harbour service 8.1939–46.

ACCORD DY tug, 640gr, 140 x 35 ft. Inglis 10.9.1957.

ACCRINGTON 1,678/10. Hired as accommodation ship 12.1915–11.18 and as rescue ship 1943–45.

ACCRUITY Cstr 465/35. Hired as cable carrier 1941–44.

ACCUMULATOR Dr 85/12. Hired 1915–19 and 2.40–10.40.

ACHELOOS (see BUSEN 7)

ACHERNAR (ex-*Chire*) Tr 256/08, 1–3pdr. Portuguese, purchased as M/S 1915. Sold 17.5.19 Cruze Bros, Gibraltar.

ACHIEVABLE Dr 89/13, 1–3pdr. Hired 1914–19.

ACHIEVABLE Dr 96/27. Hired as M/S 11.1939–1.46.

ACHILLES II Tr 225/06, 1–6pdr. Hired 1914. Sunk 26.6.18 by mine off the Shipwash.

ACHROITE Tr 314/34, 1–12pdr. Hired as M/S 8.1939–45.

ACME (ex-*Northern Light*) MFV 39net. Transferred from War Dept 3.1941. Ferry service to 1945.

ACOR (ex-*HS.69*) DY tug 300 tons, 83½ x 21½ ft. Transferred from War Dept 1918. Sold 24.3.20.

ACORN 22-gun ship. Hired 1649–54.

ACORN Dr 96/19. Hired on harbour service 9.1940–46.

ACQUIRE Dr 94/07. Hired as BBV 5.1940--45.

ACQUISITION Dr 83/13, 1–3pdr. Hired as store carrier 1915–19 and as tender 3.40. Degaussing vessel 3.41–10.43.

ACRASIA (see MOED-EN-WERK)

ACTIVE Cutter 10, 80bm. Hired 1794–1803. (In French hands 11.1800
–16.5.01 as VICTOIRE.)
ACTIVE Cutter 8, 78bm, 8–4pdr. Hired 6.1803–5.14.
ACTIVE Cutter 6, 72bm. Hired 2.1804. Renamed LORD KEITH 1804.
Captured 11.1.1808 by the French.
ACTIVE Tug 58/75. Hired on harbour service 1915–18.
ACTIVE II Dr 65/06, 1–3pdr. Hired 1915–19.
ACTIVE III Dr 81/07, 1–3pdr. Hired 1915. Sunk 15.10.17 by mine
off Milford Haven.
ACTIVE IV Tr 185/99, 1–6pdr. Hired 1916–18.
ACTON 1,288gr, 1–4in, 4–12pdr. Hired as decoy ship (Q.34) 1917.
(Also operated as HARELDA.)
AD.402 (see ST CYR)
ADAM Tr 324/19. Hired as M/S 2.40–45.
ADAMANT Dr 80/01. Hired as BBV 11.1939–41.
ADDER Tug 54/06. Hired on harbour service 2.1918–19.
ADELAIDE (ex-*Victoria*) Iron S.DY tug, 33 tons, 65 x 10 ft.
Transferred from War Dept 1.10.1891. Sold 1907.
ADELE Dr 100/15, 1–6pdr. Hired 1915–19 (base ship KINGFISHER
1918–19) and on harbour service 1941–46.
ADELE (see KINGFISHER)
ADELE Yt 327/06. Hired on examination service (RAN) 9.1939.
Wrecked 7.5.43 in collision with breakwater at Port Kembla, but listed
to 1945.
ADELPHI (see A.ROSE)
ADEPT Rescue tug 700 tons, 142½ x 33½ ft, 1–3in. Cochrane 25.8.1941.
Wrecked 18.3.42 in the Hebrides.
ADEPT (ex-*Empire Barbara*) DY tug, 274gr. Transferred from MOT and
renamed 31.5.1947. Sold 1959 Ceylon Govt.
ADEQUATE Dr 90/ -. Hired 11.1914. Sunk 2.12.16 in collision off
Kirkabista light.
ADHERENT Rescue tug 700 tons, 142½ x 33½ ft, 1–3in. Cochrane
24.9.1941. Foundered 14.1.44 in the N.Atlantic.
ADHERENT (see DILIGENT)
ADJUTANT Tug 231gr. German, captured 10.10.1914 by the cruiser
DARTMOUTH. Lost 6.2.15.
ADMIRABLE Dr 90/14. Hired 1914. Sunk 15.5.17 by Austrian forces
in the Adriatic.
ADMIRAL CRADOCK Tr 295/14. Hired 1918–19.
ADMIRAL JELLICOE Dr. Hired as BDV 3.1916–19.
ADMIRAL MITCHELL Cutter 12, 133bm. Hired 1800–01 and 8.1803
–4.05.

ADMIRAL SIR JOHN LAWFORD Tr 338/30, 1–12pdr. Hired as M/S 8.1939. Wreck dispersal 5.44. Returned 1946.

ADMIRATION Dr 77/14. Hired as water carrier 1.1915–19.

ADMIRE Dr 93/08, 1–3pdr. Hired on examination service 12.1914–19 and on harbour service 2.41–45.

ADONIS (see NORDHAV I)

ADORATION Dr 93/12. Hired as BDV 6.1915–19 and on examination service 1940–45.

ADRIA 3,809/14. Commissioned as base ship 29.1.1943. Renamed GOMBROON 12.43. Laid up 12.45.

ADRIAN (ex-*Industry*) Cutter 8, 84bm. Hired 1804–8.1810.

ADRIAN Tr 199/00, 1–6pdr. Hired 1914. Sunk 13.3.18 in collision off Harwich.

ADRIATIC Dr 147/36. Belgian, hired as A/P Tr 10.1940–6.45.

ADRIENNE LOUISE MFV 46/35. Belgian, hired as A/P vessel 10.1940. TRV 3.43–45.

ADVANCE Tr. Hired 1918–19.

ADVENTURE A.ship 26, 260bm. Hired 1650–54.

ADVENTURE MERCHANT A.ship 40, 380bm. Hired 1652–54.

ADVENTURE Brig, 6–3pdr. Hired 1756. Captured 1756 by the French L'INFERNALE.

ADVENTURE Transport 10. Hired 1814–15.

ADVENTURE DY tug 306 tons, 110 x 23 ft. Bow McLachlan 15.3.1900. Renamed TYRIAN 3.04; TYRE 3.18; SIDONIAN 1918. Sold 17.10.25 Cox & Danks.

ADVENTURE II Tr 184/06, 1–6pdr. Hired 1915–19.

ADVENTURESS Yt 362/13, 2–12pdr. Hired as A/P Yt 11.1914–18.3.19. (Served as ANGLIA in WW.II.)

ADVENTURESS Yt 322/98. Hired on examination service 13.9.1939, purchased 3.40. Sold 2.46.

ADVICE DY paddle tug 700 tons, 144 x 27 ft. London & Glasgow Co. 2.10.1899. Sold 20.10.50 J. Scott, Cork to BU.

ADVICE DY tug, 640gr, 140 x 35 ft. Inglis 16.10.1958.

ADVISABLE Dr 115/30. Hired as M/S 11.1939–45.

AEGUSA (ex-*Erin*) Yt 1,242/96. Hired as A/P Yt 1914. Sunk 28.4.16 by mine off Malta.

AEROLITE Yt 84/80. Purchased 1915. Sold 28.8.18.

AETNA DY paddle tug 530 tons. Laird 1.9.1883. Sold 19.2.1929 Young, Sunderland to BU.

AFRICA 46–gun ship. Hired 1694–96.

AFRICA Cutter. Hired 1803–04.

AFRICAN (ex-sloop DEE renamed 5.1825) Wood paddle DY tug, 263bm. Woolwich DY 30.8.1825. BU 12.1862. (See DEE in volume I.)

AFRICAN Iron S DY tug, 41bm, 57½ x 12 ft. Rennie 1866, purchased 1865. BU 1907.

AFRICANA Tr 313/30, 1–3in. Hired as M/S (SAN) 9.1939–10.4.47.

AFRICAN PRINCE Tr 125/96. Hired 1917–19.

AFRIKANDER Wh 126gr. German *Bismarck* seized 11.1914. Base ship at Simonstown 1917. Sold 2.19.

AFTERGLOW Admiralty wood Dr. Ailsa, Troon. Renamed EQUINOX 1918 and cancelled.

AFTERGLOW Admiralty wood Dr, 112gr. Chambers, Lowestoft 1919. Sold 1921, renamed *Port Richard.* Hired as AFTERGLOW, M/S, 1–3pdr, 1941–44.

AGAMEMNON II Tr 225/07. Hired 1914. Sunk 15.7.15 by mine off the Shipwash.

AGAMEMNON 7,593/29, 2–4in, 4–20mm, 400 mines. Completed as M/L 10.1940. Harbour service 1944–46.

AGAMI Tr 186/99. Hired 1918–19.

AGATE Tr 248/14, 1–6pdr. Hired 1915. Sunk 14.3.18 by mine off the Royal Sovereign light vessel.

AGATE (ex-*Mavis Rose*) A/S Tr 627 tons, 1–4in. Purchased 1935. Wrecked 6.8.41 near Cromer.

AGATHA Yt 450/05, 1–12pdr, 1–6pdr. Hired as A/P Yt 28.9.1914–15.3.19.

AGATHA II Tr 137/96, 1–3pdr. Hired as M/S 1915–19.

AGATHA DY tug, 40gr, 57 x 17 ft. Harris, Appledore 9.3.1961.

AGHIOS GEORGIOS Tug 164/16. Greek, hired as store carrier. Lost 8.6.1942 in the Mozambique Channel.

AGHIOS PANTALEIMON Aux. schooner 105/20. Greek, hired as store carrier. Lost 30.5.1941.

AGILE Tr 246/07. Hired as M/S 1914. Sunk 27.4.17 by mine off Harwich.

AGILE DY tug, 640gr, 140 x 35 ft. Goole SB 2.7.1958.

AGNES (ex-*Venus*) Lugger 6, 67bm. Hired 3.1804. Lost 3.1806 off the Texel.

AGNES Dr 60/ -. Hired on harbour service 1915–18.

AGNES DY tug, 40gr, 57 x 17 ft. Harris, Appledore 5.4.1961.

AGNES & JANET Dr 91/14. Hired 1915–19.

AGNES BUNYAN MFV 46/01. Hired as boom tender 8.1940–12.40.

AGNES DUNCAN 2,496/12. Hired as store carrier (RFA) 7.1915–19.

AGNES GARDNER Dr 96/20. Hired on harbour service 2.1941–45.

AGNES H HASTIE Tr 210/12, 1–6pdr. Hired as M/S 1914–19.

AGNES H WETHERLY Tr 229/17. Hired 1917–19 and as A/P Tr 6.40–12.45.

AGNES IRVIN Dr. Hired 1917–19.

AGNES NUTTEN Tr 183/15. Hired as mooring vessel 1915—19 and as A/P Tr, 1—6pdr, 6.40—12.45.

AGNES WICKFIELD Tr 219/09. Hired as M/S 1914—19 and as M/S 11.39—12.45.

AGRA Tr, 'Basset' class (RIN). Hooghly DK & Eng Co 18.3.1942. Sold 1946, renamed *Fritha.*

AGUIA (ex-*Knight of the Cross*) DY tug, 194gr. Purchased 1915. Sold 11.3.22.

AHMEDABAD Tr, 'Basset' class (RIN). Burn, Calcutta 28.10.1943. Sold 1947.

AH MING Tug 93/13. Hired on examination service 11.1940. Lost 1.42 to the Japanese.

AHOLA Yt 48/36. Purchased as A/P Yt 1940. Sold 11.45.

AID DY lighter, 154bm. Chatham DY 30.11.1838. BU completed 1.11.1878. (Also known as Chatham YC.3.)

AID DY tank vessel 390 tons, 115 x 21 ft. Willoughby, Plymouth 10.9.1900. Sold circa 1948.

AID DY tug, 194gr. Hired 1.1915, purchased 7.15. Sold 10.19 at Constantinople.

AID (ex-*Empire Jenny*) DY tug, 274gr, 109 x 26½ ft. Transferred from MOT 31.5.1947. Sold 1960, renamed *Irving Teak.*

AIGLE Tr 163/98. Hired 1917—19.

AIGLON (see EAGLE II)

AIGLON Tr 305/07. French A/P Tr seized 3.7.1940 at Plymouth. M/S to 1945 then examination service. Returned 7.46.

AIK LAM Cstr 155/41. Hired as M/S 1941. Repair ship 1944. Wrecked 22.3.46.

AILSA CRAIG Tr, 'Isles' class. Cook Welton & Gemmell 16.10.1943. Sold 4.46, renamed *Veslemoy.*

AIMWELL Rescue tug 'B.A.T' class. Defoe, Bay City 8.4.1942 on lend-lease. Returned 1946 to the USN.

AIREDALE DY tug 170 tons, 85 x 24½ ft. Scarr, Hessle 16.5.1961.

AIR POCKET Admiralty wood Dr, 99gr. Chambers 1918. Renamed AMBITIOUS 1919. Sold 10.20, renamed *Cineraria.*

AIRSPRITE Petrol carrier (RFA), 965gr, 204 x 33 ft. Blythswood 22.12.1942. Arrived 14.3.65 at Antwerp to BU.

AISHA Yt 117/34. Hired as HDPC 2.1940. Sunk 11.10.40 by mine in the Thames estuary.

AISNE Tr 316/15. Hired 1915—19.

AIVERN Dr 72/10. Hired 1915. Foundered 8.2.17 in the Channel.

AJAX Tug 273/94. Hired 7.1914. To War Dept 7.8.14.

AJAX II Dr 81/09. Hired 1914. Sunk 27.10.16 by German torpedo boats in the North Sea.

AKITA Tr 314/39, 1–12 pdr. Hired as M/S 8.1939–10.45.

AKRANES Tr. Hired as BDV 1915–19.

AKRANES Tr 358/29. Hired as M/S 8.1939. Sunk 4.7.41 by air attack in Bridlington Bay.

ALABURN Dr 85/12, 1–3pdr. Hired 1915–19.

ALADER YOUSANOFF Russian merchant 2,071/05 commissioned as seaplane carrier, 1–12pdr, 2–A/C, 1.1919. Transferred 8.19 to 'White' Russians on the Caspian Sea.

ALAFOSS Tr 357/29, 1–12pdr. Hired as M/S 8.1939 and later purchased. Sold 1946.

ALARM Tug 432/19. Hired as M/S 1940. Renamed ALARM II in 1.42. Returned 1946.

ALASKA Tr 135/98, 1–6pdr. Hired as M/S 1915–19.

ALASKA II Tr. Hired 1918–19.

ALASTOR Yt 340/26. Commissioned as training ship 3.1940. A/S Yt 1.41. For disposal 6.45.

ALAUNIA 14,030/25, 8–6in, 2–3in. Hired as AMC 8.1939. Purchased 8.2.44 and completed as repair ship 9.45. Arrived 10.9.57 Hughes Bolckow, Blyth to BU.

ALBANY Yt 71/30. Hired as HDPC 11.1939, purchased 5.41, fire-float 12.43. Sold 7.46.

ALBATROSS 1,414/84. Hired as supply ship and mine carrier (RFA) 5.8.1914–19.

ALBATROSS II Tr 220/06, 1–6pdr. Hired 1914–19.

ALBATROSS III Tr 151/95, 1–12pdr. Hired 1915–18.

ALBATROSS IV Dr 86/07, 1–3pdr. Hired 1915–19.

ALBATROSS V Tr. Hired 1918–19.

ALBEMARLE 48–gun ship. Hired 1664–67.

ALBERIA Tr 286/10, 1–6pdr. Hired 1914–19. (Served as ALBERIC in WW.II.)

ALBERIC Tr 286/10. Hired as M/S 4.1940. Sunk 3.5.41 in collision with the destroyer ST ALBANS off Scapa.

ALBERT Tug 61/82. Hired 8.1914–18.

ALBERTA Tr 210/07. Hired as M/S 1914. Sunk 14.4.16 by mine off Grimsby.

ALBERT FAROULT Pilot 225/38. French, seized 7.1940 at Falmouth. On examination service 1941–44.

ALBERT HULLETT Wh 250/29. Hired as M/S (SAN) 1940. Renamed LANGLAAGTE 1941. Returned 1947.

ALBERTON DY tug (RCN) 462 tons, 104 x 28 ft. Toronto 1944. Sold 1949.

ALBERT VICTOR Paddle tug 150/83. Hired on harbour service 7.1914. M/L, 8 mines, 1918–19.

ALBION Cutter 6, 76bm, 6–4pdr. Hired 1803–12.

ALBION II Tr 240/07. Hired 1915. Sunk 13.1.16 by mine off St Catherine's Point.

ALBION II Paddle 363/93, 1–6pdr. Hired as M/S 5.1915. Renamed ALBYN 1916. Returned 14.3.19.

ALBION III Yt 1,346/05, 2–12pdr, 1–6pdr. Hired as A/P Yt 2.1915–19.

ALBYN (see ALBION II)

ALBYN Yt 82/34. Hired as BBV 31.12.1940. Renamed DUNDONALD base ship 1942. Laid up 11.45.

ALCA 3,712/27, 1–4in, 6–20mm, 220 mines. Hired as M/L 11.1940–46.

ALCANTARA 15,830/14, 8–6in, 2–6pdr. Hired as AMC 10.3.1915. Sunk 29.2.16 in action with the German GREIF in the North Sea.

ALCANTARA 22,209/26, 6–6in, 2–3in. Hired as AMC 9.1939. To MWT 1943 as troopship.

ALCINOUS 6,743/00. Hired as store carrier (RFA) 8.1914–12.14.

ALCIS Tug. Hired as M/S 1942–45.

ALCMARIA Tr 148/16. Purchased as M/S 11.1939. Sold 1946. (Norwegian crew 10.40–45.)

ALCOR Dr 97/22. Hired as M/S 11.1939–9.45.

ALDER (ex-*Lord Davidson*) Tr 346/29, 560 tons. Purchased as M/S 2.1939. Grounded 22.10.41 east coast of Scotland.

ALDER LAKE Motor M/S (RCN) 255 tons, 126 x 26 ft. Midland Bt Wks 3.12.1944. To Russian navy 20.9.45.

ALDERSDALE Oiler (RFA) 17,320 tons, 464 x 62 ft. Cammell Laird 7.7.1937. Sunk 26.5.42 by air attack in the Barents Sea.

ALDGATE Boom gate vessel (dumb) 290 tons, 98 x 26 ft, 1–3in. Hong Kong & Whampoa Co 5.4.1934. Scuttled 19.12.41 at Hong Kong.

ALDIC Yt 85/31. Purchased as HDPC 1940. Sold 2.45.

ALERT Cutter 6, 120bm. Hired 1796–1815.

ALERT Cutter 6, 44bm, 6–12pdr carr. Hired 1804–13.

ALERT Cutter 10, 117bm. Hired 1812–14.

ALERT II Dr 83/07, 1–3pdr. Hired 1914–19.

ALERT III Dr 96/07, 1–3pdr. Hired 1915–20.

ALERT Cable ship 941/18. Hired 1940. Lost 24.2.45 by unknown cause in the North Sea.

ALETES Yt. American on lend-lease as A/S Yt from 1941. Returned 21.11.45.

ALEXANDER Brig, 253bm, 90 x 26 ft. Hired as discovery ship 1818–7.1.1819.

ALEXANDER COLVILLE Tr, 'Castle' type. Greenock. Cancelled 1919.

ALEXANDER DUNBAR Tr, 'Castle' type. Cancelled 1919.

ALEXANDER HILLS Tr, 'Mersey' type. Cochrane 22.5.1917. Renamed MOY 1920. Target-towing 1921; danlayer 1943. Sold 1.46.

ALEXANDER McBETH Tr, 'Mersey' type. Cochrane 1919. Sold 1919, renamed *John W Johnson.*

ALEXANDER McDOWELL Tr, 'Mersey' type. Cochrane. Cancelled 1919.

ALEXANDER MURRAY Tr, 'Mersey' type. Cochrane. Cancelled 1919.

ALEXANDER PALMER Tr, 'Castle' type. Smiths Dk 21.5.1917. Renamed NESS 1920. Sold 1922 Spanish navy.

ALEXANDER SCOTT Tr, 'Castle' type. Smiths Dk 3.8.1917. Sold 4.5.20, same name. Hired as M/S 8.39–44.

ALEXANDRA Paddle 235/80. Hired as tender 9.1915. Renamed ALEXIS, A/P vessel 1918. Returned 2.20.

ALEXANDRA II Tug 168/07. Hired 10.1914. Wrecked 28.10.15 in Hoxa Sound.

ALEXANDRA Tr, 1–6pdr. Hired 1915–19.

ALEXANDRA Tug 215/16. Hired as rescue tug 1.1918–19.

ALEXANDRA Yt (155/91?). Hired as accommodation ship 11.1940–44.

ALEXANDRITE Tr 313/33. Hired as M/S 9.1939–11.45.

ALEX GABRIELLE MFV 57/24. Belgian, hired as BBV 8.1940–7.44.

ALEX HASTIE Tr 206/14, 1–6pdr. Hired as M/S 1915–19 and as A/P Tr 10.39–1.40.

ALEXIS (see ALEXANDRA)

ALEX WATT Dr 86/13, 1–3pdr. Hired 1915–19 and as TRV 5.40–45.

ALFIE CAM Tr 282/20. Hired as M/S (RAN) 1940–45.

ALFRED Brig 10. Hired 1793–1801.

ALFRED DY craft, 90bm. Transferred from War Dept 1.10.1891. Sold 1901.

ALFRED DY barge. Fellows, Yarmouth 1901. Hulked 1943.

ALFRED Dr 96/07, 1–3pdr. Hired 1915–19.

ALFRED COLEBROOK Dr 56/12. Purchased 1940. Sunk 9.9.40 as blockship in the Richborough Channel.

ALFRED EDITH Tr 262/08. Belgian, hired 1918–19.

ALFREDIAN Tr 293/13, 1–12pdr. Hired as A/P Tr 11.1939–9.46.

ALGENIB (ex-*Neptuno*) Tr 330/07, 1–3pdr. Portuguese, purchased 1915. Sold 17.5.19 Cruze Bros, Gibraltar.

ALGERIAN 2,315/24. Hired as cable ship 1.1943–45.

ALGOA BAY Tr 270/19. Hired as M/S (SAN) 10.1939–9.12.40.

ALGOL (ex-*Maria Amalia*) Tr 213/01, 1–3pdr. Portuguese, purchased as M/S 1915. Sold 17.5.19 Cruze Bros, renamed *Rio Lima.*

ALGOMA (ex-*London-Istanbul*) 1,849/13. Belgian, hired as depot ship 1940. Renamed AMBITIOUS 1941. Returned 21.6.45.

AL HATHERA Tug 279/27. Hired as M/S 1941–45.

ALIANORA Yt 61/38. Purchased as A/P Yt 1940. Sold 11.45.

ALICE (ex-*Vincent Grech*) DY tug 253/13. Purchased 1916. Sold 9.25 at Malta.

ALICE Yt 527/30. Purchased as A/S Yt 9.1939. Accommodation ship 1941. Sold 1947.

ALICE DY tug, 40gr, 57 x 17 ft. Harris 9.3.1961.

ALICIA Yt 51/36. Hired as echo yacht 12.1939, purchased 8.41. Sold 2.46.

ALIDA Tr 270/15, 1–6pdr. Hired as M/S 1915–19 and as BDV 1.40–45.

ALIPED V Yt. Hired as HDPC 10.1939–45.

ALISDAIR Yt 120/37. Hired as HDPC 10.1939–45.

ALKANET (ex-*Anemone*) Tr 296/36. Hired as M/S 1941–43.

ALLAHABAD Tr, 'Basset' class (RIN). Hooghly Dk & Eng Co. Cancelled 3.1945.

ALLAN RAMSAY Tr 210/11. Hired 1918–19.

ALLEGIANCE (see KING SALVOR)

ALLEGIANCE Rescue tug 700 tons, 142½ x 33 ft, 1–3in. Cochrane 22.2.1943. On loan as *Allegiance 2* from 1949; *Kowloon Docks* 1955. Foundered 1.9.62 off Hong Kong.

ALLENBY (see RESULT)

ALLENWOOD Cstr 398/20. Commissioned as M/S (RAN) 9.1941. Returned 1945.

ALLERSIE Dr. Hired as BBV 1940–44.

ALL HALLOWS (ex-*Jamaica*) Tr 205/14. Hired as fuel carrier 3.1944–45.

ALLIANCE DY tug 615 tons, 145 x 29 ft. Chatham DY 23.8.1910. Sunk 19.12.41 at Hong Kong.

ALLIANCE Tug 100 tons Hired 7.1941. Lost 29.4.42.

ALLIGATOR Cutter 6. Hired 1793–1801.

ALLIGATOR Cutter 6. Hired 1799–1801.

ALLIGATOR (ex-*Stormcock*) Salvage tug 630 tons, 157½ x 25 ft. Purchased 1896. Sold 1919, renamed *Refloater*.

ALLIGATOR DY tug 395 tons, 105 x 26½ ft, 1–12pdr. Dunston, Hessle 16.10.1940. Lost 2.45 in the East Indies.

ALLIGATOR (see CHARON)

ALLOCHY Dr 96/18. Hired as hospital tender 1941–45.

ALLS WELL Dr 87/10. Hired 1915–19.

ALMA Tr 206/15. Dutch, hired as M/S (Dutch crew) 6.1940. RN crew 10.9.43–45.

ALMA A/P vessel. Hired 1944–45 in East Africa.

ALMANDINE Tr 295/32. Hired as M/S 8.1939–12.45.

ALMANZORA 16,034/14. Hired as AMC 23.8.1915–20.12.19 and as accommodation ship 1939–40.

ALMOND M/S Tr 505 tons, 150 x 27½ ft, 1–12pdr. Ardrossan DY Co 22.5.1940. Sunk 2.2.41 by mine off Falmouth.

ALNESS Tender, 70gr, 75 x 18 ft. Pimblott, Northwich 18.6.1964.

ALNMOUTH Tr 236/11, 1–6pdr. Purchased as M/S 7.1914. Sold 1919, same name.

ALNMOUTH Tender, 70gr, 75 x 18 ft. Pimblott 5.10.1964.

ALOMA Yt 66/98. Hired on examination service 4.1940–7.40.

ALONZO (ex-*Alonso*) Tr 172/06. Hired as M/S 1918–19.

ALOUETTE Cstr 570/94, 1–12pdr. Hired as fleet messenger 23.9.1914. ABS 7.15. Returned 21.11.19.

ALOUETTE (ex-*Esquimaux*) Tr 520/39, 1–4in. Hired as A/S Tr 8.1939. Sunk 19.9.42 by U-boat off Portugal.

ALOUETTE II Yt 57/30. Hired as echo Yt 5.1940–45.

ALPHA Tr 274/00, 1–6pdr. Hired 1915–19.

ALPHA II Dr 65/00. Hired in WW.I.

ALPHA II Tr 200/05, 1–3pdr. Hired as M/S 1915–19.

ALPHEUS Cstr 151/15. Hired as BBV tender 1942–45.

AL RAWDAH 3,549/11. Transferred from War Dept as accommodation ship 9.6.1941–3.46.

ALSATIAN 18,481/13, 8–4.7in. Hired as AMC 7.8.1914–4.4.19.

ALSATIAN Tr 191/99. Hired 1914–16 and 1918–19. (Known as ALSATIAN MINOR 1914–16.)

ALSATIAN DY tug 170 tons, 85 x 25 ft. Scarr, Hessle 27.7.1961.

ALSEY Tr 416/32. Hired as M/L 2.1940–46.

ALTAIR (ex-*Victoria Laura*) Tr 257/07, 1–3pdr. Portuguese, purchased as M/S 1915. Sold 12.5.19 Cruze Bros.

ALTAIR (ex-*Venetia*) Yt 505/05. Hired as A/S Yt 9.1939–45.

ALTHORPE Cutter 16, 163bm, 14–12pdr carr, 2–6pdr. Hired 1804. Renamed EARL SPENCER 1805. Foundered 8.05 in the Channel.

ALTRUIST (ex-*Speedwell*) MFV 39/94. Hired on harbour service 1.1941–44.

ALVINIA Yt 318/ -. Russian SOKOLITZA seized and commissioned 9.1918. Sold 15.7.19.

ALVIS (ex-*Transport Union*) Tr 280/18, 1–12pdr. Belgian, hired as M/S 5.1940–3.45.

ALYNBANK 5,151/25, 8–4in, 2–3in. Commissioned as A/A ship 4.1940. Sunk 6.44 as blockship, Normandy. Salved and BU 12.45.

AMADAVAT Tr 171/99. Hired 1914–16.

AMALFI Yt 124/25. Hired as HDPC 1.1940–44.

AMALIA Dr 139/17. Hired as M/S 11.1939–45.

AMALTHAEA Yt 634/81, 2–6pdr. Hired as A/P Yt 3.1915. IOLAIRE 11.18. Stranded 1.19 north Scotland.

AMARYLLIS Training ketch, 37/82. Presented 1920. Scuttled 12.6.51 off Start Point.

AMAZONE Yt 229/36, 1–6pdr. Hired on examination service 6.1940. Renamed DUNLIN 11.40. Returned 1945.

AMAZONE Cstr 250/39. Dutch, hired as BBV 9.1940–44.

AMBALA Tr, 'Basset' class (RIN). Alcock Ashdown. Cancelled 3.1945.

AMBASSADOR Tr 149/99. Hired 1917–19.

AMBASSADOR (ex-*Embassy*) Paddle 387/11, 1–12pdr. Hired as M/S 11.1939. M/S training 1944–45.

AMBER Tr 172/98. Hired 1917–19.

AMBER (ex-*Cape Barfleur*) Tr 457/34, 700 tons, 1–4in. Purchased as A/S Tr 1.1939. Sold 1945, renamed *Etonian*.

AMBER (see MMS.222)

AMBITION (ex-*Thrush*) Tr 166/02. Hired as fuel carrier 3.1944–45.

AMBITIOUS Dr 81/07, 1–3pdr. Hired 1914. Base ship 1918–19.

AMBITIOUS II Dr 90/10, 1–3pdr. Hired in WW.I.

AMBITIOUS (see AIR POCKET)

AMBITIOUS (see ALGOMA)

AMBLER Yt 261/22. Purchased as A/P Yt (RCN) 7.1940. Sold 1946.

AMBROSE 4,595/03. Commissioned as AMC 10.12.1914. Purchased 20.10.15 for conversion to depot ship. Renamed COCHRANE base ship 1.6.38. Sold 8.46, BU 11.46 Ward, Inverkeithing.

AMBROSE S/M base ship. Name borne by CARMANIA II from 1940–45 and by MFV.18 from 1945.

AMBROSE PARE Tr 326/06. French A/P Tr AMBROISE PARE seized 7.1940 at Plymouth. A/S Tr 8.40–3.46.

AMEER Tr 216/08. Hired as M/S 1914. Sunk 18.3.16 by mine off in Felixstowe.

AMENARTAS Yt 54/18. Purchased as accommodation ship 1942. Sold 8.45.

AMENITY Tr 212/08. Hired 1917–19.

AMERICA Tug 244/91. Hired on harbour service 13.9.1915. M/L, 10 mines, 1918–19.

AMERICAN SALVOR Salvage vessel 800 tons, 170 x 37 ft, 1–3in, 2–20mm. Barbour Bt Wks, New Bern NJ 27.12.1942 and on lend-lease from 9.9.43. Returned 3.10.46 to the USN.

AMETHYST II Tr 172/98. Hired 1914–15 and 1918–19.

AMETHYST III Yt 330/77, 2–6pdr. Hired as A/P Yt 3.1915–2.17.

AMETHYST (ex-*Phyllis Rosalie*) A/S Tr, 627 tons, 1–4in. Purchased 1935. Sunk 24.12.40 by mine in the Thames estuary.

AMHERST (see FORT AMHERST)

AMIABLE Dr 92/10, 1–3pdr. Hired 1914–19 and as degaussing vessel 5.40–46.

AMITY Dr 82/07, 1–6pdr. Hired 1915–19.

AMPERE Tr 154/91. Hired 1917–19.

AMPHITRITE A.ship 20, 328bm. Hired 1793–94.

AMPLIFY Tr 342/ -. Hired 1915. Wrecked 17.1.17 off Castlebay.

AMPULLA Tr 248/13. Hired as M/S 1914–19 and purchased as A/P Tr, 1–12pdr, 6.40. Sold 1946.

AMRITSAR Tr, 'Basset' class (RIN). Garden Reach 19.12.1941. Sold 1950.

AMROTH CASTLE Tr 255/13, 1–6pdr. Hired 1914–19 and as A/P Tr, 1–12pdr, 5.40. M/S 1.41–45.

AMSTERDAM 1,777/94, 1–4in, 1–12pdr. Commissioned as ABS 10.1914. Returned 29.9.19.

AMSTERDAM Tr 241/13. Dutch, hired as M/S (Dutch crew) 6.1940. Renamed ANDYK 1941. RN crew 1943–46.

AMSTERDAM Tug 368/37. Dutch, hired as rescue tug (Dutch crew) 8.1940–44.

AMULREE Yt 86/38. Hired as HDPC 1.1940. Sunk 1.6.40 in collision off Dover.

AMY Tr 270/14. Hired 1915. Sunk 11.4.17 by mine off Le Havre.

AMY Yt 416/77, 1–12pdr, 1–6pdr. Hired as A/P Yt 7.1915–3.19.

AN.1 Wh 223/26. Hired as A/P Wh 10.1940. Renamed SAMBHUR 1.41. Stranded 5.5.42 near Colombo.

AN.2 Wh 221/26. Hired as A/P Wh 11.1939. Sunk 8.11.40 by mine off Falmouth.

AN.4 Wh 223/24. Hired as A/P Wh 11.1940. Renamed IMPALA 1.41. Returned 4.46.

AN.5 Wh 246/29. Hired as A/P Wh 11.1940. Renamed OKAPI 1.41. Returned 12.45.

ANCHOR (ex-*Alert*) Tug 195/10. Hired as tender 10.1914. DY tug 5.15–3.2.19.

ANCHORITE (see PROGRESS)

ANCHOR of HOPE Dr 95/07. Hired 1915–19.

ANCHOR of HOPE II Dr 79/03. Hired 1915–19.

ANCHOR STAR Dr 82/08. Hired 1915–19.

ANCIENT (see VETERAN)

ANCONA DY tug 67 tons, 75½ x 15 ft. Scarr 2.4.1919. Reported sold 8.22 but listed 1928.

ANCRE ESPERANCE Dr 110/35. Belgian, hired as A/P Dr 10.1940. Renamed OCEAN FIRE, firefloat, 12.42. Returned 1945.

ANDANES Tr 169/99. Hired 1917–19.

ANDANES Tr 320/16. Hired as A/P Tr 5.1940. BDV 1.41–45.

ANDANIA 16,950/22, 8–6in, 2–3in. Hired as AMC 9.1939. Sunk 16.6.40 by 'UA.1' south of Iceland.

ANDELLE 1,832/22. Commissioned as M/S 10.1940. Repair ship 1943. BU 4.45.

ANDES 15,620/13. Commissioned as AMC 22.3.1915. Returned 22.10.19.

ANDRADITE Tr 313/34, 1—12pdr. Hired as M/S 8.1939—1.46.

ANDREE DUPRE Tug 285/19. Hired (RCN) 1940—46.

ANDRE-LOUIS Tr 284/07. French M/S seized 3.7.1940 at Plymouth. Returned 3.4.45.

ANDRE-MARCEL Dr 125/36. French A/P vessel seized 3.7.1940 at Southampton. A/P Dr 8.40—45.

ANDRE-MONIQUE Tr 152/37. Belgian, hired as A/P Dr 1940—45.

ANDREW ANDERSON Tr, 'Castle' type. Cook Welton & Gemmell 1919. Sold 13.2.22, renamed *Normanby*.

ANDREW APSLEY Tr, 'Castle' type, 290gr. Cook Welton & Gemmell 2.6.1919. Sold 13.10.19, renamed *Callancroft*. (Served as MILFORD EARL in WW.II.)

ANDREW JEWER Tr, 'Mersey' type, 327gr. Cochrane 1918. Renamed NITH 1920; EXCELLENT 6.22. Sold 1948, renamed *Malvern*.

ANDREW KING Tr, 'Mersey' type, 324gr. Cochrane 19.4.1917. Renamed OUSE 1920. Sunk 20.2.41 by mine off Tobruk.

ANDREW MARVEL Tr 285/12. Hired 1915—29.

ANDREW McWILLIAMS Tr, 'Mersey' type. Cochrane. Cancelled 1919.

ANDREW SACK Tr, 'Castle' type, 275gr. Smiths Dk 5.7.1917. Sold 1919, renamed *Alexandrite*. (Served as NORTH NESS in WW.II.)

ANDRINA Dr 92/11. Hired 1915—19. (Served as ROSS ARD in WW.II.)

ANDROMEDA Tr 149/98. Hired 1917—19.

ANDROMEDA Tug 658/10. Hired as M/S 1941. Sunk 18.4.42 by air attack at Malta.

ANDROMEDA Tug 134/33. In service 1942—45.

ANDRONIE CAMIEL Dr 139/36. Belgian, hired as A/P Dr 7.1940. Ferry service 1943—45.

ANDROS Tug 274/85. Purchased as DY tug 1915. Sold 8.22 at Constantinople.

ANDYK (see AMSTERDAM)

ANGELE-MARIE Tr 238/29. French M/S seized 3.7.1940 at Southampton. M/S 8.40—46.

ANGELINA Dr 86/08, 1—3pdr. Hired 1915—19.

ANGELUS Tr 304/14. Hired 1914. Sunk 28.2.16 by mine off Dover.

ANGERTON Tr 186/01, 1—6pdr. Hired 1914—19.

ANGLE Tr 222/08, 1—6pdr. Hired 1915—19.

ANGLE Tr 531/36. Hired as A/S Tr 9.1939—10.45.

ANGLIA 1,862/00. Hired as ABS 8.8.1914—5.15.

ANGLIA Tr 196/04. Hired 11.1917—19.

ANGLIA Yt 362/13. Purchased as ABV 9.1939. Sold 1946.
ANGOLIAN Tr 141/98. Hired 1918—19.
ANGORA 4,300/11, 3—4.7in, 2—6pdr, 320 mines. Hired as M/L
27.2.1915—4.19.
ANGUS Tr 179/06. Hired in WW.I.
ANIDA Tr 270/17, 1—12pdr. Hired 1917—19.
ANIMATE Dr 88/17, 1—3pdr. Hired 1917—19 and on harbour service
1941—46.
ANIMATION Dr 99/25. Hired as TRV 1940—45.
ANKH Yt 58/38. Purchased as A/P Yt 1940. Sold 9.45.
ANKING 3,470/24. Hired as depot ship 1941. Sunk 2.3.42 by Japanese
surface craft off Java.
ANN Cutter 12. Hired 1796—1801.
ANN Cutter 10. Hired 1800—02.
ANN Lugger 10, 154bm. Hired 3.1807—09.
ANNABELLE Tr 202/17. Hired as A/P Tr 11.1939. BBV 1941—12.44.
ANNA LEOPOLD MFV 53/36. French, ex-Belgian, seized 7.1940. Re-
named BLUE TIT 11.40, M/L tender; ANNA LEOPOLD 1942, harbour
service. Returned 14.11.45 to Belgium.
ANNA MARIE Yt 344/30. Hired as A/S Yt 9.1939. Renamed TORRENT
1941. Sunk 6.4.41 by mine off Falmouth.
ANNE Brig 10, 120bm, 10—12pdr carr. Hired 5.1804—7.1809.
ANNE (ex-AENNE RICKMERS renamed 5.8.1915) 4,083/11, 1—12pdr,
2—A/C. German merchant seized 1914 in the Mediterranean. Commis-
sioned as seaplane carrier 1.15. Collier (RFA) 1.18. Sold 1920, renamed
Ithaki.
ANNE Yt 121/25. Hired as HDPC 1.1940—46.
ANNE GASTON Dr. French M/S seized 3.7.1940 at Southampton.
Examination service 9.40—6.45.
ANNE MARIE MFV, 1—6pdr. Belgian, hired as A/P vessel 1940—44.
(Also known as 'P.5'.)
ANNET Tr, 'Isles' class. Cook Welton & Gemmell 25.3.1943. Wreck
dispersal 1946. Sold 28.5.58, renamed *Ulva.*
ANN FORD MELVILLE Tr 212/11, 1—6pdr. Hired 1915—19.
ANNIE Dr 94gr. Hired 1915. Destroyed 19.12.17 after grounding off
Enos.
ANNIE Dr. Belgian, hired as A/P Dr 7.1940. Renamed ANNIE II in
1943. Returned 1945.
ANNIE CUMINE Dr 80/13. Hired 1915—19.
ANNIE MATHERS Dr. Hired 1917—19.
ANNIE MELLING Tr 221/06. Hired 1915—19.
ANNIE SMITH Dr 84/07. Hired 4.1915. Sunk 9.4.18 in collision off
Lundy.

ANNIE WALKER Tr 123/90. Hired 1917–19.
ANN LEWIS Tr 216/16, 1–6pdr. Hired 1916–19.
ANN MELVILLE Tr 201/09, 1–6pdr. Hired 1915–19 and as M/S 2.40.
Fuel carrier 5.44–10.44.
ANSON Tr 211/05, 1–6pdr. Hired as M/S 1915–19 and as A/P Tr
11.39. Danlayer 5.40. Renamed COCKADE 1941; STOCKADE, water
carrier, 1944. Returned 1946.
ANT Tr 158/91. Hired 1915–19.
ANT Dr 61/04. Hired on harbour service 1915–19.
ANT Cutter 4, 27bm. Hired 7.1803. Captured 16.3.1806 by the French.
ANT Cutter 6, 48bm. Hired 7.1808–5.1810.
ANT (see ANTIC)
ANTARES (ex-*Cabo Verde*) Tr 218/06, 1–3pdr. Portuguese, purchased
as M/S 1915. Listed to 1921.
ANTARES II Tr 275/-. Sunk 2.5.1918 in collision off Gibraltar.
ANTENOR 19,150/25, 6–6in, 2–3in. Hired as AMC 8.1939–42.
ANTHONY 36–gun ship, 450bm. Hired 1649. Captured 30.11.1652 by
the Dutch.
ANTHONY ASLETT Tr, non-standard 'Mersey' type, 305gr. Cochrane
22.2.1917. Renamed ROTHER 1920. Sold 1922 Spanish navy.
ANTHONY HOPE Tr 288/13. Hired 1915. Sunk 16.11.16 by mine off
Le Havre.
ANTIC (ex-ANT renamed 1942) Rescue tug, 700 tons, 142½ x 33 ft,
1–3in, 2–20mm. Cochrane 24.3.1943. Fleet tug 1946. (On loan Dutch
navy 6.43–45.)
ANTICOSTI Tr, 'Isles' class. Collingwood SY 1.4.1942. Sold 1946, re-
named *Culoy*. (On loan RCN to 17.6.45.)
ANTICYCLONE Admiralty wood Dr, 100gr. Chambers 1918. Sold
circa 1930.
ANTIOCH II Tr 300/18. French M/S seized 3.7.1940 at Falmouth. M/S
8.40–46.
ANTOINE WILLY Dr. Belgian, hired 6.1940. Wrecked 15.12.40 near
Dartmouth.
ANTONIA 13,867/21, 18,750 tons. Hired as repair ship 9.1939,
purchased 4.42. Renamed WAYLAND 1942. Sold 1.48, BU at Troon.
ANTONIO Tr 210/08. Hired 1917–19.
ANTWERP 2,957/20. Hired as escort 12.1940–45.
ANWOTH Tr 211/15, 1–6pdr. Hired 1915–19.
ANZAC II Tr 316/16, 1–6pdr. Hired 1916–19.
AORANGI 17,490/24. Hired as accommodation ship 7.1944–46.
APLEY Tr 222/08. Hired as M/S 1914. Sunk 6.2.17 by mine off the
Isle of Wight.
APPLEBY Tender, 70gr, 75 x 18 ft. Pimblott 3.2.1965.

APPLELEAF (see TEXOL)

APPLELEAF (ex-*George Lyras*) Oiler (RFA), 22,980 tons, 525 x 68 ft. Bartram 22.4.1955, purchased 17.4.59.

APPLETREE Dr 84/07. Hired as HDPC 1.1940. Sunk 15.10.40 in collision in Oban harbour.

APT MFV. Hired on examination service 1941—45.

AQUAMARINE Tr 288/11, 1—6pdr. Hired 1915—19.

AQUAMARINE Tr 357/27. Hired as ABV 8.1939—9.44.

AQUARINE Yt 58/38. Purchased as HDPC 1940. Sold 3.46.

AQUARIUS Tr 187/05. Hired 1918—19.

AQUILLA Cstr 450/07. Hired as store carrier (RFA) 12.1915—5.1.20 and as cable ship 1941—45.

AQUITANIA 44,786/14. Hired as AMC 2.8.1914—5.9.14.

ARAB Tr 531/36. Hired as A/S Tr 9.1939—11.45.

ARABESQUE (see YESSO)

ARABIA 5,943/26. Italian, captured 1940 and used as coal hulk. Wrecked 29.8.43 in the Red Sea.

ARABIAN Tr 180/99. Hired as boom gate vessel 1914.

ARACARI Tr 245/08. Hired as M/S 1914—19 and as water carrier 1.43. Grounded 3.10.43 north of Sicily.

ARAGON 9,588/05. Hired as base ship 9.1914—16.

ARAGONITE Tr 315/34. Hired as M/S 8.1939. Sunk 22.11.39 by mine off Deal.

ARALIA Tr 229/99. Hired 1918—19.

ARAWA 14,462/22, 7—6in, 2—3in. Hired as AMC 27.8.1939—41.

ARCADY Dr 85/10, 1—6pdr. Hired 12.1914—19.

ARCADY (ex-*Rival*) Dr 96/07. Hired as M/S 11.1939—6.45.

ARCHDALE Tug 119/96. Hired 9.1915—12.15.

ARCHIMEDES Dr 83/11. Hired 9.1915—19 and as BBV 6.40. Examination service 1942—12.44.

ARCTIC Barge, 145 x 26 ft. Hired as kite-balloon vessel 1.1916, purchased 5.16. Sold 14.1.20.

ARCTIC EXPLORER Tr 501/37, 1—4in. Hired as A/S Tr 8.1939, purchased 10.39. Sold 1945. (On loan USN 3.42—10.42.)

ARCTIC HUNTER Tr 356/29, 1—12pdr. Hired as M/S 8.1939—5.45.

ARCTIC PIONEER Tr 501/37, 1—4in. Purchased as A/S Tr 8.1939. Sunk 27.5.42 by unknown cause in the Portsmouth area. Raised 1947 and sold.

ARCTIC PRINCE Tr 194/15, 1—12pdr. Hired 1915—19.

ARCTIC RANGER Tr 493/37. Purchased as A/S Tr 8.1939. Sold 7.45.

ARCTIC TRAPPER Tr 352/28, 1—12pdr. Hired as A/P Tr 5.1940. Sunk 3.2.41 by air attack off Ramsgate.

ARCTIC WHALE (Z.15) Admiralty Wh, 'Z' class. Smiths Dk 7.10.1915. Sold 20.4.20, renamed *Bermudian*. (Served as BERMUDIAN, tug, in WW.II.)

ARCTURUS (ex-*Rio Tejo*) Tr 337/10, 1—3pdr. Portuguese, purchased 1915. Sold 17.5.19 Cruze Bros.

ARDENT II Tr 228/08, 1—6pdr. Hired 1915—19.

ARDENTE Tug. Italian, hired 7.1918—19.

ARDLAW Dr 94/09, 1—3pdr. Hired 1915—19.

ARETHUSA II Cstr 480/06. Hired as fleet messenger and store carrier 29.5.1915—26.4.20.

ARFON Tr 227/08. Hired as M/S 1914. Sunk 30.4.17 by mine off St Alban's Head.

ARGO Store carrier (RFA), 854/06, 1,250 tons, 198 x 30 ft. Purchased 19.12.1917. Sold circa 1939.

ARGO Tr 174/03. Hired 1918—19.

ARGO Dr 90/38. French M/S ARGO II, seized 3.7.1940 at Southampton. M/S 12.40—2.46.

ARGON Tr 226/07, 1—6pdr. Hired 1915—19.

ARGUS Lugger 8. Hired 1792—96.

ARGUS Lugger 14. Hired 1794. Captured 12.1798 by the French privateer VENDEMIARE.

ARGYLLSHIRE Tr 540/38. Purchased as A/S Tr 9.1939. Sunk 1.6.40 by E-boat torpedo off Dunkirk.

ARIADNE II Tr 225/06, 1—6pdr. Hired 1914—19.

ARIAN Tr 221/10, 1—6pdr. Hired as M/S 1916—19.

ARIANA Tr 285/02. Hired 1917—18.

ARIANE Yt 630/98, 1—12pdr, 2—6pdr. Hired as A/P Yt 23.2.1915—25.2.16.

ARIEL II Tr 174/05, 1—6pdr. Hired 1914—19.

ARIEL Cable ship 1,479/39. Hired 1940—46.

ARIES Yt 268/80, 2—3pdr. Hired as A/P Yt 12.9.1914. Sunk 31.10.15 by mine off Leathercoat.

ARIES II Tr 250/06, 1—6pdr. Hired 1914—19.

ARIES III Tr 159/99. Hired 1918—19.

ARIGUANI 6,746/26, 1—6in, 2—MG. Hired as OBV 10.1940. Catapult ship 1941—43.

ARIMATHEA Dr 87/07. Hired 1914—19.

ARISIO M/S fitting out in 6.1940. Not traced after.

ARISTEA Tr 261/35. Hired as M/S (SAN) 1.1940—12.44.

ARISTOCRAT Lugger 22. Hired 1794—98.

ARISTOCRAT Brig. Hired 1798—1801.

ARISTOCRAT (ex-*Talisman*) Paddle 544/35, 1—3in, 4—MG. Hired as A/A ship 8.1940. Ferry service 1945—46.

ARISTOCRAT Cstr 122/32. Hired (RCN) 1944—46.

ARKWRIGHT Tr 370/30, 1—12pdr. Hired as M/S 8.1939—12.45.

ARLANZA 15,044/12. Commissioned as AMC 23.3.1915. Returned 1.6.20.

ARLETTE Yt 80/02. Hired on examination service 1940–45.

ARLETTE II Yt 163/36. Purchased for examination service 1940. Sold 12.45.

ARLEY Tr 304/14, 1–12pdr. Hired 1914–19 and as M/S 8.39. Sank in tow after mine damage 3.2.45 in the North Sea.

ARLIEUX Tr (RCN), 357gr, 130 x 25 ft, 1–3in. Vickers, Montreal 1918. Boom gate vessel 1941. Sold 1946.

ARMADALE CASTLE 12,973/03, 8–4.7in. Hired as AMC 2.8.1914–11.9.19.

ARMAGEDDON Tr 323/15, 1–6pdr. Hired 1915–19.

ARMANA Tr 375/30, 1–12pdr. Hired as M/S 6.1940–11.45.

ARMENIER Cstr 914/19. French M/L seized 3.7.1940 at Milford Haven. Harbour service 1940, then target. Scuttled 4.45.

ARMENTIERS Tr (RCN) (as ARLIEUX). Vickers, Montreal 1918. Boom gate vessel 1941. Sold 1947, renamed *A.G. Garrish,* tug.

ARMOURER Cstr 724/88. Hired as store carrier (RFA) 17.3.1918–3.4.19.

ARNDALE Oiler (RFA) 17,210 tons, 464 x 62 ft. Swan Hunter 5.8.1937. Arrived 12.4.60 in Belgium to BU.

ARNDILLY CASTLE Dr 78/08, 1–3pdr. Hired 1914–19.

ARNO Cstr 745/94. Hired as ammo. carrier (RFA) 5.2.1915–28.6.17.

ARNOLD BENNETT Tr 374/30, 1–12pdr. Hired as A/P Tr 1939. M/S 1941–7.45.

AROHA Tr, 'Castle' type (RNZN). Stevenson & Cook, Port Chalmers 8.9.1942. Sold 1946 mercantile.

ARONIA Yt 193/29. Hired as M/S 11.1939. Became base ship MARTELLO to 1945.

A.ROSE Tr 208/24. Hired as danlayer 1940. M/S and renamed SIESTA 12.40. Renamed ADELPHI fuel carrier 5.44. Returned 1945.

ARPHA Yt. Hired as ABV 11.1939–1.46.

ARRAN Tr, 'Isles' class. Cook Welton & Gemmell 16.11.1940. Sold 2.10.46, renamed *Assan Reis.*

ARRAS Tr (RCN) (as ARLIEUX). Vickers, Montreal 1918. BU 12.57.

ARREST (see BUZZARD)

ARSENAL Tr 389/33. Purchased as A/S Tr 8.1939. Sunk 16.11.40 in collision with the Polish destroyer BURZA off the Clyde.

ARTEGAL (see HENRIETTE)

ARTHUR (ex-*Venus*) Cutter 6, 70bm, 6–3pdr. Hired 6.1803. Captured 19.1.1805 by the French in the·Mediterranean.

ARTHUR CAVANAGH Tr, 'Castle' type, 277gr. Bow McLachlan 1918. Sold 1920, same name. Hired as M/S 8.1939–46.

ARTHUR HERWIN Tr, 'Strath' type, 201gr. Fleming & Ferguson 9.12.1919. Sold 10.11.19, renamed *River Lossie.* (RIVER LOSSIE in WW.II).

ARTHUR H JOHNSTON Dr 99/13. Hired 1914—19.

ARTHUR LESSIMORE Tr, 'Castle' type, 276gr. Smiths Dk 9.3.1917. Sold 1919, renamed *Avanturine*. (Served as IRVANA in WW.II.)

ARTHUR ROSE Patrol vessel (RAN). In service 1942—45.

ARTOIS (see DIGBY)

ARUM Tr 194/26. Hired as M/S (SAN) 1.1940—10.44.

ARVONIAN 2,794/05, 3—4in, 3—12pdr, 4—TT. Hired as decoy ship 6.3.1915, purchased 20.11.17. Sold 3.19. (On loan USN 11.17—1.18 as SANTEE.)

ARY (ex-*Ary Scheffer*) Cstr 642/04. Commissioned as wreck-dispersal vessel 1.1943. To MWT 12.4.46.

ASAMA Tr 284/14. Sunk 16.7.1917 by U-boat while serving as decoy vessel.

ASAMA Tr 303/29, 1—12pdr. Hired as M/S 9.1939. Sunk 23.1.41 by air attack off Plymouth.

ASCANIA 14,043/25, 8—6in, 2—3in. Hired as AMC 9.1939—42.

ASCONA Dr 138/30. Hired as M/S 9.1939—11.45.

ASH M/S Tr 530 tons, 150 x 27½ ft, 1—12pdr. Cochrane 13.11.1939. Sunk 5.6.41 by mine in the Thames estuary.

ASH LAKE Motor M/S (RCN) 255 tons, 126 x 26 ft. Midland Bt Wks. Cancelled 22.10.1945 and completed mercantile.

ASHLEAF (ex-OLGA renamed 1916) Oiler (RFA), 5,768gr. Ropner 12.9.1916. Sunk 29.5.17 by U-boat off Bishops Rock.

ASHLYN Tr 304/14, 1—6pdr. Hired 1914—19.

ASHTON Tr 144/96, 1—6pdr. Hired as M/S 1914—19.

ASH TREE 1,579/09. Hired as store carrier (RFA) 9.1916—19.

ASIA Tr 309/05. Hired as M/S 1914. Sunk 12.9.17 by mine off Bressay.

ASIA A.merchant, 4—4in. Russian, seized and commissioned 10.1918. Transferred 28.7.19 to 'White' Russians.

ASIE Tr 551/14. French A/P Tr seized 3.7.1940 at Portsmouth. A/S Tr 9.40—4.46.

ASP DY tank vessel 330 tons, 115 x 21 ft. Green, Blackwall 15.10.1890. On sale list 1.47.

ASPASIA Tr 342/16, 1—12pdr. Hired 1916—19.

A SPENCE MACDONALD Tr 195/11. Hired 1915—19.

ASPENLEAF (see SAXOL)

ASPIRANT Dr 81/08, 1—6pdr. Hired 1915—19.

ASPIRANT Rescue tug, 'B.A.T' class. Levingston SB, Orange NJ 10.10.1942 and to the RN 3.5.43 on lend-lease. Returned 1946 to the USN.

ASPIRE Dr 87/07, 1—6pdr. Hired 1.1915—19.

ASSEGAI Yt 82/76. Purchased 1915. Sold 2.11.21.

ASSIDUOUS Rescue tug 700 tons, 142½ x 33 ft, 1—3in. Cochrane 4.6.1943. DY tug 1946. Sold 9.58.

ASSISTANCE (see SALVESTOR)

ASSURANCE DY tug 300 tons, 110 x 22 ft. Bow McLachlan 18.12.1899. Sold 31.1.23 Carriden S Bkg Co.

ASSURANCE Rescue tug 700 tons, 142½ x 33 ft, 1–3in. Cochrane 23.5.1940. Wrecked 18.10.41 in Lough Foyle.

ASTER Yt 249/83, 2–3pdr. Hired as A/P Yt 25.9.1914–5.10.16.

ASTERIA Cstr 493/91. Commissioned as store carrier (RFA) 20.7.1915. Sold 22.1.21.

ASTON VILLA Tr 546/37, 1–4in. Hired as A/S Tr 9.1939. Sunk 3.5.40 by air attack off Norway.

ASTRAL Admiralty wood Dr, 100gr. Chambers 1918. Sold 6.10.21 and foundered 10.21.

ASTRAL Pilot 451/30. Belgian, hired as BBV 6.1940. Wreck location 1.44–45.

ASTRONOMER 8,401/17. Hired as boom carrier 1939. Sunk 2.6.40 by U-boat off Kinnairds Head.

ASTROS 275/17. Hired as BDV 12.1939–46.

ASTRUM SPEI Dr 84/14. Hired 1914. Sunk 9.7.16 by an Austrian cruiser in the Otranto Strait.

ASTURIAN 3,193/90. Hired as store carrier (RFA) 28.5.1918–2.12.18.

ASTURIAS 22,048/25, 8–6in, 2–3in. Hired as AMC 8.1939. Damaged and laid up 7.43. To MWT 30.5.44.

ATALANTA Yt 1,398/03, 2–3in. Hired as A/P Yt 5.6.1915–21.2.19.

ATALANTA II 486/06, 2–6pdr. Hired as M/S 3.12.1915–26.6.19 and as netlayer 1940–24.4.45.

ATALANTA III Tug 577/07. Hired as rescue tug 21.2.1915–19.

ATALANTA MFV 24/35. Hired on ferry service 1939. Renamed OPTIMIST 7.41. Returned 1945.

ATHELSTAN Tr 202/11, 1–6pdr. Hired as M/S 1914–19 and as A/P Tr 11.39–1.40.

ATHENE A/C transport 10,330 tons, 457 x 63 ft, 2–4in, 12–20mm, 40–A/C. Greenock DY Co. 1.10.1940. Sold 1945, renamed *Clan Brodie.*

ATHENIAN Tr 218/19. Hired as A/P Tr 11.1939. M/S 6.40. Fuel carrier 3.44–9.46.

ATHENS Cutter 10, 50bm. Hired 1804–05.

ATHLETE Tug 119/93. Hired 9.1915–6.16.

ATHLETE Rescue tug, 'B.A.T' class. Levingston 18.5.1943 on lend-lease. Sunk 17.7.45 by mine off Leghorn.

ATLANTA Dr 60/03. Hired as boom tender 5.1915–19.

ATLANTIC Tr 166/98. Hired 1917–19.

ATLANTIC GUIDE 1,943/24. Purchased 9.1939. Sunk 27.5.40 as blockship at Zeebrugge.

ATLANTIC SALVOR Salvage vessel 1,360 tons, 200 x 39 ft, 2–40mm, 4–20mm. Basalt Rock Co, California 24.10.1942 for lend-lease but retained by the USN as CLAMP.

L'ATLANTIQUE Tr 659/20. French A/P Tr seized 3.7.1940 at Plymouth. A/S Tr 8.40–45.

ATLAS DY tug 165 tons, 86 x 19 ft. Fleming & Ferguson 18.6.1895. Sold 1909, same name.

ATLAS DY tug 615 tons, 145 x 29 ft. Chatham DY 2.9.1909. Sold 19.5.58.

ATLAS Tug 84/72. Hired on harbour service 1.1915–7.15.

ATLASI Skid-towing M/S in service 12.1941–45.

ATMAH Yt 1,746/98. Purchased as target Yt 7.1940. Accommodation ship 1943. Sold 1946.

ATMOSPHERE Admiralty wood Dr, 101gr. Chambers 1918. Sold 2.8.21, same name.

ATMOSPHERE (see GOS.2)

ATREUS 6,645/11, 1–12pdr, 4–20mm, 192 mines. Hired as M/L 1939–45.

ATTENDANT Oiler (RFA) 1,935 tons, 200 x 34 ft. Chatham DY 5.7.1913. Sold 1934.

ATTENDANT Yt 357/13. Loss reported 11.1943.

ATTENTIF Rescue tug 672 tons. French navy tug seized 7.1940. Returned 7.45.

AUCHMEDDEN Dr 82/14. Hired 1914–19.

AUCKLAND Tr 155/99, 1–6pdr. Hired as M/S 10.14–19.

AUCUBA Tr 211/06. Hired as BDV 1915–19.

AUDREY Paddle 196/97. Purchased for ferry service 1915. Sold 7.22 New Medway SP Co.

AUDREY Tr 186/06. Hired 1917–19.

AUDREY DY tug, 40gr, 57 x 17 ft. Harris, Appledore 5.4.1961.

AU FAIT Dr 83/09. Hired 1915. Captured 25.4.16 by German destroyers off Zeebrugge.

AUK Tr 168/03, 1–6pdr. Hired as M/S 1914, renamed ANTIC 1917–19.

AUK Tr 183/01, 1–3pdr. Hired as BDV 1915–19.

AULD LANG SYNE Dr 75/06. Hired 1915–19.

AURANIA 13,984/24, 8–6in, 2–3in. Hired as AMC 8.1939. Renamed ARTIFEX repair ship 11.42 and purchased. Sold 28.12.60 to Italian shipbreakers.

AUREA Tr 270/17, 1–12pdr. Hired 1917–19.

AU RETOUR Dr 73/06. Hired 1915–19.

AURILIA Dr 87/14. Hired as M/S 11.1939. A/P Dr 9.40–45.

AURORA II Tr 225/06, 1–6pdr. Hired 1914–19.

AURORA Dr 74/06. Hired as boom tender 5.1915–19 and as M/S AURORA II in 1940. Sunk 24.5.41 by air attack at Tobruk.

AUSONIA 13,912/21, 8–6in, 2–3in. Hired as AMC 9.1939. Purchased and completed as repair ship 4.44. BU 9.65 in Spain.

AUSTRALIA Tr 238/82, 1–6pdr. Hired as BDV 1915–19.

AUSTRALIA Barge 175 tons. Purchased as BBV 29.4.1942. Sold 9.11.45.

AVAILABLE Dr 102/12. Hired on harbour service 11.1939–1.46.

AVALANCHE Admiralty wood Dr, 100gr. Chambers 1918. Sold 1930, renamed *Loch Alsh.*

AVALANCHE (see BALMORAL)

AVALON (see NORDHAV.I)

AVALON (ex-*Georgian*) 2,484/10. Hired as base ship (RCN) 1941, purchased 5.42. Laid up 3.46 and later sold.

AVANTURINE (ex-*Mendip*) Tr 412/34. Hired as A/S Tr 8.1939, purchased 11.39. Renamed SPHENE 2.40. For disposal 4.45.

AVANTURINE Tr 296/30, 1–12pdr. Hired as A/P Tr 2.1940. M/S 1941. Sunk 1.12.43 by E-boat torpedo off Beachy Head.

AVE MARIA Dr. Hired as HDPC 10.1939–4.46.

AVENGER (ex-*Aetearoa*) 15,000/14. Hired as AMC 14.12.1915. Sunk 14.6.17 by 'U.155' west of Gibraltar.

AVERSE Water carrier. French naval vessel seized 3.7.1940 at Southampton. Returned 1945.

AVIATOR Cstr 435/07. Hired as store carrier (RFA) 16.10.1914–21.1.19.

AVOCA (ex-*Avon*) 11,073/07, 8–6in, 2–6pdr. Commissioned as AMC 14.1.1916. Returned 29.10.19.

AVOCET 1,408/00. Hired as fleet auxiliary 25.1.1917. Returned 31.1.17 as unsuitable.

AVOLA Tr 255/13. Hired as M/S 8.1939–4.46.

AVON II Tr 250/07, 1–12pdr. Hired 1914–19 and as AVON A/P Tr, 1–6pdr, 5.40–12.41.

AVONDALE Dr 80/11. Hired 1914. Sunk 15.5.17 by an Austrian cruiser in the Otranto Strait.

AVONDEE Tr 202/18. Hired as fuel carrier 3.1944–10.44.

AVONGLEN Tr 275/17. Hired on examination service 8.1940. Hospital tender 1942–8.46.

AVONMOUTH Tr 139/90. Hired 1917–19.

AVON STREAM Tr 249/15. Hired as M/S 9.1939–7.45.

AVONTOWN 1,743/99. Hired as ammo. carrier (RFA) 11.2.1916–19.

AVON WATER Tr 260/30. Hired as BDV 9.1939–45.

AWANUI Cstr 170/07. Hired on examination service (RNZN) 1941–44.

AWATERE Tr, 'Castle' type (RNZN). Patent Slip Co, Wellington 26.9.1942. Sold 1946, same name.

AYACANORA Tr 147/94. Hired 1917–19.

AYRSHIRE Tr 540/38, 1–4in. Hired as A/S Tr 9.1939–10.45.

AZANIA Hired as M/S 5.1941–44.

AZARA Yt 33/36. Purchased as HDPC 10.1939. Sold 2.46.
AZARAEL Dr 94/07, 1—6pdr. Hired 1915—19.
AZUR Yt 136/29. Purchased as HDPC 11.1939. Sold 4.46.

BABIANA Tr (SAN), 262/35. Hired as M/S 9.1939—12.44.
BACCHANTE II Yt 973/91, 2—12pdr. French, hired 1.2.1915—25.2.16.
BACCHUS Store carrier (RFA) 4,000 tons, 295 x 44 ft. Hamilton 10.5.1915, purchased on stocks 22.3.15. Renamed BACCHUS II in 5.36; damaged as bombing target 11.38 and sunk 15.11.38 by gunfire of DUNEDIN 10 mls off Alderney.
BACCHUS Store carrier (RFA) 5,150 tons, 320 x 49 ft. Caledon 15.7.1936. Sold 1962, renamed *Pulau Bali.*
BACCHUS Store carrier (RFA) 7,960 tons, 350 x 55 ft. Robb 4.6.1962.
BACHAQUERO 4,890/37, 365 x 64 ft, 2—4in, 6—20mm. Converted 1941 as tank landing ship. Returned 1945.
BACKWASH Admiralty wood Dr, 99gr. Colby 1917. Sold 4.8.21, same name. (Served as MORVEN HILL in WW.II.)
BADEN POWELL Dr 93/00, 1—3pdr. Hired 1915—19.
BADEN POWELL II Tr hired 1917—19.
BADGER Cutter, 107bm. Hired 16.11.1812—13.5.1814.
BADGER (ex-schooner *Westward*) 1,686/20. Purchased 1939 as base ship. Paid off 10.46, sold 1949, renamed *African Queen.*
BADINAGE (see SABREUR)
BADORA Cstr 279/14. Hired as A/P vessel (RIN) 1939—44.
BAFFIN Tr, 'Isles' class. Collingwood SY 13.4.1942. Lent RCN to 20.8.45. Sold 1947, same name.
BAHAWALPUR (see BARODA)
BAHRAM Dr 72/24. Hired as HDPC 1940. Sunk 3.4.41 by mine off the Humber.
BAIA Tug 181/12. Italian, captured 1941. Lost in tow 3.11.42 off E.Africa.
BALAENA (Z.2) Admiralty whaler, 'Z' class. Smiths Dk 29.5.1915. Sold 20.4.20 A.J.Ashwin.
BALDUR (see ST CLAIR)
BALDUR (see SOUTHERN ISLES)
BALEINE M/S (RCN), 1—3pdr. Hired 1915—19.
BALFOUR Tr 285/12, 1—3pdr. Hired 1915. Sunk 13.5.18 in collision off the R.Sovereign light vessel.
BALGOWNIE Tr 185/02. Hired 1917—19.
BALISE (see VAILLANT)
BALLISTA Naval armament store carrier, 122gr. Yarwood, Northwich 6.10.1939.

BALMEDIE Tr 205/06. Hired 1914. Sunk 27.4.15 in collision off the Dardanelles.

BALMORAL Paddle 471/00, 1–6pdr. Hired as M/S 15.5.1915–11.6.19 and as A/A ship, 2–2pdr, 1940. Harbour service 1943–46.

BALMORAL Tr 222/16, 1–6pdr. Hired 1916–19 as M/S and as A/P vessel 11.39. Renamed AVALANCHE 6.40 as M/S. BBV 1944. Returned 1945.

BALMORAL CASTLE Tr hired as BDV 1915–19.

BALMORE 1,925/20. Hired as degaussing ship 1940. Sunk 11.11.40 by air attack in the Atlantic.

BALNA Tug 88/29. Hired as DY tug 1942–46.

BALTA Tr, 'Isles' class. Cook Welton & Gemmell 2.12.1940. Sold 12.7.46, renamed *Ching Hai.*

BALTAVIA 2,592/24. Commissioned 14.11.1939 as store carrier. Returned 1945.

BANDIT Fleet tug 840 tons, 165 x 32 ft, 1–3in, 1–20mm. Fleming & Ferguson 15.2.1938. Renamed BRITON 1947. Sold 1960.

BANDOLERO Tr 440/35. Purchased as A/S Tr 8.1939. Sunk 30.12.40 in collision with the destroyer WATERHEN off Sollum.

BANGALOW Cstr 632/39. Hired as repair ship (RAN) 1942–46.

BAN HONG LIONG Cstr 1,671/08. Hired as A/P vessel 1940–43.

BANKA Cstr 623/14. Hired as M/S 1940. Sunk 10.12.41 by unknown cause off the east coast of Malaya.

BANKVILLE Cstr 339/04. Hired as cable vessel 1942–45.

BANKWOOD (ex-*Malaya*) Yt 39/34. Hired as HDPC 1939–45.

BANN DY tank vessel 250 tons. Queenstown 19.1.1886. Sold 20.2.1908 in Jamaica.

BANN Tug 35/31. Hired for harbour service 1941–44.

BANNERET (ex-*Verbena*) Dr. Hired for harbour service 1941–45.

BANNU Tr (RIN), 'Basset' class. Shalimar D & E Co. Suspended 10.1944, cancelled 3.45.

BANSHEE Dr 49/98. Hired for harbour service 1915–19.

BANSHEE (ex-*Lord Suffolk*) Dr 115/29. Hired as M/S 11.1939–1.46.

BANTAM DY tug, 67gr, 75 x 15 ft. H.Scarr, Hessle. Completed 1920 as FAVOROLLE. Sold 22.2.21 F.T.Everard.

BAN WHATT HIN Tug (RIM), 352/85. Hired 8.1917–12.18.

BANYERS Tr 448/14. Hired 1914. Sunk 6.1.15 by mine off Scarborough.

'Bar' class boom defence vessels 730 tons, 150 x 32 ft 1–3in. 74 ordered for the RN including two cancelled, and four built for the RAN:

BARBAIN Blyth 8.1.1940.

BARBARIAN Blyth 21.10.37. Sold 27.2.46 Turkish navy.

BARBASTEL Philip 26.7.45. BU 2.65 at Haulbowline.

BARBECUE Ardrossan 19.12.44.

BARBERRY Ferguson 11.2.43. To sale list 1958.

BARBETTE Blyth 15.12.37. Sold 3.41 Turkish navy.

BARBETTE Simons 18.6.43. BU 10.65 in Belgium.

BARBICAN Blyth 14.3.38. BU 1968 Inverkeithing.

BARBOUR Blyth 9.4.41. Arrived 30.4.52 McLellan, Bo'ness to BU.

BARBOURNE Simons 4.5.42. Arrived 1.4.64 Ward, Briton Ferry to BU.

BARBRAKE Simons 29.6.42. Renamed FLEUR (SAN) 1951.

BARBRIDGE Lobnitz 8.8.41. Arrived 6.11.64 Ward, Inverkeithing to BU.

BARBROOK Blyth 28.5.38. To sale list 1958.

BARCAROLE Ardrossan 14.3.45.

BARCASTLE Blyth 28.7.38. To sale list 1962.

BARCLIFF (ex-BARWICK renamed 1940) Lobnitz 10.5.40. Arrived 13.10.67 at Antwerp to BU.

BARCLOSE Blyth 9.7.41. Arrived 8.8.62 Arnott Young, Dalmuir to BU.

BARCOCK Blyth 3.9.41. Lent Belgian navy 17.9.46—49; sold 21.6.62 Pounds, Portsmouth.

BARCOMBE Goole SB 28.7.38. Grounded 13.1.58 and not listed after 10.58.

BARCONIA Hill. Ordered 1941 and cancelled.

BARCOTE Blyth 8.2.40. Arrived 4.63 in Holland to BU.

BARCROFT Goole SB 24.9.38. Sold 21.6.62 Pounds, Portsmouth.

BARCROSS Blyth 21.10.41. Renamed SOMERSET (SAN) 1951.

BARDELL Blyth 12.1.42. Sold 1950 at Freetown.

BARDOLF Blyth 14.4.42. Arrived 10.1.64 at New Waterway to BU.

BARFAIR Lewis 21.5.38. Sold 27.2.46 Turkish navy.

BARFIELD Lewis 28.7.38.

BARFLAKE Philip 18.4.42. Sunk 22.11.43 by mine off Naples.

BARFOAM Simons 8.9.41.

BARFOIL Philip 18.7.42.

BARFOOT Lewis 25.9.42. Floating laboratory 1949.

BARFORD Simons 21.9.41.

BARFOSS Simons 17.2.42. On sale list 10.68.

BARFOUNT Simons 5.1.42. Arrived 19.8.64 at New Waterway to BU.

BARGLOW Lewis 9.11.42.

BARHILL Ferguson 26.11.42.

BARHOLM Ardrossan 31.12.42. Sold 9.62 Messrs Loti, Spezia.

BARILLA Lewis 7.1.43. Sold 23.7.58.

BARITONE Philip 3.3.45. To sale list 1958.

BARKING Lobnitz 25.9.41.

BARKIS Ferguson 29.3.45. Arrived 28.2.64 Ward, Inverkeithing to BU.

BARLAKE Blyth 10.9.40. To sale list 1962.

BARLANE Lobnitz 27.6.38. To sale list 1958.

BARLEYCORN Lewis 6.3.43. Arrived 18.12.64 Ward, Inverkeithing to BU.

BARLIGHT Lobnitz 10.9.38. Scuttled 19.12.41 at Hong Kong; raised by the Japanese 9.42 and commissioned 20.9.42 as netlayer 101; sunk 15.6.44 at Saipan.

BARLOW Simons 26.8.38. To sale list 1958.

BARMILL Blyth 16.10.40. To sale list 1958.

BARMOND Simons 24.12.42.

BARMOUTH Simons 11.10.38. Sold 8.64 Risdon Beazley, Southampton.

BARNABY Simons 8.3.43. Arrived 12.8.64 J.A.White St Davids (not BU).

BARNARD Lewis 1.7.42.

BARNDALE Lobnitz 30.11.39.

BARNEATH Lewis 17.8.42. To sale list 1958.

BARNEHURST Blyth 21.10.39. Arrived 12.10.64 Smith & Houston to BU.

BARNESS Not ordered. Cancelled 6.41.

BARNSTONE Blyth 25.11.39.

BARNWELL Lobnitz 13.2.40.

BARON Philip 11.4.44. Sold 8.57 Colombo Port Commissioners.

BARONIA Hill 21.4.41. Sold 11.2.59 at Singapore.

BAROVA Hill 5.7.41. Arrived 19.8.64 at New Waterway to BU.

BARRAGE Hall Russell 2.12.37.

BARRANCA Hall Russell 18.1.38. Arrived 5.8.64 Smith & Houston to BU.

BARRHEAD Simons 17.10.40. Sold 1964 S.Bldg Ind, Faslane.

BARRICADE (ex-EBGATE renamed 1937) Hill 7.2.38. Arrived 30.5.52 McLellan, Bo'ness to BU.

BARRIER (ex-BARGATE renamed 1937) Hill 17.5.38. To sale list 1962.

BARRINGTON Simons 15.11.40.

BARRYMORE Simons 13.2.41. To sale list 1952.

BARSING Simons 31.3.41. Sold 4.6.62 Westminster Dredging Co.

BARSOUND Simons 25.5.41. Arrived 5.1.64 at New Waterway to BU.

BARSPEAR Ferguson 25.5.43. Sold 9.62 Messrs Loti, Spezia.

BARSTOKE Simons 9.7.41. Sold 15.8.60 at Singapore.

BARTHORPE Lobnitz 22.3.40. Arrived 4.63 in Holland to BU.

BARTIZAN Ardrossan 20.5.43.

BARWIND Ferguson 22.9.42. Arrived 26.3.64 Ward, Briton Ferry to BU.

(See also KANGAROO, KARANGI, KIMBLA and KOALA)

BARALONG 4,192/01. Hired as supply ship 2.8.1914; served 1915 as decoy ship, 3–12pdr; renamed WYANDRA 9.15. Returned 1916.

BARBADOS Tr 211/05, 1–6pdr. Hired 1914–19 and as A/P vessel 11.39–1.40.

BARBADOS Tr. Hired as boom gate vessel 1915–19.

BARBARA DY tug, 40gr, 57 x 17 ft. Duston, Thorne 8.3.1963.

BARBARA COWIE Dr 82/09, 1—3pdr. Hired 1915—19.

BARBARA ROBB Tr 263/30. Hired as BDV 9.1939—12.44.

BARBARA ROBERTSON Tr 325/19. Hired as M/S 1939. Sunk 23.12.39 by U-boat gunfire north of the Hebrides.

BARBE AUGUSTE Dr 42/33. French M/S seized 3.7.1940 at Southampton M/L tender 1941—45.

BARDSEY Tr, 'Isles' class. Fleming & Ferguson 17.7.1943. Oil tank cleaning vessel 1950.

BAREILLY Tr (RIN), 'Basset' class. Shalimar. Suspended 12.1944, cancelled 3.45.

BARISAL (ex-SHOLAPUR renamed 1944) Tr (RIN), 'Basset' class. Burn, Calcutta. Suspended 10.1944, cancelled 3.45.

BARKERVILLE Harbour tug (RCN). Owen Sound, Canada 1944.

BARKOL (ex-PLA hopper No 3) Oiler (RFA), 704/98. Hired 1916—20.

BARLE Tr 283/14, 1—6pdr. Hired 1915—19.

BARLEY STALK Dr, 1—6pdr. Hired 1917—19.

BARNARD BOYLE Tr, 'Strath' type 203gr. Hall Russell 13.6.1918. Sold 3.11.21, renamed *Dulcibelle*. (Served as DULCIBELLE in WW.II.)

BARNARDO Dr 77/09, 1—3pdr. Hired 1915—19.

BARNET (ex-*Earl Haig* 324/19) Boom trawler 423 tons, 1—3in. Purchased 1933. Sold 1947.

BARNSLEY Tr 144/96. Hired 1915—15.

BARNSNESS Tr 173/07. Hired as BBV 2.1940; fuel carrier 1944. Returned 12.44.

BARODA Tr (RIN), 'Basset' class. Shalimar 22.10.1941. Renamed BAHAWALPUR (RPN) 1948; sold 22.1.59.

BARON ARDROSSAN 4,319/05. Store carrier hired 11.8.1914—18.8.16.

BARON HERRIES 1,610/07. Store carrier hired 15.8.1914. Sunk 22.4.18 by U-boat, 43 mls off Bishop Rock.

BARON ROSE Aux.schooner 529/81, 4—4.1in, 2—12pdr. Hired as decoy vessel 9.4.1918—1.19.

BARON RUZETTE Tr 214/10. Belgian hired 1917—19.

BARRA Yt 73/24. Hired as HDPC 5.1940—45.

BARRACUDA (ex-*Heinrich Jessen*) 3,335/40. Danish, hired as base ship (RIN) 1940—44.

BARRANCA 4,115/06, 1—4in, 2—12pdr. Commissioned as decoy ship (Q.3) 6.1916—5.17. (Also served as ECHUNGA.)

BARROWBY Wh 176/12. Hired 1.1.1915—19.

BARRY Paddle 398/07, Hired as M/S 29.6.1915; renamed BARRY-FIELD 1917; returned 20.11.19. (Served as SNAEFELL in WW.II.)

BARWICK Tug 418/19. American, commissioned as rescue tug1.1944, renamed BEHEST 3.44, returned 1946.

BARTONIA Dr 82/08, 1—3pdr. Hired 1916—19.

BASIL GEORGES MFV. Belgian, hired as BBV 6.1940—45.

BASSANIO Tr 268/04, 1—13pdr. Hired 1914—19.

BASSET A/S trawler 461 tons, 150 x 27½ ft, 1—4in. Robb 28.9.1935.
Sold 15.9.47, renamed *Radford.*

BASSET (see BEAGLE)

BASS ROCK Tr 169/07. Hired 1914—19.

BASTION (see BOSTONIAN)

BASUTO Tr 402/32. Hired as BDV 1.1940—11.45.

BAT DY store carrier, 75bm, 54 x 18 ft. Chatham DY 4.4.1836. Sold
26.4.1890. (Also R.Clarence YC.1.)

BAT DY tug. Hired 1943—46.

BATAVIER II 1,573/20. Dutch, hired as accommodation ship 1940—
46.

BATTENHALL 2,380/01. Hired as store carrier (RFA) 8.1914—12.14.

BATTERSOL (ex-PLA hopper 4) 704/98. Hired as oiler (RFA) 16.11.1916—
20.

BATTLEAXE (ex-Russian T.16) M/S Tr, 292gr, 130 x 23½ ft, 1—12pdr.
Smiths Dk 19.6.1916, commissioned 1918. Renamed DEE 1920. Sold
1946, renamed *Safir.*

BAY M/S Tr 505 tons, 150 x 27½ ft, 1—12pdr. Cochrane 12.12.1939.
Sold 1947, same name.

BAYANO 5,948/13, 2—6in. Hired as AMC 21.11.1914. Sunk 11.3.15
by 'U.27' off Corsewell Point, Clyde.

BAYANO 6,815/17, 4—6in, 2—4in. Hired as escort ship 9.1917—3.19.

BAYARD 220/08. Hired as decoy vessel 1917 (Q.20). Sunk 29.6.17 in
collision in the Channel.

BAYARD Tr 231/08. French, hired 1917—18.

BAY INNAUNG Tr, 'Basset' type. Irrawadi Flotilla Co, Rangoon. Laid
down 8.1941. Destroyed on stocks 3.42.

BAY LEAF (ex-BAYOL renamed 1919) Oiler 8,455gr. Sold 1919, renamed *Pyrula.*

BAY LEAF (ex-*London Integrity*) Oiler, 12,123/55. Purchased 1959.

BAYOL (ex-dummy QUEEN MARY renamed 1915, ex-*Cevic*) Oiler,
8,455/94, 500 x 60 ft. Renamed BAY LEAF 1919. Sold 1919, renamed *Pyrula.*

BAYONET (ex-BARNHURST renamed 1938) BDV 530 tons, 135 x
30½ ft, 1—3in. Blyth DD 16.3.1939. Sunk 21.12.39 by mine in the
Firth of Forth.

BAYONNE (see CH.II)

B.C.LADY MFV 77/39 M/S (RCN). Hired 1941—45.

BD/BV class boom defence and barrage vessels (dumb). BD series, 300
tons, 95 x 25 ft, 1—12pdr (boom defence) BV series, 275 tons, 95 x
25 ft, 2—12pdr (Dover barrage)

BV.1 Workman Clark 12.11.1917. Gate vessel 1941; laid up 1944.

BV.2 Workman Clark 12.11.17. Gate vessel 1941, laid up 1944.

BD.3 Workman Clark 1918. Sold 6.24 J.Jackson.

BV.4 Workman Clark 28.11.17. Renamed SANDGATE 30.6.33; scuttled 13.2.47 in deep water off Singapore.

BV.5 Workman Clark 12.11.17. Renamed PARKGATE 30.6.33; BV.5 1940; laid up 1944.

BV.6 Workman Clark 1917. Sold 28.6.27 Ward.

BV.7 Workman Clark 12.11.17. Renamed POLEGATE 30.6.33; BV.7 1940, A/A vessel; to sale list 1945.

BV.8 Workman Clark 12.11.17. Renamed SOUTHGATE 30.6.33. Sold 1946 at Singapore.

BV.9 Workman Clark 1917. Gate vessel 1941; laid up 1919. Sold 8.4.42 Ward.

BV.10 Workman Clark 1917. Gate vessel 1941–45.

BD.11 Chambers, Glasgow 1917. Sold 5.23 Ward.

BD.12 Chambers 16.11.17. Sold with BD.11.

BD.13 Chambers 13.12.17. Sold with BD.11.

BD.14 Chambers 12.4.18. Sold with BD.11.

BD.15 Scott & Co 15.11.17. Sold with BD.11.

BD.16 Scott & Co 10.12.17. Sold with BD.11.

BV.17 A.W.Robertson 14.3.18. Renamed WESTGATE 1937, gate vessel. Sold 6.8.46 at Malta.

BV.18 A.W.Robertson 12.4.18. Gate vessel 1941. Sold 28.4.47.

BD.19 Manchester DD Co 17.11.17. Sold 5.23 Ward.

BD.20 Manchester DD Co 1917. Sold with BD.19.

BD.21 Manchester DD Co 1917. Sold with BD.19.

BD.22 Manchester DD Co 1918. Sold 5.23 McLellan.

BD.23 Day Summers, Southampton 28.11.17. Sold 9.4.23 J. McWilliam.

BD.24 Day Summers 1917. Sold with BD.23.

BD.25 Day Summers 1918. Sold with BD.23.

BD.26 Day Summers 1918. Sold with BD.23.

BD.27 Thornycroft 13.4.18. Sold with BD.23.

BD.28 Thornycroft 1918. Sold with BD.23.

BD.29 Warren, Hull 1918. Sold with BD.23.

BD.30 Warren 1918. Renamed REIGATE 30.6.33 gate vessel. Sold 1958.

BV.31 Workman Clark 19.4.18. Sold 6.24 Ward.

BD.32 Workman Clark 23.5.18. Sold 5.23 McLellan.

BD.33 Workman Clark 23.5.18. Sold 5.23 McLellan.

BD.34 Workman Clark 25.5.18. Sold 6.24 J.Jackson.

BD.35 Workman Clark 28.5.18. Sold with BD.32.

BD.36 Workman Clark 28.5.18. Sold with BD.32.

BD.37 Manchester DD 1918. Sold with BD.32.

BD.38 Manchester DD 1918. Sold 9.4.23 Metals & Accessories Ltd.

BD.39 Glasgow 1918. Sold with BD.32.

BD.40 Glasgow 1918. Fate unknown.

BV.41 A.W.Robertson 6.9.18. Gate vessel 1941. Sold 10.10.47.

BV.42 A.W.Robertson 22.10.18. Gate vessel 1941; lost 22.12.43 by explosion in Leith docks.

BD.43 Chepstow 1918. Sold 9.4.23 J.McWilliam.

BD.44 Chepstow 1918. Fate unknown.

BD.45 Camper & Nicholson 1918. Sold 9.4.23 J.McWilliam.

BD.46 Camper & Nicholson 1.10.18. Renamed ROGATE 30.6.33, gate vessel. Sold 7.47 to BU.

BD.47 Chepstow 1918. Sold 9.4.23 J.McWilliam.

BD.48 Chepstow 1918. Sold 9.4.23 Metals & Accessories.

BD.49 Manchester DD 1918. Sold 9.4.23 J.McWilliam.

BD.50 Manchester DD 1918. Sold 5.23 E.Suren.

BD.51 Glasgow 1918. Sold 5.23 McLellan.

BD.52 Glasgow 1918. Sold 5.23 McLellan.

(the following eight vessels all believed cancelled:)

BD.53, 54 both Warren, Hull.

BD.55, 56 both Chepstow.

BD.57–60 all Glasgow.

BEACON STAR Dr 99/11 Hired for harbour service 5.8.1915–19.

BEAGLE DY tug 170 tons, 85 x 25 ft. Dunston, Hessle 25.2.1963. Renamed BASSET 8.67.

BEATHWOOD Tr 209/12. Hired as A/P Tr 12.39–40.

BEATRICE Tr 239/07, 1–6pdr. Hired 1914–19.

BEATRICE II Tr 173/06, 1–3pdr. Hired 1914–19.

BEATRICE III Dr 62/05. Hired 1915–19.

BEATRIX ADRIENNE MFV. Belgian, hired as A/P vessel 1940; laid up 1942–45.

BEAULIEU Tug 58/01. Hired as BDV 7.1914–19.

BEAULIEU Tender, 70gr, 75 x 18 ft. Doig, Grimsby 20.9.1963.

BEAULNE VERNEUIL Tr 268/18. French M/S seized 3.7.1940 at Plymouth. Gate vessel 1940; returned 30.3.46.

BEAULY 1,061/24. Hired 1939, commissioned 6.10.39 as decoy vessel LOOE; to MWT 20.6.41.

BEAUMARIS CASTLE Tr 275/17. Hired as M/S 2.1940–11.45.

BEAUMONT (ex-*Rose*) Cutter 10, 105bm. Hired 4.3.1804–5.3.1805.

BEAVER Gunvessel hired 30.9.1801–12.01.

BEAVER Tug 154/-. Hired 10.1914, purchased 1918. Sold 2.23.

BEAVER (ex-*Energy*) Dr 79/06. Commissioned as base ship 1939. Renamed ROYAL CHARTER 1940. Returned 1945.

BEAVER (94/22?) Commissioned as M/S 1942. Lost 5.4.42 off Ceylon.

BEAVER (ex-*Aztec*) Yt 890/02. American, commissioned 1.4.1941 (RCN). Returned 1945.

BEAVERTON Tug (RCN) 462 tons, 104 x 28 ft. Toronto 1944. Sunk 1947 in collision in the St Lawrence.

BECHEVILLE 4,228/24. Purchased 1944. Sunk 9.6.44 as blockship.

BEDDGELERT Tender, 70gr, 75 x 18 ft. Doig, Grimsby 13.11.1963.

BEDENHAM Store carrier, 1,192gr, 215 x 37½ ft. Ailsa, Troon 26.9.1938. Blown up 27.4.51 by accident at Gibraltar; wreck sold 24.6.52.

BEDFORDSHIRE Tr 443/35, 1–4in. Purchased as A/S Tr 8.1939. Lent USN 3.42; sunk 11.5.42 by U-boat off Cape Lookout, N.Carolina.

BEDLINGTON (see TERJE 3)

BEDOUIN Tr 188/02. Hired 1914. Sunk 13.2.15 by mine off Tory Island.

BEE (see THAMES)

BEECH (ex-*Lord Dawson*) M/S Tr 540/29. Purchased 2.1939. Sunk 22.6.41 by air attack north of Scotland.

BEECH LAKE Motor M/S (RCN) 255 tons, 126 x 26 ft. Vancouver SY 31.5.1945. To Russian navy 5.2.46.

BEECHLEAF Oiler (RFA), 5,861gr. Richardson Duck 26.10.1916. Sold 1919.

BEGA Tr 318/14. Hired 1914. Sunk 18.6.17 by U-boat north of Scotland.

BEGONIA II Dr 91/07, 1–6pdr. Hired 1915–19.

BEHEST (see BARWICK)

BEHEST (ex-*Empire Sophy*) DY tug 261/44. Transferred from MOT and renamed 5.47. Not listed 1948.

BELGAUM Tr 337/16, 1–6pdr. Hired 1916–19.

BELGIQUE 4,606/02. Purchased 1944. Sunk 6.44 as blockship.

BELGOL Oiler (RFA) 4,900 tons, 335 x 41½ ft. Irvine DD, Hartlepool 23.4.1917. Arrived 22.6.58 at Charlestown to BU.

BELIZE Armed vessel, 1–12pdr. Hired 1916–19.

BELLDOCK Tr 236/17. Hired as A/P Tr 11.1939–40.

BELLE Paddle 148/92. Commissioned as M/S 26.5.1917. Returned 9.1.19.

BELLE O'MORAY Dr 83/11, 1–3pdr. Hired 1914–19 and on examination service 3.40–2.46.

BELLEROPHON II Tr 184/07, 1–6pdr. Hired 1914–19.

BELLONA Sloop 18, hired 1779. Wrecked 9.1780 at the mouth of the Elbe.

BELLONA Tr 184/07, 1–6pdr. Hired 1914–19 (BELLONA III from 1915). Hired as A/P Tr 11.39, renamed EGERIA 1940, danlayer. M/S 1.41–1945.

BELLONA II Dr 82/07, 1–3pdr. Hired 1914–19.

BELMONT Tr 209/06, 1–6pdr. Hired 1915–19.

BELOS Dr 68/00. Hired 1915—18.
BELTON Tr 202/18. Hired for examination service 1940—45.
BELUGA Admiralty whaler, 'Z' class. Smiths Dk 26.6.1915. Sold
10.4.20 A.J.Ashwin.
BELUGA (ex-DOLPHYN renamed 1941) M/S 1941—43.
BELVOIR CASTLE Dr. Hired as BBV 6.1940. Laid up 1943—45.
BEMBRIDGE Tender 70gr, 75 x 18 ft. Doig, Grimsby 15.1.1964.
BEMPTON Tr 226/14. Hired 1915—19.

BEN AIGEN Dr 93/03. Hired for harbour service 12.1914—19.
BEN ALDER Dr, 1—3pdr. Hired as BDV 1915—19.
BEN & LUCY Dr 83/10, 1—6pdr. Hired 1915—19 and as M/S 10.39;
target towing 1944, returned 1945.
BEN ARDNA Tr 187/12. Hired 1914. Sunk 8.8.15 by mine near the
Elbow buoy.
BEN ARDNA Tr 226/17. Hired for examination service 8.1939. Sunk
12.5.42 in collision off the Tyne.
BEN BARVAS Tr 198/14. Hired as mooring vessel 1914—19.
BEN BHEULAH Tr 275/17. Hired as M/S 8.1939—10.45.
BEN BHRACHIE Tr 235/16, 1—6pdr. Hired as M/S 1916—19 and
3.40—12.45.
BEN BREAC Tr 235/16, 1—6pdr. Hired 1916—19 and as M/S 6.40;
fuel carrier 3.44. Returned 12.45.
BEN BUI Dr 73/10, 1—3pdr. Hired 1915—19.
BEN CHOURN Tr 197/14, 1—6pdr. Hired 1914—19.
BEN DEARG Tr or Dr hired 1917—19.
BEN DEARG Tr 280/20. Hired as M/S 8.1939—6.46.
BEN DORAN Tr. Hired as mooring vessel 1915—19.
BEN EARN Tr 235/16, 1—6pdr. Hired 1916—19 and as M/S 2.40—2.46.
BEN GAIRN Tr 234/16, 1—6pdr. Hired 11.1916—19 and as M/S 6.40.
Sunk 4.5.41 by parachute mine off Lowestoft.
BEN GLAMAIR Tr 198/14, 1—6pdr. Hired 8.1914—19.
BEN GLAS Tr 234/17, 1—6pdr. Hired 3.1917—19 and as A/P Tr 11.39;
M/S 6.40; fuel carrier 1944—10.44.
BEN GULVAIN Tr 197/14, 1—6pdr. Hired 10.1914—19 and as M/S
8.39—8.46.
BEN HEILEM Tr 196/14, 1—6pdr. Hired 1914. Wrecked 8.10.17 off
Berwick.
BEN HEILEM Tr 224/19. Hired as A/P Tr 11.39; M/S 1941—4.46.
BEN HOLDEN Tr 197/14, 1—6pdr. Hired 1914—19.
BEN HOPE Tr 160/00. Hired 1917—19.
BEN IDRIS Tr 232/31. Hired for examination service 8.1939; M/S
1941. Returned 9.45.

BEN IVER Tr 197/14, 1–6pdr. Hired as M/S 1914–19.
BEN JOHNSON Petrol carrier 228/38. Hired as water carrier (RFA) 1943–46.
BEN LAWERS Tr 176/00, 1–6pdr. Hired as M/S 1914–19.
BEN LEDI Tug. Hired 1914–19.
BEN LEDI Tr 149/98. Hired 1918–19.
BEN LORA Tr 197/13, 1–6pdr. Hired 1914–19.
BEN LOYAL Tr 183/01, 1–3pdr. Hired 1914–19.
BEN LUI Tr 155/00. Hired as boom gate vessel 1915–19.
BEN MEIDIE Tr 234/17, 1–6pdr. Hired 4.17–19 and as M/S 1.40–3.46.
BEN MY CHREE 2,651/08. Hired as seaplane carrier, 2.1.1915. Sunk 11.1.17 by shore batteries Castellorizo harbour; raised 1920, BU 1923.
BEN ROSSAL Tr 260/29. Hired as BDV 9.1939–3.46.
BEN ROY Tr 260/29. Hired as M/S 2.40–45.
BEN SADLER Petrol carrier 289/31. Hired as oiler (RFA) 1942–45.
BEN SCREEL Tr 197/15. Hired 1.15–19.
BEN TARBERT Tr 197/12. Hired as BDV 1915–19 and as A/P Tr 5.40; BDV 7.40; M/S 1941; store carrier 1944. Returned 1946.
BEN TORC Tr 199/15, 1–6pdr. Hired 1915–19 and as A/P Tr 11.39; M/S 6.40. Returned 9.46.
BEN URIE Tr 234/16, 1–6pdr. Hired 12.16–19 and as M/S 2.40–12.45.
BEN VURIE Tr 200/14, 1–6pdr. Hired 12.14–19.
BEN ZINNES Tr. Hired as BDV 1915–19.

BENACHIE Dr 96/19. Hired as M/S 10.39; S/M tender 1944. Returned 1946.
BENARES Tr (RIN), 'Basset' type. Hooghly Dk & Eng. Co. Suspended 11.1944, cancelled 3.45.
BENBECULA Tr, 'Isles' class. Cook Welton & Gemmell 28.10.1943. Sold 12.3.46, renamed *Vigilant.*
BENDISH (ex-American SANTEE renamed 4.6.1918, ex-ARVONIAN) Decoy ship, 2,794/05, 3–4in, 3–12pdr, 4–TT. Sold 3.19 as *Arvonian.*
BENDORAN 5,560/19. Purchased 1944. Sunk 9.6.44 as blockship; salved and BU 1947.
BENEFICIENT Dr 80/07. Hired 1915. Sunk 1.6.16 by gunfire in the Adriatic.
BENGAL Tr 211/05, 1–6pdr. Hired 1915–19 and 11.39. Renamed STAUNCH 1940, M/S. Fuel carrier 1944. Returned 11.44.
BENGAL II Tr 149/96, 1–6pdr. Hired 1915–19.
BENGALI Tr 455/37. Purchased as A/S Tr 8.39. Sunk 5.12.42 after petrol explosion at Lagos, W.Africa.
BENJAMIN COLEMAN Tr, 'Strath' type, 202gr. Fleming & Ferguson 2.11.1917. Sold 16.11.21, same name. Hired as A/P Tr 11.39; fuel carrier 1944. Returned 9.45.

BENJAMIN COOKE Tr, 'Castle' type, 276gr. Bow McLachlan 10.1917. Sold 1920, renamed *Emiel Vandervelde*. (Served as NAMUR in WW.II.)
BENJAMIN HAWKINS Tr, 'Mersey' type, 323gr. Goole SB 1919. Sold 17.10.19, renamed *Frobisher*. Purchased 6.33 as FASTNET, 444 tons. (qv)
BENJAMIN STEVENSON Tr, 'Castle' type, 255gr. Smiths DK 19.6.17. Sunk 18.8.17 by U-boat gunfire, northern North Sea.
BENMORE MFV. Hired as A/P vessel 2.1940—6.45.
BENODET (see CH.12)
BENONI (ex-*Pol V*) Wh (SAN), 221/25. Hired as M/S 1941—45.
BENSTROME Tr 198/14. Hired 1915—19.
BENTON CASTLE Tr 283/14. Hired 1915. Sunk 10.11.16 by mine off Dartmouth.
BENVOLIO Tr 352/30. Hired as M/S 9.39. Sunk 23.2.40 by mine off the Humber.
BERAR Tr (RIN), 'Basset' type. Hooghly Dk & Eng Co 31.7.1942. Sold 1947.
BERBERIS (ex-*Lord Hewart*) Tr, 565 tons, 1—4in. Purchased 2.1939. Sold 1945, renamed *Bergen*.
BERENGA Tr 227/17. Hired as A/P Tr 11.39. BBV 6.40, returned 9.45.
BERGEN Tr 236/07. Hired as M/S (Norwegian crew) 1940. Gate vessel (RN) 1943. Returned 1945.
BERKSHIRE Tr 133/97. Hired 1915. Sunk 15.5.15 in collision in Red Bay.
BERKSHIRE Tr 466/36. Hired as A/S Tr 10.39—11.45.
BERMAGUI Cstr 402/12. Commissioned as M/S (RAN) 11.12.39. Returned 7.45.
BERMUDA Tr 211/05, 1—6pdr. Hired 1914—19.
BERMUDIAN Tug 237/15. Hired as DY tug 1940—46.
BERN Tr, 'Isles' class. Cook Welton & Gemmell 2.5.1942. Oil-tank cleaning vessel 9.55.
BERNADETTE Tr 302/14. French M/S seized 7.1940 at Dover. BDV 11.40—12.45.
BERNARD FLYNN Tr, 'Mersey' type. Cochrane. Cancelled 1919.
BERNARD SHAW Tr 335/29. Hired as M/S 9.39—9.45.
BERRIE BRAES Dr 82/08. Hired 1915—19.
BERRIMA 11,137/13. AMC (RAN) hired 11.8.1914—7.15.
BERRY CASTLE Dr 59/01. Hired 1918—19.
BERRYHEAD Tr. Hired 1918—19.
BERSIMIS Tug 229/30. Hired (RCN) 1942—46.
BERTY Tug 73/14. Hired as DY tug 9.14—19.
BERU Tr 195/11, 1—3pdr. Hired 1914—19 and as A/P Tr 10.39—1.40.

BERVIE BRAES Tr 203/17. Hired as A/P Tr 11.39; M/S 3.40; fuel carrier 1944; returned 10.44.

BERYL Yt 1,368/98, 1−3in, 1−12pdr. Hired 11.1.1915−15.3.19.

BERYL II Tr 248/13, 2−6pdr. Hired 2.15−19.

BERYL III Dr 88/09, 1−6pdr. Hired 1915−19 and as BERYL II on examination service 6.40−45.

BERYL (ex-*Lady Adelaide*) A/S Tr 615 tons, 1−4in. Purchased 1.1939. Sold 1945, renamed *Red Knight*.

BERYL II Tr (RAN), 248/13. Hired as M/S 9.39; boom gate vessel 1944−46.

BERYL Yt 83/26. Hired as M/S 1940. Renamed DRUSILLA 10.40. Purchased 1941 as repair craft. Sold 7.45.

BESSIE DY hoy, 55bm. White, Cowes 7.1861. In service 1880. (Also known as R.Clarence YC.2.)

BESSIE DY barge 140 tons. Fellows, Yarmouth 1899. In service in 1924.

BESSIE Dr 79/03. Hired for harbour service 11.14. CROSSBOW 8.18−19.

BETSY Cutter 6, 50bm, 6−3pdr. Hired 1803−04.

BETSY Cutter 6, 60bm, 6−12pdr. carr. Hired 6.1803−12.04.

BETSY Cutter 6, 51bm. Hired 1.1806−3.1810.

BETSY Dr 86/03, 1−3pdr. Hired 1915−19.

BETSY SIM Dr 53/-. Hired 1917. Sunk 18.7.17 in collision off Haisborough light vessel.

BETSY SLATER Dr 84/11, 1−3pdr. Hired 1915−19 and as BBV 5.40−44.

BETTY DY craft, 65bm, 47 x 18 ft. Plymouth DY 1728. Fate unknown.

BETTY DY tug, 40gr, 57 x 17 ft. Dunston 12.1962.

BETTY BODIE Dr 96/18. Hired for examination service 8.1939−6.46.

BETTY HUDSON Tug 138/15. Hired as BBV 1942−44.

BETTY INGLIS Tr 104/95. Hired 1918−19 and as M/S 12.39; laid up 1940, returned 3.46.

BEVER (ex-*Hektor 10*) Wh (SAN) 252/30. Hired as M/S 10.1941. Sunk 30.11.44 by mine off Piraeus.

BEVERLEY BROOK Aux.barge 238/37. Hired as water carrier 1943−45.

BHADRAVATI Cstr 1,449/32. Hired as A/P vessel (RIN) 1939−45.

BIANCA Tr 174/05, 1−3pdr. Hired 1914−19.

BIARRITZ 2,388/15, 2−12pdr, 180 mines. Hired 2.1915−1919 as minelayer and 1942−45 as landing ship.

BIBURY Tender, 70gr, 75 x 18 ft. Doig, Grimsby 19.2.1964.

BICKERSTAFFE Paddle 213/78. Commissioned as M/S 16.4.1917, returned 1.4.19.

BIEN VENU Dr 77/10. Hired 1915−19.

BIGGAL Tr, 'Isles' class. Ferguson 4.12.1944. Sold 1947, renamed *Frankfurt-Main*.

BIGLIERI (ex-Italian G.BIGLIERI salved at Massawa). In commission as M/S 1942—46.

BILLOW Admiralty steel drifter, 96gr. Webster & Bickerton 1918. For disposal 1935.

BILLOW (see GOS.3)

BILOELA Collier (RAN) 9,200 tons, 370 x 54 ft. Cockatoo DY 10.4.1919. Sold 3.31, renamed *Wollert.*

BILSDEAN Tr 242/17. Hired as M/S 2.1940—11.45.

BINGERA Cstr 922/35. Commissioned as A/S vessel (RAN) 12.1939—46.

BIRCH Tr 215/12. Hired 1914. Sunk 23.8.16 by mine off Yarmouth.

BIRCH M/S Tr 530 tons, 150 x 27½ ft, 1—12pdr. Cook Welton & Gemmell 13.11.1939. Sale list 1947. Sold, same name.

BIRCHGROVE PARK Cstr 640/30. Commissioned as M/S (RAN) 8.1941—46.

BIRCH LAKE Motor M/S (RCN) 255 tons, 126 x 26 ft. Port Carling Bt Wks. Cancelled 22.10.1945 and completed mercantile.

BIRCHOL Oiler (RFA) 2,407 tons, 220 x 34 ft. Barclay Curle 16.6.1917. Wrecked 29.11.39 in the Hebrides.

BIRCHOL Oiler (RFA) 2,670 tons, 218 x 38 ft. Lobnitz 19.2.1946.

BIRCHTON Tug (RCN) 462 tons, 104 x 28 ft. Toronto. Building 1944.

BIRDLIP A/S Tr 750 tons, 166 x 28 ft, 1—12pdr, 3—20mm. Cook Welton & Gemmell 9.7.1941. Sunk 13.6.44 by 'U.547' off Lagos, W. Africa.

BISHOPDALE Oiler (RFA) 17,357 tons, 464 x 62 ft. Lithgow 31.3.1937.

BISHOPSGATE Boom gate vessel (dumb) 290 tons, 93 x 26 ft, 1—4in. Robb 15.11.1932. BU 8.59 Charlestown.

BISMILLAH II Air/sea rescue craft 1941—42 then laid up to 1946.

BISON Store carrier (RFA) 766 tons, 165 x 26 ft. Mordey Carney 1.11.1902. Listed to 1946.

BITTERN II Tr 207/03, 1—6pdr. Hired 1914—19.

BJERK Wh 182/12. M/S (Norwegian crew) in service 9.1940—10.45.

BJORN Wh. In service 1917—19.

BLAAUWBERG Wh 307/35. Hired as A/S vessel (SAN) 12.1940—5.46.

BLACKAMOOR 38—gun ship, 270bm. Hired 1664—67.

BLACK ARROW Yt 50/34. Hired as HDPC 1.1940—45.

BLACK BEAR (see XARIFA)

BLACKBIRD (ex-SHEPPEY renamed 11.1942) M/L trawler, ex'Isles' class. Cook Welton & Gemmell 20.2.43. Sold 1949, renamed *Goodmar.*

BLACKBURN ROVERS Tr 422/34. Hired as A/S Tr 8.1939. Sunk 2.6.40 by unknown cause in the North Sea.

BLACKCOCK Ship, 330bm. Hired 1664—67.

BLACKCOCK Tug 253/86. Hired 11.8.1914. Wrecked 18.1.18 in the White Sea.

BLACK DRAGON (ex-Danish training ship KOBENHAVN) Oil hulk, 3,400gr. Purchased on stocks 1914. Sold 9.22, renamed *Dragon.* (Also known as C.600.)

BLACK EAGLE DY craft. Listed from 1919. Sold 7.29 J.A.White.

BLACKFLY (ex-*Barnett*) Tr 482/37. Purchased as A/S Tr 8.1939. Sold 1946, renamed *Loyal.*

BLACK FROST Admiralty wood Dr, 99gr. Colby 1918. Renamed COLUMBINE 1925, base ship. Sold circa 1931, renamed *Timor.* (Served as MILLWATER in WW.II.)

BLACK ISLE Water carrier in service 1942–45.

BLACK JOKE Cutter 10. Hired 1793–1800.

BLACK JOKE Lugger 10, 109bm. Hired 5.1808. Captured 1811 by the French in the Channel.

BLACK JOKE Yt 149/19. Purchased as BBV 4.1941. Sold 12.45.

BLACK NIGHT Admiralty Wood Dr, 97gr. Colby 1918. Sold 3.10.21, same name.

BLACKOL (ex-PLA hopper 5) Oiler (RFA) 869/06. Hired 9.1916–20.

BLACK RANGER Oiler (RFA), 3,417gr, 349½ x 47 ft. Harland & Wolff, Govan 22.8.1940.

BLACKSTONE Tr 148/15. Purchased as oil carrier 10.1915. Sold 4.21 M S Hilton.

BLACKTHORN Dr 79/04, 1–3pdr. Hired 1915–19.

BLACKTHORN M/S Tr 505 tons, 150 x 27½ ft, 1–12pdr. Cook Welton & Gemmell 29.11.1939. Sold 1947, renamed *Maythorn.*

BLACKWATER (see WILLIAM INWOOD)

BLACKWHALE (Z.5) Admiralty Wh, 'Z' class. Smiths Dk 28.6.1915. Sunk 3.1.18 by mine off Fifeness.

BLAKENEY Tender, 70gr, 75 x 18 ft. Doig, Grimsby 12.5.1964.

BLANCHE Tr, 1–6pdr. Hired 1915–19.

BLANCHE MADELEINE MFV. Belgian, hired as A/P vessel 9.1940 (Polish crew); harbour service 1941. Returned 1945.

BLANCHE MARGUERITE MFV, 1–6pdr. Belgian, hired as A/P vessel 10.1940; training 1943. Returned 1945.

BLARE Admiralty steel Dr, 97gr. Brooke Marine 1919. Sold 1919, renamed *Maybird.*

BLAZER (see CHARM)

BLESSING Gunvessel. Hired 9.1801–02.

BLESSING Fishing vessel hired as decoy 6.1916–17.

BLIA MFV. Norwegian, hired 1941. Lost 11.41.

BLIGHTY Tr 325/19. Hired as M/S 1940, later purchased. Renamed PODOLE (Polish) 25.5.44.

BLINJOE 1,331/29. Dutch, hired as accommodation ship (RIN) 1944–45.

BLISSVILLE Tug (RCN) Canada 1944. Sold 1947.

BLITHESOME Dr 81/08. Hired 1914–19.

BLIZZARD Admiralty steel Dr, 97gr. Colby 1918. Sold 1919, renamed *Satinstone*. (Served as HARVEST GLEANER in WW.II.)

BLIZZARD (see GOS.4)

BLOEMENDAAL Tr 242/17. Hired as M/S (Dutch crew) 8.1940. BBV (RN) 1943; returned 1945.

BLOEMFONTEIN Dr 82/03, 1–3pdr. Hired 1915–19.

BLOMVLEI A/S Tr (SAN) 252/35. Hired 3.1940–3.45.

BLOOM Dr 87/07, 1–6pdr. Hired 1915–19.

BLOOMFIELD Dr 83/06. Hired for harbour service 11.1914. BUDLEIA 8.18–19.

BLOSSOM 30–gun ship, 300bm. Hired 1652–54.

BLOSSOM DY tank vessel 390 tons, 115 x 23 ft. Bow McLachlan 15.5.1901. BU 1961 at Gibraltar.

BLOSSOM Dr 86/07, 1–3pdr. Hired 1914–19.

BLOSSOM II Dr 58/00. Hired 10.1914–12.14.

BLOSSOM III Dr, 1–6pdr. Hired 1916–19.

BLOWPIPE Armament store carrier 250gr. In service 1947. Sold 1966 at Singapore.

BLUEBELL Dr 79/02. Hired for harbour service 11.1914–2.15.

BLUEBELL II Dr 94/07, 1–MG. Hired 1914–19.

BLUEBELL III Tr 179/04, 1–6pdr. Hired 1914–19.

BLUEBELL IV Dr 88/07, 1–3pdr. Hired 1915–19.

BLUEBELL Boom tender in service 1940. Renamed PROLIFIC 1940. Returned 1945.

BLUEBIRD Yt 80/11. Hired as danlayer 1939; harbour service 1941–44.

BLUE HAZE Admiralty steel Dr, 97gr. Brooke Marine 1919. Sold 14.7.19, same name. Hired as TRV 5.40–2.46.

BLUE RANGER Oiler (RFA), 3,417gr, 349½ x 47 ft. Harland & Wolff, Govan 29.1.1941.

BLUE SKY Admiralty wood Dr, 98gr. Colby 1918. Foundered 6.22 in the Thames estuary, perhaps mined.

BLUE TIT (see ANNA LEOPOLD)

BLUFF M/S Tr (SAN), 262/35. Hired 9.1939–12.44.

BLUSH Admiralty steel Dr. Cancelled 1919.

BLUSTER Admiralty steel Dr. Cancelled 1919.

BLUSTER (see CYCLONE)

BOADICEA II Yt 447/82, 1–12pdr, 1–6pdr. Hired 10.5.1915–15.3.19. Hired as accommodation ship 1.43–45.

BOARDALE Oiler (RFA) 17,338 tons, 464 x 62 ft. Harland & Wolff, Govan 22.4.1937. Sunk 30.4.40 after grounding near Narvik.

BOARHOUND Tug 54/82. Hired 7.1914–19.

BOARHOUND (see TERJE 2)

BOB READ Dr 95/13, 1–3pdr. Hired 1916–19.

B.O. DAVIES Pilot cutter 173/32. Hired for examination service 1940–46.

BODO (ex-*Gos 8*) Wh (Norwegian crew) 351/36. Hired as A/S vessel 1941. Sunk 4.1.43 by mine off the east coast of Scotland.

BOKSBURG (ex-*Uni III*) M/S Wh (SAN) 240/26, 1–3in. Hired 10.1941–7.46.

BOLD Rescue tug, 'B.A.T' class. Defoe SB, Bay City 21.5.42 on lend-lease. Returned 13.6.46 to the USN.

BOLD PATHFINDER Fast patrol boat 130 tons, 121 x 25½ ft, 2–40mm, 4–TT. Vosper 17.9.1951. Sold 17.5.64.

BOLD PIONEER (as BOLD PATHFINDER) White 18.8.1951. Sold 22.10.58.

BOLHAM (ex-*Sarah Colebrook*) 157/13, 2–3in. Hired as decoy vessel 3.1917–10.18.

BOLINA Tender 6, 181bm, 6–3pdr. Hired 16.7.1803. Wrecked 3.11.1807 near Perranporth.

BOMBARDIER Tr, 305gr,130 x 24 ft, 1–12pdr. Smiths DK 1.4.1915, purchased on stocks 12.14. Sold 4.5.20 Belgian govt.

BOMBARDIER Tr 750 tons, 175 x 30 ft, 1–4in, 4–20mm. Cook Welton & Gemmell 23.1.1943. Sold 1946, renamed *Norman*.

BOMBAY Tr 229/07, 1–6pdr. Hired 1915–19 and as A/P vessel 12.39–40.

BOMBAY Tr, 'Castle' type (RIM). Bombay 1919. Fate unknown.

BOMBO Cstr 540/30. Hired as M/S (RAN), commissioned 5.1941. Store carrier 1944–46.

BOMBSHELL Tug 97 tons. Philip, Dartmouth 14.4.1945.

BONA Tr 186/06. Hired 1918–19 and as fuel carrier 1944–44.

BON ACCORD Tr 214/08, 1–6pdr. Hired 1915–19.

BONA DEA Tr 322/14, 1–6pdr. Hired 1915–19.

BON AMI Dr 76/08. Hired 1915–18.

BONAR LAW Tr 285/12. Hired 1915. Sunk 27.10.15 after collision off the South Goodwin.

BONAVENTURE Ship, 260bm. Hired 1620–21.

BONAVENTURE Ship. Hired 1653. Lost 1653 by fire.

BONAVENTURE 50–gun ship. Hired 1696–97.

BONEAXE (also BONE AXE) Seized Russian Tr. Listed 11.9.1918 to 1921.

BON ESPOIR Dr 86/08, 1–57mm. Hired 1915–19.

BONETTA (ex-*Cedar*) MFV. Hired for harbour service 1940–45.

BONITO A/S Tr 670 tons, 146 x 25 ft, 1–4in, 3–20mm. Cochrane 8.10.1941. Sold 1946, renamed *Blaefell*.

BONNYVILLE Tug (RCN). Owen Sound, Canada 1944. Fate unknown.

BONO Dr 70/08, 1–57mm. Hired 1915–19.

BONTHORPE Tr (RAN) 273/17. Commissioned as A/S Tr 5.2.1940; M/S 1941–46.

BOOMERANG (see GATLING)

BOONAH Ammo. carrier (RAN) 279 tons. Williamstown DY 15.6.1951.

BORA Admiralty steel Dr. Rose St Fndry. Cancelled 1919.

BORDE 2,014/21. Purchased 18.10.1939 as M/S; repair ship 4.42; BU 4.45.

BORDER GLEN Tr 123/31. Hired 1915–16.

BORDER KING Dr 92/14, 1–3pdr. Hired 1915–19 and for harbour service 8.39–10.45.

BORDER LADS Dr 86/14, 1–6pdr. Hired 1915. Sunk 25.3.18 off the Tyne; probably torpedoed.

BOREALIS (ex-TWINKLE renamed 1918) Admiralty wood Dr. Colby 1918. Sold 1921, renamed *Brash*.

BOREALIS (ex-*Pilot No 15*) 451/30. Belgian, hired as BBV 6.1940. Sunk 10.8.40.

BOREALIS (see GOS.6)

BOREAS Tr 184/07, 1–6pdr. Hired 1914–19 and as A/P Tr 1939; renamed CUCKOO 1940. Returned 7.2.40.

BORNEO Tr 211/06. Hired 1914. Sunk 18.6.17 by mine off Beachy Head.

BORNOL (see ORANGELEAF)

BORODINO Store carrier 2,726/11. Hired 1.12.1914–28.4.19, and purchased 1940. Sunk 27.5.40 as blockship at Zeebrugge.

BORTIND Tr 328/12. Hired as M/S (Norwegian crew) 1940–1.46.

BOSCAWEN A:ship 16. Hired 1748–60.

BOSCOBEL Tr 225/06, 1–6pdr. Hired 1916–19.

BOSTONIAN (ex-*Cambrian*) 5,736/96, 3–6in. Hired as escort 11.6.1917. Sunk 10.10.17 by 'U.53' south of Start Point.

BOSTONIAN Tr 192/00. Hired 1916. BASTION 1916–19.

BOSTON SALVOR Salvage vessel 800 tons, 170 x 37 ft, 1–3in, 2–20mm. Barbour Bt Wks, New Bern 20.2.1943 and to the RN 26.1.44 on lend-lease. Wrecked by V.2 rocket at Antwerp 16.3.45.

BOSWORTH 6,672/19. Purchased 10.7.1944. Sunk 4.9.44 as blockship; raised and BU 5.49 at Troon.

BOTANIC Tr 348/28. Purchased as M/S 8.1939. Sunk 18.2.42 by air attack in the North Sea.

BOTLEA 5,119/17. Hired 9.1939, commissioned 16.9.39 as decoy ship. (Served until 1940 as LAMBRIDGE); AMC 2.41; returned 12.41.

BOULOGNE (see CH.II)

BOUNTEOUS Dr 63/-. Hired 1914. Wrecked 4.12.17 on the north shore of Rhum.

BOUNTEOUS Dr. Hired for examination service 1942–46.

BOUNTEOUS SEA Dr 56/00, 1–3pdr. Hired 1915–19 and on harbour service 1941–46.

BOUNTIFUL Dr 91/11, 1–6pdr. Hired 1916–19 and as boom tender 7.39–45.

BOUNTY DY store vessel, 44bm, 47 x 15 ft. Fishboune 1809. In service in 1842.

BOUNTY Yt 67/36. Purchased as A/P vessel 1940. Sold 12.45.

BOURNABAT Iron pad tug. Purchased 9.9.1854 at Constantinople. Wrecked 29.3.1855 at Scutari.

BOURNE (ex-*Bournemouth Queen*) Paddle 353/08, 2–6pdr. Hired as M/S 5.2.1915–5.5.20. (In WW.II as BOURNEMOUTH QUEEN.)

BOURNEMOUTH QUEEN Paddle 353/08, 2–2pdr, 4–MG. Hired as A/A ship 4.1941; accommodation ship 1.44. Returned 1945.

BOUVET Nos 1, 2, 3 and 4. Four Norwegian whalers, all 245/30, hired as M/S 3.1940–46.

BOVERTON 2,958/10. Hired as fleet auxiliary 22.10.1914–4.19.

BOVIC Tr 109/96. Hired 1914. Sunk 5.8.17 in collision off Souter Point.

BOWELL (see CAMPENIA)

BOWHEAD (Z.4) Admiralty Wh, 'Z' class. Smiths Dk 26.6.1915. Sold 20.4.20 A.J.Ashwin.

BOWLING Cstr 793/10. Hired as ammo.carrier 2.9.1914–14.2.19.

BOWNET BDV 530 tons, 135 x 30½ ft, 1–3in. Blyth DD 19.1.1939. On sale list 1958.

BOWSTRING Armament store carrier, 220gr, 115 x 22½ ft. Scarr, Hessle 27.8.1938.

BOW WAVE Admiralty steel Dr, 97gr. Brooke Marine 1919. Sold 26.6.19, same name. Hired as TRV 1940–45.

BOXER DY tug 170 tons, 85 x 25 ft. Dunston 12.12.1962.

BOXOL Oiler (RFA) 2,200 tons, 220 x 34 ft. Barclay Curle 12.7.1917. Arrived 2.9.59 Rees, Llanelly to BU.

BOY ALAN Dr 109/14, 1–3pdr. Hired 1914–19 and as M/S, 1–6pdr 11.39. Sunk 10.2.41 in collision in the Thames estuary.

BOY ALEX Dr 75/08, 1–3pdr. Hired 1915–19 and as M/S 11.39–45.

BOY ANDREW Dr 97/18. Hired as A/P vessel 1940. Sunk 9.11.41 in collision in the Firth of Forth.

BOY ARCHIE Dr 58/01. Hired 12.1914–19.

BOY ARTHUR Dr 90/07, 1–3pdr. Hired 1915–19.

BOY BEN Dr 84/06. Hired 1915–19.

BOY BILLY Dr 70/04. Hired 1915–19.

BOY BOB Dr, 1–6pdr. Hired 1916–19.

BOY CHARLES Dr 86/13, 1–3pdr. Hired 1915–19.
BOY CHARLEY Dr 83/07, 1–3pdr. Hired 1914–19.
BOY CHY Dr 78/08. Hired 1915–19.
BOY DANIEL Dr 83/12. Hired 1915–19.
BOY DAVIE Dr. Hired for examination service 1940; degaussing vessel 1942–44.
BOY EDDIE Dr 59/09. Hired 1915–19.
BOY EDWARD Dr 80/09. Hired 1915–19.
BOY ERNEST Dr 56/02. Hired 1915–19.
BOY GEORGE Dr 84/06, 1–3pdr. Hired 1915–19.
BOY GEORGE II Dr 83/06. Hired 1915–19.
BOY GEORGE III Dr 70/03. Hired 1915–19.
BOY HAROLD Dr 74/-. Hired 1915. Sunk 3.3.16 by mine off Brindisi.
BOY HECTOR Dr 81/03, 1–6pdr. Hired 1915–19.
BOY JACOB Dr 62/06, 1–6pdr. Hired 1915–19.
BOY JERMYN Dr 97/18. Hired 1940–40.
BOY JOE Dr 85/13, 1–3pdr. Hired 1915–19.
BOY JOHN Dr 87/14. Hired as M/S 12.39–7.45.
BOY PAT Yt. Hired as M/S 1939–46.
BOY PHILIP Dr 128/30. Hired as M/S 10.39. Transferred to War Dept 8.43.
BOY RAY Dr 84/10. Hired as A/P vessel 6.40; water boat 3.44, returned 1946.
BOY ROY Dr 95/11, 1–3pdr. Hired 1914–19 and 11.39. Beached after bomb damage 28.5.40, Dunkirk.
BOY ROY MFV 20/-. Hired 1941. Lost 11.2.42 by unknown cause.
BOY SCOUT Dr 80/13, 1–6pdr. Hired 10.14–19 and as M/S 11.39; BBV 1940–45.
BOY WILLIE Dr 81/07. Hired 1915–18.
BOY WILLIE Dr 66/04. Hired 1916. Renamed WILLIAM II 7.17, RAMESES 12.17–19.

BOYNDIE BURN Dr 73/10. Hired 1915–19.
BOYNE (see WILLIAM JONES) ·
BOYNE WATER Yt 81/25. Hired as HDPC 1940–45.
BRABANT Tr 280/18. Hired as M/S 8.1939–12.45.
BRACKEN Dr 66/03, 1–3pdr. Hired 1915–19.
BRACKENDALE Dr 88/16, 1–3pdr. Hired 1916–19 and as A/P vessel 1939; degaussing vessel 1940–46.
BRACKLYN Tr 303/-. Hired 1916. Sunk 11.5.17 by mine off Yarmouth.
BRACODEN Dr 81/12. Hired 1914–19.
BRACONBURN Tr 203/18. Purchased 1944. Lost 30.7.44 on passage to Scapa for use as blockship.

BRACONDALE 2,095/03. Ex-fleet collier purchased for use as decoy vessel 24.5.1917. Renamed CHAGFORD 6.17. Sunk 7.8.17 by 'U.44' in the Atlantic.

BRACONDENE Tr 235/16, 1–6pdr. Hired 2.16–19 and as M/S 8.40–8.46.

BRACONHEATH Tr 201/06, 1–6pdr. Hired 1914–19 and as danlayer 2.40; laid up 1942–44.

BRACONHILL Tr 203/19. Hired as A/P vessel 11.39; examination service 1940–7.45.

BRACONLYNN Tr 206/13, 1–6pdr. Hired 1914–19 and as A/P vessel 12.39–40.

BRACONMOOR Tr 194/17. Hired as M/S 8.39–8.46.

BRADFORD Tr 163/96. Hired 1915. Foundered 28.10.16 off the Old Head of Kinsale.

BRADFORD CITY 3,683/10. Commissioned as decoy ship 10.1915. Sunk 16.8.17 by U-boat in the Messina Strait.

BRADMAN Tr 452/37, 1–4in. Hired as A/S Tr 8.1939. Sunk 25.4.40 by air attack; salved by Germans and renamed FRIESE.

BRAE FLETT Dr 54net/02. Hired for harbour service 1941. Sunk 22.9.43 by unknown cause in the Clyde area.

BRAE HEAD Dr 85/14. Hired 5.1915–19.

BRAE LOSSIE Dr 77/01, 1–3pdr. Hired 1915–19.

BRAEMAR Tr 197/00, 1–12pdr. Hired as BDV 1914–19.

BRAEMAR Dr. Hired 1.1940–45.

BRAEMAR Tr 212/27. Purchased as danlayer 4.40. Renamed JENNIFER 1940. Laid up 1942.

BRAEMAR Yt 147/31. Hired 1940. Renamed CLORINDE 1940, HDPC. Listed to 1946.

BRAERIACH Tr 199/02. Hired 1918–19.

BRAES o'BUCKIE Dr 84/10. Hired as boom gate vessel 4.1915–19 and on harbour service 1942; water boat 1944–46.

BRAES o'ENZIE Dr 87/15. Hired 4.15–19.

BRAES o'MAR Tr 227/15, 1–6pdr. Hired 9.15–19 and as A/P vessel 1939–40.

BRAKPAN (ex-*Terje 6*) Wh 335/36, 1–4in. Hired as M/S (SAN) 3.1941–9.46.

BRAKVLEI (ex-*Hektor 4*) Wh 234/29, 1–3in. Hired as M/S (SAN) 7.1940–6.46.

BRAMBLE II Dr 91/08, 1–57mm. Hired 1915–19.

BRAMBLELEAF (ex-RUMOL renamed 1917) Oiler (RFA) 12,300 tons, 405 x 54½ ft. Lithgow 28.12.16. Torpedoed and beached 6.42 near Port Said; BU 4.53 at Spezia.

BRAMBLELEAF (ex-*London Loyalty*) Oiler (RFA), 12,133gr, 525 x 71 ft. Furness SB 16.4.1953, purchased 1959.

BRAMLEY MOOR Tug 214/16. Hired as rescue tug 15.9.1916—8.2.19.
BRANCH Dr 93/08, 1—3pdr. Hired 1914—19 and as A/S Dr 1940—45.
BRANDARIS Yt 48/37. Dutch, hired as BBV 1940—42.
BRANDENBURGH Dr 79/15, 1—3pdr. Hired 1915—19.
BRANKSEA Cstr 214/90. Purchased 1940. Sunk 10.2.40 off Girdleness
on passage to Scapa as blockship.
BRANWEN Yt 151/05, 2—6pdr. Hired 4.1.1915—12.3.17.
BRAS d'OR Tr 221/01. Hired as M/S (RCN) 10.1939. Foundered
19.10.40 in the Gulf of St Lawrence.
BRAVE Ship, 160bm. Hired 1588—89 and 1596—97.
BRAVE Lugger 12. Hired 1798. Sunk 22.4.1799 in collision with
transport *Eclipse* in the Channel.
BRAVE BORDERER Fast patrol boat 75 tons, 90 x 25½ ft, 1—40mm,
4—TT (as MTB), *or* 2—40mm, 2—TT (as MGB). Vosper 7.1.1958.
BRAVE SWORDSMAN (as BRAVE BORDERER) Vosper 22.5.58.
BRAVO Tr 137/96. Hired 1917—19.
BRAZIL BRASBY Tr, 'Strath' type. Hall Russell 31.10.1917. Sold
17.5.19, renamed *Tyrwhitt.*
BREADALBANE Tr 112/91. Hired 1917—19.
BREADWINNER Dr 93/07, 1—3pdr. Hired 1.1915—19.
BREADWINNER II Dr 88/07, 1—3pdr. Hired 1915—19.
BREAKER Admiralty steel Dr, 96gr. Brooke Marine 1919. Sold 1919,
renamed *Kathleen.* (KATHLEEN in WW.II.)
BREAM A/S Tr 670 tons, 146 x 25 ft, 1—4in, 3—20mm. Cochrane
10.12.1942. Sold 1946, renamed *Valafjell.*
BRECON CASTLE Tr 274/16, 1—6pdr. Hired 3.16—19 and as M/S
8.39—12.45.
BREDA Yt 1,431/12. Purchased 1939 as convoy leader; S/M tender
1940. Sunk 18.2.44 in collision, Campbeltown Loch.
BREDON A/S Tr 750 tons, 166 x 28 ft, 1—12pdr, 3—20mm. Cook
Welton & Gemmell 20.11.1941. Sunk 8.2.43 by U-boat in the N.
Atlantic.
BREEZE (see GUSTAVE DENIS)
BREEZE Cstr 622/33. Commissioned as M/S (RNZN) 26.10.1942.
Returned 1945.
BREME Dr 84/10. Hired on examination service 1941—45.
BRENDA Tender. Hired 1854—55.
BRENDA 123/06. Hired on examination service 1940—45.
BRENDA DY tug, 40gr, 57 x 17ft. Dunston 25.3.1963.
BRENT Tr 142/92. Hired 1917—19.
BRESAY Dr 81/08, 1—3pdr. Hired 1914—19.
BRESSAY Tr, 'Isles' class. Cook Welton & Gemmell 20.1.1942. Sold
3.46.

BRETWALDA Tr 488/25, 2–20mm. French *Administrateur de Bournat* seized 1940 and later purchased. A/S Tr. Sold 1947.

BREVIK (ex-*Kos XIII*) Wh 258/32. Hired 1940 (Norwegian crew); returned 1946 to Norway.

BRIAR ROSE MFV. Hired for ferry service 1941–45.

BRIDGET DY tug, 40gr, 57 x 17 ft. Dunston 18.1.1963.

BRIDLINGTON Tr 205/13. Hired 1917–19.

BRIGADIER M/S Tr, 305gr, 130 x 24 ft, 1–12pdr. Smiths Dk 1.4.1915, purchased on stocks 1915. Renamed BUGLER 1919. Sold 4.5.20 Belgian govt as *Pilote 6.*

BRIGADIER (ex-*Worthing*) 2,294/31. Hired as training ship 1940; landing ship 1942–46.

BRIGAND Fleet tug 840 tons, 165 x 32 ft, 1–3in. Fleming & Ferguson 8.7.1937. Sold 23.9.60.

BRIGHTER DAWN MFV. Hired for harbour service 1942–45.

BRIGHTER HOPE Dr 53/09. Hired 1915–19.

BRIGHTON Paddle 531/78. Hired as fleet messenger 29.6.1915, purchased 22.5.17. Sold 26.4.19.

BRIGHTON II Dr 75/06, 1–6pdr. Hired 1915–19.

BRIGHTON BELLE Paddle 396/00. Hired as M/S 10.1939. Sunk 28.5.40 in collision with wreck in the Downs.

BRIGHTON o'the NORTH Dr 98/14. Hired 10.1914–19 and for examination service 1941–46.

BRIGHTON QUEEN Paddle 533/97. Hired as M/S 9.1914. Sunk 6.10.15 by mine off Nieuport.

BRIGHTON QUEEN Paddle 807/05. Hired as M/S 10.1939. Sunk 1.6.40 by gunfire off Dunkirk.

BRILLIANT Cstr 657/01. Hired 17.1.1915 as ammo. carrier (RFA); transport 5.16, returned 2.19.

BRILLIANT STAR Tr 125/96. Hired 1918–19.

BRIMNES Tr 413/33, 1–4in. Hired as A/S Tr 9.39–46.

BRINE Admiralty steel Dr, 96gr. Ouse SB 15.7.1918. Sold 7.20, same name. Purchased as boom tender 1938. Sold 1950.

BRINMARIC Yt 106/38. Hired as HDPC 1940; M/S 1943, returned 1946.

BRISBANE Tr 207/03. Hired 1918–19.

BRITAIN (ex-*Britannia*) Paddle 459/96, 1–6pdr. Hired as M/S 28.1.1915–13.4.19. (Served as SKIDDAW in WW.II.)

BRITANNIA Cutter 6, 69bm, 6–3pdr. Hired 1793–96 and 1803–2.1811.

BRITANNIA 4,129/73. Hired as AMC 1885–86.

BRITANNIA II Dr. Hired 1915–19.

BRITANNIA IV Dr 63/02, 1–57mm. Hired 1915–19.

BRITANNIC (ex-MINER V renamed 1960) (see Vol.I) Cable layer (RFA) 300 tons, 110 x 26½ ft.

BRITISH Tr 406/30. Hired as M/S 8.1939–12.45.

BRITISH BEACON Oiler (RFA) 15,030 tons, 430 x 57 ft. Workman Clark 1918. Renamed OLCADES 1937. Hulk 1948. Arrived 18.4.53 Hughes Bolckow, Blyth to BU.

BRITISH CROWN Dr 85/13, 1–3pdr. Hired 1914–19 and as M/S 1941–45.

BRITISHER (ex-*Britannia*) Tug 80/02. Hired 1916, purchased 1917. Sold 2.23.

BRITISH FAIR Cutter 8. Hired 1793–1800 and 1803–04.

BRITISH FAIR Cutter 6, 71bm. Hired 6.1803–9.05 and 3.1807–4.14.

BRITISH GUIANA Tr 146/36. Hired as A/S Tr 11.1939–3.46.

BRITISH HONDURAS Tr 147/30. Hired as A/S Tr 12.1939–1.46.

BRITISH LANTERN Oiler (RFA) 15,030 tons, 430 x 57 ft. Workman Clark 1918. Renamed OLIGARCH 1937. Scuttled 14.4.46 with ammunition in the Red Sea.

BRITISH LIGHT Oiler (RFA) 13,690 tons, 420 x 54 ft. Palmer 1917. Renamed OLWEN 1937. Sold 1947, renamed *Mushtari.*

BRITISH MONARCH Dr 57/02. Hired 1915–19.

BRITISH STAR Oiler (RFA) 15,000 tons, 430 x 57 ft. Swan Hunter 1917. Renamed OLYNTHUS 1937. Disposal 1946.

BRITON Tr 196/06. Hired 1915. Sunk 21.7.15 by mine off the Longsands.

BRITON Dr 79/06, 1–6pdr. Hired 1915–19.

BRITON (see BANDIT)

BRITTANY 1,445/33, 4–20mm. Hired as netlayer 1940–45.

BRIXHAM Cstr 501/85. Hired as store carrier (RFA) 4.9.1915–8.3.16.

BROADLAND Dr 76/13, 1–3pdr. Hired 1914–19 and as A/P Dr, 1–3pdr 1.1940. Foundered 6.6.45 in the N.Atlantic.

BROCH Dr 90/08. Hired 1914–19.

BROCH HEAD Dr 85/11. Hired 1915–19.

BROCK Tr 304/14, 1–6pdr. Hired 8.1914–19 and as M/S, 1–6pdr, 2–20mm 8.39–45.

BROCKLESBY Cstr 508/12. Hired as fleet auxiliary 2.1916–18.

BRODICK Tender, 70gr, 75 x 18 ft. Doig, Grimsby 10.7.1964.

BROIL Admiralty steel Dr, 96gr. Brooke Marine 1919. Sold 1919, same name. (Served as M.A.WEST in WW.II.)

BROKE Cutter 14. Hired 1814–14.

BROMELIA Tr 242/06, 1–6pdr. Hired 1915–19.

BROMSGROVE 1,446/09. Hired as fleet auxiliary 1918–19.

BRONTES Tr 428/34. Hired as A/S Tr 8.1939–45.

BRONTOSAURUS (see YOUNG MUN)

BRONZEAXE Seized Russian trawler. Listed 9.1918–21.

BRONZEWING Tug (RAN) 250 tons, 99 x 21 ft. Morts Dk Sydney 27.8.1946.

BROOMDALE Oiler (RFA) 17,338 tons, 461 x 62 ft. Harland & Wolff, Govan 2.9.1937. BU 1.60 in Belgium.

BRORA A/S Tr, 'Isles' class. Cook Welton & Gemmell 18.12.1940. Wrecked 6.9.41 in the Hebrides.

BRORERAY A/S Tr, 'Isles' class. Cook Welton & Gemmell 17.6.1942. Renamed GWEAL 9.42. Sold 1948, renamed *Velox.*

BROTHERS Dr 65/03. Hired 1915–19.

BROTHERS GEM Dr 96/07. Hired 1915–19.

BROWN RANGER Oiler (RFA), 3,500 gr, 349½ x 47 ft. Harland & Wolff, Govan 12.12.1940.

BRUCE Tr 103/83. Hired 1917–19.

BRUCE (ex-*Manxmaid*) 1,512/10. Hired as radar training ship 10.1941. Reverted to MANXMAID 12.41, training ship. Returned 1945.

BRUCKLAY Tr 182/00. Hired 1918–19.

BRUINE French navy water carrier seized 3.7.1940 at Southampton. Returned 1945 to the French navy.

BRUINSVISCH Dr 164/29. Dutch, hired as M/S (Dutch crew) 1940; RN crew 3.44; fuel carrier 5.44. Returned 1945.

BRURAY A/S Tr, 'Isles' class. Cook Welton & Gemmell 1.6.1942. Lent Portuguese navy 8.10.43–2.7.45 as 'P.1'; sold 11.2.46 Portuguese navy as SAO MIGUEL.

BRUTUS Tr 311/06, 1–6pdr. Hired as M/S 1914–19.

BRYHER A/S Tr, 'Isles' class. Cook Welton & Gemmell 8.4.1943. Sold 1947.

B.T.B. Dr 89/11, 1–6pdr. Hired 1915–19 and as M/S 11.39–1.46.

BUBBLE Admiralty steel Dr, 96gr. Brooke Marine 1919. Sold 1919, same name. (Served as UNICITY in WW.II.)

BUCCANEER Cstr 970/90. Hired as store carrier (RFA) 20.7.1916. Purchased 1919, sold 1921.

BUCCANEER Fleet tug, 840 tons, 165 x 32 ft, 1–3in. Fleming & Ferguson 7.9.1937. Sunk 26.8.46 by accidental hit from shell during target practice.

BUCCLEUCH Tr 146/03. Hired 1917–19.

BUCENTAUR Tr 184/07, 1–6pdr. Hired as M/S 1914–19 and as A/P Tr 12.39–40.

BUCEPHALUS (see VENTURE)

BUCHAN Dr 81/08, 1–3pdr. Hired 1915–19.

BUCHANS II Tr 203/18. Hired as A/P Tr 7.1940–8.46.

BUCKIE BURN DY tug, 172gr. Purchased 1919. BU 9.58.

BUCKINGHAM Tr 172/99. Hired 1918–19.

BUCKINGHAM Tr 253/30. Hired as M/S 8.1939; BDV 2.40–12.45.

BUCKLER Dr 81/11, 1–3pdr. Purchased 11.12.1914. Sold 1919. Hired as kite-balloon vessel 1942–45.

BUDDING ROSE Dr 88/14. Hired as BDV 1914–19. One on harbour service in 1942 may be same vessel.

BUDLEIA (see BLOOMFIELD)

BUFFALO DY mooring vessel 750 tons, 135 x 27½ ft. Bow McLachlan 25.1.1916. Sunk 4.4.41 on a British mine off Singapore.

BUFFALO II Tr 230/05, 1–6pdr. Hired 1915–19.

BUGLER (see BRIGADIER)

BULAN 1,048/24. Hired as cable ship 1942–46.

BULAWAYO (see NORTHMARK)

BULLDOG Tr 148/92. Hired 1917–19.

BULLFINCH Cable ship 1,950 tons, 229 x 36½ ft, 1–4in, 4–20mm. Swan Hunter 19.8.1940.

BULLFROG Salvage vessel 895 tons, 131 x 36 ft. Purchased 1915. Sold 2.23 Carriden S Bkg Co.

BULLFROG Cable ship 1,950 tons, 229 x 36½ ft, 1–4in, 4–20mm. Swan Hunter 26.1.1944. Sold 13.9.47, renamed *Retriever.*

BULLHEAD Cable ship 1,950 tons, 229 x 36½ ft, 1–4in, 4–20mm. Swan Hunter 3.10.1944. Sold 13.9.47.

BULLSEYE Cable ship 1,950 tons, 229 x 36½ ft. Swan Hunter. Cancelled 12.1944 and completed as *Alert.*

BULLWHALE Admiralty Wh, 'Z' class. Smiths Dk 28.6.1915. Sold 6.3.20 Allen Adams & Co, renamed *Rio Casma.*

BULOLO 6,267/38, 7–6in, 2–3in, 2–4in. Hired as AMC 9.1939; landing ship 1942. Returned 4.12.46.

BULRUSH Dr 90/07. Hired 11.1914–19.

BUNGAREE 3,155/37, 2–4in, 1–12pdr, 8–20mm, 423 mines. Hired as minelayer (RAN) 10.1940, commissioned 4.6.41. For return 1946.

BUNGAY (ex-*Maidstone*) 688/26. Hired as BBV 7.1941–10.43.

BUNTING (ex-*Swallow*) 160/05. Hired as store carrier (RFA) 4.1918–19.

BUNTING (ex-*Merlin*) Yt 181/96. Hired as danlayer 1.1940. Renamed FREELANCE 1940. Paid off 1944.

BUNTING (see FREELANCE)

BUNTING (see EMPEROR of INDIA)

BURD Dr 83/04. Hired 1915–19.

BUREAUCRAT Tug 137/16. Hired for harbour service 12.1916–19.

BURGONET BDV 530 tons, 135 x 30½ ft, 1–3in. Blyth DD 14.3.1939. For sale at Malta 1958.

BURKE Tr 363/30. Hired as M/S 9.1939, later purchased; wreck dispersal 1944, sold 1.46.

BURLINGTON (ex-*Chartered*) 2,068/21. Hired as M/S 17.5.1940. Renamed SOOTHSAYER 1940, FAIRFAX 1941. Repair ship 1944–45.

BURMA Oiler (RFA) 3,945 tons. Greenock & Grangemouth Co 3.3.1911. Sold 28.6.35, BU McLellan, Bo'ness.

BURMAH Tr 168/92. Hired 1917–19.

BURNBANKS Tr 193/05. Hired as danlayer 2.1940–41.

BURNHAVEN Dr 96/18. Hired on harbour service 8.1939. TRV 1943–45.

BURNLEY Tr 275/-. Hired as M/S 1915. Sunk 25.11.16 by mine off Orfordness.

BURONG Cstr 215/21. Hired as M/S base ship 1.1944–46.

BURRA Tr, 'Isles' class. Goole SB 29.3.1941. To the Italian navy 22.1.46.

BURRABRA Ferry 458/08. Hired as A/S training ship (RAN) 12.1942–44.

BUSEN 3 Wh 210/24. Norwegian, hired as M/S 12.1940. Renamed ICICLE 9.41. Returned 1.46.

BUSEN 4 Wh 266/25. Norwegian, hired as M/S 1941. Renamed STORM-WRACK 1942. Returned 11.45.

BUSEN 6 Wh 266/25. Norwegian, hired as M/S 1941. Renamed RAIN-STORM 9.41. Returned 1946.

BUSEN 7 Wh 254/26. Norwegian, hired as M/S 1941. Renamed SILHOUETTE 9.41. Lent Greek navy 8.43–46 as ACHELOOS. Returned 2.47.

BUSEN 8 Wh 394/28. Norwegian, hired as A/S Wh 10.1941. Renamed LURCHER 1941. Returned 12.45.

BUSEN 9 Wh 384/29. Norwegian, hired as A/S Wh 10.1941. Renamed MASTIFF 1941. Returned 12.45.

BUSEN 10 Wh 374/30. Norwegian, hired as A/S Wh 1941. Renamed COLLIE 1941. Renamed PRETORIA (SAN) 5.42. Returned 11.45.

BUSEN 11 Wh 279/31. Norwegian, hired as M/S 1941. Renamed SNOWDRIFT 12.41. Lent Greek navy 7.43–46 as THASOS. Returned 1947.

BUSH Tr 222/08, 1–12pdr. Hired 1915–20 and as A/S Tr 1–12pdr, 1940. Salvage vessel 3.44 and to MWT.

BUSHWOOD 2,314/30. Purchased as M/S 1940. Degaussing vessel 1942. Store carrier 1944–11.46.

BUSK Cstr 367/06. Purchased 1939. Sunk 19.2.40 as blockship.

BUSTLER (ex-*Merry Andrew*) Wood paddle tug 217 tons, 112 x 20½ ft. Purchased 28.3.1855. Sold circa 1893.

BUSTLER (ex-*Conqueror*) Iron paddle tug 346 tons, 130 x 20 ft. Purchased 1896. Sold 11.21 at Gibraltar.

BUSTLER Rescue tug 1,118 tons, 190 x 38½ ft, 1–3in, 2–20mm. Robb 4.12.1941.

BUSY Tug 300 tons, 95 x 24 ft, 2–MG. Gulfport, Pt Arthur, Texas 3.11.1941 on lend-lease. Returned 1.47 to the USN.

BUSY BEE Dr 92/03. Hired 8.1915–19.

BUTE Tr, 'Isles' class. Goole SB 12.5.1941. Sold 3.46.

BUTSER A/S Tr 750 tons, 166 x 28 ft, 1–12pdr, 3–20mm. Cook Welton & Gemmell 29.7.1941. Sold 1946, renamed *Balthazar.*

BUTTERMERE (ex-Kos XXV purchased 26.8.1939) A/S Wh, 560 tons, 138½ x 26½ ft, 1–12pdr, 1–20mm. Smiths Dk 30.6.39. Lent USN 3.42–10.42. Sold 5.46, renamed *Tiern.*

BUZZARD Tr 199/07, 1–6pdr. Hired 1914–20.

BUZZARD II Tr 181/98. Hired 1918–19 and as boom gate vessel 1940; renamed ARREST 1941. Returned 7.45.

BUZZARD (see DOUGLAS ALEXANDER)

BYDAND Dr, 1–6pdr. Hired 1917–19. One on ferry service 1942–45 may be same vessel.

BY GEORGE Tr 225/14. Hired 1914. Sunk 7.9.17 by mine in the Aegean.

BYNG Dr 101/20. Hired as BDV 10.1939–46.

BYSTANDER Yt 72/34. Hired as echo yt 1939–46.

B.Y.M.S. Motor minesweepers built in the USA on lend-lease 1942–43. 207 tons (Nos 1–80), 215 tons (Nos 137 up), 130 x 24½ ft, 1–3in, 2–20mm. (Note: 2,000 was added to the boat numbers early in 1944). The return date in many cases was nominal, the boats being sold by the USN on station.

BYMS.1–4 Assoc Car & Fndry, Wilmington. Returned 1947.

BYMS.5–8 Wheeler, Whitestone NY. Returned 1946.

BYMS.9–14 Assoc SB, Seattle. No 10 listed to 1945; others for disposal 1.47 at Malta.

BYMS.15–16 Dashel Carter, Benton Harbour. Returned 1946 and 1947 resp.

BYMS.17–20 Bellingham Marine Rly. Nos 17, 18 at Hong Kong 7.46 to return; No 19 beached Italian coast after mining 19.9.43; No 20 for disposal 1947.

BYMS.21–24 Seattle SB Co. No 22 sunk 16.8.44 by mine off the south of France; others returned 1947.

BYMS.25–28 Ballard Marine Rly, Seattle. No 25 listed to 1945; others for disposal at Malta 1.47.

BYMS.29–30 Barbour, New Bern. No 29 returned 1947; No 30 sunk 8.10.44 by mine off Le Havte.

BYMS.31–36 Assoc Car. Nos 31,34, 36 returned 1947; No 32 returned 1948; No 33 to Greek navy 1945 as KALYMNOS; No 35 to Egyptian navy 1947 as MALEK FUAD.

BYMS.37–42 Barbour. No 37 to Italian navy 1947 as ORCHIDEA; No 38 to Dutch navy 1947 as MARSDEP; No 47 to Egyptian navy 1947 as DARFOUR; others returned 1947.

BYMS.43–54 Gibbs, Jackson. Nos 43,45 returned 1946 Nos 46,51,54 returned 1947; Nos 44,47,49 returned 1948 then to Finnish navy; Nos 48,50 to Dutch navy 1947; No 52 returned 1948; No 53 sunk 28.4.45 by mine in the Mediterranean.

BYMS.55–64 Westerguard, Biloxi. No 55 returned 1949; No 56 to Greek navy 1946 as PAXOI; Nos 57,58 returned 1947; Nos 59–62 & 64 returned 1946; No 63 returned 1948.

BYMS.65–80 Wheeler, Whitestone. Nos 65–67 to Greek navy 1944; No 68 to Greek navy 1946; Nos 69,75 to Egyptian navy 1947; No 74 to Greek navy 1944 as KASSOS and lost 15.10.44; No 78 to Greek navy 1947 as VEGAS; No 77 mined 25.10.44 off Corinth; others returned 1946–48.

BYMS.137,141,142. Astoria Marine Constr. All returned 1947 and last two to Italian navy.

BYMS.148–50 San Diego Marine Constr. No 148 returned 1946 and other two to Egyptian and Italian navies resp. in 1947.

BYMS.152–54 Campbell, San Diego. All returned 1947.

BYMS.155–57, 161–62. Berger, Manitowoc. Nos 155, 156 to Dutch navy 1947; No 157 returned 1948; No 161 returned 1946; No 162 listed to 1945.

BYMS.167–68 Dashel Carter. Returned 1948 and 1946.

BYMS.171–75, 181–82 Grebe, Chicago. Nos 171, 172 to Greek navy 1946 as KEFALINIA and KERKYRA; No 175 to Egyptian navy 1947 as TOR; others returned 1947–48.

BYMS.185–91, 194. Greenport Basin, Long Island. Nos 185,186 to Greek navy 1944; No 188 to Dutch navy 1947 as VOLKERAK; No 190 Greek SIMI 1945; No 191 Greek KOS 1944 and mined 15.10.44; No 194 to Italian navy 1947 as TULIPANO; others returned 1947.

BYMS.197, 202–06 Hiltebrant, Kingston NY. No 197 returned (1948?); No 202 returned 1947; No 206 to Italian navy 1947 as MAGNOLIA; others returned 1946.

BYMS. 207–14 R Jacob, City Island. Nos 207, 208 to France 1944 as D.354,355 resp. No 209 to Greek navy 1946; No 210 to Dutch navy 1946; No 212 to Egyptian navy 1947; others returned 1947.

BYMS.217,221 Martinac, Tacoma. Both returned 1946.

BYMS.223,225 Mojean, Tacoma. Both returned 1946.

BYMS.226,229,230,232–34 Sample, Booth Bay. No 226 returned (1948?); No 229 to Greek navy 1944; No 230 Dutch OOSTERSCHELDE 1947; others returned 1947–48.

BYMS.236,240 Stadium Yt Basin, Cleveland. No 236 returned 1946; No 240 to Greek navy 1945 as ITHAKI.

BYMS.244,246 Tacoma Boat Bldg. Both returned 1946.

BYMS.252–58 Weaver, Orange Texas. No 254 to Dutch navy 1947 as DEURLOO; No 255 sunk 5.10.44 by mine off Boulogne; others returned 1946–47.

BYMS.261,264 S Coast Co, Newport Beach Cal. Both returned 1946.
BYMS.277–78 Martinac. Both to Italian navy 1947.
BYMS.279–80 Grebe. No 279 returned 1948; No 280 to Italian navy 1947.
BYMS.282,284 San Diego Marine Constr. Both returned 1946.

C & A Dr. Hired on harbour service 1942–44.
CABALSIN Tr 222/04, 1–6pdr. German *Burhave* captured 1915. Sold 16.3.20, renamed *Star of the Orient.*
CACHALOT (Z.7) Admiralty Wh, 'Z' class. Smiths Dk 28.7.1915. Sold 1933 renamed *Gladiator.*
CACHOSIN Tr 218/12, 1–12pdr. German *Doktor Krugler* captured 1915. Sold 16.3.20, renamed *Cairnrigh.*
CACOUNA Yt 202/32. Hired as examination vessel 1940–45.
CADELLA Tr 289/13. Hired as BDV 10.1939–46.
CADET Tr 323/14. Hired 1917–19.
CADORNA Tr 255/17, 1–12pdr. Hired 7.1917–19 and as M/S 5.40–5.45.
CADUCEUS (ex-*Manxman*) 2,030/04. Hired as radar training ship 10.1941–45.
CAERPHILLY CASTLE Tr 275/19. Hired as M/S 8.1939–40.
CAERSIN Tr 128/92, 1–6pdr. German *Dora* captured 1915. Sold 17.3.20.
CAESAR A.ship hired 1642–43.
CAESAR II Tr 315/06, 2–6pdr. Hired 1914–19.
CAESAREA 1,505/10. Hired as ABS 31.10.1914–12.15. Became *Manxmaid* and served as BRUCE in WW.II.
CAILIFF Tr, 'Isles' class. Collingwood SY 30.4.1942. Lent RCN 9.42–17.6.45; sold 1946, renamed *Borgenes.*
CAIRN DY tug 170 tons, 85 x 24½ ft. Doig, Grimsby 19.1.1965.
CAIRNDALE (ex-*Erato* purchased on stocks) Oiler (RFA) 17,000 tons, 460 x 59 ft. Harland & Wolff 25.10.1938. Sunk 30.5.41 by U-boat west of Gibraltar.
CAIRNEY Store carrier (RFA), 131gr, 125 x 16½ ft. Livingstone, Hull 1915. Sold 26.2.47.
CAIRNGARTH Tug 133/13. Hired 11.1917–19.
CAIRNWELL Tr 141/95. Hired 1918–19.
CAIRO Tr 172/02, 1–6pdr. Hired as base ship 10.1914 M/S 1916–19.
CAISTER CASTLE Tr 109/14, 1–3pdr. Hired 1915–19.
CALAIS Lighter 230/03. Hired as degaussing vessel 16.12.1940–48.
CALA MARA Yt 313/98. Hired as M/S 6.1941; laid up 1943–45.

CALANTHE Yt 430/98, 2–6pdr. Hired 19.11.1914; laid up 5.17, returned 1919. Hired as examination vessel 8.39. Sunk 24.4.41 by air attack off Milos.

CALCEOLARIA Dr 92/08, 1–6pdr. Hired 1915. Sunk 27.10.18 by mine off the Elbow Lt buoy.

CALCUTTA Tr (RIN), 'Basset' class. Hooghly Dk & Eng Co 8.3.1943. Sold 1947.

CALDY Tr 222/08, 1–6pdr. Hired 1915–19 and as A/P Tr 27.11.39–22.1.40.

CALDY Tr, 'Isles' class. Lewis 31.8.1943. Wreck dispersal 1946; oil-tank cleaning vessel 1951.

CALEDONIA Tr 161/06. Hired 1915. Sunk 17.3.17 by mine off the Northumberland coast.

CALEDONIA II Dr 82/92. Hired 11.1914–12.14.

CALEDONIA Paddle 244/88. Hired as M/S 26.4.1917–18.11.19.

CALEDONIA II Tr 148/98. Hired 1917–19.

CALEDONIAN SALVOR Salvage vessel 1,360 tons, 200 x 39 ft, 2–40mm, 4–20mm. Basalt Rock Co, Napa, California 22.8.1942 and to the RN 20.5.43 on lend-lease. Returned 1946 to the USN.

CALETA Yt 138/30. Hired as HDPC 1940–45.

CALGARIAN 17,515/13. Hired as AMC 15.9.1914. Sunk 1.3.18 by 'U.19' off Rathlin Is.

CALIBAN Tr 277/19. Hired as BDV 12.1939; purchased 1943. Sold 13.12.46.

CALIFOL Oiler (RFA), 6,572gr. Raylton Dixon 2.5.1916. Renamed ROSELEAF 1917. Sold 15.7.19.

CALIFORNIA 16,792/23, 8–6in, 2–3in. Hired as AMC 8.1939–1942.

CALIPH Tr 226/06, 1–6pdr. Hired 8.14–19.

CALISTA Yt 265/02, 2–3pdr. Hired 9.1914–6.12.17.

CALISTOGA Dr 72/10. Hired 1915–19.

CALLIOPE II Tr 240/07. Hired 1914. Sunk 5.3.16 in collision off the Butt of Lewis.

CALLIOPSIS Dr 97/18. Hired for harbour service 1941–45.

CALLSIN Tr 126/96, 1–6pdr. German *Mond* captured 1915. Sold 7.4.21, same name.

CALM Admiralty steel Dr, 96gr. Duthie Torry 9.5.1918. Sold 10.8.20, renamed *John Hedley*. (Served as PRE-EMINENT in WW.II.)

CALM (see GOS.7)

CALSHOT Tender/tug 679/30. Hired on ferry service 16.12.1940–1.9.45.

CALUMSIN Tr 224/02, 1–12pdr. German *Wurzburg* captured 7.10.1915. Sold 31.12.21.

CALVAY Tr, 'Isles' class. Cook Welton & Gemmell 29.11.1943. Sold 11.46, renamed *William Fenton*.

CALVERTON Tr 214/13, 1–6pdr. Hired as M/S 11.1939. Sunk 29.11.40 by mine off the Humber.

CALVI Tr 363/30. Hired as M/S 9.1939. Sunk 29.5.40 by air attack off Dunkirk.

CALVIA Tr 304/15, 1–6pdr. Hired 1915–19.

CALVINIA Tr 191/01, 1–6pdr. Hired 1915–19 and as danlayer 1.40–12.45.

CALYPSO Tr 187/01. Hired 1918–19.

CALYX (ex-*Calypso*) 2,876/04. Hired as AMC 19.11.1914–26.6.15.

CAMBODIA Tr 284/11, 1–12pdr. Hired 1915–19.

CAMBRE Dr. French, seized 7.1940. On harbour service 1940–41 then laid up.

CAMBRIA 1,842/97. Hired as ABS 8.8.1914. Hospital ship 7.8.15.

CAMBRIA Tr 206/05, 1–6pdr. Hired 8.1914–19.

CAMBRIA Cable ship 1,960/05. Hired 1941. Sunk 8.11.45 in collision with *Almirante Ruis Luis* off Montevideo.

CAMBRIAN II Tr 191/00, 1–6pdr. Hired 1914–19.

CAMBRIAN Tr 338/24. Hired as BDV 9.1939. Sunk 30.5.40 by mine at Spithead.

CAMBRIAN SALVOR Salvage vessel 1,360 tons, 200 x 39 ft, 2–40mm, 4–20mm. Basalt Rock Co 7.9.1942 and to the RN 1.7.43 on lend-lease. Returned 1946 to the USN.

CAMBRIDGE (ex-*Cambria*) Paddle 420/95, 1–12pdr, 1–6pdr. Hired as M/S 10.1914–9.6.19. (Served as PLINLIMMON in WW.II.)

CAMBRIDGESHIRE Tr 443/35, 1–4in. Hired as A/S Tr 8.1939–45.

CAMBRISIN Tr 160/91, 1–6pdr. German *Orion* captured 9.1915. Sold 17.3.20.

CAMBUSDOON Wood MMS. A.Zoghzoghy, Beirut 1943. To Greek navy 7.43 as NAFPAKTIA.

CAMBUSKENNITH Wood MMS. A.Moosali, Beirut 1943. To Greek navy 7.43 as MONEMVASSIA.

CAMBUSLANG Wood MMS. A.Tahhab, Tripoli Syria 1.10.42. To Greek navy 1943 as AEGIALIA; to RN 3.44 as tender; sold 1946.

CAMBUSLIE Wood MMS. A.Moosali, Beirut 1943. To Greek navy 7.43 as AMVRAKIA.

CAMEL DY lighter, 100bm. In service 1851. BU completed 5.3.1877 at Chatham. (Also Chatham.YC.1.)

CAMEL Iron paddle tug, 319bm, 484 tons, 130 x 23 ft. Palmer, Jarrow 3.2.1866. Sold 3.4.1913 Ward, Preston.

CAMEL DY paddle tug 690 tons, 145 x 28 ft. Bow McLachlan 19.10.1914. BU 1962.

CAMELLIA II Dr 85/07, 1–3pdr. Hired 1915–19.

CAMEO Tr 172/98, 1–12pdr. Hired 1914–18.

CAMERATA 3,723/10. Hired as fleet auxiliary 5.8.1914—19.

CAMITO 6,611/15, 4—6in. Hired as escort ship 26.2.1918—27.3.19 and as OBV, 6,833gr, 2—6in, 1—12pdr 9.40. Sunk 6.5.41 by U-boat in the N.Atlantic.

CAMPAIGNER Tug 163/11. Hired 13.5.1915—3.7.17.

CAMPANIA II Dr 90/07. Hired 1915. Sunk 5.3.17 by unknown cause off St Abbs Head.

CAMPANIA II Tr 167/95. In service 1918.

CAMPANULA Dr 95/13, 1—6pdr. Hired 1915—19.

CAMPEADOR V Yt 213/38. Hired as A/S Yt 9.1939. Sunk 22.6.40 by mine off Portsmouth.

CAMPEADOR Yt 96/34. Hired 23.2.1940—46.

CAMPENIA Tr, 'Isles' class. Collingwood SY 1.6.1942. Renamed BOWELL 9.42; MISCOU 11.42. Sold 3.46 renamed *Cleveland*.

CAMPERDOWN Cutter 14, 159bm, 14—12pdr carr. Hired 1798—10.1804.

CAMPERDOWN Dr 97/07, 1—3pdr. Hired 1915—19.

CAMPINA Tr 290/13. Hired as A/P Tr 9.1939. Purchased 6.1940; sunk 22.7.40 by mine off Holyhead.

CAMPINE DY tug, 61gr, 75½ x 15 ft. Yarwood, Northwich 1919. Sold 8.22, renamed *Britannia*.

CAMPOBELLO Tr, 'Isles' class. Collingwood SY 19.6.1942. Foundered 16.3.43 in the N.Atlantic.

CAMPSIN Tr 130/94, 1—6pdr. German *Adjutant* captured 1915. Sold 18.2.20.

CANADA II Tr 231/86, 1—6pdr. Hired as BDV 1915—19.

CANADIAN PRINCE Tr 455/37, 1—4in. Purchased as A/S Tr 8.1939. Sold French navy 28.11.39 as La BONOISE.

CANCER Tr 230/16, 1—6pdr. Hired 1916—19.

CANDIDATE Tr 161/06, 1—12pdr. Hired 1914—19.

CANFISCO MFV 62/25. Hired (RCN) 1941—44.

CANNA Tr, 'Isles' class. Cochrane 18.11.1940. Lost 5.12.42 after accidental explosion at Lagos, W.Africa.

CANNING 5,375/96. Commissioned as kite-balloon ship 29.6.1915; depot ship 1917. Sold 12.2.20.

CANNON Armament tug, 96gr. A.Hall 30.9.1943.

CANNOSIN Tr 153/94, 1—6pdr. German *Paul* captured 1915. Sold 16.3.20.

CANTATRICE Tr 302/15. Hired 1915. Sunk 5.11.16 by mine off Yarmouth.

CANTERBURY 2,910/29. Hired as air target 6.1942 then landing ship to 1945.

CANTON 15,784/38, 9—6in, 2—3in. Hired as AMC 9.1939. To MWT 14.4.44.

CANUTE Tug 271/23. Hired as DY tug 1.7.1941–46.
CAPABLE Rescue tug 890 tons, 165 x 36 ft, 1–3in, 2–20mm. Hall Russell 22.11.1945.
CAPACITY Water boat, 55 tons. Hired 12.6.1941–46.
CAP d'ANTIFER Tr 294/20. French M/S ex-Belgian *Compass,* seized 3.7.40 at Southampton. A/P vessel 1940; M/S 1941. Sunk 13.2.44 by E-boat torpedo off the Humber.
CAP des PALMES 3,082/35. French AMC seized 9.11.1940 by the Free-French COMMANDANT DOMINE off Libreville. Free-French AMC to 1942 then to MWT.

CAPE ARGONA Tr 494/36, 1–4in. Purchased 8.1939 as A/S Tr. Sold 1945.
CAPE BARRACOUTA Tr 390/30, 1–12pdr. Hired as M/S Tr 8.1939–1.46.
CAPE BEALE MFV 47/25. M/S (RCN). Hired 9.1939–45.
CAPE CHELYUSKIN Tr 494/36, 1–4in. Purchased as A/S Tr 8.1939. Sunk 29.4.40 by air attack off the coast of Norway.
CAPE COLONY Dr 82/08. Hired 1916. Sunk 8.1.17 by mine off Harwich.
CAPE COMORIN Tr 504/36, 1–4in. Hired as A/S Tr 8.1939–45.
CAPE FINISTERRE Tr 594/39, 1–12pdr. Hired as A/S Tr 2.1940. Sunk 2.8.40 by air attack off Harwich.
CAPE HOWE 4,440/30. Commissioned as decoy ship 15.9.1939. Sunk 21.6.40 by U-boat west of Ireland while operating under the name PRUNELLA.
CAPE LEEOWIN 1,406/25. Hired as survey vessel (RAN) 8.1943–46.
CAPE MARIATO Tr 497/36, 1–4in. Hired as A/S Tr 6.1940–12.45.
CAPE MELVILLE Tr 342/29, 1–12pdr. Hired as M/S 8.1939–9.45.
CAPE NYEMETSKI Tr 422/34, 1–4in. Hired as M/S 8.1939–2.46.
CAPE PALLISER Tr 497/36, 1–4in. Hired as A/S Tr 9.1939–9.45.
CAPE PASSARO Tr 590/39, 1–4in. Hired A/S Tr 9.1939. Sunk 21.5.40 by air attack off Narvik.
CAPE PORTLAND Tr 497/36, 1–4in. Purchased as A/S Tr 9.1939. Lent Portuguese navy 8.10.43–6.8.44 as P.5; sold 1945.
CAPE SABLE 4,398/36. Commissioned 19.9.1939 as decoy vessel, operating under the name CYPRUS. AMC 2.41; to MWT 3.42.
CAPE SIRETOKO Tr 590/39. Purchased as A/S Tr 9.1939. Sunk 29.4.40 by air attack off Norway. Salved 1940 and became German GOTE; sunk 11.5.44 by air attack near Makkaur.
CAPE SPARTEL Tr 346/29, 1–12pdr. Hired as M/S 8.1939. Sunk 2.2.42 by air attack off the Humber.
CAPE TRAFALGAR Tr 326/17. Purchased 5.1940 as A/P Tr. BDV 1.41. Sold 6.1.47.

CAPE WARWICK (ex-*Compton*) Tr 516/37, 1—4in. Purchased as A/S Tr 8.1939. Lent USN 3.42—10.42. Sold 26.1.46.

CAPELLA Dr 92/11, 1—57mm. Hired 1915—19.

CAPETOWN Dr 83/08, 1—3pdr. Hired 1914. Renamed CAPO 1918. Returned 1919.

CAPETOWN II Tr 188/08. Hired 1917—19.

CAP FERRAT Dr 139/38. French M/S ex-Belgian *Jeanne Paulette* seized 3.7.1940 at Southampton. M/S to 1946.

CAP FREHEL Dr 92/31. French M/S ex-Belgian *Rene Georges*, seized 7.1940 at Southampton. Reverted to RENE GEORGES 1940; fate unknown.

CAP GRIS-NEZ Dr 67/28. French M/S ex-Belgian *Dolfijn,* seized 7.1940 at Southampton. Believed lost or reverted to DOLFIJN and fate unknown.

CAPE NEGRE Dr. French M/S ex-Belgian *Pax,* seized 3.7.1940 at Southampton. Reverted to PAX, M/S to 1944.

CAPO (see CAPETOWN)

CAPORAL PEUGEOT Dr 102/23. French M/S seized 3.7.1940 at Plymouth. Laid up to 1943 then A/P to 12.45.

CAPRICE (ex-*Holly*) Dr 79/04. Hired for examination service 1940. Renamed CAPRICORN 1943. Returned 1947.

CAPRICORNUS Tr 220/17, 1—6pdr. Hired 1917—19 and as M/S 11.39. Sunk 7.12.40 by mine off SE coast.

CAPSTONE Tr 275/17, 1—12pdr. Hired as A/P Tr 6.1940; M/S 2.42—10.45.

CAPTAIN Tr 126/92. Hired 1917—19.

CAPTAIN FRYATT Dr, 1—3pdr. Hired 1917—19.

CAPTAIN POLLEN Tr 275/17. Hired 1917—19.

CAPTIVE (ex-HANS CAPTIVE renamed 1944) Rescue tug, 766/23. German *Max Berendt* sunk 11.7.42 at Tobruk and raised by the RN 1943. Sunk 3.2.46 in Potomas Bay.

CAPTOR RCMP vessel hired for examination service (RCN) 5.9.1939. Became nominal base ship in 1943.

CARBILL Tr 242/17, 1—6pdr. Hired 1917—19.

CARBINE Armament tug 151 tons, 85 x 22½ ft. Yarwood, Northwich 19.3.1935. Transferred 1960 to Baileys (Malta) Ltd.

CARBINEER Tr, 276gr, 130 x 24 ft, 1—12pdr. Purchased 11.12.1914; Smiths Dk 15.2.15. Wrecked 18.5.16 on Crebawethan Point.

CARBINEER II (see FUSILIER)

CARBON (C.150) (ex-*John Holloway*) DY tug, 185gr, 72 x 17 ft. Purchased 1900. Sold 1947.

CARBOSIN Tr 158/96, 1—6pdr. German *Darmstadt* captured 30.9.1915. Sold 5.10.20.

CARCASS (ex-*Hibernia*) Tug 214/84. Hired as ABV 2.8.1914. Renamed HIBERNIA II in 1915.

CARCASS (ex-*Java*) Tug 128/05. Hired 21.7.1915–14.5.19.
CARDIFF CASTLE Tr 251/07, 1–12pdr. Hired 1914–19.
CARDIFF CASTLE Tr 276/19. Hired as M/S 8.1939–1.46.
CARDINAL Tr 309/12, 1–12pdr. Hired 1915–19.
CARDY Tug. Hired for DY service 1940–45.
CAREFUL Rescue tug 890 tons, 165 x 36 ft, 1–3in, 2–20mm. A.Hall
23.10.1945.
CARENCY Tr 233/16, 1–6pdr. Hired 10.1916–19 and as A/S Tr 1940;
examination service 1943–47.
CAREW CASTLE Tr 256/12. Hired 1915. Sunk 12.6.17 by mine off
Hartland Point.
CARIAD Yt 153/03. Hired as BBV 9.1940–44.
CARIBBEAN 5,820/90. Hired as AMC 19.11.1914. Accommodation
ship 6.15; foundered 26.9.15 on passage to Scapa Flow.
CARIBOU Transport (Newfoundland govt) 2,200 tons, 260 x 41½ ft.
Schiedam, Holland 10.1925. Sunk 14.10.42 by U-boat in the Cabot
Strait.
CARIBOU (ex-*Elfreda*) Yt 301/28. American, purchased as A/S Yt
(RCN), commissioned 9.10.40. Paid off 9.10.45.
CARIEDA Tr 225/13, 1–6pdr. Hired 1915–19.
CARILON Tr 226/15. Hired 1915. Sunk 24.12.15 by mine off Margate.
CARINA (ex-*Golden Eagle*) Yt 356/99. Hired as A/S Yt 1.1940–46.
CARINTHIA 20,277/25, 8–6in, 2–3in. Hired as AMC 8.1939. Sunk
7.6.40 by 'U.46' west of Ireland.
CARISBROOKE Tr 230/28, 1–12pdr. Hired as M/S 8.1939. For disposal
7.46.
CARLO 1,737/11. Purchased as ammo.hulk 14.9.1939. BU 1951.
CARLTON Tr 266/-. Hired 1915. Sunk 21.2.16 by mine off Folkestone.
CARMANIA 19,650/05, 8–4.7in. Hired as AMC 8.8.1914–6.7.16.
CARMANIA II Tr 250/07, 1–6pdr. Hired as M/L 1915–19.
CARMELA Yt 148/03. Hired as accommodation ship 12.8.1941;
purchased 1943, sold 11.45.
CARMENITA Aux.barge 109/20. Hired as BBV 12.1939. accommodation
ship 1942; for disposal 11.45.
CARMI Dr 86/03. Hired 3.1915–25.5.15.
CARMI III Dr 88/08. Hired 1915–19.
CARMINA Tug 49/15. Purchased for examination service 29.11.1939.
For disposal 1.48 at Gibraltar.
CARNARVON CASTLE 20,122/26, 8–6in, 2–3in. Hired as AMC
8.9.1939–44. (Was to have been purchased for conversion to A/C
carrier 8.42.)
CAROL Oiler (RFA) 2,178 tons, 200 x 34 ft. Devonport DY 5.7.1913.
Sold 28.6.35, BU at Bo'ness.

CAROL & DOROTHY Dr 89/05. Hired 1915–19.

CAROLINE Tr 253/30. M/S (Dutch crew) 1940. Sunk 28.4.41 by mine off Milford Haven.

CAROLINE MOLLER Tug 444/19, 1–12pdr. Hired as rescue tug 1.1940. Sunk 7.10.42 by E-boat torpedo in the North Sea.

CARONIA 19,686/04. Hired as AMC 2.8.1914–22.9.16.

CARRAIG Yt 64/10. Hired as HDPC 3.1.1940. Laid up 12.43.

CARRIGAN HEAD 4,201/01. Hired as supply ship (RFA) 4.8.1914; commissioned as decoy ship (Q.4) 1.6.16, 1–4in, 2–12pdr; escort ship, 2–6in, 2–4in from 8.17–2.19. (Also served as decoy ship SUFFOLK COAST.)

CARRIGART Dr 84/12, 1–3pdr. Hired 8.1915–19.

CARRON Wood paddle tug, 267bm, 445 tons, 130 x 21 ft. Devonport DY 31.5.1867. BU 1885.

CARRON Iron paddle DY tug 450 tons. Purchased 14.3.1888. Sold 1904. Hired 1916–19.

CARRON 2,531/06, 3,870 tons, 2–4.7in. Hired as ABS 22.11.1914–9.10.19.

CARRON 1,017/94. Purchased 1939. Sunk 3.3.40 as blockship at Scapa Flow.

CARROO Cstr 281/97. Hired (RAN) 6.1942–12.44.

CARRY ON Dr 93/19. Hired as BBV 12.1939. Sunk 17.12.40 by mine off Sheerness.

CARTARET Cutter 6, 59bm. Hired 1800–01 and 6.1803–2.1805.

CARTHAGE 14,253/31, 8–6in, 2–3in, 2–40mm. Hired as AMC 17.9.1939–10.43.

CARTIER Canadian govt survey vessel 850 tons. Swan Hunter 1910. Served as patrol vessel, 3–12pdr, 1914–19 and 1942–45.

CARTMEL Tug 304/07. Hired as rescue tug 6.1917–19.

CARTMEL Tender, 78gr. Pimblott 4.10.1967.

CARYANDA Yt 65/38. Hired as HDPC 3.9.1939–46.

CARYSFORT II Tr 243/15, 1–6pdr. Hired 6.1915–19.

CASCADE Admiralty steel Dr. Ouse SB 3.7.1918. Sold 1945.

CASORIA Tr 185/97, 1–6pdr. Hired 1914–19.

CASPIAN Tr 150/95. Hired 1918–19.

CASSANDRA Tr 174/05, 1–3pdr. Hired 1915–19.

CASSIOPEIA Dr 97/20. Hired as hospital tender 1940–45.

CASSOWARY Tr 222/98, 1–3pdr. Hired 1915–19.

CASTELNAU Tr 337/18. French M/S seized 3.7.1940 at Southampton. Returned 2.46.

CASTLE 36–gun ship, 330bm. Hired 1664–67.

CASTLE BAY Dr 108/18. Hired as M/S 11.1939–46.

CASTLE HARBOUR 730/29. Hired on examination service 1940. Sunk 16.10.42 by U-boat in the W.Indies.

CASTLEROCK Tr 259/04. Hired as A/P Tr 13.5.1940–9.45.

CASTLE STUART Dr 80/10. Hired 7.8.1914–19 and on harbour service 1941; hospital drifter 1944–45.

CASTLETON Tr 211/04. Hired as A/P Tr 11.1939–1.40.

CASTOR Tug 70/-. Hired as DY tug 11.1915–18.

CASTOR II Tr 209/16, 1–6pdr. Hired 7.1916–19.

CASTOR 199/31. Dutch, hired as BBV 21.7.1940; laid up 3.43–45.

CASWELL Tr 276/17, 1–6pdr. Hired 1.1917–19 and as M/S 2.40–46.

CAT II Yt 86/17. Hired as danlayer 9.1939–12.39.

CATANIA Yt 668/95, 2–6pdr. Hired 7.9.1914–2.19.

CATAPULT Armament tug, 184gr, 98½ x 21 ft. Yarwood 7.1944.

CATERINA Yt 81/24. Hired as HDPC 2.1940. To War Dept 1.42.

CATHAY 15,225/25, 8–6in, 2–3in. Hired as AMC 8.1939–42.

CATHERINE Dr 78/14, 2–MG. Hired as A/P vessel 1939. Foundered 8.6.42 in the Scapa area.

CATHERINE JEAN (MFV.651) MFV hired as mining tender 1943–46.

CATO 1,064/14. Hired as store carrier (RFA) 4.11.1914–21.2.15.

CATSPAW Admiralty steel Dr, 96gr. Ouse SB 6.8.1918. Foundered 31.12.19 in the Kattegat.

CAULONIA Tr 296/12, 1–6pdr. Hired 1915–19 and as A/P Tr 1940; M/S 4.42. Foundered 31.3.43 in Rye Bay after running aground.

CAUTIOUS (see PRUDENT)

CAVA Tr, 'Isles' class. Fleming & Ferguson 3.3.1941. Sold 16.5.47, renamed *Lucia Venturi.*

CAVALCADE (see COURSER)

CAVE Tr 247/02, 1–12pdr. Hired 1914–19.

CAVINA 6,907/24, 2–6in, 1–12pdr. Hired as OBV 6.8.1940–7.7.42.

CAWDOR CASTLE Dr 84/08. Hired as BDV 3.1915–19.

CAWNPORE Tr (RIN), 'Basset' class. Burn, Calcutta. Ordered 7.1942. Deferred 10.44, cancelled 3.45.

CAWSAND Tender, 78gr. Pimblott 24.1.1968.

CAYRIAN Tr 216/11. Hired 1917–19 and as A/P Tr 11.39; M/S 7.40–12.45.

CAYTON WYKE Tr 373/32, 1–12pdr. Purchased as A/S Tr 8.1939. Sunk 8.7.40 by E-boat torpedo off Dover.

CD.1–CD.100 Admiralty drifters built in Canada 1918. (See Admiralty drifters in list of classes.)

CD.54, 86–88 and 93 all lost 1920 on passage to the UK.

CD.43 lost 1921; CD.1 renamed EBBTIDE 1924; CD.82 renamed ONYX 1919. All others sold 1919–22.

CECIL COOMBES (see GEORGE AIKEN)

CECILE MAPLESON Cstr 344/24. Hired as cable layer 31.12.1941. To S.African govt 5.44.

CECILIA A.ship, 187bm. Hired 5.3.1806–12.1810.
CECIL RHODES Tr 112/91. Hired 1918–19.
CEDAR Tr 219/09, 1–6pdr. Hired 1914–19.
CEDAR (ex-*Arab*) M/S Tr, 649/33, 1–12pdr. Purchased 11.1935. Sold 7.46, renamed *Red Gauntlet.*
CEDARBERG Wh (SAN) 307/35, 1–4in. Purchased 14.3.1941. Sold 7.5.46, renamed *Uni 7.*
CEDARDALE Oiler (RFA) 17,000 tons, 460 x 59 ft. Blyhswood 25.3.1939. Sold 1.60, BU at Hong Kong.
CEDAR LAKE Motor M/S (RCN) 255 tons, 126 x 28 ft, 2–20mm. Taylor, Toronto 1.8.1945. To Russian navy 11.45.
CEDAR LEAF Tr 176/10. Hired 11.1914–19.
CEDAROL (see ROWANOL)
CEDARWOOD Survey vessel (RCN) 566 tons. Transferred from government 4.10.1948. Paid off 10.56.
CEDRIC 21,040/03. Commissioned as AMC 17.11.1914. Returned 20.1.16.
CEDRIC Tr 230/05. Hired as A/P Tr 11.1939; BBV 5.40–44.
CEDRON Dr 84/07. Hired as tender 11.1914–19.
CELANDINE II Dr 73/06, 1–3pdr. Hired 1915–19.
CELEROL Oiler (RFA) 4,900 tons, 335 x 41½ ft. Short, Sunderland 23.3.1917. Arrived 17.7.58 McLellan, Bo'ness to BU.
CELIA M/S Tr 545 tons, 150 x 28 ft, 1–12pdr, 3–20mm. Cochrane 15.9.1940. Sold 1946, same name.
CELIA DY tug, 40gr. Pimblott, Northwich 25.5.1966.
CELOSIA Dr 87/08. Hired 1915–19.
CELTIA Tr 239/07. Hired 1917–19 and as A/P Tr 25.11.39–19.1.40.
CELTIC 20,904/01, 8–6in. Hired as AMC 10.1914–11.1.16.
CELTIC PRIDE Cstr 456/10. Hired as fleet auxiliary 7.1915–1.7.20.
CELURCA Dr 94/16. Hired 1916–19.
CENSIN Tr 145/94, 1–6pdr. German *Burgermeister Smidt* captured 30.9.1915. Sold 11.5.20.
CENTURION 26–gun ship, 250bm. Hired 1588–89.
CENTURION 22–gun ship, 200bm. Hired 1620–21.
CENTURION Tr 156/04, 1–3pdr. Hired as BDV 1915–19.
CENWULF Dr 93/12. Hired 11.1914–12.14 and 8.15–19.
CEOL MARA II Yt 63/29. Hired as BBV 17.9.1940. Laid up 3.44.
CEPHEUS Tr 155/91. Hired 1917–19.
CERBERUS (ex-*Oceana*) Tug 337/89. Hired as ABV 3.8.1914–18. Renamed *Oceana,* stranded 18.10.18 at Scapa.
CERBERUS Tr 155/91. Hired 1915–15.
CEREALIA Tr 220/05. Hired 1915–19.
CERES Sloop 10. Hired 1793–94.
CERES Gunvessel. Hired 9.1801–12.01.

CERES (see CERUS)

CERESIA Tr 284/14. Hired 1914—19. (Served in WW.II as CHORLEY.)

CERISIO Tr 338/15. Purchased as M/S 9.1939. Sold 1945.

CERUS DY buoy boat, 25bm. Purchased 8.9.1830. Renamed CERES 1860. Sold 26.7.1877 at Greenock. (Also known as Devonport YC.3.)

CERVIA Tug 157/25. Hired 1942—45.

CETO Yt 185/88, 2—3pdr. Hired 8.9.1914—11.3.18.

CETO Yt 130/35. Purchased as calibrating Yt 5.1940. Sold 2.46.

CETUS Tr 139/93. Hired 1918—19.

CEVIC (see BAYOL)

CEVIC Tr 151/95. Hired 1918—19.

CEVIC (ex-*Pelican*) Tr 250/08. Hired as fuel carrier 1.1943. Water carrier 3.44—8.44.

CEYLON Tug 150/99. Hired as ABS 17.11.1914—13.3.19.

CEYLON Yt 311/91. Hired 6.1915—5.16.

CEYLONITE Tr 249/18, 1—12pdr. Hired as M/S 4.1940. For disposal 1.46.

CHAFFINCH French navy tug NACQUEVILLE seized 7.1940. M/L tug 4.41; DY tug 1944. Returned 8.45.

CHAGFORD (see BRACONDALE)

CHAINSHOT Armament tug 106 tons. Philip, Dartmouth 1946.

CHAKDINA 3,030/14, 2—3pdr. Hired as ABV 1939. Sunk 5.12.41 by Italian A/C in the eastern Mediterranean.

CHAKLA 3,081/14, 2—4in, 1—2pdr. Hired as ABV 8.1939. Sunk 29.4.41 by air attack at Tobruk.

CHALCEDONY Tr 332/11, 1—6pdr. Hired as M/S 1914—19.

CHALCEDONY Tr 357/28, 1—12pdr. Hired as A/P Tr 8.1939, later purchased. M/S 1941; sold 1945.

CHALLENGER Tr 160/97. Hired 1917—19.

CHAMBERLAIN Tr 161/05, 1—6pdr. Hired 1917—19.

CHAMISS BAY MFV 58/28. Hired as A/P vessel (RCN) 1942—45.

CHAMPAGNE (see OROPESA)

CHAMPION Cutter 6. Hired 1793—1800 and 1803—04.

CHAMPION Cutter 6, 50bm, 6—3pdr. Hired 20.6.1803. Renamed SABINA 1804; returned 31.12.04.

CHAMPION Tr. Hired as boom gate vessel 1915—19.

CHAMPION II Dr, 1—3pdr. Hired 1915—19.

CHAMPION French navy tug seized 7.1940. Rescue tug 9.40—44.

CHANCE Schooner. Hired 1805—06.

CHANCE Schooner, 132bm. Hired 6.1815—11.15.

CHANCE Dr 92/08. Hired 8.1914. Sunk 26.1.16 in collision off the Orkneys.

CHANCELLOR Tr 186/04. Hired as accommodation ship 1915—19.

CHANCELLOR Tr 156/04. Hired 1917–19.

CHANDBALI ex-Tr 362/19. Hired as A/P vessel (RIN) 1939–43.

CHANDOS Tr 200/19. Hired as A/P Tr 25.11.1939–1.40.

CHANDRAVATI Cstr 556/33. Hired as A/P vessel (RIN) 1939–40.

CHANGTE 4,324/25. Hired as store carrier (RFA) 27.8.1939–43.

CHANGTEH Tug 244/14. Hired as M/S 4.1940. Sunk 14.2.42 by air attack off Singapore.

CHANGUINOLA 5,980/12. Hired as AMC 21.11.1914–17.1.20.

CHANNEL FIRE (see GABRIELLE MARIA)

CHANTALA 3,120/20, 2–3pdr. Hired as ABV 1939. Sunk 7.12.41 by mine off Tobruk.

CHANTICLEER Tr 173/94, 1–6pdr. Hired 1914–19.

CHAR (ex-*Stranton*) Tug 149/99. Hired as ABV 17.11.1914. Sunk 16.1.15 in collision in the Downs.

CHARDE Dr 99/19. Hired as M/S 11.1939. Sunk 21.6.40 in collision off Portsmouth.

CHARITY Dr 102/01. Hired 1914. Lost 24.10.15 by unknown cause on passage Yarmouth to Poole.

CHARITY Dr 65/03, 1–3pdr. Hired 1916–19.

CHARLES 30–gun ship. Hired 1650–54.

CHARLES 32–gun ship, 269bm. Hired 1664–67.

CHARLES A.ship 16, 309bm. Hired 5.1804. Sunk 31.8.1807 by shore batteries at Copenhagen.

CHARLES Schooner 118bm. Hired 10.1811–5.1814.

CHARLES ADAIR Tr, 'Mersey' type, 316gr. Cochrane 7.6.1917. Sold 1920, renamed *Sleaford.*

CHARLES ANTRAM Tr, 'Castle' type, 290gr. Cook Welton & Gemmell 18.6.1919. Sold 1920, renamed *Edmund van Beveren.* (Served as FLANDERS in WW.II.)

CHARLES ASTIE Tr, non-standard 'Mersey' type, 295gr. Purchased on stocks; Cochrane 25.1.1917. Sunk 26.6.17 by mine off Lough Swilly.

CHARLES BARBER Tr, 'Strath' type. Hall Russell. Cancelled 1919.

CHARLES BLIGHT Tr, 'Strath' type. Hall Russell 13.3.1919. Sold 1919, same name; sunk 9.20 by mine.

CHARLES BOYES Tr, 'Castle' type, 290gr. Cook Welton & Gemmell 14.2.1918. Sold 1919, same name; hired as M/S 9.39. Sunk 25.5.40 by mine in the North Sea.

CHARLES CARROLL Tr, 'Strath' type. Montrose SY 11.4.1918. Sold 1919, renamed *River Aire.*

CHARLES CHAPPELL Tr, 'Castle' type, 296gr. Bow McLachlan 19.6.1917. Sold 1919, renamed *San Nicolas.*

CHARLES COUCHER Tr, 'Strath' type. Hawthorns, Leith. Cancelled 1919.

CHARLES DENISE Dr 114/35. Belgian, hired as BBV 1940–45.
CHARLES DONELLY Tr, 'Castle' type, 277gr. Bow McLachlan 1918.
Sold 6.20, renamed *Calydaira*. (Served as PELAGOS in WW.II.)
CHARLES DORAN (see JOHN ANDERSON)
CHARLES DOYLE Tr, 'Strath' type, 202gr. Rennie Forrest 1919. Sold
1919, renamed *Sabina*. (Served as SABINA in WW.II.)
CHARLES HAMMOND Tr, Mersey' type. Cochrane 1918. Sunk 2.11.18
in collision with destroyer MARKSMAN off Kirkaldy.
CHARLES HAY Dr 75/09. Hired 1915–19.
CHARLES HENRI Dr 110/35. Belgian, hired as A/P vessel 7.1940–9.45.
CHARLES HUTSON Barge 125/89. Hired as BBV 5.1941–12.44.
CHARLES LAWRENCE Tr, 'Strath' type. Hall Russell. Cancelled 1919.
CHARLES LEGG Tr, 'Castle' type, 275gr. J P Rennoldson 1918. Sold
1919, renamed *Roderigo*. (Served as MILFORD COUNTESS in WW.II.)
CHARLES LIVINGSTONE Pilot 434/21. Hired as examination vessel
30.7.1940–16.12.41.
CHARLES McIVER Yt 428/36. Hired as ABV 9.1939–12.45.
CHARLES PLUMIER 4,504/38. French AMC seized 22.11.1940 by the
destroyer FAULKNOR off Gibraltar. Renamed LARGS 1941, as OBV
Landing ship 10.42–12.45.
CHARLES VALIANT Tr 224/16. French M/S seized 3.7.1940 at
Southampton. M/S to 6.46.
CHARLOTTE Cutter 10. Hired 1793–1800 and 1803–04.
CHARLOTTE Schooner 11, 77bm. Hired 6.1803–6.1806.
CHARLOTTE DY tug, 50gr. Pimblott 20.10.1966.
CHARLSIN Tr 241/07, 1–6pdr. German *Esteburg* captured 5.9.1915.
Sunk 30.9.17 by U-boat in the central Mediterranean.
CHARM Tug 283/88. Hired 4.12.1914. Renamed BLAZER 1915,
examination service. Wrecked 9.11.18 in the Scilly Isles.
CHARM (see COYTOBEE)
CHARMING MOLLY Cutter 8. Hired 1796. Foundered 2.1801 on
passage from Jersey.
CHARMOUTH Tr 195/10, 1–6pdr. Hired 1914–19.
CHARON (ex-*Eclair*) Wh, 1–12pdr, 2–3pdr. Purchased 4.1915. Sold
6.3.19 at the Cape.
CHARON Rescue tug 700 tons, 142½ x 33 ft, 1–3in. Cochrane
21.11.1941. Renamed ALLIGATOR 1947, DY tug. BU 1.59 at Tipnor.
CHASSE MAREE Tr 251/20. French M/S seized 3.7.1940 at Southampton.
M/S to 1.44 then fuel carrier to 1945.
15 French chasseurs (S/M chasers) seized 3.7.1940 in the UK. CH.5–15:
107 tons, 116½ x 17½ ft, 1–75mm, 2–20mm; CH.41–43: 126 tons
and as CH.5; CH.98: 60 tons, 105 x 15½ ft, 1–75mm; CH.106: 128
tons, 137 x 17 ft, 1–75mm (the names were given in 1941).

CH.5 (CARENTAN) Seized Portsmouth. Free-French 9.40; foundered 21.12.43 in a gale in the Channel.

CH.6 Seized Portsmouth. Polish crew 8.40; foundered 12.10.42 in a gale in the Channel.

CH.7 Seized Portsmouth. Polish crew 8.40; lost with CH.6.

CH.8 (RENNES) Seized Plymouth. Free-French 9.40; sunk 13.7.42 by air attack in the Channel.

CH.10 (BAYONNE) Seized Portsmouth. Free-French 9.40; returned 1946 to the French navy.

CH.11 (BOULOGNE) Seized Portsmouth. Polish crew 8.40; Free-French 9.40; returned 1946.

CH.12 (BENODET) Seized Plymouth. Free-French 9.40–46.

CH.13 (CALAIS) Seized Portsmouth. Free-French 9.40; returned 1946.

CH.14 (DIELETTE) Seized Portsmouth. Free-French 9.40; returned 1946.

CH.15 (PAIMPOL) Polish crew 8.40; Free-French 9.40–46.

CH.41 (AUDIERNE) Seized Portsmouth. Free-French 1940–46.

CH.42 (LARMOR) Seized Portsmouth. Free-French 9.40; returned 1944 to French navy.

CH.43 (LAVANDOU) Seized Portsmouth. Free-French 9.40; returned 1944 to French navy.

CH.98 Seized Portsmouth. Laid up to 1942 then target vessel to 1945.

CH.106 Seized Portsmouth. Laid up to 1942 then Free-French harbour service to 1945.

CHASSIRON Tr 258/13. Hired as M/S 9.1939–8.45.

CHATHAM DY lighter, 73bm. Chatham DY 1734. Fate unknown.

CHATHAM Brig-sloop 10, 184bm. Hired 1793–4.95.

CHATHAM DY craft, 46bm. Rochester 1798. Fate unknown.

CHATTENDEN Armament store carrier, 1,192 tons, 230 x 25 ft. Richards IW 14.10.1943. Sold 1966.

CHATTERENO Dr 58/02. Hired 1915–19.

CHECKSIN Tr 140/95, 1–3pdr. German *Wulsdorf* captured 1915. Sold 1920.

CHEERLY Rescue tug, 'B.A.T' class. Levingston, Orange, Texas 23.7.1943 and to the RN 18.1.44 on lend-lease. Returned 19.2.46 to the USN.

CHEERY Dr 1–6pdr. Hired 1915–19.

CHERBOURGEOIS I Tug 99/03. French, seized 1940. Harbour tug 1942–5.45.

CHERBOURGEOIS III Tug 261/13. French, seized 3.7.1940 at Poole. Rescue tug to 12.45.

CHERBOURGEOIS IV Tug 296/30. French, seized 3.7.40 at Plymouth. DY tug to 4.46.

CHERRY LAKE Motor M/S (RCN) 255 tons. Taylor, Toronto. Cancelled 22.10.1945, completed mercantile.

CHERRYLEAF (ex-PERSOL renamed 1917) Oiler (RFA) 12,300 tons, 405 x 54 ft. Raylton Dixon 9.11.1916. Sold 1947, renamed *Alan Clore.*
CHERSIN Tr 218/12, 1–6pdr. German *Else Kunkel* detained 4.8.1914 at Aberdeen. Sold 16.3.20. (spelt CHIRSIN in some lists)
CHERUB DY tank vessel 390 tons, 115 x 21 ft. Hong Kong & Whampoa 1901. Lost 12.41 at Hong Kong.
CHERWELL (see JAMES JONES)
CHESHIRE 10,552/27, 8–6in, 2–3in. Hired as AMC 9.1939–12.7.43.
CHESTER Iron tank vessel, 164bm, 234 tons, 105 x 18 ft. Laird 14.3.1861. Sold 12.1925.
CHESTER II Tr 143/96. Hired 1915. Sunk 29.2.16 in collision in the Forth.
CHESTER III (ex-*Badia*) Tug 150/09. Hired as ABS 31.7.1914–7.9.17.
CHESTERFIELD 1,013/13. Hired as store carrier (RFA) 12.10.1914. Fleet messenger 6.16. Sunk 18.5.18 in the central Mediterranean.
CHESTNUT Dr 107/14. Hired 11.1918–19 and as M/S 11.39. Renamed MAIDA 1940. Sunk 16.3.40 by mine off the east coast of Scotland.
CHESTNUT M/S Tr 505 tons, 150 x 27½ ft, 1–12pdr. Goole SB 24.2.1940. Sunk 30.11.40 by mine off the North Foreland.
CHICHESTER (ex-*Arcadia*) Tug 180/95. Hired as ABS 4.8.1914–29.5.19.
CHICO (ex-*Bluebird*) Yt 75/32. Hired as echo yacht 10.1939. Laid up 16.2.45–46.
CHIEFTAIN Tr 278/05, 1–12pdr. Hired 1915–19.
CHIEFTAIN II Tr 149/99. Hired 1917–19.
CHIKARA Tr 250/08, 1–12pdr. Hired 1914–19.
CHILDERS (ex-*Norvegia*) Wh, 180gr. 2–3pdr. Purchased 1915. Sold 1919.
CHILTERN Tr 324/17, 1–12pdr. Hired as A/P Tr 5.1940–45.
CHIMAERA Dr 107/07. Hired 1918–19.
CHIMAERA Dr 87/12. Hired on examination service 8.1939–8.41.
CHIMERA Admiralty steel Dr, 96gr. Brown, Hull 1920. Sold 1920, same name. (Served as TWINKLING STAR in WW.II.)
CHINA Tr 190/93, 1–6pdr. Hired 1915–19.
CHINKOA 5,222/13. Hired as store carrier (RFA) 3.8.1914–19.12.14.
CHINTHE Tug 668/32. Hired as M/S in WW.II. Later purchased and renamed HATHI.
CHIRSIN (see CHERSIN)
CHITRAL 15,346/25, 7–6in, 3–4in, 3–3in. Hired as AMC 8.1939–44.
CHITTAGONG Tr,(RIN), 'Basset' class. Burn Calcutta. Ordered 23.9.1941, cancelled 3.45.
CHOICE Tr 165/05, 1–6pdr. Hired 1914–19.
CHOICE (ex-*Stalker*) Tr 197/99. Hired as fuel carrier 1944. Foundered 25.8.44 at Arromanches.

CHORLEY Tr 284/14. Hired as BDV 1.1940. Foundered 25.4.42 off Start Point.

CHRIS Dr 81/10. Hired 1915–19.

CHRISOBEL Dr 84/04. Hired 1915–19.

CHRISTABEL II Yt 111/28. Hired as HDPC 1940–45.

CHRISTANIA T PURDY Tr 213/17. Hired as A/P Tr 11.1939. BBV 1940–45.

CHRISTINA CRAIG Dr 86/12. Hired 1915. Sunk 15.2.18 in action off Dover.

CHRISTINA MAYES Dr 82/08. Hired 1915–19.

CHRISTINE ROSE Dr. French A/P vessel seized 3.7.1940 at Southampton. Examination service 9.40. Wrecked 10.9.41 on the coast of Argyll.

CHRISTOPHER Tr 316/11. Hired 1915. Sunk 30.3.17 by mine off Southwold.

CHRISTOPHER DIXON Tr, 'Mersey' type, 324gr. Cochrane 4.9.1917. To Irish govt 1922. (Served as LORD GAINFORD in WW.II)

CHRYSANTHEMUM Dr 82/07, 1–6pdr. Hired 1915–19.

CHRYSEA Tr 210/12, 1–6pdr. Hired 1914–19 and as BBV 4.40–1.45.

CHRYSOLITE Tr 251/16, 1–6pdr. Hired 9.1916–19 and as M/S 8.40–1.46.

CHRYSOPRASE MFV 50/02. Hired for harbour service 2.1941–4.44.

CHUB (ex-Portsmouth YC.4 renamed 17.11.1870) DY buoy boat, 66bm. Sold 23.11.1894.

CHUB DY tank vessel 340 tons, 115 x 21 ft. Lobnitz 17.2.1897. Sold 17.6.32 at Capetown.

CHUB (ex-*Vincia*) Tug 150/09. Hired as ABV 30.7.1914–15.12.19.

CHURCHSIN Tr 142/00, 1–6pdr. German *St Georg* captured 1915. Sold 11.5.20, renamed *Banks o'Dee.*

CHUTING Tug 207/21. Hired 6.1941 in China and believed lost there 1942

CICERO Tr 173/07, 1–12pdr. Hired 1914–19.

CILICIA 11,100/38, 8–6in, 2–3in. Hired as AMC 8.1939–16.2.44.

CINCERARIA Dr 99/18. Hired 1941–5.44.

CINCERIA Dr 75/11. Hired as BDV 1.1915–19.

CIRCASSIA 11,170/37, 8–6in, 2–3in. Hired as AMC 9.1939. Landing ship 1944–45.

CIRCE 778/12, 1–4in. Hired as M/S 11.1939. To the RAN and renamed MEDEA 1942. Listed to 1946.

CIRRUS Admiralty wood Dr, 98gr. Colby 1918. Sold 1928, renamed *Travellers Joy.*

CISSY Dr 60/01. Hired 1915–19.

CITRON Dr 78/11. Hired 1915–19 and as BBV 1.40–8.44.

CITY of ABERDEEN Dr 88/07. Hired 8.1914–19.

CITY of ABERDEEN Tr 194/98. Hired 1918–19 and as A/P Tr 4.12.39 –18.1.40.

CITY of BELFAST 994/93, 2–12pdr. Hired as ABS 30.10.1914–3.10.19.
CITY of BELFAST II Dr 88/07, 1–3pdr. Hired 11.14–19.
CITY of CARLISLE Tr 208/99, 1–6pdr. Hired 1915–19.
CITY of DUNDEE Tr 269/14. Hired 1914. Sunk 14.9.15 in collision off Folkestone.
CITY of DURBAN 5,945/21, 8–4in, 2–6pdr. Hired as decoy ship (BRUTUS) 9.1939. AMC 3.41–4.42.
CITY of EDINBURGH Dr 88/07, 1–3pdr. Hired 11.1914–19.
CITY of EDINBURGH II Tr 308/07, 1–6pdr. Hired 1914–18.
CITY of GLASGOW Dr 88/07, 1–3pdr. Hired 12.1914–19.
CITY of HULL Dr 88/07, 1–3pdr. Hired 1915–19.
CITY of HULL Tr 181/98. In service 1918.
CITY of LIVERPOOL Dr 88/07, 1–6pdr. Hired 11.1914. Sunk 31.7.18 by mine off the South Foreland.
CITY of LIVERPOOL Tr. Hired as boom gate vessel 1915–19.
CITY of LONDON Dr 88/07, 1–3pdr. Hired 1915–19.
CITY of LONDON 8,920/07, 8–6in, 2–6pdr. Commissioned as AMC 8.1.1916. Returned 7.19.
CITY of LONDON Tr 195/01. Hired 1918–19.
CITY of LONDON Cstr 633/27. Purchased as accommodation ship 1944. Sold 5.46.
CITY of MANCHESTER Tr 189/99. Hired as boom gate vessel 1915–19.
CITY of OXFORD 4,019/82, 7,430 tons. Purchased as dummy battleship ST VINCENT 20.10.1914. Kite-balloon ship 17.7.15; sold 1920.
CITY of PERTH Dr 88/07, 1–3pdr. Hired 1915. Base ship 1917–19.
CITY of PERTH (see WILLIAM ASHTON)
CITY of ROCHESTER Paddle 235/04. Hired as M/S 18.12.1914–27.11.19 and as M/S 12.9.39. Sunk 19.5.41 by air attack at Chatham.
CITY of SELBY Tr 284/14, 1–6pdr. Hired 1914–19.
CITY of YORK Tr 202/04. Hired as boom gate vessel 1915–19.
CIVILIAN 7,871/02. Hired as store carrier (RFA) 14.8.1914–25.8.14.
CLACHNACUDIN Dr 78/08. Hired 1915–19.
CLACTON 820/04. Commissioned as M/S 7.10.1914. Sunk 3.8.16 by 'U.73' in the Mediterranean.
CLACTON BELLE Paddle 458/90. Commissioned as M/S 16.8.1915. Hospital carrier 8.11.19–5.20.
CLAESJE Tr 229/33. Dutch M/S in service with the RN 1940–45.
CLAIRE Tr 219/07. Hired 1915–19 and as A/P Tr 25.11.39–6.2.40.
CLAN MACKAY MFV. Hired as danlayer 1940–45.
CLAN McNAUGHTON 4,985/11. Hired as AMC 19.11.1914. Foundered 3.2.15 after being mined in the N.Atlantic.
CLANS Dr 89/15. Hired 6.1915–19 and 1942–44.
CLARA Dr 66/01. Hired 20.1.1915–16.2.15.

CLARA & ALICE Dr 79/09. Hired 1915. Foundered 26.5.18 off Palermo.

CLARA SIMONNE (P.10) MFV 83/31, 1–6pdr. Belgian (Polish crew) hired as A/P vessel 8.1940–45.

CLARA SUTTON Dr 102/17. Hired 1917–19 and as boom tender 1940–45.

CLARE DY tug, 40gr, 57 x 17 ft. Pimblott 6.7.1967.

CLARIBELLE Tr 204/18, 1–12pdr. Hired as M/S 1941–45.

CLARICE (ex-*Daffodil*) Dr 94/07. Hired on harbour service 11.1939–1.44.

CLARINET (ex-*Bardolf*) Tr 257/11. Hired as BDV 12.1939; purchased 11.43, sold 1946.

CLARION Dr 100/08, 1–3pdr. Hired 1915–19.

CLAROSIN Tr 159/97, 1–6pdr. German *Sophie* captured 1915. Sold 18.2.20.

CLASSIN Tr 182/97, 1–3pdr. German *Präsident Rose* captured 1915. Sold 17.3.20, renamed *Blackhall.*

CLAUDIAN Dr 63/99. Hired 1918–19.

CLAVIS Dr 87/11. Hired 1915. Sunk 9.7.16 by Austrian cruisers in the Adriatic.

CLAVIS MFV 32/31. Dutch, hired as BBV 12.1939–11.45.

CLAYMORE II Yt 66/98. Purchased as tender 28.8.1917. Sold 6.12.19.

CLAYMORE Cstr 260/02. Purchased as boom gate vessel (RNZN) 10.1943. Sold circa 1953.

CLEARING Admiralty steel Dr, 98gr. Ailsa 28.8.1918. Sold 17.3.21, renamed *Vernal.* (VERNAL in WW.II.)

CLEARSIN Tr 135/91, 1–3pdr. German *Resie* captured 1915. Sold 18.2.20.

CLEARWATER Tender 62 tons. German LUMME seized 1945. On sale list 1958.

CLEETHORPES Paddle 273/03, 2–6pdr. Hired as A/P vessel 19.9.1916–19.4.19.

CLEMENTINA Yt 625/87, 2–6pdr. Hired 22.9.1914. Beached 5.8.15 after collision off Tor Point.

CLEMENTINA II Tr 200/03, 1–6pdr. Hired 1915–19.

CLEON Tr 266/07, 1–6pdr. Hired 1915. Sunk 1.2.18 by mine off Folkestone.

CLEON Dr -/40. Danish, seized 30.5.1940. BBV 1940; store carrier 1944–2.46.

CLEOPATRA II Tr 240/07, 1–6pdr. Hired 1914–19 and as A/P Tr 12.39. Renamed TEAZER 1940. Returned 1940.

CLEOPATRA III Tr 321/06, 1–12pdr. Hired 1915–19.

CLEVELA Tr 387/30, 1–12pdr. Hired as M/S 9.1939–5.46 (CLEVELLA in Navy List.)

CLEVELAND Tender 4, 69bm, 4—2pdr. Hired 4.1803—04.

CLEVELAND Storeship. Hired 1809—10.

CLIFFORD 487/04. Commissioned as fleet messenger 1.8.1915. Sunk 16.5.16 by U-boat near Crete.

CLIFTON Transport. Hired 1854—55.

CLIFTON Tr 242/06. Hired 1915. Sunk 18.2.17 by mine off the Daunt light vessel.

CLIFTON Tr 194/15, 1—6pdr. Hired as M/S 11.1939—3.46.

CLIFTON Tug (RCN) 462 tons, 104 x 28 ft. Canadian Bridge Co, Toronto 31.7.1944.

CLINCHER (ex-HS.41) DY tug 368/92. Transferred from War Dept 1918. Sold 24.11.20.

CLINKER DY tank vessel 390 tons, 115 x 23 ft. Willoughby, Plymouth 23.2.1901. Sold 1948.

CLIO Tr 144/96. Hired 1915—16.

CLONSIN Tr 202/11, 1—6pdr. German *Doktor Robitsch* detained 4.8.1914 at Aberdeen. Sold 1920, renamed *Birkhall.*

CLORINDE (see BRAEMAR)

CLOTILDE Tr 289/13, 1—6pdr. Hired 1914—19 and as M/S 2.1940—12.45.

CLOUD Admiralty steel Dr, 96gr. Duthie Torry 11.4.1918. Sold 1946.

CLOUDARCH (see TWINKLE)

CLOUDBANK Admiralty steel Dr. Goole SB. Cancelled 1919.

CLOUDBURST Admiralty steel Dr. Brown, Hull. Cancelled 1919.

CLOUDBURST (see POL IV)

CLOUGHSTONE Tr 233/07. Hired as BBV 12.1940. Fuel carrier 1944—4.45.

CLOUGHTON WYKE Tr 324/18, 1—12pdr. Purchased as M/S 5.1940. Sunk 2.2.42 by air attack off the Humber.

CLOVER DY tug, 101bm. Purchased 10.2.1876 in Bermuda. BU there 9.1882.

CLOVER DY tank vessel 165 tons, 86 x 19 ft. Fleming & Ferguson 1895. Sold 1910.

CLOVER Dr 83/11, 1—3pdr. Purchased as store carrier 1916. Sold 1921.

CLOVERBANK Dr 78/12. Hired 1915. Sunk 24.4.16 in action off Zeebrugge.

CLOVERBANK Dr 92/-. Hired 1917. Sunk 15.2.18 in action off Dover.

CLOVERDALE Dr 100/07. Hired as M/S 11.1939. A/P vessel 1940—12.45.

CLUNY Dr 83/08. Hired 1915—19.

CLUNY HILL Dr 86/09. Hired 1915—19.

CLUPEA Dr 83/07, 1—3pdr. Hired 1915—19.

CLYDE Newfoundland govt vessel, 440gr, 154½ x 25 ft. Inglis 1900. Wrecked 19.12.51 off Williamsport, NF.

CLYDE Tr 146/98. Hired 1915. Sunk 14.10.17 in collision off Sidmouth.
CLYDE II Dr 94/07, 1–3pdr. Hired 1915–19.
CLYNE CASTLE Tr 252/07, 1–6pdr. Hired 1914–19.
CLYNE CASTLE Tr 307/29, 1–12pdr. Hired as M/S 8.1939. Wreck dispersal 1944.–11.45.
CLYTHNESS Tr 276/20. Hired as M/S 8.1939–7.45.
CMBs Coastal motor boats (motor torpedo boats) Thornycroft design, built 1916–20.
CMB.1–13 (built 1916), CMB.40–61 (1918), CMB.112 and 121–123 (1920) all 5 tons, 40 x 8½ ft, 2–MG, 1 torpedo.
Nos 1,2,8,10,11,40,42,47 and 50 all war losses.
No 4 preserved in the Imperial War Museum; Nos 9,12 lasted up to 193ᵇ.
CMB.14–39, 62–99, 113–117 (1917–19), 118–120 (1920) all 11 tons, 55 x 11 ft, 2–4 MG, 1–2 torpedoes.
Nos 18,39,62,67,71 and 79 all war losses.
CMB.100–104 (1919) all 24 tons, 70 x 14 ft, 4–MG, 6 torpedoes and designed for minelaying.
No 102 renamed HORNET 1923 as nominal base ship. Nos 103, 104 laid up 1928 and commissioned in WW.II.
CMTB.1 Motor torpedo boat (RCN) Vosper 1939. Sold 1945.
COADJUTOR Tr 207/15, 1–6pdr. Hired as M/S 3.1915–19.
COALAXE Tr 263/10. Russian T.36 (ex-*Seis*) seized 1918 and in commission from 9.1918. Sold 11.5.20, renamed *Calicut*.
COALSIN Tr 130/92. German *Toni* captured 7.10.1915. Sold 5.10.20.
COAL TIT (ex-*Belgica*) MFV 21/25. Belgian, in service as M/L tender 16.9.1940–46.
COASTGUARD MFV 48/35. Purchased as danlayer (RNZN) 1940. Tender 1946; sold 1961.
COBBERS Tr 276/19, 1–12pdr. Hired as A/P Tr 1940. Sunk 3.3.41 by air attack in the North Sea.
COCHIN DY tug, 61gr, 75½ x 15 ft. Yarwood, Northwich 1919. On sale list 1946.
COCHIN Tr (RIN), 'Basset' class. Alcock Ashdown, Bombay. Ordered 14.11.1941, renamed KOLABA 1943 and cancelled.
COCHIN (see MULTAN)
COCHIN (ex-MULTAN renamed 1943) Tr (RIN), 'Basset' class. Burn, Calcutta 29.12.1943. Sold 1950.
COCHRANE Tr (Burma govt), 'Basset' class. Irrawadi Flotilla Co, Rangoon. Laid down 8.1941. Destroyed 3.42 on stocks.
COCKADE (see ANSON)
COCKATRICE II Tr 115/94. Hired 1914–16.
COCKCHAFER 8–gun vessel. Hired 1793. Foundered 1.11.1801 off Guernsey.

COCKER (see KOS XIX)

CODFISH (ex-*Foremost II*) Tug 123/15. Hired 1.6.1915–12.1.20.

COILA Yt 355/22. Purchased as A/S Yt 9.1939. Sold 5.47 as pilot vessel.

COLCHESTER (ex-*Felixstowe*) 1,280/18. Hired as wreck dispersal vessel 7.1941–1.46.

COLDBLAST Admiralty steel Dr, 98gr. Ailsa 19.11.1919. Sold 17.3.21, renamed *Elsie Bruce.*

COLDSNAP Admiralty steel Dr, 96gr. Duthie Torry 28.1.1918. Sold 1945, same name.

COLDSTREAMER A/S Tr 750 tons, 175 x 30 ft, 1–4in, 4–20mm. Cook Welton & Gemmell 10.12.1942. Sold 1946, renamed *Esquimaux.*

COLETTE Aux. barge 180/26. Hired as BBV 5.1940. M/S repair craft 1940–6.45.

COLEUS Dr 102/16, 1–3pdr. Hired 1916. Sunk 4.10.18 by mine off Dover.

COLIN CRAIG Tr 'Castle' type. Greenock. Cancelled 1919.

COLL A/S Tr, 'Isles' class. Ardrossan DY Co 7.4.1942. Wreck dispersal 12.45; oil-tank cleaning vessel 1950.

COLLEAGUE Tr 207/15, 1–6pdr. Hired 4.1915–19.

COLLENA Tr 293/15, 1–6pdr. Hired 5.1915–19 and purchased as BDV 1.40. Sold 7.45.

COLLIE (see BUSEN.10)

COLLIE DY tug 170 tons, 85 x 25 ft. Rowhedge IW 28.2.1964.

COLLINGDOC 1,780/25. Purchased. Sunk 3.1942 as blockship.

COLLINGWOOD Tr 179/02. Hired 1917–19 and as boom gate vessel 1940. Renamed FIELDGATE 10.40; listed to 1945.

COLNE DY tank vessel. In service 1920–21.

COLNE (see ISAAC CHANT)

COLONIAL Dr 84/08, 1–3pdr. Hired 1915–19. (Served as EASTERN DAWN in WW.II.)

COLONSAY M/S depot ship. In service 1940. Paid off 31.7.45.

COLPOYS Brig-sloop 16, 158bm, 14–12pdr carr., 2–4pdr. Hired 4.1804–07.

COLSAY Tr, 'Isles' class. Cook Welton & Gemmell 15.12.1943. Sunk 2.11.44 by human torpedo off Ostend.

COLTMAN Tr 312/07, 1–12pdr. Hired 1914–19.

COLUMBA Tr 138/93. Hired as BDV 1914. Sunk 10.3.18 by mine off May Island.

COLUMBELLA (ex-*Columbia*) 8,292/02. Hired as AMC 20.11.1914–6.6.19.

COLUMBIA Tr 266/86. Presented 1914. Sunk 1.5.15 by German destroyer torpedo off Foreness.

COLVILLE Tug (RCN). Listed 1944–50.

COMBE 2,030/12. Hired as ammo.carrier (RFA) 1915. Sunk 12.10.15 by unknown cause on passage to Archangel.

COMBER Tr 303/16. Purchased as M/S (RCN) 1942. Listed to 1945.

COMELY Dr 95/07. Hired 8.1914–19.

COMELY BANK Dr 87/14, 1–3pdr. Hired 1914–19 and as BBV 12.39–11.44.

COMET Tug. Hired as gunboat 1915. Lost 1.12.15 by grounding in the Tigris.

COMET (ex-*Tamura*) Tr 301/24. Hired as decoy vessel 9.1939. Sunk 30.9.40 by mine off Falmouth.

COMET STAR Dr 60/06. Hired 1915–19.

COMFORT Dr 60(net). Hired as danlayer 13.12.1939. Rammed in error and sunk 29.5.40 by minesweeper LYDD off Dover.

COMFORT MFV 50/03. Hired for harbour service 31.12.40–45.

COMITATUS Tr 290/19. Hired as M/S 10.1939–45.

COMMANDANT Tr 207/05. Hired 1915. Sunk 2.4.16 by mine off the Sunk light vessel.

COMMANDER EVANS Tr 344/24, 1–12pdr. Hired as A/P Tr 11.1939; danlayer 1944–8.45.

COMMANDER FULLERTON Tr 227/15. Hired 1917. Sunk 12.12.17 by German destroyers in the North Sea.

COMMANDER HOLBROOK Tr 227/15, 1–6pdr. Hired 1.1915–19 and as A/S Tr, 1–6pdr 6.40; M/S 1942–11.45.

COMMANDER HORTON Tr 227/15. Hired 1917–19 and as A/P Tr 6.40–10.40.

COMMANDER NASMITH Tr 243/15, 1–6pdr. Hired 8.1915–19 and as A/P Tr, 1–6pdr 6.40; M/S 5.42; fuel carrier 1944–5.45.

COMMILES Tr 264/18, 1–6pdr. Hired as M/S 8.1939–10.45.

COMMISSIONER Tr 161/05, 1–12pdr. Hired 1917–18.

COMMISSIONER Wood paddle tug 102/62. Hired 1918–19.

COMMODATOR Tr 281/18. Hired as M/S 8.1939–10.45.

COMMODORE Tr 138/91. Hired 1917–19.

COMMONWEAL (ex-*Commonwealth*) Tug 115/02. Hired as ABV 2.12.1914–7.6.19.

COMORIN 15,241/25, 8–6in, 2–3in. Hired as AMC 9.1939. Lost 6.4.41 by fire in the N.Atlantic.

COMOX Tr (RCN) 460 tons, 150 x 27½ ft, 1–4in. Burrard, Vancouver 9.8.1938. Sold 1947, renamed *Sung Ming*.

'Comp' class composite-built boom defence vessels ordered 1943 and laid down 1944:

COMPACT Curtis, Totnes. Cancelled 1945.

COMPANION Doig, Grimsby. Cancelled 2.45.
COMPATRIOT Doig. Cancelled 2.45.
COMPEER Doig. Cancelled 10.44.
COMPETENT Doig. Cancelled 10.44.
COMPETITOR Curtis. Cancelled 1945.
COMPLETE Wivenhoe. Cancelled 1945.
COMPLEX Wivenhoe. Cancelled 10.44.
COMPLIMENT Curtis. Cancelled 10.44.
COMPOSURE Curtis. Cancelled 10.44.

COMPANION Tr 163/03. Hired 1917–19.
COMPT H Van der BURGH Tr 200/07. Belgian, hired 1918–19.
COMPUTATOR Tr 286/19, 1–6pdr. Hired as M/S 1939. Sunk 21.1.45 in collision with destroyer VANOC in Seine Bay.
COMRADE Tr 161/06, 1–6pdr. Hired 1915–19.
COMRADES Dr 63/03. Hired 1916. Sunk 18.10.17 by mine off Cape d'Antifer.
COMRADES Dr 114/28, 1–3pdr. Hired as A/P vessel 9.1939; target towing 1944–4.46.
CONAMORE Dr 88/09, 1–3pdr. Hired 1914–19.
CONAN DOYLE Tr 314/15. Hired 1917–19.
CONCERTATOR Tr 275/17. Hired as M/S 8.1939–1.46.
CONCORD 28–gun ship. Hired 1664–67.
CONCORD Brig 6, 153bm. Hired 7.6.1803–19.5.1810.
CONCORD II Dr 81/06, 1–3pdr. Hired 1915–19.
CONCORD III Tr 236/05, 1–6pdr. Hired 1915–19.
CONCORDIA Dr 91/13. Hired 12.1914–19 and as M/S 12.39–5.46.
CONDOR II Tr 227/05, 1–6pdr. Hired 1914. Wrecked 22.11.14 in the Firth of Forth.
CONDOR Dr 84/07. Hired as tender 2.1915. Renamed RAWLINSON 8.18–19.
CONDOR II Dr 63/05, 1–6pdr. Hired 1915–19.
CONFEDERATE Tr 202/13, 1–6pdr. Hired 1914–19.
CONFEDERATE 562/06. Danish *Protector* seized 4.5.1940. Salvage vessel to 1946.
CONFIANCE (ex-*Navigator*) Iron tug 270 tons, 107 x 19 ft. Purchased 4.1885. Sold 1947.
CONFIANCE Fleet tug 760 tons, 140 x 35 ft, 1–40mm. Inglis 15.11.1955.
CONFIANCE Dr 96/30. Belgian, hired for harbour service 14.9.1940–21.9.45.
CONFIDE Dr 95/07. Hired for harbour service 1940–45.
CONFIDENT Salvage vessel 300 tons, 95 x 24 ft, 2–MG. Gulfport Co, Pt Arthur, Texas 11.12.1941 on lend-lease. Returned 1946 to the USN.

CONFIDENT Fleet tug 760 tons, 140 x 35 ft, 1–40mm. Inglis 17.1.1956.

CONFIER Dr 69/10. Hired 1914–19.

CONFLAGRATION Admiralty steel Dr, 96gr. Watson, Gainsborough 1919 Sold 29.9.20, same name.

CONGO Tr 152/97. Hired 1915–19.

CONGRE Tr 299/18. French M/S seized 3.7.1940 at Portsmouth. Free-French M/S 9.40; RN crew 1941; fuel carrier 1943. Returned 1.46 to the French navy.

CONIDAW Yt 90/39. Hired as M/S 1939–45.

CONIE Dr 85/07. Hired 2.1915–18.

CONINGSBY Tr 257/06, 1–6pdr. Hired 1914–19.

CONISTON Tr 217/04, 1–6pdr. Hired as A/P Tr 11.1939–40.

CONNAGE Dr 77/01, 1–6pdr. Hired 1915–19.

CONNARD (ex-*Concord*) Dr 65/03, 1–6pdr. Hired 1917–19.

CONNIE Tr 198/00. Hired 1917–19.

CONQUERANT Tug 70 tons. French navy tug seized 3.7.1940 at Falmouth. Served as M/S to 1945. (Spelt CONQUERANTE in most lists.)

CONQUERESS Tug 121/13. Hired as DY tug 22.1.1915. Purchased 6.10.15. Sold 6.5.53, BU at Northam.

CONQUEROR II Yt 526/89, 2–6pdr. Hired 1.2.1915. Sunk 26.9.16 by S/M gunfire off Fair Isle.

CONQUEROR Paddle tug 177/84. Hired as DY tug 1916–19.

CONQUEROR Yt 900/11, 1–4in, 1–12pdr, 4–20mm. Hired as A/S Yt 9.1939; A/A ship 1941–45.

CONQUISTADOR Tr 224/15. Hired as A/P Tr 11.1939. M/S 6.40; sunk 25.11.40 in collision in the Thames estuary.

CONRAD Tug 40/38. Egyptian, hired for harbour service 31.8.1939–25.9.45.

CONSBRO Tr 350/30. Hired as BDV 1.1940–9.45.

CONSOLATION Dr 70/06, 1–6pdr. Hired 1915–19.

CONSOLATION Dr 97/18. Hired as M/S 11.1939–9.45.

CONSORT Tr 181/09, 1–10pdr. Hired 1915–19.

CONSTANCE Lugger 12. Hired 1798–1801.

CONSTANCE Cutter 6. Hired 1799. Wrecked 12.1804 on the Irish coast.

CONSTANCE Tr 166/02. Hired 1917–19.

CONSTANCE Yt (48/11?) Hired as boom tender 1941. Renamed CLARION 1944; returned 1945.

CONSTANCY Dr 63/03, 1–3pdr. Hired 1915–19.

CONSTANT FRIEND Dr 92/12, 1–3pdr. Hired 1915–19 and as A/P vessel 6.40–6.45.

CONSTANT HOPE Dr 86/13, 1–6pdr. Hired 1915–19 and as BBV 6.40–45.

CONSTANT STAR Dr 98/11. Hired 8.1915–19.

CONSTITUTION Cutter 14. Hired 1790 and 1796. Captured 9.1.1801 by two French cutters off Portland; recaptured 10.1.1801 and returned.

CONSTITUTION Cutter 10, 120bm. Hired 4.5.1804. Sunk 26.8.1804 in action with French gunboats off Boulogne.

CONSUL Paddle 257/96. Hired for examination service 3.11.1939–23.1.41 and 8.4.44–6.11.44.

CONTENDER Tr 236/30, 1–12pdr. Hired as M/S 2.1940–10.45.

CONTRIVE Dr 95/11, 1–3pdr. Hired 1915–19 and as degaussing vessel 5.40–2.46.

CONTROL Tug. Egyptian, hired 6.1940. M/S 1943–46.

CONTROLLER Tr 201/13. Hired 1914–19 and as danlayer 1.40. BBV 1942; fuel carrier 4.44–9.44.

CONVALLARIA Dr 77/10, 1–3pdr. Hired 1915–19.

CONVALLARIA Dr 96/19. Hired as A/P Dr 4.1940–3.46.

CONVERT 20–gun ship, 180bm. Hired 1662–64.

CONWAY Tr 228/04, 1–6pdr. Hired 1915–19 and as A/P Tr 11.39–7.2.40.

CONWAY CASTLE Tr 274/16, 1–6pdr. Hired 3.1916–19 and as M/S, 1–6pdr 8.39–10.45.

COOGIE 762 tons, 1–4.7in, 2–3pdr. Hired as A/P vessel (RAN) 1914–21.

COOKSIN Tr 149/96. German *Herbert* captured 1915. Sold 17.3.20.

COOLEBAR Cstr 479/11. Commissioned as M/S (RAN) 18.12.1939. Store carrier 1944–46.

COOMASIN Tr 170/97, 1–6pdr. German *Heppens* captured 1915. Sold 11.5.20.

COOMBAR Cstr 581/12. Commissioned as M/S (RAN) 4.1941. Returned 1946.

COONGOOLA 34/-., 2–MG. Hired as A/P vessel (RAN) 1941–45.

COOT Tr 172/06, 1–6pdr. Hired 1914–19.

COPINSAY Tr, 'Isles' class. Cochrane 2.12.1940. Transferred War Dept 6.46; sold 1956, renamed *Ion.*

COPIOUS Dr 96/19. Hired as A/P Dr 12.1939–8.45.

COQUITLAM Motor M/S (RCN) 228 tons, 105 x 22 ft. Newcastle SB Co 5.1.1944. Sold 1946.

COR IV DY tug 300 tons, 93½ x 21½ ft. Ex-HS.72 112/12 transferred from War Dept 1919. Sold 21.7.20.

CORAL (ex-*Cape Duner*) Tr 455/35. Purchased as A/S Tr 30.1.1939, 705 tons, 1–4in. Wrecked 4.42 by air attack at Malta and wreck BU 1943.

CORAL BANK Dr 85/14, 1–3pdr. Hired 1914–19 and as M/S 12.39–1.46.

CORAL HAVEN Dr 82/13. Hired 1916. Sunk 15.5.17 by Austrian cruisers in the Adriatic.

CORAL HILL Dr 56/11, 1–3pdr. Hired 1915–19.
CORBRAE 1,788/35, 3,000 tons, 8–20mm. Purchased as M/S 3.1940.
Repair ship 1944; for disposal 11.46.
CORBURN 1,786/36, 3,060 tons, 8–20mm. Purchased as M/S 2.1940.
Sunk 21.5.40 by mine off Le Havre.
CORCYRA Tr 225/14. Hired 1914–19. (Stranded 20.2.15 near Bacton
and salved.) Purchased as A/S Tr 11.40; water carrier 1.42. Sold 27.8.46.
CORDELA Tr 355/30, 1–12pdr. Purchased as M/S 8.1939. Sold 1946.
CORDELIA Dr 69/02. Hired 3.12.1914–11.9.15.
CORDELIA II Yt 57/30. Hired as HDPC 1940–46.
CORDOVA 2,387/88, 1–12pdr. Purchased as boom gate vessel 1915.
Sold 29.7.19.
CORDOVA Motor M/S (RCN), BYMS.137 class. American YMS.420
purchased 30.1251.
CORELLA Tr 243/07. Hired 1915–19.
CORENA Tr 352/24, 1–12pdr. Purchased as M/S 8.1939. On sale list
4.46.
COREOPSIS II Dr 88/11, 1–3pdr. Hired 1914–19 and as examination
vessel COREOPSIS 14.9.39. Renamed OLIVINE 1939. Returned 12.45.
CORFIELD 1,797/37, 3,000 tons. Purchased as M/S 2.1940. Sunk
8.9.41 by mine off the Humber.
CORFU 14,170/31, 9–6in, 4–4in. Completed as AMC 25.11.1939. To
MWT 17.2.44.
CORGI DY tug 170 tons, 85 x 25 ft. Rowhedge IW 28.4.1964.
CORIENTES Tr 280/10. Hired 1915. Sunk 23.6.17 by mine off Malin
Head.
CORINGA Tug 294/14. Hired 1915–19 and as rescue tug 4.40. Sunk
23.6.40 by unknown cause in the N.Atlantic.
CORINSIN Tr 159/96, 1–6pdr. *Stuttgart* captured 30.9.1915. Sold
18.2.20, renamed *Corbiere*.
CORINTHIAN 3,151/38, 2–6in, 1–12pdr. Hired as OBV 9.1940.
Training ship 1944–2.45.
CORIOLANUS Tr 226/17. Hired as M/S 8.1940. Renamed CRAFTSMAN
1940/41. Returned 10.44.
CORIOLANUS M/S Tr 545 tons, 150 x 28 ft, 1–12pdr, 3–20mm.
Cochrane 2.9.1940. Sunk 5.5.45 by mine in the Adriatic.
COR JESU Dr 97/31. Hired as BBV 9.8.1940. Sunk 8.6.41 by air attack
off Alnmouth.
CORMORANT II Tr 154/91. Hired 1915–19.
CORMORANT III Dr 94/07, 1–3pdr. Hired 1915–19.
CORMORANT IV Tr 162/97, 1–6pdr. Hired 1916–19.
CORNCRAKE (see MACKEREL)
CORNELIAN Tr 222/00, 1–12pdr. Hired 1917–19.

CORNELIAN Tr 262/17. Hired as A/P Tr 1.1940. Renamed FORFEIT 1940. Returned 6.46.

CORNELIAN (ex-*Cape Warwick*) Tr 568 tons, 1—4in. Purchased as A/S Tr 11.1935. Sold 1945, renamed *Lincoln City.*

CORNELIUS BUCKLEY Tr, non-standard 'Mersey' type, 248gr. Cochrane 24.2.1917. Sold 1921, renamed *Savaria.*

CORNELIUS CARROLL Tr, non-standard 'Strath' type, 213gr. A.Hall 1918. Sold 1921, renamed *Boyne Braes.*

CORNET Tr 191/99. Hired 1918—19.

CORN RIG Dr 97/11. Hired as boom gate vessel 18.1.1915—19 and for harbour service 1942—45.

CORNSTALK Dr 73/16. Hired 1917—19.

CORNUCOPIA Dr 96/18. Hired for harbour service 1941—45.

CORONA Tr 212/12. Hired 1915—19. (Sunk by mine 23.3.16 off Ramsgate and raised.)

CORONADO 6,939/15, 4—6in, 2—4in. Hired as escort 30.9.1917—20.3.19.

CORONARIA Dr 81/11, 1—3pdr. Hired 1916—19.

CORONATA Dr 83/12. Hired 1915—19.

CORONATIA Tr 185/02, 1—6pdr. Hired 8.1914—19 and as boom gate vessel 12.39—44.

CORONATION 50—gun ship, 465bm. Hired 1664—67.

CORONATION (YC.5) DY craft, 71bm. Listed from 1831. Sold 2.12.1869 Marshall, Plymouth to BU.

CORONATION DY tank vessel 477 tons, 120 x 22½ ft. Crown, Sunderland 14.12.1937.

CORONATION Dredger 3,044/02, 4—3in, 2—2pdr. Purchased as harbour A/A ship 11.1940. Sold 9.47, renamed *Inz Wenda.*

CORONET Dr 79/03. Hired 4.8.1915—29.7.16.

CORONET (see ROBERT CLOUGHTON)

CORRY ROY Tr 327/15, 1—12pdr. Hired 1915—19.

CORSAIR Yt 2,181/30, 1—6pdr. Purchased for FAA 22.8.1940. For sale 12.48 at Bermuda.

CORSAIRE Dr 35/30. French M/S CORSAIRE II seized 3.7.1940 at Southampton. Renamed FLIBUSTIER 1941. Listed to 1944.

CORTASIN Tr. German *Sonnetag* captured 1915. Listed to 17.12.15.

CORTES 1,275/85. Hired as store carrier (RFA) 15.9.1915—1.12.15.

CORTINA Tr 213/13, 1—6pdr. Hired 1914—19 and as A/P Tr 11.39. M/S 6.40; sunk 7.12.40 in collision off the Humber.

CORUSCATION (ex-*Sapphire*) Dr 89/10. Hired as A/P Dr 5.3.1940—45.

CORVI (ex-*Mindello II*) Tr 216/09, 1—3pdr. Portuguese, purchased 1915. Sold 17.5.19, renamed *Rio Zezere.*

CORVUS Tr 140/93. Hired 1917—19.

CORYCIA Yt 250/96, 2—6pdr. Hired 25.9.1914. Purchased 11.17 as salvage vessel; sold 1.6.20.

CORYPHENE (ex-*Siluria*) Tr 207/07. Hired as fuel carrier 4.1944–1.45.
CORYTHAIX Tr 280/10. Hired 1915–19.
COSMEA Dr 96/8. Hired for examination service 1942–45.
COSMOS Dr 91/14, 1–6pdr. Hired 1915. Sunk 15.2.18 in action off Dover.
COTILLION M/S Tr 530 tons, 150 x 27½ ft, 1–4in, 3–20mm. Ardrossan DY Co 21.12.1940. Sold 28.3.47.
COTSMUIR Tr 242/15. Hired 1915. Sunk 2.2.17 by unknown cause in the North Sea.
COTSMUIR Tr 275/17, 1–12pdr. Hired as M/S 2.1940–11.45.
COTTEL (see MMS.142)
COUGAR (ex-*Breezin-Thru*) Yt 226/16. American, purchased and commissioned as A/S Yt (RCN) 11.9.1940. Paid off 26.11.45.
COULARD BANK Dr 88/10, 1–3pdr. Hired 1915–19.
COULARD HILL Dr 86/08, 1–3pdr. Hired 1915–19.
COUNCILLOR Tr 116/85. Hired 1917–19.
COUNT Tr 410/29. Purchased as BDV 1940. Sold 1945, renamed *Guttaberg*.
COUNTESS of ELGIN Cutter 8, 78bm, 8–3pdr. Hired 20.6.1803–9.5.1814.
COUNTESS of SCARBOROUGH A.ship 20. Hired 1778. Captured 23.9.1779 by the American BONHOMME RICHARD off Flamborough Head.
COUNTY of FIFE Tr 114/96. Hired 1917–19.
COUNTY of INVERNESS Dr 84/13. Hired 3.1915–(18?).
COUNTY of NAIRN Dr 81/07, 1–3pdr. Hired 1915–19.
COURAGE Dr 88/12, 1–3pdr. Hired 1914–19.
COURIER Cutter 12. Hired 1798–1801.
COURIER Cutter 12, 114bm. Hired 7.1804–8.1806.
COURONNE Dr 83/08. Hired 1914–19.
COURONNE Cstr 227/35. French M/S seized 3.7.1940 at Southampton. A/P vessel 1940; M/S 2.42; water carrier 1943. Returned 1947.
COURSER Tr 227/05. Hired as boom gate vessel 1915–19 and as M/S 9.40. Renamed CAVALCADE 4.45. Returned 31.12.46.
COURTIER Tr 181/10. Hired 1914. Sunk 6.1.16 by mine off Kilnsea.
COURTIER Tr 225/29, 1–12pdr. Hired as M/S 8.1939– 7.45.
COVE 2,734/12. Mine carrier (RFA). Hired 4.8.1914. Paid off 13.2.19.
COVENT GARDEN Dr 84/12. Hired 1915–19.
COVENTRY Merchant (rated as '6th Rate'). Purchased as Arctic discovery relief ship 12.1835; fitted out 2.1836 but probably not used. (Is also listed under the name COVE.)
COVENTRY CITY Tr 546/37, 1–4in. Hired as A/S Tr 9.1939–8.45. (On loan to the USN 3.42–10.42.)

COVERLEY M/S Tr 530 tons, 150 x 27½ft, 1–4in, 3–20mm. Ardrossan DY Co 27.5.1941. Sold 12.3.47.

COVESEA Dr 94/09. Hired 2.12.1914–19. (A/P vessel 1940–44 may be the same craft.)

COW WHALE (Z.8) Admiralty wh, 'Z' class. Smiths Dk 28.7.1915. Sold 6.3.20, renamed *Rasit.*

COYTOBEE Tug 156/02. Hired as ABS 1914. Renamed CHARM 10.4.16. Returned 20.11.19.

CRABE French navy tug seized 1940. Boom gate vessel 1940–45.

CRACKER Lugger. Hired 1797.

CRACKER DY paddle tug 700 tons, 144 x 27 ft. London & Glasgow Co 7.12.1899. Arrived 16.7.56 at Ward, Grays to BU.

CRADOSIN Tr 133/95, 1–12pdr. German *Elma* captured 1915. Sold 5.10.20, renamed *Jeannie Annette.*

CRAFTSMAN (see CORIOLANUS)

CRAIG ALVAH Dr 80/09. Hired 1915–19 and 12.39–12.45.

CRAIGBO Dr 94/09, 1–3pdr. Hired 1915–19 and on examination service 6.40–44.

CRAIG COILLEACH Tr 233/17. Hired as M/S 8.1940–46.

CRAIGELLACHIE Tr 112/96. Hired 1917–19.

CRAIGENTINNY Dr 96/19. Hired on examination service 1941–42 then laid up to 1945.

CRAIG EWAN Tr 204/10, 1–12pdr. Hired 1915–19.

CRAIG GOWAN Tr 126/97. Hired 1918–19.

CRAIGHAUGH Dr 89/14. Hired 1915–19.

CRAIGHEAD Dr 93/08. Hired 28.3.1915–19.

CRAIGIEVAR Tr 112/96. Hired 1918.

CRAIG ISLAND Tr 243/13, 1–6pdr. Hired 1915–19 and as gate vessel 11.39–45.

CRAIGMILLAR Tr. Hired 1917–19.

CRAIG MILLAR Tr 112/96. Hired 1917–19.

CRAIG MILLAR Tr 210/05. Hired as M/S 1.1940–11.45.

CRAIGMIN Dr 74/09. Hired 1915–19.

CRAIGMORE Tr 210/16. Hired 1916–19.

CRAIG MOUNT Dr 80/14. Hired 1915–19.

CRAIGNEEN Dr 90/14. Hired 1914–19.

CRAIGNOON Dr 77/08. Hired 1915. Sunk 15.5.17 in action in the Adriatic.

CRAIGOWAN Tr. Hired 1917–19.

CRAIGROY Dr 96/18. Hired as A/S Dr 12.1939–10.45.

CRAIGSIN Tr141/95. German *Blumenthal* captured 10.1915. Sold 10.20.

CRAIK Tr 219/15, 1–6pdr. Hired 4.1915–19 and on examination service 26.8.39–7.11.44.

CRAITHIE Tr 210/11. Hired 1914. Sunk 27.8.14 by mine off the Tyne.

CRAITHIE Tr 225/16. Hired 1916. Wrecked 16.12.16 on Nizam Point, Barra Head.

CRAMOND ISLAND Tr 180/10, 1–6pdr. Hired 1915–19 and as boom gate vessel 11.39. Sunk 2.4.41 by air attach off St Abbs Head.

CRANBROOK Motor M/S (RCN) 228 tons, 105 x 22 ft. Star SY 5.6.1943 For disposal 5.11.45.

CRANEFLY (ex-*Cotswold*) Tr 312/17. Hired as M/S 8.1939–1.46.

CRANNOCK Dr 84/11. Hired as A/S Dr 11.1939–1.46.

CRASSULA Tr 261/35. Hired as M/S (SAN) 22.6.1940–11.12.46.

CRATER Tr 132/96. Hired 1917–19.

CREAGH MHOR MFV 40/31. Hired as BBV 29.11.1939–9.45.

CREMYLL DY hoy, 76bm. Pembroke Dock 29.8.1836. In service in 1885

CREMYLL DY tank vessel 480 tons, 120 x 22½ ft. Crown, Sunderland 28.2.1938.

CRENELLA (see MONTCALM)

CREOLE DY tank vessel 390 tons, 115 x 21 ft. Bow McLachlan 29.8.1902 Sold 1948.

CREOLE Yt 399/27. Hired as degaussing vessel 11.1940. Renamed MAGIC CIRCLE 4.41. Returned 1946.

CREOSOL Oiler (RFA) 1,920 tons, 220 x 35 ft. Short, Sunderland 5.2.1916. Lost 1918.

CRESCENCE Cstr 255/36. Hired as A/C transport 1941–45.

CRESCENT Merchant, 140bm. Hired 1588.

CRESCENT 28–gun ship, 326bm. Hired 1649–53.

CRESCENT Dr 63/02, 1–3pdr. Hired 1915–19.

CRESCENT II Tr 200/10. Hired 1915–18.

CRESCENT MOON Admiralty steel Dr, 96gr. Duthie Torry 27.5.1918. Sold 1946.

CRESTED EAGLE Paddle 1,110/25. Hired 3.1940 as A/A ship. Sunk 29.5.40 by air attack at Dunkirk.

CRESTFLOWER Tr 367/30, 1–12pdr. Purchased 8.1939 as M/S. Foundered 19.7.40 after air attack off Portsmouth.

CREVETTE Tr 203/18. Hired as A/P Tr 11.1939–40 and as fuel carrier 5.44–10.44.

CREVICE (see KENNET)

CRICCIETH (ex-*Conqueror*) Tug 102/05. Hired as BDV 10.2.1915–19.

CRICKET Ketch, 97bm. Hired 22.7.1808. Lost 31.10.1808.

CRISPIN 5,051/35, 2–6in, 1–12pdr. Hired as OBV 8.1940. Sunk 3.2.41 by U-boat in the N.Atlantic.

CROCODILE (ex-*Flying Vulture*) DY tug 440 tons, 135 x 24 ft. Purchased 1896. Sold 5.11.24 at Gibraltar.

CROCODILE DY tug 380 tons, 105 x 26½ ft. Dunston, Hessle 2.12.1940. Grounded 3.5.46 on the Sind coast; salved and sold 1947.

CROCUS DY tug 46 tons, 55 x 11½ ft. Purchased 1897. Sold 1920.
CROMORNA Dr 85/10. Hired 1915–19.
CROMSINTr 136/96, 1–6pdr. German *Ost* captured 24.6.1915. Sold
11.5.20, renamed *Aro*.
CROSSBOW (see BESSIE)
CROSSTIDE Admiralty steel Dr. Goole SB. Cancelled 1919.
CROTON Tr 150/98, 1–6pdr. Hired 1916–19.
CROUPIER Tr 302/14, 1–6pdr. Hired 1914–19.
CROWLIN Tr, 'Isles' class. Cook Welton & Gemmell 15.11.1943. Sold 3.46.
CROWN of ARAGON 4,500/05. Hired as supply ship (RFA) 3.8.1914–
25.4.15.
CROWN of CASTILE 4,505/05. Hired as supply ship (RFA) 2.8.1914–
19.2.15.
CROWN of GALICIA 4,821/06. Hired as supply ship (RFA) 3.8.1914–
23.1.15.
CROWNSIN Tr 137/95. German *Varel* captured 7.10.1915. Sunk
4.5.16 in the Mediterranean (listed to 9.16.)
CROXBY Tr 215/11, 1–6pdr. Hired 1914–19.
CRUCIS (ex-*Bicalho*) Tr 243/11, 1–3pdr. Portuguese, purchased 1915.
Sold 17.5.19, renamed *Rio Minho*.
CRUDEN BAY Tug 125/99. Hired 1.1915–14.1.20.
CRUISER Tug 98/74. Hired for harbour service 8.7.1917–19.
CRUSOE (ex-*HS.70*) DY tug 300 tons, 83½ x 21 ft. Transferred from
War Dept 1919. Sold 6.20.
CRYSTAL Tr 149/95. Hired 1917–19.

CT boats. Controlled target boats. (Date converted-date last listed.)
CT.01 (ex-MAC.1, ex-MTB.1) 1942–44.
CT.02 (ex-DCMB.72) 1942–46.
CT.03 (ex-MAC.3, ex–MTB.3) 1942–45.
CT.04 (ex-MAC.4, ex-MTB.4) 1942–46.
CT.05 (ex-MTB.103) 1042–46.
CT.06 (ex-MAC.6, ex-MTB.19) 1942–45.
CT.07 (ex-MAC.2, ex-MTB.2) 1942–46.
CT.08 (ex-MA/SB.5) 1942–46.
CT.09 (ex-MTB.14) 1942–43.
CT.10 (ex-MTB.18) 1942–46.
CT.11 (ex-MTB.100) 1942–45.
CT.12–19 (most of these were ex-R.Air Force launches) all 1943–46.
CT.20, 21 (ex-High-speed Launches) 1943–45.
CT.22 (ex-MTB.31) 1943–46.
CT.23, 24 (ex-MTBs 34, 32) 1943–45.
CT.25 (ex.MGB.21) 1943–45.
CT.26–29 1943–45.
CT.30 No trace.

CT.31–33 (ex-Dutch mtbs TM.28–30)1943–46.

CT.34 1943–49.

CT.35 1943–46

CT.36 (ex-MTB.361) 1943–49.

CT.37 1943–47.

CT.38 (ex-MTB.353) 1943–43.

CT.39 (ex-MTB.354) 1943–47.

CT.40–43 (ex-MGBs 189, 190, 180) 1944–48.

CT.44 (ex-MTB.531) 1945 Renamed CT.8044 in 1949–57.

CT.45 (ex-MTB.537) 1945. CT.8045 in 1949–57.

CT.46. Renamed CT.8046 in 1949; renamed RCB.2 in 1949; listed 1953.

CT.47 1945–49.

CT.48 (ex-MTB.481) 7.46 converting; not completed (?).

CT.49 (ex-MTB.490) 7.46 converting; not completed (?).

CT.101–104. Built White, Cowes 1946. Renamed CT.8101–8104 in 1949; sold 1958.

CUCKOO Tr 156/96, 1–6pdr. Hired 1914–19.

CUCKOO Tr 135/94. Hired 1918–19.

CUCKOO (see BOREAS)

CUDWEED Dr 69/11. Hired 1915–19.

CUDWOSIN Tr 122/07, 1–6pdr. German *West* captured 1915. Sold 16.3.20, renamed *Karl Grammerstorf I*, tug.

CUIRASS Tr 321/15, 1–6pdr. Hired 1915–19 and purchased as BDV 12.39. On sale list 1945.

CULBASIN Tr 133/93, 1–6pdr. German *Nereus* captured 1915. Sold 5.10.20.

CULBLEAN Tr 210/11, 1–6pdr. Hired 1914–19.

CULLIST 1,030/ –. Commissioned as decoy ship 3.1917, 1–4in, 2–12pdr 2–TT. Sunk 11.2.18 by U-boat in the Irish Sea. (Also served as HAYLING JURASSIC and PRIM.)

CULLYKHAN Dr 75/10. Hired 1915–19.

CUMBRAE Tr, 'Isles' class. Cochrane 20.12.1940. To Italian navy 22.1.46 as RD.302.

CUMULUS Admiralty wood Dr, 97gr. Colby 1918. Sold 2.10.20 renamed *Boy Jermyn*. (BOY JERMYN in 1940.)

CUMULUS (ex-*Royal Sovereign*) MFV 44/36. Hired for harbour service 13.9.1939–45.

CUPID Yt. Hired in the W.Indies for examination service 10.12.1940. Served to 1943 or later.

CURLEW Fishery protection (Canadian Govt) 400 tons, 116 x 19½ ft, 3–MG. Polson, Ontario 1892. Sold circa 1920.

CURLEW Tr 125/97. Hired 1917–19.

CURRAN 1,106/00. Hired as fleet messenger 17.7.1915–3.11.15.

CURRENT Admiralty steel Dr, 96gr. Chambers 1919. Sold 10.8.20, same name. (Served as COPIOUS in WW.II.)

CURTANA Tr 354/29, 1–12pdr. Hired as M/S 8.1939–10.45.

CUTTACK Tr (RIN), 'Basset' class. Burn, Calcutta 7.1943. Sold 1946, renamed *Figura.*

CUTTY SARK Yt 828/20. Hired as A/S Yt 9.1939. S/M tender 1940–46.

CYCLAMEN Dr 94/11, 1–3pdr. Hired 1915–19.

CYCLONE Admiralty steel Dr, 96gr. Watson, Gainsborough 1919. Renamed BLUSTER 1919. Sold 19.8.21. (Served as HELEN WEST in WW.II.)

CYCLONE (see POL.VI)

CYCLONE (see GROWLER)

CYELSE Tr 237/12, 1–6pdr. Hired 1915–19 and as fuel carrier 3.43. Water carrier 1.44–3.46.

CYGNET Cutter 10, 120bm. Hired 1796–99.

CYGNET II Tr 300/07, 1–6pdr. Hired as M/S 1914–19.

CYGNET III Tr 138/93. Hired 1917–19.

CYGNI (ex-*Monchique*) Tr 207/03, 1–3pdr. Portuguese, purchased 1915. Sold 17.5.19, renamed *Rio Vouga.*

CYMRIC Aux.schooner, 226/93, 1–4in, 2–12pdr. Hired as decoy vessel 15.3.1918–4.19.

CYNARA Yt 560/13. Hired as A/S Yt 9.1939. Not listed 1940.

CYNIC Rescue tug, 472gr, 142 x 29 ft, 1–6pdr. Bow McLachlan 1917. Sold 18.2.22 renamed *Ursus.*

CYNTHIA Tr 167/97. Hired 1917–19.

CYNTHIA Paddle 225/92. Hired as M/S 1917–24.5.17.

CYPRESS Cutter. Hired 1760.

CYPRESS (ex-*Cape Finisterre*) Tr 570 tons, 1–12pdr. Purchased as M/S 11.1935. Sold 3.46, renamed *Vardberg.*

CYPRUS (see CAPE SABLE)

CYRANO Tr 214/05, 1–6pdr. Hired 1915–19.

CYRIL VERSCHAEVE Dr 114/36. Belgian, hired for harbour service 1941–45.

CYRUS FIELD Cable ship 1,288/24. Hired (RCN) 1941–46.

CYSNE II Yt 87/06. Hired as HDPC 2.1940. Accommodation ship 11.40–43.

DABCHICK (see THORNEY)

DACCA Tr, 'Basset' class (RIN). Burn, Calcutta. Ordered 23.9.1941. Deferred 12.44, cancelled 1945.

DAEDALUS Storeship. Hired 1790–95.

DAERWOOD Motor M/S (RCN) 228 tons, 105 x 22 ft. Vancouver SY 31.3.1943. To sale list 11.45.

DAFFODIL II Dr 94/07, 1–3pdr. Hired 2.1915–19. (Served as CLARICE in WW.II.)

DAFFODIL Dr 74/04. Hired for harbour service 5.15–19.

DAFFODIL Ferry 490/06. Hired as assault ship 1918–18.

DAFFODIL (ex-Train Ferry No 3) 2,678/17. Purchased as landing ship 9.1940. Sunk 18.3.45 after mine damage off Dieppe.

DAGNY Tr 138/04. Icelandic, hired as boom tender 1942–45.

DAGON Tr 250/14. Hired 1915. Sunk 8.12.16 by mine in the North Sea.

DAHINDA II Yt 57/27. Purchased as HDPC 1939. Sold 12.45.

DAHLIA II Tr 154/89, 1–6pdr. Hired 1.1915–18.

DAH PU 1,974/22. Hired 12.4.1942. Sunk 28.6.43 by U-boat at Muscat.

DAILY BREAD Dr 56/01. Hired 1915–19.

DAIMLER Tr 257/10. Hired 1914–19.

DAINTY Rescue tug, 468gr, 142 x 29 ft. Finch, Chepstow 1918. To Irish govt 1922.

DAIRLIE Dr 79/10. Hired 1915–19.

DAISY II Dr 100/08. Hired as M/S 2.1915–19 and 14.9.39–12.4.43.

DAISY III Dr 92/07. Hired 2.1915–19.

DAISY IV Dr 98/07, 1–3pdr. Hired 2.1915–19.

DAISY V Dr 77/04, 1–6pdr. Hired 3.1915–19.

DAISY VI Dr 85/06, 1–6pdr. Hired 4.1915–19.

DAISY MFV. Hired for harbour service 12.1939–45.

DAISY Dr 50/02. Hired as degaussing vessel 1.1.1941. Foundered 25.4.42 in a storm in the Clyde.

DAISY Dr. Hired for harbour service 1941–45.

DAISY Tug. Hired in the Mediterranean 10.1941. Foundered 2.1.42 on passage Alexandria-Tobruk.

DAISY Tug. Hired in the W.Indies 13.12.1942–15.4.43.

DAISY DY tug 40gr. Dunston, Thorne 28.6.1968.

DAISY BANK Dr 84/11, 1–3pdr. Hired 1915–19 and 12.39–7.44.

DAISY WOOD Dr 72/11. Hired 1915–19.

DALE Tr 199/99. Hired 8.1914–19.

DALE CASTLE Tr 246/09, 1–6pdr. Hired 1915–19 and as A/P Tr, 2–MG 5.40. Target towing 1944–3.46.

DALKEITH (ex-*Dalhousie*) Tug 741/89. Purchased as salvage vessel 3.1916. Sunk 18.5.18 by enemy action off Sardinia.

DALMATIA Tr 357/28, 1–12pdr. Purchased as M/S 9.1939. Danlayer 1944; sold 24.4.46, renamed *Westhawk*.

DALMATIAN Tr 186/00. Hired 1914–16.

DALMATIAN DY tug 170 tons, 85 x 25 ft. Doig, Grimsby 2.4.1965.

DALRIADA 758/26. Hired as wreck dispersal vessel 2.1941. Sunk 19.6.42 by mine in the Thames estuary.

DAMITO Tr 275/17. Hired as M/S 8.1939. Fuel carrier 9.43—1.46.

DAMSAY Tr, 'Isles' class. G.Brown 27.6.1942. Sold 28.8.59 Mole & Bray, Stourport; BU 1960 at Troon.

DANDINI Tr 212/17, 1—6pdr. Hired 4.1917—19.

DANDOLO Tr 207/10. Hired as fuel carrier 4.1944—45.

DANDY Rescue tug, 468gr, 142 x 29 ft. Finch, Chepstow 1919. Sold 6.21, renamed *Lagos Vulcan.*

DANE Tr 265/13. Hired 1915. Sunk 28.8.15 by mine off Aldeburgh.

DANE II Tr 346/11. Hired 1915—19 and as DANE, M/S 1.40—1.46.

DANEMAN Tr 516/37, 1—4in. Purchased as A/S Tr 8.1939. Abandoned in tow 8.5.43 after collision with ice, N.Atlantic.

DANESTON Tr 239/15. Hired as mooring vessel 1915—19.

DANIA Tr 195/04. Hired 1.1918—19.

DANIEL CLOWDEN Tr, 'Castle' type, 280gr. G.Brown 1919. Sold 8.8.19, renamed *Hannah Woodbridge.* Hired as DANIEL CLOWDEN, M/S 8.39—10.45.

DANIEL DICK Tr, 'Castle' type, 276gr. J P Rennoldson 1919. Sold 1921, renamed *Agate.* (Served as CLYTHNESS in WW.II.)

DANIEL DIZMONT Tr, 'Strath' type. Montrose SY 1919. Sold 1920.

DANIEL FEARALL Tr, 'Mersey' type, 324gr. Cochrane 2.11.1917. Renamed STOUR 1920; base ship PEMBROKE 1.9.22; STOUR 1939. Sold 7.46.

DANIEL HARRINGTON Tr, non-standard 'Castle' type, 276gr. Smiths Dk 8.2.1917. Sold 1920, renamed *Start Point.* (Served as LUCIENNE JEANNE in WW.II.)

DANIEL HENLEY Tr, non-standard 'Castle' type, 276gr. Smiths Dk 24.1.1917. Sold 9.20, renamed *Kilgerran Castle.*

DANIEL HILLIER Tr, 'Strath' type. Hawthorns, Leith 1919. Sold 1919.

DANIEL LEARY Tr, 'Castle' type, 275gr. C Rennoldson 1920. Sold 1920, renamed *Strato.*

DANIEL McPHERSON Tr, 'Mersey' type. Cochrane 1919. Sold 1919, renamed *Havardur Isfindingur.*

DANIEL MUNRO Tr, Mersey' type, 324gr. Cochrane 1919. Sold 1919, renamed *Estrella do Norte.* (ESTRELLA do NORTE in WW.II.)

DANIEL STROUD Tr 209/12. Purchased as M/S 7.1914. Sold 1919, renamed *Loch Esk.* (LOCH ESK in WW.II.)

DANMARK 8,391/25. Danish, in service as oil hulk 1942—46.

DAN O'CONNELL Dr 52/11. Hired 1916—18.

DANUBE II Tug 227/10. Hired 8.1914—19.

DANUBE III Tug 234/24. Hired for examination service 28.8.1939. Sunk 13.10.40 by mine off Sheerness.

DANUBE V Tug 241/35. Hired for examination service 28.8.39. Rescue tug 1941–11.10.45.

DANUBE VI Tug 241/35. Hired 28.8.39–20.4.45.

DAPHNE A.ship. Hired 1794–96.

DAPHNE DY tug 40gr. Dunston, Thorne 18.7.1968.

DAPPER Tug 419/15. Purchased as salvage tug 1915. Sold 3.23. Hired 25.9.40–46.

DARCY COOPER Dr 126/28. Hired for examination service 1940. Sunk 9.4.41 by air attack off Harwich.

DARDA Dr 99/11. Hired as BDV 3.1915–19 and for harbour service 30.9.39. Salvage vessel 12.41–42.

DARGLE Tr 351/14. Hired 1917–18 as decoy ship (Q.29).

DARICA Ferry 692/42. Turkish, hired 9.42–18.11.43.

'Dark' class fast patrol boats. 50 tons, 67 x 19½ ft 1–40mm, 4–TT (as MTB), or 1–4.5in, 1–40mm (as MGB).

DARK ADVENTURER Saunders Roe 28.10.1954. On sale list 1964.

DARK AGGRESSOR Saunders Roe 9.12.54. Sold 4.10.61.

DARK ANTAGONIST Saunders Roe 11.12.55. On sale list 1964.

DARK ATTACKER Saunders Roe. Cancelled.

DARK AVENGER Saunders Roe 6.9.55. Sold 1967.

DARK BATTLER Saunders Roe. Cancelled 2.5.53.

DARK BITER Saunders Roe 23.6.55. Sold 1967.

DARK BOWMAN Saunders Roe. Cancelled 1955.

DARK BUCCANEER Vosper 30.9.54. On sale list 1964.

DARK CHASER Vosper. Cancelled.

DARK CHIEFTAIN Vosper. Cancelled.

DARK CLIPPER Vosper 9.2.55. On sale list 1964.

DARK CRUSADER Vosper. Cancelled.

DARK DEFENDER Thornycroft. Cancelled.

DARK EXPLORER Thornycroft. Cancelled.

DARK FIGHTER Taylor 4.10.55. On sale list 1964.

DARK GLADIATOR Taylor 5.12.56.

DARK HERO McGruer 16.3.57. On sale list 1965.

DARK HIGHWAYMAN Vosper 29.3.55. Sold 1967.

DARK HORSEMAN McGruer. Cancelled 11.57.

DARK HUNTER Miller 18.3.54. Sold 16.4.62.

DARK HUSSAR Thornycroft 16.5.57. On sale list 1965.

DARK INTRUDER Morgan Giles 6.7.55.

DARK INVADER Morgan Giles 5.9.55. On sale list 1964.

DARK KILLER Thornycroft 26.9.56. On sale list 1964.

DARK ROVER Vosper 30.8.54. On sale list 1964.

DARK SCOUT Saunders Roe 20.3.58. Sold 4.62.

DARKDALE Oiler (RFA) 17,000 tons. Blythswood 1940. Sunk
22.10.41 by 'U.68' at St Helena.
DARKNESS Admiralty wood Dr, non-standard. Fellows 1918. Renamed
COLUMBINE 1.11.19 as base ship. Sold 1923.
DARK NIGHT Admiralty steel Dr. Goole SB. Cancelled 1919.
DARNAWAY Dr 94/18. Hired for harbour service 8.1939—9.45.
DARNETT NESS Tr 277/20. Hired as M/S 8.1939—9.45.
DAROGAH Tr 221/14. Hired 1915—19 and as A/P Tr 12.39. M/S 2.40;
sunk 27.1.41 by mine in the Thames estuary.
DARRACQ Tr 256/10, 1—6pdr. Hired 1914—19.
DART Cutter 8. Hired 1782.
DART Cutter 10, 56bm. Hired 6.1803—1.1815.
DART DY tug. Hired 31.5.1941—13.11.45.
DARTHEMA Tr 373/29, 1—12pdr. Hired as M/S 10.1939—12.45.
DARTMOUTH Tr 139/90. Hired 1917—19.
DARWEN Tr 227/16. Hired as A/P Tr 11.1939. M/S 6.40—2.46.
DASHER (see VENTURE)
DASHING SPRAY Dr 69/11. Hired 1915—19.
DATUM Dr 90/10. Hired 11.1914—12.14 and 1915; sunk 27.10.16 by
German destroyer in the Dover Strait.
DAUNTLESS Tug 109/03. Hired 2.1915—18.
DAVARA Tr 291/12, 1—6pdr. Hired 1914—19.
DAVID BLAKE Tr, 'Strath' type, 203gr. Hall Russell 13.6.1918. Sold
1921, same name.
DAVID B SUMMERS Dr 61/11. Hired 1915—19.
DAVID BUCHAN Tr, 'Strath' type, 203gr. Hall Russell 9.4.1918. Sold
10.11.19, renamed *River Ness*. (RIVER NESS in WW.II.)
DAVID CONN Tr, 'Strath' type, 202gr. Montrose SB 13.7.1918. Sold
15.11.19, renamed *River Spey*. (RIVER SPEY in WW.II.)
DAVID DILLON Tr, 'Castle' type, 275gr. J P Rennoldson 1919. Sold
28.7.19, renamed *Edouard Nierinck*. (Served as EDWARD WALMSLEY
in WW.II.)
DAVID FLETT Dr 84/12. Hired 3.1915—19.
DAVID GILLIES Tug 375/08. Hired 10.1917. Stranded 5.5.18 in the
Mediterranean.
DAVID HAIGH Tr 276/18. Purchased as M/S (SAN) 19.9.1939. BDV
12.43; sold 25.6.46.
DAVID MIFFON Tr, 'Mersey' type. Cochrane. Cancelled 1919.
DAVID OGILVIE Tr, 'Castle' type, 276gr. Smiths Dk 7.5.1917. Sold
1920, same name. Hired as M/S 9.39—7.46.
DAVY Tr 450/36. Purchased as A/S Tr 8.1939. Sold 1945.
DAWN Admiralty steel Dr, 96gr. Duthie Torry 11.6.1918. Renamed
EXPANSE 1919; sold 1920.

DAWN Yt 37/34. Hired as HDPC 1941—45.

DAYBREAK Admiralty steel Dr, 96gr. Duthie Torry 9.7.1918. Sold 1920, renamed *Ralph.Hall Caine.* (Served as ALLOCHY in WW.II.)

DAYBREAK (see KOS VII)

DAYLIGHT Admiralty wood Dr, 94gr. Fellows, Yarmouth 1918. Renamed TRADEWIND 1920. Sold 5.21.

DAYLIGHT (see GLOBE I)

DAYSPRING Admiralty steel Dr, non-standard 108gr. Fellows, Yarmouth 1917. Sold 1920, renamed *Castle Bay.* (CASTLE BAY in WW.II.)

DAYSTAR Dr. Hired 1918—19.

DEAL 691/28. Hired as BBV 5.1941—10.43.

DEAN SWIFT (ex-*Swift*) Cstr 1,141/11. Hired 7.8.1914—11.8.15.

DEBRA HUYSENNE Belgian vessel. Hired as BBV 9.1940. Harbour service 1942—45.

De BRIES Yt 69/04. In service in 1944.

DECIBEL (ex-*Bournemouth Belle*) Purchased on stocks; Bolson, Poole 21.11.1953. Trials vessel. Sold 8.58.

DECISION (see HENGIST)

De DRIE GEZUSTERS MFV 105/12. Served with the RN (Dutch crew) in WW.II.

De DRIE GEZUSTERS MFV 49/39, 1—6pdr. French, ex-Belgian, seized 7.1940. A/P vessel (Polish crew to 1942). Returned 5.10.45. (Also known as P.8.)

DEE Tr 151/93. Hired 1918—19.

DEE (see BATTLEAXE)

DEERHOUND DY tug 170 tons, 85 x 25 ft. 1967.

DEER SOUND (see PORT QUEBEC)

DEFENDER Tr 128/99. Hired 1917—19.

DEFENSOR Dr 97/20. Hired for harbour service 1940—1.46.

DEFIANCE Sloop 18. Hired 1782—85.

DEGARA LEROSA Tr, 'Mersey' type. Cochrane 1919. Sold 1919.

De HEILIGE FAMILIE Dr 114/35. Belgian, hired for harbour service 1942—45.

De HOOP Dr 91/31. Belgian, hired as BBV 31.7.1940. Renamed LIEGE 1941. Returned 1946.

De HOOP MFV 53/36. Dutch, hired as A/P vessel (Dutch crew) 7.10.1940—3.9.45.

De La POLE Tr 255/11. Hired 1915. Wrecked 4.2.16 on the Goodwins.

De La POLE Tr 290/19, 1—12pdr. Hired as A/P Tr 5.1940. M/S 1941—12.45.

DELHI Tr 171/03. Hired 1917—19.

DELIGHT 50—ton pinnace hired 1588.

DELILA Tr 202/19, 1—6pdr. Hired as A/P Tr 6.1940—1.46.

DELIVERER Dr 79/-. Hired 1915. Sunk 3.11.17 by unknown cause off Dublin.

DELIVERER Dr 94/09. Hired for harbour service 1941—44.

DELPHIN II Tr 253/38. Polish, hired for examination service (Polish crew) 9.1940—1.46.

DELPHINE Tr 250/14, 1—6pdr. Hired 1915—19.

DELPHINULA (ex-*Buyo Maru*) Oiler (RFA) 10,500 tons, 385 x 50½ ft. Listed from 1921. Hulk 1939—47; BU 9.47.

DELPHINUS Tr 257/06, 1—12pdr, 1—6pdr. Hired 1915—19 and as A/P Tr, 1—6pdr 11.39. M/S 10.40; sold 1945.

DELTA Tr. Hired 1917—19.

DELUGE (ex-Belgian *President de Leeuw*) Tug 260/08. Hired 16.12.1914—1

DEMETER (ex-*Buenos Aires*) 5,646/20. Purchased as store carrier (RFA) 6.1941. Ammo hulk 10.45; sold 1949.

DENBYDALE (ex-*Empire Silver*) Oiler (RFA) 17,000 tons, 460 x 59 ft. Blythswood 19.10.1940. Arrived 27.7.55 Hughes Bolckow, Blyth to BU. (Was broken in two by Italian frogmen at Gibraltar and repaired.)

DENFORD Dr 77/01. Hired as coal boat 8.2.1915—19.

DENIS CASEY Tr, 'Castle' type. Ailsa, Troon 1918. Sold 7.20, renamed *Cardigan Castle*.

DENNY DUFF Dr 80/12. Hired as store carrier 1915—19.

DENTARIA Tr 259/08, 1—12pdr. Hired 1914—19.

DEODAR M/S Tr 505 tons, 150 x 17½ ft, 1—12pdr. Goole SB 26.3.1940. Sold 1947, renamed *Mollex VI*.

DEO-na-MARA Yt 62/31. Hired as HDPC 10.1939—45.

DEO VOLANTE MFV, hired as A/P vessel 1.1940—6.45.

DEPARTURE BAY MFV 44/26. Hired as M/S (RCN) 1941—45.

DEPTFORD DY lighter, 71bm, 52 x 18 ft. Sheerness DY 1716. Fate unknown.

DERBY Tr 144/96. Hired 1915; DEBENEY 1918—19.

DERBY COUNTY Tr 399/38, 1—4in. Purchased as A/S Tr 8.1939. Sold 1945.

DERBYSHIRE 11,660/35, 6—6in, 2—3in. Hired as AMC 10.1939. Landing ship 1944—45.

De ROSA Dr 99/22 Belgian, hired as A/P vessel 6.40—10.45. (Also spelt De ROZA in some lists.)

DERRIMUT Ammo. carrier (RAN) 279 tons. Williamstown DY 19.10.1951.

DERVISH Tr 346/11, 1—6pdr. Hired as A/P Tr 6.1940. Sunk 9.9.40 by mine off the Humber.

DERWENT Tr 151/93. Hired 1917—19.

DERWENT (see JOHN BRICE)

DERWENTDALE Oiler (RFA) 17,000 tons, 460 x 59 ft. Harland & Wolff, Govan 12.4.1941. Landing ship 1941; oiler 1946. Sold 1.60, renamed *Irvingdale I*.

DERWENTDALE (ex-*Halcyon Breeze*) Oiler (RFA), 42,504gr. Chartered 17.6.1967.

DESIRE Dr 83/08, 1–3pdr. Hired 4.1915–19.

DESIRE (ex-Belgian *President Desire Maas*) Tug 165/12. Hired for DY service 11.12.1915. Sunk 24.1.18 by U-boat off the Yorkshire coast.

DESIREE Tr 212/12, 1–6pdr. Hired as M/S 1914–19 and as M/S 11.39. Sunk 16.1.41 by mine in the Thames estuary.

DESPATCH Iron tank vessel, 257bm, 370 tons. Maudslay, Greenwich 30.1.1869. Sold 17.5.1905.

DESPATCH Tank vessel 405 tons, 115 x 21 ft. Bow McLachlan 29.2.1904. Renamed DESPOT 1918. Sold 1946, renamed *Despote.*

DESPOT (see DESPATCH)

DESTINN Tr 226/14, 1–6pdr. Hired 1914–19 and as A/P Tr 1.1940. M/S 1.42; water carrier 9.43–8.45.

DESTINY Rescue Tug, 'B.A.T.' class. Defoe SB, Bay City 1.7.1942 on lend-lease. Returned 1946 to the USN.

DESTINY (C.10) (ex-*Oner II*) 91/37, 80 x 21 ft. DY tug. Purchased 1947. BU 1.64 Pounds, Portsmouth.

DEVANEY (ex-*Devonia*) 318/06. Fleet messenger purchased 7.11.1917. Sold 9.19, renamed *Lochiel.*

DEVANHA Tr 196/01, 1–6pdr. Hired as BDV 1915–19.

DEVERON Tr 233/05, 1–6pdr. Hired 1914–19.

DEVERONSIDE Dr 89/14. Hired 1.1915–19.

DEVON DY lighter. Chatham DY 24.9.1835. Wrecked 23.10.1868 near Penzance. (Also known as Devonport YC.4.)

DEVON DY store carrier, 124bm. Plymouth DY 1845. Fate unknown.

DEVON CITY 4,928/33. Hired as boom carrier 1940–8.4.46.

DEVON COUNTY Dr 86/10, 1–6pdr. Hired 1915–19 and as M/S 11.39. Sunk 1.7.41 by mine in the Thames estuary.

DEVONIA Cstr 99/94. Hired as DY lighter 1915–19.

DEVONIA Paddle 520/05, 1–12pdr, 1–3pdr. Hired as M/S 16.9.1914–9.6.19, and as M/S 10.39. Beached 31.5.40 after air attack at Dunkirk.

DEVONIA MFV. Hired as degaussing vessel 1941–43.

DEVONPORT DY lighter. Plymouth DY 1824. Listed 1850.

DEVONPORT DY buoy boat. Devonport DY 6.1851. Fate unknown.

DEVOTION Dr 88/10. Hired 3.1915–19 and as water carrier 1941–44.

DEW Admiralty steel Dr. 96gr. Ouse SB 1918. Sold 1921, same name. (Served as OLIVE TREE in WW.II.)

DEW (see KOS VIII)

DEWDALE Oiler (RFA) 17,000 tons, 460 x 59 ft. Cammell Laird 7.2.41. Landing ship 1941; oiler 1946; BU 12.59 in Belgium.

DEWSLAND Tr 236/07, 1–12pdr. Hired 1915–19.

DEWY EVE Dr 109/16. Hired as M/S 1.1940. Sunk 9.6.40 in collision at Scapa.

DEWY ROSE Dr 100/15. Hired as BBV 5.1940—45.
DEXTERITY Dr 87/08, 1—3pdr. Hired 1915—19.
DEXTEROUS Rescue tug 700 tons, 142½ x 33 ft, 1—3in. Cochrane 3.4.1942. Sold 23.1.47.
DEXTEROUS DY paddle tug 710 tons, 145 x 30 ft. Yarrow 21.8.1956.
DHOON Tr 275/-. Hired 1916. Sunk 24.11.16 by mine off Yarmouth.
DHOON Tr 323/15, 1—12pdr. Hired as M/S 5.1940. Renamed DHOON GLEN 1943; returned 11.45.
DIADEM II Dr 75/04, 1—3pdr. Hired 1916—19.
DIADEM Tr. Hired 1918—19.
DIAMOND II Tr 289/13, 1—6pdr. Hired 1915—19.
DIAMOND III Tr 150/94. Hired 1918—19.
DIAMOND 60—ton vessel. Hired 1588.
DIAMOND Brig 10, 191bm. Hired 1793—9.94.
DIAMOND Schooner 4. Hired 1832—33.
DIANA 80—ton vessel. Hired 1588—89.
DIANA A.ship 10, 179bm. Hired 1804—05.
DIANA Tr 172/99. Hired as BDV 1915—19.
DIANA II Tr. Hired 1916—19.
DIANE Yt 259/02, 2—6pdr. Hired 9.1914—23.11.17.
DIANE Yt 227/03. Hired as HDPC 1940—41.
DIANE LUCIE MFV 78/31. Belgian, hired as A/P vessel 17.10.1940. Degaussing vessel 1941—5.45.
DICK WHITTINGTON Dr 80/13, 1—6pdr. Hired 1914—19 and as degaussing vessel 1942—43 or later.
DIDO Tug 66/02, 1—6pdr. Hired as A/P vessel 1941—45.
DIGBY 3,966/13. Hired as AMC 22.11.1914—6.1.19. (On loan French navy as ARTOIS 24.11.15—19.7.17.)
DIGIT (ex-*Tilsitt*) Tr 422/19. Purchased as BDV 1940. Sold 1946, renamed *Eirik Jall*.
DILIGENCE (ex-*Kingfisher*) DY tug 350 tons, 102 x 23 ft. Purchased 22.3.1906. Renamed SECURITY 1914. Sold 8.2.27 Elliot Tug Co.
DILIGENCE II Dr 85/05, 1—3pdr. Hired 1915—19.
DILIGENT Cutter 6. Hired 1793—1801.
DILIGENT DY paddle tug 695 tons, 145 x 27½ ft. Barclay Curle 31.8.1898. Sold 9.10.23 Young, Sunderland.
DILIGENT Dr 80/02. Hired 7.1915—19 and as BBV 1940. Renamed SNOWFINCH 1941. Returned 1944.
DILIGENT Rescue tug 700 tons, 142½ x 33 ft. Cochrane 22.6.1940. Renamed TENACITY 11.40; ADHERENT 1947. BU 12.60.
DILIGENT (ex-*Empire Ace*) DY tug, 274/42. Transferred from MOT and renamed 5.47. Lent USN 1961 as EMPIRE ACE.
DILIMER Dr 139/16. Hired as A/P Dr 1940—45.

DILSTON 1,530/13. Hired as fleet auxiliary 2.1916—19.

DINAPORE Tr (RIN), 'Basset' class. Alcock Ashdown, Calcutta. Cancelled 3.1945.

DINGLEDALE Oiler (RFA) 17,000 tons, 460 x 59 ft. Harland & Wolff, Govan 27.3.1941. Sold 1959 as oil hulk *Royaumont.*

DINAS Tr 219/09, 1—6pdr. Hired 1914—19.

DINORAH Tr 192/03. Hired 1914—19.

DINSDALE (ex-*Empire Norseman*) Oiler (RFA) 17,300 tons. Harland & Wolff, Govan 1942. Sunk 31.5.42 by U-boat in the S.Atlantic.

DIPAVATI Cstr 840/36. Hired as A/P vessel (RIN) 9.1939—45.

DIRECTOR DY paddle tug 710 tons, 145 x 30 ft. Yarrow 11.6.1956.

DIRK Tr 181/09, 1—12pdr, 1—6pdr. Hired 1917. Sunk 28.5.18 by U-boat off Flamborough Head.

DIRKJE Tr 234/34. M/S (Dutch crew) listed 1940—45.

DISA Tr 197/24. Hired as M/S (SAN) 19.9.1939—16.5.40.

DISCOVERER 5,421/13, 4—6in. Hired as escort 16.6.1917—1.3.19.

DISCOVERY II Falkland Islands govt research ship, 1,036/30. Hired as ABV 11.1939—1941 or later.

DISPATCH Sloop 14. Hired 1764. Capsized 1780 in the St Lawrence.

DISPENSER Salvage vessel 950 tons, 150 x 35½ ft, 2—20mm. Smiths Dk 22.4.1943. On charter from 1954.

DISTANCE Admiralty steel Dr, 97gr. Chambers 1919. Sold 1919, renamed *Leonard Boyle.* (Served as DUNDARG in WW.II.)

DISTOL Oiler (RFA) 1,920 tons, 220 x 35 ft. Tyne Iron SB Co 4.3.1916. Sold 1947, renamed *Akhawi.*

DIVER Tr 207/00. Hired 1917—19.

DIVERSION (see NORMAN)

DIVETTE French DY tug seized 3.7.1940 at Southampton. Harbour service to 1945.

DIVIS Cstr 1,634/83. Hired as fleet auxiliary 29.7.1914—19.

DIXI Ketch 114/13. French merchant seized 1940. Accommodation ship 1940; degaussing vessel 1941—45.

DIXON Tr. Hired 1916—19.

DOCHET Tr, 'Isles' class. Davie, Lauzon 26.6.1942. Sold 1947, renamed *Catherine,* then German EIDER.

DOCKLEAF Oiler (RFA), 5,311gr. Bartram 11.11.1916. Sold 1919.

DOCTOR LEE Tr 307/14, 1—6pdr. Hired 1915—19 and as BDV 12.39—46.

DOGGER BANK Tr 274/12. Hired as boom gate·vessel 1915—19.

DOLDRUM Admiralty wood Dr, 94gr. Smith, Rye 1919. Sold 1919, renamed *Beatrice Eves.* (Served as GLOAMIN in WW.II.)

DOLFIJN Tr 168/20. Dutch M/S hired 1940 (Dutch crew). Renamed GOEREE 1942. Fuel carrier (RN) 1944. Returned 1945.

DOLFIJN Dr 67/28. French M/S CAP GRIZ-NEZ ex-Belgian *Dolfijn*, seized 3.7.1940 at Southampton. (May be the DOLPHYN renamed BELUGA 1941.) (see BELUGA)

DOLLAR PRINCESS Dr 74/11. Hired 1915—19.

DOLLY Lugger 8. Hired 1796—1801.

DOLLY Cutter 8, 61bm. Hired 9.7.1803—19.9.03.

DOLORES (ex-*Rainbow*) Tr 176/06. Purchased as danlayer 1.1940. On sale list 1946.

DOLPHIN A.merchant, 470bm. Hired 1650—54.

DOLPHIN Cutter 12, 93bm. Hired 1793. Purchased 4.6.1801, sold 1802.

DOLPHIN Lugger 6. Hired 1799—1800.

DOLPHYN (see DOLFIJN)

DOMINICK ADDISON Tr, 'Castle' type, 290gr. Cook Welton & Gemmell 2.4.1919. Sold 1920, renamed *Tenedos*. (Served as GADFLY in WW.II.)

DOMINICK DUBINE Tr, 'Castle' type, 277gr. J P Rennoldson 1918. Sold 1919, renamed *Emildos*.

DOMINO (see SABRA)

DOMQUE GENTILE Tr, 'Castle' type, 277gr. Ailsa, Troon 5.8.1918. Sold 1921, renamed *Hagnaby*.

DON Cstr 939/92. Hired as storage carrier (RFA) 26.8.1914—20.2.15.

DONALDA Tr 226/14, 1—6pdr. Hired 1915—19.

DONALD & DORIS Tr 149/97. Hired as BBV 1942—44.

DONNA NOOK Tr 307/16, 1—12pdr, 1—3pdr. Hired 1916—19 and as A/P Tr, 1—12pdr 11.39. M/S 1941; sunk 25.9.43 in collision with STELLA RIGEL off Harwich.

DON RODERIC Yt 56/84. Hired as fleet messenger 1914. Paid off 28.5.15.

DONSIDE Tr 182/00. Hired 1914. Sunk 7.1.17 by mine off Lowestoft.

DOOMBA Cstr 750/19, 1—4in, 1—40mm. Hired as M/S (RAN) 9.1939, later purchased. Sold 3.2.47.

DOON Tr 199/99. Hired 1917—19.

DOON (see FRASER EAVES)

DOONIE BRAES Tr 213/18, 1—3pdr. Hired as danlayer 5.1940. M/S 1942—1.45.

DOORIE BRAE Dr 94/20. Hired as A/P Dr 11.1939—45.

DORA Tr 295/00. Hired 1915—16.

DORADE Yt 87/05. Hired 1917—19.

DORADE II Yt 213/06. Hired for examination service 5.1940—45.

DORA DUNCAN Tug 126/91. Hired for harbour service 8.1915—1918.

DORANDO Tr 139/95. Hired 1916—18.

DORANDO PIETRI MFV. Hired for harbour service 1940—45.

DORCAS Tr 173/06, 1—6pdr. Hired 1914—19.

DOREEN Tr 194/03. Hired 1915—19.

DORIA Tug 150/09. Hired as ABS 30.7.1914–2.1.19 and on harbour service in WW.II.

DORIENTA Dr 101/14. Hired as M/S 9.1939–5.46.

DORILEEN Tr 226/17. Purchased as BDV 1.1940. Sold 5.46.

DORINDA Tr 270/17, 1–6pdr. Hired 1917–19 and as M/S, 1–12pdr 8.1939–11.45.

DORIS II Dr 82/07. Hired 1915–19.

DORIS Tr 122/02. Hired 1918–19.

DORIS Tr 174/97. Served in WW.II.

DORIS Paddle 84/89. Hired for harbour service 8.4.1918–17.8.18.

DORIS DY tug 40gr. Dunston, Hessle 15.10.1968.

DORIS MAUD Dr 74/14. Hired 1915–19.

DORITA Cstr 109/20. Hired as BBV 1941. Accommodation vessel 1942–44.

DOROTHY DY tug 40gr. Dunston, Hessle 28.11.1968.

DOROTHY DUKE Yt 307/18. Purchased as A/S Yt 1941. For disposal 12.45.

DOROTHY F Tr. Hired 1915–19.

DOROTHY GRAY Tr 199/08, 1–6pdr. Hired 1914–19 and as M/S 7.40. A/P Tr 1941–12.44.

DOROTHY LAMBERT Tr 299/23. Hired as M/S 2.1940–2.46.

DORSET Cutter 8. Hired 1782–1800 and 1801–02.

DOTTEREL Yt 214/87. Hired as tender 20.4.1918. Renamed DOTTER 1918; purchased 1919. Sold 7.6.22.

DOUBLE TIDE (see SIROCCO)

DOUGLAS ALEXANDER A/P vessel hired in the W.Indies 1940. Renamed BUZZARD 1941–46 as base ship.

DOURO Survey vessel. Hired 1831–33.

DOURO Tr 152/97. Hired 1918–19.

DOURSWOLD Dutch, hired as BBV 1941–44.

DOVE Sloop 10, 177bm. Hired 1793–10.94.

DOVE (YC.5) DY lighter, 135bm. Chatham DY 1828. BU completed 5.1872 at Chatham.

DOVE II Tr 168/97, 1–3pdr. Hired 1914–19.

DOVE III Dr 81/07, 1–3pdr. Hired 1915–19.

DOVER Brig 10. Hired 1794–1801.

DOVER Cutter 4, 49bm. Hired 4.11.1808–20.5.1810.

DOVER Tr 163/96, 1–6pdr. Hired 1914–19.

DOVER HILL 5,815/18. Purchased 1944. Sunk 9.6.44 as blockship at Arromanches.

DO WELL Dr 71/11. Hired 1914–19.

DOWGATE Boom gate vessel 290 tons, 98 x 26 ft, 1–3in (dumb). Hong Kong & Whampoa 24.9.1935. Scuttled 2.42 at Singapore.

DOWNIEHILLS Tr 227/16. Hired 1917–19.

DOWNPOUR Admiralty steel Dr. Goole SB. Cancelled 1919.

DOX MFV 35/31. Belgian, hired as A/P vessel 1.6.1940. Sunk 20.3.41 by air attack at Plymouth. (Belgian sources say 4.7.41; listed as at Plymouth 23.3.41.)

DRACO Tr 139/95. Hired as BDV 1915—19.

DRAGE (see DRAGON)

DRAGON DY wood paddle tug 113 tons, 85 x 17 ft. Purchased 11.7.1860. Sold 1867 at Malta.

DRAGON Tug 153/93. Hired for DY service 10.3.1915. Renamed DRAGE 1917. Returned 19.1.19.

DRAGON II Tr, 1—6pdr. Hired 1917—19.

DRAGONET BDV 530 tons, 135 x 30½ ft, 1—3in. Blyth 1.6.1939. Sold 1960, renamed *Foundation Venture.*

DRAGOON M/S Tr, 297gr, 138½ x 23½ ft, 1—3in. Purchased on stocks 11.12.1914; Smiths Dk 16.1.15. Renamed DRUMMER 1919. Sold, same name. (DRUMMER in WW.II.)

DRAINIE Dr 92/18. Hired for harbour service 1941. Water carrier 1943—47.

DRAKE 60—ton pinnace hired 1588—89.

DRAKE Hired storeship in service 1759. Foundered 1.1.1760 off Pondicherry.

DRAKE Brig 6, 130bm. Hired 1779.

DRAKE Cutter 12. Hired 1799—1801.

DRAKE Cutter 12, 130bm. Hired 9.5.1804—24.3.05.

DRAKE II Tr 207/00. Hired 1916. Wrecked 3.7.17 Garmish Bay, W. Ireland.

DRAKE III Dr 89/07, 1—6pdr. Hired 1916—19.

DRAMA Yt. Hired 1915, later purchased. Sold 1.5.19.

DRANGEY Tr 434/35. Purchased as A/S Tr 8.1939. Sold 1946.

DRANGUET Tug 70/35. French DY tug seized 7.1940 at Southampton. Served as M/S to 6.45. (Spelt DRANQUET in most lists.)

DREADAXE Tr, ex-Russian seized 1918. Listed from 9.18. Sold 1919.

DREADFUL Tug 286/12. Hired 9.5.1917, purchased 9.5.18. Sold 1920, renamed *Rumania.*

DREADNOUGHT II Tr 150/07, 1—6pdr. Hired 1917—19.

DREDGOL Oiler (RFA) 7,589 tons, 326 x 54½ ft. Simons 25.5.1918. Sold 28.6.35 Arnott Young, Dalmuir to BU.

DREEL CASTLE Dr 97/08, 1—3pdr. Hired 1915—19 and as M/S 11.39—40.

DRIFT FISHER Dr, 1—3pdr. Hired 1916—19.

DRIVER M/S Tr 207/10, 400 tons, 1—6pdr. Purchased 1910. Renamed NAIRN 6.19; sold 1920.

DRIVER DY tug, 233gr. A Hall 9.10.1942. For sale 1964 at Gibraltar.

DRIZZLE Admiralty steel Dr, 96gr. Chambers 1919. Sold 1920, same name. (Served as PILOT STAR in WW.II.)

DROBAK (see KOS IV)

DROMEDARY (see LIVELY)

DROMEDARY DY paddle tug 680 tons, 144 x 27½ ft. Barclay Curle 31.5.1894. Sold 2.23.

DROMEDARY (ex-Belgian *President Armand Grisar*) DY tug, 130gr. Purchased 23.5.1940. Listed to 1946.

DROMIO Tr 380/29, 1–12pdr. Hired as M/S 8.1939. Sunk 22.12.39 in collision north of Whitby.

DROUGHT Admiralty steel Dr. Ailsa, Troon. Cancelled 1919.

DRUMBLADE Tr 195/00. Hired as BDV 1915–19.

DRUMBLAIR Tr 196/00. Hired 1918–19.

DRUMMER (ex-DRAGOON renamed 1919) M/S Tr, 297gr. Sold 26.2.20. Hired as M/S, 1–6pdr, 8.39; A/P Tr 7.40; sunk 4.8.40 by mine off Brightlingsea.

DRUMMER BOY Tr 209/16, 1–12pdr. Hired 7.1916–19 and as A/P Tr, 1–6pdr 11.39; M/S 6.40–8.45.

DRUMOAK Tr 208/02. Hired 1914. Sunk 5.10.14 by mine off the Tyne.

DRUMTOCHTY Tr 211/15. Hired 1915. Sunk 29.1.18 by mine off Dover.

DRUSILLA Tr 250/14, 1–12pdr. Hired 1915–19.

DRUSILLA (see BERYL)

DRYPOOL Tr 331/11, 1–12pdr. Hired 1915–19.

DUBLIN Cutter. Hired 1803–04.

DUBLIN CASTLE Russian merchant, seized and commissioned 1918 on the Caspian Sea, 2–6in. Transferred 31.7.19 to 'White' Russians.

DUCHESS (ex-*Duchess of Fife*) Paddle 336/03, 2–6pdr. Commissioned as M/S 26.5.1916. Paid off 9.19, sold 1.23.

DUCHESS 314/97. Hired as M/S (RNZN) 6.40. Gate vessel 1.44; harbour service 1946–47.

DUCHESSE de BRABANT Tr 338/24. Belgian, hired as A/P Tr 7.1940–45.

DUCHESS of ARGYLL Paddle 593/06. Purchased as test vessel.

DUCHESS of BUCCHLEUCH Paddle 450/16, 2–6pdr. Hired as A/P vessel 12.7.1916, later purchased. Sold 1.23.

DUCHESS of CORNWALL Paddle 302/96. Hired as M/S 1940. Damaged 23.11.40 by air attack at Southampton and not taken over.

DUCHESS of CUMBERLAND Cutter 8. Hired 1783.

DUCHESS of CUMBERLAND Cutter 8, 66bm, 8–3pdr. Hired 1803–04.

DUCHESS of DEVONSHIRE 1,200/91, 2–12pdr. Hired as ABS 30.10.1914–6.11.19.

DUCHESS of FIFE Paddle 443/99, 2–6pdr. Hired as M/S 23.3.1916–9.12.19.

DUCHESS of FIFE Paddle 336/03. Hired as M/S 11.1939–1.45.
DUCHESS of HAMILTON Paddle 553/90. Hired as M/S 3.1915. Sunk
29.11.15 by mine off the Galloper.
DUCHESS of KENT Paddle 400/96, 2–6pdr. Hired as M/S 20.6.1916–
23.9.19.
DUCHESS of MONTROSE Paddle 322/02. Hired as M/S 15.5.1915. Sunk
18.3.17 by mine off Dunkirk.
DUCHESS of NORFOLK Paddle 381/11, 2–6pdr. Hired as A/P vessel
17.5.1916–19.4.19. (Served as AMBASSADOR in WW.II.)
DUCHESS of RICHMOND Paddle 354/i0, 2–6pdr. Hired as A/P vessel
17.5.1916. Sunk 28.6.19 by mine in the Aegean.
DUCHESS of ROTHESAY Paddle 385/94. Hired as M/S 14.10.1915–
29.3.20 and 11.39. Laid up 8.40; accommodation ship 7.42–45.
DUCHESS of YORK DY vessel, ex-army depot transferred 11.1834. Sold
21.1.1836.
DUCHESS of YORK Paddle 302/96, 2–6pdr. Hired as A/P vessel
18.5.1916, purchased 6.19. Sold 23.6.21.
DUCK DY lighter. Portsmouth DY 4.4.1833. One in service, 111bm, in
1874 (same vessel?).
DUENNA Yt 140/37. Hired as HDPC 1.1940–45.
DUKE (ex-*Duke of Devonshire*) Paddle 250/96, 2–6pdr. Hired as A/P
vessel 25.3.1916. M/S 20.4.19–31.12.20.
DUKE of ALBANY 1,997/07. Hired as ABS 30.10.1914. Sunk 26.8.16
by 'UB.27' in the North Sea.
DUKE of CLARENCE Cutter 6, 65bm. Hired 1794–1801 and 6.1803.
Wrecked 25.11.1804 Portuguese coast.
DUKE of CLARENCE 1,635/92, 2–4in, 2–12pdr. Hired as ABS
6.11.1915–4.2.19.
DUKE of CORNWALL 1,528/98, 1–4in, 1–12pdr. Hired as ABS
31.10.1914–1.2.19.
DUKE of CUMBERLAND Cutter 6, 66bm. Hired 6.1803–1.1805.
DUKE of CUMBERLAND Brig 4, 180bm. Hired as packet 1803–05.
DUKE of RUTLAND A.ship 10. Hired 1784. Foundered 30.7.1784 in
a hurricane off Jamaica.
DUKE of WELLINGTON (ex-*Duke of York*) 3,743/35. Hired 5.1942–
45.
DUKE of YORK 38–gun ship. Hired 1664–66.
DUKE of YORK Lugger 6. Hired 1794. Lost 1799.
DUKE of YORK Lugger 6. Hired 1796–1800.
DUKE of YORK Cutter 8, 82bm. Hired 1.1803–9.1810.
DULCIBELLE Tr 203/18, 1–6pdr. Hired as A/P Tr 11.1939–45.
DULCIE DORIS Dr 80/13. Hired 1915–19.
DUNAVON 235/08. Hired as cable vessel 23.4.1940–19.12.45.

DUNCLUTHA 3,973/10. Commissioned as decoy ship 23.11.1916.
Returned 5.18.

DUNCOMBE 830/ . Hired as decoy ship 8.1915–6.18.

DUNCTON A/S Tr 750 tons, 166 x 28 ft, 1–12pdr, 3–20mm. Cook
Welton & Gemmell 6.9.1941. Sold 1945, renamed *Colwyn Bay.*

DUNDALK Oiler (RCN) 950 tons, 176 x 31½ ft. Canadian Bridge Co,
Walkerville 4.7.1943.

DUNDARG Dr 96/19. Hired as boom tender 1940–45.

DUNDEE 2,707/11, 2–4in. Hired as ABS 11.10.1915. Sunk 3.9.17 by
'U.19' in the Channel.

DUNDEE Paddle tug 264/75. Hired 15.2.1918–17.3.19.

DUNDONALD (see ALBYN)

DUNDURN Oiler (RCN) 950 tons, 176 x 31½ ft. Canadian Bridge Co,
Walkerville 18.9.1943.

DUNEDIN Dr 78/10, 1–3pdr. Hired 1915–19 and for examination
service 5.40–1.45.

DUNGENESS Tr 263/14, 1–12pdr. Hired as A/P Tr 5.1940. Sunk
15.11.40 by air attack off the Norfolk coast.

DUNIRA Tr 150/01. Hired in WW.I?

DUNKERY A/S Tr 750 tons, 166 x 28 ft, 1–12pdr, 3–20mm. Cook
Welton & Gemmell 4.12.1941. Sold 1947.

DUNLEATH Tr 292/96. Store hulk 1942–45.

DUNLIN (see AMAZONE)

DUNLOGIE MFV. Hired as A/P vessel 1940–45.

DUNLUCE CASTLE 8,114/04. Purchased 9.1939 as M/S base ship.
Arrived 7.45 Ward, Inverkeithing to BU.

DUNMORE HEAD 1,682/98. Purchased as ammo.hulk 1939. BU 1951
Rees, Llanelly,

DUNNET BDV 385 tons, 125 x 26½ ft, 1–3in. Lytham SB 5.8.1936.
Sold 3.46, renamed *Kingsmoor.*

DUNNETT Tr 204/14, 1–6pdr. Hired 1918–19.

DUNOTTAR CASTLE 15,007/36, 7–6in, 2–3in. Hired 8.1939 as AMC.
To MWT 1942. (Was to have been escort carrier 7.42.)

DUNRAVEN 3,117/10, 1–4in, 4–12pdr, 2–TT. Commissioned as
decoy ship 1.7.1917. Sunk 10.8.17 by 'UC.71' in the Channel.

DUNRAVEN CASTLE Tr 276/17, 1–6pdr. Hired 1917–19 and as
M/S 3.40–9.45.

DUNVEGAN CASTLE 15,008/36, 8–6in, 2–3in. Hired as AMC 1939.
Sunk 28.8.40 by 'U.46' west of Ireland.

DURBAN Tr 152/97. Hired 1918–19.

DURGA Tr 216/11, 1–6pdr. Hired 1914–19.

DURHAM CASTLE 8,217/04. Purchased as storeship 1939. Sunk
26.1.40 by mine off Cromarty.

DURRAWEEN Tr 271/19. Hired as M/S (RAN) 7.1940–46.
DUSK Admiralty steel Dr, 96gr. Duthie Torry 9.8.1918. Sold 1920, same name. (Served as COSMEA in WW.II.)
DUSK (see ESTRELLA do MAR)
DUSKY QUEEN MFV 40/20. Hired as A/P vessel 1940. Stranded 9.1.41 near Dover.
DUSTER Tr 192/11. Hired 1914. Wrecked 17.12.17 near Portreath.
DUSTY MILLER Dr 73/11. Hired 1915–19.
DUTHIES Dr 89/14, 1–3pdr. Hired 2.1915–19 and as FAA safety vessel 8.39. Sunk 25.10.40 by air attack at Montrose.
DUTIFUL Dr 98/07, 1–MG. Hired 1.1915–19.
D W FITZGERALD Tr 235/16, 1–6pdr. Hired as M/S 1916–19 and as M/S 8.40–45.
DYNEVOR CASTLE Tr 283/14. Hired 1917–19.
DX.1–DX.25 Towed landing craft (dumb lighters) 125 tons, 98 x 20 ft. Ordered 2.1916 from Craig Taylor, Harkess, Osborne Graham, Short, Simons and Thompson. Most of them finished up as DY lighters.

E.A.B. Dr 67/10. Hired 1.1915–19.
E & F Tr 275/17. Hired as A/P Tr 5.1940. Was fitting out as BDV in 10.40; fate unknown.
EADWINE Dr 96/14, 1–6pdr. Hired 1915–19 and as A/P Dr, 1–3pdr 10.40–3.46.
EAGER Dr 102/12, 1–3pdr. Hired 1914–19 and as M/S, 2–MG, 11.39–45.
EAGLE 44–gun ship. Hired 1664–66.
EAGLE Coastguard yawl, 118bm. Built 1844. Sold 1893 at Portsmouth.
EAGLE Tug 102/83. Hired for harbour service 1.8.1914–19.
EAGLE Tr 168/99, 1–6pdr. Hired 1914. Renamed EAGLET 1916. Returned 1918.
EAGLE II Paddle 647/98. Hired as M/S 1915. Renamed AIGLON 11.15. Returned 23.7.20.
EAGLE III Paddle 441/10, 2–6pdr. Hired as M/S 2.6.1916–10.3.20. (Served as ORIOLE in WW.II.)
EAGLE Tr 146/91. Hired 1918–19.
EAGLESCLIFFE HALL 1,900/28. Accommodation ship in 1942.
EAGLESDALE Oiler (RFA) 16,819 tons, 463½ x 60 ft. Furness SB 18.11.1941. Sold 1959, renamed *N Tisar.*
EAGLET (ex-Chinese *Toewan*) Paddle, 1–32pdr. Hired 8.1855–57.
EAGLET (see EAGLE)
EARL ESSEX Tr 225/14, 1–6pdr. Hired 1914–19 and as A/P Tr 11.39. M/S 6.40–2.46.

EARL GRANARD Tr 211/04, 1–6pdr. Hired 1916–19.

EARL KITCHENER Tr 348/15, 1–12pdr. Hired 7.1915–19 and as M/S 8.39–4.46.

EARL LENNOX Tr 226/14. Hired 1915. Sunk 23.10.17 by mine off Islay.

EARL of BUCHAN Tr 227/16. Hired 1916–19.

EARL of BUTE A.ship 26. Hired 1776. Foundered 1777 in the Gulf of Florida.

EARL o'CAIRNS Tr 132/83. Hired as BBV 1942–45.

EARL of POWIS Tug 116/82. Hired 8.1914–1.17.

EARL of WARWICK Tr 208/05, 1–12pdr. Hired 2.1915–19.

EARL ROBERTS (ex-*Lord Roberts*) Paddle tug 199/00. Hired as M/S 28.7.1916. Lent USN as tug 9.18–1.19; returned 7.3.19.

EARL ST VINCENT Cutter 16. Hired 1799–1801.

EARL ST VINCENT Cutter 14, 194bm, 14–12pdr carr. Hired 5.1804–3.06.

EARL SPENCER Two 14–gun cutters, both hired 1799–01.

EARL SPENCER Cutter 12, 141bm, 12–12pdr carr. Hired 7.1803–6.14.

EARL SPENCER (see ALTHORPE)

EARLY (see WENDY)

EARLY MORN Dr 58/01. Hired 1915–19.

EARN Dr 80/03. Hired as BDV 7.1915–19.

EARNER (ex-EARNEST renamed 1943) Rescue tug 700 tons, 142½ x 33 ft, 1–3in, 2–20mm. Cochrane 3.7.43. Sold 1961 renamed *Nisos Rodos*

EARRAID (ex-GRUNA renamed 11.1941) Tr, 'Isles' class. Crown, Sunderland 18.12.41. Sold 13.3.51.

EASEDALE Oiler (RFA) 16,820 tons. Furness SB 18.12.1941. Sold 1960 as hulk.

EAST ANGLIA Dr 83/09, 1–3pdr. Hired 1.1915–19.

EASTBOURNE Tr 163/96. Hired 1917–19.

EAST BRITON Dr, 1–3pdr. Hired 1915–19.

EAST COAST Tr 192/07, 1–6pdr. Hired as M/S 1915–19 and as fuel carrier 1944–45.

EASTCOATES Tr 277/19. Hired as M/S 8.1939–45.

EASTELLA Tr 183/03. Hired 1915–19.

EASTER MORN Dr 91/09, 1–3pdr. Hired 1.1915–19.

EASTERN DAWN Dr 91/09 1–3pdr. Hired 1915–19.

EASTERN DAWN Dr 84/08. Hired as degaussing vessel 1941–45.

EASTERN ISLES (see WESTERN ISLES)

EASTER ROSE Dr 84/14. Hired as BBV 6.1940. S/M tender 1942–44.

EAST HOLME Dr 75/12, 1–3pdr. Hired 1.1915–19.

EASTORE Supply ship (RCN). Brunswick USA 1945.

EASTWARD HO Tr 162/98, 1–6pdr. Hired 1918–19.

EBBTIDE Admiralty steel Dr. Chambers, Lowestoft. Cancelled 1919.
EBBTIDE (ex-CD.1 renamed 11.24) Admiralty wood Dr. On harbour service to 1946.
E.B.C. Dr 60/09. Hired 1.1915—19.
EBENEZER Dr 83/06, 1—3pdr. Hired 1915—19.
EBLANA Cstr 808/92. Hired as fleet messenger (RFA) 31.7.1917—12.6.18.
EBONOL Oiler (RFA) 2,200 tons, 220 x 34 ft. Clyde SB 16.10.1917. Scuttled 20.12.41 at Hong Kong; salved by Japanese, renamed *Enoshina Maru*; recovered 1945 at Batavia, reverted to EBONOL. Sold 1947.
EBONOL (see ROWANOL)
EBOR Tr 165/97. Hired 1917—19.
EBOR ABBEY Tr 220/11, 1—12pdr. Hired as A/P Tr 1.1940—2.46.
EBOR JEWEL MFV 27/29. Hired as BBV 11.1939—9.45.
EBOR VALLEY A/P vessel in 1941—42.
EBOR WYKE Tr 348/29, 1—12pdr. Hired as M/S 8.1939. Sunk 2.5.45 by torpedo off the east coast of Iceland.
EBRO 8,480/15, 8—6in. Hired as AMC 23.3.1915—19.
EBRO II Tr 183/98. Hired 1915—18.
ECCLESHILL Tr 226/11, 1—6pdr. Hired as M/S 1917—19 and as BBV 2.40—1.45.
ECHO (ex-*Luda*) DY tank vessel 150 tons, 72 x 15 ft. Sunderland SB Co 4.1887 and purchased 4.87. Sold 9.10.28 Plymouth & Devonport S Bkg Co.
ECHO (ex-*Barrowby*) Wh 165/97, 180 tons, 1—12pdr, 2—3pdr. Purchased 1915. Sold 6.3.19 at the Cape.
ECHO Tr. Hired as BDV 1915—19.
ECHO Dr 97/37. French M/S seized 3.7.1940 at Southampton. Renamed RESOUND 12.40. In 1.46 to return.
ECHODALE Oiler (RFA) 17,000 tons, 460 x 59 ft. Hawthorn Leslie 29.11.1940. BU 9.61 at Spezia.
ECHUNGA (see BARRANCA)
ECILA Yt 75/32. Hired as HDPC 1.1940—41.
ECLIPSE Tr 185/99. Hired 1917—19.
ECONOMY Dr 79/06, 1—57mm. Hired 1.1915—19.
EDAY Tr, 'Isles' class. Cochrane 26.6.1941. Sold 1.47, renamed *Fjellberg*. (On loan R.Norwegian navy 8.44—19.10.44 as TROMOY.)
EDDY Admiralty steel Dr. A Hall 6.8.1918. Sunk 16.5.42 by mine off Malta.

'Eddy' class oilers (RFA), av 2,200gr, 4,160 tons, 270 x 46 ft. Ten ordered 1951—53:
EDDYBAY Caledon SB 29.11.51. BU 8.64 in Belgium.

EDDYBEACH Caledon SB 24.4.51. Sold 1964, renamed *Mykinai.*
EDDYCLIFF Blythswood SB 25.8.52. Sold 1964, same name; renamed *Knossos.*
EDDYCOVE Cancelled 1953.
EDDYCREEK Lobnitz 19.1.53. BY 2.64 at Leghorn.
EDDYFIRTH Lobnitz 10.9.53.
EDDYMULL Cancelled 1953.
EDDYNESS Blyth DD 22.10.53.
EDDYREEF Caledon SB 28.5.53. BY 1964 in Belgium.
EDDYROCK Blyth DD 16.12.52.

EDDYSTONE Tr 165/97. Hired 1918–19.
EDEN (see THOMAS JOHNS)
EDENDALE 1,659/97. Examination service 1943–46.
EDGEHILL (see WILLAMETTE VALLEY)
EDINBURGH CASTLE 13,330/10. Hired as AMC 4.9.1914–12.7.19.
Purchased as base ship 8.39; scuttled by gunfire 25.9.45 sixty miles off Freetown.
EDINBURGH CASTLE Tr 241/99. Hired as boom gate vessel 1915–19.
EDINBURGH CASTLE II Paddle 158/96. Hired as M/S 19.7.1916.
Hospital tender HC.8 from 1918; lost 24.9.19 at Murmansk.
EDINBURGH CASTLE Russian merchant commissioned 1918 as CMB carrier, 1–12pdr, 2–CMBs. Handed over 31.7.19 to 'White' Russians on the Caspian Sea.
EDISON Tr 196/96. Hired 1915. Wrecked 6.7.15 on the Isle of Lewis.
EDITH DY tug 140 tons. Malta DY, completed 3.1905. Sold 31.1.23.
EDITH Dr, 1–3pdr. Hired 1916–19.
EDITH Hired as BBV 1942–44.
EDITH M PURDY Tr 205/18. Hired as BBV 2.1940–5.45.
EDITOR Tr 169/98, 1–6pdr. Hired as M/S 1914–19.
EDUARD van VLAENDEREN Tr 324/25. Belgian, hired as A/P Tr 6.1940. Wrecked 22.1.41 off the Faroes. (Spelt EDOUARD van VLAENDEREN in some British lists.)
EDWARD VII Tr 231/06, 1–6pdr. Hired as M/S 1914. Cable repair vessel 1917–19.
EDWARD VII Paddle tug 138/01. Hired for harbour service in WW.I.
EDWARD BARKER Tr, 'Strath' type, 203gr. Hall Russell 1918. Sold 1921, renamed *Mirabelle.* (MIRABELLE in WW.II.)
EDWARD CATTELLY Tr, 'Castle' type, 278gr. Ailsa 17.3.1919. Sold 1919, renamed *Sir John Hotham.* (Served as LOCH NAVER in WW.II.)
EDWARD COLLINGWOOD Tr, 'Castle' type, 277gr. Bow McLachlan 1918. Sold 1921, renamed *Towannes.* (Served as T R FERRENS in WW.II.)
EDWARD DRUCE Tr, 'Mersey' type, 325gr. Goole SB 7.1918. Sold 1920, renamed *Girard.* (GIRARD in WW.II.)

EDWARD FLINN Tr, 'Mersey' type. Cochrane. Cancelled 1919.
EDWARD GALLAGHER Tr, 'Castle' type. C Rennoldson 1919. Sold 1919.
EDWARD GREY Tr, 'Strath' type, 199gr. Ritchie Graham 1920. Sold 1920, renamed *Suzette*. (SUZETTE in WW.II.)
EDWARDIAN Tr 295/12, 1–12pdr. Hired 1915–19.
EDWARDIAN Tr 348/31, 1–12pdr. Hired as M/S 9.39, later purchased. Sold 1.46.
EDWARD MARR Tr, 'Mersey' type. Cochrane. Cancelled 1919.
EDWARD McGUIRE Tr, 'Mersey' type, 324gr. Cochrane 17.5.1919. Sold 1919, renamed *Cape St Vincent*.
EDWARD MOONEY Tr, 'Mersey' type, Cochrane. Cancelled 1919.
EDWARD WALMSLEY Tr 276/19, 1–12pdr. Hired as M/S 8.1939–7.46.
EDWARD WILLIAMS Tr, 'Mersey' type, 324gr. Cochrane 8.5.1917. Sold 1922, renamed *Cape Trafalgar*. (CAPE TRAFALGAR in WW.II.)
EDWINA Tr 267/15, 1–6pdr. Hired as M/S 1915–19 and as A/P Tr, 1–12pdr 5.40. M/S 1941–5.45.
E.E.S Dr 91/11. Hired 1.1915–19.
EFFORT Dr 82/07, 1–3pdr. Hired 1915–19.
EGAD Tug 170/98. Hired for harbour service 12.1917–19.
EGBERT Dr. 84/10, 1–3pdr. Hired 1914–19.
EGELAND Wh 153/12. Hired as M/S 4.1941. Stranded 29.11.41 on the coast of Palestine.
EGERIA (ex-*Bellona*) Tr 184/07. Hired as A/P Tr 11.1939. Danlayer 8.40; M/S 1.41–1.45.
EGERIA Yt 50 tons. Hired (RAN) 6.1942, purchased 2.43 and renamed TASMAN. Sold 9.44.
EGERTON DY tug 337 tons, 99 x 21 ft. Cran, Leith 5.3.1908 and purchased 23.7.08. Sold 2.23, renamed *Benson*.
EGERTON (ex-*Empire Darling*) DY tug, 203gr. Transferred from MOT 5.1947. On sale list 1958.
EGILIAS AKERMAN Tr, 'Castle' type. Cook Welton & Gemmell 18.3.1919. Sold 1919, renamed *Kesteven*. (Served as COMPUTATOR in WW.II.)
EGILSAY Tr, 'Isles' class. Cook Welton & Gemmell 7.2.1942. To Italian navy 22.2.46 as RD.306.
EGLANTINE Dr 95/07. Hired 1915. GULLWING 9.17–19.
EGLISE Dr 99/14, 1–3pdr. Hired 1915–19.
EGRET Cstr 1,394/03. Hired as store carrier (RFA) 16.1.1915–6.12.18.
EGRET Tr 224/99. Hired 1918–19.
EGRETT Tr 169/99. Hired 1918–19.
EGYPT (ex-*Sphinx*) DY barge. Transferred from War Dept 1.10.1891. Listed to 1942/43.

EIDER Tr 168/99, 1–6pdr. Hired 1914–19.

EIDER II Tr 142/92. Hired 1918–19.

EILA II Yt 60/31. Hired as HDPC 5.1940–45.

EILEEN Yt 1,022/10, 2–12pdr. Hired 4.11.1914–19.

EILEEN Tug 86/79. Hired for harbour service 8.12.1914–7.7.15.

EILEEN DUNCAN Tr 223/10, 1–6pdr. Hired as M/S 1914–19 and as M/S 1.40. Sunk 30.9.41 by air attack at N.Shields; raised and BU at Blyth.

EILEEN EMMA Dr 102/14, 1–3pdr. Hired 1915–19 and as A/P Dr, 1–3pdr 11.39–4.46.

E.J.M. Dr 72/10. Hired 1915–19.

El AFFIA (ex-*Vulcan*) Tug 129/21. Hired in the E. Indies 1941–46.

ELAN II French navy DY tug seized 3.7.1940 at Southampton. BBV 8.40; target towing 12.40–45.

ELARA Tr (Ceylon Govt), 'Basset' type. Irrawadi Flotilla Co. Laid down 12.1941. Lost on stocks at the capture of Rangoon.

E. LAULAND Dr. Danish, seized 5.1940. BBV 6.40; harbour service 5.41–45.

El KEBIR Tug 129/25. Hired in the E. Indies 1941–46.

ELBE Tr 165/97. Hired 1918–19.

ELBURY (ex-*Pict*) Tr 394/25. Hired as M/S 9.1939–7.45.

ELCHO Tr 155/08, 1–3pdr. Hired as M/S 1914–19.

ELDEROL Oiler (RFA) 2,200 tons, 220 x 34 ft. Swan Hunter 10.5.1917. Arrived 1.9.59 Rees, Llanelly to BU.

ELDORADO Tr 180/02. Hired 1918–19 and as danlayer 2.40. M/S 8.40–12.45.

ELDORADO (see OPHIR)

ELEANOR Cstr 1,980/88. Hired as mine carrier (RFA) 8.1914. Sunk 12.2.18 by U-boat off St Catherines Point.

ELEANOR Tr 193/14. Hired 1915–18.

ELEAZAR Tr 111/95. Hired 1917–19.

ELECTOR Tr 169/98. Hired 1917–19.

ELECTRA II Tr 269/04, 1–6pdr. Hired 1915–19 and as A/P Tr 5.40. Boom gate vessel 1.44–2.46.

ELECTRIC Tr 183/90. Hired 1918–19.

ELEGANT Dr 84/11, 1–3pdr. Hired 1915–19.

ELENA (see VIOLA)

ELEPHANT (ex-SL.22) DY tug 56 tons, 62 x 14 ft. Built 1892, renamed 4.93. Sold 21.10.20.

ELEPHANTA Admiralty non-standard steel Dr, 107gr. Fellows, Yarmouth 1919. Sold 1920, renamed *Byng*.

ELEVATE Dr 78/01. Hired 4.1915–19.

ELEVEN Dr 77/01, 1–57mm. Hired 1915–19.

ELF DY tug 172 tons, 80 x 19 ft. Flemming & Ferguson 28.5.1896. Listed to 1905.

ELF Tr 165/97. Hired 1917—19.

ELF (ex-*Empire Belle*) DY tug 257/44. Transferred from MOT 5.1947.
Sold 1960, renamed *Mare Jonio*.

ELF KING Tr 289/13, 1—12pdr. Hired 1917—19.

ELGAR Dr 94/07, 1—3pdr. Hired 1915—19.

El HIND 5,319/38. Hired as landing ship (RIN) 1943. Lost 14.4.44 by
fire in Bombay docks.

ELIBANK Dr 96/15. Hired 4.1915—19.

ELISABETH GUILBERT (P.3) MFV 67/29, 1—6pdr. Belgian hired as
A/P vessel (Polish crew) 8.1940—42. Laid up 1943—45.

ELISE Tr 239/07, 1—6pdr. Hired 1915. Sunk 22.9.18 by mine off Blyth.

ELIZA Sloop 6, 185bm, 6—3pdr. Hired 5.1803—05.

ELIZA Cutter 8. Hired 1805—12.

ELIZA Sloop 8, 141bm. Hired 10.1806—5.1811.

ELIZA Sloop 1—18pdr carr. Hired 1821.

ELIZA & JANE A.vessel, 110bm, 4—3pdr. Hired 9.1803—10.1812.

ELIZABETH Tender 10, 161bm. Hired 3.1805—1812.

ELIZABETH A.ship, 205bm. Hired 1.1808—4.09.

ELIZABETH DY tank vessel 370 tons, 115 x 22 ft. Maudsley, Greenwich
4.3.1873. Sold 1.1921, renamed *Fawley*.

ELIZABETH 156/92, 1—7.5in howitzer, 1—4in, 2—12pdr. Hired as
decoy vessel 3.1918—11.18.

ELIZABETH ANGELA Tr 253/28, 1—12pdr. Hired as M/S 11.1939.
Sunk 13.8.40 by air attack in the Downs.

ELIZABETH THERESE Dr 156/34. French M/S seized 3.7.1940 at
Southampton. Lost 4.7.45 by unknown cause.

ELK Tr 181/02, 1—6pdr. Hired as M/S 1915—19 and as danlayer 10.39.
Sunk 27.11.40 by mine off Plymouth.

ELK II Tr 169/98, 1—6pdr. Hired 1915—19.

ELK Tr. Hired 1917—19.

ELK (ex-*Arcadia*) Yt 578/26. Commissioned as A/S Yt (RCN) 10.9.1940.
Paid off 9.4.45.

ELLA Dr 92/03 Hired 4.1915—19.

ELLA Dr 92/01 Hired 11.1915—19.

ELLEN & IRENE Dr 88/14. Hired 1914—19.

ELLERAY Cstr 1,201/05. Hired as ammo carrier (RFA) 5.11.1914—19.

ELLESMERE Tr 183/03, 1—6pdr. Hired as M/S 1916/19.

ELLESMERE (ex-*Kos XXIV*) A/S Wh 580 tons, 138½ x 26½ ft, 1—12pdr,
1—20mm. Smiths Dk 17.6.1939, purchased 26.8.39. Sunk 24.2.45 by
U-boat in the Channel.

ELLIDA Yt 360/94, 2—6pdr. Hired 9.1914—29.8.18.

ELLIE Tr. Hired 1917—19.

ELM Tr 168/99, 1—6pdr. Hired 1914—19.

ELM Tr 530 tons, 150 x 27½ ft, 1—12pdr. Inglis 12.12.1939. Sold 1946, renamed *Helm*.

El MENZALA Tr 308/17. Purchased as M/S 23.4.1940. Renamed TORNADO 7.40; TORNADO II in 8.43, water carrier. Sold 4.46.

ELMIRA Tr 197/14, 1—6pdr. Hired as M/S 1915—19.

ELM LAKE Motor M/S (RCN) 255 tons, 126 x 28 ft. Mac Craft, Sarnia 25.8.1945. To Russian navy 17.11.45.

ELM LEAF Oiler (RFA), 5,948gr. In service 1917.

ELMOL Oiler (RFA) 2,200 tons, 210 x 34½ ft. Swan Hunter 23.7.1917. On charter 1959; sold 1961.

ELNA Yt 62/38. Hired as HDPC 2.1940—46.

ELOQUENT Dr 71/11. Hired as M/S 12.1939—46.

ELPINIKI Fleet auxiliary. In service 12.1916. Sold 13.2.20 Bowen Rees & Co.

ELSAY Dr 67/01. Hired 15.10.1914—30.4.15.

ELSE Schooner, 227gr. German, captured 8.1914 in the Channel. Renamed FIRST PRIZE 9.14; sold 1914. Hired as decoy ship (Q.21) 1017 and operated under the name PRIZE 2—12pdr. Sunk 15.8.17 by 'UB.48' in the Atlantic.

ELSE RYKENS Tr 266/35. Hired as A/S tr 12.1939—11.45.

ELSIE Tr 184/96, 1—6pdr. Hired as M/S 1916—19.

ELSIE & NELLIE Dr 101/16. Hired as BBV 1.1940—2.45.

ELSIE CAM (ex-*Sophie Busse*) Tr 250/22. Hired as M/S 2.1940—1.46.

ELSWICK Tr 215/06, 1—6pdr. Hired 1915—19.

ELSWICK PARK 4,188/20. Purchased 1944. Sunk as blockship 9.6.44.

El TOVAR Yt 57/36. Hired as echo yacht 1.1940. Laid up 1942.

ELVINA Tr 201/14, 1—6pdr. Hired as M/S 1915—19.

ELY Tr 183/03, 1—3pdr. Hired 1915—19.

ELYSIAN Tr 204/12, 1—6pdr. Hired as M/S 1915—19.

ELYSIAN DAWN Dr 91/09. Hired 1914—19 and on harbour service 1940—45.

EMBERLEY (see MMS.119)

EMBLEM Dr 85/07. Hired 1.1915—19.

EMBRACE Dr 94/07. Hired 3.1915—19 and as HDPC 5.40. Grounded 2.8.40 in Loch Alsh.

EMERALD Tr 289/13, 1—12pdr. Hired 1915—19.

EMERALD II Tr 150/94. Hired 1917—19.

EMERALD III Tr. Hired 1917—19.

EMERALD WINGS 2,139/20. Purchased 1940. Sunk 1940 as blockship at Scapa. (Listed in 4.41.)

EMILE BAUDOT Cable ship 1,149/17. French AMC seized 3.7.1940 at Plymouth. In service as cable vessel 9.40—45.

EMILIA PRIMEIRO Tr 421/19. Portuguese, purchased as BDV 8.6.1940. Renamed SUNRISE 1940. Sold 17.5.46.

EMILION Tr 201/14, 1–10pdr. Hired 1915–19 and as A/P Tr 11.39.
M/S 4.40. Sunk 24.10.41 by mine in the Thames estuary.
EMILY DY barge 140 tons. Fellows, Yarmouth 1899. Listed in 1944.
EMILY DY tug 140 tons. Seath, Rutherglen 28.11.1901 and purchased
14.11.01. Sold 1.34 at Malta; repurchased by 1936; sunk 7.4.42 by air
attack at Malta.
EMILY Dr 63/03. Hired 1915–19.
EMILY BARRATT Dr 73/13. Hired as BBV 20.8.1940.
Laid up 9.44.
EMILY REAICH Dr 83/04, 1–3pdr. Hired 1915–19.
EMINENT Dr 79/10, 1–3pdr. Hired 1914–19.
EMINENT Rescue tug, 'B.A.T.' class. Defoe, Bay City 12.8.1942. Returned
1946 to the USN.
EMINENT (ex-*Empire Tessa*) DY tug, 302/46. Transferred from MOT
3.1947.
EMLEY Tr 223/11. Hired 1914. Sunk 28.4.18 by mine off May Island.
EMMA A.ship. Hired 1809–11.
EMMANUEL CAMELAIRE Tr,'Castle' type, 280gr. Ailsa 25.4.1918. Sold
1921, renamed *Presidente Francqui*. (Served as BRABANT in WW.II.)
EMPEROR Tr 181/ –. Hired 1918–19.
EMPEROR of INDIA Paddle 482/06, 2–6pdr. Hired as A/P vessel
23.5.1916. Renamed MAHRATTA 1918, returned 1920. Hired as M/S,
534gr, 1–12pdr 12.39; A/A ship 11.40; accommodation ship 1943–46.
(Was BUNTING 1944–45.)
EMPHATIC Rescue tug, 'B.A.T' class. Levingston SB, Orange Texas
18.8.1943 and to the RN 27.1.44 on lend-lease. Returned 1946 to the
USN.
EMPHATIC (ex-*Empire Joan*) DY tug, 203/43. Transferred from MOT
3.1947. Sold 1958.
EMPIRE ARTHUR 760/42. Commissioned as water carrier 10.1942.
Capsized 22.11.43 off Freetown.
EMPIRE BITTERN 8,500/02 Purchased 6.1944. Sunk 23.7.44 as
blockship, Normandy.
EMPIRE BUNTING 6,448/19. Purchased 2.1944. Sunk 9.6.44 as
blockship, Normandy.
EMPIRE DACE 716/42. Hired as ferry 7.1943 in the Mediterranean.
Sunk 1.12.44 by mine in Greek waters.
EMPIRE DEFIANCE 4,632/09. Italian *Erica* seized 6.1940. RN from
2.44. Sunk 9.6.44 as blockship, Normandy.
EMPIRE FAIRY Tug 277/42. RN from 19.5.42. Sold 1948, renamed
Nathamee.
EMPIRE FLAMINGO 4,996/20. Purchased 2.1944. Sunk 9.6.44 as
blockship, Normandy.

EMPIRE FULMAR 7,775/41. American *Hawaian Shipper* on lend-lease 11.1941–1.46.

EMPIRE JOSEPHINE Tug 274/44. RN from 4.1945. Transferred Hong Kong Govt 1946, later renamed *Yau Wing.*

EMPIRE MOORHEN 5,617/19. Purchased 2.1944. Sunk 9.6.44 as blockship, Normandy.

EMPIRE ORIOLE 6,535/41. American *Extavia* on lend-lease 11.1941–46.

EMPIRE PIERROT Listed 8.1945–1.46.

EMPIRE PINTAIL 8,252/40. American *Howell Lykes* on lend-lease 11.1941–1.46.

EMPIRE RIDLEY 6,838/41. Hired as cable ship 9.1943. Renamed LATIMER 1943. For disposal 8.45.

EMPIRE SAM Tug 274/42. RN from 3.9.1942. Transferred Hong Kong Govt 1946.

EMPIRE SEAMAN 1,927/22. German *Morea* seized 1940. RN from 5.40. Lost 4.12.40 by unknown cause.

EMPIRE SENTINEL 619/98. German *Phaedra* seized 1939. RN from 6.40; converted to wreck dispersal vessel, renamed RAMPANT 1.43. To MOT 4.46.

EMPIRE TAMAR 6,561/07. Purchased 2.1944. Sunk 9.6.44 as blockship Normandy.

EMPIRE TANA 6,148/23. Purchased 3.1944. Sunk 9.6.44 as blockship, Normandy.

EMPIRE WATERHEN 6,004/20. Purchased 2.1944. Sunk 9.6.44 as blockship, Normandy.

EMPRESS 1,690/07, 2,540 tons, 311 x 40 ft, 8–12pdr, 6–A/C. Hired 1914, commissioned 25.8.14 as Seaplane carrier. Returned 11.19.

EMPRESS Paddle 229/88. Hired as tender 1.1919–12.2.19.

EMPRESS Paddle 173/79. Hired for examination service 26.8.1939–11.1.41 and 13.3.44–8.11.44.

EMPRESS of ASIA 16,910/13, 8–4.7in. Hired as AMC 2.8.1914–20.3.16.

EMPRESS of BRITAIN 15,860/06. Hired as AMC 16.8.1914–11.5.15.

EMPRESS of JAPAN 5,940/90, 8–4.7in. Hired as AMC 13.8.1914–27.10.15.

EMPRESS of RUSSIA 16,810/12, 8–4.7in. Hired as AMC 23.8.1914–12.2.16.

EMPRESS QUEEN 1,781/40. Hired as A/A ship 5.10.1940. Renamed QUEEN EAGLE 1941. Returned 9.43.

EMPRISE (see ENTERPRISE)

EMPHYREAN Tr 215/14, 1–6pdr. Hired as M/S 1914–19 and as A/P Tr 11.39. M/S 4.40–1.45.

EMU Tr, 164/00. Hired as BDV 1915–19.

EMU Tr 154/95. Hired 1917–19.

EMU DY tug (RAN) 250 tons, 99 x 21 ft. Morts Dk, Sydney 25.6.1946.

EMULATE Dr 77/08, 1–6pdr. Hired 1915–19.

EMULATOR Dr 66/04. Hired as BDV 7.1915–19.

EMULATOR Tr 168/99. Hired 1918–19. (A vessel on harbour service 1941–42 may be this vessel.)

EMULOUS Rescue tug 1,360 tons, 147 x 33½ ft, 1–3in, 2–20mm. Camden SB, New Jersey 1.9.1943 and to the RN 2.2.44 on lend-lease. Returned 30.4.46 to the USN.

EMULOUS (ex-*Empire Spruce*) DY tug, 129/42. Transferred from MOT 3.1947. Sold 1958, renamed *Irving Oak.*

ENA MAY Dr 118/91. Hired 11.1914–16.12.14.

EN AVANT Dr 90/14, 1–3pdr. Hired 1914–19.

EN AVANT Tr 264/11. M/S (Dutch crew) 6.1940–43; RN 1.44–11.45.

ENCHANTER Rescue tug 868 tons, 160 x 34½ ft, 1–3in, 2–20mm. Cochrane 2.11.1944. Sold 1947, renamed *Englishman.*

ENCORE Tr 164/00. Hired 1918–19.

ENCORE (Rescue tug (as ENCHANTER). Cochrane 2.12.1944. On sale list 1967.

ENCOUNTER Discovery bark. Hired 1616.

ENDEAVOUR A.ship 12, 169bm. Hired 2.4.1804–10.1812.

ENDEAVOUR Tr 156/94. Hired 1915. Foundered 10.3.18 after collision with Kirkwall boom.

ENDEAVOUR II Dr 89/07, 1–25mm. Hired 1915–19.

ENDEAVOUR 82/04. Hired for harbour service (RNZN) 1942. Purchased 1943; renamed HAURAKI 1956. Sold 1963.

ENDON Tr 235/14, 1–6pdr. Hired 1915–19.

ENDSLEIGH Cstr 159/38. Purchased as experimental vessel 7.5.1943.

ENDURANCE Dr 94/07, 1–6pdr. Hired 1915–19.

ENDYMION Tr 164/00. Hired 1917–19.

ENERGETIC DY paddle tug 700 tons, 145 x 27½ ft. J.Brown 22.5.1902. Sold 15.4.53, arrived 6.53 Shaws of Kent, Rainham, Kent to BU.

ENERGETIC (ex-EMPIRE EDWARD renamed 1956) DY tug, 234/42. Transferred from MOT 1947. Sold 1965.

ENERGIE DY tug, 73gr. Belgian, hired 3.1915–19.

ENERGIE Salvage vessel, 2,800gr. Hired from MOT 1.1949–50.

ENERGY Dr 79/06. Hired 1915–19.

ENERGY Dr 45/ –. Hired 1917. Wrecked 5.3.17 in Peterhead Bay.

ENERGY DY tug 365 tons, 90 x 28½ ft. A.Hall 26.10.1942. On sale list 1964.

ENERN Wh 248/29. Hired as M/S in the W. Indies (Dutch crew) 1944–46.

ENFIELD Armament store carrier 604 tons, 131 x 25 ft. Lobnitz 5.9.1945.

ENFORCER Rescue tug (as ENCHANTER). Cochrane 22.7.1944.
BU 1963.

ENGADINE 1,676/11, 316 x 41 ft, 2–4in, 1–6pdr, 4–A/C. Hired as
seaplane carrier 11.8.1914–12.19.

ENGLISHMAN Tug 487/37. Hired as rescue tug 2.1940. Sunk 21.1.41
by air attack 40 miles west of Tory Is.

ENGLISH ROSE Tr 188/14. Hired as M/S 1914–19.

ENIGMA Rescue tug (as ENCHANTER). Cochrane 22.6.1944. Sold 1964

ENNERDALE Oiler (RFA) 17,000 tons, 462½ x 59 ft. Swan Hunter
1.1941. Landing ship, 1–4in, 1–12pdr, 4–20mm 1942; oiler 1946;
arrived 14.4.59 at Faslane to BU.

ENQUIRY Sloop. Hired 1691. Captured 13.10.1691 by the French.

ENSAY Tr, 'Isles' class. Cook Welton & Gemmell 5.3.1942. To Italian
navy 16.2.46 as RD.314.

ENTENTE CORDIALE MFV 51/37. French M/S seized 3.7.1940 in the
UK. To MWT 1940–45.

ENTERPRISE DY tug 300 tons, 110 x 23 ft. Bow McLachlan 2.10.1899.
Renamed EMPRISE 1919. Sold 1947.

ENTERPRISE Dr 100/07, 1–6pdr. Hired 9.14; ENTERTAIN 1918–19.

ENTERPRISE II Dr 84/06. Hired 1915. Sunk 8.3.16 by mine off
Brindisi.

ENTERPRISING Dr 98/14. Hired 8.1914–19. (One hired as degaussing
vessel 6.40–47 may be the same vessel.)

ENTICER Rescue tug (as ENCHANTER). Cochrane 11.3.1944. Foundered
21.12.46 in the China Sea.

ENVOY Tr 150/95. Hired 1918–19.

ENVOY Rescue tug (as ENCHANTER). Cochrane 11.3.1944. Sold 1965.

ENZIE Dr 93/08. Hired as BDV 1.1915–19 and on harbour service
1941–45.

EPHRAIM BRIGHT Tr, 'Castle' type. Cook Welton & Gemmell. Cancelled
1919.

EPHRETAH Dr 96/18. Hired as HDPC 1.1940–45.

EPIC (ex-*Heroic*) Tug 268/09. Hired as rescue tug 3.5.1917–19.

EPINE Tr 358/29. Hired as M/S 9.1939–1.46.

EPPING Tender 22/14. Hired as nominal base ship 30.8.1939. Renamed
BADGER then EPPING then FERRY PRINCE 1943. Returned 1945.

EPPING (see LEXA)

EPPING (ex-*Sou'wester*) Yt 96/91. Hired as base ship 18.6.1943, later
purchased. Laid up 7.45; sold 4.46.

EPPINGDALE Oiler (RFA) 17,000 tons. Cancelled 1939.

EPWORTH Tr 223/11. Hired 1914. Sunk 22.5.17 in collision off the
east coast.

EQUATOR Tr 168/99, 1–6pdr. Hired 1915–19.

EQUERRY Tr 369/29. Hired as M/S 8.1939–4.45.

EQUITY Tr 158/96. Hired 1917–19.

ERA Tr 168/99. Hired 1914. Sunk 11.7.16 by gunfire from three U-boats off Aberdeen.

ERA II Dr 94/07, 1–3pdr. Hired 1915–19.

ERASTUS Dr 100/08, 1–3pdr. Hired 1914–19.

ERIC STROUD Tr 213/14, 1–6pdr. Hired 1915–19.

ERIDANUS (ex-*Pelican*) Tr 205/05. Hired as fuel carrier 4.1944–11.44.

ERILLUS Tr 201/14, 1–6pdr. Hired 1915–19 and as A/P Tr 11.39–1.40.

ERIMO Tr 265/30, 1–12pdr. Hired as M/S 8.1939–8.45.

ERIN II Tr 181/03. Hired 1914. Sunk 19.10.15 by mine off the Nab.

ERIN III Dr 81/07, 1–3pdr. Hired 1915–19.

ERIN Tr 394/33. Hired as A/S Tr 1940. Blown up 18.1.42 by Italian frogmen at Gibraltar.

ERIN 5,780/32, 2–6in. Hired as OBV 30.9.1940. Renamed MAPLIN 1.41, fighter catapult ship. Returned 7.42.

ERINS ISLE Paddle 633/12, 2–6pdr. Hired as M/S 21.11.1915. Sunk 7.2.19 by mine off the Nore.

ERISKA Yt 347/02, 2–6pdr. Hired 3.6.1915–29.3.19.

ERISKAY Tr, 'Isles' class. Fleming & Ferguson 28.8.1942. Foundered 12.11.45 off Sao Jorge, Azores. (On loan Portuguese navy 8.10.43–26.6.44 as P.8.)

ERITH Tr 325/17. Hired as M/S 2.1940–6.45.

ERIVAN Oiler (RFA), 2,419/93, 285 x 39 ft. Purchased 1916. Sold 2.19.

ERMINE 1,777/12. Commissioned 16.7.1915 as fleet messenger. Sunk 2.8.17 by mine in the Aegean.

ERMINE Tr 181/03, 1–3pdr. Hired 1915–19.

ERNA Tr 330/15, 1–6pdr. Hired as M/S 1915–19 and as BDV 5.40–46.

ERNE Tr 168/99, 1–6pdr. Hired 1915–18.

ERNE (see JOHN CHIVERS)

EROICAN Tr 225/14, 1–3pdr. Hired as M/S 1915–19 and as danlayer 4.40. M/S 3.42; fuel carrier 4.44–2.45.

EROS Tr 286/07. Hired 1914. Sunk 5.9.17 by mine off Felixstowe.

EROS Tr 181/03. Hired 1917–19.

ESCALLONIA Tr 286/11, 1–12pdr. Hired 1914–19.

ESCALLONIA MFV. Hired as A/P vessel 11.1939–45.

ESCAUT 1,087/38. Hired as armament store carrier (RFA) 21.6.1940. Sunk 3/4.8.41 by air attack off Suez.

ESCORT Iron paddle DY tug, 340bm, 525 tons. Laird 26.4.1873. Wrecked 20.4.1887 on a reef near Malta.

ESCORT DY paddle tug 685 tons, 145 x 27½ ft. Fawcett, Preston 28.7.1896. Sold 31.5.22 J A White.

ESCORT Tr 165/97. Purchased as BDV 1915. Sold 1920.

ESHER Tr 235/14, 1–3pdr. Hired as M/S 1915/19.

ESKBURN Dr 90/14. Hired 1914. Foundered 30.11.16 after collision off Dover.

ESKE Tr 290/06, 1–10pdr. Hired 1916–19.

ESKIMO 3,326/10. Hired as AMC 19.11.1914–18.7.15.

ESLEA Dr 83/08, 1–6pdr. Hired 1915–19.

ESMERALDA Tr 181/03. Hired 1918–19.

ESMERALDA Yt 78/36. Hired as echo Yt 2.1940–1.47.

ESPERANCE BAY 14,204/22, 3–6in (later 7–6in, 2–3in). Hired as AMC 9.1939–41.

ESSEX Ketch. Hired 1672–75.

ESSEX II Tr 220/06, 1–6pdr. Hired 1914–19.

ESSEX III Tr 180/03, 1–6pdr. Hired 1918–19.

ESSEX MAID Yt 81/39. Hired as HDPC 10.1939–45.

ESSEX QUEEN Paddle 389/97. Hired as M/S 13.9.1939. Ambulance carrier 1.40–29.3.1943.

ESTHER A.ship. Hired 1760–62.

ESTOY Tug 101/70. Hired 2.6.1917–22.3.19.

ESTRELLA d'ALVA Tr 329/09. Portuguese, purchased 1941. Renamed SUNBURST 1942, M/S, 1–12pdr. Sold 1.46 at Kilindini.

ESTRELLA do MAR Tr 327/14. Portuguese, purchased 1941. Renamed DUSK 1942, M/S, 1–12pdr. Sold 1946, renamed *Akbari*.

ESTRELLA do NORTE Tr 341/19. Portuguese, purchased 1941. Renamed STORMCENTRE 1942, M/S, 1–12pdr. Sold 8.46.

ETESIAN Admiralty wood Dr, 94gr. Fellows, Yarmouth 1918. Sold 1920, same name. (Served as M H STEPHEN in WW.II.)

ETHEL Tr 278/07, 1–6pdr. Hired 1915–19.

ETHEL DUNCAN 2,510/12. Hired as fleet auxiliary 1.1916–19.

ETHEL NUTTEN Tr 182/06, 1–6pdr. Hired 1917–19.

ETHEL TAYLOR Tr 276/17, 1–12pdr. Hired as A/P Tr 1940. Sunk 22.11.40 by mine, Tyne area.

ETHELWULF Tr 185/03. Hired 1914–15.

ETHIOPIAN 5,424/36. Hired as boom carrier 18.5.1940–5.46.

ETHNEE Dr 86/13. Hired 1914. Wrecked 15.1.18 on the Goodwins.

ETNA Tr 189/07, 1–6pdr. Hired 1917–10.

ETOILE POLAIRE Tr 278/ –. Hired 1915. Sunk 3.12.15 by mine off the Goodwins.

ETOILE POLAIRE Dr 66/38. French M/S seized 3.7.1940 at Southampton M/S 1940; danlayer 1942–6.46.

ETON Tr 156/97. Hired as BDV 1915–19.

ETRURIA Tr 376/30. Hired as A/P Tr 5.1940. BDV 11.40–2.46.

ETRURIAN Tr 186/00, 1–6pdr. Hired 1914–19.

ETRUSCAN Tr 202/13, 1–6pdr. Hired as M/S 1915–19 and as A/P Tr 11.39. M/S 6.40; fuel carrier 4.44–11.44.

ETTRICK (see SAMUEL JAMIESON)

EUCLASE Tr 295/31, 1–12pdr. Hired as M/S 2.1940–4.46.

EUDOCIA Tr 147/91. Hired 1918–19.

EUNICE & NELLIE Dr 93/08. Hired for harbour service 7.2.1915–19.

EUNICE & NELLIE Dr 96/18. Hired as M/S 12.1939. TRV 6.43–46.

EUN MARA Yt 251/06. Hired 2.2.1915–4.5.16.

EUN MARA Yt 29/12. Hired as HDPC 6.1940. Laid up 10.45.

EUREKA Tr 165/97. Hired as BDV 1915, purchased 1916. Sold 1922.

EURIPEDES Tr 307/07, 2–6pdr. Hired 1915–19.

EUROPA Transport, 800gr. Hired 1854. Burnt 31.5.1854 by accident at sea.

EUSTON Tr 209/06. Hired 1915. Sunk 12.2.17 by mine off Hartlepool.

EUTHAMIA Tr 142/90. Hired 1918–19.

EVA Dr 88/93, 1–6pdr. Hired 1915–19.

EVADNE Tr 189/07. Hired 1915. Sunk 27.2.17 by mine off the Owers.

EVADNE Yt 581/31, 1–3in. Hired as A/S Yt 9.1939. Examination service 1943–45.

EVANGEL Tr 197/14. Hired 1916. Sunk 25.3.17 by mine off Milford Haven.

EVA WALES Tr 251/15, 1–12pdr. Hired 1.1915–19.

EVELINA Tr 202/19. Hired as A/P Tr 11.1939. Sunk 16.12.39 by mine, Tyne area.

EVELINE Tr 206/12. M/S (Dutch crew) from 7.1940. Sunk 27.1.42 in collision off Milford Haven.

EVELINE NUTTEN Tr 183/15, 1–6pdr. Hired 1915–19.

EVELYN Tr 235/06, 1–6pdr. Hired as M/S 1914–19.

EVELYN JOYCE Dr 93/12. Hired 1917–19.

EVELYN ROSE Tr 327/18, 1–12pdr. Hired as A/P Tr 12.1939. M/S 1941–45.

EVENING PRIMROSE Dr 88/11, 1–6pdr. Hired 1915–19 and as A/P Dr. 1–6pdr. 11.39–45.

EVENING STAR Yt 270/94, 2–6pdr. Hired 9.1914–2.17.

EVENING STAR II Dr 89/07. Hired 1915–19.

EVENTIDE Admiralty steel Dr. Chambers, Lowestoft. Cancelled 1919.

EVERARD Dr 82/07. Hired 1915. Sunk 15.1.16 in collision off the Tuskar Rock.

EVEREST Tr 189/07, 1–6pdr. Hired 1914–19.

EVERGREEN Tr 180/02. Hired 1918–19.

EVERTON Tr 240/15, 1–6pdr. Hired 1915–19 and as A/P Tr, 1–3pdr. 12.39–3.46.

EVESHAM Tr 239/15, 1–6pdr. Hired as M/S 1915–19 and as A/P Tr, 1–3pdr, 12.39. Sunk 27.5.41 by air attack off Gt Yarmouth; raised, BU 1946 at Troon.

EWALD Tr 209/13. M/S (Dutch crew) from 6.40—45;
E.W.B. Dr 95/11. Hired 1915—19.
EXCALIBUR Tug 143/20. German FINKENWARDER seized 1915,
commissioned 1.12.45. To MOT 1946.
EXCEL Dr 103/07, 1—3pdr. Hired 3.7.1915. BDV 1917—19.
EXCEL II Tr 157/95. Hired 1915—17.
EXCEL III Dr 86/07, 1—6pdr. Hired 1915—19.
EXCEL IV Dr 77/06. Hired 1917—19.
EXCELLENT Trawlers used as base ships (see JACKDAW, WILLIAM
LEACH and ANDREW JEWER).
EXCELLENT Dr 60/14. Hired 1915—19.
EXCELLENT Tr 103/07. Hired as BDV 1915—19.
EXCELLENT Tug. French naval HAINNEVILLE seized 7.1940. Renamed
EXPONENT 1942. Listed to 1945.
EXCELSIOR Dr 85/07, 1—6pdr. Hired 1915—19.
EXCHANGE 36—gun ship, 332bm. Hired 1664—66.
EXCHEQUER Dr 86/14. Hired as tender 4.1915—19 and on examination
service 5.40—4.46.
EXCLUDER DY tug, 549/42, 800 tons. German GOLDINGEN seized
1945. Sold 1958, renamed *Lenadil.*
EXE (see THOMAS JARVIS)
EXETER Tr 165/97. Hired 1917—19.
EX FORTIS Dr 90/14, 1—3pdr. Hired 1914—19 and as BBV 12.39—9.45.
EXHORTER DY tug, 567/37, 816 tons. German OST PREUSSEN
seized 1945. Sold 1963.
EXMOUTH II Tr 236/11, 1—3pdr. Hired 1914—19.
EXMOUTH 3,900/99. Hired as store carrier (RFA) in WW.I.
EXPANSE Admiralty steel Dr. Ailsa. Cancelled 1919.
EXPANSE (see DAWN)
EXPECTANT Dr 93/13, 1—3pdr. Hired 1915—19.
EXPECTATION Dr 77/10, 1—3pdr. Hired 1915—19.
EXPELLER DY tug, 285/42, 500 tons. German BORA seized 1945.
Sold 1969.
EXPERT Dr 100/07, 1—3pdr. Hired 1914—19.
EXPERT Tr 156/94. Hired as BDV 1914—19.
EXPERT Rescue tug 890 tons, 165 x 36 ft, 1—3in, 2—20mm. Fleming
& Ferguson 14.2.1945. Sold 1968, renamed *Nisos Myokos.*
EXPLORATOR Dr 79/09, 1—3pdr. Hired 1915—19.
EXPLORER Scottish Fishery Board vessel. Hired for examination
service 6.1940—12.4.46.
EXPONENT (see EXCELLENT)
EXUBERANT Dr 79/02, 1—3pdr. Hired 1915—19.
EXUBERANT DY tug, 172/44. German SCHULAN seized 1945. To
MOT 1946.

EXULTANT MFV. Hired as A/P vessel 1941—45.

EXWEY (ex-*Monarch*) Paddle 315/88. Hired for examination service 27.8.1939. Accommodation 1944—8.46.

EXYAHNE Tr 226/14, 1—12pdr. Hired 1915—19 and as A/P Tr 11.39. M/S 4.40—12.45.

EYRIE Dr 84/ —. Hired 1914. Sunk 2.9.14 by mine off the Outer Dowsing.

EZEKIEL JOHNSON Tr, 'Mersey' type. Cochrane. Cancelled 1919.

F & G.G Dr 85/14. Hired 1915—19.

FABIA Tug 151/19. Hired for harbour service 20.11.1939—45.

FABIOUS Barge 230 tons. Hired as BDV 7.7.1941. Sunk 16.1.43.

FAIR BREEZE Dr 92/25. Hired as A/P Dr 9.1939. Sunk 1.6.40 in collision with wreck off Dunkirk.

FAIRFAX (see BURLINGTON)

FAIRHAVEN Dr 96/19. Hired as BBV 5.1940. Foundered 5.9.44 in the N.Atlantic on passage from Iceland.

FAIR HELGA Wh 175/12. Purchased as M/S 3.8.1917. Sold 1921.

FAIR ISLE Tr 192/09. Hired 1914. Wrecked 26.12.14 in Sinclair Bay; salved and returned 1919.

FAIR ISLE Dr 97/08, 1—3pdr. Hired 1917—19.

FAIR MAGDA Wh 175/12. Purchased as M/S 3.8.1917. Sold 1921.

FAIR MAID Paddle 430/15. Commissioned as M/S 12.7.1915. Sunk 9.11.16 by mine near Cross Sand Buoy.

FAIR MAID Paddle 211/86. Hired as tender 11.1940—45.

FAIRPLAY II Tug 282/21. Hired as rescue tug 10.1939. Wrecked 2.3.40 on the Yorkshire coast.

FAIRVIEW Tr 187/09, 2—6pdr. Hired 1914—19.

FAIRWAY Tr 326/18, 1—12pdr. Hired as A/P Tr 5.1940. Danlayer 1941—3.46.

FAIR WEATHER Admiralty wood Dr, 93gr. Forbes 25.3.1918. Sold 1921, same name. Hired as A/P Dr 1.40—12.45.

FAIR WIND Admiralty steel Dr, 96gr. A Hall 6.8.1918. Sold 1921, renamed *Hawthorn Bank*. (HAWTHORN BANK 109gr in WW.II.)

FAIRY Tug. Hired 19.1.1918. Renamed FIERY 1918. Returned 29.1.19.

FAIRY KNOWE Dr 86/13. Hired for harbour service 11.1914—19 and as M/S 11.39. Target towing 1941—12.45.

FAISAN French navy tug, seized 7.1940 at Plymouth. DY tug 1940; boom gate vessel 1941—45.

FAITH Tr 135/91. Hired 1918—19.

FAITHFUL DY tank vessel 395 tons, 115 x 22 ft. Bow McLachlan 2.6.1903. Sold circa 1948.

FAITHFUL Dr 92/03, 1—3pdr. Hired 1915—19.

FAITHFUL II Dr 86/07, 1—3pdr. Hired 1917—19.

FAITHFUL DY paddle tug 710 tons, 145 x 30 ft. Yarrow 14.6.1957.

FAITHFUL FRIEND Dr 110/13, 1—6pdr. Hired 1915—19.

FAITHFUL STAR Dr 103/27, 1—3pdr. Hired as A/P Dr 9.1939—3.46.

FAITHLIE Dr 79/03. Hired for harbour service 25.7.1915—19.

FALCON Tr 154/95. Hired 1917–19.

FALCON Tug 124/92. Hired 1941–45.

FALCONET (ex-BARNHAM renamed 1938) BDV 530 tons, 135 x 30½ ft 1–3in. Blyth DD 5.12.38. Sale list 1958.

FALCONHURST Tug, 77gr. Hired 1.1918–19.

FALIE Cstr 215/19. Hired as store carrier (RAN) 10.1940–46.

FALK Wh 307/37, 1–12pdr. A/S Wh. (Norwegian crew) 11.1940. RN crew 3.41–10.46.

FALKIRK Dr 56/ –. Hired 1917. Sunk 29.10.18 in collision off Kinnairds Head.

FALLING SEA Admiralty steel Dr. Chambers. Cancelled 1919.

FALLING STAR Admiralty steel Dr, 96gr. A Hall 20.8.1918. Sold 1919, renamed *Betty Bodie*. (BETTY BODIE in WW.II.)

FALMOUTH II Tr 165/97, 1–6pdr. Hired 1915–19.

FALMOUTH III Tr 198/09. Hired 1915. Sunk 19.11.15 by mine off Dover.

FALSTAFF Tr 173/06, 1–3pdr. Hired 1915–19.

FAME Schooner. Hired 1807–12.

FAME Dr 68/ –. Hired 1916. Wrecked 22.10.16 near Poole.

FAMILIAR FRIEND Dr 92/11. Hired 1915–19.

FANCY Cutter, 43bm. Hired 10.1808–9.09.

FANCY Cutter 4, 112bm. Hired 7.1809–2.11.

FANCY Cutter, 118bm. Hired 2.1811–24.8.14.

FANCY Dr 83/06, 1–3pdr. Hired 1915–19.

FANCY Tr. Hired 1918–19.

FANDANGO A/S Tr 530 tons, 150 x 27½ ft, 1–4in, 3–20mm. Cochrane 26.3.1940. Sold 1946, same name.

FANE Tr 262/07, 1–6pdr. Hired 1914–19.

FANE Tr 310/30. Hired as M/S 8.1939. Renamed SNAKEFLY 10.39. Returned 10.45.

FANLING Yt 65/ –. Purchased as A/P Yt 16.5.1941 at Shanghai. Lost 2.42, probably captured by Japanese.

FANNY Lugger 16. Hired 1799–1801.

FANNY Cutter 181bm. Hired 1804.

FANNY (ex-Woolwich YC.14 renamed 17.11.1870) DY lighter, 168bm. Renamed Devonport YC.17 then YC.17 in 11.85. Listed 1890.

FANNY MAIR Dr 84/11. Hired 1915–19. (Served as CRANNOCK in WW.II.)

FANO MFV. Danish, seized 5.1940 for examination service. Renamed FORTITUDE 1941 as nominal base ship and on harbour service to 1945.

FARA Tr, 'Isles' class. Cochrane 27.1.1941. Sold 12.7.46.

FARADAY Tr 322/16, 1–12pdr. Hired 1917–19 and as A/P Tr, 1–6pdr, 12.39. Renamed FRANCOLIN 1941. Sunk 12.11.41 by air attack off Cromer.

FARADAY Cable ship 5,533/23. Hired as base ship 24.10.1940. Sunk
26.3.41 by air attack off St Annes Head; raised 9.41 and to MWT.

FARNBOROUGH (ex-LODORER renamed 1915) Decoy ship (Q.5),
3,207/04, 5–12pdr, 2–6pdr. Commissioned 21.10.15. Torpedoed by
'U.83' south of Ireland 17.2.17 and beached next day at Berehaven.
Purchased 22.10.17; sold 4.19, renamed *Hollypark.*

FARNE Tr, 'Isles' class. Cook Welton & Gemmell 22.4.1943. Sold 1947,
same name.

FAROUK Aux. schooner, 91gr. Hired as store carrier 6.1940. Sunk 13.6.42
by 'U.83' in the Mediterranean.

FARSUND (ex-*Kos VI*) A/S Wh, 248/29 (Norwegian crew) with the RN
7.1940–45.

FASTNET (ex-*Frobisher*) Boom Tr 444 tons, 138½ x 23½ ft, 1–12pdr.
Purchased 6.1933. Lent Dutch navy 20.2.42 and abandoned 4.42 at
Batavia.

FAUVETTE 2,644/12. Hired as store carrier (RFA) 2.1915. ABS,
19.3.15; sunk 9.3.16 by mine in the North Sea.

FAVO Dr 77/01, 1–6pdr. Hired 1915–19.

FAVORITA Tr 314/16, 1–12pdr. Hired 1917–19.

FAVORITE Cutter, 72bm. Hired 3.1807–6.1811.

FAVOROLLE (see BANTAM)

FAVOUR Dr 93/08. Hired as boom gate vessel 5.1915–19 and as HDPC
6.40–45.

FAVOURITE A.vessel, 4–2pdr. Hired 6.1803–10.1804.

FAVOURITE Cutter 6, 76bm, 6–3pdr. Hired 6.1803. Renamed
FLORENCE 1804. Returned 11.1806.

FAVOURITE Dr 94/07, 1–3pdr. Hired 1915–19.

FAVOURITE Rescue tug, 'B.A.T' class. Levingston, Orange Texas
17.2.1942 on lend-lease. Returned 27.3.46 to the USN.

FAVOURITE DY paddle tug 710 tons, 145 x 30 ft. Ferguson 1.7.1958.

FAWN Tr (210/98?). Hired 1918–19.

FAWN (ex-*Primrose*) Dr 89/15. Hired as A/S Dr 25.12.1939–45.

FAWN Tr 143/97. Hired as degaussing vessel 12.1941–45.

FEACO Dr 123/24. Hired as M/S 10.1939–11.45.

FEARLESS II Dr 81/07, 1–3pdr. Hired 11.1914–19.

FEAR NOT Dr 101/08. Hired for harbour service 1915–19 and as A/P
Dr 1941. Boom tender 1942; store carrier 1943; examination service
1944–45.

FEAR NOT II Dr 60/02. Hired 1915–19.

FEASIBLE Dr 103/12, 1–6pdr. Hired as A/P Dr 1914–19 and as M/S
11.39–8.45.

FEE des EAUX MFV. French M/S seized 3.7.1940 at Dartmouth. A/P
Dr 8.40–11.45. (Also known as MFV.2025 from 3.43–45.)

FELICIA Dr 90/07. Hired for harbour service 1915.

FELICIA Tr. Hired 1918—2.19.

FELICITAS Dr 67/10. Hired 1915. Sunk 15.5.17 by Austrian cruisers in the Adriatic.

FELIX Cstr 136/12. Hired as BBV 9.1.1941—44.

FELLOWSHIP Dr 99/14. Hired as M/S 11.1939. Lent Greek navy 10.41—46.

FELSPAR Cstr 799/08. Hired as store carrier (RFA) 1.9.1914. Ammo. carrier 1917—18.

FEMERN Wh 257/32. Norwegian, hired as M/S (Dutch crew) 1941—46.

FENELLA (ex-*Unity*) Dr 96/20. Hired for examination service 28.3.1940—11.2.46.

FENNEW Dr 85/11, 1—6pdr. Hired 1915—19. (Served as YOUNG ALFRED in WW.II.)

FENTONIAN Tr 221/12, 1—6pdr. Hired as M/S 1914—19 and as A/P Tr 11.39. M/S 7.40; fuel carrier 3.44—2.45.

FERMO Tr 175/98. Hired 1918—19.

FERN Dr 85/07. Hired 1916—19.

FERN II Dr 59/02, 1—3pdr. Hired 1916—19.

FERNDALE Dr 75/10. Hired 1915. Sunk 27.12.15 off St Annes Head.

FERNMOOR 4,972/36. Hired as boom carrier 1940—46.

FEROL Oiler (RFA) 2,178 tons, 200 x 34 ft. Devonport DY 3.10.1914. Sold 29.1.20 Anglo American Pet. Co.

FERRET A.ship18. Hired 1803—04.

FERRET Lugger, 63bm. Hired 7.1808. Captured 22.11.1808 by the French.

FERRET (ex-*Onora*) Yt 56/23. Purchased and commissioned as base ship.

FERRIBY Tr 324/12, 1—12pdr. Hired 1915—19.

FERRY BELLE Ferry 62/24. Hired for examination service 1940—45.

FERRYHILL Cstr 411/09. Hired as store carrier (RFA) 4.10.1914—19.7.15.

FERRY KING Ferry 57/18. Hired as tender 1941—45.

FERRY PRINCE Ferry 69/39. Hired for examination service 9.1939—20.5.41.

FERRY PRINCE (see EPPING)

FERTILE Dr 98/07, 1—3pdr. Hired 1915—19.

FERTILE VALE Dr 91/17. Hired as A/P Dr 12.1939. Sunk 17.7.41 in collision off the Tay.

FERTILITY Dr 89/07, 1—6pdr. Hired 1915—19.

FERTILITY Dr 96/19. Hired for harbour service 26.8.1939—45.

FERTILITY MFV 22net/33. Hired for harbour service 10.3.1941—44.

FESSONIA Yt 28/37. Hired for boom patrol 1940. Purchased 1941, sold 1946 at Alexandria.

FESTING GRINDALL Tr, non-standard 'Castle' type. Smiths Dk 9.1.1917 Sold 1920, same name.

FESTUBERT Tr (RCN), 290gr, 130 x 24 ft, 1–12pdr. Polson IW, Toronto 2.8.1917. Boom gate vessel 9.39; sold 1947, renamex_Inverleigh.

FETLAR Tr, 'Isles' class. Cochrane 7.1941. Arrived 22.6.60 at Antwerp to BU.

FEUGH Tr 227/16, 1–6pdr. Hired 1917–19.

FEZENTA Tr 228/14, 1–6pdr. Hired as M/D 1915–19 and as A/P Tr 11.39. M/S 6.40–11.45.

FEZZARA MFV 54/20. French M/S seized 7.1940. A/P vessel to 1945.

F.H.S Dr 95/08. Hired 1915–19.

FIARAY Tr, 'Isles' class. Goole SB 13.6.1942. Sold 1946, renamed *Atlas*.

FIAT Tr 314/16. Hired 1918–19.

FIAT Cstr 197/33. Dutch, hired as BBV 25.7.1940–25.3.43.

FICHOT (see MMS.238)

FIDELE French navy boom tug, seized 3.7.1940 at Southampton. Salvage vessel 9.40; mooring vessel 1941; S/M diving tender 1944–45.

FIDELIA Dr 74/03. Hired as tender 11.1914–19.

FIDELIA Tr 147/91. Hired 1918–19 and purchased as BDV 15.5.40. Sunk 5.5.41 by air attack at Lowestoft.

FIDELITY 2,450/20, 3–4in, 2–3in. French *Le Rhin* handed over 1.7.1940 by her commander. Commissioned as special service vessel 24.9.40; sunk 30.12.40 by 'U.435' in the Atlantic.

FIDGET Salvage vessel 837 tons, 150 x 28½ ft. Purchased 1915. Sold 8.21 J R Thomson.

FIDGET (ex-*Formidable*) Dr 88/17, 2–MG. Purchased as M/S 11.1939. A/P Dr 9.40; sold 1.46.

FIDGET (ex-*Empire Jonathan*) DY tug, 233/44. Renamed 5.1947.

FIELDGATE (see COLLINGWOOD)

FIERY (see FAIRY)

FIERY CROSS. Admiralty wood Dr, Forbes 1918. Sold 1932.

FIERY CROSS (see GLOBE V)

FIFER Yt 194/39. Hired as A/P Yt (RCN) 1941–46.

FIFESHIRE Tr 540/38. Hired as A/S Tr 9.1939. Sunk 20.2.40 by air attack east of Copinsay.

FIFINELLA Tr 314/17, 1–12pdr. Hired 1917–19.

FILEY Tr 226/14. Purchased 1915. Wrecked 2.10.16 on Tory Island; salved 1917; sold 1920.

FILEY BAY Tr 370/31, 1–12pdr. Hired as M/S 8.1939–3.45.

FILLA Tr, 'Isles' class. Crown, Sunderland 2.4.1942. To Italian navy 1946.

FINDON Tender, 127bm. Hired 3.1804–17.11.10.

FINESSE (see TREVO TERCEIRO)

FINLANDE Tr 1,344/37. French, seized 25.9.1940 in the Newfoundland area. Intended for Free-French, but laid up until 4.41 then to MWT. (Listed in RN to 7.46.)

FINROSS Dr 78/11. Hired 1915. Wrecked 27.11.16 near Gallipoli.

FINTRAY Tr 195/06. Hired as danlayer 2.1940. M/S 8.40–1.45.

FINWHALE (Z.13) Wh, 'Z' class. Smiths Dk 24.9.1915. Sold 6.3.20, renamed *Canadian National No 1.*

FIONA 1,611/05,1–4in, 1–12pdr. Hired as ABS 28.11.1914. Wrecked 6.9.17 on the Pentland Skerries.

FIONA (ex-*Juna*) 2,190/27, 2–4in, 3–MG. Hired as ABV 31.8.1939. Convoy service ship 1940. Sunk 18.4.41 by air attack at Sidi Barrani.

FIR Tr 530 tons, 150 x 27½ ft, 1–12pdr. Inglis 27.1.1940. Sold 1947, renamed *Vollen.*

FIREBALL Admiralty wood Dr, 93gr. Fellows, Yarmouth 1919. Sold 28.4.20, renamed *Maviston.* (Served as HOLLYDALE in WW.II.)

FIREFLY (ex-*St Just*) Tr 394/30. Hired as M/S 9.1939–10.45.

FIRELIGHT Admiralty wood Dr, 99gr. Chambers 1919. Sold 1920, renamed *Just Reward.* (JUST REWARD in WW.II.)

FIR LAKE Motor M/S (RCN) 255 tons, 126 x 28 ft. Mac Craft Co, Sarnia. Cancelled 22.10.1945 and completed mercantile.

FIRM DY paddle tug 690 tons, 144 x 27½ ft. Chatham DY 23.8.1910. Arrived 2.9.60 at Antwerp to BU.

FIRMAMENT Admiralty wood Dr 93 gr. Forbes, Fraserburgh 1918. Sold 1919, renamed *Foxglove.*

FIRMAMENT (see KOS IX)

FIRMAXE (ex-Russian T.34, ex-*Cuatro*) Tr, 292gr, 130 x 23½ ft, 1–12pd Seized and commissioned 9.1918. Sold 11.5.20, renamed *Cannanore.*

FISHER BOY Dr 91/14, 1–3pdr. Hired 1915–19 and as M/S, 1–mg, 11.3

FISHER BOY MFV. Hired as A/P vessel 10.7.1940–12.41.

FISHERGATE Tr 205/05, 1–6pdr. Hired 1915–19.

FISHER GIRL Dr 85/13, 1–57mm. Hired 1916–19 and as degaussing vessel 1940. Sunk 25.11.41 by air attack in Falmouth harbour.

FISHER LAD Dr 96/19. Hired as A/S Dr 12.1939–11.45.

FISHER LASS Dr. Hired 1918–19.

FISHER QUEEN Dr 88/16, 1–3pdr. Hired 1916–19 and as HDPC 10.40–9.46.

FISHTOFT Tr 188/01. Hired 1914–19.

FISKAREN MFV. Norwegian, hired 9.1941. Sunk 23.12.41 in collision in Belfast Lough.

FIVE Dr 84/10. Hired 1914–19.

FIZZER (ex-*Violet*) Dr 90/07. Hired 1915–19.

FLAFF Admiralty steel Dr, 98gr. Watson, Gainsborough 1919. Sold 1920, renamed *River Ugie.*

FLAME Admiralty wood Dr, 92gr. Forbes 1918. Sold 1921, same name. (Served as UBERUS in WW.II.)

FLAMER (ex-*Stanley*) DY store carrier 235 tons, 160 x 24 ft. Transferred from War Dept 1.10.1891. Sold 23.12.1913.

FLAMER (C.108) DY tug, 124gr, 75 x 17½ ft. Bowling 1915 and
purchased 3.15. Renamed YC.298 in 1943. Sold 6.48 Pounds, Portsmouth.
FLAMER DY tug 365 tons 90 x 28 ft, 1–12pdr. A.Hall 23.5.1940. On
sale list 1965.
FLANDERS Tr 289/20. Hired as M/S 8.1939–12.45.
FLANDRE Tr 226/15, 1–6pdr. Hired as M/S 9.1915–19 and as A/P Tr,
1–6pdr, 6.40. M/S 1.42–12.45.
FLARE Rescue tug, 'B.A.T' class. Levingston, Orange Texas 11.6.1943
on lend-lease. Returned 1946 to the USN.
FLARE (see ROCKLAND)
FLASH Admiralty steel Dr 97gr. Colby 16.2.1918. Sold 17.11.20,
renamed *A.J.A.*
FLASH (see GLOBE II)
FLAT CALM Non-standard Admiralty wood Dr 92gr. Forbes 1918. Sold
1930, renamed *Fircroft.*
FLATHOLM Tr, 'Isles' class. Cook Welton & Gemmell 8.5.1943. Sold
31.8.60 to BU in Belgium.
FLAUNT Rescue tug, 'B.A.T' class. Levingston 30.6.1943 on lend-lease.
Returned 1946 to the USN.
FLAUNT (see ROCK PIGEON)
FLECK Admiralty wood Dr, 99gr. Chambers 1919. Sold 1921, same
name.
FLEETWING Dr 53/03, 1–3pdr. Hired 1915–19.
FLEETWING II Tr 119/96. Hired 1917–19.
FLEETWOOD Tr 163/96. Hired 1917–19.
FLEMING Tr 356/29, 1–12pdr. Hired as M/S 8.1939. Sunk 24.7.40 by
air attack in the Thames estuary.
FLEUR de LIS Canadian Govt Yt 316/29. Commissioned as A/S Yt
(RCN) 1940–45.
Le FLIBUSTIER (see CORSAIRE)
FLICKER Tr 192/11. Hired 1915. Sunk 4.3.16 by mine off Dover.
FLICKER Admiralty steel Dr. A.Hall 21.8.1918. Sold 1935.
FLICKER (see KOS X)
FLINT Tr, 'Isles' class. G.T. Davie, Lauzon 14.7.1942. Sold 1947,
renamed *Cornelia* then W.German TRAVE.
FLINT CASTLE Tr 275/16, 1–6pdr. Hired 1916–19.
FLINTLOCK Armament store carrier, 187gr. Philip, Dartmouth 1946.
FLINTSHIRE Tr 225/16, 1–6pdr. Purchased 4.1916. Sold 5.1.26,
renamed *Taipo.* (TAIPO in WW.II.)
FLIRT Cutter 12. Hired 1799–1801.
FLIRT Cutter, 119bm. Hired 7.1803–16.1.1806.
FLIXTON Tr 201/19. Hired for examination service 8.1939–7.46.
FLOANDI Dr 114/14. Hired 1914–19.

FLO JOHNSON Dr, 1–6pdr. Hired 1917–19.

FLOODTIDE Admiralty wood Dr 88gr. Chambers. Cancelled and completed 1920 as *Marjorie Grace.*

FLOODTIDE Admiralty wood Dr CD.72 renamed 1923. Sold circa 1930.

FLORA Cutter 12. Hired 1783.

FLORA A.ship 12, 202bm. Hired 1793–95.

FLORA Cutter 14. Hired 1794. Lost 1798.

FLORA Brig 14, 148bm. Hired 1800. Wrecked 20.11.00 in the Hamoaze but listed 1801.

FLORA Dr 92/01. Hired as tender 11.1914–19.

FLORAL QUEEN MFV 21/36. Hired as A/P vessel 6.1940–2.12.43.

FLOREAT Dr 93/08, 1–3pdr. Hired 1915–19.

FLOREAT MFV. Hired as A/P vessel 6.1940–24.1.42.

FLOREAT II MFV 25/33. Hired as HDPC 11.1939–45.

FLOREAT III MFV 26/34. Hired as HDPC 11.1939–46.

FLORENCE (see FAVOURITE)

FLORENCE BRIERLEY Tr 330/18. Purchased as BDV 1.1940. Sold 8.46

FLORENCE DOMBEY Tr 182/00. Hired 1918–19.

FLORENTINO 1,822/21. Purchased 22.9.1939. Sunk 25.5.40 as blockship at Scapa Flow.

FLORIDA (ex-Gun 9) Wh 256/30. Purchased as M/S (SAN) 12.12.1940. Sold 25.3.46, renamed *Uni IX.*

FLORIDIAN 4,777/13. Hired as supply ship (RFA) 3.8.1914–10.7.16.

FLORINDA Yt 135/73. Purchased as accommodation ship 6.1940. Laid up 4.45.

FLORIO Tr 314/16, 1–12pdr. Hired as A/P Tr 1917–19 and as M/S 8.39–6.45.

FLORIS Cstr 424/12. Hired as fleet messenger 2.1918–3.4.19.

FLOTSAM Admiralty wood Dr, 100gr. Chambers 1919. Sold 2.10.20, same name.

FLOTTA Tr, 'Isles' class. Cochrane 14.2.1941. Foundered 6.11.41 after grounding 29.10.41 east Scotland.

FLOURISH Dr 83/03, 1–3pdr. Hired 1915–19.

FLOW Admiralty steel Dr, 96gr. Watson 1920. Sold 1920, same name. Hired for examination service 9.39–3.46.

FLOWER Dr 83/07. Hired 1915–19 and on harbour service 1942–45.

FLOWERGATE 5,200/11. Purchased 7.2.1944. Sunk 9.6.44 as blockship at Arromanches.

FLOWER o'MORAY Dr 84/08. Hired 12.1914–19.

FLOWING TIDE Dr 83/13. Hired 5.1915–19.

FLUELLEN Tr 545 tons, 150 x 28 ft, 1–12pdr. Cochrane 1.11.1940. Sold 2.47.

FLURRY Admiralty wood Dr, 100gr. Chambers 1919. Sold 1920, same name. (Served as GLEAM ON in WW.II.)

FLUSH Admiralty wood Dr, 97gr. Wood, Lossiemouth 1919. Sold 1920, same name. Hired as BBV 1.11.39—45.

FLUTTER Admiralty wood Dr, 99gr. Chambers. Cancelled 1919 and completed as *Animation*. (ANIMATION in WW.II.)

FLY Cutter ¹2. Hired 1796—1801.

FLY Cutter 10, 83bm. Hired 25.6.1804—9.05.

FLY Coastguard cutter, 60 bm. Buklt 1863. Hulk 1904. BU 1928.

FLY M/S Wh 180 tons, 2—3pdr. German *Sturmvogel* seized 1914, commissioned 1.15. Sold 1919.

FLY Tr 158/90. Hired 1918—19.

FLYING ADMIRAL Tr 275/17, 1—12pdr. Hired as A/P Tr 30.5.1940—31.12.41.

FLYING BREEZE Tug 387/13. Hired 2.8.1914—19 and on examination service 8.39—3.9.40.

FLYING BUZZARD Tug 200/12. Hired as DY tug 11.8.1914—6.2.19.

FLYING CORMORANT Tug 199/09. Hired as DY tug 6.1916—12.18.

FLYING FALCON Tug 184/04. Hired 6.1917—20.

FLYING FISH Cutter. Hired 1782—83.

FLYING FISH Schooner 14, 74bm. Hired 6.7.1809—5.14.

FLYING FISH (ex-*Lady Augusta*) Schooner 1, 78bm. Hired 1813, purchased 1817. Sold 31.3.1821 at Antigua.

FLYING FISH II Tug 189/82. Hired as DY tug 12.1914. Converting 1918 to minelayer, 8 mines, but not completed. Returned 1920.

FLYING FOAM Tug 217/17. Hired 2.1917—19.

FLYING FOX Tug 185/85. Hired as DY tug 7.1914—18.

FLYING KESTREL Tug 516/13. Hired 2.8.1914—19.

FLYING MIST Tug 148/92. Hired 6.1915—19.

FLYING SPRAY Tug 217/17. Hired 5.1917—19.

FLYING SPORTSMAN Tug 187/82. Hired 7.1914—3.19.

FLYING WING Tr 226/15, 1—6pdr. Hired as M/S 1915—19 and as A/P Tr 11.39. M/S 5.41—46.

FLYING WITCH Tug 142/91. Hired 6.1915—20.

FOAM Yt 39/02. Hired as tender 9.1918—4.19.

FOAM Admiralty steel Dr, 95gr. Abdela Mitchell 1919. Sold 1921, renamed *Starwort*.

FOAMCREST (see HERON)

FOGBANK Admiralty wood Dr, 95gr. Clapson 1919. Sold 1920, renamed *Dyker Lassie*.

FOGBOW Non-standard Admiralty wood Dr, 92gr. Forbes 1918. Sold 1920.

FOGBREAK Admiralty steel Dr, 95gr. Abdela Mitchell 1920. Sold 1920, renamed *Craighall*. (Served as SPES AUREA in WW.II.)

FOIL (ex-*Uberus*) MFV 36net/35. Hired as A/P vessel 23.6.1940—6.45.

FOINAVON Yt 670/19. Hired as accommodation ship 4.10.1939—45.

FOLKESTONE Lugger 12, 131bm, 12—12pdr carr. Hired 5.6.1804—3.05 and 9.8.1807—28.4.14.

FOLKESTONE 496/03, 2—12pdr. Hired as M/S 9.10.1914—31.1.20.

FONTENOY Tr 276/18. Hired as M/S 2.1940. Sunk 19.11.40 by air attack off Lowestoft.

FORAY Yt 76/29. Hired as HDPC 10.1939. Laid up 9.42.

FORBIN 7,291/22. French, seized 6.1940 at Gibraltar. To MWT 1940. Again RN 1944 and sunk 9.6.44 as blockship at Arromanches.

FORCE Tr 324/17. Hired as M/S 2.1940. Sunk 27.6.41 by air attack off the Norfolk coast.

FORCEFUL Tug 288/25, 2—20mm. Hired (RAN) 1.1942—10.43.

FORCEFUL DY paddle tug 710 tons, 145 x 30 ft. Yarrow 5.1957.

FORDE 829/19. Hired as salvage ship 11.1939. To MWT 1940 and returned 3.47. (See FORD in Vol I.)

FORECAST Dr 96/25, 1—3pdr. Hired as A/P Dr 11.1939. Sunk 10.4.44 by unknown cause at Greenock. Raised and BU 7.44.

FORELOCK Dr 89/10. Hired for harbour service 12.1914—19 and on examination service 1942. Water carrier 1944—45.

FOREMOST I Tug 123/15. Hired 6.1915—11.19.

FOREMOST III Tug 98/15. Hired 6.1915. To War Dept 11.16.

FOREMOST 22 Tug 211/24. Hired for examination service 28.8.1939—6.40.

FOREMOST 43 Cstr 227/28. Hired as supply ship 10.1941—5.43.

FOREMOST 87 Tug 163/35. Hired 4.1940—8.40.

FOREMOST Tug 143/38. DY tug in service 1943. On sale list 9.67.

FORERUNNER Dr 92/11. Hired 1915—19 and as M/S 11.39. Lost 14.10.41 in collision in the Thames estuary.

FORESIGHT II Dr 87/11. Hired 1914—19 and on harbour service 10.40—46.

FORESTER DY craft, 80bm. Listed 1827. Coastguard 3.28. Sold 1862.

FORETHOUGHT Dr 86/13, 1—3pdr. Hired 1918—19.

FORETHOUGHT Dr 77/24. Hired as HDPC 21.10.1939. Calibrating vessel 1943—45.

FORFAR (ex-*Montrose*) 16,400/21, 8—6in, 2—3in. Hired as AMC 3.9.1939. Sunk 2.12.40 by 'U.99' west of Ireland.

FORFEIT (see CORNELIAN)

FORGLEN Dr 80/09, 1—3pdr. Hired 1.1915—19.

FORION (ex-*Orion*) Tug 83/00. Hired 9.1917—19.

FORK LIGHTNING Admiralty steel Dr 97gr. Brooke 1918. Sold 20.8.20, same name.

FORMIDABLE Dr 86/13, 1—6pdr. Hired 2.1915—19.

FORSETTI Yt 56/26. Hired as BBV 5.1940—44.

'Fort' class Store carriers (RFA), average 7,200gr, 9,790 tons, 424½ x 57 ft.

FORT BEAUHARNOIS W.Coast S.Bldrs, Vancouver 1944. Arrived 8.11.62 at Spezia to BU.

FORT CHARLOTTE W.C.S.B., Vancouver 1944. For sale 1967.

FORT COLVILLE W.C.S.B., Vancouver 1943. To MOT 1946.

FORT CONSTANTINE Burrard, Vancouver 1944. Listed 1963.

FORT DUNVEGAN Burrard 28.2.44.

FORT DUQUESNE W.C.S.B., Vancouver 1944. BU 6.67.

FORT LANGLEY Victoria Mchy 1945.

FORT ROSALIE United SY, Montreal 18.11.44.

FORT SANDUSKY United SY 25.11.44.

FORT WAYNE United SY 1944. Sold circa 1948, renamed *Angusdale*.

FORT WRANGELL Burrard 1944. Sold 1948, renamed *Eastwave*.

FORT ALBERT Tr 193/06, 1–6pdr. Hired 1914–19.

FORT AMHERST 3,489/36. Hired as store carrier (RFA). Purchased 12.1951. Renamed AMHERST 1952.

FORT EDWARD Tr 208/08, 1–6pdr. Hired 1915–19.

FORT GEORGE Tr 180/02, 1–6pdr. Hired as decoy ship 1917–19.

FORTH Tug 129/83. Hired for harbour service 1.8.1914–24.3.19.

FORTITUDE (see NEPTUNE)

FORTITUDE Dr 86/03, 1–3pdr. Hired 1915–19.

FORTITUDE Tug. In service 1918–20.

FORTITUDE (ex-*Empire Charles*) DY tug 244/43, 487 tons. Transferred from MOT 3.1947. Sold 1964 to BU.

FORTOL Oiler (RFA), 4,900 tons, 335 x 41½ ft. McMillan, Dumbarton 21.5.1917. BU-1958 at Rosyth.

FORT ROBERT Tr 203/18. Hired as A/P Tr 11.1939. M/S 4.40–8.45.

FORT ROSE Tr 212/17, 1–3pdr. Hired as A/P Tr 5.1940–45.

FORT ROYAL Tr 351/31, 1–12pdr. Hired as M/S 8.1939 and later purchased. Sunk 9.2.40 by air attack off Aberdeen.

FORT RYAN Tr 255/32. Hired as BDV 9.1939–12.44.

FORTUNA Tr 259/06, 1–3pdf. Hired 1917–19 and as A/P Tr, 1–6pdr 6.40. Sunk 3.4.41 by air attack off St Abbs Head.

FORTUNATUS Dr 58/02. Hired 1918–19.

FORTUNE Cutter 10. Hired 1782.

FORTUNE Cutter 8. Hired 1797–98.

FORT WILLIAM Tr 188/03. Hired 1918–19.

FORWARD II Tr 250/06, 1–6pdr. Hired 1915–19.

FORWARD III Dr 89/07. Hired 1915. Sunk 31.3.17 by mine off the Shipwash.

FORWARD IV Dr 74/05, 1–6pdr. Hired 1915–19.

FORWARD HO Tr 269/15, 1–6pdr. Hired as M/S 1915–19.

FOSDYKE Tr 245/08, 1–6pdr. Hired 1914–19.

FOSS Tr 275/16, 1–6pdr. Hired as M/S 1916–19 and as BDV 1.40–7.46.

FOSSBECK 4,918/30. Hired as A/C transport 11.1939. Boom carrier 4.42–5.46.

FOULA Tr, 'Isles' class. Cochrane 28.7.1941. To Italian navy 2.46.

FOULNESS Tr, 'Isles' class. Lewis 23.2.1942. Oil tank cleaning vessel 1957.

FOUNTAIN DY tank vessel. Pembroke Dock 26.11.1833. Fate unknown.

FOUNTAIN Admiralty wood Dr, 95gr. Clapson 1919. Sold 1919, same name.

FOUNTAIN DY tank vessel 530 tons. Crown, Sunderland 17.1.1939. On sale list 1963.

FOUR Dr 91/07, 1–3pdr. Hired 1915–19.

FOX Three cutters hired 1783.

FOX Cutter 12, 124bm. Hired 1793. Lost 1797. (May be the cutter purchased 1794 - see Vol I.)

FOX Cutter 10, 70bm. Hired 1794–1801.

FOX Two 10–gun cutters hired 1796–1801.

FOX Cutter 8, 98bm. 8–4pdr. Hired 6.1803. Renamed FRISK 1804. Returned 5.9.1806.

FOX Cutter 8, 95 bm, 8–4pdr. Hired 6.1803–1.1805.

FOX Survey vessel. Hired 1812–16.

FOX (see LEA RIG)

FOXTROT A/S Tr 530 tons, 150 x 27½ ft. 1–4in, 3–20mm. Cochrane 23.4.1940. To War Dept 31.7.46. BU 9.51.

FOYLE (see JOHN EDMUND)

FOYLEBANK 5,582/30, 8–4in. Commissioned as A/A ship 3.1940. Sunk 4.7.40 by air attack off Portland.

FRAGRANCE Dr 72/10, 1–3pdr. Hired 12.1914–19.

FRAGRANT Dr 94/08, 1–6pdr. Hired 1915–19 and on harbour service 1941–45.

FRANCIS (ex-*Nancy*) Cutter 6, 46bm. Hired 5.1804–15.10.1805.

FRANCIS BATEY Tug 151/14. Hired as DY tug 10.1914–19.

FRANCISCO ANTONIO QUARTO (see SPIDER)

FRANCIS CONLIN Tr, 'Castle' type. Ailsa 21.1.1919. Sold 1919, renamed *Inverythan.*

FRANCIS DUNCAN 2,384/07. Hired as fleet auxiliary 24.10.1913–19.

FRANCIS FRENCH Tr, 'Mersey' type. Cochrane. Cancelled 1919.

FRANCOL Oiler (RFA) 4,900 tons, 335 x 41½ ft. Earle 18.10.1917. Sunk 3.3.42 by a Japanese squadron 300 miles south of Java.

FRANCOLIN (see FARADAY)

FRANCOLIN (ex-*Speedwell*) MFV. Hired as mine observation vessel 28.7.1940. Danlayer 1942–45. (Bore the name JACKDAW 1940–43 as nominal base ship)

FRANC TIREUR Tr 314/16, 1—6pdr. Hired as M/S 1916—19 and as A/P Tr, 1—12pdr 5.40. M/S 1941. Sunk 25.9.43 by E-boat torpedo off Harwich

FRANK Tug 76/96. Hired 5.1917—19.

FRANK DIXON Tug 133/20. Hired as DY tug (RCN) 1942—46.

FRASCATI Tr 220/14, 1—6pdr. Hired 11.1914—19.

FRASER Tr 310/07. Hired 1916. Sunk 17.6.17 by mine off Boulogne.

FRASERBURGH Dr 83/07, 1—3pdr. Hired 1915—19.

FRASER EAVES Tr, 'Mersey' type, 324gr. Cochrane 2.10.1917. Renamed DOON 10.20. Sold 1947.

FRATTON 757/25. Hired as BBV 8.1940. Accommodation ship 4.44. Sunk 18.8.44 by torpedo while at anchor in Seine Bay.

FREDERICK (see LORD NELSON)

FREDERICK BOYCE Tr, 'Strath' type. Hall Russell. Cancelled 1919.

FREDERICK BUSH Tr, 'Castle' type, 277gr. Cook Welton & Gemmell 14.3.1918. Sold 1920, renamed *Cawdor*.

FRED EVERARD Cstr 229/26. Hired as store carrier (RFA) 1941—44.

FRED SALMON Dr 102/12. Hired 1915—19. (Served as STRIVE in WW.II.)

FREEBOOTER Fleet tug 840 tons, 165 x 32 ft, 1—3in. Fleming & Ferguson 29.11.1940. Sold 1961.

FREEDOM Dr 90/07, 1—3pdr. Hired 1915—19.

FREEDOM Rescue tug (wood-built) 1,360 tons, 147 x 33½ ft, 1—3in, 2—20mm. Camden SB, New Jersey 1.10.1943 and on lend-lease from 20.3.44—4.46.

FREEDOM (see ROCKGLEN)

FREELANCE Yt 106/08. Hired as A/P Yt 28.9.1940. Renamed BUNTING 1940, base ship. Renamed FREEWILL 1940, accommodation ship. Disposal 1945.

FREELANCE (see BUNTING)

FREESIA Tr 285/11, 1—6pdr. Hired 1914—19.

FREEWILL (see FREELANCE)

FREIJA Salvage vessel 326/17. Purchased during WW.II. Sold 19.1.55 Pounds, Portsmouth.

FRENCH 133/20. Canadian govt vessel commissioned as A/S vessel (RCN) 18.9.1939—9.46.

FRERES COQUELIN Dr 185/34. French M/S seized 3.7.1940 at Plymouth. M/S to 1942 then laid up. Returned 2.46.

FRESCO DY tug 124 tons, 76 x 17 ft. Scott, Bowling 1915 and purchased 1915. Sold 3.23.

FRESCO DY tug 365 tons, 90 x 28 ft, 2—MG. A.Hall 20.6.1940. Renamed HANDMAID 1941.

'Fresh' class DY tank vessels 594 tons, 126 x 25½ ft. 14 vessels, all built by Lytham SB Co.

FRESHBROOK 5.11.1941. Sold 1963 Park Stanton & Co.
FRESHBURN 29.10.43.
FRESHENER 16.3.42.
FRESHET 6.7.40.
FRESHFORD 23.3.44. On sale list 1967.
FRESHLAKE 15.7.42.
FRESHMERE 23.11.42.
FRESHPOND 28.8.45.
FRESHPOOL 11.3.43.
FRESHSPRAY 5.3.46.
FRESHSPRING 15.8.46.
FRESHTARN 22.8.44.
FRESHWATER 23.3.40. Sold 1969.
FRESHWELL 2.7.43.

FRESHET Admiralty steel Dr 96gr. A.Hall 1918. Sold 1921, renamed
Jean Paterson. (Served as XMAS ROSE in WW.II.)
FRESHWATER Paddle 264/27. Hired on examination service 1941—44.
FREUNCHY Dr 84/ . Hired 1915. Sunk 8.1.16 by mine off Brindisi.
FREYA Tr 204/17. Hired on examination service 5.1940—45.
FRIARAGE Tr 210/30, 1—6pdr. Hired for examination service 9.1939.
A/P Tr 1940—12.45.
FRIEDA MFV 68/29. French (ex-Belgian) M/S seized 1940. A/P vessel
1940—2.46.
FRIENDLY GIRLS Dr 90/13. Hired 2.1915—19 and 1940—41.
FRIENDLY STAR Dr 58/09. Hired 2.1915—19.
FRIENDS Dr 81/06, 1—6pdr. Hired 1915—19.
FRIENDSHIP 20-gun ship. Hired 1793. Captured 1795 by the French.
FRIENDSHIP Tender 6, 175bm, 6—3pdr. Hired 8.1803—05.
FRIESLAND Tr 268/99, 1—12pdr. Hired 1915—19.
FRIESLAND Tr. Hired as M/S 1940—45.
FRIGATE BIRD Dr 84/05, 1—57mm. Hired 1916. Sunk 11.3.18 in
collision in the Mediterranean.
FRISK (see FOX)
FRISKY Rescue tug, 613gr, 155 x 31 ft. Lewis 8.1918. Sold 4.25,
renamed *Foundation Franklin.*
FRISKY Rescue tug 700 tons, 142½ x 33 ft, 1—3in, 2—20mm. Cochrane
27,5.1941. Sold 1948, renamed *Hasan.*
FRISKY (ex-EMPIRE RITA) DY tug 300/46. Transferred from MOT
1946 and renamed circa 1959.
FROLIC DY tug 79 tons, 61 x 15 ft. Bow McLachlan 1915 and
purchased 3.15. Sold 5.23 Cork Harbour Commissioners.
FRONS OLIVAE Dr 98/12, 1—3pdr. Hired 12.1914. Sunk 12.10.15 by
mine off the Elbow buoy.

FRONS OLIVAE Dr 93/16. Hired 1916–19 and as M/S 11.39–45.
FROSTAXE Tr 191/99. Russian T.41 (ex-*Atlas*) seized and commissioned in the Baltic 8.1918. Sunk 3.4.19 in collision with *Epiros* off Newhaven.
FROTH Admiralty steel Dr, 97gr. A.Hall 1918. Sold 1921, same name.
FRUITFUL Dr 89/04. Hired on harbour service 4.1915–19.

'FT' class fleet tenders 238 tons, 103 x 21 ft, 4–20mm. Built in the USA 1944, transferred on lend-lease and returned 1946, except where noted.
FT.1–4 Warren Boat Co.
FT.5, 6 H G Marr. (FT.5 bore the name TENDERFOOT from 1944.)
FT.7–10 and 21–23 Camden SB Co. (FT.7 converted to A/S repair vessel 1944 and returned 1947. Bore the name ASTRAVEL 1944–45. FT.9 radar workshop 7.45.)
FT.14, 15 and 29 Bristol Yt Co. (FT.15 transferred to Greek navy 1945.)
FT.16–19 W A Robinson. (FT.16 bore the name TENDERHEART from 1944.)
FT.25, 27 Hodgdon Bros. (FT.27 returned 1947.)
FT.30 Noank SB Co.
FT.56 builder unknown.

F.T.EVERARD Tug 124/28. Hired as DY tug 1940–46.
FUDAY Tr, 'Isles' class. Cook Welton & Gemmell 1.1.1944. Sold 1947.
FUH WO Cstr 953/22. Hired as A/S–M/S vessell 6.1940. Lost 3.42 in the Singapore area.
FUJI Tr 255/12, 1–6pdr. Hired 1915–19.
FULL MOON Admiralty wood Dr, 92gr. Forbes, Fraserburgh 25.3.1918. Sold circa 1930, renamed *Dougalls*. (Served as REIDS in WW.II.)
FULL MOON (see KOS XI)
FULMAR Tr 231/99. Hired 1915. Sunk 17.1.16 by mine off Sollum.
FUMAROLE Admiralty wood Dr, 97gr. Colby 1918. Sold 5.47.
FUME Admiralty steel Dr, 97gr. Colby 1919. Sold 1920, same name.
FUNDY M/S Tr (RCN) 460 tons, 150 x 27½ ft, 1–4in. Collingwood SY 18.6.1938. Sold 1947.
FURZE Dr 99/11, 1–3pdr. Hired 1914–19 and on harbour service 1941. Water carrier 1943–45.
FUSILIER Tr 294gr, 130 x 24 ft, 1–12pdr. Smiths Dk 1.2.1915, purchased 11.12.14. Renamed CARBINEER II 1919. Sold 26.2.20, same name. Hired as A/P Tr 5.40; BDV 1940–7.46.
FUSILIER A/S Tr 750 tons, 175 x 30 ft, 1–4in, 4–20mm. Cook Welton & Gemmell 23.12.1942. Sold 4.46, renamed *Serron*.
FUTURIST Tr 234/20. Hired as M/S (RNZN) 8.1940–45.
FYLDE Tug 256/04. Hired 1917–2.19.
FYLDEA Tr 377/30. Hired as M/S 9.1939–12.45.
FYLLA MFV. Danish, seized 5.1940. On harbour service to 1945.

GABIR Tr 219/09, 1–6pdr. Hired as M/S 1916. Sunk 24.5.18 by mine off Lowestoft.

GABRIELLE DENISE MFV. Belgian, hired as A/P vessel 7.1940. Target towing 1941–6.45.

GABRIELLE MARIA Dr 102/31. Belgian, hired as A/P Dr 1940. BBV 1941. Renamed CHANNEL FIRE, fire-float 1942. Returned 1944.

GABY Tr 210/09. Belgian, hired 1918–19.

GADFLY (ex-*Tenedos*) Tr 290/19. Hired as M/S 8.1939–9.45.

GADITANO (ex-*Barrister*) 4,750/93. Purchased as blockship 1915 but not used. Oil hulk 1916. Sold 3.32.

GADRA Tr 219/09, 1–6pdr. Hired as M/D 1915–19 and as A/P Tr 11.39–1.40. Sunk 6.1.41 while fishing.

GAEL Yt 115/04. Hired as A/P Yt 1.10.1917–19 and as HDPC 1.40. Sunk 24.11.40 by mine off the Humber.

GAELIC Schooner, 224gr, 2–12pdr. Commissioned as decoy ship 'Q.22' on 6.11.1916. Returned 9.18. (Also operated as BRIG II AND GOBO.)

GAELIC Tr 159/90. Hired 1917–19.

GAIRSAY Tr, 'Isles' class. Ardrossan DY Co 28.5.1942. Sunk 3.8.44 by explosive motor boat off Normandy.

GALATEA Lugger. Hired 1795–1805.

GALATEA 569/06. Hired on examination service 8.1940. Renamed PYGMALION 1941. Returned 1946.

GALAXY Admiralty steel Dr 96gr. Colby 1919. Sold 1919, same name.

GALE Admiralty steel Dr, 96gr. A.Hall 1919. Sold 1919, renamed *Ocean Rover*.

GALE Cstr 622/35. Hired as M/S (RNZN), commissioned 3.4.1941. Paid off 10.44.

GALILEAN Dr 72/11, 1–3pdr. Hired 1916–19.

GALLINULE Tr 238/07, 1–6pdr. Hired as M/S 1915–19 and as A/P Tr 12.39–1.40.

GALLIONS REACH Hopper 821/36. Hired as Salvage vessel 1942–2.47.

GALMA Yt 43/08. Hired on harbour service 8.1940; purchased 9.41. Laid up 1.46.

GALVANI Tr 353/29, 1–12pdr. Hired as A/P Tr 6.1940. M/S 1941–8.45.

GAMBIER Cutter 12, 109bm. Hired 6.1808–5.1814.

GAMBRI Tr 274/16, 1–6pdr. Hired 1917. Sunk 18.1.18 by mine off the Royal Sovereign light vessel.

GAMECOCK Tug 50/86. Hired 2.1915–3.18.

GAMECOCK Tr 171/05, 1–6pdr. Hired 1914–19.

GAMRIE BAY Dr 87/14. Hired as BDV 7.1915–19.

GAMTOOS Cstr 794/37. Hired as salvage vessel (SAN) 1942–46.

GANEFF Hired as M/S 1940. On examination service 1943–45.

GANGA Paddle 89/31. Hired as A/P vessel (RIN) 1939–6.46.

GANGES Transport. Hired 1854. Foundered 14.11.1854 off the Crimea.

GANILLY Tr, 'Isles' class. Cook Welton & Gemmell 22.5.1943. Sunk 5.7.44 by mine in the Channel.

GANNET (ex-*Penguin*) A/P vessel (RAN) 208 tons, 1−12pdr. Hired 1918−19.

GANTON Tr 330/14, 1−12pdr. Hired 1915−19.

GARDENIA Tr 146/91, 1−6pdr. Hired 1915−18.

GARDNER Dr 54/09, 1−3pdr. Hired 1915−19.

GARGANEY DY mooring vessel 950 tons, 168 x 36½ ft. Brooke Marine 13.12.1965.

GARMO Tr 203/00. Hired as M/S 1914. Sunk 20.12.14 by mine off Scarborough.

GARNET Tr 265/16, 1−6pdr. Hired as M/S 1916−19.

GAROLA Tr 249/12, 1−6pdr. Hired as M/S 1914−19 and as A/P Tr 11.39. M/S 6.40, fuel carrier 1.44, target towing 1944−5.46.

GARRIGILL Dr 99/14. Hired 1915−19.

GARRY (see GOLDAXE)

GARTH Hired vessel in service 12.1916−18.

GARU Tr 215/11, 1−3pdr. Hired 1915−19.

GASTON RIVIER 315 tons. French survey vessel, seized 3.7.1940. Free-French M/S 10.40; RN crew 8.41−46.

GASPE M/S Tr (RCN) 460 tons, 150 x 27½ ft, 1−4in. Morton 12.8.1938. Sold 1947.

GATESHEAD Tr, 'Isles' class. Davie, Lauzon 1.8.1942. Arrived 13.10.59 at Rotterdam to BU.

GATINAIS Cstr 389/33. French M/S seized 7.1940 at Southampton. BBV 8.40. To MWT 11.41 and sunk 3.12.42 by E-boat torpedo off Start Point.

GATLING Armament tug. Hong Kong & Whampoa DY Co 1937. Lost at the fall of Hong Kong and became Japanese. Recovered 1946, renamed BOOMERANG. Sold 17.10.51.

GATLING Armament store carrier 604 tons, 131 x 25 ft. Lobnitz 9.7.1945.

GAUL Tr 270/05, 1−6pdr. Hired as M/S 1915−19.

GAUL Tr 531/36, 1−4in. Purchased as A/S Tr 1939. Sunk 3.5.40 by air attack off Norway.

GAUNTLET Tug 149/91. Hired 1917−19.

GAVA Tr 256/20, 1−12pdr. Hired as A/P Tr 11.1939. M/S 5.42; target towing 9.42−6.46.

GAVENEY BRAE Dr 54/10. Hired 1915−19.

GAVENWOOD Dr 88/ −. Hired 1915. Sunk 20.2.16 by mine off Brindisi.

GAVINA Tr 289/15, 1−12pdr. Hired 1916−19.

GAVOTTE A/S Tr 530 tons, 150 x 27½ ft, 1−4in, 3−20mm. Cook Welton & Gemmell 7.5.1940. To Italian navy 3.46.

'Gay' class fast patrol boats. 50 tons, 67 x 19½ ft, 1–40mm, 4–TT.
GAY ARCHER Vosper 20.8.1952. Sold 24.7.63.
GAY BOMBARDIER Vosper 25.8.52. On sale list 1963.
GAY BOWMAN Vosper 19.12.52. Sold 24.7.63.
GAY BRUISER Vosper 19.12.52. Sold 31.1.62.
CAY CARABINEER Thornycroft 22.1.53. On sale list 1963.
GAY CAVALIER Taylor 23.1.53. Sold 25.7.63.
GAY CENTURION Thornycroft 3.9.52. Sold 31.1.62.
GAY CHARGER Morgan Giles 12.1.53.
GAY CHARIOTEER Morgan Giles 12.6.53.
GAY DRAGOON Taylor 28.1.53. Sold 31.1.62.
GAY FENCER McGruer 18.2.53.
GAY FORESTER McGruer 23.3.54. Sold 31.1.62.

GAYA Tr (RIN), 'Basset' class. Calcutta. Cancelled 10.1944.
GAZELLE DY tug 115 tons, 73 x 14½ ft. Purchased 4.6.1903. Sold
circa 1924, renamed *Rio Gradlon.*
GAZELLE 609/89, 2–12pdr. Hired as M/S 27.10.1914– 10.4.20.
(Operated as M/L, 50 mines 5.15–11.15.)
G.C.D Dr 77/01. Hired 1915–19.
GELERT Yt 122/81. Purchased as HDPC 11.1939. Sold 9.1.46.
GELLYBURN Dr 86/08, 1–3pdr. Hired 1915–19 and on harbour service
9.39. Water carrier 1.44–45.
GELSINA Tr 226/15. Hired 1916. Sunk 25.6.17 by mine off Girdle Ness.
GEMAS Wh 207/25. Hired as M/S 9.1939. Sunk 2.3.42 by HMAS
BALLARAT seven miles off Java to avoid capture by the Japanese.
GEMMA Tr 271/18, 1–12pdr. American, purchased 1940 as A/P Tr.
Sold 1949 in Trinidad.
GEMSBUCK (see HVAL I)
GEMUNU Tr (Ceylon govt), 'Basset' class. Irrawadi Flotilla Co, Rangoon.
Laid down 8.1941. Lost on stocks at the fall of Rangoon.
GENERA MFV 31/26. Hired as BBV 24.11.1939–12.45.
GENERAL Tr 191/98. Hired 1917–19.
GENERAL BIRDWOOD Tr 324/19, 1–12pdr. Purchased as M/S 8.1939.
Fuel carrier 1944. Sold 5.46.
GENERAL BOTHA Tr 245/16, 1–6pdr. Hired as M/S 1916–19 and as
M/S 6.40–11.45.
GENERAL COOTE Lugger 6, 49bm. Hired 3.1804–9.04.
GENERAL ELLIOT Gunvessel. Hired 9.1801–12.01.
GENERAL GORDON Tr 267/05, 1–6pdr. Hired 1917–19.
GENERAL JOFFRE Tr 194/14, 1–6pdr. Hired as M/S 1916–19.
GENERAL LEMAN Dr 86/19. Belgian, hired as BBV 5.9.1940–27.8.45.
GENERAL van der HEIJDEN 1,213/29. Dutch, hired as water carrier.
Lost 14.4.1944 by fire at Bombay.

GENERAL van SWIETEN 1,300/28. Dutch, hired as water carrier. Lost with GENERAL van der HEIJDEN.

GENERAL WHITE Dr 72/00, 1–3pdr. Hired 1915–19.

GENIUS Dr 96/19. Hired as M/S 10.1939–11.45.

GEORDIE Dr, 1–MG. Hired as A/P vessel 12.1939–5.46.

GEORGE 40–gun ship, 467bm. Hired 1665. Captured 1666 by the Dutch and burnt.

GEORGE Cutter8. Hired 1782.

GEORGE Cutter 14. Hired 1798–1801.

GEORGE Tug 277/13. Purchased 1917. Sold 1920 at Smyrna.

GEORGE V Dr 67/ –. Hired 1915. Sunk 3.6.17 by mine off Dover.

GEORGE V DY tug 224/15. Hired 1.5.1915–24.11.15.

GEORGE V MFV 41/01. Purchased for ferry service 9.1939. Sold 7.45.

GEORGE & ALBERT Dr 99/16. Hired as BBV 12.1939–1.46.

GEORGE ADGELL Tr, 'Castle' type, 290gr. Cook Welton & Gemmell 18.6.1919. Sold 1919, same name. Hired as A/P Tr 6.40. M/S 1941–1.46.

GEORGE AIKEN Tr, 'Castle' type. Cook Welton & Gemmell 19.12.1919. Renamed CECIL COOMBES 1919. Sold 1920, renamed *Highbridge.*

GEORGE ANDREW Tr, 'Mersey' type, 312gr. Cochrane 23.7.1917. Sold 1921, renamed *Lord Astor.* (Served as CRANEFLY in WW.II.)

GEORGE AUNGER Tr, non-standard 'Castle' type, 260gr. Cook Welton & Gemmell 20.9.1917. Sold 1922, same name.

GEORGE A WEST Dr 86/13, 1–3pdr. Hired 1915–19.

GEORGE BAKER Dr 96/19. Hired for harbour service 9.1939–40 and 1944–45.

GEORGE BLIGH Tr, 'Mersey' type, 324gr. Cochrane 24.3.1917. Sold 1920, same name. Hired as BDV 9.39–1.46.

GEORGE BONAVENTURE 20–gun ship, 239bm. Hired 1649–54.

GEORGE BORTHWICK Tr, 'Strath' tupe, 216gr. Hall Russell 21.6.1917. Sold 1920, same name. (Served as ANNABELLE in WW.II.)

GEORGE BROWN Tr, 'Mersey' type, 324gr. Cochrane 10.5.1917. Renamed WILLIAM DOGHERTY 1919. Sold 1920, renamed *Rosedale Wyke.*

GEORGE BURTON Tr, 'Strath' type, 203gr. Hall Russell 8.12.1917. Sold 1921, renamed *Bervie Braes.* (BERVIE BRAES in WW.II.)

GEORGE CASTLE Tr, 'Strath' type, 204gr. Williamson 8.1919. Sold 1920, renamed *Lord Tennyson.* (Served as RIVER ANNAN in WW.II.)

GEORGE CLARKE Tr, 'Castle' type, 276gr. J P Rennoldson 2.10.1917. Sold 1922, renamed *Tranio.* (Served as LADY STANLEY in WW.II.)

GEORGE CLINES Tr, 'Strath' type. Hawthorns, leith 1919. Sold 1920.

GEORGE COCHRANE Tr, 'Castle' type, 290gr. Cook Welton & Gemmell 28.6.1918. Sold 1919, same name.

GEORGE CORTON Tr, 'Castle' tupe, 277gr. Cox 1918. Sold 1921, renamed *Zencon.* (Served as NORTHCOATES in WW.II.)

GEORGE COULSTON Tr, non-standard 'Strath' type, 213gr. A Hall 27.4.1918. Sold 1921, renamed DOONIE BRAES. (DOONIE BRAES in WW.II.)

GEORGE COUSINS Tr, 'Castle' type, 276gr. Ailsa 13.6.1919. Sold 1919, same name. Hired as M/S 8.39—7.45.

GEORGE D IRVIN Tr, 194/11, 1—6pdr. Hired 1914—19 and as BDV 5.40. M/S 1.41; store carrier 1944—7.45.

GEORGE DARBY Tr, 'Castle' type, 276gr. Bow McLachlan 1918. Sold 1922, renamed *Dulby.*

GEORGE DIXON (see JOHN CAMPBELL)

GEORGE FENWICK Tr, 'Mersey' tupe, 326gr. Cochrane 1917. Sold 1922, renamed *Cape Otway.*

GEORGE FRENCH Tr, 'Strath' type, 205gr. Murdoch & Murray 1918. Sold 1920, renamed *Arlette.*

GEORGE GREENFIELD Tr, 'Castle' tupe, 280gr. G.Brown 1918. Sold 1922, renamed *Rio Mesa.*

GEORGE GREEVES Tr, 'Castle' tupe, 280gr. G.Brown 1919. Sold 1919, same name.

GEORGE HARRIS Tr, 'Castle' type, 278gr. Hepple 1918. Sold 1919, renamed *Karachi.*

GEORGE HAY Dr 82/12. Hired 1914—19.

GEORGE H HASTIE Tr 229/16, 1—6pdr. Hired 5.1916—19.

GEORGE HODGES Tr, 'Strath' type, 203gr. Hawthorns 1918. Sold 1919, renamed *Hood.*

GEORGE IRELAND Tr, 'Strath' type, 202gr. Rennie Forrest 1918. Renamed TEVIOT 1920. Sold 1923, renamed *Thursby.*

GEORGE LANE Tr, 'Strath' type, 200gr. Scott 1919. Sold 1920, renamed *River Kelvin.*

GEORGE MARTIN Tr, 'Mersey' type. Cochrane. Cancelled 1919.

GEORGE MILBURN Tr, 235gr. Hired 1916. Sunk 12.7.17 by mine off Dunmore.

GEORGE R GRAY Tug, 268gr. Hired 1917. Stranded 27.10.18 on the Garne Islands.

GEORGE ROBB Tr, 217/30, 1—12pdr. Hired as M/S 8.1939,later purchased. Sold 1.46.

GEORGE ROBINSON Tug 95/96. Hired 12.1914—19.

GEORGE R PURDY Tr 212/17. Hired for examination service 1940—10.44.

GEORGE SCOTT Tr 209/16, 1—6pdr. Hired 3.1916—20.

GEORGES Le VERDIER 308/30. French pilot vessel, seized 1940. On examination service 11.40—6.44.

GEORGE STROUD Tr 202/06, 1—6pdr. Hired 1914—19.

GEORGETTE Tr 203/18. Hired as A/P Tr 11.1939. M/S 8.40—5.46.

GEORGE WALKER Dr 65/11. Hired 1915—19.

GEORGE WESTPHAL Tr, 'Mersey' type, 324gr. Cochrane 1917. Sold 1921, renamed *Estelle Yvonne.*

GEORGIANA (see KING GEORGE)

GERARD 194/21, 1—12pdr. Hired (RAN) 4.1941—7.47.

GERBERDINA JOHANNA Tr 255/12. Dutch, served as M/S (Dutch crew) 5.1940—45.

GERMISTON (see UNI IV)

GERTRUDE (ex-*Flying Fish*) Schooner 16, 147bm. Hired 6.1804. Sunk 15.12.1804 after collision with the frigate Aigle in the Channel.

GERVAIS RENTOUL Dr 100/17, 1—3pdr. Hired as flare Dr 11.1939 then A/P to 5.46.

G.E.S Dr 60/09. Hired 1918—19.

G G BAIRD Dr 97/18. Hired for harbour service 1940—45.

GIANG BEE 1,646/08. Hired for examination service 9.9.1939. Lost 2.42 in the Singapore area.

GIBRALTAR 5,832/14. German prize *Schneefels* used as water carrier (RFA) 1.6.1915—8.16. Renamed *Polescar,* transport.

GILBERT EUGENE MFV 53/36. French M/S seized 3.7.1940 at Plymouth. A/P vessell 11.40—9.41; mining tender 1942—44.

GILDEROY Tr 153/99. Hired 1917—19.

GILLIAN Tr 206/19. Hired on examination service 8.1939—8.45.

GILLSTONE Tr, 'Isles' class. Cochrane 19.7.1943. Sold 1946.

GILLYGATE Tr 207/05, 1—12pdr. Hired 1915—19.

GILSAY (see HARRIS)

GILT EDGE Dr 88/16. Hired as M/S 11.1939. Danlayer 1943—8.45.

GIOVANNI GUINTI Tr, 'Castle' type, 277gr. Ailsa 31.5.1918. Sold 1919, renamed *Cymrea.*

GIPPSLAND Ferry 159/08. Hired as tender (RAN) 6.1942, purchased 7.44. Sold 11.46.

GIRAFE 380 tons. French boom vessel seized 1940 at Portsmouth. BDV 9.40—45.

GIRARD Tr 326/18. Purchased as BDV 6.1940. Sold 1.47.

GIRL ANNIE Dr 67/10, 1—3pdr. Hired 1.1915—19.

GIRL CHRISTINA MFV. Hired as HDPC 1940—45.

GIRL EILEEN Dr 82/10, 1—3pdr. Hired 1.1915—19.

GIRL ELLEN Dr 93/14, 2—MG. Hired as A/P vessel 12.1939—3.46.

GIRL ENA Dr 89/07, 1—3pdr. Hired 1915—19 and on harbour service 1941—45.

GIRL ETHEL Dr 88/14, 1—6pdr. Hired 1915—19 and as degaussing vessel 5.40—4.45.

GIRL EVA Dr 76/13. Hired 1915. Sunk 2.10.16 by mine off the Elbow light buoy.

GIRL EVELYN Dr 85/11. Hired for harbour service 7.1915—19.

GIRL GLADYS Dr 110/17, 1—3pdr. Hired 1917—19 and on examination service, 1—3pdr, 11.39—2.46.

GIRL GRACIE Dr 95/13. Hired 1915. Sunk 15.5.17 by Austrian cruisers in the Adriatic.

GIRL HELEN Yt 63/34? Hired as danlayer 12.1939—41.

GIRL HILDA Dr 88/07, 1—3pdr. Hired 1915—19.

GIRL KATHLEEN Dr 95/13, 1—6pdr. Hired 1916—20. (Served as UNITED BOYS in WW.II.)

GIRL LILY Dr 85/11. Hired 4.1915—19.

GIRL LIZZIE Dr 98/18. Hired on harbour service 5.1940—6.46.

GIRL MARGARET Dr 99/14, 1—6pdr. Hired as M/S 1915—19 and as M/S 11.39. Burnt out 1946? and beached in Kalkara Creek, Malta. BU 9.47.

GIRL MARJORIE Dr 92/12, 1—3pdr. Hired 1915—19.

GIRL MAY Dr 81/07, 1—3pdr. Hired 1915—19.

GIRL NANCY Dr 67/10, 1—3pdr. Hired 1916—19 and as M/S 9.40—1.46.

GIRL NORAH Dr 75/11, 1—3pdr. Hired 1915—19.

GIRL PAMELA Dr 93/12. Hired as flare Dr 11.1939. Sunk 29.5.40 in collision off Dunkirk.

GIRL PAT MFV. Hired as M/S 1940—45.

GIRL RHODA Dr 86/08, 1—2½pdr. Hired 1915—19.

GIRL ROSE Dr 86/11. Hired 1915. Sunk 15.5.17 by Austrian cruisers in the Adriatic.

GIRL VIOLET Dr 94/17, 2—MG. Hired on examination service 3.1940—12.45.

GIRL WINIFRED Dr 90/12, 1—3pdr. Hired 1915—19 and as A/P Dr, 2—MG, 12.39—12.45.

GIROFLEE Yt 59/28, 1—6pdr. Hired as A/P Yt 15.9.1939. Purchased 1941. Examination service 1941; training vessel 6.43; laid up 8.45. Sold 1946.

GIVENCHY Tr, 'Castle' type (RCN). Vickers, Montreal 1918. Sold 22.9.52 to BU in the USA.

GLACIER Admiralty wood Dr, 96gr. Forbes, Sandhaven 1918. Sold 1921, renamed *Girl Joey*.

GLACIER (ex-*Magnolia*) Tr 260/09. Hired as A/P Tr 5.1940—6.44.

GLADSTONE Tug 214/16. Hired 31.8.1916—16.12.18.

GLADYS Dr 75/06. Hired for harbour service 6.1915—19.

GLADYS Tr 286/17. Hired as BDV 11.1939—4.46.

GLADYS & ROSE Dr 72/08. Hired 1915—19.

GLADYS MAY Dr 88/07. Hired 1914—19.

GLALA Yt 51/20. Hired as HDPC 11.1939. Purchased as hospital tender 5.42; fire service 10.43. Sold 1946.

GLAMIS CASTLE Tr 204/02, 1—12pdr. Hired 1915—19.

GLARE Admiralty steel Dr. Forbes, Sandhaven. Cancelled 1919.
GLATIAN Tr 220/13, 1–6pdr. Hired 1914–19 and as M/S, 1–6pdr,
11.39–45.
GLEAM Admiralty wood Dr, 92gr. Forbes, Findochty 1918. Sold 1921,
same name.
GLEAM MFV 57/22. Hired for harbour service 1941. Sunk 15.6.44 in
collision in the Clyde.
GLEAM of HOPE Dr 72/11, 1–3pdr. Hired 1915–19.
GLEAM ON Dr 100/19, 1–6pdr. Hired as M/S 12.1939–12.45.
GLEANER Tr 131/96. Hired 1915–16.
GLEANER of the SEA Dr 91/12. Hired 1915. Sunk 27.10.16 by German
destroyers in the Dover Straits.

'Glen' class harbour tugs (RCN), 90gr. 21? built in Canada 1944–45:
GLENADA, GLENBRAE, GLENCOVE, GLENEAGLE, GLENELLA,
GLENELM, GLENFIELD, GLENHOLM, GLENKEEN, GLENMONT,
GLENMOUNT, GLENORA, GLENVALLEY, GLENWOOD all sold
1946–48.
GLENBROOK, GLENDEVON, GLENDON, GLENDYNE, GLENEVIS,
GLENLIVIT, GLENSIDE all retained in service to 1960 or later.

GLEN Aux schooner, 1–12pdr. 1–3pdr. Commissioned as decoy ship
5.4.1917–17. (Also operated as ATHOS and SYDNEY.)
GLEN Armament lighter 130 tons. In service 1926. Sunk 11.40 by mine
in the Firth of Forth.
GLEN AFTON Dr 72/06, 1–3pdr. Hired 1915–19.
GLEN ALBYN Dr 82/09, 1–3pdr. Hired 12.1914–19 and as M/D 12.39.
Sunk 23.12.39 by mine in Loch Ewe.
GLEN AVON Paddle 509/12, 1–12pdr, 1–6pdr. Hired as M/S 4.11.1914–
5.7.19 and as M/S, 1–12pdr, 4–20mm, 15.9.39. A/A ship 5.42. Foundered
2.9.44 in a gale in Seine Bay.
GLEN BERVIE Tr 224/15, 1–10pdr. Hired 1916–19.
GLEN BOYNE Tr 224/15, 1–6pdr. Hired 1915. Sunk 1.19 by mine.
GLENCLOVA Tug 119/10. In service (RCN) 1942–45.
GLEN CORRAN Dr 86/08, 1–3pdr. Hired 1915–20.
GLEN COVA Tr 161/94. Hired 1917–19.
GLENCROSS (ex-*Glen Rosa*) Paddle 306/93, 1–12pdr. Hired as M/S
12.6.1917–12.9.19.
GLENDALE (Q.23) MFV 35/40. (see SPEEDWELL II)
GLENDALE V M/S training vessel (RCN) 1942–45.
GLENEARN Dr 79/09. Hired on harbour service 3.1915–18.
GLENEARN 9,784/38. Hired as store carrier 10.1939. Landing Ship
1942. Returned 8.46.

GLEN ESK Tr 226/07, 1–6pdr. Hired 1914–19.

GLENFOYLE 1,690/13. Decoy ship, sunk 18.9.1917 by 'U.43' in the Atlantic, while operating as STONECROP.

GLENGARRY Dr 64/00. Hired 1915–19.

GLEN GOWER Paddle 553/22, 1–12pdr. Hired as M/S 15,9,1939. Renamed GLENMORE 1.42; A/A ship 7.42; accommodation ship 1.45– 6.45.

GLENGYLE 9,919/39. Hired as store carrier 1939. Landing ship 1942. Returned 7.46.

GLENGYNACK Dr 96/07. Hired 1916–19.

GLEN HEATHER Dr 95/13, 1–6pdr. Hired 1915–19 and as M/S 11.39– 11.45.

GLEN KIDSTON Tr 360/30, 1–12pdr. Hired as M/S 8.1939. A/P Tr 6.40; M/S 1941–7.45.

GLENMORE 1,656/82. Hired as fleet auxiliary 1916; later purchased. Sold 29.1.20.

GLENMORE (see GLEN GOWER)

GLENOGIL Tr 220/02. Hired as BDV 1914–19.

GLENOGIL Dr 95/94. On harbour service 1919.

GLEN PROSEN Tr 224/07. Hired 1914. Sunk 3.11.16 by mine off the Cross Sands light vessel. (GLEN PROSEEN in some lists.)

GLENROY Tr 137/95, 1–3pdr. Hired 1916–19.

GLENROY 9,809/38. Hired as store carrier 21.10.1939. Landing ship 1942. Returned 8.46.

GLEN SANNOX Paddle M/S. Hired and returned 1914.

GLEN STRATHALLAN Yt 356/28, 1–12pdr. Hired as A/S Yt 9.1939– 45.

GLENTILT Dr 61/00. Hired 1915; GLENEALY 6.18–19.

GLEN USK Paddle 524/14, 1–12pdr, 2–6pdr. Hired as M/S 28.1.1915– 5.9.19 and as M/S, 1–12pdr, 4–20mm, 16.9.39. A/A ship 5.42; accommodation ship 3.45–10.45.

GLINT Admiralty wood Dr, 95gr. Forbes, Sandhaven 1919. Sold 1921, renamed *Prospects Ahead*. (PROSPECTS AHEAD in WW.II.)

GLITTER Admiralty steel Dr, 96gr. A Hall 1918. Renamed RALEIGH, base ship 1939. Sold 1946, renamed *Ocean Raleigh*.

GLOAMING Admiralty wood Dr, 94gr. Forbes, Fraserburgh 1919. Stranded 3.21 and salved. Sold 1922, renamed *Beatrice Eves.* Hired as GLOAMIN, M/S, 12.39–3.45.

GLOAMING MFV 21net/28. Hired 24.11.1939. Sunk 20.3.41 by mine off the Humber.

GLOBE I Wh 218/25. Norwegian, hired as M/S 1941. Renamed DAYLIGHT 6.42. Returned 1945.

GLOBE II Wh 206/25. Norwegian, hired as M/S 4.1941. Renamed FLASH 6.42. Returned 11.45.

GLOBE V Wh 249/36. Norwegian, hired as M/S 4.1941. Renamed
KARMOY (Norwegian crew) 1942. Renamed FIERY CROSS (RN) 8.44.
Returned 1.47.

GLOBE VI Wh 249/35. Norwegian, hired as M/S 4.1941. Renamed
MAALOY (Norwegian crew) 1942. Sunk 27.3.44 by U-boat off Ceylon.

GLOBE VIII Wh 297/36. Norwegian, hired as M/S 4.1941. Renamed
HINNOY (Norwegian crew) 1942. Returned 1.46.

GLORIA Tr 187/07, 1–6pdr. Hired as M/S 1914–19 and as BBV 2.40–
9.44.

GLORIA II Tr 264/07, 1–6pdr. Hired 1916–19.

GLORY Cutter 4, 58bm. Hired 1804–05.

GLOSS Admiralty steel Dr, 96gr. Colby 1919. Sold 1919, same name.

GLOUCESTERSHIRE 8,124/10. Hired as AMC 12.1915–7.19.

GLOW Admiralty steel Dr, 96gr. A Hall 1918. Sold 1919, same name.
Hired as M/S 12.1939–11.45.

G.M Tr 225/10. Hired 1915–19.

G.M.H Dr 88/11. Hired 1915–19.

GO AHEAD Dr 100/19. Hired as M/S 11.1939. Sunk 18.11.40 in
collision off Sheerness.

GOATFELL (ex-*Caledonia*) Paddle 624/34, 1–12pdr, Hired as M/S
11.1939. A/A ship, 1–12pdr, 8–20mm, 6.41; accommodation ship 5.44;
A/A ship 12.44. Returned 5.46.

GOBO (see GAELIC)

GOELAND II Tr 245/15, 1–6pdr. Hired 1915–19.

GOEREE (see DOLFIJN)

GOISSA Yt 1,023/93, 2–12pdr, 1–6pdr. Hired as A/P Yt 19.2.1916.
Sunk 15.11.18 by mine in the Dardanelles.

GOLDAXE Tr, 191gr, 130 x 23½ ft, 1–12pdr. Smiths Dk 1.6.1916.
Russian T.13 seized in the White Sea and commissioned 8.18. Renamed
GARRY 10.20. Sold 1946, same name.

GOLDBELL Cstr 178/32. Hired as cable ship 9.1943–44.

GOLDCREST (ex-*Swift*) Cstr 155/04. Hired as store carrier (RFA)
4.1918–19.

GOLDDRIFT Cstr 178/32. Hired as cable ship 9.1943–44.

GOLDEN CHANCE Dr 85/14, 1–3pdr. Hired as M/S 1915–19 and as
FAA safety vessel 1940–1.46.

GOLDEN CROWN Tug 184/96. Purchased for DY service 1917. Sold
6.19 at the Cape.

GOLDEN DAWN Dr 80/13, 1–3pdr. Hired 1915–19 and on harbour
service 2.40. Lost 4.4.40 at Ardrossan.

GOLDEN DAWN Dr 85/14. Hired on harbour service 1941–3.46.

GOLDEN EAGLE 32–gun ship. Hired 1664–66.

GOLDEN EAGLE Paddle 793/09. Hired as fleet auxiliary 6.9.1918.
Conversion to M/L not completed 11.18. Returned 3.12.18. Hired as
A/A ship, 1–3in, 9–MG, 1.40. Accommodation ship 1.45. Returned 6.45.

GOLDEN EFFORT Dr 86/14, 1–6pdr. Purchased 1914. Sold 1921.
Hired as M/S 12.39. Sunk 23.9.43 by unknown cause in the Clyde.
GOLDEN EMBLEM Dr 95/18, 1–6pdr. Hired as A/P Dr 1.1940–12.45.
GOLDEN EYE DY mooring vessel 950 tons, 168 x 36½ ft. Brooke
Marine 31.3.1966.
GOLDEN FEATHER Dr 88/13, 1–3pdr. Hired 1915–19.
GOLDEN GAIN Dr 84/11. Hired 1914–19.
GOLDEN GIFT Dr 89/10, 1–3pdr. Hired 1914–19 and as flare Dr, 1–3pd
11.39. Harbour service 1941.Sunk 6.4.43 in collision in Oban Bay.
GOLDEN GLEAM Tr 191/95. Hired 1917–19.
GOLDEN GLEAM Yt 52/38. Hired as HDPC 10.1939–42.
GOLDEN HARP Dr 94/07. Hired 12.1914–19.
GOLDEN HARVEST Dr 88/14, 1–3pdr. Hired 1914–19 and as M/S
9.39–6.46.
GOLDEN HIND Yt 144/31. Hired as BBV 14.9.1940. Purchased 1.42.
Laid up 11.44 and sold 1946.
GOLDEN LILY MFV 57/12. Hired for examination service 18.7.1940.
Laid up 1943.
GOLDEN LINE Dr 99/19. Hired on harbour service 1941–1.46.
GOLDEN MILLER Dr 83/10, 1–3pdr. Hired as A/P Dr 11.1939–9.45.
GOLDEN NEWS Dr 95/14. Hired 1915–19 and as M/S 11.39–3.46.
GOLDEN RAY Dr 79/14, 1–3pdr. Hired 1915–19.
GOLDEN RING Dr 83/10, 1–6pdr. Hired 1915–19.
GOLDEN RULE Dr 65/05, 1–3pdr. Hired 1915–19.
GOLDEN SHEAF Dr 95/16. Hired 1916–19 and on harbour service
1941–6.45.
GOLDEN SPUR Dr 57/08. Hired 1915–19.
GOLDEN STRAND Dr 69/11, 1–3pdr. Hired 1915–19.
GOLDEN SUNBEAM Dr 84/20, 1–3pdr. Hired as flare Dr 11.1939.
Sunk 19.8.43 in collision off Dungeness.
GOLDEN SUNRAY Dr 94/06. Hired 2.1915–19.
GOLDEN SUNSET Dr 85/13, 1–6pdr. Hired 1915. Sunk 4.1.18 in
collision off the Shambles light vessel.
GOLDEN THYME MFV 48net. Hired as HDPC 1.1940–7.45.
GOLDEN VIEW Dr 96/18. Hired as M/S 10.1939–3.46.
GOLDEN WEST Dr 88/13, 1–3pdr. Hired 1915–19 and for harbour
service 10.40–6.45.
GOLDEN WEST MFV. Hired as degaussing vessel 10.1940. Foundered
15.1.45 in Aberdeen harbour.
GOLDFINCH (ex-*Antwerp 33*) Belgian tug hired as M/L 6.40. Renamed
GREENFINCH 1943. Returned 2.4.46.
GOLD RANGER Oiler (RFA), 3,300gr, 339½ x 48 ft. Caledon 12.3.1941.
GOLDSEEKER 206/00. Scottish Fishery Board vessel hired for examination
service 8.1914–19.

GOLIATH Tug 354/21, 3—MG. Belgian, hired as rescue tug 1940—6.45.

GOLIATH Tug. Hired in the E.Indies 1941—43.

GOMBROON (see ADRIA)

GONDIA Tug 200/27. Hired for harbour service 1940—46.

GONDOLIER Paddle 250/66. Purchased 1.1940. Sunk 3.40 as blockship.

GONZALO Tr 173/96, 1—6pdr. Hired 1915—19.

GOOD DESIGN 14—gun vessel. Hired 1797—1802.

GOOD DESIGN II Dr 79/10. Hired 1916—19.

GOOD FRIEND Dr 88/08. Hired 1915—19.

GOOD HOPE II Tr 256/14, 1—12pdr. Purchased 1914. Sold 1921.

GOOD HOPE III Dr 85/07, 1—3pdr. Hired 1915—19.

GOOD HOPE IV Dr 63/05, 1—3pdr. Hired 1915—18.

GOOD HOPE V Dr 63/02. Hired 1917—19.

GOOD LUCK Tr 294/12, 1—6pdr. Hired 1915—19.

GOOD TIDINGS Dr 98/07, 1—3pdr. Hired 1915—19.

GOODWILL DY craft, 74bm, 52 x 19 ft. Sheerness DY 1706. Fate unknown.

GOODWILL DY lighter, 115bm, 64 x 20½ ft. Chatham 1791. Fate unknown.

GOODWILL DY lighter. In service 1824. BU completed 20.8.1858.

GOODWILL MFV 43/06. Hired as A/P vessel 1.1940. Examination service 1942—43.

GOODWIN 1,570/17, 1—12pdr. Hired as guardship 1.9.1939. A/A ship 1941; convoy rescue ship 6.43—4.46.

GOOLE No 6 Tug 108/85. Hired 1917—19.

GOOLE No 7 Tug. Hired 4.1917—19.

GOOLE No 10 Tug 169/96. Hired 12.1914—19.

GOOLGWAI Tr 271/19. Hired as M/S (RAN) 10.1939—46.

GOONAMBEE Tr 222/19. Hired as M/S (RAN) 7.1940—45.

GOORANGAI Tr 223/19. Hired as M/S (RAN) 10.1939. Sunk 20.11.40 in collision with *Duntroon* off Port Phillip.

GOOSANDER Tr 238/08, 1—6pdr. Hired 1914—19 and as A/P 11.39—40. Purchased as fuel carrier 2.43. Sold 2.46.

GOPHER Tug 198/10. Hired in WW.I.

GORRIGAN Tr, 'Isles' class. Ardrossan DY Co 30.12.1943. Arrived 10.57 at Charlestown to BU.

GORSE Dr 99/11, 1—3pdr. Hired 1914—19 and as HDPC 12.39—11.45.

GOS I Wh 274/27. Norwegian, hired as training vessel MOSS (Norwegian crew) 1941. A/P Wh 1943—45.

GOS 2 Wh 247/28. Norwegian, hired as M/S 11.1940. Renamed ATMOSPHERE 9.41. Returned 12.45.

GOS 3 Wh 247/28. Norwegian, hired as M/S 11.1940. Renamed BILLOW 9 41. Returned 1945.

GOS 4 Wh 217/28. Norwegian, hired as M/S 11.1940. Renamed BLIZZARD 1940. Returned 6.45.

GOS 6 Wh 264/35. Norwegian, hired as M/S 1941. Renamed BOREALIS 9.41. Returned 10.45.

GOS 7 Wh 264/35. Norwegian, hired as M/S 11.1940. Renamed CALM 9.41. Returned 1945.

GOS 8 Wh 351/36. Norwegian, hired as A/S Wh 1941. Renamed BODO (Norwegian crew) 1941. Sunk 4.1.43 by mine off the east coast of Scotland.

GOS 9 Wh 366/37. Norwegian, hired as A/S Wh 1941. Renamed NARVIK (Norwegian crew) 1941. Returned 1945.

GOSFORTH 1,077/98. Hired as store carrier (RFA) 3.2.1917–3.11.19.

GOSHAWK II Tr 208/00, 1–6pdr. Hired 1914–19.

GOTH Tr 394/25, 1–12pdr. Purchased as M/S 8.1939. Sold 11.45.

GOULDING (ex-*R L Goulding*) Wh 224/21. Commissioned as M/S (SAN) 11.6.1940. Returned 1946.

GOUMIER Cstr 1,058/20. French A/P vessel seized 3.7.1940 at Falmouth. Ammo. store 7.40–45.

GOURKO 1,975/11. Purchased as canteen ship 7.8.1914. Sold 1919. Purchased as blockship 1940. Sunk 4.6.40 by mine off Dunkirk.

GOWAN Tr 173/05, 1–12pdr. Hired 1915–19.

GOWAN II Dr 97/07, 1–3pdr. Hired 7.1915–19.

GOWAN III Dr 84/07, 1–3pdr. Hired 1915–19 and as GOWAN, A/P Dr 12.39–4.45.

GOWAN IV Dr 86/06. Hired 1917–19.

GOWAN BANK Dr 78/10, 1–3pdr. Hired 1915–19.

GOWAN BRAE Dr 82/06. Hired 1915–20.

GOWAN CRAIG Dr 85/15, 1–3pdr. Hired 1915–19 and as M/S 12.39–6.46.

GOWAN HILL Dr 96/20. Hired on harbour service 8.1939. Sunk 7.5.41 by air attack at Greenock.

GOWAN LEA Dr 84/14, 1–57mm. Hired 1914–20.

GOZO Tr 172/02, 1–6pdr. Hired as M/S 1914–19.

GRAAF van VLAANDEREN Tr 375/25. Belgian, hired as BDV 9.1940–4.45. (Spelt GRAFF van VLANDEREN in navy lists.)

GRACE Cutter 10. Hired 1793–1801.

GRACE WETHERLEY Tr 268/17, 1–6pdr. Hired 1917–19.

GRACIE Dr 83/07. Hired 1915. Sunk 10.2.17 in collision off the Tongue light vessel.

GRACIE FIELDS Paddle 393/36. Hired as M/S 10.1939. Sunk 29.5.40 by air attack off Dunkirk.

GRACKLE Tr 191/15, 1–6pdr. Hired 1915–19.

GRAEMSAY Tr, 'Isles' class. Ardrossan DY Co 3.8.1942. Wreck dispersal 2.46; oil-tank cleaning vessel 1957.

GRAIN Tr, 'Isles' class. Cochrane 17.8.1943. To Italian navy 16.3.46.
GRAMPIAN Tr 409/30, 1–12pdr. Hired as M/S 8.1939–3.46.
GRAND DUKE Tr 327/15, 1–12pdr. Hired 1915–19.
GRANGE (ex-*AS.37*) Tug 125/80. Transferred 31.1.1915 from War Dept.
Sold 3.23.
GRANGEMOUTH 1,560/98, 2–12pdr. Hired as ABS 5.1.1915–1.4.19.
GRANITE CITY Tug 113/83. Hired 4 1918–19.
GRANSHA 1,192/01. Hired as store carrier (RFA) 16.7.1915–21.3.19.
GRANT HAY Dr 77/11. Hired 9.1914–5.15.
GRANTON N.B Tr 180/12, 1–6pdr. Hired 1914–19.
GRANUWEAL Tr 174/09, 1–6pdr. Hired 1914–19.
GRAPESHOT Armament tug, 57gr. 106tons. Philip, Dartmouth 21.7.1945.
GRAPPLER DY paddle tug 690 tons, 144 x 27½ ft. Chatham DY
4.9.1908. Arrived 20.5.57 Dover Ind Ltd to BU.
GRASMERE (see WASTWATER)
GRASSHOLM Tr, 'Isles' class. Lewis 20.4.1943. Sold 1946, same name.
GRATEFUL Dr 107/07. Hired 1915. Wrecked 25.3.16 off Tor Head.
GRATEFUL Hired vessel in service as HDPC 1.1940–3.46.
GRATITUDE Dr 60/02, 1–3pdr. Hired 1915–19.
GRATITUDE MFV. Hired on harbour service 1942–45.
GRAYLING A/S Tr 650 tons, 146 x 25 ft, 1–4in, 3–20mm. Cochrane
4.3.1942. Sold 1946, renamed *Barry Castle*.
GRAY RANGER Oiler (RFA), 3,313gr, 339½ x 48 ft. Caledon 27.5.1941.
Sunk 22.9.42 by U-boat in the Arctic.
GREAT ADMIRAL Tr 284/08. Hired 1917–19 and as A/P Tr 5.40–6.45.
GREATAXE Tr 181/99, 1–6pdr. Russian T.6 (ex-*Wostock*) seized 9.1918
in the White Sea. Sold 1920, renamed *Roslin*.
GREAT EMPEROR Tug 171/09. Hired 13.7.1917. To War Dept 9.12.17.
GREAT HEART Dr 78gr. Hired 1915. Sunk 24.9.15 by unknown cause
off Dover.
GREBE Tr 204/07. Hired 1917–19.
GRECIAN Tr 119/96. Hired 1915.
GRECIAN EMPIRE Tr 195/99, 1–12pdr. Hired 1915–19.
GRECIAN PRINCE Tr 126/99. Hired 1918–19.
GREEK FIRE Admiralty wood Dr, 94gr. Forbes, Fraserburgh 1919. Sold
1919, same name.
GREENFINCH (see GOLDFINCH and LAMA)
GREENFLY (ex-*Quantock*) Tr 441/36, 1–4in. Purchased as A/S Tr
9.1939. Sold 1945, reverted to *Quantock*.
GREEN HOWARD Tr 349/27, 1–12pdr. Hired as M/D 8.1939–3.46.
GREENOL (ex-*Hopper No 7*) 869/07. Hired as oiler (RFA) 1916–20.
GREEN PASTURES Dr, 1–6pdr. Hired 1917–19.
GREEN PASTURES Dr 97/19. Hired as M/S 12.1939. Tender 1943–11.45.

GREEN RANGER Oiler (RFA), 3,300gr, 339½ x 48 ft. Caledon 21.8.1941 Wrecked in tow 17.11.62 near Hartland Point.

GREEN SEA Admiralty steel Dr, 95gr. Colby 1919. Sold 1919, renamed *Gladys & Violet.*

GREGNESS Tr 240/17, 1–6pdr. Hired 1917–19.

GREGORY Tr 355/30, 1–12pdr. Hired as A/P Tr 8.1939. M/S 1941–7.45

GRENADA Tr 220/07, 1–6pdr. Hired 1914–19.

GRENADE (ex-*Grenadier*) Paddle 357/85, 2–6pdr. Hired 3.7.1916–23.10

GRENADIER Tr, 1–6pdr. Hired 1914–19.

GRENADIER A/S Tr 750 tons, 175 x 30 ft, 1–4in, 4–20mm. Cook Welton & Gemmell 26.9.1942. Sold 4.46, renamed *Isernia.*

GRESILLONS MFV 54/11. French M/S seized 1940. On examination service 9.40; harbour service 1944–45.

GRETA Yt 292/98, 1–6pdr. Hired as A/P Yt 8.10.1914–3.19.

GRETA II Tr 273/06, 1–6pdr. Hired as M/S 1914–19.

GRETA III Tr 168/99. Hired 1914–19.

GREY DAWN Dr 84/13. Hired 1914–19.

GREY FOX, GREY GOOSE,GREY OWL, GREY SEAL, GREY SHARK, GREY WOLF (see under SGB, steam gunboats).

GREYHOUND Cutter 12. Hired 1783.

GREYHOUND Cutter 12, 115bm. Hired 1795–99.

GREYHOUND Paddle 556/95, 2–6pdr. Hired as M/S 1.10.1915–14.5.19.

GREY MIST Yt 197/20. Hired as danlayer 11.1939 and later purchased. Target towing 1943–45. Sold 1947.

GREY SEA Admiralty steel Dr, 98gr. Brooke 1918. Sold 1919, same name.

GREY SKY Admiralty wood Dr, 96gr. Forbes, Sandhaven 1920. Sold 1920, same name. (Served as STAR of BUCHAN in WW.II.)

GRIANAIG Yt 439/04. Hired as A/P Yt 3.1916. Hospital ship 1916. Returned 1919.

GRIBB (see HEKTOR 9)

GRIFFIN 200-ton ship hired for the Armada action.

GRIFFIN Cutter 6, 71bm, 6–3pdr. Hired 1794–12.1805.

GRIFFIN Tr 183/03. Hired 1914–19.

GRIFFITH GRIFFITH Tr, 'Castle' type, 296gr. Cook Welton & Gemmell 27.8.1918. Sold 1920, renamed *Kilindini.*

GRILSE A/S Tr 670 tons, 146 x 25 ft, 1–4in, 3–20mm. Cochrane 6.4.1943. Sold 6.46.

GRIMSBY Tr 153/96, 1–6pdr. Hired 1914–18.

GRIMSBY TOWN Tr 422/34. Hired as A/S Tr 8.1939–11.45.

GRIMSTAD (see KOS XV)

GRIMWOOD (ex-*S.H Grimwood*) Wh 219/24, 1–12pdr. Hired as M/S (SAN) 5.1940–3.46.

GRINDER Wood paddle tug, 332bm, 505 tons, 120 x 25 ft. White, Cowes 21.3.1868. Sold 28.10.1919. Multilocular S.Bkg Co.

GRINDER DY tug, circa 300 tons, 120 x 24½ ft. Hong Kong. Ordered 31.8.1941 and lost on stocks at the fall of Hong Kong. Launched by Japanese 5.5.43 as NAGASHIMA. Fate unknown.

GRINDER DY paddle tug 710 tons, 145 x 30 ft. Simons 6.5.1958.

GRIPER Rescue tug 700 tons, 157 x 35 ft, 1–3in. Cochrane 16.5.1942. Sold 12.46 Singapore Harbour Board.

GRIPER DY paddle tug 710 tons, 145 x 30 ft. Simons 6.3.1958.

GRIVE 2,037/05. Hired as store carrier (RFA) 5.8.1914. ABS, 2–4.7in, 24.2.16. Torpedoed 8.12.17 and foundered 24.12.17 in the North Sea.

GRIVE (see NARCISSUS)

GRIZZLY (ex-*Machigonne*) Yt 216/09. Commissioned as A/P Yt (RCN) 17.7.1941. Paid off 30.12.44.

GROENLAND Tr 1,179/30. French A/P vessel seized 3.7.1940 at Plymouth. Laid up to 30.3.41, then to MWT.

GRONINGEN Cstr 988/02. Hired as canteen ship 5.9.1914–16.11.14.

GROSBEAK Tr 192/10, 1–6pdr. Hired 1914–19.

GROSMONT CASTLE Tr 276/17. Hired as M/S 2.1940–2.46.

GROUNDSWELL Admiralty steel Dr, 96gr. Ouse SB 17.5.1919. Sold 1919, completed as *Elie Ness.* (Served as TRUSTY STAR in WW.II.)

GROUSE Tr 167/97, 1–6pdr. Hired 1914–19.

GROVE PLACE Tug 36/19. Hired as BBV tug 1942 and purchased 17.5.43. Sold 1945.

GROWLER Rescue tug 1,118 tons, 190 x 38½ ft, 1–3in, 2–20mm. Robb, Leith 10.9.1942. On loan as *Caroline Moller* 4.47; renamed *Castle Peak* 1952; GROWLER 1957; on loan as *Welshman* 3.58–64; renamed CYCLONE 1964.

GRUINARD Tr, 'Isles' class. Crown 20.11.1942. Sold 6.46, renamed *President F.D.Roosevelt.* (Lent Portuguese navy 10.43–9.44 as P.7.)

GRUNA (see EARRAID)

GRYME 126gr. Hired as degaussing vessel (RCN) 12.1942–46.

G.S.L Dr 85/12. Hired 1915–19.

G.S.P Dr. Hired 1917? Sunk 2.2.17 in collision off the Owers.

GUARDSMAN Tug 102/05. Hired as DY tug 12.1915–19 and 19.8.39. Sunk 15.11.40 by mine off the North Foreland.

GUARDSMAN A/S Tr 750 tons, 175 x 30 ft, 1–4in, 4–20mm. Cook Welton & Gemmell 7.6.1944. Sold 1946, renamed *Thuringia.*

GUAVA (ex-*British Columbia*) Tr 134/35, 1–6pdr, 1–MG. Purchased as A/S Tr 1939. Sold 1945, reverted to *British Columbia.*

GUEDEL Cstr 233/30. French M/S seized 3.7.1940 at Falmouth. Laid up to 1942, then to MWT.

GUELDER ROSE Yt. Hired as danlayer 12.1939–45.

GUERDON Dr 89/08, 1–3pdr. Hired 1914–19.

GUIANA Tug 166/85. Hired as DY tug 7.11.1914. Sunk 29.1.18 in collision off the east coast.

GUIDE ME Dr 77/03, 1–3pdr. Hired 12.1914–19.

GUIDE ME II Dr 100/07. Hired 1915. Sunk 29.8.18 in collision off the Muglins.

GUIDE ME III Dr 87/07. Hired 1915–19.

GUIDE ME IV Dr 60/05. Hired 1916–19.

GUIDE ON Dr 91/11, 1–3pdr. Hired 1918–19 and as M/S, 2–MG, 11.39–2.46.

GUIDE US Dr 93/08. Hired as blockship 1941. Salvage vessel 1942 and to MWT.

GUIDO GEZELLE MFV 86/32. Belgian hired as BBV 29.5.1940–11.46. (spelt GUIDE GAZELLE in some lists)

GUIDING LIGHT Dr 99/11. Hired as HDPC 12.1939–6.45.

GUIDING STAR Dr 93/06, 1–3pdr. Hired 1915–19.

GUILLEMOT Tr 207/00, 1–6pdr. Hired 1914–19.

GULA Dr 81/36. Hired as danlayer 3.1940. A/P Dr 1941–6.45.

GULFOSS Tr 358/29, 1–12pdr. Purchased as M/S 8.1939. Sunk 9.3.41 by mine in the Channel.

GULF STREAM Admiralty steel Dr, 95gr. Colby 1919. Sold 1921, same name. (Served as JENNY IRVIN in WW.II.)

GULL Tr 166/97, 1–3pdr. Hired 1914–19.

GULL Tug 64/29, 1–6pdr. Hired as A/P vessel 1941–45.

GULLAND Tr, 'Isles' class. Cook Welton & Gemmell 5.8.1943. Sold 3.46.

GULLWING (see EGLANTINE)

GULZAR Yt 201/34. Hired as danlayer 11.1939. Sunk 29.7.40 by air attack in Dover harbour.

GUNBAR Cstr 501/11. Commissioned as M/D (RAN) 12.1940. Gate vessel 1943–46.

GUNNER Tr 287gr, 130 x 23 ft, 2–12pdr, 2–6pdr. Purchased 11.12.1914 Smiths Dk 16.1.15. Sold 1920, renamed *Temahani*. (Operated 1917 as decoy ship PLANUDES (Q.31), 3–12pdr, 3–6pdr, 2–TT.)

GUNNER Tr 350/27, 1–12pdr. Hired as M/S 9,1939–2.46.

GURTH Tr 226/05, 1–6pdr. Hired 1915–19.

GUST Admiralty steel Dr, 96gr. A.Hall 1918. Sold 1920, same name. (Served as BURNHAVEN in WW.II.)

GUSTAVE DENIS Dr 184/34. French M/S seized 3.7.1940 at Southampton Renamed BREEZE, A/P Dr 10.41. Returned 3.46.

GVAS 2 Wh 251/26. Norwegian, hired as A/P vessel 6.1940. Laid up damaged 12.44. Returned 6.46.

GWEAL (see BRORERAY)
GWEBARRA Dr 102/03. Hired as tank vessel 1942–45.
GWEEDORE Dr 82/13. Hired 8.1915–19.
GWENLLIAN Tr 220/11, 1–3pdr. Hired as M/S 1914–19 and as A/P
Tr 11.39. M/S 9.40–1.46.
GWMAHO Tr 276/17. Hired as BDV 11.1939–46.
GYPOL (see PEARLEAF)
GYPSY (ex-*Carlotta*) Yt 261gr. Hired as A/P depot 1.2.1941. Sunk
11.5.41 by air attack off the Tower pier.
GYPSY Hired as M/S base ship 1942–46.

HAARLEM Tr 431/38. Dutch, hired as A/S Tr 6.1940–5.46.
HAIDEE Yt 67/28. Hired (RCN) 1944–45.
HAIDERI 1,510/20. Hired as A/P vessel (RIN) 9.1939. Wrecked 2.4.43.
HAILSTORM Admiralty wood Dr, 98gr. Richards, Lowestoft 1918.
Sold 1920, same name. (Served as GIRL LIZZIE in WW.II.)
HAILSTORM (see KOS XII)
HAITAN 3,554/09. Hired as base ship 18.11.1941–6.46.
HALBERD Armament store carrier, 180gr? Bailey, Hong Kong. Ordered
30.9.1940. Fate unknown.
HALCYON II Tr 190/98. Hired 1917–19.
HALF MOON Dr 95/11, 1–6pdr. Hired 1916–19.
HALIFAX Tr 165/97. Hired 1917–19.
HALLGARTH (C.62) DY tug 175 tons, 73 x 16 ft. Purchased 3.1900.
Listed to 1943.
HALLMARK Dr 83/06. Hired as BBV 3.7.1940. Laid up 1942.
HALO Admiralty steel Dr, 95gr. A.Hall 1918. Sold 1946, same name.
HAMLET Tr 328/06, 1–6pdr. Hired 1914–19.
HAMLET M/S–A/S Tr, 545 tons, 150 x 28 ft, 1–12pdr, 3–20mm.
Cook Welton & Gemmell 24.7.1940. Sold 30.1.47, renamed *Eifonn.*
HAMMOND Tr 452/36, 1–4in. Hired as A/S Tr 8.1939. Sunk 25.4.40
by air attack at Aandalsnes, Norway. Salved and commissioned 2.42 in
German navy.
HAMOAZE DY lighter 4, 111bm, 70 x 19 ft. Plymouth 1702. Sold
11.6.1713.
HAMOAZE DY transport, 158bm, 70 x 23½ ft. Preston 1800. Became
a mortar vessel and BU 1.1843.
HAMOAZE DY lighter. Plymouth DY 17.1.1844. Fate unknown, but
may be the 153-ton vessel existing in 1871.
HAMPDEN (ex-*Southampton*) Tug 227/10. Hired 23.8.1914–19.

HAMPSHIRE Tr 425/34, 1—4in. Purchased as A/S Tr 9.1939. Sold French navy 28.11.39 as La TOULONNAISE.

HAMPTON (ex-*Hampton Ferry*) Ferry 2,839/34. Hired as M/L, 1—4in, 270 mines, 8.1939. To MWT 7.40 as ferry.

HANDMAID (see FRESCO)

HANDMAID (see SALVENTURE)

HANDSOME Dr 84/07. Hired 1915—19 and on harbour service 8.1.40—9.45.

HANDY DY tug 386 tons, 110 x 24 ft. Bow McLachlan 2.3.1915. Sold 6.20, renamed *Antonio Azambuja.*

HANDY Dr 67/03. Hired as boom tender 6.1915; DANDY 4.18—19.

HANDY MFV. Hired as store carrier 2.1944—1.46.

HANNAH Gun-brig. Hired 1798. Captured 25.10.1806 by the Spanish.

HANNAH JOLLIFFE Tug 178/00. Hired 8.1914—19.

HANNARAY Tr, 'Isles' class. Cook Welton & Gemmell 12.2.1944. Sold 1947, renamed *Wodan.*

HANNIBAL 44-gun ship, 500bm. Hired 1652—54.

HANNIBAL 46-gun ship, 450bm. Hired 1693.

HANNIBAL 16-gun vessel. Hired 1803. Wrecked 11.1804 near Sandown, Isle of Wight.

HANS CAPTIVE (see CAPTIVE)

HANTONIA 1,560/11. Hired as landing ship 3.4.1942. Accommodation ship 10.42—7.45.

HAN WO Tug 248/19. Hired as M/S 11.1940 in China. Captured by the Japanese.

HAPPY DAYS Dr 101/14. Hired 1915—19. (Served as DORIENTA in WW.II.)

HAPPY RETURN Cutter 10, 94bm. Hired 5.1804—12.04.

HARBINGER (ex-*Pioneer*) Paddle 241/05. Hired for examination service 6.1940. Training vessel 1941—46.

HARDEN 1,686/12. Hired as mine carrier (RFA) 3.8.1914—8.3.19.

HARD LINES Dr. Hired as BDV 1915—19.

HARLECH CASTLE Tr 275/16, 1—12pdr. Hired 4.1916—19 and as M/S 2.40—7.45.

HARLEQUIN A.ship 16, 185bm. Hired 20.6.1804. Wrecked 7.12.1809 near Seaford.

HARLEQUIN (ex-*Strathmore*) Paddle ferry service vessel 528 tons, 200½ x 24 ft. Purchased 20.3.1908. M/S 5.17; ferry 5.19; accommodation ship 9.42. Wrecked 9.42 on passage Chatham to Clyde; wreck sold 3.43.

HARLOW 1,795/15. Hired as fleet auxiliary 6.1915—18.

HARMATTAN Admiralty steel Dr. A.Hall 1918. Sold 1949.

HARMONY Tug 51/93. Hired 18.12.1917—3.19.

HARMONY (see UNISON)

HARO Tug 215/10. Hired (RCN) 1941—44.

HARPADO Yt 32/20. Hired as HDPC11.1939. Laid up 11.40; returned 1.42.

HARPOON Dr 98/42. Danish *Vestfart* seized and used as training vessel 1.3.1943—12.45.

HARRINGTON Tug 149/03. Hired 10.1914—15.12.14.

HARRINGTON Tug 332/89. Hired 8.1915—30.9.15.

HARRIOT (ex-*Rose*) Cutter 4, 45bm. Hired 5.1804—6.05.

HARRIS (ex-GILSAY renamed 1944) Tr, 'Isles' class. Cook Welton & Gemmell 29.1.44. Sold 24.3.47.

HARRY Dr 60/01, 1—6pdr. Hired 1915—19.

HARRY & LEONARD Dr? In service 1918—19.

HARRY EASTICK Dr 107/26. Hired on harbour service 20.10.40—11.12.45

HARRY MELLING Tr 275/19. Hired as M/S 8.1939—7.45.

HARRY ROSS Tr 183/01. Hired as boom gate vessel in WW.I.

HARSTAD (see KOS XVII)

HART 80—ton vessel. Hired for the Armada action 1588.

HART Brig 10. Hired 1800—01.

HART DY tender (ex-revenue cutter), 80bm, 55 x 19 ft, 2—6pdr. Woolwich DY 12.6.1822. Renamed YC.1 in 1864; DRAKE 17.11.1870. BU completed 6.3.1875 at Chatham.

HARTSIDE 2,740/09. Hired as fleet auxiliary 25.8.1916—2.5.18.

HARTVILLE Tug (RCN). Owen Sound 1944.

HARVEST Dr 69/76. Hired 1917—19.

HARVESTER Dr 95/14, 1—3pdr. Hired 1915—19.

HARVESTER MFV. Hired as A/P vessel 20.6.1940. Renamed RIPPLE 1940. Returned 19.12.41.

HARVEST GLEANER Dr 96/18, 1—MG. Hired as M/S 11.1939. A/P Dr 9.40. Sunk 28.10.40 by air attack off the east coast

HARVEST HOPE Dr 91/11, 1—3pdr. Hired 1914—19 and as A/P Dr 12.39—45.

HARVEST MOON Dr 72/04. Purchased 12.1939. Sunk 9.9.40 as blockship.

HARVEST REAPER Dr 95/25. Hired as M/S 12.1939—11.46.

HASCOSAY Tr, 'Isles' class. Cook Welton & Gemmell 28.3.1944. Sold 1947, renamed *Ypapandi.*

HASHEMI 634/18. Hired as A/P vessel (RIN) 12.1939—43.

HASLEMERE 756/25. Hired as BBV 22.10.1940. Accommodation ship 4.44—6.45.

HASTFEN Dr 77/ —. Hired 1.1915. Sunk 24.9.17 by mine off the Longsands.

HASTINGS CASTLE Dr 73/12. Hired 1914—19.

HASTY Iron paddle tug, 120bm, 140 tons, 90 x 17 ft. Napier, Glasgow 14.8.1867. Sold circa 1885.

HATANO Tr 255/12, 1–6pdr. Hired 1916–19.
HATANO Tr 297/25, 1–12pdr. Hired as M/S 9.1939–5.46.
HATSUSE Tr 295/27, 1–12pdr. Hired as M/S 8.1939–8.45.
HAUG I Wh 212/24. Norwegian, hired as M/S 12.1940–6.46.
HAUITI Cstr 148/11. Hired for examination service (RNZN) 1941 and later purchased. Listed on harbour service 1944–50.
HAUKEN Wh 251/26. Norwegian, hired as A/P vessel 5.1940–3.46.
HAUTAPU M/S Tr (RNZN), 'Castle' type. Stevenson & Cook, Port Chalmers 18.11.1942. Sold 1950 mercantile.
HAV Wh 249/30. Norwegian, hired as M/S 3.1940 and later purchased. To Russian navy 2.42.
HAVDUR, HAVLYN, HAVTOR Norwegian MFVs hired on harbour service 1941–45.
HAWERA Ferry 188/12. Hired as M/S (RNZN) 1942–46.
HAWFINCH Tug 50/15. French *Honfleurais* seized 1940. Minelayer 1940–6.45.
HAWK Cutter 8. Hired 1782–90.
HAWK Cutter 12. Hired 1798–1802.
HAWK Cutter 10, 124bm, 1–12pdr carr. Hired 7.1803–3.4.1805.
HAWK Tr 243/98. Hired 1917. Sunk 17.2.17 by mine in the central Mediterranean.
HAWK (see VIGILANT)
HAWTHORN Dr 93/07, 1–3pdr. Hired 1915–19.
HAWTHORN II Tr 180/02. Hired 1917–19.
HAWTHORN (ex-*Cape Guardafui*) Tr 593/30, 1–4in. Purchased as M/S 10.1935. Sold 7.47, renamed *Havborgin.*
HAWTHORN BANK Dr. Hired as boom tender 2.1940–10.45.
HAWTHORN BUD Dr 81/14. Hired as BDV 7.1915–19.
HAWTHORNDALE Dr 60/09. Hired 1918–19.
HAYBURN WYKE Tr 324/17. Hired as A/P Tr 5.1940. M/S 1941. Sunk 2.1.45 by torpedo, while at anchor off Ostend. (In navy lists as HAYBOUR WYKE.)
HAYLING Tr, 'Isles' class. Cook Welton & Gemmell 17.8.1942. Sold 11.6.46 Portuguese navy as TERCEIRA. (On loan to Portuguese navy 10.43–7.45 as P.3.)
HAZAEL Dr 85/08. Hired for harbour service in WW.i.
HAZAEL MFV 22net/33. Hired for harbour service 9.1939–12.45.
HAZARD 38–ton vessel hired for the Armada campaign.
HAZARD Cutter 6. Hired 1793–1801.
HAZE Admiralty (wood?) Dr. Forbes, Sandhave. Cancelled 1919.
HAZEL 1,241/07, 1–12pdr. Hired as ABS 14.11.1914–17.2.19.
HAZEL M/S Tr 530 tons, 150 x 27½ ft, 1–4in. Robb 27.12.1939. Sold 3.46.

HAZEL BANK Dr 77/08, 1–6pdr. Hired 1914–19.

H.D.M.Ls Motor launches. (See under MLs)

HEART of OAK Gunvessel. Hired 9.1801–12.01.

HEARTSEASE Vessel hired for the Armada campaign.

HEARTY (ex-*Merry Monarch*) Wood paddle tug, 221bm, 346 tons, 112 x 20 ft. Purchased 28.3.1855. BU 1876 at Malta.

HEARTY II Dr 83/07, 1–3pdr. Hired 1915–19.

HEATHBANK Dr 78/08. Hired 11.1914–19.

HEATHER Tr 169/04. Hired 1917–19.

HEATHER BELL Dr 91/04, 1–3pdr. Hired 1915–19.

HEATHER BELLE MFV 48/03. Hired for examination service 24.5.1940. BDV 1942–22.10.45.

HEATHER BLOOM Dr 88/11. Hired 1915–19.

HEATHER COCK Tug 182/03. Hired 2.1918–19.

HEATHER SPRIG Dr 83/13, 1–3pdr. Hired 2.1915–19 and as BBV 4.40. Harbour service 1941–8.46.

HEATHERTON Tug (RCN) 462 tons, 104 x 28 ft. Canadian Bridge Co, Toronto 29.6.1943.

HEATHERY BRAE Dr 90/10, 1–3pdr. Hired 12.1914–19 and as BBV 10.40. Harbour service 1942–44.

HEAT WAVE Admiralty wood Dr, 98gr. Richards 1918. Sold 1921, same name.

HEBBLE 904/91. Hired as ammo. carrier 26.8.1914. Sunk 6.5.17 by mine off Sunderland.

HEBE Storeship 6. Hired 1798–1801.

HEBE Sloop 16, 267bm. Hired 4.1804–30.10.1812.

HEBE Store carrier (RFA) 7,960 tons, 350 x 55 ft. Robb, Leith 7.3.1962.

HECATE Yt 471/03, 2–6pdr. Hired as A/P Yt 15.10.1914–20.3.19.

HECLA Dr 60/96. Hired 1918–19.

HECTOR 4,660/95. Hired as kite-balloon ship 1915–13.1.17.

HECTOR 11,198/23, 8–6in, 2–3in. Hired as AMC 9.1939. Bombed and burnt out 5.4.42 by Japanese aircraft at Colombo.

HECTOR Tug 175/21 (one Admiralty list gives 316/03). Dutch, hired on harbour service 16.10.1939–45.

HEILHORN Ferry 192/08. Norwegian, hired for examination service 8.1940–6.46.

HEKLA Tr 354/29, 1–12pdr. Hired as A/P Tr 5.1940. Renamed LIBERATOR 10.40. M/S 1.42–5.46.

HEKTOR (see HEKTOR 5)

HEKTOR 1 Wh 247/29. Norwegian hired as RONDEVLEI A/S Wh (SAN) 6.1940–7.5.46.

HEKTOR 2 Wh 247/29. Norwegian, hired as SMALVLEI M/S (SAN) 6.1940– 7.5.46.

HEKTOR 3 Wh 233/29. Norwegian, hired as SOETVLEI A/S Wh (SAN) 7.1940–25.6.46.

HEKTOR 4 Wh 234/29. Norwegian, hired as BRAKVLEI M/S (SAN) 7.1940–25.6.46.

HEKTOR 5 Wh 233/29. Norwegian, hired as HEKTOR M/S (SAN) 7.1940–25.6.46.

HEKTOR 6 Wh 315/29. Norwegian, hired as A/S Wh 5.41. Renamed ROODEPOORT (SAN) 30.1.42. M/S to 9.2.46.

HEKTOR 7 Wh 233/29. Norwegian, hired as M/S 20.11.1940–25.11.45.

HEKTOR 9 Wh 280/30. Norwegian, hired as GRIBB' M/S (SAN) 1941–5.4.46.

HEKTOR FRANS Dr 109/38. Belgian, hired as A/P Dr 10.1940–10.45.

HELCIA Tr 230/06, 1–6pdr. Hired 1914–19.

HELEN Yt 35/31. Hired as HDPC 11.1939–44.

HELENA Dr 87/06, 1–3pdr. Hired 1915–19.

HELENA Cstr 182/34. Dutch, hired as BBV 8.1940–8.43.

HELENA Tug 299/07. Hired (RCN) 1943–45.

HELEN ANN Dr 90/15. Hired on harbour service 4.1915–19.

HELENE Yt? Purchased in the W.Indies for examination service 11.1941. Laid up 1944.

HELEN FAUCIT Paddle tug, 45bm. Purchased 3.2.1855. Sold 1855?

HELENORA Dr 88/14. Hired 1914. Sunk 15.5.17 by Austrian cruisers in the Adriatic.

HELEN PEELE Tug 133/01. Hired 10.8.1917–1.19.

HELEN SLATER Dr 102/18. Hired on harbour service 1941–45.

HELEN WEST Dr 96/19. Hired as A/P Dr 1.1940–45.

HELEN WILSON Dr 44gr. Hired 1917? Lost 5.12.17 by fire at Oban.

HELGA Yt 323/08, 1–12pdr, 1–3pdr. Hired as A/P Yt 12.3.1915 and later purchased. Sold 1922 Irish govt, renamed MUIRCHU.

HELGIAN Tr 220/13. Hired 1915. Sunk 6.9.17 by mine in the Aegean.

HELGOLAND Brigantine, 182gr, 1–4pdr. Hired as decoy ship (Q.17) in 1917. (Also operated as BRIG.10.)

HELIER 1 Wh 357/36. Hired as A/S Wh (SAN) 25.10.1940. Renamed STANDERTON 1942. Returned 19.11.46.

HELIER 2 Wh 341/36. Hired as A/S Wh 3.1940–10.45.

HELIOPOLIS Yt 766/03. Purchased as FAA target 23.3.1940. Sold 1946.

HELIOS Tr 201/03. Hired 1917–19.

HELLESPONT Paddle tug 138 tons. Purchased as DY tug 20.4.1878. Sold 12.12.1904.

HELLESPONT DY paddle tug 690 tons, 144 x 27½ ft. Earle, Hull 10.5.1910. Sunk 4.42 by air attack at Malta.

HELLISAY Tr, 'Isles' class. Cochrane 27.3.1944. Sold 6.47, renamed *Elpis*.

HELMSMAN Cstr 458/03. Hired as ammo. carrier (RFA) 26.8.1914—19.
HELP Salvage vessel 950 tons, 150 x 36 ft, 2—20mm. Smiths Dk 5.5.1943.
Sold 1960.
HELPER Paddle tug, 173/73. Hired 1.4.1915. M/S 1.12.17—21.2.19.
HELPFUL DY tank vessel 395 tons. Bow McLachlan 30.9.1902. Sold
1.9.33.
HELPFUL Salvage vessel 300 tons, 95 x 24 ft, 2—MG. Gulfport Co, Pt
Arthur 17.1.1942 on lend-lease. Returned 3.42 to the USN and transferred
French navy 10.44.
HELPMATE Dr 76/12, 1—3pdr. Hired 1914—19.
HELVELLYN (ex-*Juno*) Paddle 642/37. Hired as M/S 28.9.1939. Wrecked
20.3.41 by air attack while fitting as A/A ship in London docks.
HELVETIA Tr 260/17, 1—12pdr. Hired 1917—19 and as A/P Tr, 1—12pdr,
6.40. M/S 4.42—9.46.
HELVIG 2,252/36, 4,600 tons, 1—12pdr, 6—20mm, 224 mines. Danish,
seized 5.1940 and completed as M/L depot ship 4.41. Seaward defence
vessel 1.45. Returned 4.46.
HEMATITE Cstr 722/03. Hired as ammo. carrier (RFA) 9.10.1914—4.19.
HENDON Tug 130/06. Hired 24.6.1915—19.
HENDON Tug 241/24. Hired as rescue tug 31.3.1940—3.7.42.
HENE CASTLE Tr 299/15, 1—6pdr. Hired 1915—19.
HENGIST (ex-DECISION renamed 1941) Rescue tug 700 tons, 142½ x
33 ft, 1—3in, 2—20mm. Cochrane 20.12.41. Sold 1965, renamed *Nisos
Crete.*
HENRIETTE Tr 204/18. Hired as A/P Tr 12.1939. Renamed ARTEGAL,
M/S, 7.40. Returned 3.45.
HENRIETTE Tr 261/06. French M/S seized 7.1940 at Southampton.
Free-French crew 9.40. Sunk 26.12.41 by mine off the Humber.
HENRIETTE MOLLER Tug 478/26. Commissioned as A/P vessel 1.9.1941
at Hong Kong. Fleet tug 1942—45; returned 7.10.46.
HENRIK CONCIENCE (P.6) Dr 90/31, 1—6pdr. Belgian, hired as A/P
Dr (Polish crew) 22.6.1940. Laid up 12.42.
HENRI LOUIS MFV 33/36. French M/S seized 3.7.1940 at Southampton.
Listed to 9.40.
HENRY BATTERSBY Tr, 'Strath' type. Hall Russell. 1919. Sold 1921.
HENRY BUTCHER Tr, 'Strath' type, 203gr. Hall Russell 26.3.1918.
Sold 1919, renamed *River Tay.*
HENRY CHEVALLIER Tr, 'Castle' type, 277gr. Bow McLachlan 1918.
Sold 1922, renamed *Albert.* Served as LIGNY in WW.II.)
HENRY COLBY Tr, 'Strath' type, Hawthorns, Leith 1919. Sold1919.
HENRY CORY Tr, 'Castle' type, 277 gr. Cox 1919. Sold 1919, renamed
Caliban. (CALIBAN in WW.II.)
HENRY CRAMWELL Tr, 'Mersey' type, 330gr. Lobnitz 1918. Sold 1922
Spanish navy, renamed XOUEN.

HENRY FLIGHT Tr, 'Strath' type, 209gr. Abdela Mitchell 1918. Sold 1921, renamed *Yesso*. (YESSO in WW.II.)

HENRY FORD Tr, 'Mersey' type, 324gr. Cochrane 18.10.1917. Sold 1921, renamed *Duperre*. (Was BOADICEA II for a time in 1919.)

HENRY GRATTON Tr, 1–12pdr. Hired as BDV 1915–19.

HENRY HARDING Tr, 'Strath' type, 203gr. Hawthorns 1918. Sold 1919, renamed *Ocean Clipper*.

HENRY JENNINGS Tr, 'Strath' type type, 201gr. Rennie Forrest 1918. Renamed URE 1920. Sold 1922, renamed *Aby*. (Served as MORAY in WW.II.)

HENRY LANCASTER Tr, 'Mersey' type, 326gr. Cochrane 1919. Sold 8.21, same name.

HENRY MARSH Tr, 'Mersey' type, 324gr. Cochrane 1919. Sold 1919, renamed *Springbok*.

HEORTNESSE Tr 198/11. Hired 1915–19.

HEPATICA Yt 92/14. Hired as accommodation ship 21.8.1940. Renamed OUTLAW 1941. To War Dept 2.42.

HERACLES Tug 225/85. Hired 3.1915–19.

HERALD Tug 387/07. Hired 8.9.1914–4.2.19.

HERALD Dr 86/07. Hired 1915–20.

HERCULANEUM DY tug, 201/05, 378 tons, 101 x 22½ ft. Purchased 1908. Sold 1927, renamed *Formby*.

HERCULES 300-ton ship hired for the Armada campaign.

HERCULES 26-gun ship. Hired in 1620.

HERCULES 34-gun ship, 480bm. Hired 1649. Captured 1.12.1652 by the Dutch.

HERCULES II Tr 165/98, 1–6pdr. Hired 1914–19.

HERCULES III Tr 238/06, 1–6pdr. Hired 1914–19.

HERCULES IV Tr 261/03, 1–6pdr. Hired 1915–19.

HERCULES Tr 255/05. Dutch, hired as M/S 6.1940–1.46.

HERDIS MFV 27net/22. Danish, seized 5.1940 and used as BBV until 8.45.

HERGA Yt 75/15. Hired as danlayer 29.9.1939. HDPC 3.40–12.7.40.

HERIOT 1,239/05. Hired as ammo. carrier (RFA) 4.1915–19.

HER MAJESTY Paddle 235/85. Hired as M/S 23.4.1917–24.6.19.

HERMATRICE Decoy ship. Sunk 3.1916 by U-boat off Boulogne.

HERMETRAY Tr, 'Isles' class. Cochrane 11.4.1944. Sold 25.4.47, renamed *Coimbra*.

HERMIA Tr 210/00, 1–6pdr. Hired 1915–19.

HERMIT (see PROGRESS)

HERO Cutter 8, 73bm. Hired 8.1804–2.05.

HERO Cutter, 110bm. Hired 5.1805–11.1811.

HERO Dr 84/06, 1–3pdr. Hired 1914–19.

HERO II Tr 173/06. Hired 1915–19.

HERO Tr 217/06, 1–6pdr. Hired 1915–19. (Served as HEROINE in WW.II.)

HEROIC 2,022/06, 2–12pdr. Hired as ABS 18.11.1914–6.7.20. (Was trooper 7.17–1.18.)

HEROINE Tug 207/09. Hired as rescue tug 5.1917–19.

HEROINE (ex-*Hero*) Tr 217/06. Hired as M/S 6.1940. Fuel carrier 4.44–11.44.

HERON Tr 233/02, 1–6pdr. Hired 1914–19.

HEROS Tug 382/19. Hired as A/S vessel (RAN) 1940. Harbour service 7.41–46.

HERRING A/S Tr 590 tons, 146 x 25 ft, 1–4in, 3–20mm. Cochrane 24.12.1942. Sunk 22.4.43 in collision in the North Sea.

HERRING FISHER Dr 76/08. Hired 1916–19.

HERRING GULL Dr 93/17, 1–6pdr. Hired 1917–19.

HERRING QUEEN Dr 72/11. Hired 1914–19.

HERRING SEARCHER Dr 99/14. Hired 1915–19.

HERRING SEEKER Dr 75/11. Hired 1915–19.

HERSCHELL Tr, 'Isles' class. G T Davie, Lauzon 5.11.1942. Sold 1946.

HERSILIA Yt 454/95, 1–12pdr. Hired as A/P Yt 11.9.1914. Wrecked 6.1.16 near Loch Torridon.

HERTFORDSHIRE Tr 458/36, 1–4in. Hired as A/S Tr 1939–45. (On loan to the USN 3.42–10.42.)

HESPER DY tank vessel 390 tons, 115 x 21 ft. Hong Kong & Wampoa Co 1901. Sold 3.23 in China.

HESPERIA (ex-HESPER renamed 1942) Rescue tug 1,118 tons, 190 x 38½ ft, 1–3in, 2–20mm. Robb, Leith 10.11.1942. Wrecked 9.2.45 on the coast of Libya.

H.E. STROUD Tr 214/15, 1–6pdr. Hired 1915–19.

HEUGH Tr 200/14, 1–6pdr. Hired 1915–19.

H.F.E Dr 58/09. Hired 1915–19.

HIBERNIA Tug 100/04. Hired 1914–19.

HIBERNIA II Tr 216/07, 1–6pdr. Hired 1914–19.

HICKOROL Oiler (RFA) 2,200 tons, 220 x 35 ft. McMillan, Dumbarton 30.11.1917. Sold 1948, renamed *Hemsley II*.

HICKORY M/S Tr 530 tons, 150 x 27½ ft, 1–12pdr. Robb 24.2.1940. Sunk 22.10.40 by mine in the Channel.

HICKORY LAKE Motor M/S (RCN) 255 tons, 126 x 28 ft. Grew Boats 6.11.1944. To Russian navy 15.8.45.

HIEDRA Dr 78/08. Hired 1915–19.

HIGHLANDER Tr 239gr, 480 tons, 118 x 23 ft, 1–6pdr. Smiths Dk 29.4.1915, purchased 14.4.15. Sold 1921, renamed *Fregate II*.

HIGHLAND LASSIE Dr 78/10. Hired 1915–19.

HIGHLAND LEADER Dr 82/12. Hired 1915–19.

HIGH TIDE Admiralty steel Dr, 95gr. Colby 1919. Sold 1921, same name. Became a French M/S, 106gr, and seized 3.7.40 at Southampton. Examination service 9.40. Foundered 30.3.45 off north Wales.

HILARIA Tr 207/98. Hired 1918–19.

HILARY 6,239/08. Hired as AMC 21.11.1914. Sunk 25.5.17 by 'U.88' west of the Shetlands.

HILARY II Dr 78gr. Hired 1915. Sunk 25.3.16 by mine near the Spit buoy.

HILARY 7,403/31, 2–6in, 1–3in. Hired as OBV 16.10.1940–26.7.42. Hired again as landing ship 3.43–3.46.

HILDA Yt 76/95. Hired as accommodation ship 1.9.1939. Renamed TOWER, base ship, 6.40. Reverted to HILDA 8.45 and laid up to 11.45.

HILDA Cstr 250/39. Dutch, hired as BBV 23.11.1940–26.6.43.

HILDA & ERNEST Dr 102/12. Hired 1914–19. (Served as AVAILABLE IN WW.II.)

HILDA COOPER Dr 127/28. Hired for examination service 9.1939. Harbour service 1944–45.

HILDASAY Tr, 'Isles' class. Cook Welton & Gemmell 29.4.1941. Wrecked 21.6.45 near Kilindini.

HILDEBRAND 6,991/11. Hired as AMC 20.11.1914–7.19.

HILDEGARD (see YEHONALA)

HILDINA Tr 276/18. Hired as M/S 8.1939–4.46.

HIMALAYA 6,929/92, 8–4.7in (8–6in, 1–A/C in 1916). Hired as AMC 8.1914, purchased 1916. Sold 4.22.

HINAU M/S Tr (RNZN), composite 'Castle' type. Senior Foundry, Auckland 28.8.1941. Listed to 1951.

HINBA Yt 154/03, 2–MG. Hired as danlayer 3.1.1940. A/P Yt 9.40–43.

HIND Cutter 14. Hired 1794–1806.

HIND Brig 8, 100bm. Hired 6.1803–8.04.

HINIESTA Yt 361/02. Hired as A/S Yt 9.1939 and later purchased. Calibrating Yt 1942. Sold 10.1.46.

HINNOY (see GLOBE VIII)

HIPI 39/09. Hired for harbour service (RNZN) 1942. Purchased 1943. Sold 1958.

HIPPOPOTAMUS (LC.5) Salvage vessel 703gr. Hired 20.2.1917, purchased 9.17. Sold 11.20.

HIRAVATI 580/30 Hired as A/P vessel (RIN) 9.1939–46.

HIRONDELLE Cutter 14. Hired 1801.

HIRONDELLE 1,648/90. Hired as store carrier (RFA) 4.8.1914–24.11.15.

HIRONDELLE 893/25. Hired as store carrier in WW.II.

HIROSE Tr 275/15. Hired 1915. Sunk 29.6.16 by mine off Aldeburgh.

HIRPA Wh 110/11, 1–6pdr. Hired 1914. Wrecked 2.1.18 near Buckie.

HITSOY MFV. Norwegian, hired as TRV 28.10.1943—18.4.45.

H J BULL Wh 569/35. Norwegian, hired as A/P Wh (Norwegian crew) 7.5.1941. Renamed NAMSOS 1942. Returned 1946.

HOAR FROST Admiralty Dr. Forbes, Sandhaven. Cancelled 1919.

HOBART Tr 172/02. Hired as boom gate vessel 1915—19.

HODDER 1,085/10. Hired as cable vessel (RFA) 18.3.1915—22.3.19. Also hired, 1,016gr, 10.40—1.9.42.

HODGEVILLE Tug (RCN). In service 1944—46.

HOLDENE Tr 274/15. Hired 1915. Sunk 2.2.17 by mine off Orfordness.

HOLDFAST DY salvage vessel 783 tons, 125 x 35 ft. Purchased 1915. Sold 3.23 Carriden S Bkg Co.

HOLDFAST (ex-*London*) 1,500/21, 1,699 tons. Hired as guardship 28.8.1939. Cable ship 11.42. Purchased 1946. Sold 1946.

HOLLAND 1,251/19. Danish, seized 5.1940. Sunk 3.6.40 as blockship.

HOLLAND Hired vessel. Listed on special service 6.1940—1.41 and as minelayer in 1942.

HOLLY Dr 90/07, 1—3pdr. Hired 1914—19.

HOLLY II Dr 79/04, 1—3pdr. Hired 1915—19.

HOLLY III Dr 93/07, 1—3pdr. Hired 1915. Sunk 11.5.18 by mine off Aldeburgh.

HOLLY (ex-*Kingston Coral*) Tr 590/30, 1—12pdr. Purchased as M/S 11.1935. Sold 1947, renamed *Dragaberg*.

HOLLYBANK Dr 78/09, 1—3pdr. Hired 1915—19.

HOLLYDALE Dr 99/14, 1—6pdr. Hired 1915—19. (Served as PECHEUR in WW.II.)

HOLLYDALE Dr 93/19. Hired for examination service 3.1940. Harbour service 1942—45.

HOLME ROSE Dr 89/13, 1—3pdr. Hired 1915—19.

HOLMSGARTH Dr 85/08, 1—6pdr. Hired 1916—19.

HOLYROOD Transport. Hired 1854—55.

HOLYROOD Tr 210/14, 1—12pdr. Hired 1915—19 and as A/P Tr 12.39—1.40.

HOMAYUN 3,363/95. Purchased as blockship 1915 and used as BDV. Sold 1919.

HOME GUARD A/S Tr 750 tons, 175 x 30 ft, 1—4in, 4—20mm. Cook Welton & Gemmell 8.7.1944. Sold 4.46, renamed *Loyal*.

HOMELAND Dr 83/08, 1—3pdr. Hired 1915—19.

HOMER Tug 157/15. Hired 1916—19.

HONDO Tr 229/12, 1—6pdr. Hired 1914—19.

HONEY BEE Dr 84/05. 1—2½pdr. Hired 1915; HONEYCOMB 10.18—19.

HONEY DEW Dr 99/11. Hired as store carrier 12.1939. Harbour service 1941—46.

HONEY DEW MFV 48net/03. Hired on harbour service 1.1941. Lost 9.11.42.

HONEYSUCKLE II Dr 73/03. Hired as store carrier 1916–19.

HONG LAM Cstr 104/28. Hired as looplayer 11.1941. Foundered 5.43 off Ceylon.

HONG PENG 4,055/99. Hired as ammo. store carrier (RFA) 27.4.42–7.46.

HONJO Tr 275/17. Hired 1917–19.

HONJO Tr 308/28, 1–12pdr. Hired as M/S 10.1939. Blown up 18.1.42 by Italian frogmen at Gibraltar.

HONNINGSVAAG Tr 487/40. German MALANGEN captured 4.1940 by Norwegian forces in Norway. A/P Tr (Norwegian crew) 6.40–45.

HONOR Dr 72/13, 1–6pdr. Hired 1915–19.

HONTESTROOM 1,857/21. Dutch, hired as convoy rescue ship (Free-French crew) 1.10.1940. To War Dept 7.41.

HOPE Lugger 12. Hired 1795. Sunk 11.1797 in collision in the Channel.

HOPE Schooner 14. Hired 1798–1800.

HOPE Sloop 4, 125bm, 4–3pdr. Hired 3.1803–8.1807.

HOPE Cutter 8, 84bm, 8–12pdr carr. Hired 10.1803–27.2.1805.

HOPE II Dr 92/07, 1–6pdr. Hired 1914–19.

HOPE III Dr 84/07, 1–3pdr. Hired 1915–19.

HOPE IV Dr 90/06, 1–3pdr. Hired 1915–19.

HOPE Dr 67/04. Hired as coal boat 5.1915–19.

HOPEFUL Dr 94/07, 1–6pdr. Hired 8.1914–19.

HOPEFUL MFV 24net/38. Hired on harbour service 9.1939–45.

HOPEWELL Ketch. Hired 1650–52.

HORACE STROUD Tr 192/07, 1–6pdr. Purchased as M/S 1914. Sold 1919. (Served as EAST COAST in WW.II.)

HORATIO Tr 174/06, 1–6pdr. Hired 1914–19.

HORATIO M/S–A/S Tr 545 tons, 150 x 28 ft, 1–12pdr, 3–20mm. Cook Welton & Gemmell 8.8.1940. Sunk 7.1.43 by Italian MTB in the western Mediterranean.

HORIZON Admiralty steel Dr. A.Hall 1918. Sold 1945.

HORNBEAM (ex-*Lord Trent*) Tr 530/29, 1–12pdr. Purchased as M/S Tr 3.1939. Sold 4.46, renamed *Rankin*.

HORNBY Tug 168/08. Hired 10.1914–5.16.

HORNPIPE A/S Tr 530 tons, 150 x 27½ ft, 1–4in, 3–20mm. Cook Welton & Gemmell 21.5.1940. To Italian navy 16.3.46.

HORNSEA Tr 305/00. Hired as boom gate vessel in WW.I.

HORSA (ex-RESCUE renamed 1942) Rescue tug 700 tons, 142½ x 33 ft, 1–3in. Cochrane 29.7.42. Stranded 16.3.43 on the east coast of Iceland.

HORTEN (see KOS II)

HORTENSIA Tr 244/07. Hired as boom gate vessel 1915–19 and as M/S 7.40–11.45.

HOSANNA Dr 132/30. Hired as M/S 11.1939–45.

HOTSPUR (see WRESTLER)

HOUBARA Tr 293/11, 1–6pdr. Hired as M/S 1915–19.

HOUDAN (see MINORCA)

HOVERFLY (ex-*Euryalus*) Tr 242/17. Hired as M/S 9.1939–15.1.45.

HOWDEN 1,020/09. Hired as ammo. carrier (RFA) 3.12.1914. To War Dept 19.3.15.

HOWE Tr 134/96, 1–6pdr. Hired 1915–18.

HOWITZER Armament vessel, 186gr, 98½ x 21 ft. Pollock, Faversham 11.11.1943.

HOXA Tr, 'Isles' class. Cook Welton & Gemmell 15.1.1941. Sold 7.46, renamed *Sung Hwei.*

HOY Tr, 'Isles' class. Cook Welton & Gemmell 1.2.1941. Sold 1946, renamed *Dunay.*

HUA TONG Ferry 280/27. Hired as M/S 11.1939. Sunk 2.42 by air attack in the Palembang river, Sumatra.

HUAYNA 1,988/93. Hired 20.4.1917 and purchased 29.11.17. Sold 1.5.19.

HUDDERSFIELD TOWN Tr 399/33. Purchased as A/S Tr 9.1939. Sold 1945.

HUDSON Sloop 10. Hired 1793–94.

HUDSON Tug 294/39. Dutch, hired for harbour service 28.6.1940–44.

HUGH BLACK Tr, non-standard 'Castle' type, 265gr. Cook Welton & Gemmell 10.5.1917. Sold 1922, renamed *Macbeth.* (Served as OGANO in WW.II.)

HUGHLI Tug 513/94. Hired as salvage vessel 23.2.1915. Foundered 15.5.19 off Nieuport.

HUGH WALPOLE Tr 498/37, 1–4in. Purchased as A/S Tr 8.1939. Sold 4.46.

HULL Tug 94/98. Hired for harbour service 4.1940. Listed to 1941.

HULLMAN Tug 171/14. Hired 1.1917–19.

HUMBER Sloop, 258bm. Hired 3.1804–4.11.

HUMBER (see WATER-RAIL)

HUMILITY MFV 50/02. Hired for ferry service 22.5.1940–10.45.

HUMPBACK (Z.9) Wh, 'Z' class. Smiths Dk 12.8.1915. Sold 6.3.20.

HUMPHREY Tr 207/17. Hired as M/S (RNZN) 9.1939–8.44.

HUNDA Tr, 'Isles' class. Ferguson 4.2.1942. Sold 5.46.

HUNGARIAN Tr 186/00, 1–6pdr. Hired as M/S 1914–19.

HUNGERFORD 5,811/13. German prize *Lauterfels* completed as distilling ship (RFA) 7.1915. Paid off 2.16.

HUNGJAO Yt 65gr. Purchased at Shanghai as A/P Yt 16.5.1941. 'Presumed lost' 3.42.

HUNTER Tr 185/03. Hired as BDV 1914–19.

HURRICANE Admiralty wood Dr, 99gr. Richards 1919. Sold 1919, same name. (Served as CHARDE in WW.II.)

HURRICANE Tug 90/38. Hired as BBV 29.11.1939. DY tug 1944—1.46.
HUSKY (ex-*Wild Duck*) Yt 360/30. Commissioned as A/S Yt (RCN)
23.7.1940. Paid off 28.8.45.
HUXLEY Tr 191/99, 1—6pdr. Hired as M/S 1915—19.
HVAL I Wh 223/27. Norwegian, hired as A/P Wh 10.1940. Renamed
ORYX, M/S, 1941; renamed GEMSBUCK 1944. Returned 1945.
HVAL V Wh 248/29. Norwegian, hired as M/S (Norwegian crew) 7.1940—
3.46.
HYACINTH II Dr 79/03, 1—3pdr. Purchased 1914. Sold 1920.
HYADES (see TAURUS)
HYAENA (ex-*Ellesmere*) Tr 183/03. Hired as M/S 4.12.1939—10.2.40.
HYDERABAD Decoy ship, 1—4in, 2—12pdr. Purchased on stocks.
Thornycroft 17.8.1917. Depot Ship 1918. Sold 5.20, renamed No.966.
HYDRA II Tr 214/06, 1—6pdr. Hired 1915—19.
HYDRA (see KEREN)
HYE LEONG Cstr 494/82. Hired as A/P vessel 19.10.1917—30.12.18.
HYPERION MFV 19net. Hired as A/P vessel 6.1940—45.
HYSSOP Dr 88/03. Hired on harbour service 1915—19.
HYTHE 509/05, 1—12pdr. Hired as M/S 10.1914. Sunk 28.10.15 in
collision with SARNIA off Cape Helles.

IAGO Tr 206/07, 1—6pdr. Hired as M/S 1915—19.
IANTHE Aux schooner, 212 gr, 5—12pdr. Hired as decoy vessel in WW.I.
IBIS Tr 168/03, 1—12pdr. Hired 1914—19.
IBIS V Tr 196/08. Belgian, hired 1917—19.
IBIS I Dr 78/25. Belgian, hired as BBV 30.8.1940. Harbour service 1942—
13.5.45.
IBIS II Dr 160/37. Belgian, hired on harbour service 8.12.1943. Fuel
carrier 1944—12.44.
ICEAXE Tr 486 tons, 131 x 23½ ft, 1—12pdr. Smiths Dk 17.7.1916.
Russian T.17 seized 8.1918 in the White Sea. Renamed KENNET 10.20.
Firefloat 1945. Sold 5.46, BU.
ICEBERG Admiralty steel Dr, 95gr. A.Hall 1918. Sold 26.7.21, same name
ICEBLINK Admiralty wood Dr, 94gr. Jones, Buckie 1919. Sold 1919,
renamed *Star Divine*.
ICEFIELD Admiralty steel Dr, 96gr. Ouse SB 5.4.1919. Sold 1919,
renamed *Jessie Watson*.
ICEFLOE Admiralty steel Dr, 96gr. A.Hall 1918. Sold 1919, renamed
Sunny Bird. (SUNNY BIRD in WW.II.)
ICELAND Tr, 1—6pdr. Hired 1918—19.
ICEPACK Admiralty steel Dr. A.Hall 12.6.1918. Sold 1922.

ICEWHALE (Z.12) Wh, 'Z' class. Smiths Dk 10.9.1915. Sold 5.10.28 Plymouth & Devonport S Bkg Co. (Was base ship OSPREY 3.24—28.)

ICEWHALE (ex-*Pandora*) Cstr 203/93. Purchased as air target 28.2.1941. Sold 10.47.

ICICLE Admiralty steel Dr. A.Hall 25.6.1918. Sold 1920.

ICICLE (see BUSEN 3)

ICTOR (ex-*Victor*) Tug 153/98. Hired 3.1918—2.19.

IDA Dr 95/07, 1—3pdr. Hired 1915—19.

IDA ADAMS Tr 275/07, 1—6pdr. Hired 1915—19.

IDAHO 58/10, 1—MG. Hired as A/P Yt 4.1915—2.2.19 and as A/P Yt 31.5.40. Air/sea rescue 1941. Laid up 11.45.

IDALIA Yt 157/34. Hired as danlayer 9.1939. Listed to 27.11.39.

IDAS Cutter 10, 142bm. Hired 10.11.1808—12.10.1812.

IDAS Cutter 10, 102bm. Hired 21.4.1809. Captured 4.6.1810 by the French.

IDENA Dr 95/07, 1—3pdr. Hired 1915—19.

I.F.S Dr 95/08. Hired 1914—19.

IJUIN Tr 257/11, 1—3pdr. Hired as M/S 1915. Sunk 22.7.18 by U-boat gunfire.

IJUIN Tr 282/20. Hired as M/S 8.1939—1.46.

IKATERE NZ Govt vessel, 43/40. Hired on examination service (RNZN) 1941—44.

ILEX Yt 131/96, 2—3pdr. Hired as A/P Yt 6.9.1914—20.7.15.

ILFRACOMBE Tr 165/97. Hired 1917—19.

ILIONA Yt 109/86. Hired on examination service 25.3.1918—2.19.

ILONA Pilot 122/96. Hired on examination service 1.10.1918—5.12.18.

ILSENSTEIN 8,216/04. Purchased 13.12.1939. Sunk 18.2.40 as blockship at Scapa Flow.

ILUSTRA Tr 448/14, 1—6pdr. Hired 1914—19.

IMBAT Admiralty wood Dr, 92gr. Jones, Buckie 1918. Sold 1921, same name. Hired on harbour service 1940. Sunk 4.2.41 in collision, Scapa Flow.

IMELDA Tr 249/14, 1—6pdr. Hired 1914—19 and as BDV 12.39. For disposal 7.46.

IMERSAY Tr, 'Isles' class. Cochrane 21.8.1944. Sold 1.59 at Malta.

IMHOFF Wh 224/27. Hired as M/S (SAN) 7.1941—5.46.

IMMINGHAM 2,083/07. Hired as accommodation ship 10.1914. Store carrier (RFA) 4.15. Sunk 6.6.15 in collision off Mudros.

IMMORTELLE (see THOMAS JONES)

IMMORTELLE (see TERJE 9)

IMPALA Yt 79/36, 1—6pdr. Hired as A/P Yt 6.1940. Renamed LAUREATE 1941, examination service to 1943.

IMPALA (see A.N.4)

IMPERATOR (see IMPREGNABLE)

IMPERIA Tr 213/12, 1–6pdr. Hired 1914–19 and as A/P Tr 11.39. Boom gate vessel 8.40–11.45.

IMPERIALIST Tr 520/39, 1–4in, 1–40mm. Hired as A/S Tr 8.1939–10.45.

IMPERIAL PRINCE Tr128/99. Hired 1918–19.

IMPERIAL QUEEN Tr 246/14, 1–12pdr. Hired 1916–19.

IMPERIOUS Tug 185/24. Harbour service 1941–46. BU 1947 at Rosyth.

IMPETUS DY tug 365 tons, 90 x 28 ft. A.Hall 25.1.1940.

IMPLACABLE II Dr 88/16. Hired 1918–19.

IMPREGNABLE Dr 108/11. Hired 1914; IMPERATOR 9.16–19.

INANDA 5,985. Hired as OBV 9.1940. Wrecked 7.9.40 by air attack while fitting out in the Royal Albert docks.

INA WILLIAM Tr 337/13. Hired 1916. Sunk 30.5.17 by mine off Berehaven.

INCHBROOM Dr 78/10, 1–3pdr. Hired 1915–19.

INCHCOLM Tr, 'Isles' Class. Cook Welton & Gemmell 3.3.1941. To War Dept 6.46.

INCHGARTH Tr 226/17, 1–6pdr. Hired 1917–19.

INCHGOWER Tr 202/19, 1–6pdr. Hired as A/P Tr 11.1939. M/S 6.40–2.46.

INCHKEITH Tr 174/06, 1–6pdr. Hired 1915–19.

INCHMARNOCK Tr, 'Isles' Class. Lewis 25.8.1941. Sold 1946, renamed *Tilthorn.* (On loan R.Norwegian navy as KARMOY 1944–9.46.)

INDIA 7,940/96. Hired as AMC 13.3.1915. Sunk 8.8.15 by 'U.22' off Norway.

INDIA Tr 215/06. Hired 1915–19.

INDIA Tr 190/94. Hired 1918–19.

INDIAN (see SIOUX)

INDIAN EMPIRE Tr 289/07, 1–6pdr. Hired 1914–19.

INDIAN STAR Tr 463/36, 1–4in. Hired as A/S Tr 8.1939–10.45.

INDIAN SUMMER Admiralty steel Dr, 97gr. Lewis 1918. TRV 1942. Sold 1947.

INDIRA Tug 637/18. Hired as M/S 23.4.1940. Sunk 15.12.41 by air attack at Hong Kong.

INDOMITABLE II Dr 83/08, 1–3pdr. Hired 1915–19.

INDRANI 3,640/88. Hired as supply ship (RFA) 4.8.1914. Sunk 27.6.15 by U-boat.

INDUSTRIOUS DY paddle tug 700 tons, 145 x 27½ ft. Barclay Curle 19.6.1902. BU 12.59 in Holland.

INDUSTRY 32–gun ship, 280bm. Hired 1650–54.

INDUSTRY Gunvessel. Hired 9.1801–12.01.

INDUSTRY Dr 100/07, 1–3pdr. Hired 8.1914–19 and as M/S 11.1939. Harbour service 1943–12.45.

INFATIGABLE Tug 1,050/98. French, seized 3.7.1940 at Plymouth.
Completed as salvage vessel 1.41. Renamed Le LUTTEUR 6.41. To
MWT 1942.
INFINITIVE Dr 103/16, 1–3pdr. Hired 1916–19.
INGENIEUR CACHIN Ferry 1,039/23. French minelayer seized 3.7.1940
at Southampton. Renamed VOLONTAIRE 1941 as Free-French depot
ship. Returned 1945.
INGENIEUR MINARD Ferry 1,273/11. French, seized 3.7.1940 at
Southampton. Laid up to 1942, then accommodation ship. Returned
27.6.45.
INGOMAR Tr 217/04. Hired 1918–19.
INKOSI 3,661/02. Hired as fleet auxiliary 12.3.1915–24.7.16.
INKOSI 6,618/37. Hired as OBV 15.8.1940. Wrecked 7.9.40 by air
attack while fitting out in the Victoria docks. Repaired and to MWT as
Empire Chivalry.
INKPEN A/S Tr 750 tons, 166 x 28 ft, 1–12pdr, 3–20mm. Cook
Welton & Gemmell 22.12.1941. Sold 1946, renamed *Stella Capella.*
INNERTON 5,276/19. Purchased 4.1944. Sunk 9.6.44 as blockship at
Arromanches.
INNISFAIL 399/12. Hired as cable repair ship (RAN) 1941–46.
INNISFREE 96/13. Purchased as water carrier (RFA) 7.9.1915. Sold
24.11.20.
INNISINVER 127/13. Purchased as water carrier (RFA) 14.8.1915.
Sold 7.20.
INNISJURA 127/13. Purchased as water carrier (RFA) 2.10.1915. Sold
1920.
INNISSHANNON 268/13. Purchased as water carrier (RFA) 16.9.1915.
Sold 2.21. Hired as BBV 1941–45.
INNISTRAHULL Purchased as water carrier (RFA) 15.9.1915. Wrecked
1916?
INNISULVA 268/14. Purchased as water carrier (RFA) 30.9.1915. Sold
13.3.20.
INNISVILLE Harbour tug (RCN). Owen Sound, Ontario 1944. Listed
1951.
INQUISITOR (see NORSEMAN)
INTABA 4,808/10. Hired as store carrier (RFA) 5.8.1914–5.1.18.
(Operated as decoy ship Q.2 from 6.16 to 7.17.)
INTEGRITY Dr 86/07, 1–3pdr. Hired 1915–19.
INTEGRITY II Dr 67/03, 1–2½pdr. Hired 1916–19.
INTEGRITY Rescue tug, 'B.A.T' class, Levingston SB, Orange Texas
28.3.1942 on lend-lease. Returned 2.46 to the USN.
INTEGRITY (ex-*Empire Cupid*) DY tug 529 tons, 107 x 27 ft.
Transferred from MOT and renamed 3.1947. Arrived 21.12.65 Ward,
Inverkeithing to BU.

INTENT Salvage vessel 300 tons, 95 x 24 ft. Gulfport, Port Arthur 19.2.1942 for lend-lease, but retained 3.42 by the USN.

INTERCEPTOR RCMP vessel, 48/34. Hired for examination service (RCN) 9.1939—44.

INTERNOS (ex-*Inter-Nos*) Dr 90/07, 1—3pdr. Hired 12.1914—19.

INTERNOS (ex-*Inter-Nos*) Dr 93/08, 2—MG. Hired as M/S 11.1939. TRV 6.43—3.46.

INTOMBI 3,903/12. Hired as store carrier (RFA) 4.8.1914—10.3.15.

INVADER (ex-RCMP vessel *Arcadian*) Hired on examination service (RCN) 5.9.1939—44.

INVERBOYNDIE Dr 89/10, 1—6pdr. Hired 1.1915—19.

INVERCAIRN Dr 94/16. Hired as A/S Dr 12.1939—11.45.

INVERCAULD Tr 262/17, 1—6pdr. Hired as M/S 7.1940—11.45.

INVERCLYDE Tr 215/14. Hired as water carrier 8.1939. Foundered in tow 16.10.42 off Beachy Head.

INVERFORTH Tr 248/14. Hired as A/P Tr 11.1939. M/S 4.40—7.45.

INVERLYON Smack 59/03, 1—6pdr. Hired as decoy vessel 2.8.1915—16.

INVERNAVIN Dr. Hired as BDV 1915—19.

INVERNESS Dr. Hired as M/S 11.1939—1.40.

INVERTAY Tr 230/16, 1—6pdr. Hired as M/S 8.1940—7.46.

INVERUGIE Dr 93/08, 1—3pdr. Hired as M/S 1915—19 and as M/S 12.39. BBV 5.40—8.45.

INVICTA 4,178/40, 1—12pdr, 4—20mm. Hired as landing ship 1940, completed 4.42. To MWT 8.10.45 as trooper.

IOLAIRE Yt 999/02, 2—3in. Hired as A/P Yt 1.3.1915. Renamed AMALTHAEA 11.18, returned 1.19. Hired as accommodation ship 9.1939, purchased 1.43. Renamed PERSEPHONE 6.45. Sold 1946.

IOLANDA Yt 1,822/08, 2—3in. Hired as A/P Yt 21.5.1915—5.2.19. (Served as WHITE BEAR in WW.II.)

IONA Tr 187/05. Hired 1918—19.

IONA Yt 279/20. Hired on examination service 9.1940. Calibrating Yt 1943. For disposal 1.46.

IONIC Tr 159/90. Hired 1917—19.

IPSWICH Tr 162/96, 1—6pdr. Hired as M/S 1914—19.

IRANIAN Tr 202/12, 1—6pdr. Hired 1915—19 and as A/P Tr 11.30—2.40.

IRAWADI Tr 238/06. Hired 1915. Wrecked 10.8.16 in the eastern Mediterranean.

IRELAND Paddle tug 245/91, 1—6pdr. Hired as M/S 1917. M/L, 10 mines, 4.18. Returned 1919.

IRENE Dr 85/07, 1—3pdr. Hired 1915—19.

IRENE II Dr 66/06, 1—3pdr. Hired 1915—19.

IRENE VERNICOS Tug 250gr. Hired 1941. Lost 6.41.

IRENE WRAY Tr 216/14. Hired 1915–19.

IRIDESCENCE Admiralty wood Dr, 92gr. Innes, Macduff 1917. Sold 1926, same name. Hired on examination service 4.1941–43.

IRIS II Ferry 490/06. Hired as landing ship 1918 for the Zeebrugge operation.

IRIS (ex-*Train Ferry No 1*) 2,683/17, 5–20mm. Purchased as landing ship 9.1940. Renamed PRINCESS IRIS 1942. Returned 6.46.

IRISHMAN Tug 99/96. Hired on harbour service 30.7.1914–19?

IRMA MFV. Danish, seized 1940. Harbour service to 1943 then mobile workshop to 1945.

IRMA ALICE MFV 77/30 Belgian, hired as A/P vessel, 1–6pdr, 10.1940–45.

IRONAXE Tr 296gr, 130½ x 23½ ft, 1–12pdr. Smiths Dk 31.8.1916 as Russian T.22. Seized 8.1918 in the White Sea and renamed. Sold 22.7.23 as salvage vessel, same name. Hired as salvage vessel 8.40–41 then to MWT.

IRONBOUND Tr, 'Isles' class. Kingston SY 14.1.1942. Sold 1946, renamed *Turoy*. (On loan RCN 10.42–17.6.45.)

IRRAWADI 1,243/13. Hired as A/P vessel (RIN) 9.1939–45.

IRVANA Tr 276/17, 1–12pdr. Hired as M/S 2.1940. Sunk 16.1.42 by air attack off Yarmouth.

IRWELL Tr 197/00. Hired 1918–19.

ISA Dr 87/14. Hired 1915–19. (Served as BOY JOHN in WW.II.)

ISA Tr 217/12. Hired 1917–19.

ISAAC ARTHAN Tr, 'Castle' tupe, 277gr. Cook Welton & Gemmell 1.5.1919. Sold 1921, renamed *Amber*. (Served as LOCH BUIE in WW.II.)

ISAAC CHANT Tr, 'Mersey' type, 330gr. Lobnitz 1918. Renamed COLNE 1920. Listed to 1946.

ISAAC DOBSON Tr, 'Strath' type. Montrose SY 1919. Sold 1919.

ISAAC HARRIS Tr, 'Strath' tupe, 204gr. Hawthorns 1919. Sold 1919, renamed *Pochard II*.

ISAAC HEATH Tr, 'Castle' tupe, 276gr. J P Rennoldson 1918. Sold 1919, renamed *Teroma*. (TEROMA in WW.II.)

ISABEL Tr 166/06. Hired 1918–19 and as M/S (Dutch crew) 1940. Fuel carrier (RN) 1944–45.

ISABELLA Discovery ship, 383bm, 110 x 28 ft. Hired 1.1818–1.1819.

ISABELLA FOWLIE Tr 196/11. Hired 1916–19.

ISCO Dr 100/07. Hired 1914–19.

ISERE Tug 107/19. French, seized 3.7.1940 at Dartmouth. On harbour service to 1945.

ISERNA Tr 198/99, 1–6pdr. Hired as M/S 1915–19.

ISIS Tr 168/99. Hired 1915–16.

ISIS Tr 175/99. Hired 1917–19.

ISLA Petrol carrier (RFA) 980 tons, 170 x 26 ft. Purchased 6.3.1907. Sold 9.9.21.

ISLAND MAGEE Cstr 227/00. Hired as store hulk 1942–45.

ISLAND PRINCE Tr 205/11, 1–6pdr. Hired 1914–19.

ISLAND QUEEN Cstr 803/16. Hired as fleet auxiliary 23.11.1916. Purchased as decoy ship, 4–12pdr, 10.12.17. Sold 6.19. (Operated as PRIVET (Q.19).)

ISLAY Tr, 'Isles' class. Smiths Dk 10.4.1941. Sold 10.46, renamed *Isly*.

ISLEFORD Store carrier (RFA) 423 tons, 150 x 25½ ft. Ardrossan DY Co 1913. Sunk 1.42 by unknown cause off Wick.

ISLE of ARRAN Paddle 313/92. Hired as M/S 30.5.1917–27.3.20.

ISLE of GUERNSEY 2,143/30. Hired and completed as FAA target 8.1940. Landing ship 1944–45.

ISLE of MAN Tr 176/05, 1–6pdr. Hired as M/S 1914–19.

ISLE of MAY 119/96. Hired on examination service 1940–44.

ISLE of SARK 2,211/32. Hired as radar training ship 22.12.1941–6.46.

ISLE of SKYE Paddle 211/86. Hired as tender 19.5.1916–10.5.19. (Served as FAIR MAID in WW.II.)

ISLE of THANET 2,701/25. Hired and completed as FAA target 11.1940. Landing ship 1943–45.

ISLE of WIGHT Tr 176/05, 1–6pdr. Hired as M/S 1914–19.

ISLESMAN 84gr. Purchased as DY tank vessel in WW.I. Sold 1921.

ISONZO (ex-*Isis*) 1,728/98. Hired as fleet auxiliary 6.1915–10.3.20.

ISRAEL ALDCROFT Tr, non-standard 'Strath' tupe, 212gr. Duthie Torry 20.6.1917. Sold 1921, renamed *George R Purdy*. (GEORGE R PURDY in WW.II.)

ISTRIA Tr 409/35, 1–4in. Purchased as A/S Tr 8.1939. Sold 1946.

ITALY Tr 145/96. Hired 1914. Sunk 3.9.16 in collision off Sunderland.

ITCHEN (see THOMAS HAGGERTY)

ITONIAN Tr 288/14, 1–6pdr. Hired 1915–19.

IVA Dr 85/08. Hired 1915–19.

IVANHOE Tr 190/98. Hired 1914. Wrecked 3.11.14 in the Firth of Forth.

IVY Dr 94/07. Hired 1914–19.

IVY Nigerian Govt Yt, 1,131/95, 1–12pdr, 2–6pdr. Commissioned 9.1914–17.

IVY II Dr 71/05, 1–3pdr. Hired 1915–19.

IVY III Dr 64/03. Hired 1915–19.

IVY GREEN Dr 76/08, 1–3pdr. Hired 1915–19.

IZAAC WALTON Tr 252/07, 1–12pdr, 1–6pdr. Hired 1914–19.

JABIRU 1,703/11. Hired as store carrier (RFA) 3.12.1914–6.5.16.

JABOO II Tr 236/15, 1–6pdr. Hired 1915–19.

J.A.C Dr 79/10. Hired 1914–19.

JACAMAR Tr 293/11. Hired 1915. Sunk 28.1.17 in collision off Folkestone.

JACANA (see TRIDENT)

JACINTA Tr 288/15, 1–6pdr. Hired 1915–19 and as A/P Tr, 1–12pdr, 5.40, later purchased. M/S 3.42; wreck dispersal 1.44. Sold 5.46.

JACINTH Tr 248/14, 1–12pdr. Hired 1916–19. (Served as INVERFORTH in WW.II.)

JACK (ex-*Jackal*) Tug 360/85. Hired 1.1.1915–19. (Stranded 9.8.17 in the Tyne, but salved.)

JACKDAW Tr 250/03, 1–6pdr. Purchased as M/S 1914. Renamed EXCELLENT, base ship, 1.18. Sold 1919, renamed *Sverholm.*

JACKDAW (see FRANCOLIN)

JACKETA Dr 96/26, 1–MG. Hired as M/S 11.1939–3.46.

JACK EVE Dr 96/19. Hired as M/S 11.1939–11.45.

JACK GEORGE Dr 98/13, 1–6pdr. Hired as M/S 1914–19 and as water carrier 1942–45.

JACK SALMON Dr 99/14. Hired 1.1915–19.

JACOB GEORGE Dr 67/10. Hired 1915–19.

JACOBUS 1,262/20. Purchased 21.5.1940. Sunk 10.6.40 as blockship at Dieppe.

JACQUELINE CLASINE Tr 206/06. Hired as M/S (Dutch crew) 1940. Fuel carrier 1944–2.46.

JACQUELINE FLORIMONDE MFV 82/32. Belgian, hired as BBV 1940. Harbour service 1941–45.

JACQUES MORGAND Dr 155/36. French M/S seized 3.7.1940 at Falmouth. A/P vessel 1940–45.

JADE (ex-*Lady Lillian*) Tr 613/33, 1–4in. Purchased as A/S Tr 1.1939. Sunk 10.4.42 by air attack at Malta.

JADE (see MMS.223.)

JAMAICA Tr 205/14. Hired 1917–19.

JAMAICA PRODUCER 5,464/34. Hired as OBV 8.1941–22.10.41.

JAMES 24–gun ship, 300bm.Hired 1649–54.

JAMES Tender 4, 85bm, 4–2pdr. Hired 12.1803–1810.

JAMES 9 85/24. Purchased 1940. Sunk 8.7.40 as blockship.

JAMES ADAMS Tr, 'Mersey' type, 326gr. Cochrane 7.7.1917. Sold 1919, renamed *Pilote 5.*

JAMES ALDRIDGE Tr, non-standard 'Strath' type, 221gr. Duthie Torry 10.2.1917. Sold 1921, same name.

JAMES ARCHIBALD Tr, non-standard 'Strath' type, 210gr. Duthie Torry 24.4.1917. Sold 1921, renamed *Nisus.*

JAMES BARRIE Tr 338/28. Hired as BDV 4.1940—11.45.

JAMES BASHFORD Tr, 'Strath' type, 202gr. Hall Russell 1919. Sold 1919, renamed *Strathrannock.* (STRATHRANNOCK in WW.II.)

JAMES BEAGAN Tr, 'Strath' type, 203gr. Hall Russell 19.10.1917. Sold 1921, renamed *Loch Blair.* (LOCH BLAIR in WW.II.)

JAMES BENTOLE Tr, 'Strath' tupe, 203gr. Hall Russell 21.6.1917. Sold 1921, renamed *Fort Robert.* (FORT ROBERT in WW.II.)

JAMES BERRY Tr, non-standard 'Castle' type, 269gr. Cook Welton & Gemmell 10.5.1917. Sold 1922, renamed *Montano.* (MONTANO in WW.II.)

JAMES B GRAHAM Tr 198/14. Hired 1914—19.

JAMES BOYLE Tr, 'Castle' type. Cook Welton & Gemmell. Cancelled 1919.

JAMES BRODIGAN Tr, 'Strath' tupe, 203gr. Hall Russell 1918. Sold 1919, same name. (Served as WOODS in WW.II.)

JAMES BUCHANAN Tr, 'Mersey' type, 324gr. Cochrane 18.9.1917. Sold 1922, renamed *Stoneferry.* (Served as FORCE in WW.II.)

JAMES BURGESS Tr, 'Castle' type, 276gr. C Rennoldson 31.8.1917. Sold 1919, renamed *Beaumaris Castle.* (BEAUMARIS CASTLE in WW.II.)

JAMES CATON Tr, 'Mersey' type, 330 gr. Lobnitz 26.8.1918. Sold 1921, renamed *Emile Pierre.*

JAMES CEPELL Tr, 'Castle' type, 281gr. G Brown 29.3.1918. Sold 1922, renamed *Cloxby.* (Served as ANTIOCH II in WW.II.)

JAMES CHAPMAN Tr, 'Castle' type, 280gr. G Brown 8.9.1917. Sold 1922, renamed *Dunsby.*

JAMES CHRISTOPHER Tr, 'Castle' type, 276gr. J P Rennoldson 1918. Sold 1919, renamed *Marsona.* (MARSONA in WW.II.)

JAMES COILE Tr, 'Castle' type. Cook Welton & Gemmell. Cancelled 1919.

JAMES CONNOR Tr, 'Castle' type, 277gr. Harkess 19.7.1917. Renamed WAVENEY 1920. Sold 1922 Spanish navy as UAD MULLIYA.

JAMES COSGROVE Tr, 'Castle' type. 277gr. Ailsa 5.3.1918. Sold 1919, same name. Hired as M/S (RNZN) 10.1939. Boom gate vessel 4.44—46.

JAMES CURRY Tr, 'Strath' type, 205gr. Murdoch & Murray 11.1917. Sold 1921, renamed *Ady.*

JAMES DINTON Tr, 'Castle' type, 277gr. Bow McLachlan 1918. Sold 1922, renamed *Scawby.* (Served as MILFORD DUKE in WW.II.)

JAMES E HUGHES Tug 293/14. Hired in the Red Sea 1943—46.

JAMES EVANS Tr, 'Strath' type, 206gr. Abdela Mitchel 1918. Sold 1922, same name.

JAMES FEAGAN Tr, 'Strath' type, 202gr. Montrose SY 1919. Sold 1919, renamed *River Earn.*

JAMES FENNEL Tr, 'Strath' type, 202gr. Fullerton 1918. Wrecked 9.7.18. Salved and sold 1919?

JAMES FLETCHER Yt 330/07, 2–6pdr. Hired as A/P Yt 25.9.1914–27.2.19.

JAMES GARRICK Tr, 'Strath' type, 202gr. Montrose SY 1919. Wrecked 16.2.20.

JAMES GILL Tr, 'Castle' type, 275gr. C Rennoldson 17.2.1919. Sold 1919, renamed *Pierre Francois Deswartes*. (Served as MILFORD DUCHESS in WW.II.)

JAMES GREEN Tr, 'Castle' type, 275gr. Smiths Dk 3.10.1917. Sold 1921, renamed *E & F*. (E & F in WW.II.)

JAMES HARTWELL Tr, 'Strath' type, 203gr. Ouse SB 1918. Sold 1921, renamed *Georgette*. (GEORGETTE in WW.II.)

JAMES HAYES Tr, 'Mersey' type, 326gr. Goole SB 1919. Sold 1919.

JAMES HINES Tr, 'Strath' type, 204gr. Hawthorns 1919. Sold 1919, renamed *Northward Ho*. (NORTHWARD HO in WW.II.)

JAMES HULBERT Tr, 'Mersey' type, 329gr. Lobnitz 1919. Sold 1919, renamed *M J Reid*. (Served as JEAN FREDERIC in WW.II.)

JAMES HUNNIFORD Tr, non-standard 'Castle' type, 276gr. Smiths Dk 24.1.1917. Sold 1919, renamed *Cremlyn*. (Served as ETHEL TAYLOR in WW.II.)

JAMES JOHNSON Tr, non-standard 'Castle' type, 276gr. Smiths Dk 8.2.1917. Renamed THOMAS DEAS 1917. Sold 1921, same name.

JAMES JONES Tr, 'Mersey' type, 327gr. Cochrane 1918. Renamed CHERWELL 1920. Sale list 1939 and laid up. BDV 1942. Sold 1946.

JAMES LAVENNY Tr, 'Castle' type, 274gr. Chambers 1919. Sold 1922, renamed *Kelby*.

JAMES LAY Tr, 'Castle' type, 278gr. Fletcher, Limehouse 1918. Sold 1919, same name. Hired as M/S 9.39–10.44.

JAMES LENHAM Tr, 'Strath' type. Hall Russell. Cancelled 1919.

JAMES LONG Tr, 'Mersey' type, 326gr. Cochrane 1919. Sold 1919, same name.

JAMES LUDFORD Tr, 'Mersey' type, 326gr. Cochrane 1918. Laid up 1921. Commissioned as A/S Tr 1930; M/S 1939. Sunk 14.12.39 by mine in the Tyne area.

JAMES M Cstr 136/15. Hired as BBV 1941. BDV 1942–46.

JAMES McDONALD Tr, 'Mersey' type, 324gr. Cochrane 1919. Sold 1919, renamed *Grand Fleet*. (Served as BARBARA ROBERTSON in WW.II.)

JAMES McLAUGHLIN Tr, 'Mersey' type, 324gr. Cochrane 1.5.1919. Sold 1919, renamed *General Birdwood*. (GENERAL BIRDWOOD in WW.II.)

JAMES MANSELL Tr, 'Mersey' type, 326gr. Cochrane 1919. Sold 1919, same name.

JAMES PEAKE Tr, 'Castle' type, 275gr. Smiths Dk 17.10.1917. Sold 1922, renamed *Aragonite*.

JAMES PITCHERS Tr 197/11. Hired 1914—19.

JAMES POND Tr, 'Castle' type, 275gr. Smiths Dk 21.5.1917. Sunk 15.2.18 by German destroyers off Dover.

JAMES REAICH Dr 78/01. Hired on harbour service 7.1915—19.

JAMES ROBERTSON Tr, 'Castle' type, 275gr. Smiths Dk 6.6.1917. Sold 1921, renamed *Capstone*. (CAPSTONE in WW.II.)

JAMES SECKAR Tr, 'Castle' type, 255gr. Smiths Dk 20.7.1917. Foundered 25.9.17 in the Atlantic. (Listed to 1921.)

JAMES SIBBALD Tr, 'Castle' type, 275gr. Smiths Dk 20.7.1917. Sold 1919, renamed *Kirkland*. (Served as OUR BAIRNS in WW.II.)

JAMES S MELVILLE Tr 211/11, 1—12pdr. Hired 1914—19.

JAMESVILLE Tug (RCN). Owen Sound, Ontario 1944.

JAMES WRIGHT Tr, 'Mersey' type, 326gr. Cochrane 1918. Sold 1921, renamed *Lord Ancaster*. (Served as LOCH MOIDART in WW.II.)

JAMNAGAR 576/24. Hired as A/P vessel (RIN) 1941—43, then to MWT as *Empire Bulbul*.

J & A Dr 98/14. Hired 1916. Sunk 4.4.18 in collision off Scarborough.

J & M MAIN Dr 89/13. Hired 1915—19.

JAN de WAELE Tr 324/25. Belgian, hired as BDV 9.1940—12.45.

JANE Lugger 14. Hired 1798—1801.

JANE Dr 104/01. Hired on harbour service 11.1914—19.

JANE ROSS Tr 184/01, 1—6pdr. Hired 1915—19.

JANET GEDDES Dr 88/09, 1—3pdr. Hired 1914—19.

JANETHA IV Yt 164/30. Hired as HDPC 1940—45.

JANET REEKIE Dr 81/08. Hired 1915—19.

JANIE SEDDON NZ Govt vessel, 126/01. Hired on examination service 5.1941. Base duty 1944. Sold 1947.

JANUS (ex-*Kilda*) Tr 243/11, 1—6pdr. Purchased as M/S 1914. Renamed KILDA 1919. Sold 1920, renamed *Tubal Cain*.

JANUS II Tr 240/05, 1—13pdr. Hired 1914—20.

JAN VIRGINIE MFV 52/31. Belgian, hired as BBV 1940. Harbour service 1944—45.

JAPAN Tr 205/04. Hired 1915. Sunk 16.8.15 by mine off the Shipwash.

JARAK Cstr 208/27. Hired as M/S. Sunk 17.2.1942 by air attack in the Singapore area.

JARDINE Tr 452/36, 1—4in. Purchased as A/S Tr 8.1939. Damaged by air attack and scuttled 30.4.40 west coast of Norway. Salved and became German CHERUSKER; sunk 1942.

JASON Sloop 20. Hired 1779. Captured 1779 by Americans.

JASON Cutter. Hired 1803.

JASON Transport. Hired 1854—55.

JASON II Yt 702/13, 2—12pdr. Hired as A/P Yt 1.2.1915—15.2.19.

JASON DY tug 85 tons. Purchased 5.2.1915. Renamed RIVAL 1937. Sold 1947.

JASPER (ex-*Rayvernol*) Tr 221/12, 1–6pdr. Purchased as M/S 1914. Sunk 26.8.15 by mine in the Moray Firth.

JASPER (ex-*Balthasar*) Tr 581/32, 1–4in. Purchased as A/S Tr 11.1935. Sunk 1.12.42 by E-boat torpedo in the Channel.

JAUNTY Rescue tug, 606gr, 155 x 31 ft. Ritchie Graham, Glasgow 1919. DY tug 1920. Sold 17.4.30, renamed *Rio Tejo*.

JAUNTY Rescue tug 700 tons, 142½ x 33 ft, 1–3in. Cochrane 11.6.1941. On sale list 1965.

JAVA Tug 114/98. Belgian, hired as DY tug 25.5.1915–19.

JAVA Tug 128/05. Hired as ABV 21.7.1915. Renamed CARCASS 1915. Returned 14.5.19. Hired on harbour service as JAVA 1940–45.

JAVELIN (ex-*Braconlea*) Tr 205/13, 1–6pdr. Purchased as M/S 1914. Sunk 17.10.15 by mine off the Longsands.

JAY Tr 144gr. Hired 1914. Sunk 11.8.17 by U-boat off Southwold.

JAY (ex-*Nautilus*) Tr 352/26. Belgian, purchased as M/L 1940. Renamed SANDMARTIN 12.44. Sold 1946.

J BURN Dr 90/13. Hired 1.1915–19.

J.C.P. Dr 73/08. Hired 1915. Sunk 22.3.18 after collision off Green Flash buoy.

JEAN Dr 94/07. Hired 1916. Sunk 17.10.17 by mine in the central Mediterranean.

JEAN Yt 86/32. Hired as despatch boat 1940–44.

JEAN EDMUNDS Tr 216/16. Hired as M/S 1.1940–9.45.

JEAN FREDERIC Tr 329/19. French A/P Tr seized 3.7.1940 at Falmouth. A/P Tr (Dutch crew) 1.41. Sunk 1.5.41 by air attack off Prawl Point.

JEANIE DEANS Paddle 635/31. Hired as M/S 10.1939. A/A ship 5.41–5.46.

JEANIE ROBERTSON Dr 93/08. Hired 1916–19.

JEANIE STEWART Tr 210/16, 1–6pdr. Hired 1916–19.

JEANNE ANTOINE MFV 50/32. French, seized 7.1940 at Falmouth. Laid up to 9.41, not listed afterwards.

JEANNE d'ARC MFV 70/29. Belgian, hired as A/P vessel 7.1940. BBV 6.42–44.

JEANNE et GENEVIEVE 620 tons. French store carrier, seized 3.7.1940 at Plymouth. Laid up to 9.41, then kite-balloon depot ship. Returned 7.46.

JEANNETTE Yt 1,023/11, 2–12pdr. Hired 18.1.1915–17.2.19.

JEANNIE Dr 83/07. Hired 1915–19.

JEANNIE II Dr 79/03, 1–3pdr. Hired 1915–18.

JEANNIE GILCHRIST Dr 93/07. Hired 1.1915–19.

JEANNIE HOWIE Dr 99/12. Hired as BBV 5.1940. Harbour service 1944–45.

JEANNIE LEASK Dr 95/09, 1–3pdr. Hired 1915–19 and as M/S 11.39. To Air Ministry 1943 as *Rexmoor.*

JEANNIE MACKAY MFV. Hired as A/P vessel 2.1940–1.46.

JEANNIE MACKINTOSH Dr 88/15. Hired as water boat 5.1915–19 and as M/S, 1–6pdr, 1940. A/P Dr 9.40–2.46.

JEANNIE MURRAY Dr 90/07. Hired 1915. Sunk 15.2.18 in action off Dover.

JEANNIES Dr 100/07. Hired 1914–19 and as M/S 12.39–40.

JEANNINE Dr 100/13. Belgian, hired as BBV 7.1940–45.

JEANNIE SIMPSON Dr 90/07. Hired 1914–19.

JEAN RIBAULT Dr 153/33. French M/S seized 3.7.1940 at Plymouth. M/S 1940. Mooring vessel 1943–45.

JELOY (see POL II and SHIANT)

JENNET (ex-*Betsy*) Cutter 6, 61bm. Hired 5.1804–11.04.

JENNET (ex-*Bunsen*) Tr 358/26. Purchased as boom Tr 4.1939. Sold 1.46, renamed *Westheron.*

JENNIFER (see BRAEMAR)

JENNY IRVIN Dr 98/19. Hired as M/S 11.1939–43.

JERAM Wh 210/27. Hired as M/S 10.1939. Captured 15.2.42 by the Japanese at Singapore. Became SUIKEI 21.

JERANTUT Wh 217/27. Hired as M/S 1940? Scuttled 8.3.1942 at Palembang.

JEREMIAH LEWIS Tr, 'Mersey' type, 324gr. Cochrane 1919. Sold 1919, renamed *Field Marshal Robertson.*

JERIA Tr 344/16. Hired 1916–19.

JERICO Tr 351/14, 1–12pdr. Hired 1915–19.

JERVIS BAY 14,164/22, 8–6in. Hired as AMC 8.1939. Sunk 5.11.40 in action with ADMIRAL SCHEER in the Atlantic.

JESBURN Dr 99/17, 1–6pdr. Hired 1917–19 and on harbour service 1942. Water carrier 1944–45.

JESSICA Tr 173/06, 1–6pdr. Hired 1914–19.

JESSIE Fleet auxiliary, 190gr. Sold 7.1923 at Constantinople.

JESSIE NUTTEN Tr 187/08. Hired 1914. Sunk 4.9.16 by mine off Lowestoft.

JESSIE TAIT Dr 84/15, 1–6pdr. Hired 1915–19 and as BDV 5.40. A/P Dr 1941; radar training 1944–45.

JESSMAR Dr 86/14. Hired 1914–19.

JESTER Yt 60/37. Hired as HDPC 10.1939–44.

JEUNE HELENE MFV 59/37. French A/P vessel seized 3.7.1940 at Plymouth. Renamed VP.19 (her French pendant number) 1940 and laid up to 1942.

JEWEL Dr 84/08. Hired as M/S 1.1940. Sunk 18.5.41 by mine in Belfast Lough.

J.H.F Dr 78/14. Hired 1915–19.

JIM McCAUSLAND Tug 262/86. Hired 2.9.1914–19.

JO Cstr 199/36. Dutch, hired as BBV 1940–42.

JOAN W.II MFV 63/37. Hired as M/S (RCN) 1941–45.

JOBOURG French navy tug, seized 1940 at Southampton. Examination service 1940. Target towing 1942–45.

JOCELYN Dr 94/15. Hired on harbour service 1940–45.

JOE CHAMBERLAIN Dr 79/03, 1–3pdr. Hired 11.1914–19.

JOFFRE Tug 260/16. Hired 11.1917–3.19.

J.O.GRAVEL (ex-*HS.45*) DY tug 300 tons. Transferred from War Dept 1918. Sold 1920.

JOHANNESBURG Tr 181/03, 1–3pdr. Hired 1915–19.

JOHANNESBURG (see SUDEROY II)

JOHN 34-gun ship, 400bm. Hired 1649–53.

JOHN Tr 221/10. Belgian, hired 1918–19.

JOHN ABBOTT Tr, non-standard 'Strath' type, 213gr. Duthie Torry 7.8.1917. Renamed JOHN MASON 1920. Sold 1921, renamed *Christiania T Purdy.*

JOHN AIKENHEAD Tr, 'Castle' type, 290gr. Cook Welton & Gemmell 19.12.1918. Sold 1919, renamed *Polly Johnson.* (POLLY JOHNSON in WW.II.)

JOHN ALFRED Dr 81/09, 1–3pdr. Hired 11.1914–19 and as M/S, 1–6pdr, 11.39. A/P Dr 9.40–6.45.

JOHN & ABIGAIL 40-gun ship, 356bm. Hired 1664–66.

JOHN & ELIZABETH Ship, 218bm. Hired 1664–67.

JOHN ANDERSON Tr, non-standard 'Castle' type, 273gr. Cook Welton & Gemmell 20.9.1917. Renamed CHARLES DORAN 1919. Sold 1922, same name. Hired as M/S 2.40–11.45.

JOHN ANDERSON 58/91. Purchased for examination service (RNZN) 1939. BU 1947.

JOHN & NORAH Dr 95/13, 1–6pdr. Hired 1915–19 and as M/S, 1–6pdr, 12.39. Examination service 1944–45.

JOHN & THOMAS 44-gun ship, 466bm. Hired 1664–67.

JOHN APPLEBY Tr, non-standard 'Mersey' type, 286gr. Cook Welton & Gemmell 30.1.1917. Sold 1922, renamed *Lois.* (LOIS in WW.II.)

JOHN ARTHUR Tr, non-standard 'Mersey' type, 286gr. Cook Welton & Gemmell 10.2.1917. Sold 1922, renamed *Gladys.* (GLADYS in WW.II.)

JOHN ASHLEY Tr, 'Castle' type, 290gr. Cook Welton & Gemmell 18.3.1919. Sold 1919, renamed *Limeslade.*

JOHN BAPTISH Tr, 'Castle' type, 290gr. Cook Welton & Gemmell 29.4.1918. Sold 1919, same name. Hired as M/S 9.1939–40.

JOHN BARRY Tr, 'Strath' type, 203gr. Hall Russell 24.7.1917. Sold 1921, renamed *Chrystabelle.*

JOHN BATEMAN Tr, 'Castle' type, 277gr. Cook Welton & Gemmell 29.5.1918. Sold 1921, renamed *Anderby.*

JOHN BELL Tr, 'Strath' type, 203gr. Hall Russell 12.2.1918. Sold 1921, renamed *John Smart.*

JOHN BENSON Tr, 'Castle' type. Cook Welton & Gemmell. Cancelled 1919.

JOHN BOMKWORTH Tr, 'Castle' type, 290gr. Cook Welton & Gemmell 29.5.1918. Renamed WEAR 1920. Sold 1922 Spanish navy as UAD RAS.

JOHN BOWLER Tr, 'Strath' type, 203gr. Hall Russell 1918. Sold 1922, renamed *Karabigha.*

JOHN BRADFORD Tr, non-standard 'Strath' type, 226gr. Hall Russell 25.4.1917. Sold 7.20, renamed *Dorleen.* (Served as BEN ARDNER in WW.II.)

JOHN BRASKET Tr, 'Strath' type, 203gr. Hall Russell 13.9.1917. Sold 1921, same name.

JOHN BRENNAN Tr, non-standard 'Castle' type, 260gr. Cook Welton & Gemmell 4.9.1917. Sold 1922, renamed *Iolite.* (Served as OSAKO in WW.II.)

JOHN BRICE Tr, non-standard 'Castle' type, 273gr. Cook Welton & Gemmell 22.8.1917. Renamed DERWENT 1920. Sold 1923, renamed *Beaulne Vernueil.* (BEAULNE VERNUEIL in WW.II.)

JOHN BRITTON Tr, 'Strath' type, 202gr. Hall Russell 1919. Sold 1919, renamed *Elsie Jessup.*

JOHN BROOKER Tr, non-standard 'Castle' type, 269gr. Cook Welton & Gemmell 9.6.1917. Sold 1921, renamed *Obsidian.* (Served as LOCH PARK in WW.II.)

JOHN BULL Cutter 14, 119bm. Hired 5.1804–11.06.

JOHN BULL Tug 165/80. Belgian, hired 12.1914. To War Dept 2.15.

JOHN BULLER Tr, 'Strath' type, 203gr. Hall Russell 1918. Sold 1919, renamed *San Pedro.*

JOHN BULLOCK Tr, 'Castle' type, 275gr. C Rennoldson 9.7.1917. Sold 1921, renamed *Filiep Coenen.* (Served as FLYING ADMIRAL in WW.II.)

JOHN BURLINGHAM Tr, non-standard 'Castle' type, 266gr. Cook Welton & Gemmell 21.4.1917. Sold 1920, renamed *Rehearo.* (REHEARO in WW.II.)

JOHN CALLAGHAN Tr, 'Strath' type, 205gr. Murdoch & Murray 7.10.1917. Sold 1921, renamed *Star of Liberty.* (STAR of LIBERTY in WW.II.)

JOHN CAMPBELL Tr, 'Castle' type, 280gr. G.Brown 1.11.1917. Renamed GEORGE DIXON 1919. Sold 1921, renamed *Lushby.*

JOHN CASEWELL Tr, 'Castle' type, 277gr. Ailsa 3.10.1917. Sold 1920, same name.

JOHN CATTLING Tr, 'Castle' type, 276gr. Bow McLachlan 1918. Sold 1920, same name. Hired as M/S 8.39–7.45.

JOHN CHATWAY Tr, 'Castle' type. Greenock. Cancelled 1919.

JOHN CHIVERS Tr, 'Castle' type, 276gr. Bow McLachlan 17.12.1917. Renamed ERNE 1920. Sold 1922 Spanish navy as UAD MARTIN.

JOHN CHURCH Tr, 'Castle' type, 281gr. Bow McLachlan 16.10.1917. Sold 1920, renamed *Antares.*

JOHN CLAVELL Tr, 'Castle' type, 276gr. Hepple 1920. Sold 1922, renamed *Denis.*

JOHN CLAY Tr, non-standard 'Strath' type, 212gr. A.Hall 16.11.1917. Sold 1921, renamed *Braconash.*

JOHN C MEIKLE Tr 194/14. Hired 1914–19.

JOHN COLLINS Tr, 'Castle' type, 277gr. Ailsa 19.11.1917. Sold 1920, renamed *Janera.*

JOHN CONDON Tr, 'Strath' type. Hall Russell. Cancelled 1919.

JOHN CONNE Tr,'Strath' type, 204gr. Hawthorns 30.5.1919. Sold 1921, renamed *Braconbush.*

JOHN COOMBE Tr, 'Castle' type. Greenock. Cancelled 1919.

JOHN COOPER Tr, 'Castle' type, 277gr. Harkess 5.7.1917. Sold 1922, renamed *Penfret.*

JOHN COPE Tr, 'Strath' type, 202gr. Rennie Forrest 1918. Sold 1919, renamed *River Garry.* (RIVER GARRY in WW.II.)

JOHN CORBETT Tr, 'Strath' type. Hall Russell. Cancelled 1919.

JOHN CORMACK Tr, 'Mersey' type, 324gr. Cochrane 4.9.1917. Sold 1922, renamed *Lord Pirrie.* (Served as CHILTERN in WW.II.)

JOHN CORWARDER Tr, 'Strath' type, 202gr. Fleming & Ferguson 20.9.1917. Sold 1919, renamed *River Nith.*

JOHN COTTRELL Tr, 'Mersey' type, 325gr. Goole SB 1919. Sold 1919, renamed *St Endellion.* (Served as BLIGHTY in WW.II.)

JOHN CREIGHTON Tr, 'Castle' type. Greenock. Cancelled 1919.

JOHN CURRAN Tr, 'Strath' type, 203gr. Montrose SY 1918. Sold 1922, renamed *Commandant Gamas.*

JOHN DAVIS Tr, 'Castle' type, 276gr. Bow McLachlan 1918. Sold 1921, renamed *Cesar de Paepe.*

JOHN DETHERIDGE Tr, 'Mersey' type. Cancelled 1919.

JOHN DIXON Tr, 'Mersey' type. Cochrane. Cancelled 1919.

JOHN DIXON (see JOHN CAMPBELL)

JOHN DONOVAN Tr 206/14, 1–3pdr. Hired 1914–19.

JOHN DORMOND Tr, 'Castle' type, 276gr. J P Rennoldson 1919. Sold 1922, renamed *Amethyst.*

JOHN DOWNIE Tr, 'Mersey' type. Cochrane. Cancelled 1919.

JOHN DUNKIN Tr, 'Strath' type, 202gr. Fleming & Ferguson 6.8.1918. Sold 1921, same name.

JOHN DUNN Tr, 'Mersey' type, 330gr. Ferguson 27.3.1918. Sold 1922, renamed *Florence Brierley*. (FLORENCE BRIERLEY in WW.II.)

JOHN DUPUIS Tr, 'Strath' type, 203gr. Abdela Mitchell 1918. Sold 1922, renamed *Ravenna*.

JOHN DUTTON Tr, 'Mersey' type, 330gr. Ferguson 17.1.1918. Sold 1922, renamed *Karlsefni*.

JOHN EBBS Tr, 'Mersey' type, 326gr. Cochrane 2.10.1917. Sold 1920, renamed *Pilote 4*.

JOHN EDMUND Tr, 'Mersey' type, 328gr. Goole SB 1918. Renamed FOYLE 1920. To War Dept 3.46. Sold 1947, renamed *Cramond Island*. (Was on loan SAN 9.21–6.34 as SONNEBLOM.)

JOHN EDSWORTH Tr, 'Strath' type, 202gr. Fullerton 1918. Sold 1919, renamed *River Leven*. (RIVER LEVEN in WW.II.)

JOHN E.LEWIS Tr 253/11. Hired 1914. Sunk 16.1.18 by mine off Harwich.

JOHN EVANS (see JOHN LEWIS)

JOHN EVELYN (ex-*Fort Lavernock*) Store carrier (RFA), 435gr, 142 x 25 ft. Purchased 1924. Sold 1946, same name.

JOHN FAIRMAN Tr, 'Strath' type, 202gr. Rennie Forrest 1918. Sold 1920, renamed *Ocean Victor*. (OCEAN VICTOR in WW.II.)

JOHN FELTON Tr, 'Mersey' type, 324gr. Cochrane 1.11.1917. Sold 1920, same name.

JOHN FISSER Tr, 'Strath' type, 202gr. Ritchie Graham 1918. Sold 1919, renamed *Joule*. (Served as MARY CAM in WW.II.)

JOHN FITZGERALD Tr, non-standard 'Strath' type, 235gr. Duthie Torry 14.12.1917. Sold 1921, same name. Hired as BDV 1.40–7.46.

JOHN FRANCOIS Tr, 'Strath' type, 203gr. Murdoch & Murray 1918. Sold 1921, renamed *Edith M Purdy*. (EDITH M PURDY in WW.II.)

JOHN GAUNTLET Tr, 'Castle' type, 290gr. Cook Welton & Gemmell 12.8.1918. Sold 1920, renamed *Nairobi*.

JOHN GEOGHAN Tr, 'Castle' type, 278gr. Ailsa 9.10.1918. Sold 1922, renamed *Miningsby*. (Served as CONGRE in WW.II.)

JOHN GILLMAN Tr, non-standard 'Castle' type, 236gr. Smiths Dk 9.1.1917. Sold 1920, same name.

JOHN GRAHAM Tr, 'Castle' type, 290gr. Cook Welton & Gemmell 27.7.1918. Sold 1921, renamed *Ruby*. (Served as EASTCOATES in WW.II.)

JOHN GRAY Tr, 'Strath' type, 203gr. Scott, Bowling 11.4.1918. Sold 1920, renamed *Fort Rona*.

JOHN GREGORY Tr, 'Castle' type. G.Brown 1919. Sold 1919.

JOHN GULIPSTER Tr, 'Castle' type, 290gr. Cook Welton & Gemmell 24.9.1918. Sold 1919, renamed *Betty Johnson*. (Served as COMITATUS in WW.II.)

JOHN G WATSON Tr 196/10. Hired 1915. Sunk 31.10.15 after collision at Stornoway.

JOHN G WATSON Tr 235/16, 1–6pdr. Hired 1916–19.

JOHN HAILE Tr, 'Strath' type, 204gr. Hawthorns 1918. Sold 1922, renamed *Tumby*. (TUMBY in WW.II.)

JOHN HEATH Tr, 'Strath' type, 202gr. Ouse SB 1919. Sold 1919.

JOHN HERD Dr 103/30. Hired on harbour service 1941–45.

JOHN HIGH Tr 228/ -. Hired 1916. Sunk 7.8.16 by mine in the White Sea.

JOHN HIGHLAND Tr, 'Mersey' type, 330gr. Ferguson 23.9.1918. Sold 1919, renamed *Ocean Ensign*.

JOHN HOWARD Tr, 'Strath' type, 202gr. Rennie Forrest 1919. Sold 1921, renamed *Evelina*. (EVELINA in WW.II.)

JOHN HUNS Tr, 'Strath' type, 202gr. Fullerton 1919. Renamed JOHN MOSS 1919. Sold 1919, renamed *Allenby*. (Served as SARAH A PURDY in WW.II.)

JOHN HUNTER Tr, 'Strath' type, 202gr. Rennie Forrest 1918. Sold 1921, renamed *Delila*. (DELILA in WW.II.)

JOHN JACKSON Tr, 'Strath' type, 202gr. Rennie Forrest 1918. Sold 1921, same name. (Served as INCHGOWER in WW.II.)

JOHN JACOBS Tr, 'Mersey' type, 325gr. Cochrane 1918. Sold 1922, renamed *Castelnau*. (CASTELNAU in WW.II.)

JOHN JEFFERSON Tr, 'Mersey' type, 324gr. Cochrane 1918. Sold 1922, renamed *St Amant*.

JOHN JOHNSON Tr, 'Mersey' type, 324gr. Cochrane 1918. Sold 1922, renamed *Cloughton Wyke*. (CLOUGHTON WYKE in WW.II.)

JOHN KENNEDY Tr, 'Strath' type. Abdela Mitchell 1919. Sold 1919.

JOHN KENTALL Tr, 'Strath' type, 204gr. Williamson 1918. Sold 1919, renamed *Wheatstone*.

JOHN KIDD Tr, 'Castle' type, 276gr. Smiths Dk 20.2.1917. Sold 9.20, renamed *Rotherslade*. (ROTHERSLADE in WW.II.)

JOHN LANGSHAW Tr, 'Strath' type, 200gr. Scott, Bowling 20.3.1919. Sold 1919, renamed *Ethel Crawford*.

JOHN LEMON Tr, 'Strath' type. Hall Russell. Cancelled 1919.

JOHN LEVER Tr, 'Strath' type. Hall Russell. Cancelled 1919.

JOHN LEWIS Tr, 'Castle' type, 275gr. C Rennoldson 1919. Renamed JOHN EVANS 1919. Sold 1920, renamed *Harry Melling*. (HARRY MELLING in WW.II.)

JOHN LINCOLN Dr 83/08, 1–3pdr. Hired 1914–19.

JOHN LYONS Tr, 'Castle' type, 276gr. Smiths Dk 23.3.1917. Sold 1922, renamed *Les Illates*.

JOHN McCONNELL Tr, 'Mersey' type. Cochrane. Cancelled 1919.

JOHN McCONNOCHIE Tug 90/79. Hired on harbour service 1.4.1918–19.

JOHN MANN Tr, 'Mersey' type, 324gr. Cochrane 1919. Sold 1919, renamed *Earl Haig.* (Served as BARNET in WW.II.)

JOHN MARSHALL Tr, 'Mersey' type. Cochrane. Cancelled 1919.

JOHN MASON (see JOHN ABBOTT)

JOHN MELEBURY Tr, 'Mersey' type. Cochrane. Cancelled 1919.

JOHN MINUTE Tr, 'Mersey' type. Cochrane. Cancelled 1919.

JOHN MITCHELL Dr 89/13. Hired 1915. Sunk 14.11.17 in collision off St Albans Head.

JOHN MOIRIS Tr, 'Mersey' type. Cochrane. Cancelled 1919.

JOHN MONDAY Tr, 'Mersey' type. Cochrane. Cancelled 1919.

JOHN MOSS (see JOHN HUNS)

JOHN MURPHY Tr, 'Mersey' type. Cochrane. Cancelled 1919.

JOHN OXLEY Australian Govt vessel, 544/27. Hired (RAN) 1942–46.

JOHN PASCO Tr, 'Mersey' tupe, 325gr. Cochrane 19.4.1917. Sold 1922, renamed *Arinbjorn Hersir.*

JOHN PAYNE Tug 145/09. Hired 7.1915–19.

JOHN PENDER Cable ship 2,336/00. Hired 6.1918–19.

JOHN POLLARD Tr, 'Castle' type, 276gr. Smiths Dk 21.5.1917. Sold 1920, renamed *Grosmont Castle.* (GROSMONT CASTLE in WW.II.)

JOHN QUILLIAM Tr, 'Mersey' type 324gr. Cochrane 12.3.1917. Sold 1920, renamed *Dana.*

JOHN ROBERT Dr 89/12. Hired 1915–19.

JOHN SANDERSON 3,274/89. Hired as mine carrier (RFA) 3.8.1914–19.

JOHN SHERBURN Tr 244gr. Hired 1915. Wrecked 6.3.15 near Dover.

JOHN S SUMMERS Dr 62/10. Hired 1915–19.

JOHN STEPHEN Tr 227/20. Hired as M/S 1.1940–11.45.

JOHN T GRAHAM Tr 198/12. Hired 1914–19.

JOHN THORLING Tr, 'Castle' type, 276gr. Smiths Dk 20.7.1917. Sold 1921, renamed *River Kent.* (Served as CONCERTATOR in WW.II.)

JOHN WATT Dr 84/11. Hired as store carrier 1915–19 and on harbour service 1941–45.

JOHN WELSTEAD Tr, 'Mersey' type, 324gr. Cochrane 1917. Sold 1922, renamed *Lord Harewood.*

JOHN WILLIAMSON Wh 159/12. Hired as M/S 5:1941. Norwegian crew 8.41. Lent Greek navy 7.43–46 as ALFIOS. Returned 1946.

JOHN WILLMENT Dr 101/32. Hired as M/S 1941–45.

JOHN WILSON Tug, 1–6pdr. Hired as A/P vessel 1941–45.

JOHN W MACKAY Cable ship 4,049/22. Hired 1942–46.

JOHN YULE Tr, 'Mersey' type, 324gr. Cochrane 24.3.1917. Sold 1921, renamed *Notre Dame de Lorette.*

JONATHAN BAZINO Tr, 'Strath' type, 203gr. Hall Russell 29.1.1919. Sold 1919, renamed *Pitstruan.*

JONATHAN BENJAMIN Tr, 'Strath' type. Hall Russell. Cancelled 1919.

JONATHAN BRONTON Tr, 'Strath' type. Hall Russell. Cancelled 1919.

JONATHAN CLARKE Tr, 'Mersey' type. Goole SB 1919. Sold 1919.

JONATHAN COLLINS Tr, 'Mersey' type, 325gr. Goole SB 1919. Sold 1919, renamed *St Minver.* (ST MINVER in WW.II.)

JONATHAN COLLIS Tr, 'Strath' type. Hall Russell. Cancelled 1919.

JONATHAN GREIG Tr, 'Strath' type, 204gr. Hawthorns 1919. Sold 1919, renamed *Strathglass.*

JONATHAN HARDY Tr, 'Strath' type, 202gr. Fullerton 1918. Sold 1921, renamed *Roche Bleue.*

JONGE JAN MFV 81/31. Belgian hired on harbour service 6.1940–11.45.

JONQUIL Tr 143/91. Hired 1918–19.

JOPORO French vedette, 51/32, seized 1940. A/P vessel 9.40–44.

JORDAENS MFV 74/29. Belgian, hired as BBV 1940. A/P vessel 1944–45.

JOSEPH Cutter 12. Hired 1796–1801.

JOSEPH Cutter 8, 98bm, 8–4pdr. Hired 6.1803–1.05 and 8.1807–7.09.

JOSEPH MFV 42/24. Belgian hired as A/P vessel 10.1940. Fire-Float 1942–11.46.

JOSEPH & SARAH MILES Tr 272/02. Hired 1.1915–19.

JOSEPH ANNISON Tr, non-standard 'Strath' type, 235gr. Duthie Torry 19.9.1917. Sold 1922, renamed *William Stephen.* (WILLIAM STEPHEN in WW.II.)

JOSEPH BARRETT Tr, 'Castle' type, 290gr. Cook Welton & Gemmell 2.11.1917. Sold 1919, renamed *Loch Morar.* (Served as TILBURYNESS, 279gr, in WW.II.)

JOSEPH BURGIN Tr, 'Strath' type, 203gr. Hall Russell 12.2.1918. Sold 1919, same name.

JOSEPH BUTTON Tr, 'Castle' type, 290gr. Cook Welton & Gemmell 17.12.1917. Sold 1919, same name. Purchased as M/S 8.39. Sunk 22.10.40 by mine off Aldeburgh.

JOSEPH COATES Tr, 'Strath' type, 205gr. Murdoch & Murray 1918. Sold 1921, renamed *Aigrette.*

JOSEPH CONNELL Tr, 'Castle' type, 280gr. G Brown 20.12.1917. Sold 1922, renamed *Hourtin.*

JOSEPH CONSTANTINE Tug 153/13. Hired for harbour service 2.5.1917–15.2.19.

JOSEPH CROSTHWAITE Tug 149/96. Hired for harbour service 31.8.1915–20.

JOSEPH CROWELL Tr, 'Castle' type. Greenock. Cancelled 1919.

JOSEPH DO Tr, 'Castle' type. Tyne. Cancelled 1919.

JOSEPH DUHAMEL Tr 928/29. French, seized 26.12.1940 in the Atlantic. Fitting as A/S Tr 3.41 but not completed. To MWT 4.41.

JOSEPH GIDDICE Tr, 'Castle' type, 280gr. G Brown 1918. Sold 1922, renamed *Oseby*.

JOSEPH GORDON Tr, 'Castle' type, 280gr. G Brown 29.6.1918. Sold 1922, renamed *Grouin-du-Cou*.

JOSEPH HODGKINS Tr, 'Castle' type, 276gr. Hepple 1919. Sold 1919, same name.

JOSEPHINE Yt, ex-Russian GORISLAVA commissioned 16.8.1918. Gone by 1920.

JOSEPHINE I (see SPARROW)

JOSEPHINE Dr 51/84. French, seized 7.1940 at Dover. Harbour service 1940–45.

JOSEPH MURRAY Tr, 'Mersey' type. Cochrane. Cancelled 1919.

JOSHUA ARABIN Tr, 'Castle' type, 290gr. Cook Welton & Gemmell 1919. Sold 1919, renamed *River Forth.* (Served as De la POLE in WW.II.)

JOSHUA BUDGET Tr, 'Strath' type, 202gr. Hall Russell 1919. Sold 1919, renamed *Mary Crowther.* (Served as OLDEN TIMES in WW.II.)

JOSHUA CARRETTS Tr, 'Strath' type. Hawthorns. Cancelled 1919.

J.S Dr 90/11. Hired 1915–19.

J T HENDRY Dr 88/08. Hired as BBV 1940–45.

J T STEPHEN Dr 82/08. Hired 1915–19.

JUBBULPORE (ex-QUETTA renamed 1944) Tr (RIN), 'Basset' class. Alcock Ashdown. Ordered 12.42, deferred 10.44, cancelled 1.45.

JUBBULPORE (see QUETTA)

JUDE (see MMS.239)

JUDITH Yt 45/26. Hired for training duty 1943–45.

JULIA Schooner 12, 156bm. Hired 7.1804–1.05.

JULIA DY store carrier, 122bm. Wright, Sittingbourne 17.1.1863 and purchased 2.1864. Ordered to BU 6.3.1871 at Sheerness. (Also known as Woolwich YC.2.)

JULIET Tr 173/06, 1–6pdr. Hired 1914–19.

JULIET M/S–A/S Tr, 545 tons, 150 x 28 ft, 1–12pdr. Cook Welton & Gemmell 2.10.1940. Sold 1947, renamed *Peterjon.*

JUNCO Tr 191/17. Hired 1917–19 and as HDPC 10.40. Target towing 1944–5.46.

JUNE ROSE Dr 96/18. Hired as M/S 10.1939. A/P Dr 1943–5.45.

JUNIATA 1,139/18. Purchased 1940. Sunk as blockship 1940.

JUNIOR (ex-*Juno*) Paddle 592/98, 1–6pdr. Hired as M/S 29.1.1915–27.6.19.

JUNIPER M/S Tr, 530 tons, 150 x 27½ ft, 1–12pdr. Ferguson 15.12.1939. Sunk 8.6.40 by the German cruiser ADMIRAL HIPPER off Norway.

JUPITER II Paddle 394/95, 1–6pdr. Hired as M/S 15.5.1915–29.5.20.

JUPITER Cstr 174/01? Dutch, hired as BBV 1941–42.
JURA Tr, 'Isles' class. Ardrossan DY Co 22.11.1941. Sunk 7.1.43 by 'U.371' in the western Mediterranean.
JUSTICE Rescue tug 1,360 tons, 147 x 33½ ft, 1–3in. Camden SB, New Jersey 18.10.1943 on lend-lease. Returned 3.46 to the USN.
JUSTICE (ex-*Empire Lola*) DY tug, 300/46. Transferred from MOT and renamed 3.1947. Sunk as target 7.67 off Bermuda.
JUSTIFIED Dr 93/25. Purchased as M/S 2.12.1939. Sunk 16.6.42 by mine off Malta.
JUSTIFIER Dr 93/25. Hired as M/S 12.1939–1.46.
JUST REWARD MFV. Hired as A/P vessel 6.1940–11.40.

KAHANUI Tug 207/26. Hired (RNZN) 1.1943–46.
KAI Wh 276/26. Norwegian, hired as M/S 8.7.1940–11.5.46.
KAI MING Launch 47/30. Hired on examination service 11.1940. Lost to the Japanese 2.42, Singapore area.
KAIWAKA Cstr 169/37. Commissioned as danlayer (RNZN) 25.5.1941. Listed to 1946.
KALAMALKA Motor M/S (RCN) 228 tons, 105 x 22 ft, 2–MG. Benson, Vancouver 29.12.1943. On sale list 11.45.
KALAN Yt 44/38. Hired as A/S Yt 10.1939, purchased 10.41. A/S training 5.41, target service 1944–46.
KALAVATI 1,408/28. Hired as A/P vessel (RIN) 10.1939. Store carrier 1944–45.
KALMIA Tr 189/94, 1–3pdr. Hired 1915. Lost 7.10.18 by fire at Stavres.
KALMIA II Tr 184/98, 1–6pdr. Hired 1916–19.
KALSO Tr 179/99. Hired 1917–19.
KAM Tug 386/38. Hired (RCN) 9.1943–45.
KAMPAR 971/15. Hired as A/S vessel 9.1939. Sunk 13.12.41 by air attack at Penang.
KANGAROO BDV (RAN) 730 tons, 150 x 32 ft, 1–3in. Cockatoo DY 4.5.1940.
KANIMBLA 10,985/36, 7–6in, 2–3in. Hired as AMC 9.1939; RAN from 1941. Landing ship, 1–4in, 2–12pdr, 10–20mm 1943. Returned 1949.
KANTARAH Barge 160dw/19. Hired as BBV 31.8.1939–44.
KAPHREDA Tr 245/11. Hired 1914. Sunk 8.6.16 by mine near the Corton light vessel.
KAPUNI Cstr 190/09. Commissioned as M/S (RNZN) 4.1941. Listed to 1946.

KARACHI Tr (RIN), 'Basset' class. Alcock Ashdown 1.12.1941. Sold 1946, renamed *Fravarta.*

KARA KARA Ferry 525/26, 1—12pdr. Hired as boom gate vessel (RAN) 1941—46.

KARANGI BDV (RAN) 730 tons, 150 x 32 ft, 1—3in. Cockatoo DY 16.8.1941.

KARANJA 9,891/31, 1—6in, 1—12pdr, 12—20mm. Hired as landing ship 24.7.1941. Sunk 11.12.42 by air attack off Bougie.

KAREN MARIE MFV 31/99. Danish, seized 1940. BBV 6.40. Sold 5.9.46.

KARMOY (see GLOBE V and INCHMARNOCK)

KASTORIA Tr 307/17, 1—6pdr. Hired 1917—19 and as A/S Tr 5.40. M/S 5.41—46.

KATE LEWIS Tr 207/16, 325 tons, 1—6pdr, 24 mines. Purchased as M/L 8.1916. Sold 1939.

KATHERINA Aux barge 127/10. Hired as BBV 5.1940—44.

KATHERINE 24—gun ship, 270bm. Hired 1649.

KATHERINE 36—gun ship, 298bm. Hired 1664—67.

KATHERINE Dr?, 2—MG. Hired as A/P vessel 3.1940—42.

KATHLEEN Yt 70/99. Hired as A/P Yt 1917—20.

KATHLEEN Yt 316/69. Hired as accommodation ship 6.1917—19.

KATHLEEN Dr 98/19. Hired as M/S 11.1939. Radar tender 1944—45.

KATHLEEN BURTON Tr 197/14. Hired 1916—19.

KATREEN Dr 104/16. Hired 1916—19.

KAUPO 2,420/88. Danish, seized 21.5.1940. Sunk 10.6.40 as block-ship.

KAYVILLE Harbour tug (RCN). Owen Sound 1944.

KEDAH 2,499/27. Hired as A/S vessel 14.12.1939. Accommodation ship 1943—6.46.

KELANA 88gr. Hired as A/S vessel 1.12.1939. Sunk 16.1.42 by Japanese air attack in Malayan waters.

KELANTAN 1,282/21. Hired as A/P vessel 18.12.1941. M/S depot ship 1944 and purchased. On sale list 2.47.

KELAT 1,849/81. Purchased as coal hulk (RAN) 1940. Sunk 19.2.42 by Japanese air attack on Port Darwin.

KELPY Tug 43/98. Hired for harbour service 6.11.1914—30.11.14.

KELT Tr 455/37, 1—4in. Purchased as A/S Tr 8.1939. Sold 1945, renamed *Camilla.*

KELVIN Tr 322/15. Hired 1915. Sunk 7.7.17 by mine off Harwich.

KENIA Tug 200/27, 1—MG. Hired for examination service 8.1939. Rescue tug 1940—1.11.45.

KENKORA II Yt 536/30. Hired as A/S Yt 1942—46.

KENNET Tr 167/99. Hired as boom gate vessel 1915—19.

KENNET (see ICEAXE)
KENNET Tug 42/90. Hired as boom tender 2.5.1940. Renamed
CREVICE 1940. Listed to 1941.
KENNYMORE Tr 225/14, 1–6pdr. Hired as M/S 1915–19 and as M/S
11.39. Sunk 25.11.40 by mine in the Thames estuary.
KENSINGTON Tr 172/00, 1–6pdr. Hired 1914–19.
KENT Cutter 14, 121bm. Hired 7.1804–29.9.04.
KENT DY craft, 114bm, 64 x 20½ ft. Woolwich DY 1811. Fate unknown.
KENT COUNTY Dr 86/11. Hired as decoy vessel 1915. Sunk 8.12.16
by mine off Lowestoft.
KENTISH HOY Aux barge 141/26. Hired as BBV 30.11.1939. Boom
tender 5.40–3.9.45.
KEPHALLINIA Schooner 1,267/93. Hired as store carrier 1941.
Foundered 13.8.41 off Alexandria.
KEREN (ex-HYDRA renamed 10.1941, ex-*Kenya*) 9,880/30, 1–6in,
1–12pdr, 12–20mm. Hired as landing ship 23.7.41; purchased 3.4.46.
On sale list 8.48.
KERNEVAL Tr 172/06. Hired as fuel carrier 10.4.1944–7.11.44.
KERNOOZER Dr 63/02. Hired 1918–19.
KERNOT 451/30. Belgian, hired on examination service 11.11.1940. To
Belgian navy 1.6.45 as training ship.
KERRERA Tr, 'Isles' class. Fleming & Ferguson 22.9.1941. Sold 1946,
renamed *Jason*. (On loan R.Norwegian navy 1944–9.46 as OKSOY.)
KERYADO Tr 252/20. French M/S seized 7.1940. Sunk 6.3.41 by
mine in the Channel.
KESSINGLAND Dr 78/08. Hired 1915–19.
KESTREL II Tr 181/98. Hired in WW.I.
KESTREL II Dr 75/06, 1–2½pdr. Hired 1914–19.
KESTREL Tug 70/97. Hired on examination service 9.10.1940. Boom
defence tug 1941–11.5.46.
KETHAILES Yt 626/03, 2–3pdr. Hired as A/P Yt 23.9.1914. Sunk
11.10.17 in collision off the Blackwater light vessel.
KEVERNE Tug 119/08. Hired on examination service 8.1939. Salvage
vessel 1942–44.
KEYSTONE (ex-*Gleaner*) MFV 19/29. Hired on harbour service 9.1939–
10.12.45.
KHARKI Oiler (RFA) 1,455 tons, 185 x 29 ft. Ex-collier 681/99,
purchased 20.3.1900. Sold 7.31 at Hong Kong.
KIAMA Dr 93/14, 1–6pdr. Hired 1914–19. (Served as GIRL ELLEN
in WW.II.)
KIAMARI Tr (RIN), 'Basset' class. Scindia SN Co. Ordered 12.1942,
deferred 10.44 and cancelled 1945.
KIANGA Cstr 338/22. Commissioned as M/S (RAN) 9.1941. Listed
to 1946.

KIA ORA MFV. Hired as A/P vessel 27.7.1940–45.

KIDDAW Dr 86/09. Hired as BBV 12.1939–7.45.

KIDWELLY CASTLE Tr 258/07, 1–6pdr. Hired 1914–19.

KIELDER CASTLE Tr 129/00. Hired 1917–19.

KIHNA Yt 574/30. Hired as A/S Yt 6.1942. S/M tender 1942–45.

KILDA (see JANUS)

KILDONAN CASTLE 9,692/99. Hired as AMC 25.3.1916–1.1.19.

KILLARNEY 2,100/93. Hired as accommodation ship 6.1940–46.

KILLDEER Tr 192/13, 1–6pdr. Hired 1914–19.

KILLEGRAY Tr, 'Isles' class. Cook Welton & Gemmell 27.5.1941. RNZN from 11.41.

KILLINGHOLME Paddle 508/12. Hired as fleet messenger 21.2.1916–21.4.17 and as kite-balloon depot 5.41–3.45.

KILMANY Dr 88/08, 1–3pdr. Hired 1915–19.

KILMANY Dr 96/25. Hired on harbour service 15.5.1940–12.45.

KILNBURN Dr 88/14, 1–3pdr. Hired 1915–19.

KILORAN Yt 277/30. Hired on examination service 11.1939. Laid up 1941; accommodation ship 8.41–44. On loan USN 12.44–6.45 and again laid up.

KIMBERLEY Tr 190/02, 1–12pdr. Hired 1914–19 and as A/P Tr 11.39. Renamed MANLY 12.39, returned 1940.

KIMBERLEY Dr. Hired as store carrier 1915–19.

KIMBERLEY II Tr 102/07, 1–3pdr. Hired 1915–19.

KIMBERLEY II (III?) Tr 181/02. Hired in WW.I.

KIMBERLEY IV Tr. Hired 1917–19.

KIMBLA BDV (RAN) 733 tons, 150 x 32 ft, 1–3in. Walker, Maryborough 11.1953. Research ship 3.56.

KIMMEROL Oiler (RFA) 2,400 tons, 220 x 35 ft. Craig Taylor, Stockton on Tees 4.4.1916. Sold 1949, renamed *Tenana*.

KINALDIE Tr 197/14, 1–6pdr. Hired 1915–19.

KINBRACE Salvage vessel 950 tons, 150 x 35½ ft, 2–20mm. A.Hall 17.1.1945.

KINCHELA Cstr 370/14. Hired as boom gate vessel (RAN) 1942–46.

KINCORTH Tr 148/09. Hired for special service 17.2.1917–18.

KINDRED STAR Dr 115/30, 1–6pdr. Hired as M/S 12.1939–2.46.

KINELLAR Tr 216/17, 1–6pdr. Hired 1917–19.

KINFAUNS CASTLE 9,664/99, 8–4.7in. Hired as AMC 8.1914–1.10.15.

KINGARTH (ex-SLEDWAY renamed 9.1944) Salvage vessel 950 tons, 150 x 35½ ft, 2–20mm. A.Hall 22.5.44.

KING ARTHUR Tr 159/98, 1–3pdr. Hired 1915–19.

KING BAY Cstr 237/38. Hired on examination service)RAN) 1940–46.

KING CANUTE Tr 195/99. Hired 1918–19.

KING DUCK Yt 70/30. Hired on air-sea rescue service 7.12.1940 and later purchased. Sold 11.45.

KING EDWARD Dr 63/01, 1–3pdr. Hired 1915–19.

KING EDWARD Tr 163/00, 1–6pdr. Hired as boom gate vessel 1915–19.

KING EGBERT Tr 159/99, 1–3pdr. Hired 1915–20.

KING EMPEROR Tr 246/14, 1–6pdr. Hired 1915–19 and as M/S 2.40. Fuel carrier 11.43–1.46.

KING ERIK Tr 228/99, 1–3pdr. Hired 1915–19.

KINGFISHER Dr 76/82. Hired 11.1914–12.14.

KINGFISHER (ex-*Alcyon*) Tr 322/15, 1–12pdr, 1–6pdr. Purchased 1915; renamed ADELE 1918, sold 1919.

KINGFISHER (see ADELE and KING SALVOR)

KING GEORGE A.ship. Hired 1794. Sunk 29.12.1794 by shore batteries at Tiburon.

KING GEORGE Cutter 12. Hired 1796–1801.

KING GEORGE Cutter 12, 128bm. Hired 1797, renamed GEORGIANA 1803. Stranded 9.1804 and burnt to avoid capture.

KING GEORGE Cutter 10, 58bm, 10–4pdr. Hired 6.1803–12.1804 and 9.1807–1814.

KING GEORGE Tr 164/01. Hired 1918–19.

KING GRUFFYD 5,063/19, 7–4in, 4–TT. Hired as decoy ship 14.9.1939. AMC 12.3.41–12.41 then to MWT. (Operated as decoy MAUNDER.)

KING HAROLD Tr 227/99. Hired 1918–19.

KING HENRY Tr 162/00. Hired 1918–19 and as boom gate vessel 5.40. A/P Tr 1941. Sunk 13.6.41 by air attack off Lowestoft.

KING HERRING Dr 100/09. Hired 1915–19.

KING LEAR Tr 311/06, 1–6pdr. Hired 1914–18.

KING ORRY 1,877/13, 2–4in. Hired as ABS 29.10.1914–28.1.19 and as ABV, 1–4in, 25.8.1939. Sunk 30.5.40 by air attack off Dunkirk.

KING RICHARD Tr 162/00, 1–3pdr. Hired 1915–19.

KING SALVOR (ex-ALLEGIANCE renamed 4.1942) Salvage vessel 1,440 tons, 200 x 38 ft, 4–20mm. Simons 18.5.42. Renamed KING-FISHER 4.54. Sold 1.61.

KINGSCOURT Tr 203/17. Hired as A/P Tr 11.1939. M/S 4.40, BBV 1944–9.45.

KINGS GREY Tr 338/15, 1–6pdr. Hired 1915–19 and as M/S, 1–12pdr, 8.39–9.46.

KING SOL Tr 486/36. Hired as A/S Tr 9.1939–12.45.

KING STEPHEN Tr 162/00. Hired as decoy ship 1915. Sunk 25.4.16 by the German destroyer 'G.41' in the North Sea.

KINGSTON Tr 162/97, 1–3pdr. Hired 1915–19.

KINGSTON AGATE Tr 464/37, 1—4in. Hired as A/S Tr 9.1939—1.46.
KINGSTON ALALITE Tr 412/33. Purchased as A/S Tr 8.1939. Sunk
10.11.40 by mine off Plymouth.
KINGSTON AMBER Tr 467/37, 1—4in. Hired as A/S Tr 9.1939—2.46.
KINGSTON ANDALUSITE Tr 415/34. Purchased as A/S Tr 8.1939.
Sold 1945.
KINGSTON BERYL Tr 356/28. Hired as ABV 9.1939. A/S Tr 3.41.
Sunk 25.12.43 by mine, north of Ireland.
KINGSTON CAIRNGORM Tr 448/35, 1—4in. Hired as A/S Tr 9.1939.
Sunk 18.10.40 by mine in the Channel.
KINGSTON CEYLONITE Tr 448/35, 1—4in. Hired as A/S Tr 9.1939,
purchased 11.39. Lent USN 2.42. Sunk 15.6.42 by mine in Chesapeake
Bay.
KINGSTON CHRYSOBERYL Tr 448/35, 1—4in. Hired as A/S Tr
9.1939—45.
KINGSTON CHRYSOLITE Tr 448/35. Purchased as A/S Tr 8.1939.
Sold 1945.
KINGSTON CORAL Tr 433/36, 1—4in. Hired as A/S Tr 9.1939—45.
KINGSTON CORNELIAN Tr 449/34. Purchased as A/S Tr 8.1939.
Sunk 5.1.40 in collision east of Gibraltar.
KINGSTON CRYSTAL Tr 433/36. Hired as A/S Tr 9.1939—45.
KINGSTON CYANITE Tr 433/36. Hired as A/S Tr 9.1939—45.
KINGSTON GALENA Tr 415/34, 1—4in. Purchased as A/S Tr 8.1939.
Sunk 24.7.40 by air attack off Dover.
KINGSTON JACINTH Tr 356/29. Hired as ABV 8.1939. A/S Tr 10.40.
Sunk 12.1.43 by mine off Portsmouth.
KINGSTON OLIVINE Tr 378/30, 1—4in. Purchased as A/S Tr 8.1939.
M/S 7.42. Sold 1945.
KINGSTON ONYX Tr 357/28. Hired as ABV 8.1939. A/S Tr 4.41.
In 9.44 for return.
KINGSTON PERIDOT Tr 356/29. Hired as ABV 8.1939. A/S Tr 4.41—
12.45.
KINGSTON SAPPHIRE Tr 356/29. Purchased as ABV 9.1939. Sunk
5.10.41 by U-boat off Gibraltar.
KINGSTON TOPAZ Tr 357/27. Hired as ABV 8.1939—11.45.
KINGSTON TURQUOISE Tr 356/29. Hired as ABV 8.1939. A/S Tr
10.40—11.45.
KINGSWAY Tr 211/05, 1—3pdr. Hired 1915—19 and as A/P Tr 11.39—
2.40.
KINGSWEAR 1,457/09. Hired as ammo. carrier (RFA) 23.11.1914—
24.3.19.
KINGUSSIE (ex-SOLWAY renamed 9.1944) Salvage vessel 950 tons,
150 x 35½ ft. Robb. Cancelled 10.44.

KINLOSS Salvage vessel 950 tons, 150 x 35½ ft, 2—20mm. A.Hall 14.4.1945.

KINSMAN Tug 119/08. Hired on examination service 3.1.1917—1.19.

KINTERBURY Armament store carrier 1,488 tons, 185 x 33 ft. Philip, Dartmouth 14.11.1942.

KINTYRE Tr, 'Isles' class. Ardrossan DY Co 21.10.1941. Sold 5.46.

KIPPER Dr 92/08. Hired 1916—19.

KIRIN Yt 202/13. Hired as BBV 13.9.1940, purchased 4.42. Sold 12.45.

KIRITONA Cstr 136/09. Hired as degaussing vessel (RNZN) 1942—46.

KIRKELLA Tr 436/36, 1—4in. Purchased as A/S Tr 8.1939. Sold 1946.

KIRKLAND Tr 224/08. Hired 1915. Sunk 20.8.17 by mine off the Shetlands.

KIRKLINTON Tr 227/16, 1—6pdr. Hired 1916—19.

KIRRIEMOOR 4,970/35, 2—12pdr. Hired as boom carrier 8.1940—6.46.

KISMET (see PROVIDENCE)

KITE II Tr 168/03, 1—6pdr. Hired 1914—19.

KITE Tug 69/02. Hired for DY service 11.1914—12.18.

KITTERN Tr, 'Isles' class. Cook Welton & Gemmell 21.8.1943. Sold 4.46.

KITTIWAKE Tr 153/91. Hired 1918—19.

KITTY Tr 181/98. Hired 1918—19.

KITTY GEORGE Dr 87/13. Hired 1916—19 and as water carrier 12.40—46.

KITTYHAWKE Yt 41/21. Hired on air-sea rescue service 22.8.1940. Firefloat 3.43. Sunk 11.4.44 in collision off Portsmouth.

KIWI Tr (RNZN) 600 tons, 150 x 30 ft, 1—4in, 1—20mm. Robb, Leith 7.7.1941. Sold 9.63 G.Sparrey, Auckland to BU.

KLIAS Cstr 207/27. Hired as M/S 7.1.1941. Scuttled 15.2.42 off Palembang to avoid capture by the Japanese.

KLO Wh 307/37. Norwegian, hired as A/S Wh 1940—9.46.

KLONDIKE Tr 155/98. Hired 1915. Sunk 4.6.16 in collision off the Owers.

KNIGHT ERRANT Tug 148/05. Hired as A/P vessel 24.10.14—19.

KNIGHT of MALTA 1,553/29. Hired as ABV 1.7.1940. Store carrier 11.40. Sunk 3.41 by enemy action.

KNIGHT TEMPLAR 7,175/05, 4—6in. Hired as escort 27.5.1917—5.2.19.

KNOT Tr 168/03. Hired 1915. Wrecked 5.11.16 on the North Carr rock.

KNOYDART Yt 45/35. Hired on harbour service 11.7.1940—12.44.

KOALA BDV (RAN) 768 tons, 150 x 32½ ft, 1—12pdr. Cockatoo DY 4.11.1939.

KODAMA Tr 255/11, 1—6pdr. Hired 1915—19.

KOLABA (see COCHIN and MULTAN)

KOMMETJE (ex-*Uni VIII*) Wh 252/30, 1—6pdr. Hired as M/S (SAN) 11.1940—3.46.

KONING ALBERT MFV 70/24. Belgian, hired as BBV 30.8.1940–9.45.
KOOKABURRA BDV (RAN) 533 tons, 135 x 30½ ft, 1–12pdr. Cockatoo
DY 29.10.1938.
KOOMPARTOO Ferry 448/22, 2–20mm. Purchased as gate vessel (RAN)
6.1942. Sold 8.6.62.
KOOPA Ferry 416/11. Hired RAN 1942–44.
KOORAH Tr 227/12, 1–3pdr. Hired 1914–19.
KOPANES Tr 351/15, 1–12pdr. Hired as A/P Tr 2.6.1940. Sunk 19.4.41
by air attack off the Tyne.
KORAB I Tr 263/38. Polish, hired on examination service 10.1940–46.
KORALEN Dr 106/35. Norwegian, hired on harbour service 10.1940–45.
(On loan USN 11.42–10.43.)
KOROWA Tr 324/19. Hired as M/S (RAN) 9.1939–46.
KORTENAER Cstr 384/30. Dutch, hired as BBV 8.1941–1.46.

'Kos' type Norwegian whalers: KOS I–VII all 248/29; KOS VIII, IX
both 248/30; KOS X–XVIII all 258/32; KOS XIX 305/36; KOS XX
356/36: KOS XXI–XXIII all 353/37.
KOS I Hired as A/P Wh 7.1940, renamed SVOLVAER (Norwegian crew)
8.7.40. Returned 6.45.
KOS II Hired on air-sea rescue (Norwegian crew). Renamed HORTEN
8.7.40. A/S Wh 1943–45.
KOS IV Hired as M/S (Norwegian crew) 7.40. Renamed DROBAK 1941.
Returned 30.6.46.
KOS V Hired on air-sea rescue 7.40 (Norwegian crew). Renamed RISOR
1941. RN 6.42; A/S Wh 1943–6.45.
KOS VI Hired as A/S Wh (Norwegian crew) 7.40. Renamed FARSUND
1941. Returned 6.45.
KOS VII Hired as M/S 11.40. Renamed DAYBREAK 9.41. Returned
1945.
KOS VIII Hired as M/S 11.40. Renamed DEW 9.41. Firefloat 5.44;
examination service 1.45–5.46.
KOS IX Hired as M/S 11.40. Renamed FIRMAMENT 9.41. Stranded
and lost 30.5.44 near Alexandira.
KOS X Hired as M/S 11.40. Renamed FLICKER 9.41. Returned 12.45.
KOS XI Hired as M/S 11.40. Renamed FULL MOON 9.41. Returned
5.46.
KOS XII Hired as M/S 11.40. Renamed HAILSTORM 9.41. Danlayer
1944–9.45.
KOS XIII Hired as M/S (Norwegian crew) 7.40. Renamed BREVIK
1941. Returned 6.45.
KOS XIV Hired as M/S (Norwegian crew) 7.40. Renamed MANDAL
1941. Wrecked 19.9.45 off Farsund.

KOS XV Hired as M/S (Norwegian crew) 7.40. Renamed GRIMSTAD 1941. Returned 1.46.

KOS XVI Hired as M/S (Norwegian crew) 7.40. Sunk 24.8.41 in collision.

KOS XVII Hired as M/S (Norwegian crew) 7.40. Renamed HARSTAD 1941. Sunk 26.2.43 by E-boats in the Channel.

KOS XVIII Hired as M/S (Norwegian crew) 7.40. Renamed VARDO 1941. Returned 1945.

KOS XIX Hired as A/S Wh1940. Renamed COCKER 9.41. Sunk 3.6.42 by 'U.331' off Bardia.

KOS XX Hired as A/S Wh 1940. Renamed MOLDE (Norwegian crew) 1941. Returned 1945.

KOS XXI Hired as A/S Wh 1940. Renamed WHIPPET 9.41. Sunk 4.10.41 by air attack in the Mediterranean.

KOS XXII Hired as A/S Wh 1.41. Sunk 2.6.41 by air attack in the eastern Mediterranean.

KOS XXIII Hired as A/S Wh 1.41. Scuttled 5.41 in Suda Bay to avoid capture.

KOSMOS Tr 231/16, 1—6pdr. Hired 1916—19.

KROOMAN Tug 61gr, 1—MG. Hired as rescue tug and on harbour service 1940?—8.45.

KRUGERSDORP (see UNI V)

KUALA 954/11. Hired as A/P vessel 22.12.1939. Sunk 14.2.42 by Japanese air attack in the Dutch East Indies.

KUDAT 1,725/14. Hired as A/P vessel 18.12.1941. Sunk 30.12.41 by air attack while fitting out at Port Swettenham.

KUDOS Tr 207/11, 1—6pdr. Hired 1915—19.

KUMU Tr 315/13, 1—6pdr. Hired 1914—19.

KUNG WO 4,636/21, 1—4in. Hired as M/L 18.1.1941. Sunk 14.2.42 by Japanese air attack, Singapore area.

KUNISHI Tr 268/17, 1—12pdr. Hired 1917—19.

KUNISHI Tr 303/27, 1—12pdr. Purchased as M/D 8.1939. Sold 4.46.

KURAMIA 335 tons. Hired as gate vessel (RAN) 2.1942, purchased 9.43. Listed in 1965.

KURD Tr 352/30, 1—12pdr. Hired as M/S 1939. Sunk 10.7.45 by mine off the Lizard.

KUROKI Tr 248/09, 1—6pdr. Hired 1915—19 and as BDV 1.40. In 7.45 to return.

KURUMBA Oiler (RAN) 8,350 tons, 366 x 45½ ft. Swan Hunter 14.9.1916. Sold circa 1946.

KUTUBTARI 237/15. Hired as A/P vessel (RIN) 1939—6.46.

KUVERA Tr 202/19, 1—6pdr. Hired as A/P Tr 7.1940—9.45.

KWANG MING Launch 37gr. Hired for examination service 1940. Reported 3.42 in Japanese hands.

KYBRA Cstr 858/26, 1—4in. Hired as A/S vessel (RAN) 7.1940—46.
KYLEMORE Paddle 319/97, 1—6pdr. Hired as M/S 11.1915—20.2.20
and as M/S 9.39. Netlayer 8.40. Sunk 21.8.40 by air attack at Harwich.
KYMRIC Tr 126/91, 1—6pdr. Hired 1916—19.

LABOUR (ex-*Labourdonnais*) Tug 362/16. Hired as DY tug 1.3.1916—
20.
LABRADOR DY tug 170 tons, 85 x 25 ft. Appledore SB Ltd. 19.7.1966.
La BRISE MFV 51/39. French, seized 1940. A/P vessel 8.40. Free-French
crew 1941—44.
LABURNUM Dr 82/07, 1—3pdr. Hired 13.11.1914—19.
LACENNIA Tr 348/31, 1—12pdr. Hired as M/S 10.1939—2.46.
LACERTA Tr 270/11. Hired as A/P Tr 6.1940. M/S 3.42—2.46.
LACONIA 18,099/12. Hired as AMC 27.10.1914—2.8.16.
LACONIA 19,695/22, 8—6in, 2—3in. Hired as AMC 9.1939. To MWT
1941 as trooper.
LADAS Tr 172/98. Hired 1918—19.
LADY ANN Lugger 12. Hired 1799—1801.
LADY AUDREY Dr 62/02, 1—3pdr. Hired 1915—19.
LADY BALTIMORE Yt 58/15. Hired (RCN) 1944—45.
LADY BERYL Tr 417/35, 1—4in. Hired as A/S Tr 9.1939. In 6.45 to
return.
LADY BLANCHE Yt 405/07. Hired 7.3.1915—20.3.19 and as A/S Yt
9.39. Accommodation ship 7.42—11.45.
LADY BRASSEY Tug 362/13. Hired as rescue tug 30.7.1914—19 and
as rescue tug, 2—MG, 20.12.39—6.46.
LADY CARMICHAEL (ex-*The Lady Carmichael*) Paddle 376/71. Hired
as M/L, 10 mines, 16.5.1918—19.
LADY CLARE Paddle 234/91. Hired as M/S 25.5.1917—24.12.18.
LADY CORY WRIGHT 2,516/06. Hired as mine carrier (RFA) 3.8.1914.
Sunk 26.3.18 by U-boat off the Lizard.
LADY CRADDOCK Commissioned as A/P vessel (RIN) 9.1939. Capsized
16.10.42 in the Hooghly.
LADY ELEANOR Tr 324/18. Hired as BDV 5.1940, purchased 11.40.
Sold 1.47.
LADY ELIZABETH Tug 165/27. Hired on harbour service 8.1939—
10.45.
LADY ELSA Tr 518/37. Hired as A/S Tr 9.1939—1.46. (On loan USN
3.42—10.42.)
LADY ENID Tr 354/29. Hired as M/S 8.1939—12.45.
LADY ESTELLE Tr 323/15, 1—6pdr. Hired as A/P Tr 1940. M/S 1.42—
45.

LADY EVELYN Paddle 320/00. Hired as M/S 4.1917–6.19.

LADY HOGARTH Tr 472/37, 1–12pdr. Hired as A/P Tr 10.1939. A/S Tr 12.40–45.

LADY ISMAY Paddle 495/11. Hired as M/S 4.11.1914. Sunk 21.12.15 by mine off the Longsands.

LADY LILIAN Tr 581/39, 1–4in. Hired as A/S Tr 1.1940. Sunk 16.3.41 by air attack west of Ireland.

LADYLOVE Tr 230/03. Hired as M/S 7.1940–10.40.

LADY MADELEINE Tr 581/39, 1–4in. Hired as A/S Tr 2.1940–2.46.

LADY MAGDALEN 82gr. Hired for harbour service 1.1918–19.

LADY MAY Yt. Hired as M/S 10.11.1942. To War Dept 7.44.

LADY MOYRA Paddle 519/05, 2–6pdr. Hired as M/S 21.11.1915–9.7.19.

LADY NELSON 7,970/28. Hired as ABV (RCN) 10.1939. Conversion not completed.

LADY OLIVE Cstr 701/13, 1–4in, 4–12pdr. Hired as decoy ship (Q.18) 24.11.1916. Sunk 19.2.17 by U-boat in the Channel.

LADY PATRICIA 1,372/16, 1–4in, 2–12pdr. Hired as decoy ship (Q.25) 6.2.1917. Sunk 20.5.17 by 'U.46' in the Atlantic while operating as PAXTON.

LADY PHILOMENA Tr 417/36, 1–4in. Hired as A/S Tr 8.1939–10.45.

LADY ROSEMARY Tr 472/37. Purchased as A/S Tr 28.5.1940. Laid up 9.45, sold 5.46, renamed *Kingston Ruby*. (On loan USN 3.42–10.42.)

LADY ROWENA Paddle 332/91. Hired as ferry 12.4.1916. M/S 12.8.17–6.2.19.

LADY SHAHRAZAD Yt 439/04. Hired as A/S Yt 9.1939, purchased 3.41. A/S training 1941. Sold 1946.

LADY SHIRLEY Tr 472/37, 1–12pdr. Hired as A/P Tr 27.5.1940. A/S Tr 1.41. Sunk 11.12.41 by 'U.374' off Gibraltar.

LADY SLATER Cstr 273/34. Hired on examination service 12.1939. Lost by fire 30.7.40.

LADYSMITH Dr 89/04. Hired 1915. Foundered 27.12.15 in a gale off Milford Haven.

LADYSMITH Tr 254/06, 1–6pdr. Hired 1915–20.

LADY SOMERS 8,194/29. Hired as OBV 10.1940. Sunk 15.7.41 by U-boat in the N. Atlantic.

LADY STANLEY Tr 276/17, 1–12pdr. Hired as A/P Tr 12.6.1940. M/S 5.41–26.9.45.

LADY SYBIL Tug 97/13. Hired on harbour service 11.1939–44.

LADY VAGRANT Yt 484/03. Hired as A/S Yt 8.1939. Renamed VRYSSIE 1940, returned 14.2.40.

LADY WINDSOR Tug 74gr. Hired 7.1914–19.

LAERTES A/S Tr 530 tons, 150 x 28 ft, 1–12pdr, 3–20mm. Cook Welton & Gemmell 16.10.1940. Sunk 25.7.42 by U-boat off Freetown.

LAESO Dr 148/28. Danish, seized 5.1940. BBV 6.40. Boom tender 1943–46.

LAGGAN (see PLADDA)

LAGUNA BELLE Paddle 617/96, 1–12pdr. Hired as M/S 9.1939. A/A ship 9.42; accommodation ship 1943–6.45. Returned 7.46.

LAHLOO Yt 55/37. Hired as HDPC 5.10.1939, purchased 9.9.41. Sold 10.1.46.

LAHORE Tr (RIN), 'Basset' class. Shalimar 20.12.1941. Sold 1946.

LAICH o'MORAY Dr 79/09. Hired 1915–19.

LAIRDS ISLE 1,783/11, 1–4in, 2–20mm. Hired as ABV 28.8.1939. Torpedo school ship 1940–1.44.

LAKE NEUCHATEL 3,859/07. Purchased 1940. Sunk 1940 as blockship. Raised 6.48 and BU.

LAMA 2,198/05, 3–4.7in. Hired as ABS 12.7.1915–17.1.18.

LAMA French navy tug seized 1940. Renamed GREENFINCH minelayer, 10.40. Reverted to LAMA 1943 and laid up. Listed to 10.43.

LAMONT (ex-*Clan Lamont*) 9,512/39, 1–4in, 1–12pdr, 1–40mm, 10–20mm. Purchased as landing ship; completed 5.1944. Renamed ARD PATRICK 8.8.45; sold 1946.

LANAKAI 105 tons. Gate vessel (RAN) on loan from the USN 12.1941–11.45.

La NANTAISE (see ST ARCADIUS)

LANARK 1,900/23. Hired as boom carrier 7.1945–8.45.

LANCASHIRE 9,650/17. Hired as accommodation ship in WW.II.

LANCELOT Tug 71/06. Hired on harbour service 10.12.1917–19.

LANCER Tr 275gr, 1–6pdr. Smiths Dk 17.12.1914; purchased 11.12.14. Renamed LANCER II 1917. Sunk 18.7.18 in collision off Brighton light vessel.

LANCER A/S Tr 750 tons, 175 x 30 ft, 1–4in, 4–20mm. Cook Welton & Gemmell 26.10.1942. Sold 1946, renamed *Stella Orion*.

LANDBREEZE Admiralty steel Dr, 94gr. Colby 1919. Sold 1919, same name.

LANDEMER Ferry 533/03. French M/L seized 3.7.1940 at Southampton. To MWT 10.40.

LANDFALL Admiralty steel Dr, 97gr. Lewis 15.6.1918. Sold 1946.

LANGDON McKENNAN Tr, 'Mersey' type, 324gr. Cochrane 1919. Sold 1919, renamed *Douglas H Smith*.

LANERCOST Tr 227/16, 1–12pdr. Hired 1916–19.

LANGLAAGTE (see ALBERT HULETT)

LANNER Dr 103/12, 1–6pdr. Hired as M/S 1915–19 and as M/S 11.39–2.46.

LANTAKA Tug 300 tons? Lost on stocks 3.1942 at Singapore.

LANYARD Armament store carrier 220gr, 115 x 22½ ft. Scarr, Hessle 19.3.1938.

LAOMEDON 6,491/12. Hired as boom carrier 3.8.1939–4.46.
LAPAGERIA Tr 174/16, 1–6pdr. Hired 1916–19 and as M/S 9.40.
Fuel carrier 1.42–2.46.
La PARISIENNE Dr 85/13. Hired 1915–19.
La PERNELLE French navy tug seized 1940 at Southampton. On
examination service 10.40; harbour service 1943–45.
L'APPEL a la MER MFV 55/36. French M/S seized 1940. Laid up
to 9.41 then A/P vessel. Paid off 3.44. (L'APPEL de la MER in some
lists.)
LAPWING II Tr 217/04, 1–6pdr. Hired 1915–19 and as LAPWING,
A/P Tr 27.11.39–1.40.
LAPWING III Tr 194/03. Hired 1915–19.
LAPWING IV Dr 89/07. Hired 1915–19.
LAPWING V Tr 152/94. Hired 1918–19.
LARCH (ex-*St Alexandra*) Tr 359/28, 1–12pdr. Purchased as M/S
3.1939. Sold 1946, renamed *Westhill.*
LARCH LAKE Motor M/S (RCN) 255 tons, 126 x 26 ft. Grew Bts
Co 8.9.1945. To Russian navy 2.11.45.
LARCHOL Oiler (RFA) 2,200 tons, 220 x 34 ft. Lobnitz 19.6.17.
Arrived 23.8.59 at Antwerp to BU.
LARCHWOLD Tr 129/96. Hired 1917–19.
LARGS (see CHARLES PLUMIER)
LARIAT Rescue tug, 'B.A.T.' class. Levingston 15.5.1942 on lend-
lease. Returned 2.46 to the USN.
LARK Lugger 14. Hired 1799–1801.
LARK II Tr 280/07, 1–12pdr. Hired 1915–19.
LARK Tr 133/91. Hired in WW.I.
LARMOR (see CH.32)
LARNE 3,808gr. Hired as store carrier (RFA) 2.9.1918–19.
LAROC Yt 87/39. Hired on examination service 9.1939–6.46.
LARSEN (ex-*A.E. Larsen*) Wh 162/24. Hired as M/S (SAN) 1.1940–
25.4.46.
LARUT 894/27. Hired as A/P vessel 18.12.1941. Sunk 22.1.42 by
Japanese air attack east of Sumatra.
LARWOOD Tr 452/36, 1–4in. Hired as A/S Tr 25.8.1939. Sunk
25.4.40 by air attack off Norway. Salved and became German
FRANKE 30.5.40. Recovered 1945, sold 1947.
La SALICOQUE Tug? French, seized 1940. Salvage vessel from
24.12.41. Diving tender 1942–45.
LASHER Admiralty steel Dr, 96gr. A.Hall 1919. Sold 1919, same
name. Hired on examination service 27.8.39. Harbour service 1942–
46.
LASSIE Dr 88/09. Hired 1915–19.

LASSIE MAIN Dr 84/10. Hired 1.1915–19 and as BBV 19.5.40–6.44.

LASSO Cable ship 903 tons, 180 x 35 ft, 1–12pdr. Thornycroft 17.3.1938. BU 1959.

LASS o'DOUNE Pilot 92/10. Hired on examination service 9.1939. Laid up 7.43.

LATIMER (see EMPIRE RIDLEY)

L'ATLANTIQUE Tr 659/20. French A/P Tr seized 3.7.1940 at Plymout. A/S Tr to 4.4.46.

LAUNCH OUT Dr 67/09. Hired 1915. Sunk 27.10.16 by German destroyers in the Dover Straits.

LAURA Tr 280/05. Hired 1917–19.

LAURA BADA Yt 150gr. Hired as A/P Yt (RAN) 1943–45.

LAURANA 400/39. Italian prize. RN as special service vessel from 9.43. Sold 15.7.46 Malta SS Co.

LAUREATE Tr 194/98. Hired 1917–19.

LAUREATE (see IMPALA)

LAUREL Wood S tug 30 tons, 55 x 11½ ft. Purchased 1897. Sold 1901.

LAUREL DY tug 30 tons. Dating from 1901. Renamed MISTLETOE 1913. Sold 3.23 to BU.

LAUREL II Tr 138/97, 1–6pdr. Hired 1914–19.

LAUREL III Dr 97/07, 1–3pdr. Hired 1915–19.

LAUREL (ex-*Kingston Cyanite*) Tr 590 tons, 1–4in. Purchased as M/S 11.1935. Sold 1948, renamed *Strathyre*.

LAUREL BANK Dr 84/08, 1–57mm. Hired 1915–19.

LAUREL CROWN Dr 81/12. Hired 12.1914. Sunk 2.6.16 by mine west of the Orkneys.

LAURELIA Dr 96/07, 1–3pdr. Hired 11.1914–19.

LAUREL LEAF Oiler (RFA), 5,631gr. Craig Taylor 30.8.1916. Sold 1919.

LAURENTIC 14,892/08. Hired as AMC 31.10.1914. Sunk 25.1.17 by mine off northern Ireland.

LAURENTIC 18,734/27, 7–5.5in, 3–4in. Hired as AMC 8.1939. Sunl 3.11.40 by 'U.99' in the N.W.Approaches.

LAURIER Canadian Govt vessel, 201/37. Commissioned as A/S vessel 12.4.1940. Paid off 11.45.

LAVAL (ex-*HS.43*) Dy tug 300 tons. Transferred from War Dept 1918? Sold 24.11.20.

LAVALEE Motor M/S (RCN) 228 tons, 105 x 22 ft. Benson 27.5.1943. For disposal 1946.

LAVANDOU (see CH.43)

LAVATERA Dr 84/13, 1–3pdr. Hired 3.1915–20 and as BBV 4.40–46.

LAVEROCK Dr 58/01. Hired 1918–19.
LAVEROCK Tr 275/17. Hired as BDV 12.1939, purchased 11.43.
Sold 3.46.
LAVINIA Tr 198/00. Hired as BDV 1915–19.
LAVINIA L Dr 73/17. Hired as BBV 12.1939. Sunk 5.6.41 by air
attack at Sheerness.
LAWRENCE HUGHSON Tr, 'Strath' type, 202gr. Rennie Forrest
1919. Sold 1919, renamed *Elloe*.
LAWRENNY CASTLE Tr 256/08, 1–12pdr. Hired 1916–19.
LAXMI Tr 310/18. Hired as A/P Tr (RIN) 1940–6.46.
LAYBURN BDV 800 tons, 160 x 34 ft, 2–40mm. Simons 14.4.1960.
LAYMOOR BDV (as LAYBURN). Simons 6.8.1959.

LCI(L) Infantry landing craft (large) 234 tons, 150 x 23 ft, 4–20mm.
220 vessels built in the USA 1942–43 and on lend-lease to the RN
and RCN. Numbers from 3 to 537.
LCI(S) Infantry landing craft (small) 63 tons, 100 x 21½ ft, 2–20mm.
Built 1943; numbered from 501. (2,000 added to the numbers in
1944.)
LCT(1)–(8) Tank landing craft (marks 1–8)
LCT(1).1–99 226 tons, 135 x 29 ft, 2–2pdr. Built 1940–41.
LCT(2).100–299 296 tons, 143 x 31 ft, 2–2pdr. Built 1942–43.
LCT(3). 300–499 350 tons, 175 x 31 ft.
LCT(3). 7001–50 625 tons. Built 1941–44.
LCT(4). 500 up 200 tons, 171 x 39 ft. Built 1942–45.
LCT(5) and (6). 2001 up. 143 tons. 112 x 33 ft, 2–20mm. 171 on
lend-lease 1942–43.
LCT(8). 4001 up 657 tons, 225 x 39 ft, 4–20mm. Built 1945–47.
Of this series, the following were renamed in 1956 and are listed in
volume I: 4001 (REDOUBT), 4038 (CITADEL), 4039 (PARAPET),
4040 (BASTION), 4044 (PORTCULLIS), 4064 (SALLYPORT) and
4099 (BUTTRESS).
The following were renamed on transfer to the War Dept in 1956:
4002 (*Agheila*), 4041 (*Abbeville*), 4061 (*Audemer*), 4062 (*Aachen*),
4073 (*Ardennes*), 4074 (*Antwerp*), 4085 (*Agedabia*), 4086
(*Arromanches*), 4097 (*Andalnes*) and 4128 (*Arezzo*).
LCF (A/A vessels) and LCG (gunboats) were converted LCTs. The
following were all small craft of from 3 to 30 tons built during WW.II:
LCA (landing craft [assault]), LCM (mechanised), LCP (personnel),
LCV (vehicle).

LEADER Dr 72/03, 1–6pdr. Hired 1915–19.
LEAD ME Dr 71/06, 1–3pdr. Hired 1915–19.

LEAM Tr 236/17, 1–6pdr. Hired 1917–19.
LEANDER Tr 276/07. Hired 1914. (Perhaps renamed LEANDROS.)
LEANDROS Tr 276gr. Sunk 6.8.1915 by mine off the North Knock.
LEA RIG Dr 83/08, 1–3pdr. Hired 1915–19.
LEA RIG MFV 21/39. Hired as HDPC 11.1939–46.
LEASOWE Ferry 734/21. Hired as BBV 7.1940–12.42.
LEBANON Dr 60/04. Hired as BDV 6.1915–19.
Le DINAN MFV. French, seized 3.7.1940 at Plymouth. A/P vessel
11.40–11.45. (Known as MFV.2020 from 3.43.)
LEEDS Tr 162/97. Hired 1918–19.
LEEDS UNITED Tr 405/33. Hired as A/S Tr 10.1939–45.
LEEFIELD Admiralty steel Dr. Ouse SB Co. Cancelled 1919.
LEEWARD Admiralty steel Dr, 97gr. Lewis 1918. Sold 1947.
LEEWAY Admiralty steel Dr. Sold 1922.
Le FRENE French navy tug seized 3.7.1940 at Plymouth. Boom gate
vessel 9.40–45. (Spelt La FRENE in some lists.)
LEGEND (ex-*Pearl*) MFV. Hired on ferry service 4.6.1940. Sunk
28.12.42 in the Scapa area.
LEGHORN DY tug, 61gr, 75½ x 15 ft. Yarwood, Northwich 1919.
Sold 3.23.
LEICESTER 1,001/91. Hired as store carrier (RFA) 12.10.1914. Sunk
12.2.16 by mine off Folkestone.
LEICESTER CITY Tr 422/34. Hired as A/S Tr 9.1939–3.46.
LEITH A.ship. Hired 1782.
LEITH Cutter 14. Hired 1798–1801.
LEITH NB Tr 203/14, 1–12pdr. Hired 1914–19.
Le KORRIGAN MFV. French, seized 1940? A/P vessel 12.42–45.
(Known as MFV.2022 from 3.43.)
Le LUTTEUR (see INFATIGABLE)
LEMBERG Tr 275/14, 1–12pdr. Hired 1915–18.
LEMNOS Dr 85/10. Hired on examination service 2.1940. Harbour
service 1941–45.
LENA MELLING Tr 274/ -. Hired 1915. Sunk 23.4.16 by mine near
the Elbow light buoy.
Le NIVOSE Dr 158/36. French M/S seized 3.7.1940 at Southampton.
A/P Dr 8.40–44.
LENOLA Yt 60/38. Hired as A/P Yt 31.5.1940, purchased 7.41. Laid
up 11.45, sold 1946.
LEO Tr 181/04. Hired 1918–19 and as A/P Tr 11.39–15.2.40.
LEOLA VIVIAN 49gr. Hired (RCN) 1940–46.
LEONARD Dr 89/00, 1–3pdr. Hired 11.1914–19.
LEONATO Tr 213/09. Hired 1917–19.
LEONIAN 5,424/36. Hired as boom carrier 8.1940–45.

LEONORA Tr 217/04, 1–6pdr. Hired 1914–19 and as A/P Tr 27.11.39.
To Air Ministry 1.41.
LEONORA Yt 38/28. Hired as A/P Yt 6.1940, purchased 9.41.
Training tender 1.42. Sold 12.45.
LEOVILLE Cstr 1,049/22. French A/P vessel seized 3.7.1940 at
Greenock. Free-French crew 20.3.41. To MWT 7.41.
LEPANTO 6,389/15, 2–6in, 2–4in. Hired as escort 8.2.1918–19.
LEPHRETO Tr 275/17, 1–12pdr. Hired as M/S 8.1939. Fuel carrier
1.44–11.44.
LEPRECHAUN Yt 100/39. Hired on examination service 10.9.1939,
purchased 1.42. Sold 9.45.
LERINA Dr 71/17. Purchased for examination service 9.1940. Sold
6.46.
LERITA Dr 79/14, 1–6pdr. Hired 1915–19.
LERWICK Dr 86/08. Hired 1915. Wrecked 27.3.16 in Yarmouth
Roads.
Le TIGER Tr 516/37, 1–4in. Purchased as A/S Tr 12.1939. Sold
10.45. (On loan USN 3.42–10.42.)
LETITIA 13,475/25, 8–6in, 2–3in. Hired as AMC 9.1939–42.
LETNA Yt 41/36. Purchased as HDPC 25.10.1939. Sold 7.46.
LETO Yt. Hired 1.9.1918–18.1.19.
LETTERFOURIE Dr 77/08. Hired 1915–19.
LETTIE Tug 89/14. Hired 4.1916–3.19 and as A/P tug 8.40. Sunk
9.11.41 by unknown cause off St Abbs Head.
LEVANTER Admiralty steel Dr. A.Hall 1918. Sold 1926.
LEVANTER (see POL II)
LEVANT MERCHANT 28-gun ship. Hired 1652. Captured 4.3.1653
by the Dutch.
LEVEN Tr. Hired in WW.I as BDV.
Le VOLONTAIRE (see INGENIEUR CACHIN)
LEWES 32-gun ship. Hired 1654–56.
LEWIS McKENZIE Tr, 'Mersey' type. Cochrane 1919. Sold 1919.
LEWIS REEVES Tr, 'Mersey' type, 324gr. Cochrane 23.6.1917. Sold
1922, renamed *Lord Hawke*.
LEWIS ROATLEY Tr, 'Mersey' type, 324gr. Cochrane 7.7.1917. Sold
1922, renamed *Stalwart*.
LEXA Yt 133/36. Hired as M/S 1.12.1939, purchased 11.42. Training
tender 1943. Sold 1946. (Bore the name EPPING for a time in 1942
as depot ship.)
LEYLAND Tr 236/17, 1–6pdr. Hired 1917–19.
LEYLAND Tr 452/36, 1–4in. Purchased as A/S Tr 9.1939. Sunk
25.11.42 in collision with merchant ship off Gibraltar.
LEYS Tr 222/15, 1–6pdr. Hired 1916–19.

LIBERATOR (see HEKLA)

LIBERIA Tr 250/06, 1–3pdr. Hired 1914–19 and as M/S 16.8.40–7.46.

LIBERTY Sloop. Hired 1768. Lost by fire 1769.

LIBERTY Cutter 6. Hired 1793–1801.

LIBERTY (ex-*Lady Margaret*) Paddle ferry 589 tons, 210 x 25 ft. Purchased 3.1908. Renamed WANDERER 1913; ROAMER 1919. Sold 1923.

LIBERTY II Dr 88/07, 1–3pdr. Hired 1915–19.

LIBERTY 895/90. Hired as ammo. carrier (RFA) 2.3.1915. Store carrier 25.7.16–15.4.19.

LIBERTY III Dr 86/03, 1–3pdr. Hired 1915–20 and as M/S 12.39–40.

LIBERTY IV Yt 1,571/08. Hired as A/P Yt 1.9.1915 then hospital ship 1915–1.19.

LIBERTY MFV. Danish, seized 4.1940. BBV 1940–45.

LIBRA Tr 211/12, 1–6pdr. Hired 1914–19 and as A/P Tr 11.39. M/S 6.40. Renamed TOCSIN 12.40. Fuel carrier 4.44–9.45.

LIBRA Tr 221/08. Dutch, hired as M/S (Dutch crew) 7.1940. RN 3.43–45.

LIBYAN Tr 202/13, 1–6pdr. Hired as M/S 1915–19 and as A/P Tr, 1–6pdr, 11.39. M/S 6.40; fuel carrier 3.44; target towing 1944–8.46.

LICHEN Dr 99/11, 1–3pdr. Hired 1914–19 and as M/S 11.39. Harbour service 1941–9.46.

LIDDOCH Tr 202/19, 1–3pdr. Hired as A/P Tr 25.11.1939–20.12.41.

LIEGE (see De HOOP)

LIFELINE Salvage vessel 950 tons, 150 x 39 ft, 2–20mm. Smiths Dk 17.8.1943.

LIFFEY (see STONEAXE)

LIGHT Dr 81/08, 1–3pdr. Hired 1915–19.

LIGHTER DY store carrier, 87bm. Portsmouth DY 1672. Sold 25.6.1713 at Portsmouth.

LIGHTER No 1 Hoy, 88bm, 61 x 18½ ft. Woolwich DY 1730. Fate unknown.

LIGHTER No 2 Hoy, 57bm. Woolwich DY 1730. Fate unknown.

LIGNY Tr 277/17, 1–6pdr. Hired as M/S 9.1940–11.45.

LILAC (ex-*Beachflower*) Tr 593 tons, 1–4in. Purchased as M/S 11.1935. Sold 1947, renamed *Robert Hewitt.*

LILACINA Dr 83/12. Hired 1915–19.

LILAVATI 293/11. Hired as A/P vessel (RIN) 1939–45.

LILIUM Dr 85/13, 1–6pdr. Hired 1916–19 and as A/P Dr 11.8.40. Sunk 28.10.41 and raised. Degaussing vessel 1941. Harbour service 1942–46.

LILY Cutter 8. Hired 1782.

LILY Dr 77/06, 1–3pdr. Hired 1915–19.

LILY & MAGGIE Dr 87/09, 1–3pdr. Hired 1915–19.

LILY BANK Dr 83/11. Hired 1914–19.

LILY JANE Dr 74/11, 1–3pdr. Hired 1915–19.

LILY MELLING Tr 246/08, 1–6pdr. Hired as M/S 1914–19.

LILY OAK Dr 84/08, 1–3pdr. Hired 1915–19 and as HDPC 1.40–45.

LILY REAICH Dr 88/08. Hired 1915. Sunk 26.2.16 by mine off Durazzo.

LIMEWOLD Tr 189/98, 1–6pdr. Hired 1914–19.

LIMOL Oiler (RFA) 2,200 tons, 220 x 35 ft. Lobnitz 18.10.1917. Arrived 23.8.59 Ward, Briton Ferry to BU.

LIMPET Mooring vessel 570 tons, 112 x 31½ ft. Purchased 1915. Sold 5.22.

LINCOLN CITY Tr 398/33. Hired as A/S Tr 9.1939. Sunk 21.2.41 by air attack off the Faroes.

LINCOLNIA Tr 138/96. Hired 1917–19.

LINCOLN SALVOR Salvage vessel 800 tons, 170 x 37 ft, 1–3in, 2–20mm. Bellingham IW 14.11.1942 and to the RN 5.11.43 on lend-lease. Returned 9.46 to the USN.

LINCOLNSHIRE Tr 432/36, 1–4in. Hired as A/S Tr 9.1939–9.45.

LINDENES MFV. Norwegian, hired on air-sea rescue 3.1941. Harbour service 1943–5.46.

LINDISFARNE Tr, 'Isles' class. Cook Welton & Gemmell 17.6.1943. Wreck dispersal 3.46. Arrived 26.4.58 at Dover to BU.

LINESMAN Tug 96/11. Hired on harbour service 13.3.1915–19.

LINGAY Tr, 'Isles' class. Cochrane 6.9.1944. Sold 1947, renamed *Tulipdale*.

LINNET Tr 142/87. Hired as BDV 9.1914–19.

LINNET Tr 134/91. Hired 1918–19.

LINN o'DEE Tr 227/15. Hired 1915–19.

LINUM Dr 77/01, 1–3pdr. Hired 1916–19.

LION Cutter 10. Hired 1793–1801.

LION Cutter 8, 97bm. Hired 8.1804–4.1805.

LION Tug. Purchased 2.1854. Sold 4.4.1854.

LION DY craft, 85bm. Purchased 2.1855. Sold 12.1.1869. (Also known as YC.5.)

LIONESS Ship. Hired 1650–52.

LIPIS 914/27. Hired as A/P vessel 13.11.1939. Sunk 13.2.42 by unknown cause off Singapore.

LISCOMB Tr, 'Isles' class. Kingston SY 23.3.1942. Sold 1946, renamed *Aalsund.* (On loan RCN to 17.6.45.)

LISETTE Yt 116/73, 3–6pdr. Hired as decoy ship 4.6.1917–26.6.18.

LISGAR Tug 210/09. Hired (RCN) 1940–46.

LISTRAC Cstr 778/07. French A/P vessel seized 3.7.1940 at Portsmout A/S vessel 8.40. Sunk 11.10.40 by gunfire in the Channel.

LIVELIHOOD Dr 84/07. Hired 1915–19.

LIVELY DY craft, 155bm. Portsmouth DY 5.1838. Renamed DROMEDARY 17.11.1870. Sold 23.11.94 at Portsmouth. (On loan War Dept 1.86–91.)

LIVELY Coastguard vessel, 100bm. Built 1840. Sold 13.5.1870 at narwich.

LIVELY II Dr 79/03, 1–3pdr. Hired 1915–20.

LIVINGSTONE Tr 213/00. Hired 1914. Sunk 12.12.17 by a German destroyer in the North Sea.

LIVONIA Dr 62/05, 1–3pdr. Hired as tender 1915–19.

LI WO 707/38. Hired as A/P vessel 6.1940. Sunk 14.2.42 by the Japanese, Singapore area.

LIZARD (see MYVERA III)

LIZZIE Tr 278/07, 1–3pdr. Hired 1914–19.

LIZZIE ANNIE Dr 87/08. Hired on harbour service 11.1914–19.

LIZZIE BIRRELL Dr 94/13, 1–3pdr. Hired 11.1914–19 and as M/S 11.39–8.46.

LIZZIE BROWN Dr 76/11. Hired 1915–19.

LIZZIE FLETT Dr 88/11, 1–3pdr. Hired 1.1915–19 and on harbour service 12.10.42–43.

LIZZIE HUTT Dr 82/08. Hired 1915–19.

LIZZIE MELLING Tr 207/04, 1–6pdr. Hired 1915–19.

LIZZIE WEST Dr 103/30. Hired on harbour service 30.8.1939–9.45.

LLANTHONY Yt 62/34. Hired on examination service 1940, purchased 5.41. Sold 12.45.

LLEWELLYN Motor M/S (RCN) 228 tons, 105 x 22 ft. Chantier Maritime 12.8.1942. Sold 1958 mercantile.

LLOYD GEORGE Dr 79/10, 1–6pdr. Hired 1915–19.

LLOYD GEORGE Motor M/S (RCN) 228 tons, 105 x 22 ft. Chantier Maritime 12.8.1942. Sold 1952.

LOBELIA Tr 184/96. Hired 1914. Sunk 19.4.17 by mine off Lough Swilly.

LOBSTER (see X.42)

LOCH ALINE 192/04. Hired on examination service 12.1939–11.45.

LOCH ALSH Tr 358/26, 1–12pdr. Hired as M/S 12.1939. Sunk 30.1.42 by air attack, Humber area.

LOCH ARD Tr 225/12. Hired 1914. Sunk 10.9.17 by mine off Lowestoft.

LOCH ASSATER Tr 210/10, 1–3pdr. Hired 1915–19 and purchased as A/P Tr 24.2.40. Sunk 22.3.40 by RN mine off the east coast of Scotland.

LOCH AWE Tr 216/09, 1–6pdr. Hired 1915–19.
LOCH BLAIR Tr 203/17, 1–6pdr. Hired as A/P Tr 6.1940–2.46.
LOCH BROOM Tr 190/07, 1–6pdr. Hired 1914–19.
LOCH BUIE Tr 221/16, 1–12pdr. Hired 1916–19.
LOCH BUIE Tr 277/19. Hired as M/S 8.1939–3.46.
LOCH CRAIG Dr 91/10, 1–3pdr. Hired 1.1915–19.
LOCH DOON Tr 189/04, 1–6pdr. Hired as M/S 1914–19.
LOCH DOON Tr 534/37, 1–4in. Hired as A/S Tr 8.1939. Sunk
25.12.39 off Blyth; probably by mine.
LOCH ERIBOL Tr 352/29, 3–MG. Purchased as M/S 8.1939. Sunk
12.10.45 in collision with *Sidney Sharman* off Start Point.
LOCH ESK Tr 209/12, 1–3pdr. Hired as M/S 1914–19 and as A/P
Tr 25.11.39–1.40.
LOCH EYE Tr 225/16. Hired 1916. Sunk 20.4.17 by mine off
Dunmore.
LOCH GARRY Tr 176/ 0. Hired 1915. Foundered 13.9.16 at
moorings, Kirkwall.
LOCH HOPE Tr 274/15. Hired as A/P Tr 12.1939–12.45.
LOCH HOURN Tr 210/12, 1–12pdr. Hired 1915–19.
LOCHIEL Tr 241/08, 1–12pdr, 1–6pdr. Hired 1917. Sunk 24.7.18
by mine or torpedo off Whitby.
LOCH INVER Tr 356/30, 1–12pdr. Hired as A/P Tr 10.1939. Sunk
24.9.40 by mine off Harwich.
LOCH KILDONAN Tr 211/07, 1–3pdr. Hired 1914–19.
LOCH LAGGAN Tr 255/30. Hired as BDV 9.1939–6.45.
LOCH LEE Tr 210/10, 1–6pdr. Hired 1915–19.
LOCH LEVEN Tr 357/28. Hired as M/S 8.1939–2.46.
LOCH LOMOND Tr 145/98. Hired 1918–19.
LOCH LONG DY tug, 145gr. Paisley 1926. Sunk 9.47 at Singapore.
LOCH LONG Tr 277/17. Purchased as BDV 2.1940. Sold 2.46.
LOCH LOY MFV. Hired on harbour service 22.12.1939–9.45.
LOCH LOYAL Tr 196/07, 1–3pdr. Hired 1914–19.
LOCH MAREE Tr 215/10, 1–6pdr. Hired 1915–19.
LOCH MELFORT Tr 440/34. Purchased as A/S Tr 8.1939. Sold 2.46.
LOCH MOIDART Tr 326/18, 1–6pdr. Hired as A/P Tr 6.1940. M/S
2.42–1.46.
LOCH MONTEITH Tr 531/36, 1–4in. Hired as A/S Tr 9.1939. S/M
escort 1941–11.45.
LOCH MORAR Tr 228/12, 1–6pdr. Hired 1914–19.
LOCH NABO Dr 76/10, 1–3pdr. Hired 1915–19.
LOCH NAVER Tr 216/05, 1–3pdr. Hired 2.1915. Sunk 13.5.18 by
mine in the Aegean.
LOCH NAVER Tr 278/19. Hired as M/S 8.1939. Sunk 6.5.40 in
collision off Hartlepool.

LOCH NEVIS Passenger 600/34. Hired as M/L 11.1940—4.44.

LOCH OSKAIG Tr 534/37, 1—4in. Hired as A/S Tr 8.1939. ABV
5.41—11.45.

LOCH PARK Tr 248/17. Hired as A/P Tr 6.1940. M/S 1941—8.45.

LOCH RANNOCH Tr 178/01. Hired as BDV 1915—19 and as M/S
1.40—11.45.

LOCH SHIEL Tr 216/09. Hired 1916. Sunk 26.9.16.

LOCH SHIN Tr 255/30. Hired as BDV 9.1939. Capsized 26.5.40 after
bomb damage off Harstad.

LOCH SPYNIE Dr 80/10, 1—3pdr. Hired 1915—19.

LOCH STROM Tr 176/03. Hired 1918—19.

LOCH TULLA Tr 423/34. Purchased as A/S Tr 8.1939. Sold 1.46.

LOCH TUMMEL Tr 228/13, 1—12pdr. Hired 1916. Foundered 14.7.18
in the Mediterranean.

LOCH WASDALE Tr 210/15, 1—6pdr. Hired 1916—19.

LODORER Fleet auxiliary. Hired 1915. (See FARNBOROUGH)

L'OEUVRE MFV 45/38. French M/S seized 3.7.1940 at Plymouth.
A/P vessel 10.40—8.45. (Known as MFV.2028 from 3.43.)

LOIS Tr 310/10, 1—6pdr. Hired 1915—19.

LOIS Tr 286/17. Hired as M/S 2.1940—11.44.

LOMBARD Tr 272/09. Hired 1916—20 and as A/P Tr 5.40. M/S
3.42—12.45.

LONDON 40-gun ship, 601bm. Hired 1650—53.

LONDON 46-gun ship. Hired 1664—66.

LONDON Sloop 10. Hired 1793—1801.

LONDON BELLE Paddle 738/93, 2—6pdr. Hired as M/S 18.3.1916—
1.5.19.

LONDON COUNTY Dr 83/09, 1—3pdr. Hired 1.1916. Lost 28.10.19.

LONDON MERCHANT 48-gun ship, 385bm. Hired 1664. Captured
1666 by the Dutch.

LONGA Tr, 'Isles' class. Cochrane 15.10.1943. Sold 1946.

LONGSCAR Tr 215/30. Hired on examination service 8.1939—45.

LONGSET Tr 275/14. Hired 1915. Sunk 6.2.17 by mine off Nells
Point.

LONG TOW Tug 358/19. Hired as salvage vessel 9.1939—11.45.

LONICERA Dr 78/11, 1—6pdr. Hired 1.1915—19.

LOODSMAN Belgian, hired as boom tender 1941—3.46.

LOODSWEZEN Pilot 134/31. Belgian, hired on examination service
8.1940—2.45.

LOOE (see BEAULY)

LOOK SHARP Dr 83/12. Hired 1915—19.

LOOKOUT 72/39. Hired as tender (RAN) 1.1943. Renamed
WATCHER 12.43. Wrecked 14.5.45 on Thursday Island.

LOON Tr 191/14, 1–6pdr. Hired 1914–19 and as BDV 3.40. Water carrier 1943–12.45.

LOOS Tr, 'Castle' type (RCN). Kingston SY 1918. Government service 1920–41. Boom gate vessel 1942–44.

LOP Admiralty Dr, 96gr. Berthon Bt Co 1919. Sold 1919, renamed *Grey Night.*

L'ORAGE Tr 580/21. French, seized 24.11.40 in the Atlantic. Special service Tr 7.41. To MWT 1942.

LORAINE Dr 96/16, 1–3pdr. Hired 1.4.1916; later purchased as store carrier. On sale list 1936.

LORANTHUS Dr 95/29. Hired on examination service 9.1939. Harbour service 1942–12.44.

LORD AIREDALE Tr 215/11, 1–12pdr. Hired 1915. Sunk 29.11.16 by mine off Harwich.

LORD ALLENDALE Tr 215/11, 1–12pdr. Hired 1915–19.

LORD ALVERSTONE Tr 247/ -. Hired 1916. Sunk 12.12.17 by a German destroyer in the North Sea.

LORD ANSON Dr 100/27. Hired on harbour service 30.8.1939–2.46.

LORD ASHBY Tr 215/11, 1–3pdr. Hired 1915–19.

LORD ASHFIELD Tr 346/29, 1–12pdr. Hired as M/S 9.1939–12.45.

LORD AUSTIN Tr 473/37. Hired as A/S Tr 9.1939. Sunk 24.6.44 by mine in Seine Bay.

LORD BARHAM Dr 92/25. Hired as M/S 11.1939–5.46.

LORD BEACONSFIELD Tr 302/15, 1–12pdr. Hired as A/P Tr 8.1939. M/S 1941–45. Wrecked 10.45 while on disposal list.

LORD BERESFORD (ex-*HS.71*) DY tug 300 tons. Transferred from War Dept 1919. Sold 20.4.20.

LORD CAVAN Dr 96/15. Hired as M/S 11.1939. Sunk 1/2.6.40 by gunfire off Dunkirk.

LORD CECIL Tr 228/16, 1–6pdr. Hired 1916–19 and as A/P Tr 11.39–29.3.40.

LORD CHARLES BERESFORD Dr 81/07, 1–6pdr. Hired 11.1914–19.

LORD CLAUD HAMILTON Dr 81/07. Hired 11.1914–19.

LORD COLLINGWOOD Dr 116/30. Hired on harbour service 9.1939–45.

LORD CROMER Dr 84/08, 1–6pdr. Hired 12.1914–20.

LORD CURZON Dr 88/17, 1–6pdr. Hired 1917–19 and as store carrier 9.39–2.46.

LORD DARLING Tr 256/14. Hired as M/S 23.8.1940. Examination service 1941–11.44.

LORD DENMAN Tr 309/ -. Hired 1915. Sunk 22.10.15 after collision in the White Sea.

LORD De RAMSEY Tr 215/11, 1–6pdr. Hired 1916–19.

LORD DUNCAN Cutter 8. Hired 1798–1901.

LORD DUNWICH Dr 75/11. Hired on harbour service 5.8.1915–19 and on examination service 22.10.40. Harbour service 1943–3.46.

LORD DURHAM Tr 215/11, 1–6pdr. Hired 1915–19.

LORD ESSENDEN Tr 464/36. Hired as A/S Tr 9.1939–10.45.

LORD FISHER Dr 89/16, 1–3pdr. Hired 1917–19.

LORD GAINFORD Tr 324/18. Hired as BDV 12.1939, purchased 23.11.43. Free-French crew 7.42–45. Sold 8.8.46 at Freetown.

LORD GEORGE Tr 229/05, 1–6pdr. Hired 1916–19.

LORD GREY Tr 215/11. Hired 1916. Wrecked 2.12.17 on the French coast.

LORD GREY Tr 346/28. Hired as M/S 12.1939–5.46.

LORD HAILSHAM Tr 445/34. Purchased as A/S Tr 8.1939. Sunk 27.2.43 by E-boat torpedo in the Channel.

LORD HALDANE Dr 91/11, 1–6pdr. Hired 1916–19.

LORD HENEAGE Tr 324/09, 1–6pdr. Hired 1.1915–19.

LORD HOOD Storeship 14, 361bm. Hired 1797–98.

LORD HOOD Dr 92/25. Hired as M/S 11.1939–3.46.

LORD HOTHAM Tr 464/36. Hired as A/S Tr 9.1939–9.45.

LORD HOWARD Dr 98/17, 1–3pdr. Hired as flare Dr 11.1939. Sunk 24.12.40 in collision in Dover harbour.

LORD HOWE Dr 75/17, 1–3pdr. Hired as flare Dr 11.1939. Training tender 1942–5.45. Returned 2.46.

LORD INCHCAPE Tr 338/24. Hired as M/S 8.1939. Sunk 25.10.40 by mine off Plymouth. Raised and purchased. Sold 8.46.

LORD IRWIN Tr 346/28. Hired as M/S 9.1939. Calibrating vessel 7.44–1.46.

LORD KEITH (ex-*Active*) Cutter 6, 71bm, 6–4pdr. Hired 2.1804. Captured 15.1.1808 by the French at Cuxhaven.

LORD KEITH Dr 116/30. Hired on harbour service 9.1939. BBV tender 8.40. A/P Dr 3.41–12.45.

LORD KITCHENER Tug 78/01. Hired for DY service 7.1915 and later purchased. Sold 8.20.

LORD KNOLLYS Tr 285/16, 1–12pdr. Hired 1916–19.

LORD LANSDOWNE Tr 289/13, 1–12pdr. Hired 1916–19.

LORD LEITRIM Dr 74/10, 1–6pdr. Hired 1915–19.

LORD LISTER Tr 285/12, 1–12pdr. Hired 1915–19.

LORD LLOYD Tr 396/33. Purchased as A/S Tr 8.1939. For disposal 9.45.

LORD LOVAT Dr 79/13, 1–6pdr. Hired 1915–19.

LORD MELCHETT Tr 347/28, 1–12pdr. Hired as M/S 8.1939. Dan-layer 4.44–5.46.

LORD MELVILLE Sloop 4, 104bm, 4–2pdr. Hired 1804–05.

LORD MERSEY Tr 326/16, 1–12pdr. Hired 1916–19. (The prototype for the Admiralty 'Mersey' type trawlers.)

LORD MIDDLETON Tr 464/36, 1–4in. Hired as A/S Tr 9.1939. For disposal 7.45.

LORD MILNER Dr 82/03, 1–3pdr. Hired 1916–19.

LORD MINTO Tr 295/14, 1–6pdr. Hired 1916–19.

LORD MULGRAVE A.ship 20. Hired 1793. Lost 1799.

LORD NELSON Cutter 14. Hired 1798–1801.

LORD NELSON Cutter 6, 69bm, 6–4pdr. Hired 1.6.1803. Renamed FREDERICK 1804. Returned 12.12.04.

LORD NELSON Cutter 8. Hired 1803.

LORD NELSON Cutter. Hired 8.1807. Wrecked 5.8.1809. near Flushing.

LORD NORTHCLIFFE Tr 228/16, 1–6pdr. Hired 1916–19 and as A/P Tr 11.39. BBV 5.40–11.45.

LORD NUFFIELD Tr 466/37. Hired as A/S Tr 9.1939–12.45.

LORD PERCY Tr 215/11, 1–6pdr. Hired 1916–20.

LORD PLENDER Tr 396/33. Purchased as A/S Tr 8.1939. For disposal 1945.

LORD RAGLAN Storeship. Hired 1854. Wrecked 1854.

LORD READING Tr 325?/16, 1–12pdr. Hired 1916–19.

LORD RIDLEY Tr 215/11. Hired 2.1915. Sunk 10.5.17 by mine off Whitby.

LORD ROBERTS Tr 293/07. Hired 1914. Sunk 26.10.16 by mine off the Shipwash.

LORD ROBERTS Dr 60/00. Hired on harbour service 7.10.1914–4.7.16.

LORD ROBERTS Tr. Hired 1918–19.

LORD RODNEY Dr 104/28. Hired as A/P Dr 9.1939. M/S 1941. To War Dept 10.43.

LORD ROTHSCHILD Tr 174/06. Hired 1918–19.

LORD ST VINCENT Schooner 16. Hired 1800–01.

LORD ST VINCENT Dr 115/29. Hired as A/P Dr 9.1939. BBV 9.40. Sunk 7.7.41 by mine in the Thames estuary.

LORD SALISBURY Tr 285/02. Hired 1915. Sunk 4.5.17. by mine off Salonika.

LORD SELBORNE Tr 247/17, 1–12pdr. Hired 1917–19 and as A/P Tr, 1–6pdr, 6.40. Sunk 31.3.41 by mine in the Humber.

LORDSHIP Tr 351/15, 1–12pdr, 1–6pdr. Hired 1916–19.

LORD SHREWSBURY Tr 167/98. Hired 1918–19.

LORD SNOWDEN Tr 444/34. Hired as A/S Tr 8.1939. Sunk 13.4.42 in collision off Falmouth.

LORD STAMP Tr 448/35. Hired as A/S Tr 8.1939. Sunk 14.10.40 by mine in the Channel.

LORD STANHOPE Tr 212/16, 1–6pdr. Hired 1916–19.

LORD STANHOPE Tr 448/35. Hired as A/S Tr 8.1939–11.45.

LORD STONEHAVEN Tr 444/34. Hired as A/S Tr 8.1939. Sunk 2.10.42 by E-boat torpedo off the Eddystone.

LORD STRADBROKE Dr 79/10. Hired 1.1915–19. (Served as OUR KATE in WW.II.)

LORD SUFFOLK Dr 115/29. Hired 11.1939. Renamed BANSHEE 1940. Returned 1.46.

LORD WAKEFIELD Tr 418/33. Purchased as A/S Tr 8.1939. Sunk 29.7.4 by air attack off Normandy.

LORD WENLOCK Dr 91/11, 1–57mm. Hired 1915–19.

LORD WIMBORNE Tr 215/11, 1–12pdr. Hired 1914–19.

LORD WOLMER Tr 214/11, 1–3pdr. Hired 1915–19.

LORD ZETLAND Dr 89/14, 1–6pdr. Hired 1915–19.

LORENZO Tr 176/06. Hired 1914. Wrecked 17.12.14 in Hoy sound.

LORINDA Tr 348/28. Hired as M/S 9.1939. Foundered 20.8.41 off Freetown after engine breakdown and fire.

LORMONT 1,561/27, 2–12pdr. Hired as guardship 1.9.1939. Sunk 7.12.40 in collision off the Humber.

LORNA Yt 484/04, 1–12pdr. 1–6pdr. Hired as A/P Yt 30.9.1914–30.12.19 and as ABV, 1–12pdr, 9.39. Listed to 5.41.

LORNA DOONE Paddle 410/91, 1–6pdr. Hired as M/S 13.12.1915–30.12.19 and as M/S 7.12.39. A/A ship 5.42, 5–20mm. Accommodation ship 9.43–46.

LOROONE Tr 214/13, 1–6pdr. Hired 1916–19.

LORRAINE Tr 277/17, 1–MG. Hired as A/P Tr 6.1940. M/S 2.41–1.46.

LOTHIAN Tr 131/04. Hired 1917–19.

LOTHIAN (ex-*City of Edinburgh*) 8,036/38, 4–4in, 20–20mm. Hired as landing ship 1944–46.

LOTIS Yt 29/36. Hired as HDPC 9.1939, purchased 9.41. Laid up 12.41. To War Dept 9.43.

LOTOS Tr 216/14, 1–12pdr. Hired 1914–19.

LOTTIE Dr 71/04. Hired on harbour service 9.1914–19.

LOTTIE LEASK Dr 94/07. Hired 1915. Sunk 18.12.15 by U-boat off Saseno Island.

LOUISA Brig 14. Hired 1799–1801.

LOUISA Sloop 4, 120bm, 4–3pdr. Hired 4.1803–05.

LOUISA Tender 8. Hired 1806–09 and 1814–15?

LOUISA DY craft, 81bm. In service 1860. BU 9.1876 at Sheerness.

LOUIS BOTHA Tr 226/16, 1–6pdr. Hired 1916–19 and as A/P Tr, 1–6pdr, 6.40–11.12.41.

LOUISE Tr 270/07, 1–6pdr. Hired as M/S 1914–19.

LOUISE–MARIE Tr 165/99. French M/S seized 3.7.1940 at Plymouth. M/S 10.40–46.

LOUVAIN (ex-*Dresden*) 1,830/97, 2–12pdr. Hired as ABS 31.10.19₁4.
Sunk 20.1.18 by U-boat in the eastern Mediterranean.
LOVANIA Tr 292/12, 1–12pdr. Hired as A/P Tr 6.1940. M/S 1941;
towing duty 1945–2.46.
LOVEDALE Dr 84/14. Hired 1915–19.
LOWTHER Tr 313/15. Hired as M/S 2.1940–1.46.
LOW TIDE Admiralty steel Dr, 96gr. Brooke 1919. Sold 1919, same
name. (Served as LOYAL FRIEND in WW.II.)
LOYAL I MFV 53/28. Hired as A/P vessel (RCN) 1941–45.
LOYAL II MFV 71/30. Hired as A/P vessel (RCN) 1941–43.
LOYAL FRIEND Dr 85/13, 1–6pdr. Hired 1915–19.
LOYAL FRIEND Dr 96/19. Hired as A/S Dr 12.1939–8.45.
LOYAL PRINCE Tr 208/13, 1–6pdr. Hired 1914–19.
LOYAL STAR Dr 95/13, 1–6pdr. Hired 12.1914–19.
LUBECK DY tug. Listed 1919. Sold 1921 at Port Said.
LUCANIA Dr 78/10. Hired 1915–19.
LUCERNE Tr 198/00. Hired 1918–19.
LUCIDA Tr 251/14, 1–6pdr. Hired 1914–19.
LUCIEN CHRISTIAN MFV 67/30, 1–6pdr. Belgian, hired (Polish crew)
as A/P vessel 22.6.1940–45. (Also known as P.11.)
LUCIEN GOUGY Dr 150/35. French M/S seized 3.7.1940 at Plymouth.
M/S 1.41. Sunk 21.2.45 by unknown cause.
LUCIENNE–JEANNE Tr 286/17. French M/S seized 3.7.1940. M/S
(Free-French crew) 8.40. RN 1941. Stranded 24.10.41, Sheerness area.
LUCKNOW Tr 171/03. Hired 1914. Sunk 18.5.17 by mine off Portsmouth.
LUCKNOW Tr (RIN), 'Basset' class. Alcock Ashdown 3.4.1942. Sold
1946.
LUCRATIVE Dr 87/14. Hired 12.1914–19.
LUCY 20–gun ship, 164bm. Hired 1649–54.
LUCY Tender. Hired 1777.
LUCY (ex-*Alert*) Lugger 16, 120bm. Hired 3.1804–3.05.
LUCY DY tug, 140 tons. Mordey Carney, Southampton 18.10.1902.
Sold 6.37 at Malta.
LUCY BORCHARDT 1,850/05. Purchased as ammo. hulk 14.9.1939.
BU 1951 at Preston.
LUCY MACKAY Dr 94/07, 1–3pdr. Hired 1915–19.
LUCY STAR 51 tons. Patrol vessel (RAN) 6.1942–7.46.
LUDALADY Tr 234/14. Hired as A/P Tr 11.1939. M/S 6.40. Sunk
22.1.41 by mine in the Humber area.
LUDA LORD Tr 224/13. Hired as A/P Tr 11.1939. M/S 5.40. Fuel
carrier 1.44–45.
LUDGATE (ex-*President Ludwig*) Tug 165gr. Belgian, hired 2.9.1917.
Stranded 15.2.18 in Wigtown Bay.

LUDGATE Boom gate vessel (dumb) 290 tons, 93 x 26 ft, 1—3in. Hong Kong & Whampoa DY 30.9.1935. Scuttled 2.42 at Singapore.

LUDHAM CASTLE Dr 66/04, 1—2½pdr. Hired 1916—19.

LUFRA Dr 84/07. Hired 12.1914—19.

LULL Admiralty steel Dr, 96gr. Lewis 1918. Sold circa 1923, renamed *Myrtle Leaf.*

LUMINARY (ex-*Kingfisher*) Tr 414/19. American, purchased as BDV 9.1940. Sold 12.46.

LUNAR BOW Admiralty steel Dr, 97gr. Lewis 15.6.1918. Sold 1945, same name.

LUNARY Yt 108/ -. Hired on air-sea rescue service 12.1940. Harbour service 1945—7.46.

LUNDY Tr 188/08. Hired 1915. Sunk 16.8.15 in collision in Suvla Bay.

LUNDY Tr, 'Isles' class. Cook Welton & Gemmell 29.8.1942. Tank-cleaning vessel 1956.

LUNE Tr 197/99. Hired as boom gate vessel 1915—19.

LUNE Tr 310/30. Hired as M/S 9.1939. Wreck dispersal 5.44 and purchased. Sold 7.46.

LUNEDA Tr 288/12, 1—6pdr. Hired 1914—19.

LUNKA 2,193/05, 1—6in, 2—4.7in. Hired as ABS 20.7.1915—22.1.19.

LUPINA Dr 88/08, 1—3pdr. Hired 8.1914—19 and on harbour service 11.30—12.45.

LURCHER Cutter 12. Hired 1796. Captured 2.1801 by a French privateer off the French coast.

LURCHER (see BUSEN 8)

LUSITANIA 3,825/71. Hired as AMC 1885—86.

LUSTRE GEM Dr 82/07. Hired 2.1915—19.

LUSTRING Dr 71/10. Hired 1.1915. Sunk 3.10.18 in collision off Hellier Holm.

LYCEA 2,338/24. Purchased 20.10.1940. Sunk 1940 as blockship at Scapa Flow.

LYDDITE (ex-*Lyd*) Tr 111/81. Hired on harbour service 24.10.1918—19.

LYDIA LONG Dr 74/18. Hired as M/S 11.1939. Harbour service 1940—45.

LYDIAN Tr 244/ -. Hired 1915. Sunk 18.9.15 by mine off the South Foreland.

LYDIARD (ex-*Loyal*) Tr 440/35. Purchased as A/S Tr 9.1939. For disposal 1.46.

LYNESS Store carrier (RFA) 15,500 tons, 524(0a) x 72 ft. Swan Hunter 7.4.1966.

LYNMOUTH Tr 140/92, 1—3pdr. Hired 1.1915—19.

LYNN (ex-*Lynx*) 609/89, 2—12pdr. Hired as M/S 27.10.1914—5.3.20.

LYNX Tug 79/05. Hired 2.8.1914—19.

LYNX II Tr 250/06, 1—6pdr. Hired 1914—19.
LYNX (ex-*Ramona*) Yt 445/22. Commissioned as A/S Yt (RCN) 26.8.1940. Paid off 7.43.
LYONESSE MFV 26/30. Hired on harbour service 6.1940—10.45.
LYONS 537/85. Hired as salvage vessel (RFA) 8.1914. Decoy ship, 4-12pdr, 5.15—11.15. Returned 12.15.
LYRA Tender 4, 112bm, 4—2pdr. Hired 6.1803—1812.
LYRA (ex-*Caledon*) Yt 30/36. Hired on examination service 6.1940. Firefloat 12.41—3.46.
LYRE BIRD Dr 80/02, 1—3pdr. Hired 1915—19.
LYRIC (ex-*Sonnet*) Barge 220dw/28. Hired as BBV 5.1940—5.45.
LYSANDER II Tr 264/03, 2—3pdr. Hired 1914—19.
LYSANDER III Tr 174/98, 1—6pdr. Hired 1916—18.
LYSANDER 66gr. Commissioned as patrol vessel (RAN) 2.1942. For disposal 11.45.
LYSISTRATA Yt 2,089/00, 2—4in. Russian YAROSDAVNA seized 1918. In commission 1918—19.
LYTTELTON Tug 292/07. Hired on examination service (RNZN) 1942—45.

MAALOY (see GLOBE VI)
MAAS III 227gr. Purchased as store carrier 29.1.1940. To MOT 29.3.47.
MABEL VERA Dr 98/12. Hired on harbour service 9.1915—19.
M.A.C 1—7 (see MTBs 1—5, 19 and 40K)
MACAU 1,665/03. Purchased 1941. Sunk 9.12.41 as blockship in Anking harbour. (Spelt MACAO in the loss list.)
MACAW Tr 187/09, 1—6pdr. Hired 1914—19. (Vessel on harbour service 1943—45 may be the same.)
MACBETH Tr 311/06, 1—12pdr. Hired 1914—19.
MACBETH M/S—A/S Tr 545 tons, 150 x 28 ft, 1—12pdr, 3—20mm. Goole SB 3.10.1940. Sold 1947, same name.
MACDONALD RCMP vessel, 210gr. Commissioned as A/P vessel (RCN) 11.10.1939. Returned 1945.
MACDUFF Tr 179/06, 1—3pdr. Hired 1915—19.
MACE Dr 96/19. Hired on harbour service 8.1939—45.
MACEDONIA 10,512/04. Hired as AMC 2.8.1914—11.18.
MACFARLANE Tr 285/08, 1—6pdr. Hired 1915—19.
MACKAYS Dr 83/08. Hired 1915—19.
MACKENZIE Tr, 1—6pdr. Hired as M/S 1914—19.

MACKEREL A/S Tr 670 tons, 146 x 25 ft. Cochrane 6.3.1942. Renamed CORNCRAKE 11.42 and completed as M/L, 700 tons. Foundered 25.1.43 in a gale in the N.Atlantic.

MACKEREL SKY Admiralty wood Dr, 92gr. Noble 1919. Sold 1921, renamed *Drainie*. (DRAINIE in WW.II.)

MACKLEAY Tr 317/13, 1–12pdr. Hired 1917–19.

MACSIN Tug 293/19. Hired on examination service (RCN) 1940–46.

MADDEN Tr 237/17. Hired as M/S 2.1940. Wreck dispersal 3.44–4.46.

MADELEINE–CAMILLE MFV 74/37. French (ex-Belgian), seized 7.1940. BBV 10.40–10.45.

MADELEINE HUBERTINE Dr 115/31. Belgian, hired as A/P Dr 8.10.1940. Harbour service 1942–9.45.

MADIS Dr 79/09. Hired 1916–19.

MADRAS Wood paddle tug (RIM) 197 tons, 123 x 21 ft. Blackwall 1876. Listed to 1892.

MADRAS Tr (RIM), 'Castle' type. Burn, Calcutta 1919. Laid up 12.41. Renamed or sold 1942.

MADRIGAL Yt 125/01. Purchased 1914. Sold 28.10.19.

MADURA Tr, (RIN), 'Basset' class. Garden Reach 22.12.1942. Sold 1946.

MAELSTROM Admiralty wood Dr, 96gr. Berthon Bt Co 1919. Sold 1921, renamed *Fairhaven*. (FAIRHAVEN in WW.II.)

MAFEKING Tr 181/03, 1–6pdr. Hired as M/S 1915.

MA FRENE Dr 92/13, 1–3pdr. Hired 1.1915–19.

MAGDA 2,351/88, 1–12pdr. Hired as boom gate vessel 1915, later purchased. Sold 29.7.19.

MAGDALEN Dr 94/07, 1–6pdr. Hired 1915–19.

MAGDALEN Tr, 'Isles' class. Midland SY 7.3.1942. Sold 14.4.46, renamed *Maroy*. (On loan RCN to 17.6.45.)

MAGEDOMA Yt 138/31. In commission (RCN) 1944–46.

MAGGIE BRUCE Dr 76/11, 1–3pdr. Hired 1915–19.

MAGGIE COWE Dr 91/14, 1–3pdr. Hired 1915–19 and on harbour service 1942–45.

MAGGIE GAULT Dr 91/10, 1–3pdr. Hired 1917–19 and on harbour service 6.1940–4.45.

MAGGIE LOUGH Tug 129/08. Hired as salvage vessel 8.1940–42.

MAGGIES Dr 85/07. Hired 1915–19.

MAGIC CIRCLE (see CREOLE)

MAGNET (ex-*Knight of the Cross*) Fleet tug 430 tons, 136 x 22½ ft, 4–3pdr. Purchased 22.4.1885. Sold 1.5.20.

MAGNET II Dr 60/03. Hired 24.9.1915–19.

MAGNET III Dr 92/08, 1–3pdr. Hired as BDV 1915–19.

MAGNET (ex-BARNSLEY renamed 1938) BDV 530 tons, 135 x 30½ ft, 1–3in. Smiths Dk 22.11.38. On sale list 1958.

MAGNETA Tr 322/15, 1–6pdr. Hired 1915–19.

MAGNIFICENT III Dr 93/09. Hired 11.1914–19 and as MAGNIFICENT III on harbour service 11.39–11.44.

MAGNIFICENT Dr 68/03. Hired 6.1915–19.

MAGNOLIA Tr 213/97. Hired 1916–19.

MAGNOLIA III Tr 184/98, 1–6pdr. Hired 1915–19.

MAGNOLIA (ex-*Lord Brentford*) Tr 557 tons, 1–4in. Purchased as M/S 11.1935. Sold 1.48 at the Cape; BU at Mombasa.

MAGPIE DY tug 40 tons. Purchased 1902. Listed to 1923. (Also known as C.63 from 1903.)

MAGPIE II Tr 278/03, 1–6pdr. Hired 1915–19.

MAGPIE III Tr 156/96. Hired 1918–19.

MAHELAH Yt 137/98. Hired as accommodation ship 3.1940, purchased 7.41. Laid up 9.45, sold 1946.

MAHRATTA (see EMPEROR of INDIA)

MAIDA (see CHESTNUT)

MAID MARION Yt 506/38. Hired as A/S Yt 9.1939. S/M tender 3.44 and purchased; A/P depot ship 1945–46. For disposal 1.47.

MAID of HONOUR Yt 487/07, 2–12pdr. Hired as A/P Yt 4.1915–19.

MAID o'MORAY Dr 84/11. Hired 3.1915–19.

MAID of THULE Dr 97/17. Hired 1917–19.

MAIMAI Tr (RNZN), 'Castle' type. Stevenson & Cook, Port Chalmers 25.2.1943. Sold 1946.

MAIMIE Yt 112/14. Hired as BBV 11.1949, purchased 7.41. Laid up 11.44; sold 1945?

MAINE (ex-*Swansea*) Hospital ship (RFA) 4,540 tons, 315 x 40 ft. Presented 29.6.1901. Sold 6.7.14 after stranding.

MAINE (ex-*Heliopolis*) Hospital ship (RFA) 8,785 tons, 390 x 53 ft. Purchased 7.3.1913. Sold 7.3.16.

MAINE (ex-*Panama*) Hospital ship (RFA) 10,100 tons, 401 x 58½ ft. Purchased 1920, converted 1921. Arrived 8.7.48 McLellan, Bo'ness to BU.

MAINE (ex-*Empire Clyde*, ex-Italian *Leonardo da Vinci*). Transferred from MOT and renamed 1.1.1948. Sold 26.4.54.

MAINE Hospital ship (RFA) 10,000 tons. Barclay Curle. Laid down 2.1952, cancelled 6.52.

MAIRI Yt 65/11, 1–3pdr. Hired 1.4.1915 and later purchased. Sold 8.8.19.

M.A. JAMES Cstr 125/00. Hired as BBV 8.1940–44.

MAJESTA Yt 170/99. Purchased as HDPC 1940. Accommodation ship 1943. Sold 1946.

MAJESTIC Tug 157/98. Hired 1915–19.

MAJESTIC II Paddle 408/01. Hired as A/P vessel 23.5.1916. Foundered 28.7.16 near Oran.

MAJESTIC III Dr. Hired 1917–19.

MAJESTIC IV Dr. Hired 1917–18.

MAJESTIC II Tr 159/ 0. Hired 1917–19.

MAJESTIC Hired in the E.Indies as boom tender 1940–47.

MAJESTY Dr 84/08, 1–6pdr. Hired 11.1914–19 and as A/P Dr 3.40–9.46.

MA JOIE II Yt 39/21. Hired as HDPC 12.1939, purchased 5.41. Sold 12.45.

MALACCA 211/27. Hired as M/S 12.1939. Scuttled 18.2.42 in the Tjemako river, Sumatra.

MALACOLITE Tr 248/17. Hired as M/S 8.1939–9.45.

MALAHNE Yt 458/37. Hired as air target 9.1939, purchased 10.41. Laid up 7.45, sold 1946.

MALINES 2,969/22. Hired as escort 11.1940. Sunk in the Mediterranean 19.7.42 and salved 1.43. Returned 1944.

MALLINA 3,461/09. Hired as fleet auxiliary 1916–19.

MALOJA 20,914/23, 8–6in, 2–3in. Hired as AMC 11.9.1939–11.41.

MALTA Iron paddle DY tug 530 tons. Laird 21.1.1875. Sold 1.21 J W Houston.

MALTA Tr 138/97. Hired 1914. Sunk 1.9.15 by mine off the Shipwash.

MALVERNIAN 3,133/37, 2–6in, 1–12pdr. Hired as OBV 24.8.1940. Sunk 19.7.41 by air attack in the N.Atlantic.

MAMARI 7,924/11. Hired 7.9.1939 and purchased as dummy A/C carrier HERMES 28.9.39. Hit a wreck 2.6.41 in the Wold Channel and torpedoed 4.6.41 by E-boat and sunk.

MAMMOUTH French navy tug, seized 3.7.1940 at Plymouth. BBV 8.40; target towing 1944–45.

MANAGEM Yt 205/88, 1–12pdr. Egyptian, hired 1.1917–19.

MANCHESTER Storeship. Hired 1814–15.

MANCHESTER CITY 5,600/37, 1–4in, 1–12pdr, 4–20mm, 317 mines. Hired as M/L base ship 1939–45.

MANCHESTER SPINNER 4,767/18. Purchased 3.1944. Sunk 9.6.44 as blockship at Arromanches.

MANCO 2,984/08. Hired as supply ship (RFA) 10.12.1914. A/P depot ship 4.15–10.15.

MANDA Tr 150/98. Hired 1918–19.

MANDAL (see KOS XIV)

MANDARIN DY mooring vessel 950 tons, 168 x 36½ ft. Cammell Laird 17.9.1963.

MANELA 8,303/21. Hired as seaplane depot ship 1939. To RAF Coastal Command 10.41 as accommodation ship.

MANFORD (see PENHURST)

MANGROVE M/S Tr 530 tons, 150 x 27½ ft, 1–12pdr. Ferguson 15.2.1940. Sold 11.2.46 Portuguese navy as FAIAL. (On loan Portuguese navy 8.10.43–27.6.45 as P.2.)

MANICA 4,120/00. Hired as kite-balloon ship 11.3.1915, later purchased. Sold 1920.

MANISTEE 5,368/21, 2–6in, 1–12pdr. Hired as OBV 14.9.1940. Sunk 24.2.41 by U-boat in the N.Atlantic.

MANITOULIN Tr, 'Isles' class. Midland SY 23.4.1942. Sold 1946, renamed *Ran*. (On loan RCN to 17.6.45.)

MANLY Iron paddle tug 188 tons, 100 x 17 ft. Rennie, Greenwich 23.4.1868. Sold 26.1.1912.

MANLY (see KIMBERLEY)

MANNOFIELD Tr 206/05. Hired 1918–19.

MANOORA 10,856/34, 6–6in, 2–3in. Hired as AMC (RAN) 14.10.1939. Landing ship, 1–12pdr, 6–40mm, 2.43. Returned 1946.

MANOR Tr 314/13, 1–6pdr. Hired 1914–19 and as A/S Tr 8.1939. Sunk 9.7.42 by E-boat torpedo in the Channel.

MANOU Yt 223/12. French, seized 7.1940. BBV 8.40. To War Dept 1.45.

MAN o'WAR Tr 517/36, 1–4in. Hired as A/S Tr 9.1939–2.7.45.

MANSFIELD Tr 165/97. Hired 1917–19.

MANTUA 10,885/08. Hired as AMC 8.1914–26.12.19.

MANUKA Tr, composite 'Castle' class (RNZN). Mason, Auckland 23.9.1941. Sold 1946.

MANX ADMIRAL Tr 219/12. Hired as boom gate vessel 1915–19.

MANX BEAUTY MFV 24/37. Hired on examination service 5.1940–45.

MANX BRIDE Dr 61/10. Hired on harbour service 1914.

MANX FAIRY MFV 24/37. Hired on examination service 5.1940. Base ship PLEIADES 1944–45.

MANX HEATHER Yt 57/04. Hired on harbour service 2.1941–45.

MANX HERO Tr 221/10, 1–6pdr. Hired 1914. Sunk 10.3.15 by mine in the Mediterranean.

MANX HERO Tr 236/16, 1–6pdr. Hired 1916–19.

MANX KING Tr 235/16, 1–6pdr. Hired 1916–19.

MANX LAD MFV 24/37. Hired on examination service 7.1940. Sunk 16.8.40 by mine off Holyhead.

MANX LASS MFV 24/37. Hired on examination service 6.1940–45.

MANXMAID (see BRUCE)

MANXMAN 2,048/04, 2–4in, 1–6pdr, 8–A/C. Purchased as seaplane carrier 4.1916. Sold 12.2.20 Isle of Man SP Co. (Served as CADUCEUS in WW.II.)

MANX PRINCE Tr 221/10, 1–6pdr. Hired as M/S 1914–19 and as A/P Tr 12.39. M/S 6.40. Sunk 28.11.40 by mine off the Humber.

MANX QUEEN Tr 234/15. Hired 1915. Wrecked 1.3.16 on Filey Brigg.

MANYEUNG Ferry 371/33. Hired as M/L 8.1939. Not listed after 12.41, probably lost at Hong Kong.

MANZANITA Dr 93gr. Hired 1916. Wrecked 6.9.16 in the Adriatic.

MAPLE (ex-*St Gerontius*) Tr 357/29, 550 tons, 1—4in. Purchased as M/S Tr 2.1939. Sold 1946, renamed *Sumatra.*

MAPLE LAKE Motor M/S (RCN) 255 tons, 126 x 26 ft. Clare SB. Ordered 4.8.1944. Cancelled 18.9.44.

MAPLELEAF (see MOUNT ROYAL)

MAPLIN (see ERIN)

MARACAIO (see MEROPS)

MARAMA Yt 33/31. Hired as HDPC 6.1940, purchased 9.41. Training tender 1943—45. Sold 4.46.

MARANO Tr 245/16. Hired as A/P Tr 11.1939. M/S 6.40—1.45.

MARA SMITH Dr 88gr. Hired 1915—19.

MARAUDER Fleet tug 840 tons, 165 x 32 ft, 1—3in, 2—MG. Fleming & Ferguson 9.11.1938. Rescue tug 11.39—46. Sold 1958, renamed *Emerson K.*

MARAUDER MFV. Hired as M/S (RCN) 1941—45.

MARAVEL (ex-*Chelsea*) Yt 295/26. American, purchased as A/S Yt 1940. Sold 1946.

MARCELLA Yt 160/87. Hired as ABS 6.7.1915. Sunk 24.3.16 in collision in the Downs.

MARCELLE MFV 64/25. Belgian, hired as BBV 6.8.1940. Sunk 10.11.40 by mine in the Bristol channel.

MARCEL—PIERRE MFV 50/31. French, seized 1940. A/P vessel 1.41. Laid up 4.43.

MARCHIONESS of BREADALBANE Paddle 246/90. Hired as M/S 30.4.1917—21.1.19.

MARCHIONESS of BUTE Paddle 246/09, 2—6pdr. Hired as M/S 27.10.1915, purchased 23.10.17. Trooper 1.19. Sold 16.1.23 Ward, Inverkeithing.

MARCHIONESS of LORNE Paddle 295/91, 2—6pdr. Hired as A/P vessel 19.6.1916. M/S 4.19—20.

MARCHWOOD DY tug 140 tons. Dundee SB Co 1902. Sold 1948.

MARCIA Schooner, 73bm. Hired 8.1804—12.04.

MARCIA MFV 36/28. Hired as BBV 22.2.1940—11.45.

MARCONI Tr 261/03, 1—12pdr. Hired 1916—19.

MARCONI Tr 322/16. Hired 1917—19 and as M/S 3.40. Sunk 20.9.41 in collision off Harwich.

MARE Dr 92/11, 1—3pdr. Hired 1915—19 and as M/S, 2—MG, 11.39—10.45.

MARETTA Tr 350/29. Hired as M/S 9.1939—11.45.

MARGARET Dr 115gr. Purchased 11.1914. Sunk as blockship? 16.12.14.

MARGARET DUNCAN Tr 224/13, 1—6pdr. Hired 1915—19.

MARGARET HAM Tug 113/13. Hired 9.1915—12.18.

MARGARET HOBLEY Aux schooner 119/68. Hired as BBV 22.8.1940–
44.
MARGARET HYDE Dr 161/20. Hired as M/S 11.1939–4.45.
MARGARET ROSE Tr 348/12. Purchased as BDV 3.1940. Laid up 7.46.
Sold 1946?
MARGARET WEATHERLEY Tr 211/11. Hired as BDV 1915–19.
MARGATE Tr 161/96. Hired 1916. Sunk 24.4.17 by U-boat off Spurn
Point.
MARGIT 2,490/03. Hired as decoy ship 12.1915–3.16.
MARGO III Yt 33/33. Hired as kite-balloon vessel 6.1940, purchased
9.41. Sold 4.45.
MARGUERITA Dr 96/19. Hired on harbour service 11.1939–10.45.
MARGUERITE Tr 151/95. Hired 1917–19.
MARGUERITE MARIE LOUISE Dr 85/31. Belgian, hired as A/P Dr
7.10.1940. Target towing 1943; TRV 1944–12.45.
MARIA Tender 4, 154bm, 4–3pdr. Hired 4.1803–09.
MARIA Sloop 6, 176bm. Hired 6.1803–05.
MARIA Schooner,104bm. Hired 12.1813–7.14.
MARIA DY barge 80 tons. Crampton, Portsmouth 1899. Listed to 1937.
MARIA Tr 407/29, 855 tons, (deep), 166 x 27 ft. German AUGUST
WRIEDT captured 7.1941. Commissioned as wreck dispersal vessel 3.42.
Handed over 6.51 to BU.
MARIA ELENA Dr 146/32. French M/S seized 3.7.1940 at Portsmouth.
M/S to 11.45.
MARIA ELIZABETH Dr 164/29. Dutch, M/S (Dutch crew) 1940. Fuel
carrier (RN crew) 3.44–45.
MARIA GIOVANNA Aux schooner 255gr, 400 tons. Italian, captured
1.1.1941 by DAINTY off Bardia. Store carrier. Lost by grounding
22.11.41 off Tobruk but listed to 6.42. (Spelt MARIA di GIOVANNI
in the Loss List.)
MARIA JOAO Yt 317/94. Purchased as calibrating Yt 12.1939.
Armament store carrier 1.44. Sold 3.46.
MARIA LUDOVICA Dr 129/31. Belgian, hired as A/P Dr 9.10.1940–
9.45.
MARIA R OMMERING Tr 216/14. Dutch, hired as M/S (Dutch crew)
1940. RN crew 4.43. Returned 1946.
MARIE Dr 60/05. Hired 1915–19.
MARIE JOSE ROSETTE Tr 139/36. Belgian, hired on harbour service
8.12.1943. Fuel carrier 3.44–2.45.
MARIE LOUISE Tr 140/08. Belgian, hired 1918–19.
MARIE LOUISE Tr 258/18. Belgian, hired as BDV 10.1940–1.46.
MARIE–LOUISE 117/98. French, seized 1940 (in West Africa?).
Boom tender 6.40–46.

MARIE LOUISE MACKAY Cable 1,378/22. Hired 5.1941–12.45.
MARIE THERESE ANDREE MFV 39/31. French, seized 1940 at Southampton. Fate unknown.
MARIE THERESE DEBRA MFV 38/22. Belgian, hired as A/P vessel 11.10.1940–8.44.
MARIGNAM (ex-*Teal,* ex-*Marignam*) Tr 408/19, 1–12pdr. American, purchased 9.1940 as BDV. Renamed TEAL 10.40. Sold 12.3.46, renamed *Wulkan.*
MARIGOLD Pinnace, 30bm. Hired 1588.
MARIGOLD Dr 95/18. Hired on harbour service 11.1939. MARIGOLD II 1940. Returned 1945.
MARINA Yt 34/35. Hired on examination service 30.8.1939, purchased 6.41. Foundered 6.6.44 in a storm.
MARINER Dr 88/07, 1–3pdr. Hired 1916–19.
MARINUS Dr 84/11. Hired as BBV 12.1939–4.46.
MARION Tr 129/91, 1–3pdr. Hired 1914. Sunk 23.2.18 by mine off Malta.
MARION II Tr 119/91. Hired 1917–19.
MARIPOSA 3,806/14. Purchased 3.1944. Sunk 9.6.44 as blockship.
MARIS STELLA Tr 285/07. French M/S seized 3.7.1940 at Southampton. Boom gate vessel 1940–45.
MARIS STELLA MFV 79/31. Belgian, hired as A/P vessel 8.10.1940–45.
MARISTO Tr 287/14, 1–12pdr. Hired 1916–19.
MARITANA Dr 97/07. Hired 1916–19.
MARJORIE M HASTIE Tr 244/30. Hired as M/S 6.1940–11.45.
MARKSMAN Tug 78/14. Hired on harbour service 11.1915–19.
MARLBOROUGH Tr 213/07. Hired as BDV 1916–19 and as A/P Tr 11.1939–3.1.40. Hired again 1945–7.46.
MARLIS 115/31. Hired (RCN) 1941–46.
MARLOES Tr 220/11, 1–6pdr. Hired 1914–19.
MARMION DY tug 100 tons, 65 x 15 ft. Purchased 3.1900. Sold 22.7.20. (Also known as C.112.)
MARMION II Paddle 409/06, 1–6pdr. Hired as M/S 15.5.1915–27.5.20 and as M/S MARMION, 1–12pdr, 10.39. Wrecked 9.4.41 by air attack at Harwich.
MARMORA 10,509/03. Hired as AMC 3.8.1914. Sunk 23.7.18 by 'U.B.64' south of Ireland.
MARNE II Tr 257/15, 1–6pdr. Hired 1915–19.
MARON 6,487/30, 2–6in, 1–3in, 1–12pdr. Hired as OBV 7.8.1940–29.6.42.
MARQUES de ESTELLA Wh 158/11. Norwegian, hired as salvage vessel 27.7.1942–18.4.46.

MARQUIS Barge 200dw. Hired as BBV 26.8.1940. Store hulk 8.42–45.

MARRAWAH Cstr 472/10. Commissioned as M/S (RAN) 3.9.1941–9.46 (lent USN 12.42–8.45.)

MARSA (ex-*Mars*) Paddle 317/02. Hired as M/S 22.9.1916. Sunk 18.11.17 in collision off Harwich.

MARSDALE 4,890/40, 2–6in, 1–12pdr, 6--MG. Hired as OBV 18.8.1940–14.6.42.

MARSDEN Tug 131/06. Hired 24.6.1915. Wrecked 31.10.15 in Suvla Bay.

MARSDEN Tug 195/17. Hired 1917–19.

MARSHFORT Decoy ship. In service 1917–12.18.

MARSH TIT (ex-*Leopold Nera*) MFV 58/37. Belgian, hired as M/L 16.9.1940–22.3.46.

MARSONA Tr 276/18, 1–6pdr. Hired as M/S 30.8.1939. Sunk 4.8.40 by mine off Cromarty.

MARTHE Tr 234/13. Hired 1917–19.

MARTICOT (see MMS.121)

MARTIN II Tr 242/97. Hired 1914–18.

MARTINDALE Yt (RAN), 56/32. Hired 1941–46.

MARTINET BDV 530 tons, 135 x 30½ ft, 1–3in. Smiths Dk 8.12.1938. On sale list 1958.

MARTINETTA Yt 115/29. Hired for A/S training 29.4.1940, purchased 11.41. Sold 2.46.

MARTIS 2,483/94. Purchased 1940. Sunk 1940 as blockship at Scapa Flow.

MARTON Tr 232/05. Hired 1916–19.

MARVELLOUS Dr 82/08, 1–3pdr. Hired 1915–19.

MARY 30-gun ship. Hired 1650–53.

MARY Two ships of 252bm. Hired 1664–67.

MARY 6th Rate 12, 105bm. Hired. Wrecked 18.3.1690 in Wicklow Bay.

MARY DY hoy, 50bm. Plymouth 1712. Fate unknown.

MARY Cutter 12. Hired 1800. Foundered 2.1805 in the Channel.

MARY Cutter 8, 100bm, 6–12pdr carr., 2–3pdr. Hired 8.1803–12.04.

MARY Victualling vessel, 54bm, 37 x 16½ ft. Muddle, Gillingham 1801. Fate unknown.

MARY Sloop 6, 211bm, 6–3pdr. Hired 4.1803–9.08.

MARY Cutter, 78bm. Hired 4.1809–4.12.

MARY Victualling vessel. Woolwich DY 5.1838. Listed in 1875.

MARY Tr 256/06. Hired 1914. Sunk 5.11.14 by mine off Yarmouth.

MARY Dr 65/02. Hired on harbour service 1915–16.

MARY ADELINE Dr 73/10. Hired 1.1915–19.

MARY A HASTIE Tr 244/30, 1–12pdr. Hired as A/P Tr 12.1939. M/S 1941–45.

MARY A PURDY Tr 202/19. Hired as BBV 2.1940–10.44.
MARY B MITCHELL Aux schooner 210/92, 1–12pdr, 2–6pdr. Hired as decoy ship (Q.9) 25.4.1916–3.19. (Also operated as MARY JOSE, NEPTUN, MARIE THERESE, JEANNETTE and EIDER.)
MARY BOWIE Dr 79/11, 1–3pdr. Hired 1915.
MARY CAM Tr 202/18. Hired as M/S (RAN) 5.1942. Sold 5.48.
MARY COWIE Dr 86/08, 1–3pdr. Hired 1915–19.
MARY HERD Dr 96/19. Hired as water carrier 5.1940–10.45.
MARY J MASSON Dr 80/13. Hired as degaussing vessel 5.1940–47.
MARYLAND Dr 61/02. Hired as store carrier 1915–19.
MARY MALTMAN Dr 79/08. Hired 1915–19.
MARYNTHEA Yt 900/11, 2–12pdr. Hired as A/P Yt 4.2.1915–8.2.19.
MARY REID Dr 77/08. Hired 1915–19.
MARY STEPHEN Dr 89/06, 1–3pdr. Hired 1916–19.
MARY STURGEON MFV 20net/33. Hired as HDPC 11.1939. To War Dept 4.42.
MARY SWANSTON Dr 96/20. Hired on harbour service 10.1939–1.46.
MARY TAVY DY tug, 182gr, 93 x 23½ ft. Philip, Dartmouth 1918. Sold 1947, renamed *Danny*.
MARY WATT Dr 96/18. Hired as tender 8.1939–46.
MARY WETHERLEY Tr, 1–6pdr. Hired 1916–19.
MARY WHITE Tr 271/35. Hired as BDV 1.1940–2.46.

MA/SB. 1–39 Motor anti-submarine boats. All built by British Power Boat Co, Hythe 1939–41:
MA/SB. 1–5 19 tons, 60 x 13 ft, 2–MG. Built 1939.
MA/SB.3 mined and beached 28.2.41 in the Suez Canal.
MA/SB.5 renamed CT.08 controlled target in 1942, sold 1946. Others all sold 1945.
MA/SB.6–21 23 tons, 70 x 20 ft, 2–MG. Built 1939–40. All converted to motor gunboats MGB.6–21 in 1940.
MA/SB.22–39 20 tons, 63 x 15 ft, 2–MG. Built 1941. All on air-sea rescue duty from 1941 and on sale list in 7.45 except MA/SB.30, sunk 14.12.41 after fouling the Humber boom.

MASCOT Dr 66/02, 1–3pdr. Hired 1916–19.
MASHOBRA 8,324/20. Hired as base ship 2.10.1939. Bombed and beached 25.5.40 at Narvik.
MASONA Tr 297/15. Hired as BDV 12.1939, purchased 11.43. Sold 1946.
MASTER (see QUICKLY)
MASTERFUL Rescue tug, 'B.A.T' class. Levingston 5.6.1942 on lend-lease. Returned 3.46 to the USN.

MASTERFUL (ex-*Empire Lawn*) DY tug 254/42. Transferred from MOT and renamed 3.1947. On sale list 1958.

MASTER JOHN MFV 29/33. Hired as BBV 12.1939—1.46.

MASTERPIECE Dr 82/07, 1—3pdr. Hired 1.1915—19.

MASTIFF M/S Tr 520 tons, 150 x 27½ ft, 1—4in. Robb, Leith 17.2.1938. Sunk 20.11.39 by mine in the Thames estuary.

MASTIFF (see BUSEN 9)

MASTIFF DY tug, 152gr. Appledore SB Ltd 12.12.1966.

MASTODONTE French navy tug 954 tons. Seized 7.1940 at Plymouth. Rescue tug 8.40. To MWT circa 10.41.

MASTWING Tr 199/08, 1—6pdr. Hired 1914—19.

MATAFELE Cstr 335/38. Hired as store carrier (RAN) 1.1.1943. Sunk 7.44 by Japanese S/M in the Coral Sea.

MATA HARI 1,020/15. Hired as A/P vessel 1.9.1939. Sunk 28.2.42 by Japanese A/C in the Sunda Strait.

MATAI 1,050/30. Commissioned as M/S (RNZN) 1.4.1941. Returned 1946.

MATCHLOCK Armament tug, 70gr. Hong Kong 1940. Sunk 1942 by mine off Canton.

MATCHLOCK Armament store carrier, 187gr. Philip 1946.

MATHILDE SIMONNE Dr 88/31. Belgian, hired as A/P Dr 10.1940. Degaussing vessel 8.42—8.46.

MATTHEW 35-gun ship. Hired for the Armada campaign.

MATTHEW BERRYMAN Tr, 'Castle' type. Cook Welton & Gemmell. Cancelled 1919.

MATTHEW CASSADY Tr, 'Castle' type, 278gr. Ailsa 18.12.1918. Sold 1919, renamed *Inverdon*.

MATTHEW CROOKE Tr, non-standard 'Strath' type, 212gr. A.Hall 2.10.1917. Sold 1921, renamed *Fort Rose*. (FORT ROSE in WW.II.)

MATTHEW FLINDERS Govt vessel 1,180/17. Hired (RAN) 1941—46.

MATTHEW FLYNN Tr, 'Castle' type, 275gr. Hepple 1918. Sold 1921, renamed *Amiral Marquer*. (Served as COMMILES in WW.II.)

MATTHEW HARTLEY Tr, 'Strath' type, 202gr. Rennie Forrest 1919. Sold 1919, renamed *Wyberton*.

MAUD Tug 63/00, 1—6pdr. Hired as A/P vessel 11.1940—9.44.

MAUN Tr 271/06, 1—6pdr. Hired 1914—19.

MAVIS Yt 260/03. Hired for ferry service 9.7.1917—26.5.19.

M.A.WEST Dr 96/19. Hired on examination service 1.9.1939. Sunk 14.5.41 by air attack off the Norfolk coast.

MAXIM Armament store carrier 604 tons, 134 x 25 ft. Lobnitz 6.8.1945.

MAXIMUS Tr 236/98, 1—6pdr. Hired 1915—19.

MAX PEMBERTON Tr 334/17, 1—12pdr. Hired 1917—19.

MAY 257/27. Hired as cable looplayer 4.1940—1.46.

MAYBERRY Dr 77/01. Hired on harbour service 11.1914–31.12.16 and 1918–19.

MAYCREST 5,923/13. Purchased 1944. Sunk 4.8.44 as blockship, Normandy.

MAYFLOWER Ship, 200bm. Hired for the Armada campaign.

MAYFLOWER Discovery vessel. Hired 1593–94.

MAYFLOWER Ship, 300bm. Hired 1649. Seized by Royalists 1650 at Lisbon.

MAYFLOWER Dr 97/07, 1–57mm. Hired 1915–19.

MAYFLOWER MFV 54net. Hired as A/P vessel 3.1.1940. Renamed MEMENTO 7.40. Returned 9.45.

MAZURKA A/S Tr 530 tons, 150 x 27½ ft, 1–4in, 3–20mm. Ferguson 28.11.1940. Sold 3.46.

MEAD 606/19. Hired as cable ship 5.5.1942–27.8.44.

MEANDER MFV 53/34. Hired (RCN) 1940–46.

MECHANICIAN 9,044/00, 2–6in, 2–4in. Hired 4.1917, commissioned as escort 20.6.17. Sunk 20.1.18 by 'UB.35' in the Channel.

MECKLENBURG 2,907/22. Dutch, hired as accommodation ship 1941–44.

MEDA (see ML.1301)

MEDEA Yt 137/04. Hired as BBV 4.1941. Purchased as accommodation ship 9.42. Sold 11.45. (Norwegian crew 1.12.42–3.43.)

MEDEA (see CIRCE)

MEDIAN Tr 217/19. Hired as A/P Tr 11.1939–8.2.40.

MEDIATOR Tr 178/12. Hired 1914. Sunk 2.1.16 by mine off Hornsea.

MEDIATOR Rescue tug 1,118 tons, 190 x 38½ ft, 1–3in, 2–20mm. Robb 21.6.1944. DY tug 1946. Sold 1968.

MEDLER (ex-*The Mermaid*) Paddle 118/91. Hired as M/L, 10 mines, 1918–28.3.19.

MEDOC Cstr 1,166/30. French A/P vessel seized 3.7.1940 at Plymouth. Free-French crew 8.40. Sunk 26.11.40 by torpedo in the Channel.

MEDUSA II Yt 627/06, 1–12pdr, 1–6pdr. Hired as A/P Yt 12.1.1915–22.3.19 and as MEDUSA, A/S Yt, 9.39. Renamed MOLLUSC 11.39. Sunk 17.3.41 by air attack off Blyth.

MEDUSA 793/13. Hired as M/S 11.1939. To RAN and renamed MERCEDES 1942. Returned 8.46.

MEDWAY DY vessel, 116bm, 68 x 20½ ft. Chatham 1796. Listed in 1815.

MEDWAY DY store carrier, 167bm, 72 x 23½ ft. Sheerness DY 30.9.1830. Foundered 25.11.1832 in a storm off Port Royal, Jamaica.

MEDWAY DY tug, 309gr. Hired 6.11.1914–6.12.18.

MEDWAY QUEEN Paddle 318/24. Hired as M/S 9.9.1939. M/S training 1.44–1.46.

MEG (see ZEDWHALE)

MEG II Dr 82/06. Hired 1.1915–19.

MEKONG Yt 899/06, 2–6pdr. Hired as A/P Yt 14.4.1915. Wrecked 12.3.16 north of Filey Brigg.

MELAMPUS (ex-*Prince of Wales*) 400/22. Hired as base ship 6.1941–12.9.42.

MELBOURNE Tr 466/36. Purchased as A/S Tr 10.1939. Sunk 22.5.40 by air attack near Narvik.

MELCOMBE REGIS Paddle 253/92. Hired as M/S 1.12.1917. Ferry service 5.19–31.5.20.

MELINGA Cstr 536/28. Hired (RAN) 1945–46.

MELINKA Dr 77/11, 1–3pdr. Hired 1915–19.

MELISANDE Yt 367/83. Hired 1918–19 and as A/P depot ship 10.39. Purchased 8.41. Sold 1945.

MELISSA Yt 52/16. Hired as A/P repair vessel 9.1939, purchased 9.41. Laid up 5.43. Sold 1945?

MELITA Yt 44/30. Hired on harbour service 11.1940–45. (Was base ship MONCK II in 1944.)

MELODY Admiralty steel Dr, 97gr. Crichton Thomson, Kings Lynn 1920. Sold 1920, renamed *Rose Duncan*.

MELODY (ex-*Celandine*) MFV 45net/03. Hired on harbour service 1.1941–1.46.

MELORA Yt 52/36. Hired as HDPC 11.1939, purchased 3.42. Examination service 1942; harbour service 1943. Sold 3.46.

MEMLING Dr 129/31. Belgian, hired as BBV 3.7.1940. Laid up 7.42. Returned 10.45.

MEMENTO (see MAYFLOWER)

MENA Tr 234/14. Hired 1915–19.

MENELAUS 4,672/05. Hired as kite-balloon ship 5.5.1915. Ammo. carrier (RFA) 6.17–29.1.18.

MENESTHEUS 7,787/29, 2–4in, 12–20mm, 410 mines. Hired as M/L 14.12.1939, completed 6.40. Amenity ship (red ensign) 2.45–7.46. Returned 8.46.

MERA Yt 293/86, 1–12pdr, 1–6pdr. Hired as A/P Yt 8.12.1914–25.3.19.

MERASHEEN (see MMS.122)

MERBREEZE Dr 117/31. Hired as M/S 11.1939–47.

MERCEDES Collier (RFA) 9,930 tons, 351 x 15 ft. Purchased 1902. Sold 7.20.

MERCEDES (see MEDUSA)

MERCURY Paddle 378/91, 2–6pdr. Hired as M/S 21.12.1915–24.1.20.

MERCURY Paddle 621/34. Hired as M/S 9.1939. Sunk 25.12.40 south of Ireland; hit one of her own mines.

MERION 11,620/02. Purchased as blockship 30.5.1915 but converted into dummy battlecruiser TIGER. Sunk 1915 by U-boat.

MERISIA Tr 291/11, 1—6pdr. Hired 1914—19.

MERLIN DY tug 24 tons, 54½ x 12½ ft. Waterman, Plymouth 23.2.1895, purchased on stocks. Sold 1919.

MERLIN Tr 172/06, 1—3pdr. Hired 1914—20.

MERLIN II Tr 186/99, 1—6pdr. Hired 1915—19.

MERLIN Yt 195/97. Hired for harbour service 22.4.1917—19.

MEROPS Brigantine, 1—4in, 2—12pdr. Hired as decoy vessel (Q.28), 1.1917—18. (Also served as MARACAIO.)

MEROR Tr 250/05, 1—6pdr. Hired 1915—19 and as M/S 9.40. Sunk 3.10.43 by mine, Humber area.

MERRICKVILLE Tug (RCN). Owen Sound, Ontario 1944. Sold 1946?

MERRIMAC Tug 226/18. Hired 2.1918—12.18.

MERRYDALE Tr 225/06, 1—6pdr. Hired 1915—19.

MERSE Tr 296/14. Hired 1915. Sunk 22.5.17 by mine off Bute.

MERSEY Cstr 546/-. Hired as store carrier (RFA) 17.9.1914—6.17.

MESSENGER DY mooring vessel 750 tons, 135 x 27½ ft. Bow McLachlan 22.2.1916. Sold circa 1950 at Malta.

MESSINES Tr, 'Castle' type (RCN). Polson IW 6.6.1917. To Canadian Transport Dept 1920 at lightship No 3.

METEOR DY paddle tug 530 tons, 128 x 25 ft. Laird 5.9.1883. Renamed PERSEVERANCE 1914. Sold 31.1.23 Carriden S Bkg Co.

METINDA 300/90. Hired as salvage vessel 10.1939, purchased 6.40. Sold 1947.

METOPA Yt 29/37. Hired as A/P Yt 6.1940, purchased 6.41. Sold 1946.

MEUSE Tr 217/04. Hired 1917—19.

MEWSLADE Tr 275/16, 1—6pdr. Hired 1916—19 and as M/S 3.40—4.46.

MEWSTONE Tr, 'Isles' class. Cook Welton & Gemmell 16.9.1943. Sold 14.4.46.

MFVs Motor fishing vessels built during WW.II for use as tenders. Some were fitted as minesweepers 1945—46.

MFV 1—442 50 tons, 61½ x 18 ft, 1—MG. 261 ordered in the UK, 85 in South Africa, 96 in Australia, of which, 100 were cancelled. 64 were still in service in 1963.

MFV 501—520 Vessels hired or purchased 1942 in Canada. All for disposal 1945—46.

MFV 601—995 28 tons, 45 x 15½ ft, 1—MG. 263 ordered 1942—45 in the UK, 19 in South Africa, 12 in Bermuda and 20 in the eastern Mediterranean, of which, 87 were cancelled. 31 still in service in 1963.

MFV 1001—1258 114 tons, 69 x 20 ft, 1—MG. 227 ordered 1943—45 of which, 18 were cancelled. 35 in service 1963.

MFV 1501–1610 200 tons, 90 x 22½ ft, 1–MG. 100 ordered 1943–45
of which, 7 were cancelled. 7 in service 1963.
MFV 2001–2047 Numbers given in 3.1943 to existing hired vessels
and listed to 1945–46.

MGB Motor gunboats built 1940–44.
MGB 6–21 (see MA/SB.6–21)
MGB 40–45 24 tons, 63 x 15 ft, 5–MG. British Power Boat Co 1940.
MGB 44 & 45 renamed S.2 & 3 (Polish crews) in 1944. All for disposal
1945.
MGB 46 32 tons, 5–MG. B.P.B Co 1940. For disposal 10.45.
MGB 47, 48 39 tons, 70 x 16½ ft, 1–20mm, 8–MG. White 1940. MGB
48 renamed S.1 (Polish crew) in 1944. Both for disposal 1945.
MGB 50–67 28 tons, 1–20mm, 8–MG. B.P.B Co 1940–41. For disposal
1945.
MGB 68 34 tons and MGB 69–73, 30 tons. All Higgins on lend-lease
1940. Returned 1946 to the USN.
MGB 74–81 47 tons, 69 x 21 ft, 2–20mm, 5–MG. B.P.B Co 1942.
Became MTBs 1943.
MGB 82–93 45 tons, 77 x 20 ft, 1–20mm, 4–MG. Elco Co on lend-lease
1941. Two war losses, others returned 1946.
MGB 98, 99 French MA/SBs seized 1940. Both war losses.
MGB 100–106 30 tons. Higgins, on lend-lease 1941. Returned 1946 to
the USN.
MGB 107–176 37 tons. B.P.B Co 1942. Became MTBs in 1943.
MGB 177–192 46 tons, 78 x 20 ft, 2–20mm, 8–MG. Higgins 1942 and
on lend-lease 1944. MGB 180, 189, 190 & 192 became CT.43, 40, 41, 42,
controlled targets in 1944.
MGB 312–335 (ex-MLs 312–335 renamed 8.41) 72 tons. Five war losses,
others for disposal 10.45.
MGB 501–509 95 tons, 110 x 20 ft, 9–MG, 2–TT. Camper & Nicholson
(except MGB 501, Vosper) 1942. MGB 501 war loss, others became
mercantile cargo carriers 1943.
MGB 510 75 tons, 100½ x 19 ft. Not completed.
MGB 511–518 115 tons, 110 x 22 ft, 2–6pdr, 4–20mm, 4–TT Camper
& Nicholson 1944. Renamed MTB 5511–5518 in 1947.
MGB 601–798 became MTBs on completion except Nos 601, 641–44,
648, 658, 659 and 663 lost as MGBs.

M.H.BUCHAN Dr 101/17. Hired 1917–19 and 8.39–6.45.
M.H.STEPHEN Dr 94/18. Hired as M/S 11.1939. Examination service
6.41; firefloat 1.44–12.44.
MICHAEL ANGELO Tr 285/11, 1–6pdr. Hired 1916–19.

MICHAEL BRION Tr, 'Strath' type, 202gr. Hall Russell 1919. Sold 1919, renamed *Sturdee.*

MICHAEL CLEMENTS Tr, 'Mersey' type, 324gr. Cochrane 21.8.1917. Sunk 8.8.18 in collision off St Catherines Point.

MICHAEL GING Tr 'Castle' type, 280gr. G Brown 11.5.1918. Sold 1922, same name.

MICHAEL GRIFFITHS Tr, 'Castle' type, 290gr. Cook Welton & Gemmell 5.9.1918. Sold 1921, same name. Hired as M/S 8.39. BDV 1.44–45.

MICHAEL McDONALD Tr, 'Mersey' type, 324gr. Cochrane 17.5.1919. Sold 1919, renamed *Kanuck.*

MICHAEL MALONEY Tr 'Castle' type, 276gr. Smiths Dk 7.5.1917. Stranded 19.2.20 at Egersund, Norway.

MICHIGAN 4,930/87. Purchased as dummy battleship COLLINGWOOD 28.10.1914. Sunk 12.15 as blockship in the eastern Mediterranean.

MIDAS Dr 89/10, 1–3pdr. Hired 2.1915–19 and as flare Dr, 1–3pdr, 11.39. A/P Dr 9.40. Sunk 3.2.41 in collision off Dungeness.

MIDHAT MFV 54/31. Hired as A/P vessel 8.1939. M/S 1941. Returned 8.43.

MIDNIGHT SUN Admiralty non-standard wood Dr, 97gr. Richards, Lowestoft 1918. Sold circa 1930.

MIGNONETTE Dr 96/07. Hired on harbour service 2.1915–19.

MIGRANT Yt. Hired as A/S Yt 9.1939, purchased 7.41. For disposal 6.45.

MIGRANT Yt 19/34. Hired on harbour service 9.1939–44.

MIKADO Tr 265/05, 1–6pdr. Hired 1916–19.

MIKASA Tr 274/15, 1–6pdr. Hired 1916–19 and as A/P Tr 12.39–2.40 and again 11.4.44–10.44.

MILDENHALL Tr 466/36, 1–4in. Purchased as A/S Tr 9.1939. To French navy 28.11.39 as L'AJACCIENNE.

MILETUS Tr 313/15, 1–12pdr. Hired 1916–19. (Served as LOWTHER in WW.II.)

MILEWATER Tug 283/88. Hired 11.8.1917–23.1.19.

MILFORD COUNTESS Tr 275/19. Hired as M/S 8.1939–46.

MILFORD DUCHESS Tr 275/19. Hired as M/S 8.1939–12.44.

MILFORD DUKE Tr 277/18. Hired as M/S 8.1939. BDV 4.40 and purchased. Laid up 7.46 and later sold.

MILFORD EARL Tr 290/19. Hired as M/S 8.1939. Sunk 8.12.41 by air attack off the east coast of Scotland.

MILFORD KING Tr 275/17. Hired as A/P Tr 12.1939. M/S 4.40; fuel carrier 3.44–7.45.

MILFORD PRINCE Tr 278/20. Hired as M/S 8.1939. Danlayer 4.44–12.45.

MILFORD PRINCESS Tr 301/24. Hired as M/S 9.1939–9.45.

MILFORD QUEEN Tr 280/17. Hired as M/S 8.1939–12.45.

MILICETE Yt 66/06. Hired (RCN) 1944–45. (Spelt MILICETTE in navy lists.)

MILKY WAY Admiralty wood Dr, 92gr. Noble 1919. Sold 1919, same name.

MILLBURN Dr 85/14, 1–3pdr. Hired 1.1915–19.

MILL o'BUCKIE Dr 99/14. Hired 2.1915–19 and on harbour service 9.39–8.45.

MILLWATER Dr 100/18. Hired on examination service 5.1940–8.45.

MINALTO Tr, 'Isles' class. Cook Welton & Gemmell 3.7.1943. Sold 1947.

MINCARLO Tr, 'Isles' Class. Ardrossan DY Co 28.3.1944. Sold 1946. (On loan R.Norwegian navy 10.44–9.46 as TROMOY.)

MINDFUL Rescue tug, 'B.A.T' class. Levingston 7.2.1943 on lend-lease. Returned 5.46 to the USN.

MINERVA Cutter 10. Hired 1793–1801.

MINERVA Cutter 6, 68bm, 6–3pdr. Hired 6.1803–12.04.

MINERVA Tender 4, 87bm, 4–2pdr. Hired 3.1804–05.

MINERVA II Paddle 315/93, 2–6pdr. Hired as A/P vessel 19.6.1916. M/S 20.4.19–7.4.20.

MINERVA III Tr 222/00. Hired 1917–19.

MINERVA IV Tr 142/00. Hired 1917–19.

MINGARY Yt 639/99, 1–13pdr. 1–6pdr. Hired as A/P Yt 29.1.1915–23.3.19.

MINIA 2,061gr. Hired as cable vessel (RFA) 7.7.1918–10.2.19.

MININGSBY Tr 245/08, 1–6pdr. HIred 1914–18.

MINION Ship, 200 bm. Hired for the Armada campaign.

MINION Armament tug, 97 tons, 72 x 18½ ft. Philip, Dartmouth 22.5.1940. On sale list 1960.

MINNA Scottish Fishery Board vessel. Hired 8.1914–19.

MINNA Scottish Fishery Board vessel, 390/39. Hired on examination service 8.1940. Special service 1943–46.

MINNIE de LARINAGA 5,046/14. Hired for special service 1940. Wrecked 8.9.40 by air attack in London docks. Purchased and sunk 5.2.41 as blockship at Dover.

MINNIE MOLLER 377/09. Hired as M/S 2.1940. Lost 31.12.41 at Hong Kong.

MINO Tr 168/03, 1–6pdr. Hired 1915–19.

MINONA Yt. 249/06, 2–6pdr. Hired as A/P Yt 7.10.1914–19 and on examination service 11.39, purchased 9.41. Base ship 1941. Laid up 1.46.

MINORCA DY tug. Rowhedge IW 1919. Renamed HOUDAN 1919. Sold 28.4.24, renamed *Erich.*

MINORU Tr 260/09, 1–12pdr. Hired 1914–20.

MINSTER 707/24. Hired a netlayer 29.8.1940. Sunk 8.6.44 by mine in Seine Bay.

MINT Dr 96/12. Hired as BDV 2.1915–19 and as water boat 11.39–46.

MINUET A/S Tr 530 tons, 150 x 27½ ft, 1–4in, 3–20mm. Ferguson 1.3.1941. To Italian navy 2.46.

MINX DY tank vessel 390 tons, 115 x 23 ft. Cox, Falmouth 13.6.1900. On sale list 1946.

MIRABELLE Tr 203/18, 1–3pdr. Hired as A/P Tr 11.1939. Fuel carrier 1944. Sunk 17.9.44 in collision.

MIRAGE Admiralty steel Dr, 97gr. Lewis 1918. Sold 1921 renamed *Thorn Tree.*

MIRAGE (ex-*Verity*) Yt 41/38. Hired as HDPC 10.1939, purchased 8.41. Laid up 3.46, sold 1946?

MIRAGE 175gr. French, seized 7.1940. Water boat 8.40–9.45.

MIRAMAR Yt 70/30. Hired (RAN) 9.1939–8.45.

MIRANDA II Yt 942/10, 2–12pdr. Hired as A/P Yt 9.1.1915–25.2.19.

MIRANDA III Tr 173/06, 1–6pdr. Hired 1916. Wrecked 14.1.18 in Pelwick Bay.

MIRIEL Yt 65/98. Hired on harbour service 13.8.1917–19.

MIRROR Cable ship 1,850/23. Hired 1941–44.

MISCOU (see CAMPENIA)

MISOA 4,800/37. Hired as tank landing ship 31.12.1940, commissioned 10.7.41. Returned 1945.

MIST Admiralty steel Dr, 97gr. Lewis 21.11.1918. To War Dept 1943.

MISTLETOE (see LAUREL)

MISTLETOE Dr 79/04, 1–6pdr. Hired 1914–19.

MISTLETOE MFV 46/90. Hired as A/P vessel 12.1939–46.

MISTRAL Admiralty wood Dr, 99gr. Richards 1919. Sold 1919, renamed *Golden Line.* (GOLDEN LINE in WW.II.)

MISTRESS ISA Dr 99/15. Hired on harbour service 1.1940–9.43.

MITCHELL BAY MFV 31/37. Hired as M/S (RCN) 1939–45.

MITRES Tr 250/17, 1–6pdr. Hired 1917–19 and as A/P Tr 1–6pdr 6.40. Salvage vessel 1941–11.45.

MIURA Tr 257/11, 1–6pdr. Hired 1914. Sunk 23.8.15 by mine off Yarmouth.

MIURA Tr 275/16, 1–6pdr. Hired 1916–19.

MIXOL Oiler (RFA) 4,326 tons, 270 x 38½ ft. Greenock & Grangemouth Co 17.6.1916. Sold 1947, renamed *White Rock.*

MIZPAH Dr 77/01. Hired 1915–19.

MIZPAH II MFV 47/29. Hired on harbour service 1.1941–10.45.

M.J.HEDLEY 449/91. Commissioned as decoy ship 6.1918. Capsized 4.10.18 in Barry Dock.

ML 1–50 Motor launches, 34 tons, 75 x 12 ft, 1–3pdr. Ordered 3.1915 from Elco, Bayonne NJ.

ML 51–550 37 tons, 86 x 12 ft, 1–13pdr. Elco 1915.

ML 551–580 42 tons, Elco 1918.

29 war losses, and of the remaining 551 boats, a total of 52 survived until 1921 and the last six were sold 1926–27.

MLs built 1940–44: Fairmile 'A' type, 57 tons, 110(oa) x 17½ ft, 1–3pdr, 2–MG. 'B' type, 73 tons, 112(oa) x 18ft, 1–3pdr, 2–MG. 'C' type, 72 tons, 110(oa) x 17½ ft, became MGBs. 'D' type, 90 tons, 115(oa) x 21 ft, became MGBs/MTBs.

ML 050–129 (ex–01–080 and known as Q.050–129 until 1944) 'B' type (RCN). Built in Canada 1941–44 and for disposal 1945 except MLs 106, 116, 121 and 124, renamed PTC 706, 716, 721 and 724 in 1949 and listed to 1954.

ML 100–111. 'A' type. Built 1940; 4 war losses; rest sold 1946.

ML 112–311, 336–600, 891–933, 2001, 4001–04. 'B' type. Built 1940–44 including 114 boats built abroad. 47 war losses; eight Canadian-built, transferred to the USN 1942; eight boats cancelled; Nos 362–65, 388–89 and 432–35 not traced after the fall of Singapore where they were building. Most were sold 1946–48 except 46 boats which lasted to 1950. 22 boats listed in 1956 and one (ML 2571 [ex–571]) listed in 1963. (Note: 2000 was added to the boat number of survivors in 1949. MLs 492–500 and 511–533 completed as air-sea rescue boats RML 492 etc. MLs 380–83, 390–91, 412–421, 436–441 and 474–77 were RIN; 400–11 RNZN; 424–31 RAN.)

ML 1001–1555 Average 50 tons, 70 x 15 ft, 4–MG. Built 1940–44, 142 abroad including 54 on lend-lease. 24 war losses; 45 boats cancelled; 6 boats not traced after the fall of Singapore; most of the rest were sold 1946–48. All boats renamed HDML (harbour defence MLs) in 1944 and survivors renamed SDML (seaward defence MLs) in 1949 except MLs 1001, 1053, 1081, 1085, 1091, 1393, and 1411 renamed SML 1–7 (survey MLs) in 1946 and SML 321–327 in 1949. ML 1301 renamed MEDA, survey ML, in 1949 and SDML 3516 (ex-HDML 1387) renamed MEDUSA, survey ML in 1961. (Note: MLs 1100–04, 1109–20 and 1261–68 were RIN; 1183–94 and 1348–51 RNZN; 1197–04 and 1330–32 SAN; 1321–29, 1338–47 and 1352–59 RAN.)

M.MORAN (ex-*HS.42*) DY tug. Transferred from War Dept 1918. Sold 7.11.19.

MMS 1 and 2 Motor minesweepers, 32 tons, 75 x 14 ft. Thornycroft, Hampton 1937. To Turkish navy 1939, renamed KAVAK and CANAK.

MMS 51 Motor minesweeper 24 tons. Built 1938. Renamed MTB 100, motor torpedo boat, 1939. Renamed CT.11, controlled target in 1942. Listed to 1945.

MMS 1–118 and 123–313 Motor minesweepers built 1940–44. 165 tons, 105 x 23 ft, 2–MG. (1500 added to numbers in 1951.)

(MMS 141, 142, 238–41 renamed BURIN, COTTEL, FICHOT, JUDE, QUIRPON and ST BARBE respectively 1944 as danlayers.)

MMS 119–122 216gr, 116 x 26 ft, 2–MG. Stone, St Johns NF 1.1941 and purchased on stocks. Renamed EMBERLEY, ODERIN, MARTICOT and MERASHEEN respectively 1941. All on sale list 1946.

MMS 1001–1090 255 tons, 126 x 26 ft, 2–20mm. Built 1943–45.

Builders: Bolson, Poole: MMS 46, 58, 281, 304. Camper & Nicholson, Gosport: 1001, 1002. Clapson, Barton: 50, 135, 263, 280, 305. Curtis, Looe: 24, 25, 27, 42, 43. Curtis, Par: 26, 28, 74, 75, 139, 140, 149, 150, 167–70, 224–28, 268–71, 282, 285–86, 292–98, 1032–34, 1040, 1078–80. Doig, Grimsby: 116–18, 179, 229, 1022, 1026, 1042, 1081–82.

E.Angian Constr.Co: 71–73, 1005, 1007–08, 1027, 1046, 1074, 1085–8 1089. Forbes, Peterhead: 2, 20, 79–81, 209, 230, 1013, 1045. Forbes, Sandhaven: 12, 33, 59–60. Harris, Appledore: 9, 38, 92, 165, 210, 1014, 1031. Herd & Mackenzie: 4, 21, 53–54, 211, 1015–16, 1047. Humphrey & Smith, Grimsby: 180, 212–13, 1023, 1025, 1043. Husband, Marchwood: 7, 22, 137–38, 262, 309. Husband, Southampton: 23, 29, 65–67. Irvin, Peterhead: 3, 55, 136, 278, 299, 302, 208. Macduff E & SB: 13, 32, 61–62, 214, 232, 275–76.Morris, Gosport: 5, 49, 89–91, 109–12, 274, 287–89. Noble, Fraserburgh: 10, 11, 18, 34, 35, 55, 56, 133–34, 208(ex-Forbes), 215, 219, 277, 301, 306–07, 1017, 1021, 1024, 1048–49. Philip, Dartmouth: 30, 88, 175, 216, 300, 1030, 1090. Reekie, Anstruther: 31, 64, 1018, 1041. Reekie, St Monance: 14, 63, 217, 260. Richards, Lowestoft: 1, 8, 19, 39–41, 44, 45, 68–70, 76, 77, 78 (ex-Curtis, Looe), 176–78, 1006, 1037–38. Rowhedge IW: 36, 37, 1084. Upham, Brixham: 6, 47, 48, 173–74, 218, 231, 272, 283, 303, 1019–20, 1029. Wivenhoe SY: 15–17, 82–87, 113–15, 1009–12, 1028, 1044, 1083.

Bahamas: 194–95. Beirut: 310, 313. Burma: 147, 156, 161–64.Canada: 99–108, 1050–73. Cayman Is: 259. Ceylon: 143–46. Hong Kong: 95, 96, 123–24. India: 97, 98 (ex-Burma), 129–32, 148 (ex-Burma), 151–55 (ex-Burma), 157–60. Jamaica: 222–23. Newfoundland: 141–42. Singapore: 51, 52, 93, 94, 125–28, 166. Tel Aviv: 311–12.

Cancelled boats: 208, 210, 235, 258–59, 262, 264, 273, 299, 306. Boats not listed as building after Japanese invasions: 123–128, 156, 161–64, 166. War losses: 39, 51, 52, 55, 68, 70, 77, 89, 93, 94, 101, 117, 168, 170, 180, 227, 229, 248, 257, 278, 288, 1016, 1019.

The following survived the year 1948:

MMS 1, 5, 46, 53, 310, 313, all lent Greek navy 1946–51 and sold 1955–57.

MMS 58 Lent Greek navy 1946–51, lost by fire 4.54.

MMS 10 Lent Italian navy 1946–50, renamed TRV.20 in 1950. Sold 1952.

MMS 32, 34, 35, 48, 49, 50, 99–102, 104–06, 135, 167, 172, 185 lent Italian navy 1946–50. Sold 1954–56.

MMS 36, 56, 57. Sold 1958. MMS 69 sold 1954.

MMS 79, 83, 84, 86 sold 1956–59. MMS 109–10 sold circa 1954.

MMS 129, 131, 132 (all RIN) renamed MUJAHID (RPN), GHAZI (RPN) and BARQ respectively 1947.

MMS 144 Sold 1957.

MMS 154 (RIN). Made a DY craft 1960.

MMS 181 BU 5.58.

MMS 182, 187. Lent Belgian navy 1946–51. BU 1955.

MMS 190, 191, 193. Lent Belgian navy 1946–51. Sold 1950–55.

MMS 217, 224, 228, 236. Sold 1956–58.

MMS 222 Renamed AMBER 1949. Sold 1955 in Bermuda.

MMS 223 Renamed JADE 1949. Damaged 2.51 in a storm and scuttled 24.2.51 off Bermuda.

MMS 233, 261 Renamed ST DAVID and VENTURER respectively 1948. For disposal 1956.

MMS 263 For disposal 1953.

MMS 266 Lent Belgian navy 1946. Returned; sold 1955.

MMS 271, 272 Sold 1958.

MMS 275 Renamed NEPTUNE 1949, nominal base ship. Sold circa 1953.

MMS 283, 286 Sold 1957.

MMS 288 Foundered 2.10.52.

MMS 285, 289 Renamed ISIS and THAMES respectively as RNVR tenders 1950. Sold 1955 and 1958.

MMS 290, 291, 294, 296, 297, 301, 307 all sold 1954–58.

MMS 1001, 1002, 1003, 1011 renamed DGV 400–403 1955 as degaussing vessels. DGV 402 for disposal 1963.

MMS 1027 Lent Belgian navy 1946–51. Sold 1956.

MMS 1017, 1030, 1034 Renamed CURZON, HUMBER and KILMOREY 1949 as RNVR tenders. Reverted 1952, sold 1956–58.

MMS 1037 Foundered 26.2.49; raised. Sold 1951.

MMS 1038, 1042, 1044, 1060, 1061 Sold 1955–58.

MMS 1048, 1075, 1077, 1090. Renamed GRAHAM, MERSEY, MONTROSE, BERNICIA 1949 as RNVR tenders. Sold 1956–58.

MMS 1089 Renamed FORTH 1950; KILLIECRANKIE 1951 as RNVR tenders. Sold 1958.

MOA Tr (RNZN) 600 tons, 150 x 30 ft, 1–4in, 1–20mm. Robb, Leith 15.5.1941. Sunk 7.4.43 by Japanese A/C off Guadalcanal.

MOED–EN–WERK Dr 108/31. Belgian, hired 4.1940. Renamed ACRASIA, danlayer, 9.40. Returned 1947.

MOIRA MFV 21net/33. Hired on harbour service 1.1940, purchased 3.42. Laid up 1.46, later sold.

MOLDAVIA 9,500/03,8–6in. Hired as AMC 27.11.1915, purchased 1.16. Sunk 23.5.18 by 'UB.57' in the Channel.

MOLDE (see KOS XX)

MOLE Dredger 206gr, 1–6in. Hired as gunboat 1914–15.

MOLLUSC (see TRINCULO)

MOLLUSC (see MEDUSA)

MOLLY 18-gun ship. Hired 1781. Captured 10.1782 by the French SEMILANTE off Madeira.

MOLLYMAWK Tr 242/99. Hired 1917–19.

MOLLYMAWK Yt 61/95. Hired as degaussing tender 1942–46.

MOLLYMAWK DY tug (RAN) 250 tons, 99 x 21 ft. Poole & Steel, Sydney 3.5.1946.

MONA Hired decoy ship. Blown up 4.7.1917 to avoid capture off Cape Passaro.

MONARCH II Dr 82/07, 1–3pdr. Hired 1915–20.

MONARCH III Tr 235/04, 1–6pdr. Hired 1916–19.

MONARCH IV Tr 130/95. Hired 1917–19.

MONARCH Tug 123/83. Hired 7.1914–18.

MONARCH Cable ship 1,150/16. Hired 1917–19 and 1942–45.

MONARCH Yt 62gr. Hired as ML depot ship 6.1941, purchased 11.41. Sold 1945.

MONARCHY (ex-*Monarch*) Paddle 315/88. Hired as M/S 5.5.1917–23.8.19. (Served as EXWEY in WW.II.)

MONARDA Dr 109/16, 1–3pdr. Hired 1916–19 and as M/S 11.39. Foundered 8.11.41 in the Thames estuary.

MONA's ISLE Paddle 1,564/82, 1–3pdr. Purchased as netlayer 28.9.1915. Sold 6.8.19 Ward, Morecambe to BU.

MONA'S ISLE 1,688/05, 2–4in, 1–12pdr. Hired as ABV 27.8.1939. A/A guardship 10.40; accommodation ship 3.42. To return 11.43.

MONDARA Cstr 359/21. French M/S seized 3.7.1940 at Southampton. Cable looplayer 11.40. Laid up damaged 6.42. Returned 1945.

MONGYR Tr 'Basset' class (RIN). Alcock Ashdown. Ordered 12.1942, cancelled 12.44.

MONICA 300/32. Dutch, hired as water carrier 27.5.1940–12.7.45.

MONICA Barge 128/06. Hired as degaussing vessel 4.1941–45.

MONIMIA Tr 374/29, 1–12pdr. Hired as M/S 8.1939–11.45.

MONIQUE–ANDREE Tr 221/19, 1–65 mm. French M/S seized 3.7.1940 at Plymouth. M/S 11.40–4.46.

MONIQUE–CAMILLE Tr 277/35. French M/S seized 3.7.1940 at Southampton. A/P Tr 9.40–3.46.

MONITOR Dr 68/06. Hired on harbour service 12.1914–19.

MONKEY DY tank vessel 330 tons, 115 x 23 ft. Lobnitz 21.12.1896. Wrecked 26.4.42 by air attack in Malta DY. Wreck BU 4.43 locally.

MONOWAI 10,852/24, 8–6in, 2–3in. Hired as AMC (RNZN) 23.10.1939 –43.

MONS Tr 163/96. Hired 1917–19.

MONSOON Yt 432/97, 2–12pdr. Hired as A/P Yt 10.5.1915–13.2.19.

MONSOON (see TRADEWIND)

MONTANO Tr 269/17. Hired as A/P Tr 3.5.1940. M/S 3.42; fuel carrier 3.44–1.46.

MONTBLETTON Dr 76/10. Hired 2.1915–19.

MONTCALM 5,478/97. Hired as dummy battleship AUDACIOUS 10.1914. Purchased 29.1.16, converted to oiler (RFA); renamed CRENELLA 18.11.16. Sold 22.10.19 Anglo-Saxon Pet. Co.

MONTCLARE 16,314/22, 7–5.5in, 3–4in. Hired as AMC 28.8.1939. Purchased as depot ship 2.6.42, 21,550 tons, 546 x 70 ft, 4–4in, 19– 20mm. Arrived 3.2.58 Ward, Inverkeithing to BU.

MONTCOFFER Dr 53/09. Hired 1915–19.

MONTE CARLO Dr 96/31. Belgian, hired as A/P Dr 9.10.1940. Harbour service 1942–10.45.

MONTENOL Oiler (RFA) 4,900 tons, 335 x 41½ ft. Gray, Sunderland 5.7.1917. Scuttled 21.5.42 after being torpedoed in the N.Atlantic.

MONTEZUMA 7,345/99. Hired as dummy battleship IRON DUKE 2.11.1914. Purchased 7.7.15, converted to oiler (RFA) and renamed ABADOL. Renamed OAKLEAF 7.2.17. Lost 25.7.17.

MONT JOLI 275/39. Hired (RCN) 1941–46.

MONTROSE 7,207/97. Purchased as blockship 28.10.1914. Wrecked 28.12.16 on the Goodwins.

MOOIVLEI Tr 252/35. Commissioned as M/S (SAN) 13.11.1939. Returned 3.45.

MOOLTAN 20,952/23, 2–3in. Hired as AMC 9.9.1939–1.41.

MOONBEAM Admiralty steel Dr, 97gr. Lewis 1918. Sold circa 1923, renamed *Skimmer*.

MOONBEAM Oiler (RCN). Listed 1940–47.

MOONFLEET Salvage tug, 145gr, 100 x 20 ft. Edwards, Millwall 2.10.1917. Sold 20.7.23, renamed *Salvage Chief.*

MOONLIGHT Admiralty wood Dr, 93gr. Richards. Cancelled and completed as *Carry On.* (CARRY ON in WW.II.)

MOONLIGHT 100/13. Hired as store hulk 1.1940–11.45.

MOONRISE Admiralty wood Dr, 92gr. Richards. Renamed ASCENDANT, cancelled and completed mercantile.

MOONRISE (ex-*Marioute*) Tr 318/18. Purchased as M/S 1940. Boom gate vessel 9.43. Sold 5.46.

MOONSET Admiralty steel Dr, 96gr. Brooke 1919. Sold 1919, renamed *Flora Taylor*.

MOONSHINE Admiralty steel Dr, 97gr. Lewis 4.9.1918. Sold circa 1924.

MOONSHINE (see POLO NORTE)

MOONSTONE (ex-*Lady Madeleine*) A/S Tr, 390/34, 615 tons, 1−4in. Purchased 1.1939. Sold 1946, renamed *Red Lancer*.

MOONYEEN Yt 34/37. Hired as HDPC 6.1940−45.

MOOR 3,688/82, 6in guns. Hired as AMC 1885−86.

MOOR DY mooring vessel, 720 tons, 138 x 29 ft. Bow McLachlan 1919. Sunk 8.4.42 by mine at Malta.

MOORBERRY DY mooring vessel 1,000 tons? Taikoo DY. Ordered 10.6.1941. No record of laying down.

MOORBURN DY mooring vessel 1,000 tons, 160 x 34 ft, 1−12pdr, 2−20mm. Goole SB 16.4.1942.

MOORCOCK DY mooring vessel (as MOORBURN). Goole SB 27.6.1942. Sold 4.63, BU at Troon.

MOORDALE DY mooring vessel 720 tons, 138 x 29 ft. Bow McLachlan 15.8.1919. Sold 1961.

MOORESS DY mooring vessel 720 tons, 1,006 (deep), 135 x 30 ft. Goole SB 16.9.1943.

MOORFIELD DY mooring vessel 1,000 tons, 149 x 37 ft, 1−12pdr. Simons 28.4.1941.

MOORFIRE DY mooring vessel (as MOORESS). Devonport DY 24.5.1941. BU 3.63 White, St Davids Harbour.

MOORFLY DY mooring vessel (as MOORBURN). Goole SB 14.7.1942. On sale list 1963.

MOORFOWL DY mooring vessel (as MOORDALE). Bow McLachlan 11.9.1919. On sale list 1963.

MOORGATE Boom gate vessel (dumb) 345 tons, 99 (oa) x 29 ft, 1−3in. Bow McLachlan 28.7.1931. On sale list 5.58.

MOORGRASS DY mooring vessel (as MOORBURN). Goole SB 25.7.1942. On sale list 1963.

MOORGRIEVE DY mooring vessel (as MOORBURN). Goole SB 4.9.1944. On sale list 1963.

MOORHEN DY mooring vessel (as MOORBURN). Goole SB 30.9.1943.

MOORHILL DY mooring vessel (as MOORDALE). Bow McLachlan 12.9.1919. Listed to 1961.

MOORILYAN Yt 1,349 tons, 1−4.7in, 2−3pdr. Commissioned as A/P Yt (RAN) 23.5.1918. Sold 1921.

MOORLAKE DY mooring vessel (as MOORDALE). Bow McLachlan 10.11.1919. Sold 1946 in the East Indies.

MOORLAND DY mooring vessel 720 tons, 135 x 31 ft. Simons 22.11.1938.

MOOR MYRTLE DY mooring vessel (as MOORBURN). Goole SB 15.3.1945. On sale list 1963.

MOORPOUT BDV (as MOORBURN). Chatham DY 24.7.1944. On sale list 10.68.

MOORSIDE DY mooring vessel (as MOORBURN). Goole SB 25.8.1945. BU 3.63 White, St David's Harbour.

MOORSMAN BDV (as MOORBURN). Chatham DY 24.7.1944.

MOORSTONE DY mooring vessel (as MOORDALE but 140 x 29 ft). Sold 1949 at Malta.

MOORVIEW DY mooring vessel (as MOORDALE). Bow McLachlan 1919. Wrecked 21.3.20 near Lands End.

MOORWIND DY mooring vessel 1,000 tons? Singapore Harbour Board. Ordered 18.8.1941. No record of being laid down.

MOOSE Tug 208/15. Hired as rescue tug 2.10.1915–19.

MOOSE (ex-*Cleopatra*) Yt 263/30. Commissioned (RCN) 8.9.1940. Paid off 24.8.45.

MOPSA Tr 206/07, 1–6pdr. Hired 1916–19.

MORAG Yt 30/29. Hired as A/P Yt 6.1940, purchased 10.41. Sold 12.45.

MORAVIA Tr 306/17, 1–6pdr. Hired 1917–19 and as A/P Tr, 1–6pdr, 8.40. M/S 1941. Sunk 14.3.43 by mine in the North Sea.

MORAY Tr 201/15, 1–6pdr. Hired 1915–19.

MORAY Tr 206/18, 1–3pdr. Hired as danlayer 4.1940. Water boat 1942. Foundered 13.3.43 off Milford Haven. (Raised?)

MORAY GEM Dr 73/11. Hired as BDV 5.2.1915–19.

MORAY ROSE Dr 96/19. Hired on harbour service 8.1939–2.46.

MORAY VIEW Dr 93/09. Hired as hospital Dr 3.1940–2.46.

MORDRED Yt. Purchased 1918. Sold 1921.

MOREA 10,890/08. Hired as AMC 3.1916–5.7.17.

MOREA 1,968/18. Italian prize. Sunk 16.8.1940 as blockship.

MORETON BAY 14,193/21, 7–6in, 2–3in. Hired as AMC 27.8.1939–9.41.

MORGAN JONES Tr, 'Castle' type, 278gr. Fletcher, Limehouse 10.3.1918. Sold 1919, same name. Hired as A/P Tr, 1–12pdr, 6.40–6.45.

MORMOND HILL Dr 98/08. Hired 1915–19.

MORN Admiralty steel Dr, 97gr. Crichton Thomson 1920. Sold 1920, renamed *Homefinder*. (Served as DEFENSOR in WW.II.)

MORNING STAR Tr 145/00. Hired as boom tender 1915–19.

MORNING STAR Dr 97/07. Hired 1915. Sunk 8.1.16 by mine in the Mediterranean.

MORNING STAR II Dr 84/06, 1–3pdr. Hired 1915–19.

MORNING STAR III Dr 90/07. Hired 1915–19.

MORNING STAR IV Dr 84/07, 1–3pdr. Hired 1915–19.

MORNING STAR V Dr 68/04, 1—3pdr. Hired 1915—19.

MORNING STAR VI Tr 120/95. Hired 1917—19.

MORNING STAR Yt 49/23. In Service 1942—45.

MOROCOCALA Tr 265/15. Hired 1916. Sunk 19.11.17 by mine off the Daunt Rock light.

MORRIS DANCE A/S Tr 530 tons, 150 x 27½ ft, 1—4in, 3—20mm. Goole SB 6.8.1940. Sold 1947.

MORRISON Dr 80/09, 1—3pdr. Hired 1915—19.

MORRISTON Sloop, 164bm. Hired 4.1804—9.1812.

MORTAR Armament store carrier, 186gr, 98½ x 21 ft. Pollock, Faversham 16.9. 1943. TRV 1962.

Mortar Floats and mortar vessels (see under MV).

MORVEN Tr 198/02, 1—6pdr. Hired 1915—19.

MORVEN HILL Dr 99/18. Hired on harbour service 10.1940—3.46.

MORVINA Tr 226/14, 1—6pdr. Hired 1915—19.

MOSS Dr 99/11, 1—3pdr. Hired as BDV 1914—19.

MOSS (see GOS 1)

MOTAGUA 5,966/12, 6—6in, 2—3pdr. Hired as AMC 21.11.1914—18.12.19.

MOUFLON French navy tug, seized 3.7.1940 at Southampton. Harbour service 1940—45.

MOUNT ARD Tr 255/31. Hired as BDV 9.1939—45.

MOUNT KEEN Tr 358/36. Hired as M/S 8.1939—1.46.

MOUNT ROYAL 7,044gr. Hired as dummy battleship MARLBOROUGH 10.1914. Converted to oiler (RFA) 1915, renamed RANGOL. Purchased 10.7.16, renamed MAPLELEAF 7.11.16. Sold 12.7.19, renamed *British Maple*.

MOURINO 2,200/06. Purchased as ammo. hulk 15.9.1939. Fate unknown.

MOUSA Tr, 'Isles' class. Goole SB 1.6.1942. To Italian navy 2.46.

MOY (see ALEXANDER HILLS)

MOYLE 1,761/07. Purchased as blockship 21.5.1940. Reported as sunk as blockship 1940 but listed as special service vessel to 8.42.

MTBs Motor torpedo boats built from 1936. Mostly armed with 4—8 MG, 2—TT.

MTB 1—12, 14—19. 22 tons, 60 x 13 ft. BPB Co, Hythe 1936—38. No.1 (ex—7), 2—4, became MAC. 1—4, minesweeper motor attendant craft in 1941 and CT 1, 7, 3 and 4 in 1942; Nos 14, 18 became CT.09, 10 in 1942 and No.19 (ex—1) became MAC.6 then CT.06 in 1942. No. 7 (ex—13) and all others were war losses.

MTB 20—23, 29—30. 36 tons, 70 x 15 ft. Vosper 1938—40. Nos 21—23 sold Roumania 1939. Four war losses.

MTB 24—28. Thornycroft, Hampton 1938—40. Two war losses.

MTB 31–40 and 40K, 57–66. 40 tons. Vosper 1940. 40K became
MAC.7 in 1941; Nos 31, 32, 34 renamed CT.22–24. Three lost by air
attack while building and three other war losses.
MTB 41–48, 201–12, 246–57. 33–41 tons. White 1940–41. Six war
losses.
MTB 49–56. 52 tons, 75½ x 16½ ft. Thornycroft 1941. All became
War Dept target boats 1941.
MTB 67, 68, 213–17, 327–31. 17 tons. Thornycroft 1940–41. Seven
war losses.
MTB 69, 70, 218–221. 35 tons; MTB 71, 72 25 tons; MTB 73–98 47
tons. All Vosper type (various builders). Nos 69, 70 became CT.18 and
19 in 1943. Five war losses.
MTB 100 (see MMS.51)
MTB 101 22 tons. White. MTB 102, 103 32 tons. Vosper. MTB 104–07
10 tons, Thornycroft. MTB 108, 109 Vosper. No 103 became CT.05 in
1942. Two war losses.
MTB 258–68 32 tons. Elco on lend-lease. Three war losses, others
returned 1946 to the USN. (No 258 was originally BPB Co, Hythe 1939
and transferred to the USN as prototype for Elco boats.)
MTB 269–74. Built USA on lend-lease to the RN and RCN, except No
272 retained by the USN.
MTB 275–306, 363–78, 396–411. 37 tons, 72½ x 19 ft. USA 1942–
44 on lend-lease. Five war losses, others returned 1947 to the USN except
No 361 renamed CT.36 in 1944.
MTB 307–26. 45 tons, 1–20mm, 4–MG, 2–TT. Elco on lend-lease,
except Nos 317–26 retained by the USN. Six war losses; others returned
1947.
CMTB 1 (RCN), MTB 332–43. 32 tons, 70 x 20 ft. BPB Co, Montreal
1941. One war loss.
MTB 344–46. Thornycroft, Hampton.
MTB 347–62, 379–95. 45 tons. Vosper type (various builders 1943)
No 361 became CT.36 in 1943. Five war losses.
MTB 412–18. 46 tons, 2–20mm, 5–MG, 2–TT. BPB Co, Hythe. Two
war losses.
MTB 419–23. 35 tons, 78 x 20 ft, 1–40mm, 1–20mm, 4–MG, 2–TT.
Higgins on lend-lease 1943. (Nos 419, 420 retained by the USN.)
MTB 424–29. 47 tons, 1–6pdr, 2–20mm, 2–TT. White. Renamed
S.5–10 on loan to Polish navy.
MTB 430–500, 502–09, 519–22. Average 41 tons. BPB Co 1942–44
(ex-MGBs). Nos 459–66, 485–86, 491 were RCN. Nos 481, 490 became
CT. 48–49 in 1946. 13 war losses.
MTB 523–37. 49 tons, 1–6pdr, 2–20mm, 4–MG, 2–TT. Vosper
1944–45. Nos 531, 537 became CT.44, 45 in 1945. Nos 534–36
cancelled.

MTB 601–798. 95 tons, 100 x 21 ft, 2–20mm, 9–MG, 2–TT. Fairmile 'D' type, various builders 1942–43. (ex–MGBs, nine being lost as MGBs.) 26 war losses and seven lost in a gale 30.1.46 in the Mediterranean. Most of the above MTBs were sold 1945–47. Those that survived to 1949 comprised:
MTB 1001, 1002 (ex-386, 392)
MTB 1023–27, 1029–30, 1032–33 (ex-523–27, 529–30, 532–33)
MTB 1505–09, 1519, 1521–22 (ex-505–09, 519, 521–22)
MTB 1570, 1580, 1588, 1596, 1598 (ex-470, 480, 496, 498)
MTB 1601–02 (ex-538–39)
MTB 5001–03, 5007–09, 5015, 5020, 5031–33, 5035–37 (ex-780 up)
MTB 5208, 5212, 5230 (ex-German S.208, 212, 130)
MTB 5511–18 (ex-MGB 511–18).
In 1956, MTB 1002 was a hulk, 1026, 1601 and 5212 were on sale list; only 5001–02, 5015, 5020, 5035–36 and 5514 survived to 1958.

MUDO Cstr 218/30. Dutch, hired as BBV 6.1940–10.45.
MULAN Cstr 249/31. Dutch, hired on examination service 8.1940. Torpedo school tender 1941–46.
MULL Tr, 'Isles' class. Cook Welton & Gemmell 27.3.1941. To War Dept 4.46.
MULLET (ex-*Express*) Paddle tug, 49bm, 1–32pdr. Purchased 9.3.1855. Sold 21.7.56.
MULLET A/S Tr 680 tons, 150 x 27½ ft, 1–4in. Cochrane 14.8.1942. Sold 1946, renamed *Neath Castle*.
MULLION Yt 40/38. Hired 7.1940, purchased for canteen service 1.42. Laid up 1.44, sold 1.46.
MULTAN (see COCHIN)
MULTAN (ex-COCHIN, ex-KOLABA) Tr, 'Basset' class (RIN). Scindia SN Co 23.5.1944. Sold 1946.
MURAENA Yt 330/07. Hired as accommodation ship 8.1940–47.
MURIA Tug 192/14. Hired 1940. Sunk 8.11.40 by mine off the North Foreland.
MURIEL STEVENS Yt 97/25. Hired as BBV 5.1940, purchased 11.41. Sold 3.46.
MURITAI 7,280/10. Hired as store carrier (RFA) 3.8.1914–12.2.15.
MURITAI Ferry 462/23. Hired as M/S (RNZN) 8.1940–46.
MURK Admiralty steel Dr, 97gr. Lewis 1918. Sold 1920, renamed *Girl's Friend*. (Served as TRUST in WW.II.)
MURMANSK Tr 348/29, 1–12pdr. Hired as A/P Tr 8.1939. Abandoned 17.6.40 after grounding at Brest.
MUROTO Tr 340/31. Hired as M/S 8.1939–11.44.
MURRAY STEWART Govt tug, 234/18. On examination service (RCN) 1.1940–1.46.

MUSCA Tug 75/22. Hired as A/P vessel 7.1940, purchased 5.43. For disposal 10.45.

MUSCOVIA MERCHANT Storeship, 322bm. Hired 4.1703. Captured 10.4.1703 by the French.

MUSETTE Yt 52/34. Hired as HDPC 9.1942, purchased 2.43. To War Dept 9.43.

MUSGRAVE Tug 220/97. Hired 12.1915—12.16.

MUSK ROSE (ex-*Rosebud*) MFV 25/19. Hired on examination service 7.1940—46.

MUSQUASH Tug 198/10, 1—3pdr. Hired as A/P vessel 1915—19.

MUTIN Yt? 54/27. French, seized 1940. Special service 1.41. Pilot vessel 1944—2.45.

MV 1—22. Mortar vessels. Numbers given to named vessels on 19.10.1855. (see DRAKE, SINBAD, BLAZER, GROWLER, HAVOCK, MANLY, MASTIFF, PORPOISE, SURLY, FLAMER, FIRM, HARDY, RAVEN, CAMEL, MAGNET, BEACON, CARRON, GRAPPLER, REDBREAST, ROCKET, PROMPT and PICKLE in Volume I.)

MV 23—56 Wooden mortar vessels, 168bm, 75 x 23½ ft. Six built by Lungley, Deptford:

MV 23 169bm, launched 24.4.1856. Became a DY mooring lighter in 3.65.

MV 24 169bm. 24.4.56. Renamed HARPY 12.3.61, revenue vessel. BU completed 12.10.72 at Chatham.

MV 25 169bm. 4.56. Became DY mooring lighter 3.65.

MV 26 171bm. 4.56. Mooring lighter 10.62. BU 1.66 Castle & Beech.

MV 27 22.5.56. Became Chatham YC.8, mooring lighter in 11.57.

MV 28 168bm. 22.5.56. Became coastguard watch vessel No 38 by 1870. Sold 18.10.78, BU at Poole.

Six by Thompson:

MV 29 169bm. 3.5.56. Coastguard WV.21 on 25.5.63. Sold 12.1906 to BU.

MV 30 19.7.56. Fate unknown.

MV 31 167bm. 6.10.56. Coastguard WV.9 in 5.63. To War Dept 6.70.

MV 32 3.9.56. BU completed 16.5.60 at Chatham.

MV 33 15.11.56. Woolwich YC.9 in 11.56; Sheerness YC.27 in 1870. Listed to 1901.

MV 34 1.11.56. Woolwich YC.10 in 11.56; Sheerness YC.28 in 1870. BU completed 3.73 at Sheerness.

MV 35 Hoad Bros 25.2.56. BU completed 10.65 by Marshall, Plymouth.

MV 36 Hoad Bros 25.3.56. BU completed 9.65 Marshall.

MV 37 Inman 22.3.56. Became Devonport YC.24 by 1867.

Six by Scott & Long:

MV 38 168bm. 23.2.56. Coastguard WV.4 on 28.5.64. BU 1901.
MV 39 168bm. 8.3.56. WV.8 on 28.5.64. Sold 23.6.97 to BU.
MV 40 169bm. 8.4.56. BU completed 7.67 at Haslar.
MV 41 168bm. 22.4.56. WV.32 in 7.63. Sold 19.2.81.
MV 42 167bm. 16.6.56. WV.14 on 6.6.67. MV.42 1870. Sold 12.77, BU at Southampton.
MV 43 167bm. 23.6.56. WV.12 on 6.2.64. Sold 11.98.
MV 44 169bm. Hessell & Holmes 11.3.56. WV.21 by 1865. BU 1865 Marshall, Plymouth.
Four by Harvey, Ipswich:
MV 45 169bm. 21.3.56. Became WV.22 and BU 1865.
MV 46 169bm. 4.56. WV.10 on 25.5.63. Sold 30.5.93 to BU.
MV 47 169bm. 7.4.56. Became a bathing place for BOSCAWEN training ship 7.66. Sold 21.12.92.
MV 48 170bm. 28.5.56. Accommodation for workmen at Chatham DY 10.62 and beached there 1.64.
Four by Patterson, Bristol:
MV 49 169bm. 28.2.56. WV.19 in 1864 and WV.22 in 5.67. Sold 11.11.98.
MV 50 169bm. 5.4.56. Coastguard 2.64. WV.17 in 1866. Sold 12.87 Castle to BU.
MV 51 168bm. 18.6.56. WV.13 in 1864. Sold 4.8.83 Castle to BU.
MV 52 167bm. 14.7.56. WV.16 on 6.2.64. Lent to Customs 10.71. BU 5.94.
MV 53 172bm. Briggs, Sunderland 24.3.56. BU 8.65 Marshall, Plymouth.
MV 54 172bm. Briggs, Sunderland 24.3.56. Became Devonport YC.12 in 1866. BU 1893.
MV 55 168bm. White, Cowes 15.6.56. WV.6 on 9.10.65. Sold 18.6.81.
MV 56 167bm. White, Cowes 21.6.56. WV.22 on 8.10.64. WV.19 in 1868. BU completed 31.3.74 at Sheerness.

Iron mortar floats Nos 101–50, 102–105bm, 60 x 20 ft.
No 101 Samuda, Poplar 24.11.55. Became coal pontoon 1871.
No 102 Scott Russell, Millwall 24.11.55. Became Chatham YC.53, dredger, 29.9.65.
No 103 Laird 13.11.55. Became Haulbowline YC.3 in 8.65. (See CUPID in Vol.I.)
Eight by Mare, Blackwall:
No 104 23.2.56. Renamed STEADY (Deptford YC.1), store carrier, 9.65. Listed 1873.
No 105 23.2.56. Coal hulk 1864. Listed 1893.
No 106 23.2.56. Woolwich YC.6, mooring lighter 1.66.
No 107 23.2.56. Became WV.7 then WV.42 in 3.76. Sold 5.1.91.

No 108 20.3.56. Woolwich YC.7 in 6.66.

No 109 20.3.56. Became a 'bridge' to THUNDERBOLT at Chatham.

No 110 20.3.56. Deptford YC.4, store carrier 1866, later renamed TRUSTY. Listed 1874.

No 111 4.56. Became YC.7 in 1863.

No 112 Builder unknown. 4.56. Pembroke YC.17 by 1867.

No 113 Builder unknown. 5.4.56. Lighter 1857.

Ten by Mare, Blackwall:

No 114 19.4.56. Made a DY barge 5.72.

No 115 19.4.56. Became torpedo lighter No 2 on 19.7.76.

No 116 24.4.56. Listed to 1871.

No 117 24.4.56. Made a coal pontoon 5.72.

No 118 8.5.56. 'Bridge' to THUNDERBOLT by 1875.

No 119 5.56. Made a lighter 7.56.

No 120 17.5.56. Made a lighter 7.56.

No 121 21.5.56. Made a DY tank vessel 7.56.

No 122 21.5.56. Lighter 7.56; pier hulk 8.72.

No 123 4.6.56. Woolwich YC.8 in 1866. Hulked by 1879 at Chatham.

Ten by Scott Russell:

No 124 8.5.56. To War Dept 15.7.71.

No 125 5.7.56. Became torpedo lighter No 1 on 19.7.76.

No 126 14.6.56. Coal pontoon 7.69. Portsmouth YC.47 in 7.79.

No 127 14.6.56. Chatham YC.53 in 5.74.

No 128 4.6.56. Hulk at Chatham by 1870.

No 129 30.8.56. Coal pontoon 7.69. Portsmouth YC.48 in 7.79.

No 130 5.7.56. Fate unknown.

No 131 5.7.56. Coal pontoon 7.69. Portsmouth YC.49 in 7.79.

No 132 5.7.56. Hulked 2.68 at Chatham. Listed 1898.

No 133 5.9.56. Fate unknown.

No 134 5.9.56. Coal pontoon 7.69. Portsmouth YC.50 in 7.79.

No 135 10.9.56. Fate unknown.

15 by Laird:

No 136 6.3.56. Became Chatham YC.49, tank vessel 5.72.

No 137 6.3.56. Woolwich YC.12 in 8.66.

No 138 11.3.56. Chatham YC.28, lighter, 12.56. Torpedo lighter No 3 on 19.7.76. To War Dept. 12.86.

No 139 11.3.56. Hulk at Chatham in 1870. To War Dept 8.71.

No 140 25.3.56. Coal pontoon 12.67. Portsmouth YC.43 in 7.79.

No 141 25.3.56. Portsmouth YC.41, barge, 10.67.

No 142 26.3.56. Portsmouth YC.19 on 4.2.67.

No 143 26.3.56. Portsmouth YC. 23 on 4.2.67.

No 144 5.4.56. Malta YC.4 mooring vessel, 9.67.

No 145 9.4.56. Portsmouth YC.34, coal hulk, 1866.

No 146 9.4.56. Coal pontoon 4.68. Portsmouth YC.44 in 7.79.

No 147 14.4.56. Completed 9.66 as gunnery tender for EXCELLENT. Listed 1896.

No 148 17.4.56. Portsmouth YC.13, barge, 12.61.

No 149 17.4.56. Coal pontoon 4.68. Portsmouth YC.45 in 7.79.

No 150 17.4.56. Coal pontoon 4.68. Portsmouth YC.46 in 7.79.

MYNA Tr 328/12, 1—6pdr. Hired 1915—19.

MYOSOTIS MFV 29/37. Hired on harbour service 1.1940—9.45.

MYRIS Yt 29/35. Hired as echo Yt 2.1940, purchased 9.41. Laid up 3.45. Sold 1945?

MYRLAND Tr 324/18. Norwegian, captured from Germans 6.3.1941 at Lofoten. M/S 5.41. Firefloat 1944—46.

MYRTLE (ex-*St Irene*) Tr 357/28, 550 tons, 1—12pdr. Purchased as M/S 3.1939. Sunk 14.6.40 by mine in the Thames estuary.

MYRTLE SPRIG Dr 77/10. Hired 1915—19.

MYSTIC (ex-*HT.12*) DY tug. Transferred from War Dept 1918. Sold 2.23.

MYVERA III Yt 22/35. Hired on examination service 1940—45. (Bore the name LIZARD 1942—45 as base ship.)

NAB WYKE Tr 348/30, 1—12pdr. Hired as M/S 8.1939—3.46.

NACQUEVILLE French DY tug, seized 3.7.1940 at Southampton. M/L 11.40 and renamed CHAFFINCH. Tug 1944—8.45.

NADINE Tr 150/98. Hired 1914. Sunk 1.9.15 by mine off the Shipwash.

NADINE Tr 247/19. French M/S seized 3.7.1940 at Falmouth. M/S 12.40—45.

NADIR Admiralty non-standard wood Dr, 95gr. Richards 1918. Sold 1921, renamed *Salpa*. (SALPA, 99gr, in WW.II.)

NAGPUR Tr, 'Basset' class (RIN). Burn, Calcutta 11.3.1944. Not completed.

NAIADE Tr 240/07. Belgian, hired 1917—19.

NAIRANA 3,547gr, 3,070 tons, 315 x 45½ ft, 4—12pdr, 7—A/C. Denny 1916 and purchased as seaplane carrier. Sold 1920.

NAIRANA II Tr 225/13, 1—6pdr. Hired 1916—19 and as A/P Tr 11.39—2.40.

NAIRN Yt 489/13, 1—3in, 1—6pdr. Hired as A/P Yt 15.4.1915—3.3.19.

NAIRN (see DRIVER)

NAIRNSIDE Dr 84/12. Hired on harbour service 24.11.1914—19 and as M/S, 2—MG, 11.39. A/P Dr 9.40. Ferry service 7.42—6.45.

NALDERA 15,092/18, 8–6in, 2–7.5in howitzers. Hired as escort
29.5.1918–14.3.19.

NAMBUCCA 489/36. Commissioned as M/S (RAN) 10.1.1940. To the
USN 1943–45. Lost 12.45 while on disposal.

NAMSOS (see H J BULL)

NAMUR (ex-*Emil Vandervelde*) Tr 274/17, 2–MG. Belgian, hired as
A/P Tr 5.1940, purchased 11.43. BDV 12.40. Renamed PALISADE
1944. Laid up 7.46 and later sold.

NANCY Cutter 6. Hired 1793. Lost 1794.

NANCY Cutter 6. Hired 1793. Captured 3.1801 by a French privateer
in the Channel.

NANCY HAGUE Tr 299/11, 1–6pdr. Hired 1916–19 and as BDV 4.40,
purchased 11.43. Laid up 6.46, later sold.

NANERIC 5,609/95, 2–6in, 2–4in, 2–11in howitzers. Hired as escort
7.12.1917–19.

NANOOSE (see NOOTKA)

NAPIA Tug 155/14. Hired on examination service 6.12.1939. Sunk
20.12.39 by mine off Ramsgate.

NARANI Cstr 381/14. Hired as M/S (RAN) 12.1940–3.46.

NARCISSUS Cutter 12. Hired 1795–1801.

NARCISSUS Yt 816/05, 2–12pdr. Hired as A/P Yt 13.1.1915–
27.2.19 and as FAA target 9.39. Renamed GRIVE 1940. Sunk 1.6.40
by air attack off Dunkirk.

NARVAL Tr 211/10. Belgian, hired 1916. Foundered 26.11.16 in the
North Sea.

NARVIK (see GOS.9)

NASCOPIE Icebreaker 2,521/12. Hired as RFA 1916–19.

NASIK Tr, 'Basset' class (RIN). Shalimar, Calcutta 24.5.44. Sold 1950.

NASPRITE Petrol carrier (RFA), 965gr, 204 x 33 ft. Blythswood,
Glasgow 28.11.1940. Arrived 5.2.64 in Belgium to BU.

NATAL II Tr 208/03, 1–3pdr. Hired 1914–19 and as A/P Tr 11.39.
Boom gate vessel 9.40–6.45.

NATALIA Wh 238/25. Hired as M/S (SAN) 4.1940–6.46.

NATHANIEL COLE Tr, 'Castle' class, 275gr. Smiths Dk 20.2.1917.
Foundered 6.2.18 in Lough Swilly.

NAUTILUS II Tr 257/05, 1–6pdr. Hired 1916–19.

NAUTILUS Dr 64net/29. Hired as danlayer 12.1939. Sunk 29.5.40 by
unknown cause at Dunkirk.

NAUTILUS Tr 290/13. Hired as M/S (RIN) 1941–46.

NAUTPUR Cstr 718/74. Hired as fleet auxiliary 26.2.1915. Boom gate
vessel 1917–19.

NAVICULA Yt 43/29. Hired as HDPC 10.1939, purchased 8.41.
Training vessel 1945. Sold 3.46.

NAZARENE MFV 21net/19. Hired as A/P vessel 7.1940–10.45. (On loan USN 10.43–6.45.)

NAZARETH Tr 291/18. French A/P Tr seized 1940 at Plymouth. M/S 12.40–8.45.

NDOVU Tug 279/28. Hired as M/S 1941–47.

NEAPTIDE Admiralty steel Dr, 96gr. Ouse SB 1919. Sold 1919, same name.

NEATH CASTLE Tr 225/-. Hired 1916. Sunk 14.8.16 in collision off the Orkneys.

NEATH CASTLE Tr 275/16, 1–12pdr. Hired 1917–19.

NEAVE Tr, 'Isles' class. Cook Welton & Gemmell 16.7.1942. Wreck dispersal 3.46. Sold 1.7.51.

NEBB Wh 250/30. Norwegian, hired as M/S 1941. Danlayer 1944–45.

NEBULA Admiralty steel Dr, 97gr. Rose St Fndry, Inverness 1918. Sold 1921, renamed *Nacre*. (Served as CALLIOPSIS in WW.II.)

NEBULA (see VESTFOLD I)

NEGRO Tr 402/32, 1–12pdr. Hired as M/S 9.1939–2.45.

NEIL GOW Tr 255/14, 1–12pdr. Hired 1914–19.

NEIL MACKAY Tr 266/35. Hired as A/S Tr 11.1939–10.45.

NEIL SMITH Tr, 'Castle' type, 275gr. Smiths Dk 5.7.1917. Sold 1921, same name. Hired as M/S 8.1939–9.44.

NELLIE BRADDOCK Tr 314/13. Hired 1914–19.

NELLIE BYWATER Aux. ketch 115/73. Hired as degaussing vessel 7.1940. Fuel carrier 1944–45.

NELLIE DODDS Tr 220/11. Hired 1914–19.

NELLIE McGEE Dr 93/08. Hired 1914, later purchased. Sold 1922. Hired as water carrier 5.40–6.45.

NELLIE REID Dr 94/07, 1–6pdr. Hired 1.1915–19.

NELSON Cutter 12. Hired 1799–1806.

NELSON Cutter 10, 124bm. Hired 7.1804–5.05.

NELSON Dr 71/06, 1–3pdr. Hired 1.1915–19.

NEMEA (ex-*Hercules*) Tug 145gr. Hired 6.1915–3.19.

NEMESIS (see SOUTHERN ISLES)

NEPAULIN (ex-*Neptune*) Paddle 378/92. Hired as M/S 7.12.1915. Sunk 20.4.17 by mine off Dunkirk.

NEPTOR (ex-*Neptuno*) Tug 326/15, 478 tons. Purchased 8.11.1915. Sold 1920.

NEPTUNE 20-gun ship, 280bm. Hired 1620–21.

NEPTUNE Lugger 6. Hired 1796. Run down and sunk 1798 off Beachy Head.

NEPTUNE Cutter 6. Hired 1798–1801.

NEPTUNE Sloop 4, 113bm, 4–3pdr. Hired 18.7.1803–03.

NEPTUNE Sloop 4, 107bm, 4–3pdr. Hired 11.8.1803–04.

NEPTUNE Tender 10. Hired 1806–14.

NEPTUNE Target tug 470 tons, 135½ x 25 ft. Purchased 1904. Renamed FORTITUDE 1909. Sold 31.1.23 Carriden S Bkg Co.

NEPTUNE (C.211) DY tug. Listed 1918–23.

NEPTUNIAN Tr 315/12, 1–6pdr. Hired 1915. Lost 27.10.18.

NEREE Tr 230/09. Belgian, hired 1916–19.

NERINE Tr 197/25. Hired as M/S (SAN) 16.12.1939–26.10.44.

NERISSA II Tr 173/06, 1–6pdr. Hired 1916. Wrecked 28.2.18 off Lemnos.

NERO (ex-*N.E.R. No 3*) Tug 177/15. Hired 10.1915–19.

NESMAH Dr 87/11, 1–3pdr. Hired 1.1915–19.

NESS (see ALEXANDER PALMER)

NESSIE MFV 46net. Hired as boom Dr 6.1940–2.46.

NESS POINT Tug 85/37. Hired as A/P vessel 7.1940–45. (Bore the name MARTELLO in 1945 as base ship.)

NESSUS French navy tug 590 tons. Seized 3.7.1940 at Plymouth. Salvage vessel 11.40. To MWT 1944.

NETHERBY HALL 4,461/05. Hired as store carrier (RFA) 3.8.1914–22.1.15.

NETRAVATI 1,540/08. Hired as A/S vessel (RIN) 1939–45.

NETSUKIS Dr 85/13, 1–3pdr. Hired 1914–19 and as flare Dr, 1–3pdr, 11.39. TRV 7.43–4.46.

NEVES Dr 122/31. Hired on harbour service 10.1939–10.45.

NEVILLE Tug (RCN). Owen Sound, Ontario 1944.

NEWBRIDGE Tr 228/06. Hired 1915. Sunk 19.11.17 after collision off Prawl Point.

NEW COMET Tr 177/10. Hired 1915. Sunk 20.1.17 by mine off Orfordness.

NEW COMET Tr 244/15. Hired as A/P Tr 11.1939. M/S 5.40; fuel carrier 12.43. Returned 12.45.

NEW DAWN Dr 93/08, 1–3pdr. Hired 1.1915. Sunk 23.3.18 by mine near the Needles.

NEWHAVEN II Tr 162/97. Hired 1917–19.

NEWHAVEN NB Tr 182/09, 1–6pdr. Hired 1914–19 and as M/S 2.40–2.45.

NEWLAND Tr 245/03, 1–6pdr. Hired 1916–19 and 5.40–6.40.

NEWLYN Dr 61/-. Hired on harbour service 1.1915–3.15.

NEWMARKET 833/07, 2–12pdr. Hired as M/S 8.10.1914. Foundered 7.17 in the eastern Mediterranean.

NEW MOON Admiralty steel Dr, 95gr. Rose St Fndry 1919. Sold 1920, renamed *Milnes*. (Served as UGIE VALE in WW.II.)

NEW ROSELAND River stmr 70/35. Hired as A/P vessel 6.1940, purchased 6.42. BBV 7.42. Laid up 10.45.

NEW SPRAY Dr 70/12, 1–3pdr. Hired 2.1915–19 and as BBV 12.39. Foundered 3.1.41 in a gale off Sheerness.

NEW ZEALAND Tr 290/98. Hired as BDV 1915–19.

NEXUS Dr 86/07, 1–3pdr. Hired 1915. Sunk 13.3.18 by mine in the Thames estuary.

NGUVU Tug 179/25. Hired as M/S 9.1939. Survey vessel 1943–46.

NIBLICK Tr 154/91. Hired 1917–19.

NIBLICK Tr 255/17, 1–6pdr. Hired as A/P Tr 6.1940. M/S 1941; danlayer 1944–8.45.

NICHOLAS COUTEUR Tr, 'Mersey' type. Cochrane 1919. Sold 1919.

NICHOLAS DEAN Tr, 'Mersey' type, 331gr. Ferguson 11.3.1918. Sold 1921, renamed *Notre Dame de France.*

NIGEL (see UNI II)

NIGELLA Dr 77/01, 1–3pdr. Hired 1915–19.

NIGERIA 3,755/01. Hired as store carrier (RFA) 8.11.1916. Depot ship 1917–18.

NIGHTFALL Admiralty non-standard wood Dr, 94gr. Richards 4.7.1918. Sold 1921, same name.

NIGHT HAWK Tr 287/-. Hired 1914. Sunk 25.12.14 by mine in the North Sea.

NIGHT HAWK Tr 307/15, 1–6pdr. Hired 1916–19 and as A/P Tr 6.40. M/S 1941–8.46.

NIGHTINGALE Ship, 160bm. Hired 1588–89.

NIGHT RIDER Tr 327/15. Purchased as BDV 1.1940. Laid up 7.46. Sold 2.47.

NILDESPERANDUM Dr 91/03, 1–3pdr. Hired 1915–19.

NILE Cutter. Hired 1799–1801.

NILE Brig 16. Hired 1799–1800.

NILE Lugger 16, 170bm, 14–12pdr carr., 2–3pdr. Hired 26.4.1804–10.06.

NILE Cutter 12, 166bm. Hired 5.1804–12.06.

NIMBLE Cutter 6, 70bm, 6–3pdr. Hired 1803–14.

NIMBLE (ex-*Morecambe Queen*) Iron paddle tug, 92bm. Purchased 1.5.1855. Sold 8.56 Turkish Govt.

NIMBLE (ex-*Roslin Castle*) Ferry (RFA) 651 tons, 185 x 26 ft. Purchased 3.1908. Sold 11.10.48 at Chatham.

NIMBLE Rescue tug 890 tons, 165 x 36 ft, 1–3in, 2–20mm. Fleming & Ferguson 4.12.1941. DY tug 1946.

NIMBUS Admiralty non-standard wood Dr, 98gr. Richards 1918. Sold 1921, renamed *Girl Bella.*

NIMBUS (see VESTFOLD II)

NIMROD Cutter 8. Hired 1794–1802.

NIMROD Cutter 6, 72bm. Hired 6.1803–5.14.

NINA Dr 83/04. Hired 1.1915. Sunk 2.8.17 off Prawle Point, probably mined.

NINE SISTERS Dr 92/10. Hired 1916—19.

NINON Yt 68/06. Hired as BBV 10.1940, purchased 6.41. Laid up 3.42.

NINUS Tr 292/12, 1—6pdr. Hired 1915—19.

NIRVANA I Yt 32/92. Hired as HDPC 3.1940—45.

NIRVANA II Yt 20/35. Hired as HDPC 6.1940—45.

NITH (see ANDREW JEWER)

NITINAT Canadian fishery vessel 135/39. Commissioned (RCN) 1939—45.

NIVERNAIS Cstr 390/34. French M/S seized 3.7.40 at Plymouth. A/P vessel 9.40. To MWT 7.6.41.

NIVONIA Wh 175/12. Hired 3.8.1917—19.

NIVOSE (see Le NIVOSE)

NOBLE NORA Wh 160/12, 1—6pdr. Purchased 6.1917. Sold 3.19. Hired as M/S 3.41. To Greek navy 9.43 as SPERCHEIOS. (Norwegian crew 8.41—9.43.)

NOBLES MFV 20net/32. Hired as HDPC 11.1939. Renamed ANITA 1940. Returned 5.45.

NOCTURNE Yt 43/37. Hired on harbour service 1941—45.

NODE Admiralty steel Dr, 96gr. Colby 1918. Sold circa 1923, renamed *Tiger's Eye.* (Served as GOLDEN VIEW in WW.II.)

NODZU Tr 257/11, 1—12pdr. Hired 1916. Sunk 1.19 in collision with a wreck in the Bristol Channel.

NODZU Tr 303/29. Hired as M/S 9.1939—11.45.

NOEL DY tank vessel 350 tons. Listed 1918—47.

NOGI Tr 257/08, 1—6pdr. Hired 1.1915—19.

NOGI Tr 299/23. Hired as M/S 8.1939. Sunk 23.6.41 by air attack off Norfolk.

NOIR (see RION)

NONETA Yt 49/35. Hired as HDPC 2.1940, purchased 10.41. Laid up 6.45. Sold 1.46.

NOOGANA Tr 237/14, 1—3pdr. Hired 1915—19.

NOONDAY (ex-*Argosy*) MFV 27net/36. Hired as A/P vessel 1941—4.46.

NOONTIDE Admiralty Dr, 97gr. Colby 11.6.1918. Target towing 1944. Sold 11.6.48, same name.

NOODSVAARDER Tug 179/97. Dutch, hired as A/P vessel 1940 (Dutch crew?). Danlayer 1944—45.

NOOTKA Tr (RCN) 460 tons, 150 x 27½ ft, 1—4in. Yarrow, Esquimalt 26.9.1938. Renamed NANOOSE 1944. Sold 1947.

NORA Coaling craft (RFA), 615gr. Listed 1932—7.39.

NORA NIVEN Tr 163/07. Purchased as danlayer (RNZN) 10.1942. Sold 1944.

NORBRECK Tr 201/05, 1—6pdr. Hired 1916—19.

NORBREEZE Dr 96/20. Hired as netlayer 10.1939—46.

NORD Tug 101/05. Hired 1915—19.

NORDENFELT Armament store carrier 604 tons, 134 x 25 ft. Lobnitz 30.11.1945.

NORDHAV I Tr 644/15, 1—6pdr. Norwegian, hired as A/P Tr 6.1940. Renamed AVALON 9.40; ADONIS 6.41. Sunk 15.4.43 by E-boat torpedo off Lowestoft.

NORDHAV II Tr 425/13. Norwegian, hired 1940 as M/S. Sunk 10.3.45 by U-boat off Dundee.

NORDKAPP Tr 243/37. Hired as A/P Tr 4.1940—45 (Norwegian crew).

NORDKYNN MFV 47/24. Hired on harbour service 11.1940—2.46 (Norwegian crew).

NORDLAND Tr 393/22. German prize, BDV 4.1940. Laid up 1.46, later sold.

NOREEN Dr 79/14, 1—6pdr. Hired 1915—19.

NORFOLK Cutter 8. Hired 1807—12.

NORFOLK COUNTY Dr 83/08. Hired 1915—19 and on examination service 11.39—45.

NORFORD SUFFLING Dr 86/14. Hired 1.1915—19 and on harbour service 7.41. For return in 6.45; lost 7.3.46.

NORGROVE Tug 227/10. Hired on harbour service 12.1941—7.45.

NORHAM CASTLE Dr 93/99. Hired 1916—16.

NORINA Tr 270/17. Hired as BDV 1.1940, purchased 11.43. Sold 5.47.

NORLAN Dr 90/14, 1—3pdr. Hired 2.1915—19 and as boom tender, 3.40—12.45.

NORLAND Tr 302/16. Hired as A/P Tr 5.1940. M/S 1943—10.45.

NORMAN II Tr 346/11, 1—12pdr. Hired 1915—19.

NORMAN III Tr 120/94. Hired 1916—19.

NORMAN Tug 222/29. Hired as rescue tug 26.8.1939. Renamed DIVERSION 1940. Returned 27.11.45.

NORMAN (see THE NORMAN)

NORMAN WILSON Dr 96/19. Hired as BBV tender 11.1939. Harbour service 1944—9.46.

NORNA Scottish Fishery Board vessel, 457/09. Hired 1914—19 and on examination service 8.40—7.46.

NORNES Dr. Norwegian, hired 4.1941. Sunk 14.8.43 by unknown cause in Icelandic waters.

NORSAL 168/21. Hired (RCN) 1940—45.

NORSE Tr 279/41, 1—6pdr. Hired 1915—19.

NORSE Tr 351/30. Hired as M/S 8.1939—11.44.

NORSEMAN Yt 325/90. Hired on examination service 1940. Renamed INQUISITOR 1941. Returned 1944.

NORSEMAN Cable ship 1,844/23. Hired 1941–46.

NORTH CAPE Tr 122/89. Hired 1918–19.

NORTHCOATES Tr 277/18. Hired as M/S 8.1939. Foundered in tow 2.12.44 in the Channel.

NORTHERN CHIEF Tr 655/36, 1–4in. Hired as ABV 8.1939. A/S Tr 1942–7.45. (On loan USN 2.42–10.42.)

NORTHERN DAWN Tr 655/36, 1–4in. Hired as A/S Tr 8.1939–2.46.

NORTHERN DUKE Tr 655/36, 1–4in. Hired as ABV 8.1939. A/S Tr 1942–1.46. (On loan USN 2.42–10.42.)

NORTHERN FOAM Tr 655/36, 1–4in. Hired as ABV 8.1939. A/S Tr 1942–11.45.

NORTHERN GEM Tr 655/36, 1–4in. Hired as A/S Tr 8.1939–11.45.

NORTHERN GIFT Tr 655/36, 1–4in. Hired as ABV 8.1939. A/S Tr 1942–10.45.

NORTHERN ISLES Tr 655/36, 1–4in. Hired as ABV 8.1939. A/S Tr 1942. Stranded 19.1.45 near Durban. (On loan USN 2.42–10.42.)

NORTHERN LIGHT MFV 27net. Hired as M/S 1.1940–44.

NORTHERN LIGHTS Admiralty steel Dr, 98gr. Rose St Fndry 1919. Sold 1919, renamed *Sunnyside Girl*. (SUNNYSIDE GIRL in WW.II.)

NORTHERN PRIDE Tr 655/36, 1–4in. Hired as A/S Tr 8.1939–11.45.

NORTHERN PRINCESS Tr 655/36, 1–4in. Hired as ABV 8.1939. Sunk 7.3.42 by unknown cause in the western Atlantic. (On loan USN from 2.42.)

NORTHERN REWARD Tr 655/36, 1–4in. Hired as ABV 8.1939. A/S Tr 1942–1.46. (On loan USN 2.42–10.42.)

NORTHERN ROVER Tr 655/36, 1–4in. Hired as ABV 8.1939. Sunk 10.39 by unknown cause north of Scotland.

NORTHERN SCOT Dr 90/11, 1–3pdr. Hired 1916–19 and as store carrier 2.1940–27.11.44.

NORTHERN SKY Tr 655/36, 1–4in. Hired as ABV 9.1939. A/S Tr 1942–9.45.

NORTHERN SPRAY Tr 655/36, 1–4in. Hired as A/S Tr 9.1939–9.45.

NORTHERN SUN Tr 655/36, 1–4in. Hired as ABV 8.1939. Convoy rescue Tr 9.43–12.45.

NORTHERN TRAVELLER 1,926/45. Hired as store carrier (RFA) 16.5.1946–1.3.47.

NORTHERN WAVE Tr 655/36, 1–4in. Hired as A/S Tr 9.1939–9.45.

NORTHESK II Dr 100/13. Hired 1915–19 and as NORTHESK on harbour service 10.1939–12.45.

NORTH HAVEN Dr 100/18. Hired on harbour service 8.1939–11.45.

NORTH KING Tr 194/06. Hired 1914–19.

NORTH KING II Tr 271/06, 1–12pdr. Hired 1914–19.

NORTH LAKE Tug 103gr. Hired (RCN) 6.1943–45.

NORTHLAND 2,055/11. American, on lend-lease as accommodation ship 1.1942–44.

NORTHLYN Tr 324/19. Hired as BDV 10.1939, purchased 12.43. Sold 7.3.47.

NORTHMAN Tr 192/11, 1–6pdr. Hired 1914–19 and as A/P Tr 7.40. Base ship 1.42–6.45. Returned 3.46.

NORTHMARK Oiler (RFA) 15,000 tons, 549 x 72 ft. German NORDMARK seized 1945. Renamed BULAWAYO 1947. Arrived 4.10.55 at Dalmuir to BU.

NORTH NESS Tr 275/17, 1–12pdr. Hired as A/P Tr 11.1939–7.46.

NORTH QUEEN Tr 195/06, 1–6pdr. Hired 1914–19.

NORTH STAR II Yt 924/93, 2–3in. Hired as A/P Yt 28.10.1915–4.3.19.

NORTH STAR III Tr 188/07, 1–6pdr. Hired 1914–19. (Known as NORTH STAR until 1916.)

NORTHUMBRIA Tr 211/06. Hired 1914. Sunk 3.3.17 by mine in the Firth of Forth.

NORTHWARD Tr 204/06, 1–6pdr. Hired 1915–19 and as A/P Tr 11.1939–25.1.40.

NORTHWARD HO Tr 204/19. Hired as A/P Tr 11.1939. M/S 6.40–2.46.

NORTHWIND Yt 235/30. Hired as calibrating Yt 9.1939, purchased 5.41. Laid up 10.45, sold 1946.

NORVEGIA Wh 182/12. In service in 1915.

NORWICH CITY Tr 541/37, 1–4in. Hired as A/S Tr 9.1939–4.46. (On loan USN 2.42–10.42.)

NOSS HEAD MFV 22net. Hired on harbour service 1.1940, purchased 3.42. Sunk 9.9.43 by unknown cause but listed as at Freetown to 7.44.

NOTRE DAME de FRANCE Tr 433/31. French A/P Tr seized 3.7.1940 at Plymouth. A/S Tr 1.41–12.45. (Dutch crew 1941.)

NOTRE DAME de la SALETTE Dr. French A/P Dr seized and laid up. Harbour service 4.1944–4.45.

NOTRE DAME de LOURDES Dr 76/11. French A/P Dr seized 3.7.1940 at Southampton. Harbour service 1940–12.45.

NOTRE DAME de MONT LIGEON Tr 234/99. French, seized 1940. Boom gate vessel 10.40–10.45.

NOTTS COUNTY Tr 541/38, 1–4in. Hired as A/S Tr 9.1939. Sunk 8.3.42 by mine or U-boat south of Iceland.

NOVELLI Tr 226/26, 1–6pdr. Hired 1916–19.

NOVICE Yt? 22gr/34. French, seized 1940 at Southampton. Boom tender 1941–45.

NOX Cutter 14. Hired 1798–1801.

NUBIA Tr 196/03. Hired 1917–19. (Served as WEAZEL in WW.II.)

NUBIA Tug. Listed as rescue tug 10.1940–2.41.

NUBIAN (ex-*Procida*) 2,265/71. Purchased as coal hulk 20.12.1900.
Sold 15.7.12 at Simonstown. (Known as C.370 from 1904.)
NUCULA (ex-*Soyo Maru*) Oiler (RFA) 9,830 tons, 370 x 48½ ft.
Purchased 7.4.1915. Listed to 1936.
NUEVO CALDAS Dr 106/30. Hired on harbour service 5.1941–2.46.
NUEVO MATARO Dr 106/30. Hired on harbour service 5.1941–2.46.
NUGGET 405/89. Hired as fleet messenger 7.1915. Sunk 31.7.15 by
'U.28' gunfire SW of the Scillies.
NULCHIRA Cstr 272/08. Hired as A/P vessel (RIN) 1939–43.
NULLI SECUNDUS Dr 104/17. Hired 1917–19.
NUMITOR Tr 242/08, 1–6pdr. Belgian, hired 1916. Sunk 20.4.18
by mine in the North Sea.
NUNTHORPE HALL (see SEAMEW)
NYKEN Dr 111/20. Norwegian, hired on harbour service 1.1941.
Damaged beyond repair 10.12.41, west Scotland area.
NYLGHAN Tr 261/08. Hired 1915–19.
NYMPH Cutter 10, 160bm, 1–12pdr carr., 10–4pdr. Hired 6.1803–
12.04 and 9.1807–4.14.
NYMPHE Sloop 10. Hired 1793–94.
NYROCA 1,295gr, 1–4in, 2–12pdr. Hired as decoy ship (Q.26)
31.1.1917–27.7.18.
NYULA Yt 52/36. Hired as HDPC 3.1940. Sunk 2.5.41 in collision
off the Tyne.

OAK (ex-*St Romanus*) M/S Tr 357/28, 545 tons, 1–4in. Purchased
3.1939. Sold 3.46.
OAK APPLE Dr 98/10, 1–2½pdr. Hired as BDV 1914–19 and as
TRV 6.40–45.
OAK LAKE Motor M/S (RCN) 255 tons, 126 x 26 ft. Clare SB. Ordered
4.8.1944. Cancelled 18.9.44.
OAKLAND Dr 67/10, 1–3pdr. Hired 1.1915–19.
OAKLEA MFV. Hired on harbour service 1.1940–46.
OAKLEAF (see ABADOL)
OAKOL Oiler (RFA) 1,925 tons, 220 x 34 ft. Gray 22.9.1917. Sold
29.1.20, renamed *Orthis*.
OAKOL Oiler (RFA) 2,670 tons, 218 x 38 ft. Lobnitz 28.8.1946.
OAKWOLD Tr 129/95. Hired 1918–19.
OASIS (ex-*Al Suez*) Tr 207/98. Egyptian, purchased as A/P Tr 1941.
Sold 1946.
OBERON Dr 86/07. Hired 1915–19.
OBTAIN Dr 105/17, 1–3pdr. Hired 1917–19 and on harbour service
2.40–10.45.

OBURN Dr 93/12, 1—3pdr. Hired 1915—19. (Served as GIRL PAMELA in WW.II.)

OBUS Armament store carrier, 122gr. Yarwood, Northwich 2.11.1939.

OCEANA (see CERBERUS)

OCEAN ANGLER Dr 84/11, 1—3pdr. Hired 1915—19.

OCEAN BREEZE Dr 112/27. Hired as M/S 9.1939, purchased 6.43. To War Dept 8.43.

OCEAN BRINE Tr 227/15. Hired as BDV 11.1939. A/P Dr 4.41—11.44.

OCEAN COMRADE Dr, 1—3pdr. Hired 1916—19.

OCEAN CREST Dr 99/14, 1—3pdr. Hired 1914—19.

OCEAN CREST II Dr 88/11. Hired 1914—19.

OCEAN EAGLE Tug 420/19. Hired as M/S (RCN) 1941—44.

OCEAN EDDY Tr 231/29. Hired as BDV 1.1940—2.46.

OCEAN FAVOURITE Dr 99/13, 1—6pdr. Hired 1914—19.

OCEAN FIRE (see ANCRE ESPERANCE)

OCEAN FISHER Dr 96/14, 1—3pdr. Hired 1914. Sunk 16.6.18 by mine in the North Sea.

OCEAN FISHER Tr 205/19. Hired on examination service 4.1940—8.45.

OCEAN FOAM Dr 90/11, 1—3pdr. Hired 11.1914. Sunk 7.10.18 in collision off Penzance.

OCEAN GAIN Dr 77/15, 1—6pdr. Hired 4.1915—19 and as A/P Dr 12.39. Degaussing vessel 4.41—3.46.

OCEAN GIFT Dr 91/07, 1—3pdr. Hired 2.1915—19 and as reserved blockship 6.40—3.45.

OCEAN GLEANER Dr 86/13, 1—3pdr. Hired 1915—20.

OCEAN GUIDE Dr 75/14, 1—6pdr. Hired 1914—19 and as A/P Dr 12.39. Degaussing vessel 6.40—2.46.

OCEAN HARVEST Dr 95/13, 1—6pdr. Hired 1914—19.

OCEAN HOPE Dr 81/12, 1—3pdr. Hired 1914—19.

OCEANIC 17,274/99. Hired as AMC 9.8.1914. Wrecked 8.9.14 on Foula, Shetlands.

OCEANIC II Tr 235/98, 2—3pdr. Hired 1914—19.

OCEANIC III Dr 99/07. Hired 1914—19.

OCEANIC IV Tr 168/96. Hired 1918—19.

OCEANIC Barge 120/03. Hired as cable layer 1943. To War Dept 2.46.

OCEAN LASSIE Dr 96/19. Hired 8.1939—3.40.

OCEAN LIFEBUOY Dr 131/29. Hired as M/S 11.1939—1.46.

OCEAN LOVER Dr 96/19. Hired as M/S 3.1940. A/P Dr 1941—45.

OCEAN LUX Dr 125/30. Hired as M/S 11.1939—45.

OCEAN PEARL MFV. Hired on harbour service 1939—45.

OCEAN PILOT Dr 95/13, 1—3pdr. Hired 1914—19 and as hospital tender 9.1939—6.45.

OCEAN PIONEER Dr 90/15, 1—6pdr. Hired 4.1915—19 and as M/S 5.40. Degaussing vessel 1941—46.

OCEAN PLOUGH Dr 99/12. Hired 1914. Sunk 27.8.16 by mine off Lowestoft.
OCEAN PRIDE Dr 95/11. Hired 1.1915–19. and as A/P Dr 6.1940–2.45.
OCEAN PRINCE Tr 203/02. Hired as BDV 1914–19.
OCEAN PRINCESS Tr 203/02, 1–6pdr. Hired 11.1914–19.
OCEAN QUEEN Tr 289/06, 1–6pdr. Hired 12.1914–19.
OCEAN RAMBLER Dr 96/14, 1–3pdr. Hired 1914–19.
OCEAN RANGER Dr 88/07. Hired as TRV 7.1940–1.46.
OCEAN REAPER Dr 101/12, 1–3pdr. Hired 1914–19.
OCEAN RETRIEVER Dr 95/12, 1–6pdr. Hired 1914–19 and as A/P Dr 4.40. Sunk 22.9.43 by mine in the Thames estuary.
OCEAN RETRIEVER II Dr 94/14. Hired 1914–19.
OCEAN REWARD Dr 95/12, 1–3pdr. Hired 1914–19 and 12.39. Sunk 28.5.40 in collision off Dover.
OCEAN ROAMER Dr 90/17, 1–6pdr. Hired 1917–19.
OCEAN ROVER Yt 383/19. Purchased as TRV 11.1939. Calibrating Yt 1943. Laid up 8.45, later sold.
OCEAN SALVOR Salvage vessel 1,440 tons, 200 x 38 ft, 4–20mm. Simons 31.8.1943. Sold 1960, renamed *British Recovery*.
OCEAN SCOUT Dr 86/13. Hired 8.1915–19 and as A/P Dr 11.39. TRV 6.40–12.45.
OCEAN SEARCHER Dr 83/12, 1–3pdr. Hired 1915–19.
OCEAN'S GIFT MFV 52/06. Belgian, hired 10.1940–45.
OCEAN SPRAY Dr 82/12, 1–3pdr. Hired 1.1915–19 and as A/P Dr, 2–MG, 12.39–2.46.
OCEAN SPRITE Dr 96/19. Hired on harbour service 8.1939–45.
OCEAN STAR Dr 92/07. Hired 1.1915. Sunk 26.9.17 off the Nab, probably mined.
OCEAN STAR Dr. Hired 12.1940–45.
OCEAN SUNLIGHT Dr 131/29. Hired as M/S 11.1939. Sunk 13.6.40 by mine off Newhaven.
OCEAN SWELL Admiralty steel Dr, 96gr. Brooke 1919. Sold 1920, same name. Hired as netlayer 10.39–8.45.
OCEAN TOILER Dr 98/15. Hired as A/P Dr 4.1940–1.46.
OCEAN TREASURE Dr 92/13, 1–3pdr. Hired 1914–19 and as A/P Dr 5.40–3.46.
OCEAN VICTOR Tr 202/18. Hired as A/P Tr 11.1939–2.40.
OCEAN VIEW Tr 248/30. Hired as M/S 2.1940–12.45.
OCEAN VIM Dr 125/30. Hired as M/S 9.1939. Harbour service 1943–46.
OCTAVIA Tr 173/06. Hired 1918–19.
OCTOROON Tr 195/14, 1–6pdr. Hired 1915–19.
ODBERG Wh 351/36. A/S Wh (SAN) 5.1941–6.46.
ODERIN (see MMS.120)
ODYSSEUS Tanker 147/18. Hired as DY water boat 11.1942–1.46.

OFFA II Tr 313/13, 1–12pdr. Hired 1915–19.

OGANO Tr 265/17. Hired as A/P Tr 5.1940. M/S 1942–7.44.

OHM Tr 302/15. Hired as M/S 8.1939–12.45.

OKAPI (See AN.5)

OKINO Tr 241/14. Hired 1914. Sunk 8.3.15 by mine in the Dardanelles.

OKINO Tr 311/17, 1–12pdr. Hired 1917–19 and as BDV 1.40–1.46.

OKSOY (see POL VI and KERRERA)

OKU Tr 248/09. Hired 1916–19.

OKU Tr 303/29. Hired as M/S 8.1939–45.

OLCADES (see BRITISH BEACON)

OLD COLONY 3,364/07. Purchased and commissioned 6.1918. Sold 3.20 at Chatham.

OLDEN TIMES Tr 202/19. Hired as A/P Tr 11.1939–20.2.40.

OLDHAM Tr 165/98, 1–6pdr. Hired 1915–19.

OLEANDER Oiler (RFA) 15,350 tons, 442 x 57 ft. Pembroke Dk 26.4.1922. Sunk 8.6.40 in Harstad Bay, Norway, after damage by air attack.

OLEANDER (ex-*Helicina*) Oiler (RFA), 12,167gr, 17,000 tons, 550 x 70 ft. Swan Hunter 1945. Sold 1947, renamed *Helicina*.

OLEANDER Oiler (RFA) 32,200 tons, 610 x 84 ft. Swan Hunter 19.11.1964.

OLIGARCH (see BRITISH LANTERN)

OLIPHANT Oiler (RFA). Purchased on stocks 10.1915; Irvine 15.8.16. On charter from 25.11.16.

OLIVAE Dr 107/15. Hired as M/S 11.1939–11.45.

OLIVE Dr , 1–3pdr. Hired 1915–19.

OLIVE II Dr 89/06, 1–3pdr. Hired 1915–19.

OLIVE III Dr 83/06, 1–3pdr. Hired 1915–19.

OLIVE IV Tr 328/07? Hired 1916–19.

OLIVE M/S Tr 530 tons, 150 x 27½ ft, 1–4in. Hall Russell 26.2.1940. Sold 1948, renamed *Samba*.

OLIVE CAM Tr 281/20. Commissioned as M/S (RAN) 6.10.1939. Sold 5.46.

OLIVE LEAF Dr 82/07, 1–6pdr. Hired 1915–19.

OLIVER PICKIN Tr, 'Castle' type, 275gr. Smiths Dk 21.5.1917. Sold 1922, renamed *Fermo*. (Served as DAMITO in WW.II.)

OLIVE TREE Dr 96/18. Hired as A/P Dr 11.1939–9.45.

OLIVIA Yt 105/83. Purchased 1917. Sold 28.12.18.

OLIVINE Tr 285/05, 1–6pdr. Hired 1915–19.

OLIVINE (see COREOPSIS)

OLNA Oiler (RFA) 15,220 tons, 442 x 57 ft. Devonport DY 21.6.1921. Beached 18.5.41 on the coast of Crete after being bombed.

OLNA Oiler (RFA) 17,000 tons, 550 x 70 ft. Swan Hunter 28.12.1944. Sold 1966, BU in Spain.

OLNA Oiler (RFA) 32,200 tons, 610 x 84 ft. Hawthorn Leslie 28.7.1965.

OLVINA Tr 425/34. Hired as A/S Tr 8.1939—12.45.

OLWEN (see BRITISH LIGHT)

OLYMPIA Oiler (RFA), 7,513gr. Vickers, Barrow. Laid down 10.7.1913. Launched as *Santa Margherita* under management. Sold 15.7.19.

OLYMPIA Tr 261/17, 1—12pdr. Hired 1917—19 and as M/S 12.39—10.45.

OLYMPIC 46, 439/11. Hired as AMC 3.1917—19.

OLYMPUS Dr 58/10. Hired 1915—19.

OLYNTHUS (see BRITISH STAR)

OLYNTHUS Oiler (RFA) 32,200 tons, 610 x 84 ft. Hawthorn Leslie 10.7.1964.

OMBRA Yt 275/02. Hired as A/P Yt 9.1914—3.19 and as danlayer 10.39, purchased 5.41. Sold 1945.

ONE ACCORD Dr 102/27. Hired as M/S 11.1939—46.

ONETOS Tr 217/13, 1—6pdr. Hired 1914—19 and as A/P Tr 11.39. M/S 6.40; wreck dispersal 4.44—1.46.

ONORA Yt 56/23. Hired on examination service 6.1940, purchased 9.41. A/P Yt 5.41. Sold 1947. (Bore the name FERRET for a time as base ship.)

ONS WELZIJN Dr 73/30, 1—6pdr. Belgian, hired as A/P Dr 31.7.1940—43 or later. (Polish crew in 1940 and also known as P.12.)

ONTARIO Tr 208/07, 1—3pdr. Hired 1914—19.

ONWARD DY coal vessel 640 tons, 130 x 25 ft. Purchased 26.3.1900. Sold circa 1947. (Known also as C.4 from 1905)

ONWARD Tr 266/08. Hired 1915. Sunk 11.7.16 by U-boat off Aberdeen.

ONWARD II Tr 209/05. Hired 1915—19 and 11.39—1.40.

ONWARD III Dr 94/07, 1—6pdr. Hired 1917—19 and as ONWARD, examination service 7.40—11.44.

ONWARD III Yt 31/34. Hired as HDPC 6.1940, purchased 11.41. Sold 4.46.

ONYX II Tr 248/13, 1—6pdr. Hired 1915—19.

ONYX (ex-CD.82 renamed 15.7.1919) Admiralty wood Dr. DY service 1919. Sunk 21.3.47 in DY basin.

OOSTCAPPELLE Cstr 751/21. Hired as A/P vessel (RIN) 1939—45.

OOSTEWAL Wh 179/26. Hired as M/S (SAN) 1.1940—5.46.

OPHIR 6,942/91. Hired as Royal yacht 1901—02 and as AMC 26.1.15, purchased 26.2.15. Laid up 7.19, sold 8.21 to BU.

OPHIR II Tr 213/06, 1—6pdr. Hired 1914—19 and as A/P Tr OPHIR II in 11.39—2.40.

OPHIR III Tr 230/03, 1—12pdr. Hired 1915—19.

OPHIR Cable ship 500/07. Hired as armament store carrier 10.1940. Renamed ELDORADO, cable ship, 1943—3.46.

OPTIMIST (see ATALANTA)

OPTIMISTIC Dr 94/07. Hired on harbour service 9.1914—19.

OPULENT (ex-*Ophir*) Cable ship 500/07. Hired 12.1917–18.6.19. (Served as OPHIR in WW.II.)

ORACLE (ex-*Osprey*) Yt 625/29. Purchased as A/S Yt 9.1939. Radar trials 1943. Burnt out 29.1.44 off Liverpool. Arrived 14.5.48 Ward, Preston to BU.

ORAMA 12,927/11. Hired as AMC 4.9.1914. Sunk 19.10.17 by 'U.62' south of Ireland.

ORANAISE Tr 738/19 French A/P Tr seized 3.7.1940 at Portsmouth. Free-French crew to 9.40. BDV 12.40–1.46.

ORANGELEAF (ex-BORNOL renamed 1917) Oiler (RFA) 12,300 tons, 405 x 54½ ft. Thomson, Sunderland 26.10.16. Sold 4.47, arrived 25.1.48 Ward, Briton Ferry To BU.

ORANGELEAF (ex-*Southern Satellite*) Oiler (RFA), 12,481gr, 525 x 71 ft. Furness SB 8.2.1955 and hired 1959.

ORANSAY Yt 52/04. Hired 7.1918–4.19.

ORARA 1,297/07, 1–4in. Commissioned as M/S (RAN) 9.10.1939. Depot ship 1945–46.

ORBITA 15,678/15. Hired as AMC 21.6.1915–12.8.19.

ORCA (ex-*Cachalot*) Yt 98/35. Hired as A/P Yt 9.1940, purchased 11.41. Accommodation ship 2.43. Laid up 10.45.

ORCADES Tr 270/11. Hired 1914. Sunk 14.4.16 by mine off Grimsby.

ORCHY 1,090/30, 1–12pdr. Hired as decoy ship 10.1939. To MWT 18.6.41. (Operated as ANTOINE.)

ORCOMA 11,571/08. Hired as AMC 23.3.1915–11.10.19.

ORD HILL Dr 90/10. Hired on harbour service 3.1915–19.

ORFASY Tr, 'Isles' class. A.Hall 17.3.1942. Sunk 22.10.43 by U-boat off West Africa.

ORIANA Yt 172/96. Hired as A/P Yt 22.9.1914–11.17.

ORIANA Rescue tug, 'B.A.T' class. Gulfport Co, Port Arthur Texas 15.8.1942 on lend-lease. Returned 1946 to the USN.

ORIANA (ex-*Empire Frieda*) DY tug 295/46. Transferred from MOT 5.1947. Sunk 19.1.48 by mine off the Essex coast.

ORIANDA Tr 273/14. Hired 1914. Sunk 19.12.14 by mine off Scarborough.

ORIENT (see SAMPSON)

ORIENT II Dr 93/11, 1–57mm. Hired 1915–19.

ORIENTAL STAR Tr 427/34, 1–4in. Purchased as A/S Tr 8.1939. To French navy 28.11.39 as La SETOISE.

ORIOLE Tr 172/07, 1–6pdr. Hired 1914–19.

ORIOLE (ex-*Eagle III*) Paddle 441/10. Hired as M/S 11.1939. Experimental M/L 1941–43; accommodation ship 1943–8.45.

ORION II Dr 70/06, 1–6pdr. Hired 1915–19.

ORIZABA Tr 233/08, 1–3pdr. Hired as boom gate vessel 1915–19 and as M/S 8.40. Fuel carrier 3.44–45.

ORLANDO Tr 276/07. Hired 1914. Wrecked 14.3.15 at Stornoway.

ORLIONOCH Russian merchant, 1,406/88, seized 1918 on the Caspian and commissioned as seaplane carrier 1918, 2–4in, 2–A/C. Handed over 24.8.19 to 'White' Russians on the Caspian.

ORMONDE Tr 250/06, 1–6pdr. Hired 1914–19 and as A/P Tr 11.39. M/S 11.40. Sunk 16.2.41 by air attack off the east coast of Scotland.

ORNEN III Wh 251/30. Norwegian, hired as A/P and M/S Tr 1.1940–12.45.

ORONSAY Tr, 'Isles' class. Cochrane 30.10.1943. Sold 1946.

OROPESA 5,370/95, 6–6in, 2–3pdr. Hired as AMC 22.11.1914. Renamed CHAMPAGNE 2.12.15 on loan French navy. Returned 27.7.17. Sunk 9.10.17 by 'U.96' in the Atlantic.

OROPESA II Tr 327/14, 1–6pdr. Hired as M/S 1914–19.

OROTAVA 5,980/89, 5–6in, 2–6pdr. Hired as AMC 19.11.1914–31.10.16.

ORPHESIA Tr 273/07. Hired 1915. Sunk 22.7.17 in collision with wreck off Alexandira.

ORPHEUS Tr 228/05, 1–6pdr. Hired 1914–19 and as M/S 6.40–1.46.

ORPINGTON DY tug. Rowhedge IW 1919. Sold 8.23.

ORSAY Tr, 'Isles' class. Cochrane 1.1.1945. Completed as danlayer. Oil tank cleaning vessel 1956. Sold 3.9.57.

ORSINO Tr 172/06. Hired as M/S 1914. Sunk 28.9.16. by U-boat off Stromness.

ORTHOS Tr 218/13. Hired 1914. Sunk 9.4.17 by mine off Lowestoft.

ORTOLAN 1,727/02. Hired as supply ship (RFA) 5.8.1914–14.4.16.

ORUBA 5,971/89. Purchased as dummy battleship ORION 28.10.1914. Sunk 1915 as breakwater in Kephala Bay, Imbros.

ORVICTO Tr 226/16, 1–6pdr. Hired 1916–19 and as danlayer, 1–3pdr, 4.40. A/P and examination service 11.40–10.45.

ORVIETO 12,130/09, 4–4.7in, 1–3pdr, 600 mines. Hired as M/L 6.1.1915–4.16. AMC 6.16–19.10.19.

ORYX (see HVAL I)

OSAKO Tr 260/18, 1–12pdr. Hired as M/S 3.1940–12.45.

OSBORNE STROUD Tr 209/12, 1–6pdr. Purchased 7.1914. Sold 1920, same name. (Served as BEATHWOOD in WW.II.)

OSCAR ANGELE MFV 79/31. Belgian, hired as A/P vessel 29.10.1940–10.45.

OSCAR AUGUSTE MFV 72/30, 1–6pdr. Belgian, hired as A/P vessel 17.6.1940 (Polish crew). Lost 29.4.41. (Also known as P.2.)

OSIRIS 1,728/98. Hired as AMC 5.8.1914. Fleet messenger 10.10.14; depot ship 11.4.15–19. (OSIRIS II 1916.)

OSIRIS III Tr 173/98. Hired 1917–19.

OSMANIEH 4,041/06. Hired as fleet messenger 12.5.1916. Sunk 31.12.17 by mine off Alexandria.

OSPRAY II Tr 259/11, 1–12pdr. Hired 1915–19.

OSPREY Dr 106/84. Hired on harbour service 12.8.1914–16.12.14.

OSPREY Dr 82/07, 1–3pdr. Hired 1915–16.

OSPREY III Tr 332/05. Hired 1915–19.

OSPREY (see ICEWHALE)

OSTA Tr 230/15, 1–6pdr. Hired 1915. M/L, 24 mines, 1917–19. Hired as A/P Tr 11.39. M/S 5.40; BBV 1.44–11.44.

OSTRICH II Tr 244/03, 1–6pdr. Hired 1915. M/L, 24 mines, 6.16–19.

OSTRICH III Tr 148/89. Hired 1917–19.

OSTRICH Tr 146/91. Hired 1918–19.

OSWALDIAN Tr 249/17, 1–12pdr. Hired 1917–19 and as A/P Tr, 261gr, 5.40. Sunk 4.8.40 by mine in the Bristol Channel.

OSWY Dr 95/16, 1–3pdr. Hired 1917–19.

OTHELLO Tr 201/07, 1–3pdr. Hired 1914–19 and as A/P Tr 11.39. Boom gate vessel 8.40. Sunk 11.4.41 by mine in the Humber.

OTHELLO II Tr 206/ -. Hired 1915. Sunk 31.10.15 by mine off Leathercoat.

OTHELLO M/S–A/S Tr, 545 tons, 150 x 28 ft, 1–12pdr, 3–20mm. Hall Russell 7.10.1941. To Italian navy 3.46.

OTHONNA Tr 180/99. Hired 1915. Sunk 20.4.17 by mine off Fife Ness.

OTRANTO 12,128/09, 4–4.7in. Hired as AMC 4.8.1914. Wrecked 5.10.18 on Islay, after collision with *Kashmir*.

OTTER Tug 165/87. Hired 10.1914–15.

OTTER Yt 154/03. Purchased 1916. Sold 31.7.19.

OTTER (ex-*Conseco*) Yt 416/21. Commissioned (RCN) 4.10.1940. Lost 26.3.41 by fire off Newfoundland.

OTTILIE Tr 226/14, 1–6pdr. Hired 1915–19.

OTTOMAN EMPIRE Tr 162/91. Hired 1917–19.

OTWAY 12,077/09. Hired as AMC 11.11.1914. Sunk 23.7.17 by 'UC.49' in the Minch.

OUR ALLIES Dr 91/15, 1–57mm. Hired 1915–19.

OUR BAIRNS Tr 275/17. Hired as M/S 12.1939. Fuel carrier 1.44; target towing 1945–7.46.

OUR FRIEND Dr 86/13. Hired 1915–19.

OUR JOHN MFV 24net. Hired as A/P vessel 7.1940–3.46.

OUSE Tr 167/00. Hired as BDV 1915–19.

OUSE (see ANDREW KING)

OUTLAW (see HEPATICA)

OUTLINE Admiralty steel Dr, 96gr. Brooke 1919. Sold 1919, same name.

OUTPOST (ex-*Vidette*) Tr 240/05. Hired as fuel carrier 3.1943–45.

OVERDALE WYKE Tr 338/24, 1–12pdr. Purchased as M/S 7.1939. To Ceylon Govt 1940. Listed to 1946.

OVERFALL Admiralty steel Dr, 97gr. Colby 1918. Sold circa 1923, same name. Hired as M/S 11.39. Target towing 1943–10.45.

OVERTON Cstr 426/11. Hired as fleet messenger 26.9.1915. Store carrier (RFA) 10.20–21.

OWEN McMANNERS Tr, 'Mersey' type. Cochrane. Cancelled 1919.

O-WE-RA Yt 498/07. Hired as A/P Yt 10.5.1940–46.

OWL (ex-*Cuckoo*) Wood S.DY tug, 10bm. Transferred from War Dept 1.10.1891. Sold 7.02.

OWL II Tr 169/03, 1–6pdr. Hired 1914–19.

OWL III Tr 117/96. Hired 1918–19.

OXNA Tr, 'Isles' class. Inglis 26.1.1943. To War Dept 16.7.46, same name.

OXWICH CASTLE Tr 251/07, 1–6pdr. Hired 1.1915–19.

OYAMA Tr 257/08, 1–12pdr. Hired 1914–19.

OYAMA Tr 340/31. Hired as M/S 26.8.1939–8.11.39.

OYSTERMOUTH CASTLE Tr 283/14, 1–6pdr. Hired 1917–19 and as ABV 5.40. M/S 1941–1.46.

OZONE Admiralty steel Dr, Rose St Fndry 1919. Sold 1920, renamed *Girl Georgia.*

PACHMARI Tr, 'Basset' class (RIN). Calcutta. Ordered 12.1942, cancelled 1944.

PACIFIC Cable ship 1,570/03. Danish, seized 6.1940. Cable repair ship to 1946.

PACIFICO 687/05. Purchased 22.9.1939. Sunk 4.6.40 as blockship at Dunkirk.

PACIFIC SALVOR Salvage vessel 1,360 tons, 200 x 39 ft, 2–40mm, 4–20mm. Basalt Rock Co, Napa 24.10.1942 for lend-lease, but retained by the USN as GEAR.

PACKICE Admiralty wood Dr, 95gr. Smith, Buckie 1917. Sold 1921, renamed *Murray Clan.* (Served as UTILISE in WW.II.)

PACKICE (see VESTFOLD III)

PADMAVATI Cstr 252/04. Hired as A/P vessel (RIN) 1939–45.

PADUA (ex-*Princess of Wales*) Paddle 163gr. Hired as A/P vessel 5.6.1917. Ferry service (RFA) 1919–21.4.20.

PAHAU Tr, 'Castle' type (RNZN). Stevenson & Cook 3.4.1943. Sold 1949.

PAIMPOL (see CH.15)

PAISIBLE Dr 90/11. Hired 1915–19.

PAKEHA 7,900/10. Hired as dummy battleship REVENGE 9.1939–6.41.

PALADIN Tug 336/13. Hired as rescue tug 17.11.1914–31.1.19. (PALADIN II from 1916.)

PALENCIA Tug 95/16. Hired on harbour service 9.1939–1.46.

PALISADE (see NAMUR)

PALMA 7,632/03. Hired as store carrier (RFA) 2.8.1914–5.3.15.

PALMOL Oiler (RFA) 1,925 tons, 220 x 34 ft. Gray, Sunderland 14.11.1917. Sold 29.1.20, renamed *Invercosrie.*

PALOMARES 1,896/38, 4,540 tons (deep), 6–4in, 4–20mm. Hired as A/A ship 8.1940, purchased 30.10.41. Fighter-direction ship 1943. Sold 4.46.

PALUMA 45/42. Purchased as patrol vessel (RAN) 4.1942. Sold 5.46.

PAMELA Tr 331/11. Hired 1915–19.

PAMELA Yt 30/22. Hired as A/P Yt 7.1940. To War Dept 11.41.

PAMPANO M/S Tr 680 tons, 160 x 28 ft, 1–12pdr, 4–20mm. Ilha Viana, Rio de Janeiro 11.6.42 for the RN but transferred Brazilian navy 8.42 at MATIAS de ALBUQUERQUE.

PAMPERO Admiralty steel Dr, 96gr. A.Hall 1919. Sold 10.19, renamed *Edalba.* (Served as ACORN in WW.II.)

PANDORA Yt 49/15. Hired on air-sea rescue 5.1942–45.

PANGKOR 1,208/29. Hired as A/P vessel 25.9.1939–5.46. (On loan RIN from 1944.)

PANOPE Yt 122/28. Hired as BBV 9.1940, purchased 9.41. Laid up 11.44, sold 12.45.

PANOPIA Dr 77/08, 1–3pdr. Hired 2.1915–19.

PANORAMA (ex-*Rocroi*) Tr 408/19. American, purchased as BDV 1.1940. Sold 11.3.46. (In French hands 30.10.42–23.11.42 after stranding in the Saloum river, West Africa.)

PANSY Ship hired for the Armada campaign 1588.

PANSY Dr 91/07. Hired 1915–19. (Pansy II 1916.)

PANSY III Dr 67/03, 1–3pdr. Hired 1916–19.

PANSY Dr 72/02. Hired on harbour service 1.1917. Wrecked 20.1.17.

PAPAKURA Yt 33/12. Hired as BBV 6.1940, purchased 10.41. Kite-balloon tender 7.42. Sold 10.45.

PAPATERA M/S Tr, as PAMPANO. Ilha Viana 7.42. Became Brazilian FELIPE CAMARAO 8.42.

PARADIGM Dr 94/20. Hired as degaussing vessel 2.1940–3.46.

PARADOX Dr 73/10. Hired 1.1915–19.

PARAGON Ship. Hired 1602–03.

PARAGON II Dr 83/06, 1–3pdr. Hired 1915–19 and as BBV 5.40. Mooring vessel 1943–45.

PARAMOUNT Dr 95/11, 1–6pdr. Hired 12.1914–19 and as M/S 11.39. Harbour service 1944–1.46.

PARATI M/S Tr, as PAMPANO. Ilha Viana 11.6.42. Became Brazillian FERNANDES VIERA 8.42.

PARGO M/S Tr, as PAMPANO. Ilha Viana 26.8.42. Became Brazilian HENRIQUE DIAS 8.42.

PARGUST (ex-*Vittoria*) 2,817/07, 1–4in, 4–12pdr, 2–TT. Hired as decoy ship 22.3.1917, purchased 8.17. Reverted to VITTORIA 1918, sold 3.19. (On loan USN 10.17–4.18.)

PARIS 1,774/13, 1–4in, 1–12pdr, 1–6pdr, 140 mines. Hired as M/L 14.11.1914–4.19.

PARKGATE (see BV.5 under BD vessels)

PARKMORE Tr 199/15, 1–6pdr. Hired 1915–19.

PARKSVILLE Tug (RCN). Listed 1944–51.

PARKTOWN (see SIDNEY SMITH and SUDEROY I)

PARRAMATTA Tr 168/91. Hired 1914 and 1918–19.

PARTHIAN Tr 202/11, 1–3pdr. Hired 1914–19. (PARTHIAN II from 1916.)

PARTRIDGE 1,461/06, 2–12pdr. Hired as ABS 15.11.1914–12.7.20. (PARTRIDGE II from 1916.)

PARU M/S Tr, as PAMPANO. Ilha Viana. Launched as Brazilian BARRETO de MENEZES.

PARVATI 1,548/27. Hired as A/P vessel (RIN) 1939. Lost 30.4.41 in the Red Sea area.

PAD de LOUPE II Yt 98/20. Hired as BBV 7.1940, purchased 11.41. Sold 3.46.

PASSEREAU Tr 137/92. French M/S seized 1940 at Southampton. Naval service to 1943.

PASSING Tr 459/13, 1–6pdr. Hired 1914–19.

PAT CAHERTY Tr, 'Strath' type, 202gr. Rennie Forrest 1918. Sold 1921, renamed *Kirby*. (Served as BUCHANS II in WW.II.)

PATERSON Cstr 446/20. Hired as M/S (RAN) 1941–46.

PATHFINDER Yt 53/84. Hired on harbour service 6.1940, purchased 10.41. Renamed PATROL 1941. Lost 21.10.44 in a storm, Clyde area.

PATHWAY Dr 56/15. Hired as BBV 12.1939. Training tender 1941–42.

PATIA 6,103/13. Hired as AMC 21.11.1914. Sunk 13.6.18 by 'UC.49' in the Bristol Channel.

PATIA 5,355/22, 2–6in. Hired as OBV 10.1940. A/C catapult ship 3.41. Sunk 17.4.41 by air attack off the Northumberland coast.

PATIENCE Dr 108/31. Belgian, hired as BBV 8.8.1940. Examination service 1942; traffic control 1944–8.45.

PAT MERRYGAN Tr, 'Mersey' type. Cochrane. Cancelled 1919.

PATNA Tr, 'Basset' class (RIN). Hooghly DK & Eng Co, Calcutta 1.9.1942. Sold 1946.

PATRICIA CAM Tr. Hired as M/S (RAN) 1941. Sunk 1.43 by Japanese air attack off Wessel Island, Pacific.

PATRICIA McQUEEN Tug 58/11. Hired (RCN) 1942–46.

PATRICIAN 7,470/01. Hired as dummy battlecruiser 30.11.1914, purchased 1915. Renamed TEAKOL oiler (RFA) 1915. Renamed VINELEAF 1917. Sold 12.7.19, renamed *British Vine.*

PATRICK BORROW Tr, 'Strath' type, 202gr. Montrose SY 1918. Sold 1919, renamed *River Don.*

PATRICK BOWE Tr, 'Castle' type, 290gr. Cook Welton & Gemmell 17.1.1918. Renamed TEST 1920. Sold 1922 Spanish navy as UAD TARGA.

PATRICK CULLEN Tr, 'Castle' tupe, 276gr. Ailsa 31.3.1919. Sold 1919, renamed *Briarlyn.*

PATRICK DEVINE Tr, 'Strath' type, 202gr. Rennie Forrest 1919. Sold 1921, renamed *Yolanda.* (Served as SEDOCK in WW.II.)

PATRICK DONOVAN Tr, 'Castle' type, 276gr. J P Rennoldson 1920. Sold 1920, renamed *Loch Nevis.*

PATRICK MITCHELL Tr, 'Mersey' type, 324gr. Cochrane 16.4.1919. Sold 1919, renamed *Kelvin.*

PATRIE Tr 754/20. French A/P Tr seized 3.7.1940 at Southampton. A/P Tr 8.40. Boom gate vessel 2.44—1.46.

PATROCLUS 11,314/23, 6—6in, 2—3in. Hired as AMC 9.1939. Sunk 4.11.40 by 'U.99' west of Ireland.

PATROCLUS Rescue tug, 'B.A.T' class. Levingston 15.5.1943 on lend-lease. Returned 6.46. to the USN.

PATROL (see PATHFINDER)

PATTI Tr 339/29, 1—12pdr. Hired as A/P Tr 11.1939. M/S 1941—1.46.

PATUCA 6,103/13, 6—6in, 2—3pdr. Hired as AMC 21.11.1914. Kite-balloon ship 1915—12.18.

PAUL EMILE JAVARY 2,471/26. French, seized 29.6.1940 at Milford Haven. MWT 7.40—10.42. Training ship 10.42—43.

PAULINA Yt 317/94, 2—6pdr. Hired as A/P Yt 11.7.1916—19.

PAULINE Tr 133/99. Hired 1917—19.

PAUL RYKENS Tr 466/35, 1—4in. Hired as A/S Tr 11.1939—12.45.

PAUL THERESE MFV 96/30. Belgian, hired as BBV 30.8.1940—10.45.

PAVLOVA Tr 342/12, 1—6pdr. Hired 1914—19.

PAX Dr. French CAP NEGRE, ex-Belgian *Pax* seized 3.7.1940 at Southampton. Harbour service 4.41. M/S 1.42—5.45.

PAXIDANE MFV. Danish *Pax* seized 1940. Harbour service to 6.45.

PAXTON Dr 92/11, 1—6pdr. Hired 1.1915—19 and as flare Dr 11.1939. Beached 28.5.40 at Dunkirk after bomb damage.

PAXTON (see LADY PATRICIA)

PAX VOBISCUM Dr 84/13. Hired 2.1915—19. (Served as SCOTCH THISTLE in WW.II.)

PAYNTER Tr 472/37. Hired as A/S Tr 9.1939—9.45.

PEACE Dr 83/07, 1—3pdr. Hired 1915—19.

PEACEMAKER Dr 89/11, 1—6pdr. Hired 1915—19 and as A/P Dr 4.40—45.

PEARL Ship. Hired for the Armada campaign 1588.

PEARL 32–gun ship. Hired 1664–67.

PEARL Tr 198/99, 1–6pdr. Hired 1914–19.

PEARL II Tr 289/13, 1–12pdr. Hired 1915–19.

PEARL III Dr 72/06, 1–57mm. Hired 1915–19.

PEARL (ex-*Dervish*) A/S Tr 649 tons, 1–4in. Purchased 9.10.1935. Sold 18.4.46, renamed *Westella*.

PEARLEAF (ex-GYPOL renamed 1917) Oiler (RFA) 12,300 tons, 405 x 54½ ft. Gray 12.9.16. Arrived 23.12.47 Hughes Bolckow, Blyth to BU.

PEARLEAF Oiler (RFA) 23,900 tons, 535 x 72 ft. Blythswood 15.10.1959.

PEARY Tr 289/13, 1–12pdr. Hired 1915–19.

PEBBLE Cstr 477/90. Hired as fleet messenger 24.7.1915. Purchased as RFA 23.5.19. Sold 8.20.

PECHEUR Dr 67/ -. Hired 1915. Sunk 3.4.16 in collision.

PECHEUR Dr 99/14. Hired as netlayer 10.1939–7.45.

PEEL CASTLE 1,474/94, 2–12pdr. Hired as ABS 28.10.1914–28.1.19.

PEEL CASTLE MFV 21/30. Hired 7.1940–9.45.

PEEWIT (ex-*Plover*) Tug 245/81. Hired 9.1914–19.

PEGASUS Tr 219/17, 1–12pdr. Hired 1917–19.

PEGGY Lugger 8. Hired 1796. Captured 1799 by the French.

PEGGY Dr 100/07, 1–3pdr. Hired 9.1914–19.

PEGGY NUTTEN Tr 193/07, 1–6pdr. Hired 1916–19 and as BBV 2.40. Fuel carrier 3.44–11.44.

PEKEN Tr 228/07, 1–6pdr. Hired 1914–19 and as M/S 7.40–8.45. (Spelt PEKIN in most WW.I lists.)

PEKIN (ex-training ship *Arethusa*) Hired as accommodation ship 1940–45.

PELAGIA Dr 84/00. Hired 1915. Sunk 28.11.16 by mine off the Nab.

PELAGOS Tr 231/ -, 1–6pdr. Hired 1916–19.

PELAGOS Tr 277/18, 1–12pdr. Hired as A/P Tr 5.1940. M/S 6.41–6.45.

PELEGRIME M/S Tr, as PAMPANO. Ilha Viana 1942. Became Brazilian VIDAL de NEGREIROS 8.42.

PELICAN Ship. Hired 1588–89.

PELICAN Tr 248/08, 1–6pdr. Hired 1914–19.

PELICAN II Tr 205/05, 1–12pdr. Hired 1916–19.

PELLAG II Yt 44/37. Hired as HDPC 2.1940. Lost 10.6.40 at Dunkirk.

PELTER DY tank vessel 370 tons. Maudslay, East Greenwich 16.7.1867. Sold 11.7.1905.

PELTER DY tank vessel 405 tons, 115 x 21 ft. Day Summers, Southampton 19.3.04. On sale list 1946.

PELTON Tr 358/25. Hired as M/S 8.1939. Sunk 24.12.40 by E-boat torpedo off Yarmouth.

PEMBROKE (see DANIEL FEARALL)

PEMBROKE CASTLE Tr 153/98. Hired 1917–19.

PENCHATEAU Cstr 995/20. French A/P vessel seized 7.1940 at Plymouth. Storeship to 5.41 then to MWT.

PENELOPE Cutter 18. Hired 1795. Captured 7.7.99 by the Spanish schooner Del CARMEN.

PENELOPE Tr 149/95. Hired in WW.I.

PENFELD French DY tug seized 3.7.1940 at Plymouth. DY tug to 1946.

PENGAWAL Tug, Hired 1940. Sunk 14.2.42 by Japanese air attack off Singapore.

PENGUIN Tr 190/02, 1–6pdr. Hired 1914–19.

PENGUIN Tr 151/95. Hired on harbour service 1915–19.

PENGUIN II Tr 123/91. Hired 1918–19.

PENHALLOW (ex-*Century*) 4,318/13. Hired as decoy ship 10.1915–6.17.

PENNAN Dr 64/10. Hired 1915–19.

PENNARD CASTLE Tr 259/06, 1–6pdr. Hired 1914–19.

PENRICE CASTLE Tr 255/13, 1–3pdr. Hired 1915–19.

PENRHYN Aux. barge 120/80. Hired as BBV 8.1940–44.

PENSHURST 1,191/06, 1–12pdr, 2–6pdr, 2–3pdr. Hired as decoy ship (Q.7) 9.11.1915. Sunk 25.12.17 by 'U.110' in the Bristol Channel. (Also operated as MANFORD.)

PENTLAND FIRTH Tr 485/34, 1–4in. Purchased as A/S Tr 8.1939. Lent USN 2.42, sunk 19.9.42 in collision off New York.

PERCH ROCK Ferry 766/29. Hired as BBV 7.1940–42.

PERDITA Cstr 543/10, 1–12pdr, 1–6pdr, 100 mines. Hired as M/L 7.8.1915–21.8.19.

PERDRANT Tr 311/19. French M/S NOTRE DAME d'ESPERANCE seized 1940 at Plymouth. M/S to 1945.

PEREGRINE Ship 30, 300bm. Hired 1649. Captured 4.3.1653 by the Dutch.

PEREGRINE 1,681/92. Hired as store carrier (RFA) 4.8.1914–23.11.15.

PEREGRINE 2,514/ -. Purchased as store hulk 1914. Sold 20.3.22.

PERFECTIVE MFV 57/35. Hired on harbour service 11.1939–7.45.

PERICLES Tr 208/10. Hired 1918–19.

PERIDOT (ex-*Manchester City*) Tr 398/33. Purchased as A/S Tr 8.1939. Sunk 15.3.40 by mine off Dover.

PERIHELION Tr 215/14, 1–6pdr. Hired as M/S 1914–20.

PERILIA Dr 83/12. Hired 1.1915–19.

PERILIA Dr 98/18. Hired as M/S 11.1939–2.46.

PERLA Tug 88/24. Hired as A/P vessel 8.1939. Listed at Hong Kong to 12.41.

PERSEPHONE (see IOLAIRE)

PERSEPHONE (ex-DY hopper W.24) 725 tons/04. Converted to cable carrier 4.1943. Listed to 1945.

PERSEVERANCE Wood paddle DY tug 540 tons. Devonport DY 19.2.1875. Sold 27.4.1911 Cox, Falmouth to BU.

PERSEVERANCE (see METEOR)

PERSEVERANCE (ex-*Imara*) DY tug 437 tons, 109 x 28½ ft. Purchased 1932. Listed 1960.

PERSEVERE MFV 20/37. Hired as A/P vessel 11.1939. Sunk 27.10.40 by mine in the Firth of Forth.

PERSIAN EMPIRE Tr 195/99. Hired 1915–19.

PERSIMMON Tr 255/11. Listed 1914–15.

PERSIMMON (ex-PAMPAS renamed 1944, ex-*Parramatta*) Landing ship 12,864 tons, 425 x 61 ft. Harland & Wolff 1943, returned 8.46.

PERSISTENT Dr 96/88. Hired as store carrier 9.3.1918–19.

PERSOL (see CHERRYLEAF)

PERT (ex-*Plover*) DY tank vessel 320 tons. Purchased 1896. Sold 14.5.1907.

PERT DY paddle tug 690 tons, 145 x 28 ft. Thornycroft 5.4.1916. On sale list 1962.

PERTH 2,060/15, 3–4.7in. Hired as ABS 27.8.1915–22.12.18.

PERTHSHIRE 5,865/93, 9,336 tons. Purchased 28.10.1914 as dummy battleship VANGUARD. Water carrier (RFA) 1915, oiler 1919, store carrier 1921. Sold 26.2.34, BU in Italy.

PERUGIA 4,348/01. Hired as decoy ship (Q.1) 18.4.1916. Sunk 3.12.16 by 'U.63' in the Gulf of Genoa.

PESHAWAR Tr, 'Basset' class (RIN). Alcock Ashdown 2.5.1942, not completed. Sold circa 1954.

PESHAWUR 7,634/05. Hired as store carrier (RFA) 3.8.1914–2.5.15.

PESSAC Cstr 775/07. French A/P vessel seized 3.7.1940 at Plymouth. To MWT 10.41.

PET Smack 48/06, 1–3pdr. Commissioned as decoy ship 8.1915–16.

PETER BARRINGTON Tr, 'Strath' type, 202gr. Hall Russell 13.3.1919. Sold 1920, renamed *Cariama II*.

PETER BLUMBERRY Tr, 'Castle' type, 290gr. Cook Welton & Gemmell 18.10.1917. Sold 1921, renamed *Ingouville*.

PETERBOROUGH Tr 162/97, 1–3pdr. Hired 1914–19.

PETER CAREY Tr, 'Castle' type, 280gr. G.Brown 25.6.1919. Sold 1920, renamed *Cicely Blanche*. Hired as PETER CAREY, M/S, 8.39–9.45.

PETER DOBBIN Tr, 'Strath' type, 203gr. Williamson 1918. Sold 1921, renamed *Philippe*. (PHILIPPE in WW.II.)

PETER HALL Tr, 'Castle' type, 278gr. Ailsa 6.11.1918. Sold 1921, renamed *Transport Union*. (Served as ALVIS in WW.II.)

PETER HENDRICKS Tr 266/35. Hired as A/S Tr 11.1939–2.46.

PETER HOFFMAN Tr, 'Mersey' type, 329gr. Lobnitz 1919. Sold 1919, renamed *K.M. Hardy*.

PETER JONES Tr, 'Mersey' type. Cochrane. Cancelled 1919.

PETER KILLIN Tr, 'Castle' tupe, 276gr. Duthie Torry 1919. Sold 1919, renamed *Beaurieux*. (Served as SIR JOHN LISTER in WW.II.)

PETER LOVITT Tr, 'Castle' type, 276gr. Smiths Dk 9.3.1917. Sold 1921, renamed *Lowdock*.

PETER MAGEE Tr, 'Mersey' type. Cochrane 1919. Sold 1919, renamed *Lord Ernle*.

PETER NELL Yt 48/24. Hired as echo Yt 12.1939, purchased 9.41. Sold 2.46.

PETERUGIE Dr 80/15. Hired on harbour service 7.1915—19.

PETREL Tr 187/02. Hired 9.1914—11.14.

PETREL Dr 86/07, 1—3pdr. Hired 1916—19.

PETREL (ex-*HS.40*) DY tug. Transferred from War Dept 1918. Sold 18.6.20.

PETREL IV Tug 80 tons/32. French seaplane tender seized 1940 at Portsmouth. BBV tender 1940—44. DY tug 1944—46.

PETRELLA Petrol carrier 1,024 tons, 155 x 28 ft. Dunlop Bremner, Glasgow 16.2.1918. Sold 1946 at Alexandria.

PETROBUS Petrol carrier (as PETRELLA). Dunlop Bremner 8.11.1917. Arrived 24.2.59 Ward, Grays to BU.

PETROLEUM Oiler (RFA) 9,900 tons, 370 x 48½ ft. Swan Hunter 18.11.1902, purchased 3.05. Handed over 26.2.37 to Ward in part payment for *Majestic* (CALEDONIA).

PETRONEL Water carrier (RFA) (as PETRELLA). Dunlop Bremner 27.4.1918. Sold 6.47.

PETRONELLA 2,770/27. Dutch, hired as water carrier 4.1943. Sunk 15.10.44 by mine off Piraeus.

PETUNIA II Tr 209/99, 1—6pdr. Hired 1.1915—19.

PETUNIA III Tr 180/98. Hired 1917—19.

PEUPLIER French DY tug seized 1940. DY tug 7.40. Degaussing vessel 1941. Sunk 30.4.41, Plymouth area. Reported under salvage 6.41.

PEVENSEY CASTLE Dr 101/13, 1—6pdr. Hired 1915—19.

PEVERIL 1,459/04. Hired as decoy ship (Q.36) 18.2.1915. Sunk 6.11.17 by 'U.63' off Gibraltar. (Also operated as PUMA.)

P.FANNON Tr 211/15, 1—6pdr. Hired 1915—19.

PHASE Admiralty wood Dr, 96gr. Smith, Buckie 1919. Sold 1919, same name. Hired on harbour service 10.39. M/S 1944—2.46.

PHILANTE Yt 1,686/37. Hired as FAA Yt 9.1939, purchased 9.10.41. A/S training 11.40. Sold 1947.

PHILIPPE Tr 203/18, 1—3pdr. Hired as danlayer 4.1940. A/P Dr 9.40—12.41.

PHILLIP GODBY Tr, 'Castle' type, 290gr. Cook Welton & Gemmell 24.9.1918. Sold 1919, same name.

PHILOL Oiler (RFA) 2,200 tons, 210 x 35 ft. Tune Iron SB Co 5.4.1916.
Oil hulk 1956. Sold 1967.

PHILORTH Dr 100/07. Hired 1916–19.

PHINEAS BEARD Tr, 'Castle' type, 278gr. Cook Welton & Gemmell
17.11.1917. Sold 1919, same name. Hired as M/S 8.1939. Sunk 8.12.41
by air attack off the east coast of Scotland.

PHINGASK Dr 97/08, 1–6pdr. Hired 1.1915; base ship JULIUS 10.19–20.

PHOEBE (ex-*Betsy*) Cutter 10, 84bm. Hired 5.1804–3.05.

PHOEBE II Tr 278/07, 1–6pdr. Hired 1914–19.

PHOEBE III Tr 178/06. Hired 1917–19.

PHOENIX Ship 34, 330bm. Hired 1649–53.

PHOENIX Cutter 10. Hired 1794–1801.

PHOENIX Lugger 14. Hired 1799–1801.

PHOENIX Cutter 8, 79bm. Hired 6.1803–4.05.

PHOENIX Tender. Hired 1809–12.

PHOSPHORUS Admiralty steel Dr, 96gr. A.Hall 1918. Sold 1919,
renamed *Ocean Sprite*. (OCEAN SPRITE in WW.II.)

PHRONTIS Tr 288/11, 1–6pdr. Hired 1914–19 and as A/S Dr 5.40.
M/S 1943–1.46. (Belgian crew in 1942.)

PHYLLIS Tr 158/12. Purchased as danlayer (RNZN) 10.1942. Paid off
2.44. Sold 1945?

PHYLLIS BELMAN Tr 211/15. Hired 1915–19.

PHYLLISIA Tr 324/18. Hired as BDV 12.1939–7.46. (On loan
Portuguese navy 9.10.43–19.8.45 as B.1.)

PHYLLIS MARY Dr 94/17, 1–6pdr. Hired 1917–19 and as TRV
5.40–1.46.

PHYLLIS ROSE Dr 88/09. Hired as A/P Dr 4.1940–11.45.

PICKLE Wh 167gr, 180 tons, 2–3pdr. German *Sturmvogel* seized 1914.
Sold 1920.

PICT Tr 462/36, 1–4in. Purchased as A/S Tr 8.1939. Sold 1946.

PICTON CASTLE Tr 245/11. Hired 1915. Sunk 19.2.17 off Dartmouth.

PICTON CASTLE Tr 307/28, 1–12pdr. Hired as M/S 8.1939–12.45.

PIERCY BRETT Tr, 'Strath' type. Aberdeen. Cancelled 1919.

PIERRE-ANDRE Tr 307/21. French A/P Tr seized 3.7.1940 at
Portsmouth. A/P Tr 8.40. M/S 4.42–1.46.

PIERRE DESCELLIERS Dr 153/33. French M/S seized 3.7.1940 at
Southampton. A/P Dr 8.40. Laid up 6.42. Sunk 13.8.42 by air attack
at Salcombe.

PIERRE-GUSTAVE Tr 218/23. French M/S seized 3.7.1940 at
Southampton. M/S 11.40–3.46.

PIGEON II Tr 166/97, 1–6pdr. Hired as M/S 1914–19.

PILOT DY tug 615 tons, 145 x 29 ft. Chatham DY 2.9.1909. Arrived
27.3.60 in Holland to BU.

PILOT ME Dr 83/09, 1–3pdr. Hired 1915–19.

PILOT ME MFV. Hired as A/P vessel 7.1940. BBV 1941–45.

PILOT STAR Dr 92/07, 1–3pdr. Hired 11.1914–19.

PILOT STAR Dr 96/19. Hired on harbour service 11.1939–46.

PILOT US Dr 95/18. Hired as store carrier 8.1939–3.46.

PILOTWHALE (Z.14) Admiralty Wh, 'Z' class. Smiths Dk 24.9.1915. Sold 20.4.20, same name.

PIMPERNEL Dr 88/09, 1–6pdr. Hired 1916–19.

PINE M/S Tr 530 tons, 150 x 27½ ft, 1–12pdr. Hall Russell 25.3.1940. Sunk 31.1.44 by E-boat torpedo off Selsey Bill.

PINE LAKE Motor M/S (RCN) 255 tons, 126 x 26 ft, 2–20mm. Port Carling Bt Wks 1945. To Russian navy on completion 20.9.45.

PINEWOLD Tr 141/98. Hired 1918–19.

PINGOUIN French navy tug 700 tons. Seized 7.1940 at Portsmouth. BBV 8.40. Target towing 1943–45.

PING WO 3,105/22. Hired 1941. To RAN 22.5.42. Training ship (RAN) 1944, repair ship 1946. Returned 6.46.

PINTADE French navy tug 700 tons. Seized 7.1940 at Portsmouth. BBV 8.40. Target towing 1943–45.

PINTAIL Tr 199/08, 1–6pdr. Hired 10.1914–19.

PINTAIL BDV 950 tons, 168 x 36½ ft. Cammell Laird 3.12.1963.

PIONEER II Yt 399/14, 1–12pdr, 1–6pdr. Hired as A/P Yt 21.10.1915–14.3.19.

PIONEER III Dr 95/93. Hired on examination service 1915–19.

PIONEER Tr 121/01. Hired in WW.1.

PIONEER MFV 43/00. Hired as water carrier 1941. Training tender 1944–45.

PIPER MFV 51/02. Hired on harbour service 1.1941–45.

PIROUETTE A/S Tr 530 tons, 150 x 27½ ft, 1–4in, 3–20mm. Goole SB 22.6.1940. Sold 7.46, renamed *Tridente*.

PISCATOR Dr 55/99. Hired 1915–19.

PISCATOR II Dr 83/07, 1–6pdr. Hired 1915–19.

PISCATORIAL II Dr 93/16. Hired 1916. Lost 29.12.17.

PISCES Dr 94/07. Hired on harbour service 10.1914–19.

PITBLAE Dr 93/08, 1–3pdr. Hired as BDV 1.1915–18.

PITFOUR Tr 227/16, 1–6pdr, 24 mines. Hired as M/L 1917–19.

PITGAVENY Dr 88/09, 1–3pdr. Hired 1915–19.

PITSTRUAN Tr 206/13. Hired 1914. Sunk 13.4.17 by mine off Noss Head.

PITSTRUAN Tr 211/30. Hired as M/S 5.1940. Fuel carrier 1944–11.44.

PITT Brig 12. Hired 1809–12.

PITTENDRUM Dr 84/13. Hired 1915–19.

PITULLIE Dr 99/07, 1–3pdr. Hired 1915–19.

PLACEO Dr 83/10. Hired 1915—19.

PLACIDAS FAROULT 136/27. French, seized 6.1940 at Salcombe. Boom gate vessel 8.40. Broke from moorings at Salcombe 30.10.40, stranded then foundered 1.11.40.

PLADDA 1,334gr, 1—4in, 2—12pdr. Hired as decoy ship (Q.24) 16.1.1917—18. (Also operated as LAGGAN.)

PLADDA Tr, 'Isles' Class. Cook Welton & Gemmell 16.4.1941. Sold 1947. (On loan Rangoon Port Commissioners 5.46—10.46.)

PLAINSVILLE Tug (RCN). Owen Sound 1944. Listed 1958.

PLANET BDV 530 tons, 135 x 30½ ft, 1—3in. Lobnitz 26.12.1938. On sale list 1958.

PLANTAGENET BDV, (as PLANET). Lobnitz 23.2.1939. Sold 1959 Metal Industries as tug.

PLAYMATES Dr 93/07, 1—57mm. Hired 1915—19.

PLAYMATES Dr 93/25. Hired as M/S 10.1939—10.45.

PLEASANCE Dr 80/09. Hired 11.1914—12.14 and 12.15—19.

PLEASANTS Dr 86/13. Hired 1915—19.

PLEIADES Dr 90/07, 1—2½pdr. Hired 1915—19.

PLEIADES (see MANX FAIRY)

PLETHOS Tr 210/13, 1—12pdr. Hired 1915. Sunk 23.4.18 by mine off Montrose.

PLETO Tug 135/01. Hired on harbour service 12.1939—12.44.

PLINLIMMON (ex-*Cambria*) Paddle 436/95, 1—12pdr. Hired as M/S 13.9.1939. A/A ship, 1—12pdr, 3—2pdr, 7.42. Accommodation ship 1.44—11.46.

PLOUGASTEL French DY tug seized 1940 at Plymouth. Mine watching 1941—45.

PLOUGH Dr 95/12. Hired on harbour service 12.1914—19.

PLOUGH Dr 95/20. Hired on harbour service 9.1939—3.46.

PLOUGH BOY Dr 102/12, 1—57mm. Hired 1915—19 and as M/S 2.12.39, purchased 10.41. Sold 20.5.47 to BU.

PLUMER Dr 113/19. Hired as M/D 11.1939—7.45.

PLUMGARTH Tug 164/08. Hired on harbour service 1.6.1916—19.

PLUMLEAF (ex-TRINOL renamed 1917) Oiler (RFA) 12,300 tons, 405 x 54 ft. Swan Hunter 4.8.16. Sank to deck level 4.4.42 after Italian air attack at Malta and used as oiling jetty. Raised 11.46 and BU.

PLUMLEAF Oiler (RFA) 24,920 tons, 534 x 72 ft. Blyth SB 29.3.1960.

PLUMPER Wood S.tug 25 tons, 56 x 25½ ft. Transferred from War Dept. 1891. Sold 12.7.1910.

PLUNGER (see TRITON)

PLYM DY craft, 76bm. Built 1842. Sold 2.12.1869.

PLYM Tr 193/04, 1—6pdr. Hired 1917—19.

PLYMOUTH DY storeship, 103bm, 59 x 20 ft. Plymouth DY 1779. BU 1798.

PLYMOUTH DY craft, 166bm, 70 x 23½ ft. Franks Quarry, Plymouth 1798. Listed 1805.

PLYMOUTH Lugger 16. Hired 1797–1801.

PLYMOUTH DY pitch boat, 42bm. Plymouth 1806. Fate unknown.

PLYMOUTH DY lighter. Listed 1875. Sold 17.5.1904. (Also known as Devonport YC.6.)

PLYMOUTH SALVOR Salvage vessel 800 tons, 170 x 37 ft, 1–3in. American Car & Fndry, Wilmington 21.4.1943 on lend lease, but retained by the USN as WEIGHT.

PLYMOUTH TRADER Aux. barge 122/16. Hired as cable depot ship 27.8.1939. Laid up 7.42–45.

POCHARD Tr 146/89. Hired 1.1918–19.

POET CHAUCER DY tug, 239gr, 105 x 25 ft. Bailey, Hong Kong 8.10.1919. Lost 19.12.41 at Hong Kong.

POET LANGLAND DY tug (as POET CHAUCER). Bailey, Hong Kong 1919. To F.M.S Govt 23.6.20.

POINTER Tr 198/06, 1–6pdr. Hired 1915–19 and as M/D 1.40–12.45.

POINTER DY tug, 152gr. Appledore SB 30.1.1967.

POINTZ CASTLE Tr 283/14, 1–12pdr. Hired 1915–19 and as M/S 8.39–4.45.

POL I Wh 205/26. Norwegian, hired as M/S (SAN) 7.10.1941. Renamed RANDFONTEIN 1942. Returned 7.4.46.

POL II Wh 240/26. Norwegian, hired as M/S 4.1941. Renamed JELOY (Norwegian crew) 1942. Renamed LEVANTER (RN crew) 8.44. Returned 8.46.

POL IV Wh 240/26. Norwegian, hired 4.41. Renamed TROMOY (Norwegia crew) 1942. Renamed CLOUDBURST (RN crew) 8.44. Returned 1946.

POL V Wh 221/25. Norwegian, hired as M/S (SAN) 1941. Renamed BENONI 3.42. Returned 4.46.

POL VI Wh 254/35. Norwegian, hired as M/S 10.1940. Renamed OKSOY (Norwegian crew) 1942. Renamed CYCLONE (RN crew) 8.44. Returned 4.46.

POL VII Wh 338/36. Norwegian, hired as M/D 17.11.1942–7.7.43.

POLAR 5 Wh 278/31. Hired as M/D 3.1940–11.45.

POLAR 6 Wh 263/25. Hired as M/D 3.1940–45.

POLARIS (ex-*Southern Cross*) MFV 50/41. Survey vessel (RAN) 1944–46.

POLAR PRINCE Tr 194/15, 1–6pdr. Hired 1915–19.

POLEAXE Tr, 304gr, 136 x 24 ft, 1–12pdr. Russian T.19 seized and commissioned 8.1918. Sold 22.7.21, renamed *Dorbie*.

POLEGATE (see BV.7 under BD vessels)

POLITA Aux. barge 109/20. Hired as BBV 12.1939. Accommodation ship 1942–11.45.

POLKA A/S Tr 530 tons, 150 x 27½ ft, 1–4in, 3–20mm. Hall Russell 29.1.1941. Sold 3.4.46.
POLLACK A/S Tr 670 tons, 146 x 25½ ft, 1–4in, 3–20mm. Cochrane 22.4.1943. Sold 4.46, renamed *Cardiff Castle*.
POLLY DY tug, 79½ x 14½ ft. Bailey, Hong Kong 1916. Sold 5.31 at Hong Kong. (Also known as C.410.)
POLLY BRIDGE Cstr 403/16. Hired as fleet messenger 22.3.1918–21.12.18.
POLLY JOHNSON Tr 290/19. Hired as M/S 8.1939. Sunk 29.5.40 by air attack at Dunkirk.
POLO NORTE Tr 344/17, 1–12pdr. Portuguese, purchased 1941 as M/S. Renamed MOONSHINE 1942. Sold 1.45.
POLSHANNON 6,121/10. German prize *Birkenfels* commissioned as oiler (RFA) 3.9.1915. Sold 4.7.21.
POMEROL Cstr 1,166/30. French A/P vessel seized 3.7.1940 at Plymouth. A/P 9.40. To MWT 9.6.41.
POMONA 14-gun vessel. Hired 1797–1801.
POMONA Tr 161/99, 1–12pdr. Hired 1914–19.
POOL FISHER Cstr 605/21. Hired as boom carrier (RFA) 22.8.1940–1.46.
POONA Tr, 'Basset' class (RIN). Garden Reach 2.4.1942. Sold 1946, renamed *Firishta*.
POONAH Tr 171/03. Hired 1914. Sunk 18.8.15 in collision.
POPINJAY (ex-*Thistle*) MFV. Hired as A/P vessel 2.1940–1.46.
POPLAR LAKE Motor M/S (RCN) 255 tons, 126 x 26 ft. Star SY 10.5.1945. To Russian navy 9.1.46.
POPPY Dr 76/02. Hired on harbour service 7.1915; RECLUSE 8.18–19.
PORCHER (ex-PROCHER renamed 10.1942) Tr, 'Isles' class. Midland SY 26.5.42. To War Dept 3.47, same name. (Listed as PROCHER to 1944 and under both names to 1946.)
PORPOISE Nigerian Govt paddle tug, 2–12pdr, 1–3pdr. In commission as gunboat 1915–17.
PORTADOWN (see PROCTOR)
PORTAFERRY (see PROBE)

'Porte' class BDVS (RCN). 430 tons (deep), 125½ x 26 ft, 1–40mm.
PORTE DAUPHINE Pictou Fndry 4.1952. Canadian coastguard 1963.
PORTE de la REINE Victoria Mcy 28.12.51.
PORTE QUEBEC Burrard DD Co 28.8.51.
PORTE ST JEAN G T Davie 21.11.50.
PORTE ST LOUIS G T Davie 22.7.52.

PORTHLEVEN (see PRODIGAL)

PORTHOS 326gr. Hired as boom tender 11.1940–44.

PORTIA Cstr 494/06. Hired as fleet messenger 23.7.1915. Sunk 2.8.15 by U.28' in the Atlantic.

PORTIA II Yt 527/06, 1–12pdr, 1–6pdr. Hired as A/P Yt 8.10.1914–1.4.19.

PORTIA III Tr 178/95. Hired 1917–19.

PORTIA (see UNITIA)

PORTISHAM (see PROCTOR)

PORT JACKSON Tr 197/14. Hired 1917–19.

PORT JACKSON (see PRODUCT)

PORTMADOC (see PROFESSOR)

PORT NAPIER 9,600/40, 2–4in, 4–20mm, 550 mines. Hired as M/L 1940. Lost by fire 27.11.40 in Loch Alsh.

PORT NATAL (see PROMISE)

PORTOBELLO (see PROPHET)

PORTPATRICK (see PROTEST)

PORT QUEBEC 8,490/39, 2–4in, 4–20mm, 550 mines. Hired as M/L 1940. Renamed DEER SOUND, repair ship, 1.1.45 and purchased. Sold 1946.

PORTREATH (see PROWESS)

PORT ROYAL (see PROOF)

PORTRUSH (see PROPERTY)

PORTSDOWN A/S Tr 760 tons, 165½ x 28 ft, 1–12pdr, 3–20mm. Cook Welton & Gemmell 24.9.1941. Sold 10.4.46, renamed *Sollum.*

PORTSMOUTH Tr 178/03, 1–12pdr. Hired 1.1915–19.

PORT STANLEY (see PRONG)

PORTWEY Tug 94/27. Hired on harbour service 1942–46.

PORTZIC French navy tug seized 3.7.1940 at Plymouth. Mine-watching 1940–45.

POSEIDON Dr 96/13. Hired as tender 12.1914–19 and on examination service 10.39. Degaussing vessel 1944–6.45.

POSEIDON 94/24. Hired as A/P vessel 8.1939. Listed until the fall of Hong Kong.

POST BOY (ex-*Le Royal*) Tr 316/41. Hired as M/S 10.1940–7.46.

POULMIC French navy tender 350 tons. Seized 3.7.1940 at Plymouth. Mine-watching (Free-French crew) 8.40. Sunk 6.10.40 by mine off Plymouth.

POURQUOIS PAS Dr 45/13. French, seized 1940. A/P vessel 11.40–44.

.POUYER QUERTIER Pilot 159/11. French M/S seized 3.7.1940 at Southampton. Examination service 1941–44.

POWIS CASTLE Tr 275/16, 1–6pdr. Hired as M/S 1916–19 and as M/S 2.40. A/S training 1943, target towing 1945.

POYANG 2,873/41. Hired as store carrier (RAN) 12.5.1942–11.45.

POZARICA 1,893/38, 4,540 tons, 6–4in, 8–20mm. Purchased as A/A ship 20.6.1940. Sunk 13.2.43 by air attack off Bougie; raised and BU 1951 in Italy.

PRABNAVATI Cstr 556/33. Hired as A/S vessel (RIN) 8.1939. Sunk in error 8.12.41 by GLASGOW off the coast of India.

PRATTLER (see RATTLER)

PRECEPT Netlayer 1,016 tons, 169 x 34½ ft, 1–3in, 2–20mm. Barbour Bt Wks, New Bern 11.4.1944 on lend-lease. Returned 4.1.46 to the USN.

PRECISE (ex-USS BOXELDER) Netlayer (as PRECEPT). Barbour Bt Wks 20.7.1944 on lend-lease. Returned 14.12.45 to the USN.

PRE–EMINENT Dr 96/18. Hired on harbour service 10.1939–46.

PREFECT Tr 302/15, 1–12pdr. Hired 1916–19. (Served as NORLAND in WW.II.)

PREFECT Netlayer (as PRECEPT). American Car & Fndry Wilmington 8.3.1944 on lend-lease. Returned 28.12.45 to the USN.

PREMIER Tr 253/08, 1–6pdr. Hired as M/S 1915–19.

PREMIER II Dr 71/06, 1–3pdr. Hired 1916–19.

PREMIER Paddle 129/1846, 1–6pdr. Hired on examination service 10.1918–25.4.19.

PRESENTER Dr 106/15. Hired 1918–19.

PRESENT FRIENDS Dr 89/14, 1–6pdr. Hired 1915–19.

PRESENT FRIENDS Dr 84/19. Hired 6.1940–2.46.

PRESENT HELP Dr 82/11, 1–3pdr. Hired 1914–19 and as A/P Dr 12.39. S/M tender 1942–46. (Bore the name VARBEL for a time as base ship.)

PRESERVER Depot ship (RCN) 3,450 tons, 265 x 43 ft, 1–12pdr. Marine Industries 21.12.1941. Sold 4.1.46 Peruvian navy as MARISCAL CASTILLA.

PRESIDENCY Tr 257/07, 1–12pdr. Hired 1915–19.

PRESIDENT BRIAND Tr 227/32. French M/S seized 3.7.1940 at Southampton. M/S 9.40. To MWT 1941.

PRESIDENT HERRIOT MFV. French M/S seized 3.7.1940 at Southampton A/P vessel 11.40–43.

PRESIDENT JOHN P BEST Tug 125/00. Belgian, hired on harbour service 23.9.1915–19 and 4.42–45.

PRESIDENT THEODORE TISSIER French survey ship 965 tons. Seized 3.7.1940 at Falmouth. Free-French training ship 8.40. French navy 1945.

PRESIDENT WARFIELD 1,814/28. American, on lend-lease as accommodation ship 1.1943–5.44.

PRESS HOME Dr 77/08. Hired 1915–19.

PRESTIGE Dr 81/07, 1–3pdr. Hired 1915–19.

PRESTIGE Composite Tr, 284/44, 128 x 26 ft. Purchased 1953 for conversion to degaussing vessel but not completed. Sold 1958 at Chatham. (Was to have been renamed DGV.404.)

PRESTOL Oiler (RFA) 4,900 tons, 335 x 41½ ft. Napier & Miller 4.9.1917. Arrived 8.6.58 White, St Davids to BU.

PRESTON Dr 84/06, 1–6pdr. Hired 1916–19.

PRESTON NORTH END Tr 419/34, 1–12pdr. Hired as A/S Tr 9.1939–11.45.

PRETEXT (ex-PROTECT renamed 9.1943, ex-USS SATINWOOD) Netlayer (as PRECEPT). American Car & Fndry 23.5.1944. Returned 11.45 to the USN. Became *John Biscoe* and purchased 8.56 as research ship ENDEAVOUR (RNZN). On sale list 11.61.

PRETORIA Tr 283/06, 1–6pdr. Hired 1915–19 (Listed to 1.19 but in mercantile loss list as sunk 10.7.17.)

PRETORIA Tr 159/00. Hired 1917–19.

PRETORIA (see BUSEN 10)

PRETORIA CASTLE 17,392/38, 8–6in, 2–12pdr. Hired as AMC 2.10.193 Purchased 16.7.42 and completed as A/C carrier 9.4.43, 4–4in, 20–20mm, 15–A/C. Sold 26.1.46 renamed *Warwick Castle*.

PREVALENT Smack 42/13 1–12pdr. Hired as decoy ship 1.1917–2.19.

PREVENTER (ex-USS SEAGRAPE) Netlayer (as PRECEPT). American Car & Fndry 9.8.1944 on lend-lease. Returned 10.1.46 to the USN.

PRIDE of BUCHAN Dr 86/08. Hired 1915–19.

PRIDE of BUCKIE Dr 79/10. Hired 1915–19.

PRIDE o' FIFE Dr 83/07. Hired 1915–19.

PRIDE of FILEY Dr 87/07. Hired 1915–19.

PRIDE of MORAY Dr 50/09. Hired as water boat 1915–19 and on harbour service 1.41–2.46.

PRIMATE Tug 35/26. Hired on harbour service 6.1942–10.45.

PRIME Dr 101/14, 1–3pdr. Hired 2.1915–19 and on harbour service 10 39–6.45.

PRIMEVERE Dr 100/14. Hired 1915–19 and on harbour service 12.39–45.

PRIMORDIAL Dr 97/17. Hired on harbour service 8.1939–45.

PRIMROSE Ship, 200bm. Hired for the Armada campaign.

PRIMROSE II Dr 87/07, 1–3pdr. Hired 8.1915–19.

PRIMROSE III Dr 89/15? Hired 1915–19.

PRIMROSE Tug 150gr? In service 1916–18.

PRIMROSE Tr. Hired as BDV 1916–19.

PRIMROSE BAY Dr 79/10. Hired as BDV 7.1940. TRV 3.43–6.45.

PRINCE 2,710/1854. Hired as store carrier 7.1854. Lost 14.11.54 in a storm in the Black Sea.

PRINCE (see The PRINCE)
PRINCE ABBAS 2,030/92. Hired as ABS 5.6.1915–11.16.
PRINCE ALBERT Dr 64/02. In service 1915.
PRINCE BAUDOUIN 3,050/34. Belgian, hired as air target 7.1940–7.41
and as landing ship, 2–12pdr, 6–20mm, 1.43–13.10.45.
PRINCE CHARLES 2,950/30, 2–12pdr, 6–20mm. Hired as landing ship
21.9.1940–21.12.44.
PRINCE CONSORT Tr 155/90. Hired 1918–19.
PRINCE DAVID 6,890/30, 4–6in, 2–3in. Hired as AMC (RCN) 26.11.1939
purchased 1.40. Landing ship, 4–4in, 1–40mm, 12.43. On sale list 1.46;
sold, renamed *Charlton Monarch.*
PRINCE de LIEGE Tr 324/26. Belgian, hired as BDV 9.1940–45.
PRINCE EDWARD Sloop 14. Hired 1793–94.
PRINCE EDWARD (ex-*Prince of Wales*) Paddle 1,568/-, 1–3pdr.
Purchased as netlayer 28.1.1915. Sold 12.2.20.
PRINCE HENRY 6,893/30 4–6in, 2–3in. Commissioned as AMC (RCN)
25.5.1940. Landing ship, 2–4in, 6–20mm, 1.44. Sold 1946 renamed
Empire Parkestone.
PRINCE LEO Tr 218/13, 1–6pdr. Hired 1915–19 and as A/P Tr 11.39.
BBV 6.40–8.44.
PRINCE LEOPOLD 2,938/39. Belgian, hired as air target 22.9.1940.
Landing ship, 2–12pdr, 6–20mm, 1941. Sunk 29.7.44 by U-boat in the
Channel.
PRINCE PALATINE Tr 256/14, 1–12pdr. Hired 1914–19.
PRINCE PHILIPPE 2,938/39. Belgian, hired as air target 24.7.1940.
Landing ship, 2–12pdr, 6–20mm, 1941. Sunk 15.7.41 in collision with
Empire Wave off the west coast of Scotland.
PRINCEPS Tr 264/11, 1–6pdr. Hired 1916–19.
PRINCE ROBERT 6,892/30, 4–6in, 2–3in. Hired as AMC (RCN)
26.11.1939, purchased 5.2.40. A/A ship, 10–4in, 4–20mm, 6.43.
Sold 10.46, renamed *Charlton Sovereign.*
PRINCE SALVOR Salvage vessel 1,440 tons, 200 x 38 ft, 4–20mm.
Goole SB 8.3.1943. Sold 1965.
PRINCESS 8,689/05. German prize *Kronprinzessin Cecile* hired as
dummy battleship AJAX 10.1914. AMC, 8–6in, 9.1.16–11 9.17.
PRINCESS (see The PRINCESS)
PRINCESS Yt 730/24. Hired as A/S Yt 9.1939. Sunk 11.1.40 in
collision in the Bristol Channel.
PRINCESSA 58/21. Hired on examination service 8.1939. To War
Dept 12.41.
PRINCESS ALBERTA 1,586/05. Hired as fleet messenger 4.10.1915.
Sunk 21.2.17 by mine near Mudros.
PRINCESS ALICE Tr 225/14, 1–6pdr. Hired 1915. Sunk 6.3.18 in
collision in the Mediterranean.

PRINCESS AUGUSTA Cutter 8, 71bm, 8–4pdr. Hired 7.1803–5.1814.
PRINCESS BEATRICE Tr 214/-. Hired 1914. Sunk 5.10.14 by mine
off the Belgian coast.
PRINCESS BEATRICE Paddle 253/80. Hired as M/S 23.4.1917–26.6.19.
PRINCESS CHARLOTTE Schooner 8, 96bm, 8–12pdr carr. Hired 1804–
08.
PRINCESS ELIZABETH Paddle 338/27, 1–12pdr. Hired as M/S 22.9.1939
A/A ship, 1–12pdr, 3–20mm, 6.42–3.46.
PRINCESS ENA 1,198/06, 3–12pdr. Hired as decoy ship 30.4.1915.
Fleet messenger 4.10.15–6.7.20.
PRINCESS HELENA Paddle 246/83. Hired as M/S 8.8.1914–9.1.15.
PRINCESS IDA Ferry 45gr. Hired as mine-recovery vessel 4.1942,
purchased 11.42. Renamed BIRNBECK 1942–45 as nominal base ship.
PRINCESS IRENE 5,934/14, 2–4.7in, 2–12pdr, 2–6pdr, 500 mines.
Hired as M/L 20.1.1915. Blown up 27.5.15 by accident in Sheerness
harbour.
PRINCESS IRIS (see IRIS)
PRINCESS JULIANA Tr 266/05, 1–6pdr. Hired 1914–19.
PRINCESS LOUISE Tr 106/98. On harbour service in WW.I.
PRINCESS LOUISE 1,986/-. Hired as fleet auxiliary 3.3.1915–4.1.18.
PRINCESS LOUISE II Tr 289/05, 1–6pdr. Hired 1915–19.
PRINCESS MARGARET 5,934/14, 5,070 tons, 2–4in, 2–3in, 400
mines. Hired as M/L 26.12.1914, purchased 14.6.19. Sold 30.5.29 to BU.
PRINCESS MARIE JOSE Tr 274/15, 1–6pdr. Hired 1916–19.
PRINCESS MARIE JOSE (see SOUTHERN ISLES)
PRINCESS MARY Tr 225/14, 1–12pdr. Hired 1915–19? and as M/S
2.40–9.45.
PRINCESS MARY II Paddle 326/11, 2–6pdr. Hired as A/P vessel
17.5.1916. Sunk 2.8.19 by mine in the Aegean.
PRINCESS MAUD 1,566/02. Hired as fleet messenger 5.5.1916–4.2.18.
PRINCESS MAY Paddle 1,123/92. Purchased as accommodation ship
1914. Sold 26.1.20.
PRINCESS of WALES Cutter 10, 106bm, 10–12pdr carr. Hired 1797–
1802 and 7.1803–5.14.
PRINCESS of WALES Paddle 163gr. Hired on harbour service 15.6.1917–
19.
PRINCESS OLGA Tr 245/16, 1–6pdr. Hired 1916; sunk 14.6.18.
PRINCESS ROYAL Cutter 8. Hired 1793. Captured 7.1798 by a French
privateer in the North Sea.
PRINCESS ROYAL II Tr 213/13, 1–6pdr. Hired as M/S 1914–19.
PRINCESS ROYAL Tug 105/88. Hired on harbour service 23.6.1915–
19.

PRINCESS VICTORIA 1,687gr. Hired as fleet messenger 1914—5.15.

PRINCESS VICTORIA Tr 272gr. Hired 1915. Sunk 7.11.15 in collision off Ushant.

PRINCESS VICTORIA Tr 245/16 1—6pdr. Hired 1916—19.

PRINCESS VICTORIA 2,197/39, 1—4in, 244 mines. Hired as M/L 9.1939. Sunk 19.5.40 by mine off the Humber.

PRINCETOWN 6,060/02. German prize *Prinz Adalbert* commissioned as repair ship 17.12.1914. Sold 23.12.16.

PRINCE VICTOR Tr 207/10, 1—6pdr. Hired 1915—19 and as fuel carrier 2.44—29.11.44.

PRINCE WILLIAM A.ship 14, 307bm. Hired 1797—1801 and 5.1804—11.1812.

PRINCIPAL Dr 91/08, 1—6pdr. Hired 1914—19 and on harbour service 4.40—3.46.

PRINS ALBERT 2,938/37. Belgian, hired as air target 24.7.1940. Landing ship 2—12pdr, 6—20mm, 1941—6.46.

PRINS BOUDEWIJN Dr 84/30. French, ex-Belgian, siezed 7.1940 at Plymouth. A/P Dr 11.40—8.45.

PRINSES ASTRID 2,950/30. Belgian, hired 28.9.1940. Landing ship 1941—4.45.

PRINSES BEATRIX 4,135/39, 2—12pdr, 6—20mm. Dutch, hired as landing ship 8.1940—4.46.

PRINSES JOSEPHINE CHARLOTTE 2,950/31, 2—12pdr, 6—20mm. Belgian, hired as landing ship 28.9.1940—25.10.45. (In most lists as PRINSES J.CHARLOTTE.)

PRISCILLA Yt 273/88. Purchased 1917. Sold 31.7.19.

PRIVET (see ISLAND QUEEN)

PRIZE (see ELSE)

PROBE (ex-PORTAFERRY renamed 1943) M/S Tr, 345gr, 550 tons, 134 x 26 ft, 1—12pdr, 3—20mm. Alfeite DY, Lisbon 24.10.1942. Sold 6.46, renamed *Polo Norte.*

PROBUS Brigantine 179/1865, 2—12pdr, 2—6pdr. Hired as decoy ship (Q.30) 7.1915—18. (Also operated as READY and THIRZA.)

PROCEED Dr 64/01, 1—3pdr. Hired 1915—19.

PROCHER (see PORCHER)

PROCTOR (ex-PORTISHAM, ex-PORTADOWN renamed 1943) M/S Tr, 345gr, (as PROBE). Alfeite 23.10.1942. Sold 6.46, renamed *Arrabida.*

PROCYON Tr 196/03. Hired as BDV 1917—19.

PROCYON MFV 30/38. Hired on harbour service 11.1939—1.46.

PRODIGAL (ex-PORTHLEVEN renamed 1943) M/S Tr (as PROBE). Cia Uniao Fabril, Lisbon 26.4.1941, completed as M/S repair ship, 3—20mm, 2—MG. Sold 6.46.

PRODUCT (ex-PORT JACKSON renamed 1943) M/S Tr. (as PROBE).
Uniao Fabril 12.4.1941. Completed 2.43 as M/S repair ship. To Greek
navy 7.46 as HERMES.
PRODUCTIVE Dr 73/06, 1–3pdr. Hired 1916–19.
PROFESSOR (ex-PORTMADOC renamed 1943) M/S Tr, 334gr (as
PROBE). Uniao Fabril 28.5.1942. Sold 6.46, renamed *Algenib*.
PROFICIENCY Dr 82/13. Hired on harbour service 2.11.1914–19.
PROFICIENT Dr 58/10. Hired on examination service 11.1940. Stranded
19.12.40 near Whitby.
PROGRESS DY water carrier. Hired 1915–19.
PROGRESS II Dr 84/07, 1–3pdr. Hired 1915–19.
PROGRESS DY mooring vessel 750 tons, 135 x 27½ ft. Simons 24.1.1916.
Renamed ANCHORITE 1916, HERMIT 1944. BU 2.48 at Rosyth.
PROLIFIC Dr 60/06. Hired 1918–19.
PROLIFIC (see BLUEBELL)
PROME 7,043/30. Hired as mine carrier (RFA) 9.1940–9.46.
PROMISE (ex-PORT NATAL renamed 1943) M/S Tr, 334gr. (as PROBE).
Uniao Fabril 20.9.1941. Sold 6.46, renamed *Aldebaran*.
PROMOTIVE Dr 78/08. Hired on harbour service 11.1914–19 and as
M/S 12.39. Sunk 23.12.39 by mine in Loch Ewe.
PROMPT Iron paddle tug, 120bm, 140 tons, 90 x 17 ft. Napier 1867.
Sold 9.1922 at Malta.
PROMPT (see WARDEN)
PRONG (ex-PORT STANLEY renamed 1943) M/S Tr, 312gr, 525 tons,
129 x 27½ ft, 1–12pdr, 3–20mm (wooden hull). A.Monica, Aveiro
Portugal 14.7.1942. Sold 6.46, renamed *Sjostkirk*.
PROOF (ex-PORT ROYAL renamed 1943) M/S Tr, 336gr, (as PRONG).
A.Monica 14.7.1942. Sold 6.6.46.
PROPERTY (ex-PORTRUSH renamed 1943) M/S Tr, 341gr, 540 tons (as
PRONG). A.Monica 28.8.1942. Sold 12.6.46, same name.
PROPHET (ex-PORTOBELLO renamed 1943) M/S Tr, 336gr (as PRONG).
A.Monica 2.4.1942. Sold 6.46.
PROSIT Dr 77/06, 1–3pdr. Hired 1.1915–19.
PROSPECT Dr 58/02. Hired 1918–19.
PROSPECT Tr, 'Isles' class. Midland SB 16.6.1942. To War Dept
15.8.46, same name.
PROSPECTIVE Dr 75/10, 1–3pdr. Hired 1916–18.
PROSPECTIVE II Dr 85/18. Hired 1918–19.
PROSPECTO MFV 40/28. Hired as HDPC 11.1939. To MWT 5.43.
PROSPECTS AHEAD Dr 95/19. Hired as M/S 12.1939–1.46.
PROSPERITY Dr 72/06, 1–6pdr. Hired 1915–19.
PROSPERITY II Dr 64/01. Hired 1915–19.
PROSPEROUS 44–gun ship, 600bm. Hired 1649. Captured 28.2.1653
by the Dutch.

PROSPEROUS Rescue tug 700 tons, 143 x 33 ft, 1—3in, 1—20mm.
Cochrane 29.6.1942. On sale list 11.64.

PROTEA (see TERJE 7)

PROTECT Dr 98/07. Hired 1915. Sunk 16.3.17 by mine off Dover.

PROTECT (see PRETEXT)

PROTECT ME Dr 88/08. Hired 1915—19.

PROTECTOR Tr 161/04. Hired 1915—18.

PROTECTOR Dr 58/02. Hired on harbour service in 1918.

PROTEST (ex-PORT PATRICK renamed 1943) M/S Tr, 336gr (as
PRONG). M.M.B.Monica, Aveiro 12.8.1941. Sold 6.46.

PROVIDENCE 24—gun ship, 275bm. Hired 1649—54.

PROVIDENCE Cutter 10. Hired 1800—01.

PROVIDENCE Sloop 16, 291bm. Hired 5.1804—9.1812.

PROVIDENCE MFV. Hired on examination service 2.5.1940. Renamed
KISMET 1940—44.

PROVIDER DY tank vessel 395 tons, 115 x 21 ft. Bow McLachlan
10 2.1903. On sale list 1946.

PROVIDER Dr 99/07. Hired 1915—19.

PROVIDER Depot ship (RCN) 3,450 tons, 265 x 43 ft, 1—12pdr.
Marine Industries 12.6.1942. On sale list 1946.

PROVIDER Oiler (RCN) 22,000 tons, 523 x 76 ft. Davie SB, Lauzon
5.7.1962.

PROVOST Dr. Hired as BDV in WW.I.

PROVOST (see PROWESS)

PROWESS (ex-PROVOST, ex-PORTREATH renamed 1943) M/S Tr,
343gr (as PRONG). M.M.B.Monica 21.2.1943. Sold 6.46.

PRUDENCE Pilot 258/06. Hired on examination service 1.1941.
Calibrating vessel 1942—3.45.

PRUDENT DY tug 325 tons, 125 x 24½ ft. Bow McLachlan 17.5.1905.
Sold 10.27 Ward to BU.

PRUDENT Rescue tug 700 tons, 143 x 33 ft, 1—3in, 2—20mm. Cochrane
6.8.1940. Renamed CAUTIOUS, DY tug, 1947. Sale list 1964. Sold,
renamed *Rivtow Lion*.

PRUNELLA (see CAPE HOWE)

PUFF Admiralty steel Dr, 96gr. Brooke 1920. Sold 1920, same name.
(Served as GOWAN HILL in WW.II.)

PUFFIN Tr 199/07, 1—6pdr. Hired 1914—19.

PUGWASH Tug 229/30. Hired (RCN) 1941—45.

PUMA (see PEVERIL)

PUNCHER (ex-*HT.1*) DY tug. Transferred from War Dept 1918. Sold
22.7.20.

PUNGENT (see TYRIE)

PUNNET (ex-*Cape Matapan*) Tr 320/25, 556 tons, 140 x 24 ft, 1—12pdr.
Purchased as BDV 16.4.1939. Sold 21.1.46.

PURFOL (ex-PLA *Hopper No. 7*) 869gr. Commissioned as oiler (RFA) 9.9.1916—20.

PURI Tr, 'Basset' class (RIN). Alcock Ashdown. Ordered 12.1942, deferred 10.44, cancelled.

PURIRI Tr, 'Castle' type (RNZN). Stevenson & Cook, Port Chalmers 1941. Sunk 14.5.41 by mine off Auckland.

PURSUIT Dr 79/03, 1—3pdr. Hired 1916. Sunk 22.4.18 in collision off Penzance.

PURSUIT (ex-*Pearl*) MFV. Hired as TRV 3.1940—46.

PURUNI Tr 295/05. Hired 1917—19.

PYGMALION (see GALATEA)

PYROPE Tr 295/32, 1—12pdr. Hired as M/S 8.1939. Sunk 12.8.40 by air attack in the Thames estuary.

'Q' numbers given to decoy ships in WW.I:

Q.1—9 (see PERUGIA, INTABA, BARRANCA, CARRIGAN HEAD, FARNBOROUGH, ZYLPHA, PENSHURTS, VALA and MARY B. MITCHELL)

Q.10—16 (see BEGONIA, TAMARISK, TULIP, AUBRIETIA, VIOLA, SALVIA and HEATHER in Volume I)

Q.17—32 (see HELGOLAND, LADY OLIVE, ISLAND QUEEN, BAYARD, ELSE, GAELIC, SPEEDWELL II, PLADDA, LADY PATRICIA, NYROCA, WARNER, MEROPS, DARGLE, PROBUS, GUNNER and QUICKLY)

Q.35, 36 (see RULE and PEVERIL)

Q.E.F Dr 89/07. Hired 1915—19.

QUADRILLE A/S Tr 530 tons, 150 x 27½ ft, 1—4in, 3—20mm. Hall Russell 15.3.1941. Sold 6.6.46, renamed *Elsa*.

QUAIL II Tr 265/06. Hired 1914—16.

QUAIL III Tr 162/-. Hired 1915. Sunk 23.6.15 in collision off Portland.

QUANNET (ex—*Dairycoates*) Tr 350/26. Purchased as BDV 5.1939. Sold 1.46.

QUARTZITE Cstr 160/32. French auxiliary, seized 3.7.1940 at Salcombe. BBV 8.40. To MWT 6.41.

QUASSIA Tr 207/99. Hired 1918—19.

QUEBEC SALVOR Salvage vessel 800 tons, 170 x 37 ft, 1—3in, 2—20mm. Bellingham IW 10.5.1943 for lend-lease but retained by the USN as VALVE.

QUEEN A.ship 20. Hired 1778 and 1793—94.

QUEEN Sloop 10. Hired 1793—94.

QUEEN Cutter 14. Hired 1794–1801.

QUEEN Bomb tender. Hired 1801–02.

QUEEN Cutter, 131bm. Hired 11.1804–1.05.

QUEEN Tug 169/83. Hired on harbour service 30.7.1914–19.

QUEEN II Tr 161/00. Hired 1914–19.

QUEEN III Dr 93/06, 1–6pdr. Hired 1915–19.

QUEEN IV Paddle 345/02, 2–6pdr. Hired as A/P vessel 17.5.1916. M/S 4.19–25.11.20.

QUEEN (see The QUEEN)

QUEEN ALEXANDRA Tr 231/01. Hired 1918–19 and as M/S 14.9.40–6.10.40.

QUEEN CHARLOTTE Cutter 12, 140bm. Hired 1800–01 and 5.1804–5.05.

QUEEN CHARLOTTE Cutter 6, 60bm, 6–12pdr carr. Hired 1803–12.

QUEEN CHARLOTTE Cutter 10, 76bm, 2–12pdr carr., 8–4pdr. Hired 1803–14.

QUEEN EAGLE (see EMPRESS QUEEN)

QUEEN EMMA 4,135/39, 2–12pdr, 6–20mm. Dutch *Koningin Emma* hired as landing ship 8.1940–4.46.

QUEEN EMPRESS Paddle 411/12, 2–6pdr. Hired as M/S 25.10.1915–30.6.20 and as M/S 27.10.39. A/A ship, 4–20mm, 9–MG, 1942. Laid up 5.44, returned 9.45.

QUEEN MOTHER Dr 126/16, 1–6pdr. Hired 1916–19.

QUEEN of BERMUDA 22,500/33, 7–6in, 2–3in. Hired as AMC 30.8.1939–4.43.

QUEEN of KENT Paddle 798/16, 1–12pdr. Hired as M/S 12.9.1939. Miscellaneous service 1.44–12.7.46.

QUEEN of THANET Paddle 792/16, 1–12pdr. Hired as M/S 12.9.1939. Accommodation ship 1.44; salvage duty 1945–7.6.46.

QUEEN of the FLEET Dr 96/17, 1–3pdr. Hired 1917–19 and on examination service 4.40. Mine recovery 3.45–11.45.

QUEEN of the MAY Pilot 240/95. Hired as calibrating vessel 8.1943–12.45.

QUEEN of the NORTH Paddle 590/95. Hired as M/S 29.3.1916. Sunk 20.7.17 by mine off Orfordness.

QUEEN of the USK Tug 91/85. Hired on harbour service 20.1.1918–19.

QUEEN SALVOR Salvage vessel 800 tons, 170 x 37 ft, 1–3in, 2–20mm. Bellingham IW 30.6.1943 for lend-lease but retained by the USN as VENT.

QUEENSVILLE Tug (RCN). Owen Sound, Ontario 1944. Listed 1958.

QUEEN VICTORIA 1,568/87, 1–3pdr. Hired as netlayer 28.1.1915, purchased 8.15. Sold 12.5.20 to BU.

QUEENWORTH 2,047/25. Hired as M/S 13.2.1940, purchased 17.5.40. Sunk 9.5.41 by air attack in the North Sea.

QUENCHER 75gr. Hired as water boat 6.1918—4.19.

QUENTIN ROOSEVELT French fishery protection vessel 585 tons, seized 3.7.1940. A/S vessel 1940. Training ship 1.43—6.45.

QUERCIA Tr 288/12, 1—12pdr. Hired 1915—19 and as fuel carrier 8.42. Water boat 3.44—46.

QUERNMORE 7,302/98, 3—6in. Hired as escort 29.6.1917. Sunk 31.7.17 by U-boat north of Ireland.

QUEST Tr, 1—6pdr. Hired 1917—19.

QUEST Wh 214/17. Norwegian, hired 11.1940. Water carrier 1943—10.45.

QUESTER Tug 70/99. Hired on harbour service 2.1918—2.19.

QUETTA (ex-JUBBALPORE renamed 1944) Tr, 'Basset' class (RIN). Scindia SN Co, Bombay. Ordered 7.1942. Cancelled 1945.

QUETTA (see JUBBALPORE)

QUICKLY Tr 242/97, 3—12pdr. Hired as decoy ship (Q.32) 7.1915—18. (Also operated as MASTER.)

QUICKSAND Admiralty steel Dr, 97gr. Colby 1918. Sold 1921, same name. (Served as EPHRETAH in WW.II.)

QUICKSET Dr 78/09. Hired 1916—19.

QUICKSTEP 1,446/09. Hired as ammo. carrier (RFA) 8.11.1914—23.4.18.

QUIET WATERS Dr 117/31. Hired as A/P Dr 9.1939. Target towing 1944—2.46.

QUINCE Tug 170 tons. Hired as M/L, 8 mines, 1918—19.

QUINTIA Dr 90/14, 1—3pdr. Hired 1915—19 and as degaussing vessel 5.40—46.

QUIRPON (see MMS.240)

QUI SAIT Dr 83/09. Hired 1915—19.

RAASAY (see SHEPPEY)

RACCOON (ex-*Halonia*) Yt 358/31. Commissioned (RCN) 12.1940. Sunk 7.9.42 by U-boat in the Gulf of St Lawrence.

RACE FISHER Cstr 493/92. Hired as ammo. carrier (RFA) 11.1.1915. Fleet messenger 29.7.15. Wrecked 25.3.19 in the Mediterranean.

RACER II Dr 84/06. Hired 1915—19.

RACHEL FLETT Dr 91/14. Hired as A/P Dr 12.1939. Harbour service 10.40—1.46.

RACIA (ex-*Ocean*) Tug 410/95. Purchased in WW.I. Sold 23.6.20.

RADIANT II Dr 95/07, 1—3pdr. Hired 1916—19.

RADIANT Yt 550/27. Hired as A/S Yt 9.1939. Radar training 1941—6.45.

RADIATION Admiralty steel Dr, 96gr. Ouse SB 1920. Sold 1920, renamed *Agnes Gardner.* (AGNES GARDNER in WW.II.)

RADNOR CASTLE Tr 275/17. Purchased as M/S 8.1939. Arrived 17.5.47 Ward, Briton Ferry to BU.

RAETIA Tr 295/12, 1–12pdr. Hired 1915–19 and as M/S, 2–MG, 8.39. Fuel carrier 3.44–2.46.

RAGLAN CASTLE Tr 274/15, 1–12pdr. Hired 1915–19.

RAGLAN CASTLE Tr 280/19. Hired as M/S 8.1939, later purchased. Sold 9 47 Ceylon Govt.

RAHMAN Wh 209/26. Hired as M/S 9.1939. Sunk 1.3.42 by unknown cause at Batavia.

RAINBAND Admiralty steel Dr, 96gr. Ouse SB 17.6.1919. Sold 1920, renamed *Craiglea.*

RAINBOW Tr 176/06, 1–3pdr. Hired 1915–19. (Served as DOLORES in WW.II.)

RAINDROP Tr 167/12, 1–3pdr. Hired 1914–19.

RAINSTORM Admiralty wood Dr, 97gr. Colby 1918. Sold 1921, same name.

RAINSTORM (see BUSEN 6)

RAIT CASTLE Dr 84/12. Hired on harbour service 11.1914–19 and on harbour service 1942–45.

RAJAH Tr 172/99, 1–6pdr. Hired 1914–18.

RAJEA 300gr. Hired as store carrier 10.1941. Depot ship 1944–5.46.

RAJPUTANA 16,644/26, 8–6in, 2–3in. Hired as AMC 9.1939. Sunk 13.4.41 by 'U.108' west of Ireland.

RALCO Tr 228/12, 1–12pdr, 1–6pdr. Hired 1914–18 and as A/P Tr 11.39–22.1.40.

RALEIGH (see GLITTER)

RAMBLER DY paddle tug 690 tons, 145 x 27½ ft. J.Brown 21.12.1908. Sold 1953 to BU.

RAMBLER ROSE Dr 81/10. Hired on examination service 3.1940–4.46.

RAMBLING ROSE Dr 59/09. Hired 1915–19.

RAMDAS Cstr 406/35. Hired as A/P vessel (RIN) 9.193. A/S training 1945–6.46.

RAMESES Tr 155/94. Hired as nominal depot ship 1917–18.

RAMIER French navy tug 685 tons. Seized 7.1940 at Southampton. A/P vessel 8.40. BBV 11.40. Salvage vessel 1.43. To MWT 1943.

RAMILLIES 2,935/92. Hired as mine carrier (RFA) 3.8.1914–30.8.16.

RAMNA Wh 108/08, 1–6pdr. Hired 1915, later purchased. Sold 13.11.19.

RAMPANT (see EMPIRE SENTINEL)

RAMPUR Tr, 'Basset' class (RIN). Calcutta 19.7.1941. Renamed LAHORE (RPN) 1948. Sold 22.1.59.

RAMSEY (ex-*The Ramsey*) 1,443/95, 2–12pdr. Hired as ABS 28.10.1914. Sunk 8.8.15 by the German METEOR off the Firth of Forth.

RANCHI 16,738/25, 8–6in, 2–3in. Hired as AMC 27.8.1939–2.43.

RANDFONTEIN (see POL.I)

RANEE Tr 194/00. Hired 1918–19.

RANGOL (see MOUNT ROYAL)

RANNAS Dr 85/07, 1–3pdr. Hired 1915–19.

RANPURA 16,688/25, 8–6in, 2–3in. Hired as AMC 6.9.1939. Purchased 1943 converted to repair ship 18,250 tons, 20–20mm. Arrived 25.5.61 at Spezia to BU.

RAPIDE III Tug 85/80. French, seized 1940. Boom tender 1940–45.

RAPIDOL Oiler (RFA) 4,900 tons, 335 x 41½ ft. Gray 23.4.1917. Sold 13.3.48, renamed *Louise Moller*.

RATA Cstr 974/29. Hired as M/S (RNZN) 11.1940. Paid off 11.10.43.

RATAPIKO Tr 247/12, 1–12pdr. Hired 1914–19 and as M/S 7.40–12.45.

RATHVEN Dr 87/08, 1–6pdr. Hired 1915–19.

RATHVEN BURN DY tug, 51gr, 69 x 16 ft. McGregor, Kirkintilloch 1919. Listed to 1946.

RATNAGIRI Cstr 590/35. Hired as A/S vessel (RIN) 9.1939–46.

RATTLER Cutter 10. Hired 1793–96.

RATTLER (ex-*Splint*) Wh 136/12, 1–6pdr. Norwegian, purchased 4.1915. Renamed PRATTLER 7.16. Sold 6.3.19.

RATTLER Tr 149/91. Hired 1917–19.

RATTRAY Tr 182/00. Hired 1914–15 and 1917–19.

RAUB 1,161/26. Hired as M/S 18.9.1939. A/P vessel 12.41. Sunk 22.1.42 by Japanese air attack on the east coast of Sumatra.

RAVEN II 4,678/03, 1–12pdr, 2–A/C. German *Rabenfels* seized 8.1914 in the Mediterranean, commissioned as seaplane carrier 12.6.15, renamed 8.15. Became collier 1917, renamed *Ravenrock*.

RAVEN III Tr 131/97. Hired 1916–19.

RAVENSWOOD Paddle 345/91, 1–6pdr. Hired as M/S 26.5.1915–28.3.19 and as A/A ship, 3–20mm, 5–MG, 20.8.41, purchased 14.11.42. Laid up 11.4.45. (Was RINGTAIL 9.43–44 as nominal base ship.)

RAWALPINDI 16,697/25, 8–6in, 2–3in. Hired as AMC 9.1939. Sunk 23.11.39 by the German SCHARNHORST south of Iceland.

RAWCLIFFE 866/06. Hired as ammo. carrier (RFA) 1.3.1915–12.3.19.

RAY Admiralty non-standard wood Dr, 86gr. Stephen, Banff 1917. Sold 14.10.27.

RAYMOND Tr 221/10. Belgian, hired 1917–19.

RAYMOND Tr 131/30. Belgian, hired as BBV 8.1940. Target towing 11.42–11.45.

RAYMONT Tr 226/16, 1–6pdr. Hired 1916–19 and as A/P Tr 11.39.
M/S 8.40, store carrier 4.44–3.46.

RAY of HOPE Dr 98/25. Hired as M/S 11.1939. Sunk 10.12.39 by mine
in the Thames estuary.

RAYON d'OR Tr 342/12. Hired as M/S (RCN) 1939–45.

REALITY Dr 87/11, 1–3pdr. Hired 1.1915–19.

REALIZE Dr 108/14, 1–3pdr. Hired 1.1915–19.

REAPER Dr 90/07, 1–6pdr. Hired 12.1914–19.

REAPER II MFV 51/02. Hired on harbour service 1.1941. Renamed
PIPER 1944. Returned 10.45.

REBOUNDO Tr 278/20. Hired as M/S 9.1939–12.45.

REBUFF (ex-*Speedwell VI*) MFV 34net. Hired as boom tender 3.1.1940–
11.45

RECEPTIVE Dr 86/13. Hired 8.1915–19 and as A/P Dr 4.40. Sunk
3.7.41 by mine in the Thames estuary.

RECEPTO Tr 245/13. Hired 1914. Sunk 16.2.17 by mine in Tees Bay.

RECLAIM Dr 95/13, 1–6pdr. Hired 11.1914–19.

RECLAIM (see SALVERDANT)

RECLAIMER 296/85. Hired as salvage vessel 20.3.1915–26.2.16.

RECOIL Tr 344/38. German *Blankenburg*. A/S Tr 6.40. Sunk 28.9.40
in the Channel, probably mined.

RECOMPENSE Dr 58/02, 1–3pdr. Hired 1915–19.

RECONO Tr 248/16, 1–6pdr. Hired 1916–19 and as A/P Tr 11.39. M/S
6.40. BBV 1.45–7.45.

RECORD Dr 67/04. Hired 1918–19.

RECORDER Cable ship 2,276/02. In service 1942–46.

RECORDO Tr 230/10, 1–3pdr. Hired as M/S 1915–20 and as A/P Tr
11.39–8.2.40.

RECORD REIGN Ketch 184/97. Hired as decoy ship 10.1917–12.18.

RECOVERY DY mooring vessel 735 tons, 135 x 27½ ft. Fleming &
Ferguson 26.2.1907. Sold 25.8.23.

RECOVERY (ex-*Chivelstone*) Tug 194/99, 105 x 24 ft. Purchased as DY
tug 1902. Sold 1905, same name.

RECOVERY (see ROVER)

RECRUIT Dr 94/15. Hired as BDV 1.6.1915–19.

REDBREAST 1,313/08. Hired as fleet messenger 17.7.1915. Sunk
15.7.17 by 'UC.38' in the Mediterranean.

REDCAP (ex-*Ocean Transport?*) 313/10? Fitting as M/S in Trinidad
1.1943–5.44.

RED DRAGON (ex-*Y d'Draig Goch*) 952 tons. Purchased as store hulk
in WW.I. Listed to 1946.

RED GAUNTLET II Paddle 277/95. Hired as M/S 4.6.1916, purchased
30.7.17. Sold 22.4.19.

RED GAUNTLET Tr 338/30, 1–12pdr. Hired as M/S 8.1939. Sunk 5.8.43 by E-boat torpedo in the North Sea.

REDPOLE (ex-*Racehorse*) Wood paddle DY tug, 360bm. Purchased on stocks 4.1855; Plymouth 9.5.55. Sold 1871 at Devonport.

REDRIFT Dr 97/08, 1–3pdr. Hired 1.1915–19.

REDSHANK (ex-TURBOT renamed 11.1942) M/L Tr 680 tons, 146 x 25 ft. Cochrane 28.8.42. Arrived 9.7.57 Young, Sunderland to BU.

RED SKY Admiralty wood Dr, 94gr. Stephen, Banff 1918. Sold 1921, same name. Hired as M/S 11.39. Examination service 1941. Harbour service 1944–3.46.

REDSTART 904/80, 1–6pdr. Hired as fleet auxiliary 24.2.1915. Boom gate vessel 1917–19.

REDSTONE 3,110/18. Purchased 1940. Sunk 2.5.40 as blockship at Scapa Flow.

REDWALD Dr 80/12, 1–3pdr. Hired 1914–19.

REDWOOD (ex-*St Rose*) M/S Tr 555 tons, 140 x 24 ft, 1–4in. Purchased 3.1939. Sold 1946.

REED Dr 99/11, 1–3pdr. Hired 1914–19 and as M/S 9.39. A/P Dr 8.40. Sunk 7.11.40 by mine in the Thames estuary.

REEVE Tr 172/05, 1–6pdr. Hired as M/S 1914–19.

REFLECT Dr 78/08. Hired on examination service 2.1941–3.45.

REFLECTION Admiralty steel Dr. Stephen, Banff. Cancelled 1919.

REFORMO Tr 242/99. Hired on harbour service 2.1941–46.

REFRACTION Admiralty wood Dr, 93gr. Stephen, Banff 1918. Sold 1921, same name. Hired as M/S 11.39–3.45.

REFUNDO Tr 258/17, 1–6pdr. Hired 1917–19 and as A/P Tr 11.39. M/S 6.40. Sunk 18.12.40 by mine off Harwich.

REGAIN Dr 87/14, 1–3pdr. Hired 1915–19.

REGAL Tr 212/06, 1–6pdr. Hired 1915–19.

REGAL Tr 409/33. Purchased as A/S Tr 8.1939. Sold 7.45.

REGARD Tug 144/38. Listed as DY tug from 1959. Sold 1966, BU in Belgium.

REGARDO Tr 248/15, 1–6pdr. Hired 1915–19 and as A/P Tr 11.39. M/S 5.40. Fuel carrier 1.44–12.45.

REGENT Store carrier (RFA) 19,000 tons, 600 x 77 ft, 2–40mm. Harland & Wolff 9.3.1966.

REGENT BIRD Dr 88/09. Hired as BDV 4.1915–19 and on examination service 8.39. Harbour service 1942–12.45.

REGINA 60/1866. Hired as fleet auxiliary 5.1915–19.

REGINA Tug 40/87. Hired 1916–18.

REGINA Tr 125/91. Hired 1917–19.

REGINA STELLA Dr 84/10. Hired as store carrier 3.1940–45.

REGISTAN 5,886/30, 2–6in, 1–3in. Hired as OBV 13.9.1940–11.41.

REHEARO Tr 266/17. Hired as M/S 9.1940–1.46.

REIDS Dr 92/18, 1–6pdr. Hired as A/P Dr 12.1939–12.45.

REIGATE (see BD.30)

REIGHTON WYKE Tr 465/37. Hired as A/S Tr 8.1939–12.45.

REINDEER 1,281/97, 2–12pdr. Hired as M/S 2.10.1914, later purchased. Sold 3.1.20.

REINDEER II Tr 192/02, 1–6pdr. Hired 1916–19.

REINDEER (ex-*Mascotte*) Yt 337gr/26, 1–12pdr. American, commissioned (RCN) 25.7.1940. For disposal 10.45.

REINE des FLOTS Tr 608/23. French A/P Tr seized 3.7.1940 at Portsmouth. A/S Tr (Free-French crew) 8.40. To French navy 1946.

REJOICE Dr 83/15, 1–3pdr. Hired 1915–19.

RELEVO Tr 176/12. Hired 1915. Wrecked 30.12.16 at El Arish.

RELIANCE II Tr 203/04, 1–6pdr. Hired 1915–19.

RELIANCE III Dr 75/04. Hired 1915–19.

RELIANCE Dr 66/03. Hired on harbour service 5.1915–19.

RELIANT (ex-*London Importer*) 7,938/23, 17,000 tons, 450 x 58 ft. Purchased as store carrier (RFA) 24.3.1933. Sold 4.48, renamed *Anthony G.*

RELIANT (ex-*Somersby*) 5,898/54, 13,730 tons, 440 x 61 ft. Purchased as store carrier (RFA) 1957.

RELONZO Tr 245/14, 1–12pdr. Hired 1915–20 and as A/P Tr 11.39. M/S 5.40. Sunk 20.1.41 by mine off Liverpool.

REMAGIO Tr 174/13, 1–3pdr. Hired 1915–18.

REMARGO Tr. Hired 1917–19.

REMARKO Tr 245/14. Hired 1915. Sunk 3.12.16 by mine off Lowestoft.

REMEMBRANCE 3,660/10. Hired as decoy ship 10.1915. Sunk 14.8.16 by 'U.38' in the Mediterranean.

REMEMBRANCE Dr 82/10, 1–3pdr. Hired 1916–19.

REMEXO Tr 231/12, 1–6pdr. Hired 1915–19 and as A/P Tr 11.39. M/S 6.40. BBV 1944–12.45.

REMILLO Tr 266/17, 1–3pdr. Hired as danlayer 4.1940. A/P Tr 9.40. Sunk 27.2.41 by mine off the Humber.

REMINDO Tr 256/17. Hired 1917. Sunk 2.2.18 by unknown cause off Portland.

REMO Tr 209/00, 1–6pdr. Hired 1.1915, later purchased. Sold 1921.

RENAISSANCE Dr 104/14, 1–6pdr. Belgian, hired as A/P Dr (Polish crew) 18.6.1940. RN crew 1942–11.45. (Also known as P.1.)

RENARD (ex-*Winchester*) Yt 466/16. American, commissioned as A/S Yt (RCN) 5.1940. Laid up 11.45, sold 1947 as floating power station.

RENARRO Tr 230/13, 1–3pdr. Hired 1915. Sunk 10.11.18 by mine in the Dardanelles.

RENASCENT Dr 100/26. Hired as M/S 11.1939. Echo vessel 1943—1.46.
RENCO Tr 230/10, 1—6pdr. Hired 1915—19.
RENE Dr 89/14, 1—3pdr. Hired 1915—19 and on harbour service 1.1940—5.46.
RENE de BESNERAIS Tug 219/31. French, seized 3.7.1940. BBV 9.40. Harbour tug 1.41. To MWT 1944.
RENE—GEORGES Dr 92/31. French CAP FREHEL, ex-Belgian René-Georges seized 3.7.1940 at Southampton. A/P Dr 1940. Fate unknown.
RENNES (see CH.8)
RENNET (ex-*Deepdale Wyke*) Tr 335/28, 567 tons, 2—MG. Purchased as BDV 5.1939. Sold 11.1.46, renamed *Red Archer*.
RENOVATE Dr 81/09, 1—6pdr. Hired 1.1915—19.
RENOVELLE MFV 27net/30. Hired on examination service 7.1940—8.42
RENOVO Tr 170/04. Hired 1917—19.
RENOWN II Tug 54/79. Hired 7.8.1914—19.
RENOWN Dr 86/04, 1—3pdr. In service 1918.
RENZO Tr 230/13, 1—6pdr. Hired as M/S 1914—19 and as A/P Tr 11.39. M/S 5.40—10.45.
REO II Wood tug 129/31. Hired as skid M/S (RCN) 1941—45.
REPERIO Tr 230/07. Hired as BDV 1915—19.
REPLENISH Dr 83/13, 1—3pdr. Hired 1916—19.
REPLY Tug 20/09. Hired 9.1939—2.46.
REPORTO Tr 230/08, 1—6pdr. Hired 1.1915—19 and as A/P Tr 27.11.39 —3.2.40.
REPRO Tr 230/10, 1—6pdr. Hired 2.1915. Sunk 26.4.17 by mine off Todd Head.
RESCUE Tug 357/04. Hired as salvage tug 23.3.1915—19.
RESCUE (see HORSA)
RESEARCH MFV 43net/03. Hired as BDV 9.1940. Store carrier 1943—45.
RESERCHO Tr 258/17. Hired 1917—19.
RESERVE Rescue tug, 'B.A.T' class. Levingston 18.7.1942 on lend-lease to the RAN. Purchased 1946. On sale list 1961.
RESISTANCE Dr 85/31. Belgian, hired as A/P Dr 7.10.1940—3.46.
RESMILO Tr 258/17, 1—12pdr. Hired 1917—19 and as M/S 9.40. Sunk 20.6.41 by air attack at Peterhead.
RESOLUTE Dr 82/07, 1—3pdr. Hired 1915—19.
RESOLUTE Salvage vessel 300 tons, 95 x 24 ft. Gulfport, Port Arthur Texas 26.3.1942 for lend-lease, but retained by the USN.
RESOLUTION Lugger 10. Hired 1795—1801.
RESOLUTION Cutter, 86bm. Hired 8.1807—5.1814.
RESOLVE Rescue tug 1,400 tons, 175 x 34 ft, 1—12pdr. Ayrshire Co, Irvine 30.7.1918. On sale list 1950. (On DY service 1919—39 and 1945—49.)

RESOLVE (ex-*Empire Zona*) DY tug, 290/46. Renamed 1949.

RESOLVO Tr 231/13, 1–6pdr. Hired 1915–20 and as M/S 11.39. Mined 12.10.40 in the Thames estuary and beached near Sheerness.

RESONO Tr 230/10. Hired 1915. Sunk 26.12.15 by mine near the Sunk light.

RESOUND (see ECHO)

RESOURCE DY mooring vessel 735 tons, 135 x 26½ ft. Bow McLachlan 7.6.1910. Sold 6.24.

RESOURCE II Yt 1,000/1865. Hired as depot ship 1.10.1915. Lost by fire 12.11.15 in Southampton harbour.

RESOURCE Store carrier (RFA) 19,000 tons, 600 x 77 ft, 2–40mm. Scotts 11.2.1966 (named 8.2.66).

RESPARKO Tr 248/16. Hired 1916–19 and as A/P Tr 11.39. M/S 4.40. Sunk 20.8.40 by air attack at Falmouth.

RESPLENDENT Dr 100/14. Hired 31.3.1915–19.

RESPOND Rescue tug (as RESOLVE). Ayrshire Co 21.11.1918. DY tug 1919. Sold 1956 at Malta, BU in Italy.

RESPONDO Tr 209/05. Hired 1917–19.

RESPONSO Tr 228/12. Hired 1914. Wrecked 31.12.15 on Sanday Island.

RESTART Dr 79/12, 1–3pdr. Hired 1915–19 and as A/P Dr 1–3pdr, 10.40–5.46.

RESTFUL Salvage vessel 950 tons. A.Hall. Cancelled 10.1944.

RESTIVE (see RESTLESS)

RESTIVE Rescue tug 700 tons, 143 x 33 ft, 1–3in. Cochrane 4.9.1940. For disposal 1964.

RESTLESS DY paddle tug 700 tons, 144 x 27½ ft. Day Summers 7.6.1902. Renamed RESTIVE 1916. Sold 6.37.

RESTLESS WAVE Dr 84/07. Hired 1916–19 and as A/P Dr 7.40–10.45.

RESTORE Dr 93gr. Hired 1915. Sunk 12.10.15 by U-boat in the Adriatic.

RESTORE Dr 87/11. Hired as BBV 5.1940. Harbour service 1944–4.46.

RESTRIVO Tr 245/14, 1–3pdr. Hired as M/S 1914–19 and as A/P Tr 11.39. M/S 4.40–1.45.

RESULT Dr 63/03. Hired as tender 1.1915; ALLENBY 8.18–19.

RESULT Aux.schooner 122/93, 2–12pdr, 2–TT. Hired as decoy ship 29.11.1916–17.

RESURGE Dr 100/18. Hired on harbour service 9.1940–46.

RESURGENT (ex-*Chungchow*) 9,403/51, 14,400 tons, 450 x 63 ft. Purchased as store carrier (RFA) 1953.

RETAINER (ex-*Chungking*) 9,393/50 and as RESURGENT, purchased 1952.

RETAKO Tr 245/14, 1–3pdr. Hired 1915–19 and as A/P Tr 11.39. M/S 6.40–2.45.

RETORT Rescue tug (as RESOLVE). Day Summers 1918. DY tug 1919. On sale list 12.57.

RETRIEVER Dr 90/07, 1–3pdr. Hired 1914–20. (RETRIEVER II from 1917.)

RETRIEVER Tr 138/91. Hired in WW.I.

RETRIEVER Cable ship 674/09. Hired (red ensign) 1942–46.

RETRIEVER (see URANIA)

RETRUDO Tr 178/13, 1–6pdr. Hired 1915–19.

RETURNO Tr 244/14, 1–6pdr. Hired 1915–19 and as A/P Tr 12.39. M/S 6.40. Fuel carrier 3.44–45.

REVELLO Tr 230/08, 1–3pdr. Hired 1915–19 and as A/P Tr, 1–6pdr, 11.39. M/S 7.40–43.

REVELSTOKE Motor M/S (RCN) 228 tons, 105 x 22 ft. Star SY 3.11.1943. On sale list 12.57.

REVENGER Tug 245/05. Hired 3.8.1914. Capsized 23.4.19 in St Bride's Bay.

REVERBERATION Admiralty wood Dr, 97gr. Colby 1918. Sold 1919, same name. Hired as flare Dr, 1–3pdr, 11.1939. A/P and harbour service 8.40–2.45.

REVILLE French DY tug seized 1940 at Southampton. Fitting as examination service vessel 1.41, not listed 1942. (Spelt REVEILLE in most lists.)

REVIVE Yt 95/22. Hired as BBV 7.1940, purchased 11.41. Accommodati ship 2.45. Sold 3.46.

REVUE Tug 245/39. Hired as DY tug 10.1939–46.

REWARD Dr 79/06, 1–3pdr. Hired 1916–19.

REWARD Rescue tug 1,118 tons, 190 x 38½ ft, 1–3in. Robb, Leith 31.10.1944.

REWGA Dr 34net/37, 2–MG. Hired as danlayer 2.1940. Harbour service 1941–45.

REZALA Yt 79/21. Hired as HDPC 10.1939, purchased 3.42. Laid up 6.45, later sold.

R.H. DAVIDSON Tr 210/16. Hired 1916–19.

RHIANNON Yt 137/14. Hired as A/P Yt 15.9.1914. Sunk 20.7.15 by mine off the Longsands.

RHINOCEROS Salvage vessel 706/97. Hired 26.2.1917–10.11.20.

RHODA (ex-*Industry*) Cutter 6, 46bm. Hired 4.1804–12.04.

RHODES Hopper 550 tons dw, hired as boom gate vessel 1.1940–43.

RHODESIA Tr 193/99. Hired 1915. Wrecked 19.4.15 near Stornoway.

RHODORA Yt 709/29. Hired as A/S Yt 9.1939. Sunk 7.9.40 in collision in the Bristol Channel.

RHONE Tr 117/93. Hired 1914–18.

RHOUMA Yt 337/02, 2–6pdr. Hired as A/P Yt 1.10.1914–2.4.19.

RHU 254/40. Hired as M/L 22.10.1941. Captured 15.2.42 by the Japanese at Singapore.

RIALTO Tr 139/97, 1–6pdr. Hired as M/S 1.1915–19.

RIAN Cstr 232/34. Dutch, hired as BBV tender 5.1940. To MWT 4.43.

RIANO Tr 212/06, 1–6pdr. Hired 1915–19 and 4.44–10.44.

RIANT Dr 95/19. Hired as M/S 11.1939. Foundered 25.1.40 in a storm off the west coast of Scotland.

RIBBLE II Tr 197/00, 1–6pdr. Hired 1.1915–19.

RIBBLE Tr 193/04, 1–6pdr. Hired 1917–19.

RIBY Tr 214/10. Hired as BDV 1915–19.

RICHARD & MARTHA 46-gun ship, 500bm. Hired 1653–54.

RICHARD BACON Tr, 'Castle' type, 290gr. Cook Welton & Gemmell 2.11.1917. Sold 1921, renamed *Hagnaby*. (Served as COMMODATOR, 281gr, in WW.II.)

RICHARD BAGLEY Tr, non-standard 'Castle' type, 269gr. Cook Welton & Gemmell 9.6.1917. Sold 1922, renamed *Malacolite.*

RICHARD BAIVE (BANE?) Tr, 'Castle' type. Cook Welton & Gemmell. Cancelled 1919.

RICHARD BENNETT Tr, non-standard 'Strath' type, 227gr. Hall Russell 17.5.1917. Sold 1921, same name. Hired as M/S (SAN) 15.9.39–10.5.40.

RICHARD BOWDEN Tr, 'Strath' type, 202gr. Hall Russell 11.4.1919. Sold 1919, renamed *Cissie Scratchard.*

RICHARD BRISCOLL Tr, 'Strath' type, 203gr. Hall Russell 9.10.1918. Sold 1921, renamed *Braconburn.* (BRACONBURN in WW.II.)

RICHARD BULKELEY Tr, 'Mersey' type, 324gr. Cochrane 21.8.1917. Lent USN 1918 and lost 1919 in their service.

RICHARD COLLIVER Tr, 'Mersey' type, 331gr. Lobnitz 1918. Sold 1922, renamed *Laurette.*

RICHARD CROFTS Tr, 'Castle' type, 290gr. Cook Welton & Gemmell 13.6.1918. Sold 1920, same name. Hired as M/S 8.39–8.45.

RICHARD CUNDY Tr, 'Castle' type, 276gr. Ailsa 12.8.1919. Sold 1920, renamed *River Clyde.* (RIVER CLYDE in WW.II.)

RICHARD DORRODALE Tr, 'Mersey' type. Goole SB. Cancelled 1919.

RICHARD HEAVER Tr, 'Strath' tupe, 202gr. Fullerton 1918. Sold 1920, renamed *Forthvale.*

RICHARD IRVIN Tr 197/09, 1–6pdr. Hired as M/S 2.8.1914–19.

RICHARD JEWELL Tr, 'Mersey' type, 312gr. Cochrane 6.8.1918. Sold 1922, renamed *Lord Knaresborough.* (Served as FAIRWAY in WW.II.)

RICHARD LEE BARBER Tug 122/40. Hired as rescue tug 1.1944–7.45.

RICHARD ROBERTS Tr, 'Castle' type, 275gr. Smiths Dk 6.6.1917. Sold 1920, same name.

RICHARD WELFORD 1,349/08, 1–12pdr. Hired as ABS 5.1.1915–28.2.19.

RICHMOND Tr 162/97. Hired 1918–19.

RICHMOND CASTLE Tr 178/01, 1–6pdr. Hired 1914–19.

RIFSNES Tr 431/32, 1–12pdr. Hired as M/S 8.1939. Sunk 20.5.40 by air attack off Ostend.

RIFT Admiralty wood Dr, 94gr. Smith, Buckie 7.1920. Sold 1920, renamed *Doorie Brae.* (DOORIE BRAE in WW.II.)

RIG Dr 96/11. Hired as tender 4.1915–19 and as M/S, 2–MG, 12.39. A/P Dr 8.40–11.45.

RIGGER Paddle 574/74. Purchased as store hulk in WW.I. Sold 23.10.19 Burntisland S Bkg Co.

RIGHTO Tr 278/20. Hired as M/S 9.1939–11.44

RIGHTWHALE Admiralty Wh, 'Z' class. Smiths Dk 10.9.1915. Sold 6.3.20, renamed *Rio Tambo.*

RIGOLETTO Tr 212/06, 1–12pdr. Hired 1915–19 and as BBV 4.40. Fuel carrier 4.44–7.45.

RILETTE Tr 212/17, 1–12pdr. Hired 1917–19.

RIME Admiralty wood Dr, 93gr. Stephen, Banff 1919. Sold 1921, same name. Hired as M/S 12.39–11.45.

RIMU Tr 'Castle' type (RNZN), composite-built. Seager, Auckland 9.9.1941. Sold 1955 to BU; hull sunk 21.8.58 as bombing target off Cuvier Island.

RIMUTAKA 16,575/23. Hired as AMC 8.1939–9.39 (not suitable).

RINALDO II Tr 163/00, 1–6pdr. Purchased as M/S 1914. Sold 1921.

RINGWOOD 755/26. Hired as netlayer 9.1941–6.46.

RINOVIA Tr 429/31. Hired as M/S 8.1939. Sunk 2.11.40 by mine off Falmouth.

RINTO Tr 169/00, 1–6pdr. Hired 1914–19.

RION Yt 324/28. Hired as A/S Yt 9.1939. Renamed NOIR 6.44. For return 6.45.

RIO NERVION Tug. In service as M/S 1944–46 in the East Indies.

RIPARVO Tr 230/13, 1–3pdr. Hired 1915. Sunk 2.11.18 in collision in the Mediterranean.

RIPPLE DY tank vessel. Morts Dock, Sydney 1.1887. Listed in 1909 as a hulk.

RIPPLE DY tank vessel 390 tons. Foster & Minty, Balmain NSW 1904. To RAN 1.7.13. Listed to 1925.

RIPPLEDYKE (ex-*Empire Tesbury*) Petrol carrier (RFA), 975/46. Transferred from MOT 1952. Sold 3.60.

RISBAN Tug 159/24. French, seized 3.7.1940. Mine-watching 1940. Harbour tug 1942–45.

RISING SEA Admiralty wood Dr, 97gr. Colby 1918. Sold 1921, same name. Hired on harbour service 9.39–1.46.

RISING SUN Dr 81/06, 1–6pdr. Hired 1915–19.

RISKATO Tr 248/15, 1–6pdr. Hired 1915–19 and as A/P Tr, 1–12pdr, 6.40–5.46.

RISOR (see KOS V)

RISTANGO Tr 178/13, 1–6pdr. Hired 1915–19 and as boom gate vessel 6.40. Sunk 14.11.40 in collision with the Sheerness boom.

RIVAL II Dr 95/07, 1–3pdr. Hired 2.1915–20 and as RIVAL, M/S, 11.39. Renamed ARCADY 4.40. Danlayer 1943–6.45.

RIVAL (see JASON)

RIVER ANNAN Tr 204/19. Hired as BDV 11.1939–11.45.

RIVER CLYDE 3,913/05. Purchased as landing ship 12.4.1915. Sold 2.20 at Malta, renamed *Angela*.

RIVER CLYDE Tr 276/19. Hired as M/S 8.1939. Sunk 5.8.40 by mine off Aldeburgh.

RIVER ESK Tr 203/18, 1–12pdr. Hired as A/P Tr 6.1940–7.45.

RIVER FISHER Cstr 457/99. Hired as fleet messenger 19.7.1915–19.9.19.

RIVER GARRY Tr 203/18. Hired on examination service 8.1939–7.45.

RIVER LEVEN Tr 202/18. Hired on examination service 8.1939. Escort 1942. Fuel carrier 4.44–3.45.

RIVER LOSSIE Tr 201/19, 1–6pdr. Hired as A/P Tr 6.1940–2.45.

RIVER NESS Tr 203/18. Hired as A/P Tr 11.1939–2.40.

RIVER SPEY Tr 202/17, 1–3pdr. Hired as danlayer 4.1940. M/S 1941–45.

RIVERTON Tug (RCN) 462tons, 104 x 28 ft. Montreal 15.1.1944.

RIVER TYNE 1,525/20. Purchased as blockship 1940. Sunk 10.6.40 at Dieppe.

RIVER YTHAN Tr 161/05. Listed 3.1940–6.40 as 'to be requisitioned'. Not used.

RIVIERA 1,676/11, 2–4in, 1–6pdr, 4–A/C. Hired as seaplane carrier 11.8.1914–31.5.19. (Served as LAIRDS ISLE in WW.II.)

RIVIERE Tr 226/16, 1–6pdr. Hired 1916–19 and as BBV 4.40–4.44.

RIVULET (see SPABECK)

R.L.GOULDING (see GOULDING)

R.MACKAY Dr 73/10. Hired 1915–19.

RMLs (see MLs 492–500 and 511–533)

R.NICHOLSON Tug 200/91. Hired 8.1914–19.

ROAMER (see LIBERTY)

ROAMER Yt 47/26. Hired on examination service 6.1940 purchased 10.41. Sold 1.46.

ROBEDA Yt 28/39. Hired as HDPC 9.1939, purchased 11.41. Sold 10.45.

ROBERT BARTON Tr, 'Mersey' type, 324gr. Cochrane 28.8.1917. Sold 1922, renamed *Hayburn Wyke*. (HAYBURN WYKE in WW.II.)

ROBERT BETSON Tr, non-standard 'Castle' type, 266gr. Cook Welton & Gemmell 21.4.1917. Sold 1919, renamed *Remillo*. (REMILLO in WW.II.)

ROBERT BOOKLESS Tr, 'Mersey' type, 324gr. Cochrane 23.7.1917. Sold 1921, renamed *Gris Nez*.

ROBERT BOWEN Tr, 'Castle' type, 290gr. Cook Welton & Gemmell 14.3.1918. Sold 1919, same name. Hired as M/S 8.39. Sunk 9.2.40 by air attack off Aberdeen.

ROBERT CAHILL Tr, 'Mersey' type, 307gr. Goole SB 1920. Sold 1921, renamed *Pierre-André*. (PIERRE-ANDRE in WW.II.)

ROBERT CLOUGHTON Tr, 'Castle' type, 275gr. Bow McLachlan 18.12.1917. Ferry service 1919–22 then laid up. Renamed CORONET, BDV, 1–3in, 1933. BU 1953 Pollock Brown, Northam.

ROBERT DARBY Tr, 'Mersey' type. Cochrane. Cancelled 1919.

ROBERT DAVIDSON Tr, 'Castle' type, 275gr. C.Rennoldson 30.11.1917 Sold 1919, renamed *Augustine Isabelle.*

ROBERT DOUBLE Tr, 'Mersey' type, 326gr. Goole SB 1918. Sold 1922, same name.

ROBERT DRUMMOND Tr, 'Mersey' type, 330gr. Ferguson 4.5.1918. Sold 1922, renamed *Salmonby.*

ROBERT DUNDAS Store carrier (RFA) 900 tons, 210 x 35 ft. Grangemouth DY Co 28.7.1939.

ROBERT FAIRCLOTH Tr, 'Strath' type, 206gr. Abdela Mitchell 1918. Sold 1919, renamed *Humphrey*. (HUMPHREY in WW.II.)

ROBERT FINLAY Tr, 'Mersey' type, 325gr. Goole SB 1919. Sold 1919, renamed *Viscount Allenby.*

ROBERT FOREST Tug 33/95. Hired on harbour service 7.8.1916–19.

ROBERT GIBSON Tr, 'Strath' type, 203gr. Scott, Bowling 12.2.1918. Sold 1921, same name.

ROBERT HARDING Tr, 'Strath' type, 204gr. Hawthorns, Leith 1918. Sold 1921, renamed *Henriette*. (HENRIETTE in WW.II.)

ROBERT HASTIE Tr 210/12, 1–6pdr. Hired 1915–19 and as A/P Tr, 1 3pdr, 11.39. Air-sea rescue 1941–1.46.

ROBERT MIDDLETON Store carrier (as ROBERT DUNDAS). Grangemouth DY Co 29.6.1938.

ROBERT MURRAY Tr, 'Mersey' tupe, 324gr. Cochrane 28.6.1919. Sold 1922, renamed *Northlyn*. (NORTHLYN in WW.II.)

ROBERT SMITH Tr 211/15. Hired 1915. Sunk 20.7.17 by unknown cause in the Atlantic.

ROBERT STROUD Tr 219/30. Hired as M/S 8.1939–4.46.

ROBIN Dr 86/03, 1–3pdr. Hired 1914–19.

ROBIN II Tr 169/04, 1 6pdr. Hired 1915–19.

ROBINA 306/14. Hired as A/P vessel 1915–19 and on examination service 8.39. Harbour service 1942–46.

ROBIN HOOD Yt 50/36. Hired as HDPC 10.1939–10.45.

ROBINIA Tr 208/00. Hired 1918–19.

ROBINSON (ex-*C.P. Robinson*) Wh 196/27. Hired as M/S (SAN) 16.6.1940–4.46.

ROB ROY Tr 153/98. Hired 1914–15.
ROBUST DY paddle tug 690 tons, 145 x 28 ft. Bow McLachlan 24.9.1907.
On sale list 1955.
ROCHE BONNE Tr 258/13. Hired as M/S 2.1940. Sunk 7.4.41 by air
attack off the Lizard.
ROCHE CASTLE Tr 214/10, 1–12pdr. Hired 1915–19.
ROCHESTER DY craft, 154bm. Chatham DY 26.11.1833. BU 4.1877
at Chatham. (Also Chatham YC.2.)
ROCHESTER Tr 165/98, 1–3pdr. Hired 1914–19.
ROCHE VELEN Tr 208/18. French M/S seized 7.1940. M/S 11.40. A/P
Tr 3.45–12.45.
ROCHOMIE Dr 79/10. Hired on harbour service 7.1940–2.46.
ROCKALL Dr 114/30. Belgian, hired as M/S 7.1940. Boom tender 1943.
Harbour service 1944–9.45.

'Rock' class tugs, 233gr, 105 x 30 ft. Built in Canda for the MWT and
transferred to the RN in 1946:

ROCKCLIFFE Midland SY, Ontario 1945. Sold 1947, renamed *Taikoo
Cheong.*
ROCKFOREST Canadian SB Co, Kingston 1945. Sold 1947.
ROCKGLEN Canadian SB Co 1945. Renamed FREEDOM 1947.
ROCKLAND Midland SY 1945. Renamed FLARE 1947. On sale list
1959.
ROCKMOUNT Midland SY 1945. Sold 1948, renamed *Sabre.*
ROCKPIGEON Canadian SB Co 1945. Renamed FLAUNT 1947. On
sale list 1959.
ROCKPORT Midland SY 1945. Sold 1947, renamed *Tapline 1.*
ROCKWING Midland SY 1945. Sold 1948, renamed *Tapline 2.*
RODINO Tr 230/13, 1–12pdr. Hired 1915–19 and as A/P Tr 11.39.
M/S 4.40. Sunk 24.7.40 by air attack off Dover. (In some lists as RODINA.)
RODNEY Tr 246/06, 1–6pdr. Hired 1915–19. (RODNEY III from 1917.)
RODNEY II Dr 80/07. Hired 1915–19.
RODNEY Tug 48/87. Hired on harbour service 1917–19.
RODOSTO Tr 174/13, 1–3pdr. Hired 1915–19.
RODRIGO Tr 169/00. Hired 1918–19.
ROEBUCK A.ship, 280bm. Hired 1649–51.
ROEBUCK II 1,094/97, 1–12pdr. Hired as M/S 2.10.1914. Renamed
ROEDEAN 12.14. Sunk 13.1.15 by mine at Longhope.
ROEBUCK 776/25. Hired as BBV 22.10.1940–10.10.45. (ROEBUCK
II from 1942.)
ROEDEAN (see ROEBUCK)
ROGATE (see BD.46)

ROGER BECK Pilot 114/24. Hired on examination service 8.1939–3.42.

ROGER BLONDE Dr 82/31. Belgian, hired as BBV 8.1940–10.45.

ROGER DENISE MFV 73/30. Belgian. Fitting as A/P vessel in 11.1940. Not listed 1.41.

ROGER-JULIETTE Cstr 169/16. French, seized 1940 at Belfast. A/P vessel 10.40–11.45.

ROGER-PIERRE MFV. French, seized 1940. Firefloat 2.41–6.45.

ROGER ROBERT Dr 97/22. Belgian, hired as A/P Dr 10.1940. Examinatio service 7.42–9.45.

ROI LEOPOLD Dr 100/36. Belgian, hired on harbour service 8.12.1943–9.45.

ROLAND Tr 159/99. Hired 1917–19.

ROLANDO Tr 120/96. Hired 1914–19.

ROLL CALL Rescue tug (as RESOLVE). Ferguson 2.8.1918. Sold 8.22, renamed *Romsey*.

ROLLETTA Yt 95/09. Hired as HDPC 9.1940. Degaussing vessel 1942–12.45.

ROLLICKER DY tug (as RESOLVE). Ferguson 16.1.1919. Sold 12.6.22. Repurchased 1933. BU 6.52 Clayton & Davie.

ROLLICKER (see ROVER)

ROLLS ROYCE Tr 238/06. Hired as M/S 7.1940–46.

ROLULO Tr 170/09. Hired 1915. Wrecked 27.5.15 on the Isle of Lewis.

ROMA Yt 62/88. Hired as gunnery tender 5.12.1917–19.

ROMAN Tug 108/06. Hired on harbour service 8.1939–1.46. (served as ROMANCE in WW.I.)

ROMAN (see The ROMAN)

ROMANCE (ex-*Roman*) Tug 108/06. Hired on examination service 6.1.1917–19.

ROMAN EMPIRE Tr 182/98, 1–6pdr. Hired 1.1916–19.

ROMANY ROSE Dr 88/24, 2–MG. Hired as A/P Dr 12.1939. Degaussing vessel 1944–9.45.

ROMARA Yt 66/34. Hired as HDPC 6.1940–11.45.

ROMEO M/S-A/S Tr 545 tons, 150 x 27½ ft, 1–4in, 3–20mm. Inglis 20.3.1941. Sold 1946.

ROMILLY Tr 214/05, 1–12pdr. Hired 1916–19.

ROMSEY Tug 509/30. Hired on examination service 1942–8.45.

ROMULUS Tr 169/85. In service as boom gate vessel 1915.

RONA Scottish Fishery Board vessel 180/38. Hired on examination service 9.1939–3.46.

RONALDSAY Tr, 'Isles' class. Cochrane 14.2.1941. Sold 27.8.46, renamed *Dah Lai*.

RONAY Tr, 'Isles' class. Cochrane 15.2.1945, completed as danlayer. Arrived 13.4.67 at Troon to BU.

RONDEVLEI (see HEKTOR 1)

RONDO Tr 117/93. Hired 1915. Wrecked 3.3.15 in the Shetlands.

RONONIA Tr 213/13, 1–6pdr. Hired 1915–19.

RONSO Tr 248/15, 1–6pdr. Hired 1915–20 and as A/P Tr, 1–6pdr, 11.39. M/S 4.40. Fuel carrier 3.44.–3.46.

ROODEPOORT (see HEKTOR 6)

ROODE ZEE Tug 468/38. Dutch, hired 1941 (Dutch crew). Rescue tug 1.43. Sunk 24.4.44 by E-boat torpedo off Dungeness.

ROOKE Dr 84/08. Hired 11.1914. Sunk 3.8.16 in collision off Deal.

ROOSEVELT Dr 97/07. Hired on harbour service 7.1915–19.

RORQUAL (Z.10) Admiralty Wh, 'Z' class. Smiths Dk 12.8.1915. Sold 6.3.20.

ROSA Tr 242/04, 1–6pdr. Hired 1.1915–19.

ROSA (ex-*Desire*) Dr 83/08. Hired as A/P Dr 11.1939. Sunk 11.9.43 Clyde area; raised. Sold 4.44.

ROSA ARTHUR Dr 114/36. Belgian, hired as A/P Dr 10.1940–9.45.

ROSABELLE Yt 614/01, 1–3in, 2–6pdr. Hired as A/P Yt 28.1.1915–17.3.19 and purchased as ABV 9.39. Sunk 11.12.41 by 'U.374' in the Gibraltar Straits.

ROSALEEN 409/08. Hired as fleet messenger 22.7.1915–10.11.20.

ROSALIND II Tr 174/05, 1–3pdr. Hired 1916–19.

ROSALIND M/S-A/S Tr 545 tons, 150 x 27½ ft, 1–4in, 3–20mm. Inglis 3.5.1941. RNVR, Kenya 8.46. On sale list 1958.

ROSAURA Yt 1,552/05. Hired as ABV 5.11.1939. Sunk 18.3.41 by mine off Tobruk.

ROSE Cutter 10. Hired 1793. Captured 13.10.1800 by the Dutch in the Ems.

ROSE II Cutter 8. Hired 1793–1801.

ROSE Cutter 6, 52bm, 6–3pdr. Hired 6,1803–12.04.

ROSE (ex-*Nizam*) Tr 243/07, 1–6pdr. Purchased as M/S 3.1910. Sold 5.10.20, renamed *Aby*.

ROSE Dr 81/07. Hired as coal boat 1.1915–19.

ROSE II Tr 213/07. Hired 1914. Sunk 23.4.17 by mine in Belfast Lough. (ROSE II listed 6.17-19.)

ROSE III Dr 88/07, 1–3pdr. Hired 1915–19.

ROSE IV Tr 218/11, 1–6pdr. Hired 1915–19 and as danlayer ROSE 3.40. Renamed ROSETTE M/S 1940–11.45.

ROSE V Dr 91/07. Hired 1916.

ROSEACRE Dr 92/18. Hired on harbour service 9.1939–6.45.

ROSEBAY Dr 98/18. Hired on harbour service 1940–9.45. (Bore the name PYRAMUS for a time as nominal base ship.)

ROSEBINE Dr 72/01. Hired on harbour service 8.1915–19.

ROSE BUD Dr 100/07. Hired 1.1915–19 and as M/S 11.39–3.46.

ROSEDALE Dr 87/07, 1–3pdr. Hired 1917–19.

ROSEDEN (ex-*Kittiwake*) MFV 24net/30. Hired 11.1939–7.45.

ROSEHALL Dr 72/09, 1–2½pdr. Hired 1915–19.

ROSE HAUGH Dr 92/18. Hired as M/S 11.1939. Degaussing vessel 6.40–46.

ROSEHEARTY Dr 82/13. Hired 1915–19.

ROSE HILDA Dr 116/30. Hired as M/S 11.1939–4.46.

ROSELEAF (see CALIFOL)

ROSE MARIE MFV. Hired on harbour service 12.1939, purchased 7.42. Laid up at Trincomalee 1.46.

ROSE MARIE Yt 37/26. Hired as HDPC 11.1939, purchased 9.41. Harbour service 1941. Laid up 7.46.

ROSEMMA Dr 92/12, 1–6pdr. Hired 1916–19 and as BBV 1.40–4.45.

ROSEMONDE Tr 364/10. French M/S seized 3.7.1940 at Southampton. M/S 11 40. Sunk 22.1.42 by U-boat in the Atlantic.

ROSE o'DOUNE Dr 64/10. Hired as tender 12.1914–19.

ROSE of ENGLAND Tr 222/08, 1–6pdr. Hired 1.1915–19 and as A/P Tr 11.30–1.40. Hired again as M/S 9.40–1.46.

ROSETTA Tr 236/07, 1 6pdr. Hired 1915–19.

ROSETTA Dr 74/90. Hired as degaussing vessel 2.1941. Lost 13.10.44.

ROSETTE (see ROSE)

ROSE VALLEY Dr 100/18. Hired on examination service 10.1939. Sunk 16.12.43 in collision, probably in the Forth area. (Listed to 7.45.)

ROSEVEAN Tr, 'Isles' class. Cook Welton & Gemmell 17.7.1943. Sold 3.46.

ROSIE Dr 84gr. Hired 1915. Sunk 26.8.16 by air attack in the Adriatic.

ROSITA Yt 119/00. Purchased 1918. Sold 14.8.20.

ROSS ARD Dr 92/11. Hired as M/S 11.1939–10.44.

ROSSKEEN Tr 196/06, 1–12pdr. Hired 1914–19.

ROSSLAND Motor M/S (RCN) 228 tons, 105 x 22 ft. Vancouver SY 14.8.1943. On sale list 1946.

ROSS NORMAN Wood cstr 297/37. Hired as M/S (RCN) 1941. Degaussing vessel 8.41. Skid M/S 1943–44.

ROTHA MFV 84/37, 1–6pdr. Hired as danlayer 2.1940. A/P Dr 8.40. Renamed ELFIN 1941 as nominal base ship. Paid off 1946.

ROTHER (see ANTHONY ASLETT)

ROTHERSLADE Tr 276/17, 1–6pdr. Hired as A/P Tr 6.1940. M/S 6.41–5.46.

ROTO Tr 170/04, 1–6pdr. Hired 1915–19.

ROTTERDAM Tr 231/16. M/S (Dutch crew) 6.40. M/S (RN) 6.43–7.46.

ROULE French DY tug seized 3.7.1940 at Southampton. BDV 8.40–8.45.

ROULETTE Dr 81/07, 1–3pdr. Hired 1915–19.

ROUMELIA (ex-*Roma*) 181/03. Hired as store carrier 3.1918–4.19.

ROUNDSHOT Armament tug, 57gr 97tons. Philip 14.6.1945.

ROUSAY Tr 'Isles' class. Goole SB 20.12.1941. Sold 1948, renamed *Tova.*

ROVENSKA Yt 693/04, 1–12pdr, 1–6pdr. Hired as A/P Yt 14.4.1915–30.3.19.

ROVER Lugger 14 Hired 1798–1801.

ROVER DY tug 620 tons, 145 x 29 ft. Chatham DY 12.10.1908. Renamed ROLLICKER 1929; RECOVERY 3.34. Arrived 18.9.57 at Cork to BU.

ROWAN 1 493/09, 2–12pdr, 1 3pdr. Hired as ABS 14.11.1914–7.7.17 and 11.7.18–15.6.20.

ROWAN M/S Tr 530 tons, 150 x 27½ ft, 1–12pdr. Smiths Dk 12.8.1939. Sold 1946 renamed *Maiken.*

ROWANOL (ex-CEDAROL renamed 1946, ex-EBONOL renamed 1945) Oiler (RFA) 2,670 tons, 218 x 38 ft. Lobnitz 15.5.46.

ROWAN TREE Dr 91/17, 1–MG. Hired as M/S 1.1940. A/P Dr 9.40. Sunk 21.11.41 after grounding at the entrance to Lowestoft harbour.

ROWCLIFFE Sloop 18. Hired 1793–1801.

ROWSAY Tr 207/12. Hired 1917–19.

ROWSLEY Tr 213/12, 1–6pdr. Hired 1915–19.

ROXANO Tr 228/07, 1–3pdr. Hired as M/S 1915–19 and as A/P Tr, 1–6pdr, 11.39. BBV 10.40. Fuel carrier 4.44.–5.45.

ROYAL BANK Dr 90/06. Hired 1915, later purchased. Sold 1921.

ROYAL BRITON Tug 99/85. Hired 5.1916–8.16.

ROYAL BURGH Dr 78/11. Hired 2.1915–19.

ROYAL CHARTER (see BEAVER)

ROYAL DAFFODIL Ferry 591/34. Hired as air target 10.1939–40.

ROYAL EAGLE Paddle 1.539/32. Hired as accommodation ship 23.10.1939. A/A ship, 6–20mm, 6–2pdr, 2.40–16.5.46.

ROYALIST A.ship 16. Hired 1794–98.

ROYALIST Tr 183/98. Hired 1917–19.

ROYALLIEU Tr 211/07, 1–12pdr. Hired 1915–19 and as A/P Tr 11.1939. M/S 8.40–11.45.

ROYAL MARINE A/S Tr 750 tons, 175 x 30 ft, 1–4in, 4–20mm. Cook Welton & Gemmell 22.7.1944. Sold 11.4.46, renamed *Sisapon.*

ROYAL NORMAN Tug 144/81. Hired 5.7.1918–19.

ROYALO Tr 248/16, 1–6pdr. Hired 1916–19 and as A/P Tr 11.39. M/S 4.40. Sunk 1.9.40 by mine south of Cornwall.

ROYAL PEARL (ex-*Pearl*) Paddle 171/97. Hired as M/S 16.4.1917–19.5.19.

ROYAL RUBY (ex-*Ruby*) Paddle 171/97. Hired as M/S 16.4.1917–19.5.19.

ROYAL SAPPHIRE (ex-*Sapphire*) Paddle 223/98. Hired as M/S 16.4.1917–31.10.18.

ROYAL SCOT 1,726/10, 1–4in, 3–12pdr. Hired as ABS 28.10.1914–12.1.19.

ROYAL SCOT 1,444/30. Hired as air target 8.11.1939–41.

ROYAL SCOTSMAN 3,244/36. Hired store carrier (RN) 10.1940. Landing ship 1942–3.45.

ROYAL ULSTERMAN 3,244/36. Hired as store carrier (RN) 30.6.1941. Landing ship 1942–11.45.

ROYDUR Wh 174/11. Hired as M/S 9.1939–11.44.

ROYSTERER DY tug, (as RESOLVE). Thornycroft 4.2.1919. BU 12.54 in Italy.

RUBENS Tr 320/37. Belgian, hired as A/S Tr 8.1940. Sunk 13.2.41 by air attack in the Western Approaches.

RUBY Tr 198/99. Hired 1915. Wrecked 24.11.15 in Grandes Bay, Crete.

RUBY Tr 251/16, 1–6pdr. Hired 1916. Sunk 17.10.17 by U-boat off Ushant.

RUBY (ex-*Cape Bathurst*) Tr 420/33, 568 tons, 1–4in. Purchased as A/S Tr 18.10.1935. Sold 30.4.46, renamed *Caretta.*

RUBY MFV 46net/02. Hired as ferry 1.1941. Wrecked 9.10.42 at Scapa.

RUBY GEM Dr 76/11, 1–3pdr. Hired 1915–19.

RUDILAIS Tr 282/20. Hired as M/S 9.1939–1.46.

RUFF Tr 169/04, 1–6pdr. Hired 1914–19.

RUGBY Tr 274/16, 1–6pdr. Hired 1916–19 and as A/P Tr, 1–12pdr 5.40. M/S 3.42. Fuel carrier 12.43–5.46.

RUISSEAU French navy tank vessel, 350/22, seized 7.1940. Water carrier (Free-French crew) 8.40–11.45.

RUKMAVATI 266/04. Hired as A/P vessel (RIN) 1940–46.

RULE Hired as decoy vessel (Q.35) 1917–18.

RULER of the SEAS Dr 86/09. Hired 1917–18. (Served as KIDDAW in WW.II.)

RUMBA A/S Tr 516 tons, 150 x 27½ ft, 1–4in, 3–20mm. Inglis 31.7.1940 Sold 1947, same name.

RUMOL (see BRAMBLELEAF)

RUNA Yt 95/04. Hired 7.1918–19.

RUNDHORN Dr 98/07. Norwegian, hired on examination service (Norwegian crew) 6.1940. Listed 1941.

RUNNEL Admiralty wood Dr, 97gr. Colby 1918. Sold 1920, same name.

RUNNER (ex-*Champion*) Paddle tug 146/86. Hired on harbour service 7.1914–19.

RUNSWICK BAY Tr 349/29. Hired as M/D 8.1939–7.46.

RUPERT Tr 114/92. Hired as M/S 1914–16.

RUSHCOE Tr, 1–12pdr. Hired 1915–19.

RUSKHOLM Tr, 'Isles' class. Goole SB 4.2.1942. Handed over 2.9.49 Portuguese navy as BALDAQUE da SILVA.

RUSSELL II Tr 246/06, 1–3pdr, 24 mines. Purchased as M/L 1915.
Sold 1920, same name.
RUTHENIA (ex-*Lake Champlain*) 7,208/00, 11,850 tons, 446 x 52 ft.
Purchased as dummy battleship KING GEORGE V 1.11.1914. Water
carrier (RFA) 1915, oiler 1920. Oil hulk at Singapore from 26.3.31.
Captured there by the Japanese, renamed *Choran Maru*.
RUTHIN CASTLE Tr 275/16. Hired 1916. Sunk 21.4.17 by mine off
the Yorkshire coast.
RUTLANDSHIRE Tr 458/36, 1–4in. Hired as A/S Tr 10.1939. Bombed
and ran aground 20.4.40 at Namsos, Norway. Salved by Germans 8.41,
renamed UBIER. (Sunk 6.12.42.
RYDE Paddle 603/37, 1–12pdr. Hired as M/S 27.2.1940. A/A ship,
1–12pdr. 3–20mm, 7.42–7.45.
RYPA MFV 31/19. Norwegian, hired on harbour service 2.1941. Sunk
12.4.41 in Loch Ewe.
RYSA Tr, 'Isles' class. Cochrane 15.3.1941. Sunk 8.12.43 by mine off
Maddalena.

SABINA (ex-*Champion*) Cutter 6, 50bm. Hired 6.1803–12.04.
SABINA Tr 202/19. Hired as A/P Tr 7.1940–45.
SABINE Tr 111/88. Hired 1917–19.
SABINE Tug 488/17, 1–12pdr, 2–MG. American, purchased as rescue
tug 1940. BU 1950 at Gateshead.
SABRA Wh 245/30, 1–12pdr. Purchased as M/S 3.1940. Renamed
DOMINO 1941. Sold 6.45.
SABREUR Tr 188/16, 1–6pdr. Hired 1916–19 and as A/P Tr 12.1939.
M/S 6.40. Renamed BADINAGE 1941. Laid up 1944–45.
SABRINA Yt 513/99, 2–6pdr. Hired as A/P Yt 5.2.1915–25.3.19.
(SABRINA II from 1916.)
SACHEM 5,354/93, 3–6in. Hired as escort 28.5.1917–28.3.19.
SAFR el BAHR Yt 669/94, 2–3in. Egyptian, hired as A/P Yt 23.8.1915–
22.4.19.
SAGENITE Cstr 712/05. Hired as ammo. carrier (RFA) 7.9.1914–19.
SAGITTA Yt 756/08, 2–12pdr, 1–6pdr. Hired as A/P Yt 5.12.1914–
16.2.18 and as ABV 11.39, purchased 10.41. Sold 1946.
SAGITTAS Yt 32/26. Hired (RAN) 9.1941, purchased 9.42. Sold 9.47.
SAHRA Wh 355/36. Hired as M/S 10.1941–44.
SAILOR KING Dr 89/14, 1–6pdr. Hired 1915–19 and on mine
recovery 3.40. M/S 1943–12.45.
ST ABBS Dr 92/95. Hired 1917–19.
ST ABBS Rescue tug, 'Saint' class. Ferguson 17.12.1918. DY tug 1919;
target towing 1939. Sunk 1.6.40 by air attack at Dunkirk.

ST ACHILLEUS Tr 484/34, 1—4in. Hired as A/S Tr 8.1939. Sunk 31.5.40 by mine in the Dunkirk area.

ST ADRIAN (ex-*St George*) Yt 387/27. Hired on examination service 9.1939, purchased 5.42. Calibrating Yt 1941. Sold 9.11.45 Trinity House.

ST AETHENS Dr 76/14. Hired 1.1915—19.

ST AGNES Tr 205/08, 1—6pdr. Hired 1914—19.

ST AGNES Tr, 'Isles' class. Lewis 19.5.1943. Sold 3.46, renamed *Thor*.

SAINT-ALAIN Name given to ML.247 while on loan to the Free-French 7.1941—42.

ST AMANDUS Tr 400/33. Purchased as A/S Tr 7.1939. To French navy 1940 as CANCALAIS.

ST ANDRONICUS Tr 398/33. Purchased as A/S Tr 8.1939. To French navy 1940 as LORIENTAISE.

ST ANNE Rescue tug, 'Saint' class. Ferguson 15.4.1919. Sold 10.22, same name. Hired on examination service (RCN) 1.40—43.

ST ANTHONY 452/36. Hired as A/P vessel (RIN) 1939—45.

ST ANTHONY Tug (RCN) 840 tons, 2—40mm. St John DD 14.5.1956.

ST APOLLO Tr 580/40, 1—4in. Hired as A/S Tr 2.1940. Sunk 22.11.41 in collision with destroyer SARDONYX off the Hebrides.

ST ARCADIUS Tr 399/34. Purchased as A/S Tr 8.1939. To French navy 1940 as La NANTAISE. Seized 3.7.40 at Portsmouth. In 6.45 for return to French navy; sunk 8.7.45 in collision with *Helencrest* in the channel.

ST ARISTELL Rescue tug, 'Saint' class. Crabtree, Yarmouth 1920 and laid up. Sold 7.4.26, same name.

ST ARVANS Rescue tug, 'Saint' class. Day Summers 1919. Sold 25.8.23. (Served as OCEAN EAGLE in WW.II.)

ST ATHAN Rescue tug, 'Saint' class. Day Summers 1919. Sold 17.11.24, same name.

ST ATTALUS Tr 399/34. Purchased as A/S Tr 7.1939. To French navy 1940 as La HAVRAISE.

ST AUBIN Rescue tug, 'Saint' class. Harland & Wolff, Govan 1918. Sold 12.4.24, same name. Hired as M/S 2.40. Laid up 1943.

ST AUSTELL Rescue tug, 'Saint' class. Cancelled 1919.

ST AYLES Dr 78/06. Hired 1915—19.

ST BARBE (see MMS.241)

ST BEES Rescue tug, 'Saint' class. Harland & Wolff, Govan 1918. Sold 7.22, renamed *Henry Burton*.

ST BLAZEY Rescue tug, 'Saint' class. Cran & Somerville, Leith 16.1.1919. DY tug 1919. Condemned 12.7.46; sunk 1947 as target off Bermuda.

ST BONIFACE Rescue tug, 'Saint' class. Cancelled 1919.

ST BONIFACE (ex-ST FERGUS renamed 1919) Rescue tug, 'Saint' class. Fleming & Ferguson 16.6.19. To New Zealand Govt 18.3.25, renamed TOIA 15.4.26. RNZN 1939—47. Sold 1955.

ST BOSWELLS Rescue tug, 'Saint' class. Cran & Somerville 2.5.1919. Sunk 12.6.20 by mine off Terschelling.

ST BOTOLPH Rescue tug, 'Saint' class. Livingstone & Cooper, Hessle 1918. Laid up 1919. Sold 29.12.26 renamed *Kumaki*.

ST BREOCK Rescue tug, 'Saint' class. Cancelled 1919.

ST BREOCK (ex-ST JAMES renamed 1920) Rescue tug, 'Saint' class. Hong Kong & Whampoa 10.11.1919. DY tug 1920. Sunk 14.2.42 by Japanese air attack off Sumatra.

ST BRIAC 2,312/24. Hired as air target 7.6.1941. Sunk 12.3.42 by mine off Aberdeen.

ST BRIDGET Rescue tug, 'Saint' class. Cancelled 1919.

ST BUDEAUX Rescue tug, 'Saint' class. Cancelled 1919.

ST CATHAN Tr 565/36, 1—4in. Hired as A/S Tr 9.1939. Lent USN 2.42; sunk 11.4.42 in collision off S. Carolina.

ST CATHERINE Rescue tug, 'Saint' class. Livingstone & Cooper 6.3.1919. Laid up 1920. Sold 30.4.26, renamed *Canadian National II*.

ST CELESTIN Tr 352/25. Hired as BDV 9.1939—6.46.

ST CHARLES Tug (RCN) 840 tons, 2—40mm. St John DD 10.7.1956.

ST CLAIR Tr 255/03, 1—6pdr. Hired 1915—19 and as M/S 6.40. Renamed SUNSPOT 15.9.40 and purchased. Sold 5.47.

ST CLAIR 1,637/37. Hired 7.1940. Renamed BALDUR base ship 1940. Reverted to ST CLAIR as rescue ship 10.43. Returned 8.45.

ST CLAUDE Rescue tug, 'Saint' class. Cancelled 1919.

ST CLAUDE (ex-ST MARY renamed 1919) Rescue tug 'Saint' class. Livingstone & Cooper 1919. Laid up 1920. Sold 10.25, renamed *Lindfield*.

ST CLEARS Rescue tug, 'Saint' class. Livingstone & Cooper 1919. DY tug 1919. Sold 1948.

ST CLEMENT Rescue tug, 'Saint' class. Ferguson 21.8.1919. Sold 6.21; resold 11.21 Spanish navy as CICLOPE.

ST CLOUD Tr 189/99. Hired 1917—19.

ST COLOMB Rescue tug, 'Saint' class. Crichton, Chester 22.9.1918. Wrecked 16.1.20.

ST COLUMBA 827/12. Hired as base ship 1940—46.

ST COMBS Dr 90/08, 1—3pdr. Hired 1915—19.

ST COMBS HAVEN Dr 89/14. Hired 1.1915—19.

ST CUTHBERT Tr 311/15, 1—12pdr. Hired 1916—19.

ST CYR Tr 315/15, 1—12pdr. Hired 1916—19.

SAINT-CYR Dr. French M/S seized 3.7.1940 at Plymouth. Renamed AD.402 (her French pendant number) 1941. Listed to 1943.

ST CYRUS Rescue tug, 'Saint' class. Crichton 1919. Fleet tug 1920. Signal school 9.39; rescue tug 5.40. Sunk 22.1.41 by mine off the Humber.

ST DAY Rescue tug, 'Saint' class. Taikoo DY Co 20.11.1918. DY tug 1919; fleet tug 1942. Sold 4.48, renamed *Ursus*.

ST DENIS Tr 294/15, 1–12pdr. Hired 1916–19.

ST DOGMAEL Rescue tug, 'Saint' class. Taikoo DY Co 1918. DY tug 1919. Sold 10.50.

ST DOMINIC Rescue tug, 'Saint' class. Hong Kong & Whampoa 1919. Sold 12.11.19 at Hong Kong, same name. Hired 1940. Sunk 18.12.41 by unknown cause in the China Seas.

ST DOMINICA (ex-*Devonia*) Yt 338/95. Hired on examination service 10.1939, later purchased. Laid up 1944. Sold 7.48.

ST DONATS Tr 349/24. Hired as M/S 8.1939. Sunk 1.3.41 in collision off the Humber.

SAINTE-BERNADETTE de LOURDES Dr. French M/S seized 3.7.1940 at Southampton. Fate unknown.

SAINTE-DENISE-LOUISE MFV 42/35. French M/S seized 3.7.1940 at Plymouth. Laid up to 10.41 then Free-French to 1944. (Also known as MFV.2014 from 7.42–6.43.)

SAINTE-ELIZABETH MFV 42/32. French M/S seized 3.7.1940 at Southampton. Fate unknown.

ST ELMO Tr 314/14, 1–12pdr. Hired 1915–19.

ST ELMO'S LIGHT Admiralty wood Dr, 94gr. Innes, Macduff 1918. Sold 1921, renamed *Sweet Promise.* (SWEET PROMISE in WW.II.)

ST ELOI Tr, 'Castle' type (RCN). Polson IW 2.8.1917. Government *Lightship No 20* from 1920. Boom gate vessel (RCN) 1941–44 as ST ELOI.

ST ELSTAN Tr 564/37, 1–4in. Hired as A/S Tr 9.1939–12.45.

ST ELVIES Paddle 567/96, 2–6pdr. Hired as M/S 4.3.1915–8.5.19.

ST ENODER Rescue tug, 'Saint' class. Cancelled 1919.

ST ENODER (ex-ST OSYTH renamed 1919) Rescue tug, 'Saint' class. Day Summers 1919. Sold 9.6.25, renamed *Garm.*

ST ERTH Rescue tug, 'Saint' class. Murdoch & Murray 28.2.1919. Sold 9.25, renamed *Heros.* (HEROS in WW.II.)

ST ETIENNE Rescue tug, 'Saint' class. Cancelled 1919.

ST EWE Rescue tug, 'Saint' class. Murdoch & Murray 1.4.1919. Laid up 1919. Sold 11.10.26, renamed *Alarm.* (ALARM in WW.II.)

ST FAGAN Rescue tug, 'Saint' class. Lytham SB 1919. Target-towing 3.20. Sunk 1.6.40 by air attack at Dunkirk.

ST FAITH Rescue tug, 'Saint' class. Lytham SB 1919. Sold 6.21, same name.

ST FERGUS (see ST BONIFACE)

ST FINBARR Rescue tug, 'Saint' class. Fleming & Ferguson 7.7.1919. Sold 6.23, renamed *Franklin.*

ST FINELLA Rescue tug, 'Saint' class. Cancelled 1919.

ST FINTAN Rescue tug, 'Saint' class. Fleming & Ferguson. Cancelled 1919.

ST FLORENCE Rescue tug, 'Saint' class. Crichton 19.3.1919. Sold
14.11.24, renamed *Kyuquot.*
ST GENNY Rescue tug, 'Saint' class. Crichton 28.5.1919. Fleet tug
1919. Foundered 21.1.30 in the Western Approaches.
ST GEORGE Yt 871/90. Hired 3.3.1915. Renamed ORIFLAMME
6.18; WALLINGTON base ship 10.18—3.19.
ST GERMAIN Tr 307/07, 1—6pdr. Hired 1916—19.
ST GERVAIS Rescue tug, 'Saint' class. Cancelled 1919.
ST GILES Rescue tug, 'Saint' class. Ferguson 14.5.1919. Sold 7.22,
renamed *Khalifa.* Hired as ST GILES, A/S vessel (RAN) 1939—42 and
target towing 1945—46.
ST GORAN Tr 565/36. Hired as A/S Tr 9.1939. Sunk 3.5.40 by air
attack at Namsos.
ST GRACE Rescue tug, 'Saint' class. Cancelled 1919.
ST GREGORY Rescue tug, 'Saint' class. Cancelled 1919.
SAINT-GUENOLE Name given to ML.245 while on loan to the Free-
French 7.1941—7.42.
ST HELIER 1,885/25, 6—20mm. Hired as landing ship 4.1941—45.
ST HELIERS Rescue tug, 'Saint' class. Ferguson 26.6.1919. Sold
23.6.20, same name.
ST HILARY Rescue tug, 'Saint' class. Lytham SB 1919. Laid up 1920.
Sold 7.4.26.
ST HUBERT Tr 349/16, 1—6pdr. Hired 1916—19.
ST ISSEY Rescue tug, 'Saint' class. Napier & Miller 1918. Fleet tug 1919.
Sunk 28.12.42 by unknown cause off Benghazi.
ST IVES Tr 325/09. Hired 1915. Sunk 21.12.16 by mine off Falmouth.
ST JACOB A.ship, 255bm. Hired 1664—66.
ST JAMES (see ST BREOCK)
ST JAN BERCHMANS Tr 114/35. Belgian, hired as A/P Tr 27.9.1940.
Harbour service 7.42—11.45.
ST JOAN Yt 27/29. Hired on air-sea rescue 6.1940—11.45.
ST JOHN Tug (RCN) 840 tons, 2—40mm. St John DD 14.5.1956.
ST JOHNS Tr 208/10, 1—6pdr. Hired 1915. Sunk 3.6.18 by U-boat
off Tory Island.
ST JOSEPH Motor M/S (RCN) 228 tons, 105 x 22 ft. Newcastle SB
14.9.1943. On sale list 1946.
ST JULIEN Tr, 'Castle' type (RCN). Polson IW 6.6.1917. Sold 1921?,
renamed *Centennial.*
ST JUST Rescue tug, 'Saint' class. Napier & Miller 1918. DY tug 1919;
fleet tug 1930. Sunk 11.2.42 by Japanese air attack off Singapore.
ST KATHARINE Tr 337/27. Hired on examination service 10.1939.
Accommodation ship 1.44—1.46.
ST KENAN Tr 565/36. Hired as A/S Tr 9.1939—2.46.

ST KEVERNE Rescue tug, 'Saint' class. Cancelled 1919.

ST KEYNE Rescue tug, 'Saint' class. Murdoch & Murray 12.6.1919. Laid up 1920. Sold 18.6.26 Brazilian navy as TIMES.

ST KILDA Tr 187/14. Hired 1918—19.

ST KILDA Tr, 'Isles' class. A.Hall 29.5.1942. Sold 10.46, renamed *Glaes Compaen.*

ST KITTS Rescue tug, 'Saint' class. Murdoch & Murray 24.6.1919. Laid up 1920. Sold 3.2.26, renamed *Uco.*

ST LAWRENCE Tr 196/99. Hired 1917—19.

ST LEONARD Tr 296/12, 1—6pdr. Hired 1914—19.

ST LEONARD II Tr 210/13. Hired 1916—19.

ST LOMAN Tr 565/36. Hired as A/S Tr 9.1939—7.46. (On loan USN 3.42—10.42.)

ST LOUIS Tr 233/00, 1—10pdr. Hired 1917—19.

ST LUCIA Tr 186/07. Hired 1918—19.

ST MABYN Rescue tug, 'Saint' class. Livingstone & Cooper 1919. Laid up 1920. Sold 3.5.26. (Served as CAROLINE MOLLER in WW.II.)

ST MAGNUS 1,311/24. Hired as guardship 31.8.1939—7.8.40.

ST MALO Tr 335/11, 1—6pdr. Hired 1915—19.

ST MARGARETS Cable ship 1,950 tons, 229 x 36½ ft, 1—12pdr, 2—20m Swan Hunter 13.10.1943.

ST MARTIN Rescue tug, 'Saint' class. Livingstone & Cooper 1919. Target-towing 1921; fleet tug 1939; target-towing 1941. Sold 11.46.

ST MARY Dr 99/98. Hired 1917—19.

ST MARY (see ST CLAUDE)

ST MAURICE Tr 251/02, 1—6pdr. Hired 1914. Purchased as M/L, 24 mines, 5.18. Sold 1921.

ST MAWES Tug 80/17. Hired on harbour service 1.6.1917—20 and on examination service 9.39. Harbour service 1942—47.

ST MELANTE Tr 358/27, 1—12pdr. Hired as M/S 9.1939—8.45.

ST MELLONS Rescue tug, 'Saint' class. Harland & Wolff, Govan 1918. DY tug 1919; rescue tug 1939. Sold 8.7.49 to BU.

ST MICHAEL Yt 63/03. Hired as degaussing vessel 3.1940, purchased 3.42. Laid up 7.45. Sold 1945?

ST MINVER Rescue tug, 'Saint' class. Day Summers 1919. Laid up 1920. Sold 23.4.25, renamed *Abeille 22.* (ABEILLE 22 in WW.II.)

ST MINVER Tr 325/19, 1—12pdr. Hired as M/S 9.1939, later purchased. Fuel carrier 4.44. Sold 1946.

ST MODWEN Yt 1,023/11. Hired as A/S Yt 9.1939, purchased 7.41. Sold 1945.

ST MONANCE Rescue tug, 'Saint' class. Hong Kong & Whampoa 11.9.1919. DY tug 1920. Sold 4.48.

ST NECTAN Tr 565/37, 1—12pdr. Hired as A/P Tr 4.1940. A/S 1.41—4.46.

ST OLAVES Rescue tug, 'Saint' class. Harland & Wolff, Govan 1919. Sold 12.6.22, same name. Hired as rescue tug 12.39. Grounded 21.9.42 near Duncansby Head.

ST OLIVE Tr 234/14. Hired as M/S 3.1940—4.45.

ST OMAR Rescue tug, 'Saint' class. Ferguson 15.9.1919. DY tug 1920; fleet tug 1942; DY tug 1945. Sold 4.48.

SAINT ORAN 249/23. Hired as looplayer 4.1940—46.

ST OSYTH (see ST ENODER)

ST OWEN Rescue tug, 'Saint' class. Cancelled 1919.

ST PHILIP Rescue tug, 'Saint' class. Cancelled 1919.

ST PIERRE MFV 23net/37, 1—6pdr. Belgian, hired as A/P vessel 22.6.1940. Training tender 1943—44. Returned 5.45. (Also known as P.4.)

SAINT-PIERRE II Tr 265/04. French M/S seized 3.7.1940 at Plymouth. Lost 29.7.40, cause and place not given.

ST ROCHE Rescue tug, 'Saint' class. Cancelled 1919.

ST ROLLUX Rescue tug, 'Saint' class. Cancelled 1919.

ST RONAN Name used by ML.123 while on loan to the Free-French 1941—42.

ST SAMPSON Rescue tug, 'Saint' class. Hong Kong & Whampoa 1919. Sold 4.22, purchaser defaulted. sold 8.6.22, same name. Hired as A/P vessel 2.40. M/S 1941. Foundered 7.3.42 in the Red Sea.

ST SEIRIOL 928/14, 2—6pdr. Hired as M/S 5.3.1915. Sunk 25.4.18 by mine off the Shipwash.

ST SILIO 314/36. Hired on examination service 1940—46.

ST SUNNIVA 1,368/31. Hired as guardship 29.8.1939. Accommodation ship 9.40; rescue ship 9.42. Lost 22.1.43 in the N.Atlantic, probably iced-up and capsized.

ST TEATH Rescue tug, 'Saint' class. Walker, Sudbrook 29.5.1919. Laid up 1920. Sold 2.6.26 Brazilian navy as PARANA.

ST TRILLO Paddle 164/75. Hired as M/S 4.1917—19.

ST TUDNO 2,326/26. Hired as depot ship 9.1939—47.

ST TUDY Rescue tug, 'Saint' class. Walker, Sudbrook 11.11.1919. Laid up 1920. Sold 16.7.26.

ST VINCENT A.ship. Hired 1798—1802.

ST VINCENT Cutter 14. Hired 1806.

ST VINCENT II Tr 186/07, 1—12pdr. Hired 1914—19.

ST WISTAN Tr 567/37, 1—12pdr. Hired as A/P Tr 11.1939. A/S Tr 1.41—5.46.

SAINT-YVES Name given to ML.246 while on loan to the Free-French 7.1941—42.

ST ZENO Tr 608/40, 1—4in. Purchased as A/S Tr 3.1940. Listed to 5.46. (On loan USN 2.42—10.42.)

SAKARA Hired as boiler-cleaning vessel 9.1941—45.

SALACON Tr 211/05. Hired 1918—19.

SALADIN Barge 220gr. Hired as BBV 5.1940—44.

SALAMANDER 14-gun vessel, 110bm. Hired 1588 for the Armada campaign.

SALAMANDER (ex-*Krabben*) Wh 174/12, 1—12pdr, 2—3pdr. Purchased 4.1915. Sold 6.3.19.

SALLY Sloop 12. Hired 1797—1801.

SALLY A.ship 16. Hired 1806—07.

SALOME Tr 252/08, 1—12pdr. Hired 1915—19.

SALOPIAN (ex-*Shropshire*) 10.549/26, 6—6in, 2—4in,2—3in. Hired as AMC 9.1939. Sunk 13.5.41 by 'U.98' in the N.Atlantic.

SALPA Dr 99/18. Hired as M/S 12.1939—4.46.

SALSETTE Tr, 'Castle' type (RIM), composite-built. Bombay 1918. Listed to 1921.

SALTARELO A/S Tr 515 tons, 150 x 27½ ft, 1—4in, 3—20mm. Robb 6.8.1940. Sold 4.8.46 Portuguese navy as SALVADOR CORREIA.

SALTASH II 90dw/1864. Hired as degaussing vessel 1942—45.

SALTMARSHE 930/07. Hired as ammo. carrier (RFA) 7.3.1915—21.11.1

SALVAGE DUKE Salvage vessel 1,440 tons, 200 x 38 ft, 4—20mm. Simons 1.11.1943. To Turkish navy 1948 as IMROZ.

SALVAGE KING Tug 1,164/25. Hired 1940. Stranded 12.9.40 west of Duncansby Head.

SALVALOUR Salvage vessel (as SALVAGE DUKE). Goole SB 2.11.1944.

SALVATOR Yt 766/03, 2—12pdr. Hired as A/P Yt 5.3.1915—29.3.19.

SALVEDA Salvage vessel 1,250 tons, 185 x 34½ ft, 4—20mm. Cammell Laird 9.2.1943. Laid up 1966.

SALVENTURE (ex-HANDMAID renamed 7.1942) Salvage vessel (as SALVAGE DUKE). Simons 24.11.42. To Greek navy 1950 as SOTIR.

SALVERDANT Salvage vessel (as SALVAGE DUKE). Simons launched 12.3.1948 as RECLAIM, S/M rescue vessel.

SALVESTOR (ex-ASSISTANCE renamed 4.1942) Salvage vessel (as SALVAGE DUKE). Simons 28.8.42.

SALVICTOR Salvage vessel (as SALVAGE DUKE). Simons 11.3.1944.

SALVIGIL Salvage vessel (as SALVAGE DUKE). Smiths Dk 30.4.1945. Lent mercantile 1960; sold 5.65.

SALVIKING Salvage vessel (as SALVAGE DUKE). Simons 22.12.1942. Sunk 14.2.44 by U-boat in the Indian Ocean.

SALVINI Tr 226/16, 1—6pdr. Hired 1916—19 and as BBV 4.40. Fuel carrier 4.44—11.44.

SALVIOLA Salvage vessel (as SALVAGE DUKE). Simons 9.7.1945. To Turkish navy 9.59 as IMROZ (ii).

SALVO DY tug 400 tons, 121 x 24 ft. Purchased 19.3.1901. Sold 10.22. (Also known as C.61 from 1905.)

SALVO (ex-*Kestrel*) Tug 161/18, 1–MG. Hired as M/S 8.1939, purchased 14.2.40. Sold 11.45.

SALVONIA Tug 571/39, 1–12pdr. Hired as rescue tug 9.1939–10.45.

SAMAKI Yt 20/33. Hired as HDPC 5.1940, purchased 10.41. Laid up 8.45, sold 1946.

SAMARITAN 80gr. Hired as water boat 5.1940–47.

SAMBHUR (see AN.1.)

SAMBRE Firefloat in service 1945–47.

SAMBUR 776/25. Hired as BBV 1940. Renamed TOREADOR 1942. Laid up 1943.

SAMPSON A.ship, 300bm. Hired for the Armada campaign.

SAMPSON 40-gun ship. Hired 1650. Lost 4.3.1653 in action in the Mediterranean.

SAMPSON Iron paddle DY tug 530 tons, 128 x 25 ft. Laird 31.1.1877. Renamed ORIENT 1918. Sold 8.6.23 at Malta.

SAMPSON Tug 191/02? Hired as M/S in the E.Indies 1941–43.

SAM RICHARDS Dr 88/13. Hired 1915–19.

SAMSON Tug 232/93. Hired as DY tug 1.1918–19.

SAMSON (see SAMSONIA)

SAMSON DY tug, 850gr, 165 x 37 ft. A.Hall 14.5.1953.

SAMSONIA (ex-SAMSON renamed 1942) Rescue tug, 1,118 tons, 190 x 38½ ft, 2–40mm. Robb 1.4.1942. On charter 1948–52 as *Foundation Josephine*. DY tug 1952.

SAMUEL BAKER Tr, non-standard 'Strath' type, 194gr. Hall Russell 7.6.1917. Sold 1921, renamed *Braconmoor*.

SAMUEL BARKAS Tr, 'Strath' type, 216gr. Hall Russell 13.9.1917. Sold 1919, same name.

SAMUEL BENBOW Tr, 'Strath' type, 203gr. Hall Russell 9.7.1918. Sold 1921, same name. Commissioned as M/S (RAN) 5.9.1940. Sold 24.5.46.

SAMUEL CUNNINGHAM Tr, 'Strath' type. Aberdeen. Cancelled 1919.

SAMUEL DAWSON Tr, 'Castle' type, 276gr. J.P. Rennoldson 1919. Sold 1921, renamed *San Juan*.

SAMUEL DOWDEN Tr, 'Mersey' type, 324gr. Cochrane 18.9.1917. Sold 1922, renamed *Royal Regiment*. (Served as SEA MIST in WW.II.)

SAMUEL DRAKE Tr, 'Castle' type, 276gr. Bow McLachlan 1918. Sold 1922, renamed *Rhodolite*. (Served as SOUTHCOATES in WW.II.)

SAMUEL GASBY Tr, 'Strath' type, 199gr. Ritchie Graham 1920. Sold 1921, same name. (Served as SOUBRETTE in WW.II.)

SAMUEL GREEN Tr, 'Castle' type, 280gr. G.Brown 30.4.1919. Sold 1919 as yacht *Aries*.

SAMUEL HAMPTON Tr, 'Strath' type. Ouse SB 1919. Sold 1919.

SAMUEL JAMESON Tr, 'Mersey' type, 324gr. Cochrane 1918. Renamed ETTRICK 10.20. Sold 1926, renamed *Loughrigg*. (Served as PHYLLISIA in WW.II.)

SAMUEL LOVITT Tr, 'Strath' type. Hall Russell. Cancelled 1919.

SAMUEL MARTIN Tr, 'Mersey' type, 324gr. Cochrane 28.6.1919. Sold 1920, renamed *Field Marshall Plumer.*

SAMUEL SPENCER Tr, 'Castle' type, 275gr. Smiths Dk 17.9.1917. Sold 1921, renamed *Flash.*

SAMURAI Tr 221/14, 1–6pdr. Hired 1915–19.

SANCROFT (ex-*Empire Baffin*) 6,978/41. In service as cable layer 1.1944–45.

SANDA Yt 351/06. Hired as A/P Yt 26.1.1915. Sunk 25.9.15 by gunfire off the Belgian coast.

SANDA Tr, 'Isles' class. Goole SB 12.7.1941. RNZN 1942. On sale list 1958.

SANDBOY (see STRENUOUS)

SANDGATE (see BV.4 under BD vessels)

SANDIP Cstr 285/15. Hired as A/P vessel (RIN) 1939–45.

SANDMARTIN (see JAY)

SANDOWAY Cstr 291/15. Hired as A/P vessel (RIM) 1916–19 and 1940–43.

SANDOWN Paddle 684/34, 1–12pdr. Hired as M/S 10.1939. A/A ship, 1–12pdr, 2–2pdr, 7.42. Accommodation ship 1945–46.

SANDOY MFV 49/40. Norwegian, hired as ferry 9.1940. Lost 11.12.42, cause and place not given. probably in Iceland.

SANDRAY Tr, 'Isles' class. Cook Welton & Gemmell 5.10.1944, completed as danlayer. Sold 15.12.60 mercantile.

SANDRINGHAM Tr 179/05, 1–12pdr. Hired 1917–19.

SANDRINGHAM Tr 254/30. Hired as M/S 8.1939–1.46.

SANDRINGHAM Ferry 42/00. Hired on examination service 9.1939. To War Dept 1.41.

SANDSTORM Admiralty steel Dr, 96gr. A.Hall 1918. Sold 1921, renamed *Accord.* (ACCORD in WW.II.)

SANDSTORM (see VESTFOLD V)

SANDWICH Cutter 8. Hired 1782–83.

SANDWICH Cutter 12, Hired 1798. Captured 14.6.99 by the French. Recaptured 15.10.1803 and returned.

SANDWICH Lugger 14. Hired 1798–1801.

SANDWICH Lugger 14, 167bm. Hired 5.1804–8.04 and 5.1808–5.14.

SANGARIUS Tr 211/15, 1–3pdr. Hired as A/P Tr 12.1939–2.12.41.

SANKATY Ferr. Minelayer (RCN). In service 1940–46.

SAN PATRICIO 9,712/15. Hired as water carrier (RFA) 14.5.1915. Oiler 1.16–11.18.

SANSERIT Tr 212/16, 1–6pdr. Hired as M/S 1917–19.

SANSON Tr 231/07. 1–6pdr. Hired 1915–19 and as A/P Tr 11.39. M/S 6.40; fuel carrier 6.44–9.46.

SANSONNET Tr 212/16. Hired as A/P Tr 11.1939–2.40.

SANS PEUR (ex-*Trenora*) Yt 821/33. Commissioned as A/S Yt (RCN) 10.1939. Training ship 1944. Paid off 6.47.

SANTA Wh 355/36. Hired as M/S 10.1941. Sunk 23.11.43 by mine off Sardinia.

SANTA MARIA MFV 86/36. Hired as A/S (RCN) 9.1939–44.

SANTA MARIA MFV 75/36. Belgian hired as BBV 8.1940–9.45.

SAN TOMAS MFV 63/38. Hired (RCN) 9.1939–45.

SANTORA Dr 90/11, 1–3pdr. Hired 1915–19.

SAON Tr 386/33. Purchased as A/S Tr 9.1939. Sold 1945.

SAPHO Cstr 136/20. French, seized 7.1940 at Cardiff. MWT. 7.40. RN 10.42 as degaussing vessel. Returned 3.46.

SAPPER Tr, 276gr, 130 x 24 ft, 1–12pdr. Smiths Dk 1.2.1915, purchased 11.12.14. Foundered 29.12.17 off the Owers light vessel.

SAPPER A/S Tr 750 tons, 175 x 30 ft, 1–4in, 4–20mm. Cook Welton & Gemmell 11.11.1942. Sold 4.46, renamed *Cape Gloucester*.

SAPPHIRE Dr 95/07. Hired on harbour service 4.12.1914–19.

SAPPHIRE II Yt 1,421/12, 1–4in, 1–12pdr. Hired as A/P Yt 8.1.1915–20.2.19.

SAPPHIRE III Tr 156/03, 1–6pdr. Hired as M/S 1916–18.

SAPPHIRE (ex-*Mildenhall*) 421/35, 608 tons, 1–4in. Purchased as A/S Tr 1935. Sold 9.4.46, renamed *Dunsby*.

SAPPHO Yt 327/35. Hired as guardship 11.1939. Sunk 30.9.40 off Falmouth, probably by mine.

SARA Dr 62/02. Hired 1916–19.

SARABANDE A/S Tr 530 tons, 150 x 27½ ft, 1–4in, 3–20mm. Inglis 29.8.1940. Sold 3.46.

SARAH Tr 135/99. Hired 1917–19.

SARAH ALICE Tr 299/11. Hired 1914–19.

SARAH A PURDY Tr 202/19. Hired as BBV 2.1940–6.45.

SARAH HIDE Tr 162/21, 1–MG. Hired as M/S 11.1939–1.46. (Spelt SARAH HYDE in most lists.)

SARAH JOLLIFFE Tug 333/90. Hired as DY tug 8.3.1915–19.

SARAH MARIAN Dr 89/11. Hired 1915–19.

SARBA Tr 315/13, 1–12pdr. Hired 1915–19 and as BDV 11.39, later purchased. Sold 27.9.46.

SARDIUS Tr 213/92, 1–12pdr. Hired 1915–18.

SARDIUS II Tr 206/00, 1–6pdr. Hired 1915. Wrecked 13.2.18 in Pendower Cove.

SAREPTA Dr 89/06, 1–6pdr. Hired 1.1915; WELCOME FRIEND 6.18–19.

SAREPTA (ex-German FRIEDA PETERS) TRV 465/20, 150 x 27½ ft. Listed from 1949.

SARGASSO (ex-*Atlantis*) Yt 216/26. Hired as danlayer 10.1939. Sunk 6.6.43 by mine off the Isle of Wight.

SARGON Tr 297/13, 1–6pdr. Hired as M/S 1914–19 and as M/S 8.39–7.45

SARK Tr 145/95. Hired 1917–19.

SARKA Wh 355/36. Hired as M/S 10.1941. Danlayer 4.44–2.46.

SARNA Wh 268/30. Hired as M/S 3.1940. Sunk 25.2.41 by mine in the Suez canal.

SARNIA 1,498/10, 1–12pdr. Hired as ABS 14.11.1914. Sunk 12.9.18 by U-boat off Alexandria.

SARONTA Tr 316/17, 1–6pdr. Hired as A/P Tr 6.1940. M/S 1.41–12.45.

SARPEDON II Tr 344/16, 1–12pdr. Hired 1916–19 and as SARPEDON A/P Tr, 1–12pdr, 6.40. M/S 1.42–7.45.

SARRAIL Tr 255/17, 1–6pdr. Hired 1917–19.

SASEBO Tr 255/13, 1–6pdr. Hired 1915–19.

SASEBO Tr 308/28, 1–12pdr. Hired as M/S 8.1939–2.46.

SATA Tr 340/31. Hired as M/S 8.1939–12.45.

SATISFACTION 40-gun ship, 363bm. Hired 1664–67.

SATISFACTION A.ship 20. Hired 1782–83.

SATSA Wh 355/36. Hired as M/S 10.1941. Danlayer 4.44–12.45.

SATURN Tr 230/16, 1–6pdr. Hired as M/S 1916–19 and as A/P Tr 11.39. M/S 6.40; fuel carrier 3.44–12.45.

SATURN Tr 292/20. Hired as M/S in the W. Indies 1.42–43.

SATURNUS Cstr 200/35. Dutch, hired as BBV 17.6.1940. Wrecked 1.5.41 on the Isle of Man.

SATYAVATI Cstr 295/11. Hired as M/S (RIN) 9.1939–45.

SAUCY Rescue tug, 579gr. 155½ x 31 ft. Livingstone & Cooper 1918. Sold 12.4.24, same name. Hired as rescue tug 1939. Sunk 4.9.40 by mine in the Firth of Forth.

SAUCY Rescue tug 700 tons, 142½ x 33 ft, 1–3in. Cochrane 26.10.1942. On sale list 1964.

SAUMAREZ Cutter 10, 106bm. Hired 9.1804–4.05.

SAUNTER Tank vessel 143/16. Hired as water boat 12.1939–47.

SAURIAN Tr 219/16, 1–6pdr. Hired as M/S 1916–19 and as A/P Tr, 1–12pdr, 6.40–11.45.

SAUTERNES 1,049/22. French A/P vessel seized 3.7.1940 at Plymouth. A/P vessel 8.40. Lost 17.12.41, cause and place not given.

SAUVEUR du MONDE Dr 76/29. French, seized 3.7.1940. A/P Dr 11.40. Laid up 1943. Returned 7.45.

SAVITRI Tr 212/17. Hired as M/L, 24 mines, 1917–19.

SAWFLY (ex-*Tenby Castle*) Tr 307/28. Hired as M/S 8.1939–10.45.

SAXOL (see TYROLIA)

SAXON Tr 239/07, 1–12pdr. Hired 1914–19.

SAXON II Tr 119/94, 1–6pdr. Hired 1.1915–18.

SAXON Pilot 139/95. Hired as guardship 28.7.1917–26.1.19.

SAXON Aux.barge 106/98. Hired as BBV 1939–45.

SAXONIA Tr 197/00. Hired as A/P Tr 11.1939–24.1.40.

SAXON PRINCE Tr 237/06. Hired 1915. Foundered 28.3.16 off Dover.

SAXON QUEEN Cable ship 482/38. Hired (red ensign?) 1941–44.

SAYONARA Yt 581/80, 2–14pdr. Hired as A/P Yt 25.6.1915–11.10.18.

SAYONARA Yt 762/11. Hired as ABV 9.1939, purchased 7.41. Laid up 8.45, sold 1946.

SCADAUN Yt 157/14, 1–6pdr. Hired as A/P Yt 7.10.1914–2.3.19.

SCALBY WYKE Tr 443/35. Hired as A/S Tr 10.1939–10.45.

SCALPAY Tr, 'Isles' class. Cook Welton & Gemmell 2.6.1942. Wreck dispersal 3.46. Sold 1947 mercantile.

SCANDINAVIA Tank vessel 456/05. Hired (RFA) 9.11.1914–5.10.19.

SCANIA Dr 88/16. Hired 1916–19.

SCARAVAY Tr, 'Isles' class. Cook Welton & Gemmell 22.10.1944, completed as danlayer. Sold 11.46.

SCARBA Tr, 'Isles' class. Cook Welton & Gemmell 26.6.1941. RNZN 1942. On sale list 1958.

SCARBOROUGH Paddle 142/1866. Hired as water boat in WW.I.

SCARBOROUGH Tr 162/97. Hired 1915–19.

SCARLET THREAD Dr 96/19. Hired on harbour service 9.1939–9.46.

SCARRON Tr 296/13, 1–6pdr. Hired 1915–19 and as A/P Tr, 2–MG, 6.40. M/S 1941–12.45.

SCATERIE 41/26. Hired (RCN) 1942–46.

SCAWFELL (ex-*Jupiter*) Paddle 642/37, 1–12pdr. Hired as M/S 10.1939. A/A ship, 1–12pdr, 6–20mm, 1941–45.

SCEND Admiralty wood Dr, 97gr. Colby 1918. Sold 1919, renamed *Girl Hazel*.

SCEPTRE (ex-*Virginia*) MFV. Hired as HDPC 10.1939. Renamed ORB 1943. Returned 1945.

SCHELDE Tug 359/26, 1–MG. Dutch, hired as rescue tug (Dutch crew) 8.1940. Sank in the Clyde and under salvage in 1.44.

SCHIEHALLION Tr 198/ -. Hired 1914. Sunk 9.6.15 by mine in the Mediterranean.

SCHIEHALLION Tr 225/16, 1–6pdr. Hired 1916–19.

SCHIEVAN Yt 439/97. Hired on examination service 11.1939, purchased 4.42. Degaussing vessel 1941. To R.Norwegian navy 9.45.

SCHIPPERKE Tr 331/11, 1–6pdr. Hired 1916–19.

SCINTILLA Admiralty steel Dr, 96gr. Ouse SB 1920. Sold 1920, renamed *Asparagus*. (Served as MARY SWANSTON in WW.II.)

SCOMBER Tr 321/14, 1–6pdr. Hired 1915–19 and purchased as BDV 5.40 Sold 2.47.

SCOOPER Tr 195/00. Hired 1915–19.

SCORPIO Tr 145/88. Hired 1917–19.

SCOT Tr 202/07, 1–6pdr. Hired 1915–19.

SCOT II Dr 79/03, 1–6pdr. Hired 1915–19.

SCOTCH MIST Admiralty steer Dr. Goole SB. Cancelled 1919.

SCOTCH THISTLE Dr 84/13. Hired as M/S 11.1939. Mine-recovery 5.40. Stranded 7.10.40 in the Thames estuary.

SCOTIA Paddle tug, 268bm, 132 x 21 ft. Green, Blackwall 20.6.1863, purchased 28.11.63. Sold 1900.

SCOTIA 1,872/02, 1–12pdr. Hired as ABS 8.8.1914–1.8.17.

SCOTIA Tug 136/93. Hired in WW.I.

SCOTIA Tr 149/91. Hired 1918–19.

SCOTIA II Yt 34/09. Hired as boom tender 11.1939, purchased 12.41. Laid up 10.45, sold 1946.

SCOTLAND Tr 152/97. Hired 1918–19.

SCOTOL Oiler (RFA) 2,200 tons, 220 x 35 ft. Tyne Iron SB Co 23.6.1916. Sold 11.47, renamed *Hemsley I.*

SCOTSMAN DY tug 172 tons, 110 x 20 ft. Purchased 11.1901. Sold 19.4.21 at Simonstown. (Also known as C.371 and was to have been renamed SCOTTISH in 3.19.)

SCOTSMAN Dr 88/07, 1–3pdr. Hired 1.1915–19.

SCOTSTOUN (ex-*Caledonia*) 17,046/25, 6–4in. Hired as AMC 8.1939. Sunk 13.6.40 by 'U.25' in the North-west Approaches.

SCOTT Tr 288/ -, 1–6pdr, 24 mines. Hired as M/L 1915. Sunk 22.10.15 by mine off the Tongue light vessel.

SCOTT HARLEY 620/13. Purchased as M/S 19.2.1941. Sunk 3.3.42 by unknown cause in the Indian Ocean.

SCOTTIE Tug 50/30. Hired as DY tug 10.1942–8.46.

SCOTTISH (see SCOTSMAN)

SCOTTISH Tr 558/37, 1–4in. Hired as A/S Tr 10.1939. ABV 12.40–3.45.

SCOTTISH CHIEF Dr 78/10. Hired 1915–19.

SCOUR Admiralty wood Dr, 98gr. Colby 1918. Sold 1920, renamed *Cheviotdale.*

SCOURGE (ex-*Lea Rig*) Dr 83/08. Hired as M/S 11.1939. Renamed SKYROCKET 1942. Returned 5.46.

SCOUTER Tr 195/00. Hired 1915–19.

SCRUTATOR (ex-*Avondale*) MFV 29net. Hired on examination service 6.1940. Harbour service 1943–12.45.

SCUD Admiralty wood Dr, 97gr. Colby 1919. Sold 1920, renamed *Fleurbaix.*

SCYTHE (ex-*Baltic*) Tug 100/15? Belgian, hired as M/S 12.1939, purchased 14.2.40. Boom tender 1944. Sold 20.5.47.

S.D.J Dr 100/12. Hired 1915–19.

SDMLs (see MLs)

SEA ANGLER Yt 23gr. Hired as M/S tender 7.1940. Lost 19.5.41 by fire in the Plymouth area.

SEABELLE II Yt 1,057/27. Hired as A/P Yt 9.1939. Base ship 1942. A/S Yt (RIN) 10.44–19.5.46. (SEABELLE from 1942.)

SEABIRD Dr 41/96. Hired in WW.I.

SEABORN Dr. Hired 12.1939. Nominal depot ship 11.40. Renamed VENTURE II in 9.41.

SEABREEZE Admiralty steel Dr. A.Hall 22.11.1918. Sold 1946.

SEABY Tug, Hired as skid M/S 4.1941–7.45.

SEADOG (see STALWART)

SEAFARER MFV 20net/38. Hired as A/P Dr 11.1939–6.45.

SEAFAY Yt 210/02, 2–6pdr. Hired as A/P Yt 26.9.1914–3.2.19.

SEAFLOWER (ex-*Ospray II*) Tr 275/08, 560 tons, 1–6pdr. Purchased as M/S 4.1909. Renamed SEAROVER 1919. Sold 1920, renamed *Heinrich Beerman.*

SEAFLOWER (ex-*Boadicea*) Yt 447/82. Hired as danlayer 11.1939. BU 12.46.

SEAFOG Admiralty steel Dr, 96gr. Webster & Bickerton 1918. Sold 1921, renamed *Selimus.*

SEAGEM Tug 92/39. Hired as armament tug 8.1939. Sunk 30.10.40 by unknown cause.

SEA GIANT Tug 508/20, 1–12pdr. American, purchased as rescue tug 1940. Sold 3.5.48.

SEA GIANT DY tug, 850gr, 165 x 37 ft. A.Hall 2.6.1954.

SEA GLEANER Dr 94/07. Hired as reserve blockship 7.1940–3.44.

SEAHAWK Tr 169/98. Hired 1917–19.

SEA HOLLY Dr 95/18. Hired as M/S 11.1939. Danlayer 1943–3.4.46.

SEAHORSE Fleet tug 670 tons, 160 x 26 ft, 1–12pdr. Laird 7.7.1880. Sold 1.5.20.

SEAHORSE II Yt 106/91. Hired 1917–11.12.18.

SEAHORSE III Tr 229/01. Hired 1918–19.

SEA KING Tr 321/16. Hired 1917–20 and as M/S 8.1939. Sunk 9.10.40 by mine off Grimsby.

SEALARK II Tr 182/98, 1–6pdr. Hired 1.1915. Sunk 30.9.18 in collision off St John's Point.

SEALION Tr 231/02, 2–6pdr. Hired 1914–19.

SEALYHAM (see TERJE 5)

SEALYHAM DY tug, 152gr. Appledore SY 29.3.1967.

SEAMAN Tug 369/24, 1–12pdr. Hired as rescue tug 12.1939–11.45.

SEAMEW (ex-*Nunthorpe Hall*) Tr 248/09, 510 tons, 1–6pdr. Purchased as M/S 4.1909. Reverted to NUNTHORPE HALL 1919. Sold 4.5.20, renamed *Gines Cerda.*

SEA MIST Admiralty steel Dr. Goole SB. Cancelled 1919.

SEA MIST (ex-*Duncan*) Tr 324/17. Hired as M/S 2.1940–10.12.45.

SEA MIST 35/39. Hired as patrol vessel (RAN) 6.1941, purchased 7.42. Sold 1.46.

SEA MONARCH Tr 329/15, 1–12pdr. Hired 1916–19 and as BDV 1.40, later purchased. Laid up 7.46, sold 31.1.47.

SEA PRINCE Tug 97/85. Hired 19.7.1915–19.

SEARANGER Tr 263/14, 1–12pdr. Hired 1915–19.

SEARCHER Dr 59/08, 1–3pdr. Hired 2.1915–19.

SEAROVER (see SEAFLOWER)

SEA SALVOR Salvage vessel 1,440 tons, 200 x 38 ft, 4–20mm. Goole SB 22.4.1943.

SEA SEARCHER Tr 263/14, 1–6pdr. Hired 1915–19.

SEA SWEEPER Tr 329/15, 1–12pdr. Hired 1915–19.

SEAWARD HO Tr 263/14, 1–12pdr. Hired 1915–19.

SECURITY (see DILIGENCE)

SECURITY (ex-*Empire Roderick*) DY tug, 233/46, 470 tons. Transferred from MOT and renamed 3.1947.

SECUTA Yt 54/37. Hired as HDPC 12.1939–4.46.

SEDDON Tr 296/16, 1–6pdr. Hired 1916–19 and as A/P Tr 6.40. M/S 1941–2.46.

SEDGEFLY (ex-*Norman*) Tr 520/39, 1–4in. Hired as A/S Tr 9.1939. Sunk 16.12.39 by mine off the Tyne.

SEDOCK Tr 202/20. Hired as A/P Tr 11.1939–2.40.

SEDULOUS Dr 100/12, 1–47mm. Hired 1915–19 and as BBV 5.40. Examination service 9.40–10.45.

SEEKINGJAO Yt. Purchased 7.1941 at Hong Kong. Listed there to 3.4.42.

SEINE Tug 308/08, 2–MG. Dutch, hired as rescue tug (Dutch crew) 1940–44.

SEKSERN Wh 249/30. Hired as M/S (SAN) 10.1940–4.46.

SELAMA 291/14. Hired as A/P vessel (RIN) 1939–43.

SELBY Dr 75/03. Hired 1916. Sunk 15.5.17 in action in the Adriatic.

SELECT Dr 74/10, 1–3pdr. Hired 1.1915. Sunk 16.4.18 in collision.

SELINA Dr 98/07, 1–47mm. Hired 1915–19.

SELIS Wh 166/18. Norwegian, hired as M/S in the W. Indies 11.1940–7.41.

SEMIRAMIS Tr 246/07, 1–12pdr. Hired 8.1914–19.

SEMITA Yt 37/35. Hired as HDPC 10.1939–11.45.

SEMLA Wh 217/24. Hired as M/S 12.1941. Examination service 1942–45. Sold 3.46.

SEMNOS Tr 216/14, 1–3pdr. Hired 1915–19 and as A/P Tr, 1–3pdr, 11.39–12.41.

SENATEUR DUHAMEL Tr 913/27. French, seized 28.12.1940 in the Atlantic. A/S Tr, 1–4in, 1.41. Lent USN 2.42. Sunk 6.5.42 in collision off Wilmington.

SENATOR Tr 211/05. Hired 1915. Sunk 21.5.17 by mine off Tory Island.

SENTINEL STAR Dr 102/16. Hired 1917–19.

SERAPION Tr 195/00. Hired 1917–19 and as A/P Tr 11.39–27.1.40.

SERBOL Oiler (RFA) 5,042 tons, 335 x 41½ ft. Caledon SB Co, Dundee 7.7.1917. Arrived 30.6.58 Hughes Bolckow, Blyth to Bu.

SERENE Dr 86gr. Hired 1916. Sunk 15.5.17 in action in the Adriatic.

SERENINI MFV 53/35. French HDPC seized 7.1940 at Southampton. Harbour service 1.41–43.

SERENITY Dr 81/08, 1–3pdr. Hired 1916–19.

SERFIB Tr 210/17, 1–6pdr. Hired 1917–19.

SERGIE Russian merchant, seized 1918 on the Caspian and converted to CMB carrier, 1–12pdr, 2–CMBs. Transferred 24.8.19 to 'White' Russians on the Caspian Sea.

SERIOLA Yt 58/38. Hired as HDPC 10.1939, purchased 5.41. Sold 12.45.

SERVITOR Oiler (RFA) 1,935 tons, 200 x 34 ft. Chatham DY 26.5.1914. Sold 9.22.

SERVITOR (ex-*Captain A.Letzer*) Tug 44gr. Belgian, hired as M/S 12.1939, purchased 14.7.40. Listed to 1944.

SESAME Rescue tug 700 tons, 142½ x 33 ft, 1–3in. Cochrane 1.10.1943. Sunk 11.6.44 by E-boat torpedo off Normandy.

SESOSTRIS Tr 293/15, 1–12pdr. Hired 1916–19.

SETHON Tr 295/16, 1–6pdr. Hired 1916–19 and as A/P Tr, 1–6pdr, 6.40. M/S 1941–10.45.

SETTER Tr 171/99, 1–6pdr. Hired 1916–19. (SETTER II from 1917.)

SETTER (see TERJE 4)

SETTSU Tr 231/12, 1–6pdr. Hired 1914–19.

SETTSU Tr 301/24. Hired as BDV 12.1939–45.

SET WEATHER Admiralty wood Dr, 97gr. Colby 1918. Sold 1919, same name.

SEVRA Wh 253/29. Hired as M/S 3.1940. Sunk 6.11.40 by mine off Falmouth.

SGB 1–9 Steam gunboats 165 tons, 138 x 20 ft, 6–MG, 2–TT. Rearmed: 250 tons, 1–3in, 2–6pdr, 6–20mm, 2–TT.

SGB 1, 2. Thornycroft. Ordered 8.11.1940, cancelled 1941.

SGB 3 Yarrow 28.9.41. Renamed GREY SEAL 1943. Sold 1949.

SGB 4 Yarrow 25.9.41. GREY FOX 1943. Sold 1949.

SGB 5 Hawthorn Leslie 27.8.41. GREY OWL 1943. Sold 1949.

SGB 6 Hawthorn Leslie 17.11.41. GREY SHARK 1943. On sale list 1947.

SGB 7 Denny 25.9.41. Sunk 19.6.42 in action in the Channel.

SGB 8 Denny 3.11.41. GREY WOLF 1943. On sale list 1948.

SGB 9 White 14.2.41. GREY GOOSE 1943. On sale list 1955.
SGB 10–50 and 351–359. Projected 1941, not ordered.

SHACKLETON Tr 288/13, 1–3pdr, 24 mines. Purchased as M/L 4.1915.
Sold 1920.
SHADE Admiralty wood Dr, 96gr. Colby 1919. Sold 1921, same name.
SHADOW Admiralty wood Dr, 95gr. Stevenson & Asher, Banff 1918.
Sold 1921, renamed *Pilot Us*. (PILOT US in WW.II.)
SHAKO (ex-*Hercules*) Tug 121/13. Hired as M/S 8.1939, later purchased.
Sold 11.45.
SHALIMAR Yt 114/03. Hired as danlayer 9.1939. BDV 1942–43.
SHAMA Tr 191/18. Hired 1918–19.
SHAMROCK DY tank vessel 118 tons, 74 x 13½ ft. Pearse, Stockton on
Tees 11.8.1873. Renamed ST PATRICK 1.11.17. Transferred Irish Govt
15.5.23.
SHAMROCK Tr 184/99. Hired 1917–20 and as A/P Tr 11.39. BDV
5.40–12.44.
SHANDWICK Tr 166/12, 1–6pdr. Hired 1914–19 and as danlayer 1.40.
M/S 9.40–1.46.
SHANNON MFV. Hired on harbour service 6.1940–9.45.
SHAPINSAY Tr, 'Isles' class. Cochrane 29.3.1941. Sold 10.8.46, renamed
El Hascimy.
SHARK Tug 163/91. Hired 26.10.1914. Lent USN 30.9.18–19.
SHAWVILLE Tug (RCN). In service 1944–45.
SHEEN Admiralty steel Dr, 98gr. Brooke, Lowestoft 11.5.1918. TRV
1943. Sold 1946, renamed *Good Tidings*.
SHEERNESS WATERBOAT DY hoy, 69bm, 54 x 16 ft. Sheernes DY
1698. BU 1723.
SHEERNESS WATERBOAT (see SUPPLY)
SHEERNESS LONGBOAT Towing vessel, 27bm, 42 x 12½ ft. Sheerness
DY 1724. Listed 1747.
SHEERNESS WATERBOAT (ex-*Duke of Cumberland*) DY hoy, 86bm,
55 x 20 ft. Purchased 10.1747. Fate unknown.
SHEERNESS Cutter 10, 100bm. Hired 7.1802–3.05.
SHEERNESS Cutter 8, 8–4pdr. Hired 1800–01.
SHEERNESS DY craft, 42bm. In service 1865–74. (Also known as
Woolwich YC.5.)
SHEERNESS Wood paddle tug, 233bm, 123 x 20½ ft. Purchased 16.6.1863
Sold 3.4.1906.
SHEERNESS MFV 21net. Hired as BBV tender 6.1940–45.
SHEET LIGHTNING Admiralty wood Dr, 92gr. Innes, Macduff 1918.
Sold 1921, renamed *Roseacre*. (ROSEACRE in WW.II.)
SHEILA Yt 80/04. Purchased in WW.I. Sold 7.7.20. Hired as M/S repair
ship 1.40, purchased 11.41. Laid up 11.45, sold 1946.

SHEILA Dr 83/07, 1–3pdr. Hired 1915–19.

SHELDON Tr 288/12, 1–6pdr. Hired 1915–19 and as A/P Tr, 2–MG, 5.40. M/S 3.42; fuel carrier 3.44–1.45.

SHELOMI Tr 175/12, 1–6pdr. Hired 1915–19.

SHEMARA Yt 588/99, 1–12pdr, 1–6pdr. Hired as A/P Yt 13.9.1914–5.3.19.

SHEMARA Yt 834/38. Hired as A/S Yt 9.1939. A/S training 1941–3.46.

SHEPHERD BOY Dr 81/13, 1–3pdr. Hired 1.1915–19.

SHEPHERD LAD Dr 100/25. Hired on harbour service 8.1939–4.46.

SHEPPERTON (ex-*Shepperton Ferry*) 2,839/35, 1–4in, 2–20mm, 270 mines. Hired as M/L 8.1939. Wrecked by air attack at Belfast 5.5.41.

SHEPPEY (ex-RAASAY renamed 1942) Tr, 'Isles' class. Cook Welton & Gemmell 1.4.42. To War Dept 1946, same name.

SHEPPEY (see BLACKBIRD)

SHERA Wh 253/29. Hired as M/S 3.1940. To Russian navy 2.42. Capsized 9.3.42 on passage in the Barents Sea.

SHERATON Tr 283/07. Hired as BDV 1915–19 and as A/P Tr, 1–6pdr, 6.40–45.

SHETLAND Dr 77/03, 1–3pdr. Hired 1915–19.

SHIANT Tr, 'Isles' class. Goole SB 9.8.1941. Sold 1946, renamed *Artemis*. (On loan R.Norwegian navy 1944–9.46 as JELOY.)

SHIELBURN Tr 212/11. Hired 3.1944–10.44.

SHIELD Dr 96/07, 1–6pdr. Hired 1915–19.

SHIELDS Dr 72/01, 1–2½pdr. Hired 1916–19.

SHIKA Wh 251/29. Hired as M/S 3.1940. To Russian navy 2.42.

SHIKARI Tr 221/14, 1–6pdr. Hired 1915. Base ship 1917–19.

SHILA Wh 189/26. Hired as danlayer 2.1940. Target-towing 2.43–3.46.

SHILLAY Tr, 'Isles' class. Cook Welton & Gemmell 18.11.1944, completed as danlayer. Sold 9.58 to BU in Italy; became mercantile.

SHILLONG Tr, 'Basset' class (RIN); Burn, Calcutta 22.9.1942. Sold 1946, renamed *Fatima*.

SHIMMER Admiralty wood Dr, 97gr. Colby 1918. Sold 1921, same name.

SHIONA Yt 112/38. Hired on examination service 9.1939. Harbour service 1943–9.46.

SHIPMATES Dr 82/11, 1–6pdr. Hired 1915–19 and as flare Dr, 1–3pdr, 11.39. A/P Dr 8.40: Sunk 14.11.40 by air attack in Dover harbour.

SHIPWAY (see SWIN)

SHOLAPUR (see BARISAL)

SHOOTINGSTAR Admiralty non-standard wood Dr, 98gr. Colby 1918. Sold circa 1929, same name.

SHOOTING STAR (see VESTFOLD 6)

SHOVA Wh 180/12. Hired as danlayer 4.1940. Mooring vessel 7.42; target-towing 1.43–3.46.

SHOWER Admiralty steel Dr, 96gr. Brooke 1918. Sold 14.8.45, same name.

SHRAPNEL (see STIFF)

SHU KWANG 782/24. Hired as A/S vessel 1940. Sunk 13.2.42 by Japanese air attack in the Dutch E.Indies.

SHULAMITE Customs vessel 122/30. In commission on examination service (RCN) 5.1941–46.

SHUN ON Paddle 112/16. Hired as A/P vessel 11.1941. Lost 2.42 at Singapore. (Spelt SHUN AN in Loss List.)

SHUN WO 220/17. Hired as skid M/S 10.1940. Listed at Hong Kong until its loss to the Japanese.

SHUSA Wh 251/29. Hired as M/S 3.1940. To Russian navy 2.42 and lost 20.11.42 in their service.

SIALKOT Tr, 'Basset' class (RIN). Alcock Ashdown. Ordered 7.1942, laid down 2.44, cancelled 1945.

SIAM DUFFY Tr, 'Castle' type, 276gr. Bow McLachlan 1918. Sold 1921, renamed *Edouard Anselle.* (Served as FONTENOY in WW.II.)

SIANGWO 2,595/26. Hired as A/S vessel 1940. Beached in the Dutch E. Indies after attack by Japanese A/C 13.2.42.

SICYON Tr 283/06, 1–6pdr. Hired 1914–19.

SICYON Tr 344/30. Hired as M/S 9.1939–7.46.

SIDMOUTH Tr 220/06, 1–6pdr. Hired 1914–19.

SIDNEY SMITH Wh 250/29. Commissioned as M/S (SAN) 2.1941. Renamed PARKTOWN 2.42. Sunk 21.6.42 by Italian MTBs in the central Mediterranean.

SIDONIAN (see ADVENTURE)

SIESTA (see A.ROSE)

SIGFRA Wh 356/37. Hired as A/S Wh 12.1941, later purchased. Sold 3.46.

SIGISMUND (see SIMOUN)

SIGNA Wh 190/26. Hired as danlayer 2.1940–2.45.

SIGNET BDV 530 tons, 135 x 30½ ft, 1–3in. Blyth DD 3.5.1939. On sale list 1958.

SIGRID Yt 30/25. Hired on harbour service 6.1940, purchased 11.41. Laid up 9.45, sold 1946.

SILANION Tr 199/03, 1–6pdr. Hired 1916–19.

SILANION Tr 366/30. Hired as BDV 1.1940–12.45.

SILESIA Wh 175/12. Purchased 1917. Sold 1920.

SILHOUETTE Admiralty wood Dr, 100gr. Colby 1918. Sold circa 1929, renamed *Honora Evelyn.*

SILHOUETTE (see BUSEN 7)

SILICIA Tr 250/13, 1–6pdr. Hired 1914–19 and as M/S 8.39. Sunk 8.5.41 by mine off the Humber.

SILJA Wh 251/29. Hired as M/S 3.1940. To Russian navy 2.42. Returned and sold 3.47.

SILT Admiralty wood Dr, 100gr. Herd & Mackenzie, Findachty 1918. Sold 1921, renamed *Rose Valley*. (ROSE VALLEY in WW.II.)

SILURIA Tr 207/07. Hired 1917–19.

SILVA Wh 224/24. Hired as danlayer 5.1940. Harbour service 1942 and purchased. Laid up 3.46, sold 1946.

SILVERAXE Tr 270/08, 1–6pdr. Russian T.33 (ex-*Trece*) seized in the White sea and commissioned 8.1918. Sold 1920.

SILVERBEAM Tug 60gr. Hired as DY tug 2.1940–47.

SILVER CLOUD Yt 88/30. Hired 8.1940, purchased 9.41. Sold 6.46.

SILVER CREST Dr 94/28. Hired as M/S 10.1939. FAA vessel 1.44–2.46.

SILVERDALE Dr 62/07, 1–3pdr. Hired 1915–19.

SILVER DAWN Dr 95/25, 1–6pdr. Hired as mine-recovery vessel 11.1939. A/P 9.40–10.45.

SILVERFIELD Cstr 436/15. Hired as fleet messenger 4.8.1915–7.6.20.

SILVERFORD Dr 85/11. Hired on harbour service 1.15. A/P Dr 1917–19.

SILVER FOX Yt 59/37. Hired as HDPC 9.1939, purchased 11.41. Fire-float 2.44. On sale list 5.46.

SILVER GREY MFV 20net/32. Hired as HDPC 11.1939–9.45.

SILVER HERRING Dr 86/11. Hired 1915–19.

SILVER KING Dr 81/07, 1–6pdr. Hired 1915–19.

SILVER LINE Dr 92/12, 1–3pdr. Hired 1914–19 and as HDPC 11.39–23.12.41.

SILVER MIST Yt 37/30. Hired on harbour service 8.1942, purchased 1.43. Sold 7.46.

SILVEROL (ex-*Hopper No 8*) 869/07. Hired as oiler (RFA) 10.1916–20.

SILVER PEARL Dr 71/11. Hired 1915–19.

SILVER PRINCE Dr 108/13. Hired on harbour service 8.1915–19 and on harbour service 11.40, purchased 1.41. Sold 15.9.47. (Base ship SKIRMISHER 1.41–45.)

SILVER QUEEN Dr 84/10, 1–6pdr. Hired 1.1915. Sunk 15.2.18 in action off Dover.

SILVERSCALE Dr 91/11, 1–6pdr. Hired 1.1915–19.

SILVER SEAS Dr 117/31. Hired as M/S 11.1939. Harbour service 7.42–9.45.

SILVER SKY Dr 96/19. Hired on harbour service 12.1939. Examination service 1941–44; water boat 3.44–1.46.

SILVER SPRAY Dr 61/07. Hired 1915–19 and as M/S 12.39–6.40.

SILVER TAY MFV. Hired 4.1940, purchased 4.41. Lost 7.43.

SILVERY DAWN Dr 95/07, 1–6pdr. Hired 1915–19.

SILVERY HARVEST Dr 86/ -. Hired 1915. Sunk 16.5.18 in collision off Berry Head.

SILVERY WAVE Dr 96/ -. Hired 1915. Wrecked 13.11.15 in Crow Sound

SIMBRA Wh 356/37. Hired as A/S Wh 12.1941, later purchased. Sold 9.46.

SIMEON MOON Tr, 'Mersey' type, 324gr. Cochrane 31.5.1919. Sold 1920, renamed *General Rawlinson*.

SIMERSON Tr 248/13, 1–6pdr. Hired 1915–19 and as A/P Tr, 1–6pdr, 7.40–6.46.

SIMLA Tug 144/98. Hired 7.1914–7.15.

SIMOON 2,222/14. Hired as fleet auxiliary 1.1916–19.

SIMOUN Yt 308/97. Hired as ABS 30.5.1916. Renamed SIGISMUND 4.18. Returned 10.3.19.

SIMPSON Tr 261/17, 1–6pdr. Hired 1917–19 and as A/P Tr, 1–6pdr, 6.40. M/S 5.42–12.45.

SIN AIK LEE 198/28. Hired as M/S 9.1939. Lost 2.42 in the Singapore area.

SINCERE Dr 92/16, 1–3pdr. Hired 1916–19.

SINCERITY Cutter 6. Hired 1793–1804.

SINDONIS (ex-*Soudanese*) Tr 440/34, 1–4in. Purchased as A/S Tr 8.1939. Sunk 29.5.41 by air attack at Tobruk.

SINGAPORE Tr 159/00. Hired 1918–19.

SINGLETON ABBEY 2,467/15. Hired as fleet auxiliary 4.7.1915–19.

SIOUX Tug 340/17. French M/L seized 3.7.1940 at Portsmouth. BBV 8.40. Boom gate vessel 3.42. Renamed INDIAN 1944. Returned 1945.

SIR AGRAVAINE M/S Tr 440 tons, 126 x 24 ft, 1–12pdr, 1–20mm. Lewis 5.3.1942. Sold 4.46, same name.

SIR BEVOIS Tug 338/16. Hired on examination service 8.1939. Sunk 20.3.41 by air attack off Plymouth.

SIR BRIAN Tug 146/93. Hired 3.1918–3.19.

SIR CHARLES FORBES Paddle vessel, 141bm, 130 x 18½ ft. Purchased as tank vessel 10.1.1861. Renamed WATERMAN 1861. Sold 1862, renamed *Nagasaki Maru*.

SIR DONALD Tender. Transferred from War Dept 1906. Foundered 28.3.06 in tow of CIRCE in the Irish Sea.

SIREN Yt 48/98. Hired as HDPC 2.1940, purchased 8.41. Harbour service 7.43; laid up 1.46. Sold 1946?

Sir E.P. WILLS 162/37. Hired on examination service 9.1939. Target-towing 1943–8.45.

SIR FRANCIS DRAKE Tender 478/08. Hired as tug 7.1914–1.19 and on examination service 8.39. Ferry 1941–6.46.

SIR GALAHAD M/S Tr (as SIR AGRAVAINE). Hall Russell 18.12.1941. Danlayer 1944. Sold 4.46, renamed *Star of Freedom*.

SIR GARETH M/S Tr (as SIR AGRAVAINE). Hall Russell 19.1.1942. Sold 11.4.46, renamed *Star of the East*.

SIR GEORGE MURRAY Lighter 120dw. Hired as degaussing vessel 2.1940–1.48.
SIR GERAINT M/S Tr (as SIR AGRAVAINE). Lewis 15.4.1942. Sold 4.46, renamed *Star of the South.*
SIR HUGH BELL Paddle tug 175/13. Hired 6.1915–20.
SIRIUS Dr 91/31. Belgian, hired as A/P Dr 6.1940–12.41.
SIR JAMES RECKITT Tr 324/09, 1–12pdr. Hired 1915–19.
SIR JOHN BAKER Ferry 43/10. Hired on examination service 8.1939. Laid up 7.42–7.9.44.
SIR JOHN FRENCH Tr 351/15, 1–12pdr. Hired 1916–19.
SIR JOHN HAWKINS Tender 939/29. Hired on ferry service 7.1.1941–10.45.
SIR JOHN LISTER Tr 281/19. Hired as M/S 9.1939–8.45.
SIR JOSEPH PEASE Tug 180/96. Hired on DY service 7.1915–20.
SIR KAY M/S Tr (as SIR AGRAVAINE). Hall Russell 26.10.1942. Sold 10.4.46, renamed *Star of the North.*
SIR LAMORAK M/S Tr (as SIR AGRAVAINE). Hall Russell 23.11.1942. Sold 4.46, renamed *Braconbank.*
SIR LANCELOT M/S Tr (as SIR AGRAVAINE). Lewis 4.12.1941. Danlayer 1944. Sold 4.46, same name.
SIR MARK SYKES Tr 307/14, 1–12pdr. Hired 1915–19.
SIROCCO Admiralty wood Dr, 97gr. Colby 1919. Renamed DOUBLE TIDE 1919. Sold 1920, renamed *Cat's Eye.*
SIROCCO Admiralty steel Dr. Ailsa. Cancelled 1919.
SIRRA Wh 251/29. Hired as M/S 3.1940–4.46.
SIR RICHARD GRENVILLE Tender 896/31. Hired on examination service 8.1939. Ferry service 1941–1.46.
SIR THOMAS Tug 184/98. Hired 3.1918–1.19.
SIR THOMAS PASLEY Brig 16. Hired 1800. Captured 9.12.1800 by two Spanish gunboats in the Mediterranean.
SIR THOMAS PASLEY Cutter 14. Hired 1801–02.
SIR TRISTRAM M/S Tr (as SIR AGRAVAINE). Lewis 17.1.1942. Sold 1947.
SIR WALTER RALEIGH Tender 478/08. Hired as tug 7.1914–1.19 and on examination service 8.39. Fleet tender 3.41. Mining tender 1.42–8.46.
SIR WILLIAM HILARY Yt 40/29. Hired on air-sea rescue 10.1940, purchased 11.41. On sale list 9.46.
SISAPON Tr 326/28. Hired as M/S 9.1939. Sunk 12.6.40 by mine off Harwich.
SISTER ANNE Yt 250/29. Hired as accommmodation ship 9.1940, purchased 5.41. Laid up 12.45, sold 1946?
SITA 91/28. Hired as A/P vessel (RIN) 1940–43.

SITAKHOOND 280/10. Hired as A/P vessel (RIN) 1939–43.

SIXTEEN Dr 78/01. Hired 1915–19.

SKELWITH FORCE Cstr 562/08. Hired as fleet messenger 9.1915–7.16

SKERNE Tr 150/91. Hired 1917–19.

SKIBO CASTLE Dr 81/10. Hired as store carrier 9.1914–19.

SKIDDAW (ex-*Britannia*) Paddle 483/96, 1–12pdr. Hired as M/S 11.1939. A/A ship 8.42–7.45.

SKILFUL DY tug 300 tons. Taikoo DY Co. Ordered 15.5.1941. Listed as building until the fall of Hong Kong.

SKILPAD (see SPINDRIFT)

SKIPPER Cstr 356/04. Hired as ammo. carrier (RFA) 9.1914–19.

SKIPTON (ex-*Skipjack*) 1,167/10. Hired as ammo. carrier (RFA) 7.8.1914–22.2.19.

SKOKHOLM Tr, 'Islea' class. Cook Welton & Gemmell 29.9.1943. Sold 1946, renamed *Skogholm.*

SKOMER Tr, 'Isles' class. Lewis 17.6.1943. Wreck dispersal 1946; oil tank cleaning vessel 1956.

SKUDD 3 Wh 245/29. Norwegian, hired as M/S 6.1940. Sunk 27.8.41 by air attack at Tobruk.

SKUDD 4 Wh 247/29. Norwegian, hired as M/S 6.1940. Renamed SPATE 3.4.44. Returned 10.45.

SKUDD 5 Wh 265/30. Norwegian, hired as M/S 6.1940. Renamed SURGE 3.4.44. Returned 10.45

SKUDD 6 Wh 323/30. Norwegian, Hired as M/S 6.1940. Renamed SLEET 3.4.44. Returned 11.45.

SKYE Tr, 'Isles' class. Robb, Leith 17.3.1942. Arrived 29.5.58 McLellan, Bo'ness to BU.

SKYLARK Coastguard vessel, 70bm, 55½ x 17 ft. Built 1868. Renamed DELIGHT 28.7.84. Sold 4.4.1905.

SKYLARK Yt 36/32. Hired as balloon tender 6.1940, purchased 11.41. Examination service 1.42. Lent Clyde pilots 2.44, laid up 6.45.

SKYLINE Admiralty steel Dr. Fellows, Yarmouth. Cancelled 1919.

SKYRACK (ex-*Pilote 18*) Pilot 423/37. Belgian, hired as A/P vessel 29.6.1940–5.45.

SKYROCKET (see SCOURGE)

SLAINS CASTLE Dr 81/08. Hired 1915–19.

SLASHER Tr 195/00, 1–3pdr. Hired 1916–19.

SLAV 2,275/13. Hired as fleet auxiliary 1.1916–19.

SLAVOL Oiler (RFA) 4,900 tons, 335 x 41½ ft. Greenock & Grange-mouth Co 21.4.1917. Water carrier 1941. Sunk 26.3.42 by 'U.205' north-east of Sollum.

SLEBECH Tr 222/08. Hired as M/S 1915–19 and as M/S 12.39. Fuel carrier 3.43; water carrier 1.44–1.46.

SLEDWAY (see KINGARTH)

SLEET Admiralty steel Dr, 97gr. Brooke 1918. Sold 20.8.20, same name. (Served as CONSOLATION in WW.II.)

SLEET (see SKUDD 6)

SLEUTH (ex-*Ena*) Yt 104/01, 108 tons, 1–3pdr. Hired as A/P Yt (RAN) 1915–20.

SLEUTH (see VIGILANT)

SLIEVE BEARNAGH Paddle 383/94, 1–6pdr. Hired as M/S 24.2.1915, purchased 23.10.17. Sold 16.1.23 Ward, to BU.

SLIEVE FOY Tug 154/10. Hired as rescue tug 21.7.1915–20.

SLOGAN (ex-*Samson*) Tug 110/26, 1–MG. Belgian, Hired 11.1939 as M/S, purchased 14.2.40. Listed to 1943.

SLUGA Wh 251/29. Hired as M/S 3.1940–4.46.

SLUNA Tr, 'Isles' class. Cochrane 14.4.1941. Sold 7.46, renamed *Shun Wa*.

SMALVLEI (see HEKTOR 2)

SMEATON Tender 369/83. Hired as tug 7.1914–17 and on examination service 9.39. Laid up 1942–47.

SMEW Tr 249/07, 1–6pdr. Hired 1916–19.

SMILAX Dr 81/10, 1–3pdr. Hired 1915–19.

SMILING MORN MFV 23net. Hired on harbour service 7.1940–9.45.

SMITH SOUND MFV 22net/40. Hired as M/S (RCN) 1941–45.

SMLs (see under MLs)

SMOKE CLOUD Admiralty steel Dr. Goole SB. Cancelled 1919.

SNAEFELL 1,368/10, 2–12pdr, 1–2pdr. Hired as ABS 24.11.1914. Sunk 3.6.18 by 'UB.105' in the Mediterranean.

SNAEFELL (ex-*Waverley*) Paddle 466/07, 1–12pdr. Hired as M/S 10.1939. Sunk 5.7.41 by air attack off the Tyne.

SNAKEFLY (see FANE)

SNAP (ex-*Boy John*) MFV 39net. Hired as danlayer 12.1939–12.43.

SNIDER Armament store carrier 604 tons, 134 x 25 ft. Lobnitz 16.11.1945. Sold 1964.

SNIPE Tr 146/97. Hired as BDV 1915–19.

SNOWDON Paddle 338/92, 1–6pdr. Hired as M/S 31.12.1915–31.5.19.

SNOWDRIFT Admiralty steel Dr, 97gr. Lewis 1918. Sold 1921, renamed *Fifeness*. (Served as G.G.BAIRD in WW.II.)

SNOWDRIFT (see BUSEN 11)

SNOWDROP II Dr 94/07, 1–3pdr. Hired 1915–19.

SNOWDROP III Dr 62/05, 1–3pdr. Hired 1915–19.

SNOWDROP IV Dr 63/01, 1–2½pdr. Hired 1916–19.

SNOWFINCH (see DILIGENT)

SNOWFLAKE Admiralty steel Dr, 96gr. Webster & Bickerton 1919. Sold 1919, renamed *C.S.D.* (Served as MARY HERD in WW.II.)

SNOWSTORM Admiralty steel Dr. Goole SB. Cancelled 1919.

SOAR Tr 219/15, 1–6pdr. Hired 1916–19.

SOBKRA Wh 433/37. Hired as A/S Wh 10.1941–9.46.

SOCIETY 30-gun ship. Hired 1650–54.

SOCIETY 36-gun ship, 330 bm. Hired 1664–67.

SOETVLEI (see HEKTOR 3)

SOIKA Wh 313/25. Hired as M/S 4.1940–10.45.

SOIZIC Dr 72/37. French M/S seized 3.7.1940 at Plymouth. A/P Dr 11.40. Sunk 20.3.41 by enemy action.

SOJOURNER Dr. Hired as A/S Dr 1.1940–6.45.

SOLDIER PRINCE Tr 156/01. Hired as M/S 1914–19.

SOLENT 1,474/10. Hired as fleet auxiliary 1918–19.

SOLITAIRE (ex-*Schelde*) Tug 91/04, 2–MG. Hired as M/S 1939, purchased 1941. Capsized 20.6.44 in a storm off the Normandy coast.

SOLOMON Tr 357/28. Hired as M/S 8.1939. Sunk 1.4.42 by mine north of Cromer.

SOLON Tr 295/12, 1–6pdr. Hired 1914–19.

SOLON Tr 348/31, 1–12pdr. Hired as M/S 11.1939–1.46.

SOLSTICE Admiralty wood Dr, 98gr. Herd & Mackenzie 1918. Sold 1921, same name. Hired as M/S 11.39. S/M tender 5.43–9.46.

SOLVRA Wh 433/37. Hired as A/S Wh 1.1942–9.46.

SOLWAY Tug 103/86. Hired as DY tug 9.10.1917–19.

SOLWAY (see KINGUSSIE)

SOMERSET (see BARCROSS)

SOMERVILLE Tr 149/91. Hired 1918–19.

SONA Yt 555/22. Purchased as A/S Yt 9.1939. Accommodation ship 9.40. Sunk 4.1.42 by air attack at Poole

SONAVATI 1,638/36. Hired as A/S vessel (RIN) 1939–46.

SONDRA Wh 433/37. Hired as A/S Wh 12.1941–10.45.

SONIA (ex-*Limburg*) Tug 294/16. Dutch, hired 11.1917–19.

SONNEBLOM (see JOHN EDMUND)

SONNEBLOM (see TERJE 8)

SONNET BDV 530 tons, 135 x 30½ ft, 1–3in. Blyth DD 12.7.1939. Arrived 22.4.59 in Holland to BU.

SONNY BOY Dr 83/31, 1–6pdr. Belgian, hired on harbour service 30.6.1940–8.45.

SOOTHSAYER (see BURLINGTON)

SOPHIE FRANCOIS Dr 73/30. Belgian, hired as A/P Dr 8.10.1940. Harbour service 1942–10.45.

SOPHIE MARIE 1,138/23. Hired as A/P vessel (RIN) 1939. Sunk 19.3.42 by mine off the Andaman Islands.

SOPHOS Tr 217/14, 1–3pdr. Hired 1915–19.

SOPHRON Tr 195/03. Hired 1916. Sunk 22.8.17 by mine off the Firth of Tay.

SORANUS Tr 250/06. Hired as M/S 10.1940–10.45.
SORCERESS Yt 328/87. Hired 17.12.1914–26.2.15.
SORRENTO 2,892/12. Hired as store carrier (RFA) 2.8.1914–22.3.15.
SORSRA Wh 433/37. Hired as A/S Wh 12.1941–9.46.
SOTRA Wh 313/25. Hired as M/S 9.1939. Sunk 29.1.42 by 'U.431' off Bardia.
SOUBRETTE Tr 199/20. Hired on examination service 8.1940–4.45.
SOUTHAMPTON SALVOR Salvage vessel 800 tons, 170 x 37 ft, 1–3in, 2–20mm. Bellingham IW 23.1.1943 and to the RN 12.43 on lend-lease. Returned 10.46 to the USN.
SOUTHCOATES Tr 276/18, 1–12pdr. Hired as A/P Tr 6.1940–11.45.
SOUTHEND BELLE Paddle 617/96, 1–6pdr. Hired as M/S 2.4.1916–8.11.19.
SOUTHERN BARRIER Wh 344/36. Hired as M/S (SAN) 1.10.1940–5.46.
SOUTHERN BREEZE Wh 344/36. Hired as A/S Wh 3.1940–1.46.
SOUTHERN CHIEF Wh 295/26. Purchased as M/S 3.1940. Sold 2.46.
SOUTHERN CROSS Yt 357/33, 1–4in. Purchased on examination service (RAN) 1941. Sold 26.10.46.
SOUTHERN CROSS Yt 40/30? Purchased as A/P Yt 10.4.1942. Sold 1946.
SOUTHERN FIELD Wh 250/29. Hired as M/S 3.1940–4.46.
SOUTHERN FLOE Wh 344/36. Hired as A/S Wh (SAN) 3.1940. Sunk 11.2.41 by mine off Tobruk.
SOUTHERN FLOWER Wh 328/28. Hired as A/S Wh 3.1940. Sunk 3.3.45 by U-boat off Iceland.
SOUTHERN FOAM Wh 295/26. Hired as M/S 3.1940–1.46.
SOUTHERN GEM Wh 593/37. Hired as A/S Wh 3.1940–4.45.
SOUTHERN ISLES Wh 344/36. Hired as A/S Wh (SAN) 1940–5.46.
SOUTHERN ISLES (ex-*Princess Marie Jose*) 1,821/22. Belgian, hired 17.9.1940 as A/S training ship. Renamed NEMESIS 3.41; BALDUR base ship 10.43; NEMESIS 1945. For return 8.45.
SOUTHERN MAID Wh 344/36. Hired as A/S Wh 3.1940, purchased 20.1.41. To SAN 13.3.41. Sold 7.5.46.
SOUTHERN PRIDE Wh 582/36. Hired as A/S Wh 3.1940. Wrecked 16.6.44 in Sierra Leone.
SOUTHERN PRINCE 10,917/29, 2–4in, 7–20mm, 560 mines. Completed as M/L 15.6.1940. Accommodation ship (red ensign) 10.44. Sold 1.4.47.
SOUTHERN SEA Wh 344/36. Hired as A/S Wh 3.1940, purchased 20.1.41. To SAN 30.1.45. Sold 7.5.46.
SOUTHERN SHORE Wh 328/28. Hired as M/S 3.1940. A/S Wh 6.40–1.46.
SOUTHERN SPRAY Wh 319/25. Hired as A/S Wh 3.1940–11.45.

SOUTHERN STAR Wh 340/30. Hired as A/S Wh 3.1940–1.46.

SOUTHERN WAVE Wh 320/25. Hired as A/S Wh 3.1940–12.45.

SOUTHESK Dr 93/12. Hired 1915. Sunk 7.7.17 by mine in Auskerry Sound.

SOUTHGATE (see BV.8 under BD vessels)

SOUTHLAND 2,081/08. American, To the RN on lend-lease as accommodation ship 3.1942. Returned 1944 to the USA.

SOUTHMARK Oiler (RFA), 8,053/38. German DITTMARSCHEN seized 1945. To USN 1947.

SOUTH SEA Tr 322/13. Commissioned as M/S (RNZN) 12.8.1940. Sunk 19.12.42 in collision with *Wahine*.

SOUTHSEA Paddle 825/30, 1–12pdr. Hired as M/S 2.1940. Mined and beached 16.2.41 off the Tyne.

SOUTH TYNE Dr 79/04. Hired 1915–19.

SOUTHWARD Tr 225/07. Hired 1918–19.

SOUTHWARD HO Tr 204/19. Hired as fuel carrier 3.1944–2.45.

SOUVENIR (ex-*Wrestler*) Tug 120/14, 2–MG. Hired as M/S 1939, purchased 1940. Laid up 7.43. To MWT 8.44.

SPA Tank vessel 1,220 tons, 160 x 30 ft. Philip 11.10.1941.

SPABECK (ex-RIVULET) Tank vessel (as SPA). Philip 21.6.1943.

SPABROOK Tank vessel (as SPA). Philip 24.8.1944.

SPABURN Tank vessel (as SPA). Philip 5.1.1946.

SPACE Admiralty steel Dr. Goole SB. Cancelled 1919.

SPACE (see SPLASH)

SPALAKE Tank vessel (as SPA). Hill, Bristol 10.8.46.

SPANIARD Tr 455/37, 1–4in. Purchased as A/S Tr 8.1939. Lost 5.12.42 by explosion and fire at Lagos.

SPANIEL (see TERJE 1)

SPANIEL DY tug, 152gr. Appledore SY 12.4.1967.

SPAPOOL Tank vessel (as SPA). Hill 28.2.1946.

SPARK Admiralty steel Dr. Goole SB. Cancelled 1919.

SPARKLER DY tug 210 tons, 90 x 22 ft. Northwich 19.2.1940. Sold 11.6.57, renamed *Alfred Lamey*.

SPARKLING STAR Dr 90/06. Hired 2.1915–19.

SPARROW (ex-*Josephine I*) Tr 226/08, 550 tons, 1–12pdr. Purchased as M/S 4.1909. Reverted to JOSEPHINE I in 1919. Sold 4.5.20, renamed *Orion*.

SPARSHOLT 127/15. Hired as mooring vessel 2.1940. Sunk 13.3.42 by mine off Shoeburyness.

SPARTAN Tr 120/93. Hired on harbour service 27.11.1914–19.

SPATE Admiralty wood Dr, 96gr. Dunston 1918. Sold 1919, same name. (Served as MARGUERITA in WW.II.)

SPATE (see SKUDD 4)

SPEAR Armament store carrier, 250gr. Listed 1947–64.

SPECTRUM Admiralty steel Dr, 97gr. Brooke 27.3.1918. Sold 1920, same name. Hired on harbour service 9.39–8.45.

SPECULATION Dr 83/11, 1–3pdr. Hired 2.1915–19.

SPECULATOR Lugger 10, 93bm, 10–4pdr. Hired 1794–1801 and 8.1803–9.13.

SPEEDWELL A.ship, 80bm. Hired for the Armada campaign 1588.

SPEEDWELL Lugger 14. Hired 1797–1801.

SPEEDWELL Bomb tender 5. Hired 1801–02.

SPEEDWELL II Tr 273/99, 1–12pdr, 1–6pdr. Hired as decoy ship (Q.23) 1915. Wrecked 15.7.18 in Mounts Bay.

SPEEDWELL III Dr 96/07, 1–6pdr. Hired 5.1915–19. (Served as ALTRUIST IN WW.II.)

SPEEDWELL Dr 79/03. Hired as BDV 4.8.1915; GODSPEED 4.18–19.

SPEEDWELL IV Tr? In WW.I.

SPEEDWELL V Dr 92/11. Hired 1915. Stranded 28.10.16 near Greenore Point.

SPEETON Tr 205/13. Hired 1915. Sunk 31.12.15 by mine off Lowestoft.

SPERANZA Dr 86/11, 1–3pdr. Hired 1915–19 and as A/P Dr, 2–MG, 12.39–8.46.

SPERCHEIOS (see NOBLE NORA)

SPES AUREA Dr 95/20. Hired on harbour service 10.1939–5.45.

SPES MELIOR Dr 96/19. Hired on harbour service 10.1939–4.46.

SPEY BAY Dr 86/07, 1–3pdr. Hired 1915–19.

SPHENE (see AVANTURINE)

SPHINX II Dr 77/07, 1–3pdr. Hired 1916–19.

SPIDER Lugger 18. Hired 1794. Lost 4.4.1796 in collision with RAMILLIES 74.

SPIDER Cutter 10, 114bm, 10–12pdr carr. Hired 8.1803–12.04.

SPIDER (ex-*Assyrian*) Tr 271/06, 1–6pdr. Purchased as M/S 4 1909. Wrecked 21.11.14 near Lowestoft. Salved? Listed to 1919.

SPIDER (ex-*Francisco Antonio Quarto*) Circa 130gr. Purchased at Gibraltar as degaussing vessel 1941. Sold 25.6.46.

SPINA Wh 190/26. Hired as danlayer 2.1940–3.45.

SPINDRIFT Tr 926 tons, 160 x 26 ft. German POLARIS captured 4.1940. A/S training 6.40. M/L 1.42. To SAN 1946, renamed SKILPAD 1951. On sale list 1958.

SPINEL Cstr 509/93. Hired as fleet messenger 6.10.1915–29.6.20.

SPINET (ex-*St Merryn*) Tr 352/24. Hired as BDV 9.1939–45.

SPITFIRE III Yt 142/38, 2–MG. Hired as danlayer 10.1939. A/P Yt 9.40; laid up 12.41; firefloat 1.44. Purchased 1.45. Sold 1.46.

SPLASH Admiralty wood Dr, 96gr. Dunston 1920. Renamed SPACE 1920. Sold 1920, same name.

SPOONDRIFT Admrialty steel Dr. Rose St Fndry. Cancelled 1919.

SPORTSMAN Cstr 572/14. Hired as store carrier (RFA) 3.1918–2.19.

SPOSA Wh 316/26. Hired as A/S Wh 4.1940–4.45.

SPRAY Tug 118/07. Hired as M/S (RCN) 1941–45.

SPRAYVILLE 485/20. Hired as cable ship 9.1943–45.

SPRIGHTLY Rescue tug, 'B.A.T' class. Levingston 7.8.1942 on lend lease. Sold RAN 1944.

SPRIG o' HEATHER Dr 86/14. Hired as BBV 4.1940–2.46.

SPRINGBANK 5,155/26, 8–4in, 6–20mm. Hired as A/A ship 11.1939. Sunk 27.9:41 by 'U.201' in the N.Atlantic.

SPRINGDALE 1,579/37, 2–12pdr. Purchased as M/S 1940. Deperming vessel 1941–46.

SPRINGS (see UNI.I)

SPRINGTIDE Admiralty wood Dr. Jones, Buckie. Cancelled 1919.

SPRINGTIDE 1,579/37, 2–12pdr. Purchased as M/S 1940. Deperming vessel 1941–46.

SPRINGWELL Tr 286/17, 1–6pdr. Hired 1917–19.

SPRITE DY tug 172 tons, 80 x 19 ft. Fleming & Ferguson 4.6.1896. Sold 1906.

SPRITE DY paddle tug 690 tons, 145 x 28 ft. Thornycroft 23.8.1915. Arrived 27.3.60 in Holland to BU.

SPRUCE LAKE Motor M/S (RCN) 255 tons, 126 x 26 ft, 2–20mm. Star SY 10.7.1945. To Russian navy 19.3.46.

SPRUCOL Oiler (RFA) 1,925 tons, 220 x 34 ft. Short, Sunderland 4.7.1917. Sold 29.1.20, renamed *Juniata.*

SPRY Rescue tug, 507gr, 141½ x 29 ft. Livingstone & Cooper 1918. Sold 1.23, renamed *Lagos Atlas.*

SPUME Admiralty steel Dr. Banff. Cancelled 1919.

SPURS Tr 399/33. Purchased as A/S Tr 8.1939. Sold 1945.

SPURT Admiralty steel Dr, 96gr. Pimblott, Northwich 1919. Sold 1919, renamed *Craigentinny.* (CRAIGENTINNY in WW.II.)

SQUALL Admiralty wood Dr, 100gr. Chambers 1918. Sold 1920, same name.

SQUALL (see VESTFOLD X)

STADACONA Yt, 682/99. 1–4in, 1–12pdr. Purchased as A/P Yt (RCN) 1916. Became base ship at Halifax.

STAFFA Tr, 'Isles' class. Robb 15.6.1942. To Italian navy 1.46.

STAFNES Tr 456/36. Purchased as A/S Tr 8.1939. On sale list 7.45.

STAG Cutter 14, 131bm. Hired 1794–1801.

STAG Cutter 6, 57bm. Hired 3.1804–12.04.

STALBERG Tr 358/29. Hired as BDV 1,1940–11.45.

STALKER Tr 197/99, 1–6pdr. Hired 1915–19. (Served as CHOICE in WW.II.)

STALWART DY tug 244 tons, 95 x 22 ft. Ardrossan DD Co 1916, purchased on stocks. Renamed SEADOG 1918. Sold 31.12.19, renamed *Aghios Georgios.*

STALWART II Tr 333/14, 1–12pdr. Hired 1917–19.
STALWART (ex-*Theodor Woker*) Tug, 620gr, 146½ x 33 ft, 1–12pdr. Inglis 25.3.1939 and hired from S.African Govt 9.39 as rescue tug. Returned 1941.
STANDARD Tr 162/99. Hired 1917–19.
STANDARD COASTER Cstr 150/27. Hired as skid M/S (RCN) 5.1941–44.
STANDERTON (see HELIER 1)
STANDFAST (see STEADFAST)
STANISLAS POUMET MFV 96/31. French naval, seized 1940 at Greenock. Degaussing vessel 11.40–45.
STANLEY WEYMAN Tr 288/13, 1–6pdr. Hired 1915–19.
STAR XVI Wh 249/30. Norwegian, hired as M/S (RCN) 1941–11.45.
STARLIGHT Admiralty wood Dr, 94gr. Stevenson & Asher 1918. Sold 1921, renamed *Starlight Rays*. (In WW.II.)
STARLIGHT RAYS Dr 94/18. Hired as M/S 11.1939. Examination service 6.41; S/M tender 4.44; harbour service 5.45–7.46.
STAR of BRITAIN Tr 228/08. Hired as M/S 1914–19 and as M/S 6.40. Fuel carrier 3.44–3.46.
STAR of BUCHAN Dr 81/ -. Hired 1915. Sunk 20.10.15 by mine off the Nab.
STAR of DEVERON Tr 220/15. Hired as A/P Tr 11.1939. M/S 5.40. Sunk 30.9.41 by air attack off North Shields.
STAR of FAITH Dr 94/15. Hired 1915–19.
STAR of FREEDOM Tr 258/11. Hired 1.1915. Sunk 19.4.17 by mine off Trevose Head.
STAR of FREEDOM Tr 226/17. Hired as BDV 12.1939. Store carrier 5.41–7.46.
STAR of HOPE Dr 62/04. Hired on harbour service 10.1914–19.
STAR of HOPE MFV 56/02. Hired as HDPC 12.1939–7.45.
STAR of INDIA Yt 735/88. Hired as A/S Yt 7.1940, purchased 4.41. Examination service 9.42; accommodation ship 3.43. On sale list 5.46.
STAR of LIBERTY Tr 205/17. Hired on examination service 9.1940–1.46.
STAR of LIGHT Dr 84/12. Hired on harbour service 10.1940–2.46.
STAR of ORKNEY Tr 273/36. Hired as M/S 8.1939–9.46.
STAR of PENTLAND Tr 239/15. Hired as M/S 1.1940–5.46.
STAR of the EAST Tr 218/12, 1–6pdr. Hired 1914–19.
STAR of the EMPIRE Tr 219/13. Hired 1914–19.
STAR of the ISLES Tr 217/12, 1–6pdr. Hired as M/S 1914–19.
STAR of the NORTH Tr 192/03, 1–6pdr. Hired 1914–19.
STAR of the OCEAN Tr 203/03. Hired as BDV 1914–19.
STAR of the REALM (ex-*Nordstjernan*) Tr 325/17. Purchased as BDV 17.2.1940. Sold 6.46.

STAR of the SOUTH Tr 182/03. Hired 1918—19.
STAR of the WAVE Tr 205/03, 1—6pdr. Hired 1916—19.
STAR of the WAVE Tr 234/17. Hired as M/S 3.1940—12.45.
STAR of THULE Dr, 1—3pdr. Hired 1915—19.
STATELY Dr 72/04, 1—2½pdr. Hired 1915—19.
STATESMAN 6,153/95. Hired as store carrier (RFA) 4.8.1914—7.3.15.
STAUNCH DY barge, 131bm. Sheerness DY 10.7.1854. Sold 10.5.70.
(Also known as Deptford YC.2.)
STAUNCH (see BENGAL)
STAUNTON Tr 283/08, 1—6pdr. Hired as M/S 1914—20 and as A/P Tr,
1—6pdr, 6.40. Sunk 28.7.40 by mine in the Thames estuary.
STAVELY 1,041gr. Hired as store carrier (RFA) 10.1914—7.16.
STEADFAST (ex-*Ohio*) 625 tons, 118½ x 35 ft. American, purchased
and completed as mooring vessel 1.1916. Renamed STANDFAST 6.11.17.
Sold 5.22.
STEADY (ex-*Powerful*) Iron paddle tug, 78bm. Purchased 26.3.1855.
Sold 21.7.56 at Constantinople.
STEADY DY mooring vessel 758 tons, 135 x 27½ ft. Simons 30.3.1916.
Mined 17.7.40 off Newhaven; wreck sold 15.10.42.
STEADY HOUR Yt 50/40. Hired (RAN) 7.1941. Lost by fire 3.3.45 at
Darwin.
STEAMAXE Tr, 1—12pdr. Russian T.12, seized 9.1918 in the White Sea.
Grounded 1.11.19 near Inchkeith, salved and sold 1921.
STEENBERG Wh 250/29. Hired as M/S (SAN) 1940—5.46.
STEEPHOLM Tr, 'Isles' class. Lewis 15.7.1943. Arrived 18.6.60 in Belgium
to BU.
STEFA Wh 253/29. Hired as M/S 3.1940, later purchased. To Russian
navy 2.42. Returned; sold 5.47.
STELLA CANOPUS Tr 418/36. Hired as A/S Tr 10.1939—11.45.
STELLA CAPELLA Tr 440/37, 1—4in. Purchased as A/S Tr 8.1939.
Sunk 11.3.42 by U-boat off Iceland.
STELLA CARINA Tr 440/36, 1—12pdr. Hired as A/P Tr 11.1939. A/S
Tr 3.41—5.45.
STELLA DORADO Tr 416/35. Purchased as A/S Tr 8.1939. Sunk 1.6.40
by E-boat torpedo off Dunkirk.
STELLA LEONIS Tr 345/28. Hired as M/S 9.1939. Danlayer 4.44—7.46.
STELLA ORION Tr 417/35. Hired as M/S 9.1939. Sunk 11.11.40 by
mine in the Thames estuary.
STELLA PEGASI Tr 441/35, 1—12pdr. Hired as A/S Tr 9.1939—6.45.
STELLA POLARIS Tr 498/36. Hired as A/S Tr 5.1940—10.45.
STELLA RIGEL Tr 358/26, 1—12pdr. Hired as M/S 9.1939. Danlayer
4.44—7.45.
STELLA SIRIUS Tr 404/34. Purchased as A/S Tr 9.1939. Sunk 25.9.40
by French air attack at Gibraltar.

STELLENBERG Wh 250/29. Hired as M/S (SAN) 1940–5.46.

STEPHEN 4,435/10. Hired as store carrier (RFA) 5.1918–19.

STEPHEN FOLEY Tr, 'Mersey' type. Cochrane. Cancelled 1919.

STEPHEN FURNESS 1,712/10. Hired as depot ship 1.12.1914; store carrier 5.15; ABS, 2–4.7in, 3.16. Sunk 13.12.17 by 'UB.64' in the Irish Sea.

STEPHEN KENNEY Tr, 'Strath' type, 205gr. Abdela Mitchell 1919. Sold 1919, renamed *Witham*. (WITHAM in WW.II.)

STEPHENS Dr 89/11. Hired on harbour service 11.1939–4.46.

STERNUS Dr 93/25. Hired as M/S 1941?–9.45.

STERNWAVE Admiralty steel Dr, 96gr. Pimblott 1919. Sold 1920, renamed *Summer Rose*. (SUMMER ROSE in WW.II.)

STEWART BOYLE Tr 197/11. Hired as M/S 1914–19.

STIFF French DY tug, seized 3.7.1940 at Southampton. Harbour service 10.40–6.45. (Bore the name SHRAPNEL as base ship 1942–45.)

STINA Wh 251/28. Hired as M/S 3.1940–2.46.

STIRLING CASTLE Paddle 271/99. Hired as A/P vessel 18.5.1916. Blown up 26.9.16 off Malta, cause unknown.

STOBO CASTLE DY tug, 280gr, 104 x 27½ ft. Cran, Leith 1917 and purchased 1917. Sold 8.63 to BU. (Also known as C.102.)

STOCKADE (see ANSON)

STOCKFORCE (ex-*Charyce*) Cstr 732/05, 2–4in, 1–12pdr. Hired as decoy ship 1.1918. Damaged in action with 'U.98' and sank in tow 30.7.18 off Bolt Head.

STOIC (ex-Chilian PILOTO SIBBALD purchased on stocks) Fleet tug 885 tons, 142 x 29 ft. Bow McLachlan 3.1915. Resold 5.20 Chilian navy.

STOKE (ex-*Security*) Tug 189/04. Hired 1943–46.

STOKE CITY Tr 422/35, 1–4in. Hired as A/S Tr 9.1939–2.46.

STONEAXE M/S Tr, 292gr, 130 x 23½ ft, 1–12pdr. Smiths Dk 1.6.1916. Russian T.14, seized 8.1918 in the White sea. Renamed LIFFEY 10.20. Sold 1947.

STONECHAT Tr, 'Isles' class, completed as M/L, 580 tons. Cook Welton & Gemmell 28.8.1944. BU 1967 at Dalmuir.

STONECROP (see GLENFOYLE)

STONEFLY (ex-*Malayan*) Tr 238/30. Hired as M/S 8.1939–9.45.

STORA Wh 341/29. Hired as A/S Wh 6.1940–45. (Foundered 1.6.41, raised 3.42.)

STORK 2,029/04. Hired as store carrier (RFA) 16.8.1914–18.8.15.

STORK Tug 278/05. Hired 3.1917–19.

STORMBIRD (ex-*Stormcock*) Tug 215/85. Hired as DY tug 13.8.1914–20

STORMCENTRE Admiralty wood Dr, 99gr. Chambers 1918. Sold 1922, same name. (Served as NORTHAVEN in WW.II.)

STORMCENTRE (see ESTRELLA do NORTE)

STORMCOCK Fleet tug 580 tons, 155½ x 25 ft. Purchased 24.9.1882. Sold 7.3.22.

STORMCOCK Tr 151/92. Hired 1917–19.

STORMCOCK Tug 99/84. Hired 7.1917–19.

STORMCOCK (ex-*Capetown*) Tr 188/08. Hired as M/S 12.1939–18.1.40.

STORMCOCK (see STORMKING)

STORMKING (ex-STORMCOCK renamed 1943) Rescue tug 700 tons, 142½ x 33 ft, 1–3in, 2–20mm. Cochrane 24.11.1942. Renamed TRYPHO DY tug, 1947. Sold 7.1.59, renamed *Melanie Fair.*

STORMWRACK Admiralty wood Dr, 98gr. Stevenson & Asher 7.8.1918. Sold circa 1926, renamed *Perilia.* (PERILIA in WW.II.)

STORMWRACK (see BUSEN4)

STORNOWAY Tr 208/10, 1–3pdr. Hired 1915–19.

STOUR (see DANIEL FEARALL)

STRADBROKE (ex-*Stradbroke II*) Yt 115/28. Hired as A/P Yt (RAN) 1941–43.

STRATHAFTON Tr 209/13, 1–3pdr. Hired 1914–19.

STRATHAIRLIE Tr 193/05, 1–6pdr. Hired 1915–19.

STRATHALLADALE Tr 199/08, 1–6pdr. Hired 1915–19 and as fuel carrier 4.44–10.44.

STRATHALLAN Tr 175/00. Hired 5.1915–19. (Decoy ship 5.15–16.)

STRATHALVA Tr 215/17, 1–12pdr. Hired 1917–19.

STRATHATHOL Tr 209/12, 1–12pdr. Hired 1914–19.

STRATHAVON Tr 202/06, 1–6pdr. Hired as M/S 1914–19 and as BBV 12.40–11.45.

STRATHBEG Dr 95/07. Hired on harbour service 12.1939–4.46.

STRATHBLANE Tr 186/01. Hired as accommodation ship 1915–19.

STRATHBORVE Tr 216/30, 1–12pdr. Hired as M/S 8.1940. Sunk 6.9.41 by mine off the Humber.

STRATHBRAN Tr 212/15, 1–6pdr. Hired 1916–19.

STRATHCARRON Tr 209/13, 1–12pdr. Hired 1914–19.

STRATHCLOVA Tr 210/13, 1–6pdr. Hired 1914–19.

STRATHCLUNIE Tr 211/13, 1–6pdr. Hired 1915–19.

STRATHCOE Tr 215/16, 1–6pdr. Hired as M/S 1916. Purchased and converted to M/L, 24 mines, 8.18. Sale list 1939. Harbour service 1942; fuel carrier 9.43. Sold 4.46.

STRATHDEE Tr 193/06, 1–6pdr. Hired 1915–19.

STRATHDERRY Tr 193/11. Hired as M/S 1914. BDV 1917–19. Hired as danlayer 2.40. A/P Tr 9.40–11.41.

STRATHDEVON Tr 212/15, 1–6pdr. Hired as M/S 1915–19 and as M/S 1.40. A/P Tr 9.40–1.46.

STRATHDON Tr 155/91. Hired 1918–19.

STRATHEARN Tr 152/98. Hired 1915–19. (Decoy ship 5.15–17.)
STRATHEBRIE Tr 210/14, 1–6pdr. Hired as BDV 1914. Base ship 1917–1
STRATHEDEN Tr 210/06, 1–6pdr. Hired 1915–19.
STRATHELLA Tr 210/13, 1–6pdr. Hired 1915–19 and as A/P Tr 7.40.
Foundered 1.7.44 in Icelandic waters; raised and returned 1945.
STRATHELLIOT Tr 211/15, 1–6pdr. Hired 1915–19 and as danlayer,
1–6pdr, 1.40. A/P 9.40; store carrier 1942–1.46.
STRATHERRICK Tr 210/06, 1–6pdr. Hired 1914–19.
STRATHFINELLA Tr 192/10, 1–12pdr. Hired 1914–19 and 4.44–10.44.
STRATHGAIRN Tr 211/15, 1–6pdr. Hired 1916–19.
STRATHGARRY Tr 202/06. Hired 1915. Sunk 6.7.15 in collision off Scapa
STRATHGARRY Tr 202/24, 1–3pdr. Hired as danlayer 4.1940. A/P Tr
9.40. Mooring vessel 8.42–12.45.
STRATHGELDIE Tr 192/11, 1–6pdr. Hired as M/S 1914–19.
STRATHISLA Tr 193/05. Hired as mooring vessel 1915–19.
STRATHISLA II Tr 154/94. Hired 1917–19.
STRATHLEE Tr 215/17, 1–6pdr. Hired 1917–19.
STRATH LENE Dr 81/06. Hired on harbour service 1.1915–19.
STRATHLETHEN Tr 192/11. Hired as BDV in WW.I.
STRATHLOCHY Tr 212/16, 1–6pdr. Hired 1.1916–19.
STRATHLOSSIE Tr 193/10, 1–6pdr. Hired 1914–19.
STRATHLUI Tr 199/08, 1–6pdr. Hired 1916–19.
STRATHMAREE Tr 210/14. Hired as BDV 1915–19 and as A/P Tr, 1–3pd
11.39. Store carrier 1942–11.45.
STRATHMARTIN Tr 210/14, 1–6pdr. Hired 1915–19 and as fuel carrier
3.44–9.44.
STRATHMORAY Tr 209/12, 1–6pdr. Hired as M/S 1914–19.
STRATHMORE Dr 56/ -. Hired 1917. Lost 20.8.18 by fire in Lough Swilly.
STRATHNETHY Tr 211/ -, 1–6pdr. Hired as M/S 1914–19.
STRATHORD Tr 195/06, 1–3pdr. Hired 1914–19.
STRATHRANNOCH Tr 215/17. Hired 1917. Sunk 6.4.17 by mine off
St Abbs Head.
STRATHRANNOCH Tr 202/19, 1–3pdr. Hired as danlayer 4.1940.
A/P 8.40. Mooring vessel 1943–46.
STRATHRYE Tr 212/16, 1–12pdr. Hired 1916–19.
STRATHSPEY Tr 202/06, 1–6pdr. Hired 1915–19 and as BDV 11.39–
4.5.42.
STRATHTUMMEL Tr 210/11, 1–6pdr. Hired 1914–19.
STRATHUGIE Tr 210/14, 1–3pdr. Hired as M/S 1914–19 and as danlayer
1.40. M/S 9.40–9.45.
STRATHURIE Tr 210/11, 1–3pdr. Hired as M/S 1916–19.
STRENUOUS DY paddle tug 690 tons, 144 x 27½ ft. Thornycroft
7.12.1912. Renamed SANDBOY 3.18. Sunk 27.6.47 as a target off Bermuda

STRENUOUS Dr 77/11. Hired on harbour service 23.11.1914–19 and harbour service 2.40–1.46. (STRENUOUS II from 1942.)

STRENUOUS Tr 166/04. Hired as BDV 1915–19.

STREPHON Tr 250/13, 1–12pdr. Hired 1915–19 and as M/S 8.40–2.46.

STRIJDT voor CHRISTUS MFV 73/38. Belgian, hired as A/P vessel 28.6.1940. To MWT 4.42.

STRIVE Dr 102/12, 2–MG. Hired as M/S 11.1939–12.45.

STROMA Tr, 'Isles' class. Hall Russell 19.11.1941. To Italian navy 3.46.

STROMNESS Store carrier (RFA) 15,500 tons, 490 x 72 ft, 2–40mm. Swan Hunter 16.9.1966.

STRONGHOLD Tug 150/31. Hired on harbour service 5.1940–3.46.

STRONSAY Tr 207/11, 1–6pdr. Hired 1915–19.

STRONSAY Tr, 'Isles' class. Inglis 4.3.1942. Sunk 5.2.43 by mine in the western Mediterranean.

STRYMON Tr 198/99. Hired as M/S 1915. Sunk 27.10.17 by mine off the Shipwash.

STUART PRINCE 1,948/40, 4,129 tons, 304 x 44 ft, 24–30mm. Smiths Dk 9.3.1940, completed as A/A landing ship. Returned 1945.

STUDENT PRINCE MFV 57/35. Hired as A/P vessel 12.1939. BBV 6.40–10.45.

STURDEE Tr 202/19. Hired as A/P Tr 11.1939–2.40.

STURDY DY paddle tug 690 tons, 144 x 27½ ft. Thornycroft 12.11.1912. Renamed SWARTHY 1917. Arrived 24.3.61 Haulbowline to BU.

STURTON Tr 251/20. Hired as M/S 8.1939. Fuel carrier 4.44–10.44.

STYX (ex-*Etoile*) Wh 164/15, 1–12pdr, 2–3pdr. Purchased 4.1915. Sold 6.3.19.

SUBLIME Dr 86/07, 1–3pdr. Hired 1.1915–19.

SUBLIME II Dr 86/03, 1–3pdr. Hired 1916–19 and as SUBLIME, on examination service 10.39. Harbour service 1.43–11.45.

SUCCEED Dr 77/03. Hired on harbour service 1.1915–19.

SUCCESS A.ship 30, 240bm. Hired 1650–54.

SUCCESS II Dr 88/04. Hired as BDV 11.1914–19.

SUCCESS MFV 20net. Hired as HDPC 7.1940. Renamed SUCCESSFUL 1943. Listed to 7.45.

SUCCESSION Tr 212/16, 1–6pdr. Hired 1916–19.

SUCCOUR (see SUN III)

SUCCOUR Salvage vessel 950 tons, 150 x 36 ft, 2–20mm. Smiths Dk 18.8.1943.

SUDEROY I Wh 220/25. Norwegian, hired as M/S (SAN) 23.11.1942, renamed PARKTOWN' Returned 4.46.

SUDEROY II Wh 228/25. Norwegian, hired as M/S (SAN) 20.8.1942 renamed JOHANNESBURG. Returned 4.46.

SUDEROY IV Wh 252/30. Norwegian, hired as M/S 8.1940. RCN 6.41–11.45.

SUDEROY V Wh 252/30. Norwegian, hired as M/S 8.1940. RCN 41–11.45.
SUDEROY VI Wh 254/29. Norwegian, hired as M/S 8.1940. RCN 3.41–
11.45.
SUFFOLK COUNTY Dr 88/07, 1–3pdr. Hired 1915–19.
SUILVEN (ex-*Caledonia*) MFV 40/37. Hired on examination service
11.1939–2.45.
SUI WO 2,672/96. Hired as boom defence accommodation ship 1941.
Lost 2.42 in the Singapore area.
SUKHA Wh 251/29. Hired as M/S 3.1940–11.45.
SULARA Yt 94/24. Hired as HDPC 11.1939–45.
SULBY Tr 287/09, 1–6pdr. Hired 1914–19.
SULLA Wh 251/28. Hired as M/S 3.1940. To Russian navy 2.42. Lost
24.3.42 in the Barents Sea on passage.
SULTANA Wood paddle tug, 96bm. Purchased 1855 at Constantinople.
Sold 22.9.1856 at Pera.
SUMA Tr 284/14. Hired 1917–19.
SUMA Tr 302/27, 1–12pdr, 1–20mm. Purchased as M/S 8.1939. Sold
3.46.
SUMAR Yt 447/26, 1–12pdr. American, purchased as A/S Yt 1941.
Examination service 1943. Sold 1946.
SUMBA Wh 251/29. Hired as M/S 3.1940, later purchased. To Russian
navy 2.42–47. To MOT 3.47.
SUMMER ROSE Dr 96/19. Hired as M/S 10.1939. Sunk 13.10.40 by
mine off Sunderland.
SUMMERTON Dr 83/12. Hired 1915–19.
SUN II Tug 197/09. Hired as DY tug 8.1914–19 and on harbour service
8.39–9.45.
SUN III Tug 197/09. Hired as DY tug 8.1914. Renamed SUCCOUR
1915–19. Hired as SUN III, A/P tug, 2–MG, 8.39–8.45.
SUN IV Tug 200/15. Hired 2.1916–3.16.
SUN V Tug 200/15. Hired as A/P tug, 2–MG, 12.1939–4.46.
SUN VI Tug 139/02. Hired as DY tug 1940. Renamed SUNVI 1941–45.
SUN VII Tug 202/18. Hired 9.1939. Sunk 6.3.41 by mine off the North
Knob buoy.
SUN VIII Tug 196/19. Hired as A/P tug 10.1939–4.46.
SUN IX Tug 196/20. Hired 11.1939. Sunk 21.12.40 by mine in the Thames
estuary. Raised 6.42 and laid up.
SUN X Tug 196/20. On harbour service 8.1942–1.48.
SUN XII Tug 183/25. Hired 8.1942–6.45.
SUNBEAM I Dr 75/04, 1–6pdr. Hired 9.1914. Sunk 16.4.18 in collision
at Inchkeith.
SUNBEAM II Dr 85/16, 1–3pdr. Hired 1916–19 and as danlayer 11.1939.
TRV 8.40–11.45.
SUNBEAM IV Tr 133/91. Hired 1917–19.

SUNBEAM II Yt? 659/29? Hired as accommodation ship 1942—45.

SUNBEAM Oiler (RCN). Ex-hopper purchased 12.1940. Sold 1947.

SUNBURST Admiralty steel Dr, 97gr. Lewis 1918. Sold 1921, renamed *Boy Andrew.* (BOY ANDREW in WW.II.)

SUNBURST (see ESTRELLA d'ALVA)

SUN CLOUD Tr 213/12, 1—6pdr. Hired as M/S 1914—19.

SUNDERLAND Tug 172/14. Hired on harbour service 4.12.1915—22.3.19

SUNDOWN Admiralty steel Dr. A.Hall 22.11.1918. Wrecked 30.8.39 at Sullom Voe, Shetlands.

SUNFISH Tug 70/07. Hired as DY tug 11.1940—8.46.

SUNFLOWER II Yt 39/35. Hired as A/P Yt 8.1940, purchased 10.41. To War Dept 12.41.

SUNFLOWER IV Yt 27/38. Hired as M/S 11.1939, purchased 2.42. Laid up 10.44. Sold 1945?

SUNHILL 837/95. Hired as accommodation ship 23.9.1915—6.20.

SUNIK 5,017/15. Hired as water carrier (RFA) 13.1.1915. Oiler 8.16—19.

SUNLIGHT Tr 168/94. Hired 1917—19.

SUNLIGHT Admiralty wood Dr, 98gr. Chambers 1918. Sold 1921, renamed *Hannah Taylor.*

SUNLIGHT Tr 203/18. Hired as A/P Tr 11.1939. M/S 5.40. Wreck dispersal 4.44—2.46.

SUNNY BIRD Dr 96/18. Hired on harbour service 10.1939. TRV 5.43—1.46.

SUNNYSIDE Dr 80/10. Hired 1916—19.

SUNNYSIDE GIRL Dr 98/19. Hired as A/S Dr 12.1939—2.46.

SUNNY VALE Dr 84/13. Hired for the FAA 9.1939. TRV 7.42—1.46.

SUNRISE Tr 167/91. Hired 1918—19.

SUNRISE Admiralty wood Dr, 94gr. Stevenson & Asher 1919. Sold 1921, renamed *Taalhina.* (Served as TILLY DUFF in WW.II.)

SUNRISE (see EMILIA PRIMEIRO)

SUNSET Admiralty steel Dr. Webster & Bickerton 6.1918. Tender 1920. M/S 1940. Wercked 1.4.42 by air attack at Malta; BU 7.43.

SUNSHINE Tr 167/00. Hired as M/S 1915—19.

SUNSHINE II Dr 89/07. Hired 1917—19.

SUNSHINE III Dr 60/05. Hired 6.1917—19.

SUNSPOT Admiralty wood Dr, 99gr. Herd & Mackenzie, Findochty 1919. Sold 1920.

SUNSPOT (see ST CLAIR)

SUNVI (see SUN VI)

SUPERB Dr 61/01. Hired on harbour service 1916—18.

SUPERMAN Tug 359/33, 1—12pdr. Hired as rescue tug 11.1939—12.45.

SUPERMAN DY tug, 850gr, 165 x 37 ft. A.Hall 23.11.1955.

SUPERNAL Dr 83/10, 1—3pdr. Hired 1.1916—19.

SUPPLY A.ship 34, 308bm. Hired 1688. Wrecked 11.1.1690 at High
Lake.
SUPPLY DY hoy 4, 94bm, 63 x 18 ft. Chatham DY 4.1691. Renamed
SHEERNESS WATERBOAT 1722. BU 1747.
SUPPLY DY hoy 4, 122bm, 72 x 20 ft. Chatham DY 1725. Fate unknown.
SUPPLY DY tank vessel 250 tons, 104 x 19½ ft. Laird 11.8.1881. Sold
4.1908, renamed *Sea Fern.*
SUPPLY DY tank vessel 405 tons, 115 x 21 ft. Cox, Falmouth 10.1.1910.
Sold 10.47, renamed *Rosina M.*
SUPPLY (see TIDE AUSTRAL)
SUPPORT Dr 99/07. Hired as BDV 2.1915–19.
SUPPORTER Dr 88/14, 1–3pdr. Hired 2.1915–19 and as A/P Dr 12.39.
Hospital Dr 1943. Stranded 5.11.44 off Newhaven.
SUREAXE Tr 195/07, 1–6pdr. Russian T.31 (ex-*Uno*)seized 8.1918 in
the White Sea. Sold 11.5.20, same name. Hired for target-towing 8.42–
11.45.
SURF Yt 560/02, 2–12pdr. Hired as A/P Yt 2.1915–4.19 and as ABV,
1–12pdr, 1.39. Sunk 6.4.41 by air attack at Piraeus.
SURF Cstr 390/98. Hired (RCN) 1941–46.
SURF PATROL (ex-*Tatri*) Oiler (RFA) 15,800 tons, 445 x 60½ ft.
Bartram 7.2.1951, purchased 14.7.51.
SURF PILOT (ex-*Yung Hao*) Oiler (RFA), 10.519/38? Purchased 4.1951
but not used. Laid up and listed to 1958.
SURF PIONEER (ex-*Beskidy*) Oiler (RFA) 15,800 tons, 445 x 60½ ft.
Bartram 23.4.1951, purchased 14.7.51.
SURGE Admiralty wood Dr, 99gr. Chambers 1919. Sold 1919, renamed
Resurge. (RESURGE in WW.II.)
SURGE (see SKUDD 5)
SURLY (ex-*Silver Crest*) MFV 21net/34. Hired as HDPC 11.1939. Harbour
service 1941–46.
SURMOUNT Dr 96/12. Hired on harbour service 1.1915–19.
SURPRISE Yt 1,322/96. Russian RAZSVET seized and commissioned
24.9.1918. Renamed as despatch vessel 6.3.20. Sold 4.6.23. Hired as
A/P Yt 12.39, purchased 8.41. A/S Yt 8.40. Burnt and capsized 28.2.42
at Lagos.
SURSAY Tr, 'Isles' class. Cook Welton & Gemmell 16.12.1944, completed
as danlayer. Arrived 15.4.67 at Troon to BU.
SUSAN (ex-*Fairy*) Armament vessel 95 tons. Transferred from War Dept
1.10.1891. Fate unknown.
SUSANNA Dr 83/ -. Hired 1915. Foundered 14.12.15 off Milford Haven.
SUSANNAH JANE Yt 92/37. Hired as HDPC 1.1940, purchased 12.41.
Sold 1.46.
SUSARION Tr 261/16, 1–12pdr. Hired 1917–19 and as A/P Tr, 1–12pdr,
6.40. Sunk 7.5.41 by air attack off the Humber.

SUSETTA Cstr 339/04. Hired as fleet messenger 10.7.1915—31.7.19.
SUSSEX COUNTY Dr 83/08, 1—3pdr. Hired 1914, later purchased.
Sold 1921, same name. Hired as A/P Dr, 1—3pdr, 11.39—45.
SUSSEX OAK Tender, 124bm. Hired 3.1804. Captured 2.1808 by the French.
SUSTAIN Dr 93/08. Hired on harbour service 3.1940—8.46.
SUTHERNESS Tr 269/15, 1—6pdr. Hired as A/P Tr 6.1940. M/S 2.42—9.45.
SUVA 2,229/06, 3—4.7in. Hired as ABS 20.7.1915—19.12.19.
SUZANNE ADRIENNE Dr 82/31. Belgian, hired as A/P Dr 17.6.1940. To Air Ministry 11.43.
SUZETTE Tr 199/20. Hired as A/P Tr 11.1939—2.2.40.
SVANA Wh 268/30. Hired as M/S 4.1940. Sunk 8.4.42 by Italian air attack at Alexandria.
SVEGA Wh 253/29. Hired as M/S 3.1940. To Russian navy 2.42.
SVOLVAER (see KOS I)
SWALLOW (ex-*General Skinner*) DY tug 144 tons, 80 x 18 ft. Transferred from War Dept 1906, renamed 11.06. Sold 3.15, renamed *Leon & Tony*.
SWALLOW Tr 243/97, 1—6pdr. Hired as M/S 1914. Sunk 29.3.18 in collision off Whitby.
SWALLOW Tr 204/06, 1—6pdr. Hired 1914—19.
SWALLOW II Tr 200/00. Hired 1914—19.
SWALLOW III Dr 87/04, 1—3pdr. Hired 1915—19 and as reserve blockship 7.40—6.45.
SWAN Cutter 14. Hired 1799—1801.
SWAN Cutter 10, 119bm, 10—12pdr carr. Hired 8.1803. Captured 25.4.1811 by the French.
SWAN Tr 239/02, 1—6pdr. Hired as M/S 1914—19 and as M/S 3.40. Boiler-cleaning tender 1941—45.
SWAN II Dr 96/04. Hired 1914—19.
SWAN III Tr 270/07, 1—6pdr. Hired as M/S 1915—19.
SWAN MFV 44/00. Hired on harbour service 1.1941—45.
SWANLEY 4,641/03. Hired as store carrier (RFA) 24.2.1915—10.8.16.
SWANLEY Yt? Hired on examination service 10.1939. Listed to 1.42, believed captured by the Japanese at Singapore.
SWANSEA CASTLE Tr 256/12. Hired 1918—19 and as M/S 7.40—2.46.
SWARTBERG Wh 220/23. Hired as M/S (SAN) 10.1939—5.46. (Spelt ZWARTBERG in mercantile lists.)
SWARTHY (see STURDY)
SWEEPER Tr 395/13, 1—6pdr. Hired 1914—19.
SWEET PEA Dr 73/12. Hired 1915—19.
SWEET PROMISE Dr 94/19. Hired as M/S 11.1939. To Air Ministry 12.43.

SWELL Admiralty wood Dr, 93gr. Routh & Waddingham, Winteringham 1919. Sold 1921, same name.

SWIFT Sloop 10. Hired 1793–94.

SWIFT Cutter 12. Hired 1796–1801.

SWIFT Cutter 14. Hired 1799–1801.

SWIFT Cutter 10, 77bm. Hired 14.6.1803. Captured 3.4.1804 by the French privateer ESPERANCE in the Mediterranean.

SWIFT Cutter 8, 100bm, 8–12pdr carr. Hired 16.6.1803–13.1.1806.

SWIFT II Dr 101/07, 1–3pdr. Hired 1915–19.

SWIFT MFV 25/24. Hired as A/P vessel 7.1940. Renamed SWIRL 1944–45.

SWIFT WING Dr 98/12, 1–3pdr. Hired 1915–19 and as M/S 11.39–46.

SWIN (ex-SHIPWAY renamed 8.1944) Salvage vessel 950 tons, 150 x 36 ft, 2–20mm. A.Hall 25.3.44.

SWIRL Admiralty wood Dr, 99gr. Chambers 1919. Sold 1921, same name.

SWIRL (see SWIFT)

SWITHA Tr, 'Isles' class. Inglis 3.4.1942. Wreck dispersal 9.45. Oil-tank cleaning vessel 1950.

SWONA Wh 313/25. Hired as M/S 4.1940, later purchased. Danlayer 1944. Sold 15.2.47.

SWORD DANCE A/S Tr 530 tons, 150 x 27½ ft, 1–4in, 3–20mm. Robb 3.9.1940. Sunk 5.7.42 in collision in the Moray Firth.

SYBIL MARY Cstr 270/21. Hired as store carrier (red ensign) 5.1943–8.45.

SYCAMORE (ex-*Lord Beaverbrook*) M/S Tr 362/30, 573 tons, 1–4in. Purchased 1935. Danlayer 1945. Sold 10.7.46, renamed *Drattur*.

SYDOSTLANDET Wh 258/35. Hired as A/S Wh (SAN) 1940. Wrecked 6.4.42 near the mouth of the Umgeni river.

SYLHET Tr, 'Basset' class (RIN). Scindia SN Co, Bombay. Ordered 12.1942, cancelled 12.44.

SYLVANA Yt 487/07. Hired as danlayer 12.1939, purchased 11.42. M/S depot ship 1944. Sold 1945?

SYLVIA Tr 213/98. Hired as BDV in WW.I.

SYLVIA 1,429/94. Hired on examination service 9.1918–10.18.

SYMBOL Tug 119/14. Hired 9.1915–6.16.

SYRIA Cstr 750/98. Hired 11.1914–7.16.

SYRIAN Tr 324/18. Hired as A/P Tr 10.1939. Renamed TYPHOON 6.40, ABV. M/S 1.42–5.45.

SYRIAN Tr 298/19. Norwegian, hired as M/S (Norwegian crew) 6.1940–1.46.

SYRINGA Tr 243/05, 1–13pdr. Hired 1914–19. (SYRINGA II from 1917.)

SYRINGA (ex-*Cape Kanin*) M/S Tr 574 tons, 1–4in. Purchased 1935. Sale list 1946, sold, renamed *Davaar Island*.
SYVERN Wh 307/37, 1–75mm. Hired as A/S Wh 10.1940. Sunk 27.5.41 by air attack between Crete and Alexandria.

TABARCA 2,624/09. French, seized 7.1940 at Falmouth. Sunk 18.6.41 as blockship in Kirk Sound.
TACSONIA Tr 243/05, 1–6pdr. Hired 1.1915–19.
TAEPING MFV 49net/37. Hired as tender 11.1939–2.46.
TAGALIE Tr 210/12, 1–6pdr. Hired as M/S 9.1914–19.
TAHAY Tr, 'Isles' class. Cook Welton & Gemmell 31.12.1944, completed as danlayer. Sold 7.63, BU at Troon.
TAIPO Tr 247/14. Hired 1915. Sunk 24.6.17 by mine off the Royal Sovereign light vessel.
TAIPO Tr 225/16. Hired as A/P Tr 11.1939. M/S 5.40. Fuel carrier 4.44–11.44.
TAITS Dr 93/07. Hired 1915. Sunk 15.5.17 in action in the Adriatic.
T A JOLLIFFE Tug 199/01. Hired 8.1914–20.
TAKLA MFV 43/28. Hired as M/S (RCN) 9.1939–45.
TALIESIN Tug 79/83. Hired on harbour service 9.1914–19.
TALLA (ex-*Talisman*) Paddle 279/96. Hired as M/S 6.1917–10.19.
TALLY HO Tr 216/00, 1–6pdr. Hired 1915–19.
TALONA Dr 38gr. Danish, seized 5.1940. BBV 1940–45.
TAMARISK (ex-*St Gatien*) Tr 352/25, 545 tons, 1–4in. Purchased as M/S 8.1939. Sunk 12.8.40 by air attack in the Thames estuary.
TAMBAR Cstr 456/12. Commissioned as M/S (RAN) 7.11.1939. Listed to 1943.
TAMORA Tr 275/20. Hired as M/S 8.1939–3.46.
TAMPEON Armament tug, 178gr. Yarwood, Northwich 14.7.1938. On sale list 1964.
TAMURA Tr 280/17, 1–6pdr. Hired 1917–19.
TANAGER Tr 192/10, 1–3pdr. Hired 1915–19.
TANCRED Rescue tug, 'B.A.T' class. Gulfport, Port Arthur Texas 1.1.1943 on lend-lease. RAN 1943 and purchased. Transferred 1947 Govt Salvage Board.
TANGALOOMA Yt 21/23. Hired (RAN) 10.1942, purchased 2.43. Sold 3.46.
TANGO A/S Tr, 530 tons, 150 x 27½ ft, 1–4in, 3–20mm. Smiths Dk 29.11.1940. Sold 7.46, renamed *Ramskapelle*.
TANJORE Tr 168/83, 1–3pdr. Hired as M/S 1914–19.
TANJORE Tr? Hired as A/P vessel (RIN) 1941. Stranded 6.42 in Indian waters.

TAPAH 208/26. Hired as M/S 9.1939. Presumed lost 9.3.42 in the Singapore area.

TARA (ex-*Hibernia*) 1,862/00. Hired as ABS 8.8.1914. Sunk 5.11.15 by 'U.35' in Sollum Bay.

TARANA Tr 347/32. French M/S seized 3.7.1940 at Southampton. A/P Tr 1940. Laid up 10.45. Returned 5.46.

TARANAKI Tr 247/12, 1—12pdr. Hired 1914—19. (Operated as decoy ship in 1915.)

TARANSAY Yt 175/30. Hired as danlayer 10.1939, purchased 12.41. Examination service 1941. M/S depot 1944—7.46.

TARANTELLA A/S Tr 530 tons, 150 x 27½ ft, 1—4in, 3—20mm. Smiths Dk 27.1.1941. Renamed TWOSTEP 2.43. To Italian navy 2.46.

TARBATNESS Store carrier (RFA) 15,500 tons, 490 x 72 ft, 2—40mm. Swan Hunter 27.2.1967.

TARLAIR Dr 80/08. Hired 1.1915—19. (Base ship from 1917).

TARTAN Tr 202/12, 1—6pdr. Hired 1915—19 and as A/P Tr, 1—3pdr, 11.39. M/S 3.42—7.45.

TARTAR Cutter 12. Hired 1794—1801.

TARTAR Puffer 89/97. Hired as store carrier 9.1939—2.46.

TARTARIN Tr 288/31. French M/S seized 3.7.1940 at Southampton. A/P Tr 10.40. M/S 6.42—10.45.

TARV 158/11. Hired as mining tender 10.1918—19.

TASAJERA 3,952/38, 6—20mm. Hired as tank landing ship 1941—45.

TASMANIA Tr 146/91. Hired 1918—19.

TAURUS Yt 373/80. Hired on harbour service 10.1914—15.10.17.

TAURUS Tr 128/83. Hired 1918—19.

TAURUS Tug 107/31. M/S 1941. Renamed HYADES 1943. Listed to 1945.

TAWHAI Composite Tr, 'Castle' type (RNZN). Seager Bros, Auckland 20.7.1943, not completed. Sold 1946.

TAY & TYNE 556/09, 1—4in, 2—12pdr, 1—TT. Hired as decoy ship 28.6.1917. Purchased 26.9.17 and converted to store carrier (RFA). Renamed INDUSTRY 1920. Sold 31.10.24.

TAYMOUTH Tr 137/99. Hired 1917—19.

TAYRA Tug 105/26. Hired on harbour service 9.1939. Boom tender 1943—9.44.

TAYSIDE Tr 137/99. Hired 1917—19.

TEAKOL (see PATRICIAN)

TEAKOL Oiler (RFA) 1,925 tons, 220 x 34½ ft. Short, Sunderland 17.8.1917. Sold 29.1.20, renamed *San Dario.*

TEAKOL Oiler (RFA) 2,670 tons, 218 x 38 ft. Lobnitz 14.11.1946.

TEAL Tr 165/97. Hired 1915. Wrecked 2.1.17 off Buckie.

TEAL 131gr. Hired as BDV 15.11.1917—2.19.

TEAL (see MARIGNAM)

TEA ROSE Dr 84/11, 1−3pdr. Hired 1915−19 and on harbour service 1.40−12.45.

TEAZER (see CLEOPATRA)

TEHANA Tr 333/29, 1−12pdr. Hired as M/S 8.1939. Wreck dispersal 1944−3.46.

TEHERAN (ex-*Persia*) 3,596/83. Purchased as coal hulk 16.9.1917. Sold 1919.

TEKOURA Tr 368/29. Hired as A/S Tr 10.1939−8.45.

TELEGRAPH Brig 14. Hired 1798. Foundered 14.2.1801 in a gale off Cape Ortegal.

TELEMACHUS Cutter 18. Hired 1796−1801.

TELEMACHUS Cutter 10, 40bm. Hired 1803−04.

TEMPO 1,379/11. Hired as ammo. carrier (RFA) 11.1914−3.19.

TEN Dr 84/10. Hired 1.1915−19.

TENACITY Tug 69gr. Hired as DY-tug 12.1914−19.

TENACITY (see DILIGENT)

TENBY Tr 215/13, 1−6pdr. Hired 1915−19.

TENBY CASTLE Tr 256/08, 1−12pdr. Hired 2.1915−19. (Decoy ship 6.15−17.)

TENDERFOOT (see FT.5)

TENDERHEART (see FT.16)

TENGGAROH A/P Yt listed at Singapore 12.1941. Lost there in 2.42.

TENIERS Dr 74/29. Belgian, hired as BBV 30.8.1940. Harbour service 1942−9.45.

TERJE 1 Wh 335/36. Hired as A/S Wh 4.1940. Renamed SPANIEL 1941. Returned 4.46.

TERJE 2 Wh 335/36. Hired as A/S Wh 4.1940. Renamed BOARHOUND 1941. Returned 1945.

TERJE 3 Wh 335/36. Hired as A/S Wh 4.1940. Renamed BEDLINGTON 1941. Returned 9.45.

TERJE 4 Wh 335/36. Hired as A/S Wh 6.1940. Renamed SETTER 1941. Returned 10.45.

TERJE 5 Wh 335/36. Hired as A/S Wh 4.1940. Renamed SEALYHAM 1941. Returned 6.45.

TERJE 6 Wh 335/36. Hired as M/S (SAN) 3.1941. Renamed TERJE 9.41; renamed BRAKPAN 4.43. Returned 11.46.

TERJE 7 Wh 335/36. Hired as A/S Wh (SAN) 6.1941. Renamed PROTEA 1941. Returned 12.46.

TERJE 8 Wh 335/36. Hired as A/S Wh (SAN) 8.1941. Renamed SONNEBLOM 1941. Returned 11.46.

TERJE 9 Wh 335/36. Hired as A/S Wh (SAN) 11.1941. Renamed IMMORTELLE 1941. Returned 12.46.

TERKA Cstr 420/25. Hired as M/S (RAN) 1940. Water carrier 1944. Foundered 26.3.44 off Madang.

TERMINIST Yt 92/12. Hired as accommodation ship 3.1941, purchased 10.41. Sold 2.46.

TERN Tr 199/07. Hired as M/S 1914. Wrecked 23.2.15 in Loch Erribol.

TERN (ex-*Hopeful*) MFV 27/29. Hired as firefloat 10.1939—44.

TEROMA Tr 276/19. Hired as M/S 8.1939—45.

TERPSITHEA 157/19. Hired as store carrier 8.1941. Sunk 29.4.42 by mine off Famagusta.

TERRIER Lugger 6. Hired 1798—1800.

TERRIER (ex-*Viking*) DY tug. Purchased 12.3.1913. Sold 1948.

TERRIER Tr 179/05, 1—12pdr. Hired 1914—19.

TERRITORIAL Dr 80/09, 1—3pdr. Hired 1915—19.

TERVANI Tr 457/14. Hired 1914. Sunk 5.12.16 by mine off Orfordness.

TERVANI Tr 409/30, 1—12pdr. Hired as A/P Tr 10.1939. M/S 1941. Sunk 7.2.43 by the Italian S/M ACCIAIO off Algeria.

TESSIE Dr 87/11, 1—3pdr. Hired 1914—19 and as TRV 5.40, purchased 5.42. Sold 1946.

TEST II Dr 91/07, 1—3pdr. Hired 1914—19.

TEST (see PATRICK BOWE)

TETRARCH (see The TETRARCH)

TETTENHALL Tr 227/05. Hired 1916. Sunk 23.5.17 by mine off Lowestoft.

TEUTON Tr 141/98. Hired 1915—18.

TEUTONIC 9,984/89, 8—6in. Hired as AMC 5.9.1914, purchased 6.8.15. Troopship 1.19. BU 1922.

TEVIOT (see GEORGE IRELAND)

TEVIOTBANK 5,087/38, 1—4in, 1—12pdr, 2—20mm, 280 mines. Hired as M/L 9.1939—45.

TEWERA Tr 335/30, 1—12pdr. Hired as M/S 8.1939—46.

TEXADA Tr, 'Isles' class. Midland SY 27.7.1942. Sold 3.46.

TEXAS Pilot 301/19. American, purchased as A/P Tr 1940. Sunk 19.7.44 in collision off Jamaica.

TEXOL Oiler (RFA) 12,300 tons, 405 x 54 ft. Workman Clark 11.1916. Renamed APPLELEAF 1917. BU 12.47.

THAINS Dr 87/14. Hired 4.1915—19.

THAIS Iron paddle DY tug, 302bm, 118 x 22 ft. Laird 2.1856. Sold 2.12.1869.

THALABA (ex-*Atlantis*) Yt 61/39. Hired on air-sea rescue 10.1940. Training ship 1943—45. Sold 1.46.

THALASSA Yt 696/24. Hired as ABV 6.1942, purchased 9.42. Trials vessel 1944—45.

THALIA (ex-*Protector*) Yt 185/04. Purchased as danlayer 3.1940. Sunk 11.10.42 in collision off the Lymn of Lorne, W.Scotland.

THAMES A.ship 16. Hired 1806–08.

THAMES DY store carrier 320 tons, 112 x 19 ft. Sunderland 1880. Renamed BEE 1884; DY YC.128 in 1915. Listed to 1921.

THAMES Tug 32/97. Hired 6.11.1914. Foundered 16.2.18 off the east coast of Scotland.

THAMES Tug 624/38, 1–12pdr. Dutch, hired as rescue tug (Dutch crew) 6.1940–44.

THAMES QUEEN Paddle 517/98, 1–12pdr. Hired as M/S 14.9.1939. A/A ship 4.42–2.47.

THANE of FIFE Ferry 457/10. Hired as A/A ship 7.1940, not converted. Tender 1942–45.

THANET Tr 172/02. Hired as water carrier 1916–19.

THASOS Tug 130/97. Greek, hired as M/S 5.1940–43.

THAW Admiralty wood Dr, 93bm. Rose St Fndry, Inverness 1919. Sold 1920, same name. Hired on harbour service 12.39–2.46.

THEBAN Tr 202/13, 1–6pdr. Hired 1914–19.

THE BOYS Dr 92/14, 1–6pdr. Hired 1.1915–19 and as A/P Dr, 1–3pdr, 11.39. Foundered 14.11.40 in a storm in the Downs.

THE BRAE Dr 77/08, 1–3pdr. Hired 8.1914–19.

THE COLONEL Dr 92/08. Hired 1915–19.

THEIR MERIT Tr 275/19. Hired as M/S 8.1939–11.45.

THELE Yt 67/38. Hired as HDPC 11.1939, purchased 2.43. Laid up 6.45. Sold 1946?

THE MAJESTY Dr 99/14. Hired 1915–19.

THE MILLER Cstr 118/32. Hired as BBV tender 10.1940. Water boat 1943–8.45.

THEMIS Tug 54/09. Hired 8.1917–20.

THENDARA Yt 147/37. Hired as BBV 9.1940–9.45.

THE NORMAN Tr 225/08, 1–6pdr. Hired 1916–19.

THE PRINCE Dr 77/04, 1–3pdr. Hired 1916–19.

THE PRINCESS Dr 77/04, 1–3pdr. Hired as BDV 1915–19.

THE PROVOST Dr 93/08. Hired 1.1915–19 and as A/P Dr 12.39–6.45.

THE RAMSEY (see RAMSEY)

THERESA BOYLE Tr 224/15. Hired 1915–19.

THERMOL Oiler (RFA) 4,326 tons, 270 x 38½ ft. Caledonian SB Co, Greenock 29.4.1916. To MOT 8.11.46.

THERMOPYLAE Dr 84/13, 1–3pdr. Hired 2.1915–19 and as A/P Dr 12.39–4.46.

THE ROMAN Tr 224/09, 1–6pdr. Hired as M/S 1914–19 and as A/P Tr 12.39. M/S 7.40. Fuel carrier 3.44–8.46.

THE TETRARCH Tr 225/13, 1–3pdr. Hired as M/S 1914–19.

THE THRONE Dr 99/13. Hired 1915–19.

THETIS Lugger 12. Hired 1798–1800.

THE TOWER Tr 201/19. Hired as A/P Tr 11.1939. BBV 6.40–2.45.

THE VICEROY Cstr 477/05. Hired as fleet messenger 7.1915–6.16.

THEWAY Tr 263/31. Hired as BDV 9.1939–7.45.

THIEPVAL Tr, 'Castle' type (RCN). Kingston SY 1918. Wrecked 27.2.30 in Barclay Sound, Vancouver.

THIRLMERE A/S Wh 560 tons, 138½ x 26½ ft, 1–12pdr, 1–20mm. Smiths Dk 5.7.1939 and purchased 26.8.39. Sold 24.5.46, renamed *Kos XXVI*.

THIRTY Dr 79/02. Hired 8.1915–19.

THIRTY--FOUR Dr 84/00. Hired on harbour service 11.1914–19.

THIRTY–TWO Dr 79/02. Hired on harbour service 8.1915–19.

THISTLE DY vessel, 100bm. Purchased 1.8.1857 in China. Sold 1869 at Hong Kong. (Also known as Hong Kong YC.1.)

THISTLE Ferry (RFA) 160 tons. Purchased 9.10.1902. Transferred Irish Govt 1921.

THISTLE Yt 544/81. Hired 10.10.1914–11.6.15.

THISTLE II Dr 87/07, 1–6pdr. Hired 1915–19.

THISTLE III Dr 70/04, 1–6pdr. Hired 1915–19. (FY.1433)

THISTLE Dr 70/04. Hired 1918–19. (FY.2740)

THISTLE IV Dr 71/-. Hired 1915. Sunk 30.6.15 in collision off Great Orme's Head.

THISTLE IV Tr 228/06, 1–3pdr. Hired 1915–19.

THISTLE V Dr 79/04. Hired 1915–18 and as A/P Dr 4.40. Examination service 9.40. Sunk 8.5.41 by mine off Lowestoft.

THISTLE Tr 178/04, 1–3pdr. Hired as BDV in WW.I.

THOMAS ADNEY Tr, 'Castle' type. Cook Welton & Gemmell 2.4.1919. Sold 1919.

THOMAS ALEXANDER Tr, 'Castle' type, 290gr. Cook Welton & Gemmell 18.7.1919. Sold 1920, renamed *Etoile Polaire III*.

THOMAS ALLEN Tr, 'Castle' type, 290gr. Cook Welton & Gemmell 18.7.1919. Sold 1920, renamed *Theopile Massart*. (Served as MILFORD PRINCE 278gr, in WW.II.)

THOMAS ALTOFT Tr, 'Castle' type, 290gr. Cook Welton & Gemmell 2.6.1919. Sold 1920, same name. Hired as M/S 8.39–4.46.

THOMAS & LUCY 34–gun ship. Hired 1653–55.

THOMAS ANSELL Tr, non-standard 'Strath' type, 210gr. Duthie Torry 21.5.1917. Sold 1921, same name.

THOMAS ATKINSON Tr, 'Mersey' type, 324gr. Cochrane 8.5.1917. Sold 1922, renamed *Cavendish*. (Served as ERITH in WW.II.)

THOMAS BAILEY Tr, 'Mersey' type, 324gr. Cochrane 4.8.1917. Sold 1922, renamed *Pamxon*.

THOMAS BARCLAY Tr, 'Strath' type, 203gr. Hall Russell 9.10.1918. Sold 1921, renamed *John Morrice.*

THOMAS BARTLETT Tr, 'Castle' type, 290gr. Cook Welton & Gemmell 29.5.1918. Sold 1920, same name. Hired as A/P Tr 11.39. M/S 5.40. Sunk 28.5.40 by mine off Calais.

THOMAS BEECHING Dr 99/12. Hired 8.1915–19.

THOMAS BILLINGCOLE Tr, 'Strath' type, 202gr. Hall Russell 2.5.1919. Sold 1919, renamed *Saltaire.*

THOMAS BIRD Tr, 'Strath' type, 203gr. Hall Russell 24.7.1917. Sold 1919, renamed *River Tweed.*

THOMAS BLACKHORN Tr, non-standard 'Castle' type, 269gr. Cook Welton & Gemmell 7.7.1917. Sold 1922, renamed *Alexandrite.*

THOMAS BOMKWORTH Tr. Listed 1919–21. (Believed to be error for JOHN BOMKWORTH.)

THOMAS BOOTH Tr, 'Castle' type, 277gr. Cook Welton & Gemmell 14.2.1918. Sold 1920, same name.

THOMAS BOUDIGE Tr, 'Castle' type, 290gr. Cook Welton & Gemmell 15.8.1919. Sold 1921, renamed *Jade.* (Served as DARNETT NESS in WW.II.)

THOMAS BRAUND Tr, 'Strath' type. Hall Russell. Cancelled 1919.

THOMAS BRYAN Tr, 'Strath' type, 216gr. Hall Russell 16.8.1917. Sold 1921, same name.

THOMAS BUCKLEY Tr, non-standard 'Castle' type, 249gr. Cook Welton & Gemmell 7.7.1917. Sold 1922, renamed *Ceylonite.* (CEYLONITE in WW.II.)

THOMAS BURNHAM Tr, 'Strath' type, 203gr. Hall Russell 9.9.1918. Sold 1921, renamed *Floribelle.*

THOMAS CALTRAFFE Tr, 'Strath' type. Hawthorns, Leith. Cancelled 1919.

THOMAS CHAMBERS Tr, 'Castle' type, 277gr. Bow McLachlan 1.12.1917. Sold 1922, renamed *Prosper.* (Served as LORRAINE in WW.II.)

THOMAS CLAYTON Tr, 'Strath' type. Hawthorns. Cancelled 1919.

THOMAS COLLARD Tr, 'Strath' type, 215gr. Fleming & Ferguson 11.7.1917. Sunk 1.3.18 by U-boat north of Rathlin Island.

THOMAS CONNOLLY Tr, 'Castle' type, 290gr. Cook Welton & Gemmell 29.11.1917. Sold 1919, same name. Hired as BDV 11.39. Sunk 12.12.40 by mine at Sheerness.

THOMAS COPSEY Tr, 'Strath' type. Hall Russell. Cancelled 1919.

THOMAS CORNWALL Tr, 'Mersey' type, 324gr. Lobnitz 1918. Sunk 29.10.18 in collision off Flamborough Head.

THOMAS COWELL Tr, 'Strath' type, 204gr. Hawthorns 1919. Sold 1919, renamed *Dudley NB.* (Served as SOUTHWARD HO in WW.II.)

THOMAS CROFTON Tr, 'Castle' type, 276gr. Bow McLachlan 18.6.1917. Sold 1920, renamed *Revesby*. (Served as GWMAHO in WW.II.)

THOMAS CRUIZE Tr, 'Mersey' type, 330gr. Lobnitz 1918. Sold 1919, renamed *Celerina*.

THOMAS CURR Tr, 'Strath' type. Hall Russell. Cancelled 1919.

THOMAS CURRELL Tr, 'Strath' type, 204gr. Williamson, Workington 1919. Sold 1919, same name. Commissioned as M/S (RNZN) 16.10.39. Returned 11.45.

THOMAS DANIELS Tr, 'Castle' type, 279gr. Bow McLachlan 1918. Sold 1921, renamed *Jan Volders*.

THOMAS DEAR Tr, 'Strath' type, 203gr. Williamson 1918. Sold 1921, renamed *Ninette*.

THOMAS DEAS (see JAMES JOHNSON)

THOMAS DENNISON Tr, 'Strath' type, 201gr. Fleming & Ferguson 27.10.1919. Sold 1920, same name. (Served as THE TOWER in WW.II.)

THOMAS DOWDING Tr, 'Castle' type, 275gr. C.Rennoldson 16.11.1917. Sold 1922, renamed *Leonato*. (Served as BEN BHEULA in WW.II.)

THOMAS EVISON Tr, 'Strath' type, 202gr. Fullerton 1918. Sold 1921, renamed *Jeannie M Robertson*. (Served as AVONDEE in WW.II.)

THOMAS FOLEY Tr, 'Strath' type, 202gr. Ritchie Graham, Glasgow 1918. Sold 1920, renamed *River Tummel*. (Served as BELTON in WW.II.)

THOMAS GOBLE Tr, 'Castle' type, 275gr. Smiths Dk 17.10.1917. Sold 1921, renamed *Cotsmuir*. (COTSMUIR in WW.II.)

THOMAS GOODCHILD Tr, 'Strath' type, 200gr. Ritchie Graham 1919. Sold 1919, same name. (Served as CHANDOS in WW.II.)

THOMAS GRAHAM Tr, 'Strath' type, 203gr. Scott, Bowling 6.6.1918. Sold 1921, same name. (Served as SUNLIGHT in WW.II.)

THOMAS GRANT Store carrier (RFA) 409 tons, 108 x 25½ ft. Hill, Bristol 11.5.1953. Sale list 1960.

THOMAS GREEN Tr, 'Castle' type, 275gr. C Rennoldson 28.5.1919. Sold 1920, renamed *Ebor Elect*. (Served as CAERPHILLY CASTLE in WW.II.)

THOMAS HAGGERTY Tr, 'Strath' type, 202gr. Ouse SB 1918. Renamed ITCHEN 1920. Sold 1926, renamed *River Endrick*. (Served as MARY A PURDY in WW.II.)

THOMAS HANKINS Tr, 'Castle' type, 276gr. J.P Rennoldson 1918. Sold 1919, same name.

THOMAS HENRIX Tr, 'Strath' type, 203gr. Hawthorns 1918. Sold 1921, renamed *Crevette*. (CREVETTE in WW.II.)

THOMAS JAGO Tr, 'Mersey' type, 324gr. Cochrane 31.7.1918. Sold 1922, renamed *St Valery*.

THOMAS JARVIS Tr, 'Mersey' type, 324gr. Cochrane 1918. Renamed EXE 1920. On sale list 1926.

THOMAS J CARROLL Cstr 149/37. Hired as skid M/S in the West Indies 11.1940–12.45.

THOMAS JOHNS Tr, 'Mersey' type, 324gr. Cochrane 1918. Renamed EDEN 1920; IMMORTELLE (SAN) 1921; EDEN (RN) 1934. On sale list 1939, listed as laid up, to 1941.

THOMAS LAUNDREY Tr, 'Castle' type, 276gr. J.P Rennoldson 1918. Sold 1920, renamed *Tees Bay*.

THOMAS LAVERICKS Tr, 'Strath' type. Hall Russell. Cancelled 1919.

THOMAS LAWRIE Tr, 'Castle' type, 274gr. Chambers 1919. Sold 1922, renamed *Somersby*.

THOMAS LEEDS Tr, 'Castle' type, 276gr. Duthie Torry 1919. Sold 1919, same name. Hired as M/S 8.39–11.45.

THOMAS MALONEY Tr, 'Mersey' type, 324gr. Cochrane 16.4.1919. Sold 1920, renamed *St Neots*. (Served as ADAM in WW.II.)

THOMAS MATTHEWS Tr, 'Mersey' type, 324gr. Cochrane 1919. Sold 1919, renamed *Earl Beatty*.

THOMAS ROBINS Tr, 'Castle' type, 275gr. Smiths DK 3.9.1917. Sold 1920, renamed *Cheriton*.

THOMAS STRATTEN Tr 309/14. Hired 1917. Sunk 20.10.17 by mine off the Butt of Lewis.

THOMAS SUTTON Tr 211/16. Hired 1916–19.

THOMAS THRESHER Tr, 'Mersey' type, 324gr. Cochrane 1918. Sold 1922, renamed *Syrian*. (SYRIAN in WW.II.)

THOMAS TWINEY Tr, 'Castle' type, 275gr. Smiths Dk 20.7.1917. Sold 1921, renamed *Clyro*.

THOMAS WHIPPLE Tr, 'Mersey' type, 324gr. Cochrane 1918. Sold 1922, renamed *Lord Lascelles*.

THOMAS W IRVIN Tr 201/11. Hired 8.1914. Sunk 27.8.14 by mine off the Tyne.

THOMAS W IRVIN Tr 209/16, 1–12pdr. Hired 2.1916–19.

THOMAS YOUNG Tr 194/14. Hired 2.1915–19.

THOMOND Cstr 127/00. Hired 3.1918–19.

THOMSONS Dr 91/07, 2–MG. Hired as M/S 11.1939. A/P Dr 8.40–2.46.

THORA MFV 37/30. Danish, seized 5.1940. BBV 6.40. Sunk 26.4.43 in collision with boom at Grimsby.

THORBRYN Wh 305/36. Norwegian, hired as A/S Wh 11.1940. Sunk 19.8.41 by German air attack off Tobruk.

THORGRIM Wh 305/36. Norwegian, hired as A/S Wh 11.1940. Sunk 8.4.42 by Italian air attack at Alexandria.

THORNEY Tr, 'Isles' class. Cook Welton & Gemmell. Renamed DABCHICK 11.1942 and launched 9.3.43 as M/L Tr. Renamed PENYU (Malaysian navy) 5.54.

THORNOL (ex-*Empire Tegyika*) Oiler (RFA), 1,598gr. Transferred from MOT 1947. Sold 7,48, renamed *Caroline M.*

THORNTON Tr 225/05, 1–6pdr. Hired 1915–19.

THORNTREE MFV 43/40. Hired on harbour service 4.1944–8.45.

THORNWICK BAY Tr 437/36. Purchased as A/S Tr 8.1939. Sold 4.45.

THORODD Wh 422/19. Norwegian, hired as M/S 4.1940–45. (Norwegian crew from 1941.)

THORVARD Wh 249/30. Norwegian, hired as A/P Wh 4.1940–45. (Norwegian crew 1941–43.)

THREE Dr 87/08, 1–3pdr. Hired 1915–19.

THREE BOYS Dr 84/10. Hired 1.1915–19.

THREE KINGS Dr 98/12, 1–3pdr. Hired 1915–19 and as M/S, 1–MG, 11.39–45.

THREE THREE THREE (ex-*333*) Yt 69/36. Hired as HDPC 11.1939. Renamed TREFOIL 1941–45.

THRIFT Dr 81/07. Hired 4.1915–19.

THRIFTY Tr 139/16. Hired as M/S 12.1939–4.46.

THRIVE Dr 81/04, 1–3pdr. Hired 1916–19.

THROSK Armament store carrier 1,488 tons, 185 x 33 ft. Philip, Dartmouth 1943.

THRUSH II Tr 264/06, 1–6pdr. Hired 1914–19.

THRUSH III Tr 166/02. Hired 1915–19.

THRUSH IV Tr 134/93. Hired 1917–19.

THRUSH Dr 92/07. Hired 1915–19 and on harbour service 11.39–4.46.

THULE ROCK Dr 98/17. Hired 1917–19. (Served as LORD HOWARD in WW.II.)

THUNDERBOLT Admiralty wood Dr, 95gr. Innes 1919. Sold 1920, renamed *Ina Adam.*

THUNDERCLAP Admiralty steel Dr, 96gr. A.Hall 1918. Sold 1919, renamed *Zena & Ella.* (Served as MACE in WW.II.)

THUNDERSTONE Tr 225/13, 1–3pdr. Hired as M/S 1915–19 and as BBV 4.40–4.46.

THURINGIA Tr 297/13. Hired 1915. Sunk 11.11.17 off Youghal, probably by torpedo.

THURINGIA Tr 396/33. Purchased as A/S Tr 8.1939. Sunk 28.5.40 by mine in the North Sea.

THYRSUS Dr 75/10. Hired 1.1915–19.

TIBERIO Aux. schooner 237/02. Italian, captured 1.1.1941 by DAINTY near Bardia. Store carrier 1941. Foundered 23.12.41 off the coast of Egypt.

TIDAL RANGE Admiralty wood Dr, 99gr. Colby 1920. Sold 1920, same name.

TIDAL WAVE Admiralty steel Dr. A.Hall 1919. Sold 1919.

TIDE AUSTRAL Oiler (RAN) 26,000 tons, 550 x 71 ft, 6–40mm. Harland & Wolff 1.9.1954. Renamed SUPPLY 7.9.62. (On loan to the RN until 9.62.)

TIDEFLOW (see TIDERACE)

TIDEPOOL Oiler (RFA) 25,930 tons, 550 x 71 ft. Hawthorn Leslie 11.12.1962.

TIDERACE Admiralty wood Dr. Routh & Waddingham. Cancelled 1919.

TIDERACE Oiler (RFA) 26,000 tons, 550 x 71 ft. Thompson 30.8.1954. Renamed TIDEFLOW 28.6.58.

TIDERANGE Oiler (as TIDERACE). Laing 1.7.1954. Renamed TIDE-SURGE 6.58.

TIDEREACH Oiler (as TIDERACE). Swan Hunter 2.6.1954.

TIDERIP Admiralty wood Dr, 100gr. Chambers 1919. Sold 1919, renamed *Kentish Belle*.

TIDESET Admiralty steel Dr. Howden Dk. Cancelled 1919.

TIDESPRING Oiler (as TIDEPOOL). Hawthorn Leslie 3.5.1962.

TIDESURGE (see TIDERANGE)

TIEN HSING Tug 269/35? Hired as harbour tug 1942. Foundered 26.10.43 in the Red Sea. (In loss list as TIENTSIN.)

TIEN KWANG 781/25. Hired as A/S vessel 10.1939. Lost 2.42 in the Singapore area.

TIERCEL Yt 489/13. Hired as ABV 9.1939, purchased 10.41. Accommodation ship 1941; target 1943. Laid up 8.45.

TIGER A.ship, 200bm. Hired for the Armada campaign.

TIGRE Cutter 14, 46bm. Hired 10.1809–11.09.

TILBURYNESS Tr 279/18. Hired as M/S 9.1939. Sunk 1.11.40 by air attack in the Thames estuary.

TILLERMAN Oiler 220/31. Hired as water boat 8.1939–47.

TILLY DUFF Dr 94/19. Hired as M/S 11.1939. Harbour service 1943–8.46.

TIMOTHY BRANNON Tr, 'Strath' type, 203gr. Hall Russell 30.4.1918. Sold 1919, renamed *Keyes*. (Served as BUCHANS II in WW.II.)

TIMOTHY CRAWLEY Tr, 'Castle' type, 277gr. Ailsa 4.10.1917. Sold 1920, renamed *Loch Long*. (LOCH LONG in WW.II.)

TINA NUTTEN Tr 187/11, 1–6pdr. Hired 1915–19.

TIRADE (ex-*Transportador*) Tr 209/99. Portuguese, purchased as A/P Tr 5.1942. Sold 3.46.

TIREE Tr, 'Isles' class. Goole SB 6.9.1941. Wreck dispersal 1946. Sold 8.60 to BU in Belgium.

TITAN Yt 103/35. Hired as HDPC 9.1939. Lent Watt's School 12.43–45.

TITAN 574/28? Hired as M/S. Listed at Singapore 1940–2.42.

TITANIA Dr 92/06. Hired on harbour service 10.1914—19.

TITHONUS (ex-*Titania*) 3463/08, 2—6in, 2—6pdr. Hired as ABS 14.3.1916. Sunk 28.3.18 by U-boat in the North Sea.

TIVERE Paddle tug. Purchased 13.11.1855. Lost 3.12.1855.

TOBAGO Tr 160/99 Hired 1917—20.

TOCOGAY Tr, 'Isles' class. Cook Welton & Gemmell 7.2.1945, completed as danlayer. Sold 11.58 at Malta.

TOCSIN (see LIBRA)

TOERN Wh 248/29. Norwegian, hired as M/S 1942—46.

TOGO Dr 76/05, 1—3pdr. Hired 1.1915—19.

TOIA (see ST BONIFACE)

TOKEN Dr 89/14. Hired as tender 12.1914—19 and as A/P Dr 12.39. Wrecked 23.12.41 in Skerry Sound, Orkney.

TOKIO Tr 295/07. Hired 1914. Sunk 12.12.17 in action in the North Sea.

TOKIO II Tr 221/06, 1—6pdr. Hired 1914—19 (On loan Japanese navy 6.17—12.18) and as A/P Tr, 1—6pdr, 12.39. M/S 7.40; fuel carrier 3.44—1.46. (Spelt **TOKYO II** in navy lists 1940—46.)

TOLGA Cstr 418/25. Commissioned as M/S (RAN) 30.12.1940. Water carrier 1944—46. Scuttled 30.4.46 off New Guinea.

TOM TIT Tr 169/04. Hired as M/S 1914. Wrecked 26.12.14 at Peterhead.

TONBRIDGE 682/24. Hired as netlayer 10.1940. Sunk 22.8.41 by air attack off Yarmouth.

TONGKOL Tr 292/26. Commissioned as M/S (RAN) 4.10.1939. Sold 9.44.

TONNEAU 178/02. French navy water carrier seized 3.7.1940 at Southampton. Returned 1945.

TOORIE Cstr 414/25. Hired as M/S (RAN) 11.1940—1.43.

TOPAZ Tr 142/95. Hired 1916.

TOPAZ Tr 251/16, 1—6pdr. Hired 1917—19.

TOPAZE (ex-*Melbourne*) Tr 421/35, 608 tons, 1—4in. Purchased as A/S Tr 11.1935. Sunk 20.4.41 in collision with the battleship RODNEY off the Clyde.

TOQUADE Yt 107/23. In service as netlayer base ship 1940—41.

TORBAY Dr 83/10, 1—3pdr. Hired 1915—19 and as TORBAY II, A/P Dr, 1—3pdr, 11.39. Sunk 1.11.40 by air attack off Dover.

TORCHBEARER (ex-*Bluebell*) Barge 120dw. Hired as degaussing vessel 1.1941—8.46.

TORDO MFV 35/40. Hired for M/S training (RCN) 1941—45.

TORDONN Wh 314/25. Norwegian, hired as M/S (SAN) 11.1940—5.46.

TOREADOR (see SAMBUR)

TORFRIDA Tr 115/81. Hired 1917—19.

TORNADO (see El MENZALA)

TORONTO Tr 205/15, 1–6pdr. Hired 1916–19.

TORRENT (see ANNA MARIE)

TORR HEAD 5,911/94. Hired as store carrier (RFA) 15.8.1914–14.9.14.

TORRY (ex-*AS.39*) DY tug. Transferred from War Dept 1918? Sold 3 23.

TORTOISE DY lighter. Listed 1850. BU 2.1863 at Devonport.

TORTOISE DY lighter, 163bm. Allen & Warlow, Pembroke 9.2.1864. BU completed 2.12.1874 at Devonport. (Also known as Devonport YC.7.)

TORTOISE DY tank vessel 330 tons. Lobnitz 4.3.1897. On sale list 1946.

TORTOISE Dr 94/08. Hired 1915–16.

TORTUGUERO 5,285/21, 2–6in. Hired as OBV 1941–42.

TOSCA Cstr 449/08. Hired as ammo. carrier (RFA) 9.12.1914–17.8.16.

TOUCHSTONE Tr 173/07, 1–6pdr. Hired 1914–18 and as M/S 3.40–41.

TOUCHWOOD Dr 84/11. Hired 1914–19.

TOURACO Tr 245/08, 1–6pdr. Hired 1914–19.

TOURMALINE Tr 289/05, 1–6pdr. Hired 1916–19.

TOURMALINE (ex-*Berkshire*) Tr 430/35, 641 tons, 1–4in. Purchased 11.1935. Sunk 5.2.41 by air attack off the North Foreland.

TOURTEAU French survey vessel, seized 3.7.1940 at Southampton. M/S 9.40; boom gate vessel 1942–45.

TOWER (see HILDA)

TOWHEE Tr 199/08. Hired 1914. Sunk 15.6.17 by unknown cause in the Channel.

TOWY Tender 199gr, 1–6pdr. Hired as A/P vessel 6.1917–2.19.

TOXTETH DY tug, 148gr, 92 x 20 ft. Purchased 21.11.1901. Sold 17.10.30, renamed *Cleadon*. (Also known as C.111.)

TR.1–60 'Castle' type trawlers built 1917–18 in Canada for the RN. TR.1–36 and two others were on loan to the RCN until 1919 and TR 37, 39, 40, 51, 52, 55, 56, 58, 59 and 60 on loan to the USN until 8.19. TR.18 became Canadian Govt light vessel No.25; TR.58 wrecked 20.11.20 in Barra Sound; others sold 1919–20.

Builders. TR.1–6 Port Arthur SY 1917–18; TR.7–12 Collingwood 1918; TR.13,14 Thor IW, Toronto 1918; TR.15–18 Polson IW 1918; TR.19,20 Kingston SB 1918; TR.21–31 Vickers, Montreal 1918; TR. 32–34 Govt SY, Sorel 1918 (TR.33 transferred Polson IW); TR. 35, 36 Davie SB 1918; TR.37–44 Port Arthur SY 1918–19; TR. 45–50 Davie SB 1919; (TR. 47–49 transferred Anderson, Vickers and Anderson resp.); TR. 51–53 Anderson 1918–19; TR. 54 Kingston SB 1918; TR. 55, 56 Collingwood 1918; TR.57 Kingston SB 1919, TR. 58–60 Tidewater SB 1919.

TRADEWIND Admiralty steel Dr. Howden Dock. Cancelled 1919.

TRADEWIND (see DAYLIGHT) Hired as BBV 1940. Renamed MONSOON 1943, harbour service. Returned 11.45.

TRANG Wh 205/12. Hired as M/S 11.1939. Abandoned 14.2.42 off Singapore.

TRANIO Tr 275/18. Hired as M/S 11.1939. Sunk 26.6.41 by air attack while in tow in the North Sea.

TRANQUIL Tr 294/12. Hired as M/S 4.1940. Sunk 16.6.42 in collision off Deal.

TRANSEAS 1,499/24. Purchased 1.1940. Sunk 25.5.40 as blockship at Zeebrugge.

TRANSFER (ex-*Transit*) Tug 169/84. Hired 8.1918–20.

TRANSIT Dr 83/07. Hired 1915. Sunk 15.5.17 in action in the Adriatic.

TRANSPORTER 1,554/11. Hired as fleet auxiliary 3.1916–1.20.

TRANSVAAL Tr 250/16, 1–6pdr. Hired 1917–19 and as A/P Tr. 12.39. Fuel carrier 1942. Foundered 18.11.44 in a gale in the Channel.

TRANSVAALIA Wh 160/12, 1–6pdr. Hired as A/P Wh 6.1917–3.19 and as M/S 4.41–46. (Norwegian crew 8.41–8.43 and Greek crew as EUROTAS 8.43–45.)

TRANSYLVANIA 16,923/25, 8–6in. Hired as AMC 8.1939. Sunk 10.8.40 by 'U.56' north of Ireland.

TRANTOR (ex-*Trent*) Tug. Hired 11.1917–19.

TRAVANCORE Tr, 'Basset' class (RIN). Garden Reach 7.7.1941. For sale 1.47. Sold, renamed *Forma*.

TRAVELLER (ex-*Stormcock*) Fleet tug 700 tons, 161 x 24½ ft, 4–3pdr. Purchased 22.4.1885. Sold 1.5.20 Crichton Thompson. (Sunk 27.6.03 in collision with EURYALUS and raised 7.1.04.)

TREASURE Dr 96/07, 1–3pdr. Hired 1915–19.

TREBOULISTE Dr 119/33. French, seized 1940. Special service Dr 1940–45. (Also known as MFV.2032 from 7.43.)

TREERN Wh 247/29. Hired as M/S (SAN) 1941. Sunk 12.1.45 by mine off the east coast of Greece.

TREFOIL Oiler (RFA), 4,060 tons, 280 x 39 ft. Pembroke Dock 27.10.1913. Sold 28.6.35 McLellan, Bo'ness to BU.

TREFOIL (see THREE THREE THREE)

TRENT Discovery sloop, 250bm, 89 x 26 ft. Ex-whaler, hired 1.1818–19.11.1818.

TRENT Tr 218/04, 1–6pdr. Hired 1914–19.

TRENT 5,541/00, 2–12pdr. Hired as fleet messenger 6.3.1915–23.1.19.

TREVO TERCEIRO Tr 296/12, 1–12pdr. Portuguese, purchased as M/S 1940. Renamed FINESSE 1942. Sold 1946.

T.R.FERRENS Tr 306/13, 1–6pdr. Hired 1915–19.

T.R.FERRENS Tr 279/18. Hired as M/S 8.1939–45.

TRIAD Yt 1,413/09, 2,354 tons, 1–12pdr, 4–3pdr. Hired as A/P Yt 1.1915, purchased 19.6.15. Sold 5.33 at Bombay.

TRIBUNE Tr 302/15, 1–6pdr. Hired 1916–19.

TRICHINOPOLY Tr, 'Basset' class (RIN). Burn, Calcutta. Ordered 7.1942, cancelled 10.44.

TRIDENT II Dr 80/02. Hired 1915–19.

TRIDENT Yt 60/08. Hired on examination service 9.1940. Renamed JACANA 1940. Training tender 1944–45.

TRIER Tr 324/01, 1–10pdr. Hired 1915–19.

TRINCULO Wood S.DY tug, 41bm, 54 tons. Sheerness DY 15.1.1873. On sale list 1902.

TRINCULO DY mooring vessel 750 tons, 135 x 26 ft. Fleming & Ferguson 20.11.1915. Renamed MOLLUSC 1916. Sold 12.22, renamed *Yantlett.*

TRINGA 2,154/13. Hired as store carrier (RFA) 28.11.1914–24.6.15.

TRINITY NB Tr 203/14. Hired 1914–19.

TRINOL (see PLUMLEAF)

TRIPLE ALLIANCE Dr 87/24. Hired on harbour service 11.1939–7.46.

TRITELIA Tr 210/16. Hired as A/P Tr 12.1939–7.45.

TRITON Tr 230/-, 1–3pdr. Hired 1915–18.

TRITON Tug 173/00. Hired as DY tug 3.1918. Renamed PLUNGER 1918. Returned 1920.

TRITON Tr 230/07. Hired as A/P Tr 12.1939–40 and as fuel carrier 2.44. Renamed WRANGLER 1944. Returned 1945.

TRITONIA Dr 115/30. Hired as M/S 11.1939–1.46.

TRIUMPH II Dr 90/07, 1–3pdr. Hired 1915–19.

TRIUMPH III Dr 90/07. Hired 1915–19. (One of these last two served as BBV 3.40–44.)

TRIUMPH VI MFV 46/03. Hired as store carrier 1941. Sunk 15.12.44 in collision, Rosyth area.

TRODDAY Tr, 'Isles' class. Cook Welton & Gemmell 3.3.1945, completed as danlayer. Sold 30.9.50 at Malta.

TROGON Tr 182/07, 1–6pdr. Hired 1914–19.

TROJAN Tr 141/98, 1–6pdr. Hired 1915–19 and as boom gate vessel 1940–45.

TROMOY (see POL IV, EDAY and MINCARLO)

TRONDRA Tr, Isles' class. Lewis 4.10.1941. Wreck dispersal 1.46. Arrived 11.57 Charlestown to BU.

TROOPER M/S Tr, 206gr, 117 x 22 ft, 1–6pdr. Smiths Dk 29.4.1915, purchased 4.4.15. Sold 25.10.20, renamed *Eider II.* (Served as ALMA in WW.II.)

TROPHY Dr 83/11, 1–3pdr. Hired 1915–19 and on harbour service 11.39–1.46.

TROPIC Admiralty wood Dr, 91gr. Rose St Fndry, Inverness 1919. Sold 1922.

TROUBADOUR (ex-*Warrior*) Yt 1,245/24. Hired as A/S Yt 6.1940, later purchased. Accommodation ship 1942. Sold 1947.

TROUBRIDGE A.ship 16. Hired 1805—10.

TROUP AHEAD Dr 86/13, 1—3pdr. Hired 1915—19 and as M/S 12.39—7.46.

TROVE Dr 83/08. Hired on harbour service 1915—19.

TRUE ACCORD Dr 92/21, 2—MG. Hired as M/S 12.1939. A/P Dr 8.40. Sunk 26.12.40 in collision off Yarmouth.

TRUE BLUE Brig, 115bm. Hired 11.1807—3.09.

TRUE BRITON Schooner 12, 183bm. Hired 12.1812—6.14.

TRUE FRIEND Dr 83/09, 1—3pdr. Hired 1915—19 and as A/P Dr, 1—3pdr, 10.40—2.46.

TRUE REWARD Dr 93/13. Hired as boom tender 8.1915—19 and as degaussing vessel 5.40—1.46.

TRUE VINE Dr 95/07. Hired 8.1914—19 and as boom tender 7.40. Reserve blockship 1941—9.45.

TRUMPETER Tr 192/13, 1—3pdr. Hired 1914—19.

TRUNNION Armament tug, 178gr, 90 x 23 ft. Yarwood 19.5.1938. On sale list 11.63.

TRUST Dr 97/18. Hired as boom tender 11.1939. A/S Dr 1941—45.

TRUSTFUL Dr 94/07, 1—3pdr. Hired 12.1914—19.

TRUSTFUL II Dr 95/07, 1—3pdr. Hired 1915—19 and on harbour service 12.39—1.46 (as TRUSTFUL).

TRUSTFUL (see TRUSTY)

TRUST ON Dr 79/11. Hired 1.1915—19.

TRUSTY DY paddle tug, 319bm, 570 tons, 130 x 23 ft. Palmer, Jarrow 14.2.1866. Renamed TRUSTFUL 6.11.1917. Sold 8.9.20 W.J.Webb.

TRUSTY STAR Dr 96/20, 1—3pdr. Hired as M/S 11.1939, purchased 10.41. Sunk 10.6.42 by mine off Malta.

TRV.1—8 Torpedo recovery vessels 235 tons, 95 x 21 ft, 1—20mm.

TRV.1 Watson, Gainsborough 4.4.1942.

TRV.2 Rowhedge IW 1.4.42. On charter 1950 as *Island Commodore,* later sold.

TRV.3 Richards, Lowestoft 23.1.43. BU 1969 at Newhaven.

TRV.4 Rowhedge IW 20.2.43.

TRV.5 Watson 23.2.43. Listed to 1946.

TRV.6 Watson 27.4.45.

TRV.7 Watson 6.10.45. Transport 1948. Sold 1954?

TRV.8 Watson 17.4.46. On charter 1952 as *Arrowhead.*

TRV.20 (ex-MMS.1510, ex-MMS.10 renamed 1951).

TRY AGAIN Dr 97/07. Hired on harbour service 12.1914—19.

TRYGON Tr 289/08. Hired as M/S 1914. Sunk 30.3.15 in collision in the Clyde.

TRYPHENA Dr 69/06, 1—6pdr. Hired 1915—19.

TRYPHON (see STORMKING)

TUBEROSE Dr 67/09. Hired 1915. Sunk 31.8.16 by mine off Lowestoft.

TUGELA Tr 233/00. Hired 1916. Sunk 26.6.16 by mine off Lowestoft.

TUI Tr (RNZN) 600 tons, 150 x 30 ft, 1—4in. Robb, Leith 26.8.1941. Survey ship 1955.

TUIRANGI 114/08. Hired on examination service (RNZN) 1942—45.

TULIP Dr 88/07, 1—3pdr. Hired 1915. Sunk 23.8.18 in collision off St Anthony. (TULIP II from 1916.)

TULIP II MFV 34net. Hired on harbour service 4.1940—45.

TUMBY Tr 204/18, 1—3pdr. Hired as A/P Tr 11.1939. M/S 3.42—4.45.

TUNA Cstr 662/07. Hired as store carrier (RFA) 1940. Burnt at Aden and loss reported 9.41.

TUNG WO 1,337/14. Hired as A/P vessel 1940. Abandoned 13.12.41 as the result of enemy action.

TUNISIAN Tr 238/30. Hired as BDV 10.1939. Sunk 9.7.42 by mine off Harwich.

TURBOT (see REDSHANK)

TURCOMAN Tr 455/37, 1—4in. Purchased as A/S Tr 8.1939. On sale list 8.45.

TURFFONTEIN (see VESTFOLD VIII)

TURMOIL Oiler (RFA) 4,060 tons, 280 x 39 ft. Pembroke Dock 7.3.1917. Sold 28.6.35 McLellan, Bo'ness to BU.

TURMOIL Rescue tug 1,118 tons, 190 x 38½ ft, 1—3in, 2—20mm. Robb 14.7.1944. Sold 1965, renamed *Nisos Kerkyra*. (On charter 1946—57.)

TURQUOISE Cstr 486/92. Hired as fleet messenger 22.7.1915. Sunk 31.7.15 by gunfire of 'U.28' in the Atlantic.

TURQUOISE Tr 164/96. Hired 1918—19.

TURQUOISE (ex-*Warwickshire*) Tr 430/35, 641 tons, 1—4 in. Purchased as A/S Tr 11.1935. Sold 1946, renamed *St Oswald*.

TURTLE Iron S.tug, 37bm, 57½ x 12 ft. Dudgeon 23.1.1864, purchased 1865. Foundered 17.4.1873 at moorings at Ascension.

TUSCAN Tr 178/05. Hired 1918—19.

TUSCARORA Yt 591/97. Hired as A/S Yt 1.1940—45.

TWEED 1,777/07. Hired as fleet auxiliary 1.1916—19.

TWEENWAYS Dr 92/20. Hired as M/S 12.1939—45.

TWELVE Dr 77/01. Hired 1915—19.

TWENTE Tug 239/37. Hired 1940. Sunk 12.6.40 by enemy action at Le Havre.

TWENTY SIX, TWENTY EIGHT and TWENTY NINE Drifters, all 77/01. Hired 1915—19.

TWINKLE Admiralty wood Dr, 96gr. Colby 1919. Renamed CLOUD-ARCH 1919. Sold 1921.

TWINKLE (see BOREALIS)

TWINKLING STAR Dr 95/20. Hired as BDV 9.1939—10.45.

TWO Dr 91/07. Hired 12.1914—19.

TWO BOYS Dr 91/11. Hired 1915—19.

TWO BOYS MFV 28net/27. Hired on examination service 7.1940—45.

TWOSTEP (see TARANTELLA)

TYKE DY tug 95/11, 76½ x 17½ ft. Purchased 12.1.1912. On sale list 7.47.

TYNE PRINCE Tr 206/09, 1—6pdr. Hired 1914—19.

TYNET Dr 97/07. Hired 1915—19.

TYNE WAVE Tr 121/91. Hired 1918—19.

TYNWALD 2,376/37, 6—4in, 4—20mm. Purchased as A/A ship 4.1940, completed 11.41. Sunk 12.11.42 by the Italian S/M ARGO off Bougie.

TYPHOON Admiralty steel Dr, 96gr. A.Hall 1918. Sold 1919, renamed *Ocean Lassie*. (OCEAN LASSIE in WW.II.)

TYPHOON (see SYRIAN)

TYPHOON Fleet tug 1,380 tons (deep), 188 x 38½ ft. Robb 14.10.1958.

TYRANT Yt 149/30, 1—6pdr. Hired as A/P Yt 1940. Examination service 1943; training tender 1944—46.

TYRE (see ADVENTURE)

TYRIAN (see ADVENTURE)

TYRIE Dr 93/08, 1—6pdr. Hired 1.1915—19 and on examination service 3.40. Renamed TRENCHANT 1942; PUNGENT 1943. Returned 2.45.

TYROLIA 7,535/99, 11,850 tons. Hired as dummy battleship CENTURION 8.1914, purchased 11.14. Renamed SAXOL, oiler (RFA), 9.6.16; ASPENLEAF 10.16. Sold 12.9.19 Anglo—Saxon Petroleum Co.

UBEROUS Dr. Hired 1915—19.

UBEROUS Dr 92/18. Hired as M/S 12.1939. Grounded 11.1.41 in the Foyle.

UBERTY Dr 93/12, 1—3pdr. Hired 1915—19 and as M/S, 2—MG, 11.39. A/P Dr 8.40. Sunk 8.5.41 by air attack off Lowestoft.

UGIE BANK Tr 205/13. Hired as BDV 1914—19 and as A/P Tr 12.39—3.40. Hired as fuel carrier 3.44—10.44.

UGIE BRAE Dr 88/15, 1—6pdr. Hired 1916—19 and as A/P Dr 12.39. Degaussing vessel 6.40—4.46.

UGIE VALE Dr 95/19. Hired on harbour service 11.1939—7.45.

UHDEA Tr 191/06. Hired 1914—18.

UIVER Tr 200/02. Dutch, hired as M/S (Dutch crew) 8.40. RN crew 11.42. Returned 11.45.

UKI Cstr 545/23, 1–12pdr. Hired as M/S (RAN) 10.1939–10.44.

ULLSWATER (ex-*Kos.XXIX*) A/S Wh 555 tons, 138½ x 26½ ft, 1–12pdr, 1–20mm. Smiths Dk 31.8.1939, purchased 26.8.39. Sunk 19.11.42 by E-boat torpedo in the Channel.

ULNA Yt 167/09. Hired on examination service (RCN) 1939.

ULSTER Tr 185/97. Hired as BDV 1915–19.

ULSTER MONARCH 3,791/29, 1–12pdr, 4–20mm. Hired as landing ship 10.1940. Store carrier 10.41; landing ship 8.42–10.45.

ULSTER PRINCE 3,791/30. Hired as store carrier 1940. Wrecked by air attack 25.4.41 while aground off Nauplia.

ULSTER QUEEN 3,791/29, 6–4in, 2–3in. Hired as A/A ship 8.1940. Fighter-direction ship 1943–4.46.

ULVA Tr, 'Isles' class. Cook Welton & Gemmell 30.7.1942. Sold 4.46, renamed *Salvo*.

ULYSSES Tr 165/89, 1–6pdr. Hired as M/S 1916–18. (ULYSSES II from 1917.)

ULYSSES Tug 118/95. Hired on harbour service 5.1917–7.17.

UMBRIEL (ex-*Haussa*) Yt circa 100/39. Hired as A/P Yt 5.1940–45.

UMGENI 2,622/98. Hired as store carrier (RFA) 23.12.1914–17.4.16.

UMTALI 2,622/96. Hired as store carrier (RFA) 3.1.1915–10.4.16.

UMVOTI 5,183/03. Purchased 1940. Sunk 29.7.40 as blockship. Raised and BU 1943 by Ward at Folkestone.

UNDAUNTED Iron paddle tug (Indian) 470 tons, 160 x 25 ft. Dumbarton 1865. Listed to 1891.

UNDAUNTED Tr 141/95. Hired 1918–19.

UNDERTOW Admiralty steel Dr, 96gr. Scott, Bowling 1919. Sold 1921, same name. (Served as SPES MELIOR in WW.II.)

UNDERWING (ex-*Goodman*) 1,570/17. Hired as decoy vessel 5.1917–12.18.

UNI I Wh 249/30. Hired as M/S 11.1940. Renamed SPRINGS (SAN) 6.42. Returned 5.46.

UNI II Wh 250/30. Hired as M/S 3.1941. Renamed NIGEL (SAN) 9.41. Returned 5.46.

UNI III Wh 240/26, 1–3in. Hired as M/S 3.41. Renamed BOKSBURG (SAN) 10.41. Returned 7.46. (Listed 1.47.)

UNI IV Wh 197/23. Hired as M/S 3.41. Renamed GERMISTON (SAN) 8.41. Returned 5.46.

UNI V Wh 198/23. Hired as M/S 3.1941. Renamed KRUGERSDORP (SAN) 6.41. Returned 5.46.

UNICITY Dr 96/19. Hired as M/S 12.1939. Capsized 31.1.42 off Blyth. Raised and BU 10.43.

UNICORN Tr/Dr 124/95, 1–3pdr. Hired 1915–19.

UNIFLOROUS Dr 78/11. Hired 1914–19.

UNIO 1,773/02. Hired as fleet auxiliary 1915–19.

UNION Cutter 8. Hired 1782.

UNION Brig 12. Hired 1793. Blown up 18.12.1793 at the evacuation of Toulon.

UNION Cutter 14. Hired 1800–01.

UNION Tender, 130bm. Hired 1.1809–2.1811.

UNION Dr 84/07, 1–3pdr. Hired 1915–19.

UNISON Dr 79/10. Hired as BDV 4.1915–19 and on harbour service 1.40. Renamed HARMONY 1943. Listed to 1944.

UNITED BOYS Dr 95/13, 1–3pdr. Hired as A/P Dr 11.1939. M/S 1941–9.45.

UNITED BROTHERS Tender 4, 143bm, 4–3pdr. Hired 6.1803. Captured 6.1.1807 by a French privateer off the Lizard.

UNITIA Tr 296/13, 1–6pdr. Hired as M/S 1914–19 and as A/P Tr, 2–MG, 5.40. M/S 5.41. Renamed PORTIA 1941. Returned 1.46.

UNITY 80–ton vessel hired for the Armada campaign.

UNITY A.ship, 240bm. Hired 1649–54.

UNITY Transport, 68bm. Chatham 1665. Sold 1712. (Also known as UNITY HORSEBOAT.)

UNITY II Dr 88/04, 1–3pdr. Hired 1914–19.

UNITY III Dr 80/07, 1–3pdr. Hired 1.1915–19.

UNITY IV Dr 56/02, 1–3pdr. Hired 1915–19.

UNIVERSE Paddle tug 143/75. Hired 1917–19.

UNIVERSE MFV 67/42. Hired (RCN) 6.1942–1.46.

UNST Tr, 'Isles' class. Ferguson 28.5.1942. To Italian navy 1.46.

UPLIFTER Salvage vessel 950 tons, 150 x 35½ ft, 2–20mm. Smiths Dk 29.11.1943.

UPNOR Armament store carrier 600 tons, 142 x 24 ft. Bow McLachlan 30.3.1899. Listed to 1952.

UPOLU 1,141/91. Hired as depot ship 8.1914–12.14.

URALBA Cstr 603/42. Hired (RAN) as tender 7.1942–45.

URANA Tr 308/14, 1–6pdr. Hired 1914–19.

URANIA Tr 226/07, 1–6pdr. Hired 1914–19.

URANIA Tr 869/30. French, seized 9.1.1941 off Gibraltar. Renamed RETRIEVER 9.41 and completed 11.41 as A/S Tr. Returned 7.46.

URE (see HENRY JENNINGS)

URGENT DY tank vessel 425 tons, 110 x 25 ft. Cox, Falmouth 19.10.1910. Hulked 1950; sold by 1957.

URIE Tr 226/17, 1–6pdr. Hired 1917–19.

URKA Tr 249/17, 1–12pdr. Hired 1917–19.

URMSTON GRANGE Hired as transport 10.1899–12.1900 and purchased 1914. Sunk 1914 as blockship at Scapa.

URSULA Dr 88/00, 1–3pdr. Hired 1915–19. (URSULA II from 1917.)
URVILLE French DY tug seized 3.7.1940 at Southampton. Free-French crew 10.40. Returned 8.45.
USEFUL DY tug 27 tons. Listed 1919. Sold 1923.
USEFUL DY tug 92 tons, 70 x 16 ft. Philip, Dartmouth 17.4.1935. Sold 1959.
USKSIDE 2,209/12. Hired as fleet auxiliary 24.8.1914–28.1.19.
UTILISE Dr 94/18. Hired as M/S 12.1939–3.46.
UT PROSIM Dr 91/25, 1–3pdr. Hired as A/P Dr 11.1939. Sunk 2.3.43 by long-range gunfire, Dover harbour.
UTVAER Dr 171/14. Norwegian, hired as M/S 10.1940–45.

VACEASAY Tr, 'Isles' class. Cook Welton & Gemmell 17.3.1945, completed as danlayer. Sold 1967.
VACUNA Yt 48/98. Hired as A/P Yt 9.1939–45.
VADNE Ferry 75/39. Hired on examination service 9.1939. Harbour service 1.43–1.46.
VADURA Yt 109/26. Hired as BBV 12.1940, purchased 1.42. Laid up 7.42.
VAGRANT Yt 484/03, 1–12pdr, 1–6pdr. Hired as A/P Yt 25.9.1914–1.2.19.
VAGRANT Rescue tug, 'B.A.T' class. Levinston 1.3.1943 on lend-lease. Returned 3.46 to the USN.
VAGRANT (ex-*Empire Titania*) DY Tug 258/43, 528 tons. Transferred from MOT 5.1947. On sale list 12.67.
VAILLANT Tr 916/21. French patrol vessel seized 3.7.1940 at Sheerness. A/P Tr 8.40. Boom gate vessel 3.42 and renamed BALISE. Returned 1946. (Free-French crew to 5.41.)
VAL Dr 93/09. Hired 1916–19.
VALA 1,016/93. Hired as decoy vessel (Q.8) 8.1915. Sunk 21.8.17 by 'UB.54' in the Atlantic.
VALDA Yt 36/28. Hired as echo Yt 1.1940–44.
VALDORA Tr 251/16. Hired as A/P Tr 11.1939. Sunk 12.1.40 by air attack off Cromer.
VALENA Yt 882/08. Hired as A/S Yt 8.1939–45.
VALENTIA Tr 164/98. Hired 1918–19.
VALENTINE BOWER Tr, 'Castle' type, 275gr. C.Rennoldson 1.10.1917. Sold 1921, renamed *Malvolio*. (Served as MILFORD KING in WW.II.)
VALE of CLYDE Tr 223/08, 1–12pdr. Hired 1914–19.
VALE of FORTH Tr 226/16, 1–6pdr. Hired 1916–19.
VALE of FRUIN Tr 211/15, 1–6pdr. Hired 1915–19.

VALE of LENNOX Tr 233/09, 1–6pdr. Hired 1916–19.
VALE of LEVEN Tr 223/07. Hired 1915. Sunk 10.7.17 in collision in the Channel.
VALE o'MORAY Dr 89/11, 1–3pdr. Hired 1916–19.
VALERIA Tr 189/98. Hired 1917–19.
VALERIAN MFV 53/23. Hired on harbour service 9.1940–45.
VALESCA Tr 188/16, 1–6pdr. Hired 1916–19 and as A/P Tr 11.39. M/S 7.40; wreck-location 12.41–12.45.
VALETTE Cutter 14. Hired 1800–01.
VALHALLA Yt 1,490/92. Hired 20.6.1916. Repair ship 1917–19.
VALIANT Lugger 14. Hired 1794–1801.
VALIANT II Yt 2,184/93, 4–12pdr. Hired as A/P Yt 18.11.1914– 6.2.19.
VALINDA Cstr 143/33. Hired (RCN) 1942–46.
VALKYRIE Dr 88/04. Hired on harbour service 7.1915–19. (VALKYRIE II from 1917.)
VALKYRIEN Salvage vessel 343/07. Danish, seized and commissioned 19.1.1943. Returned 1946.
VALLAY Tr, 'Isles' class. Cook Welton & Gemmell 10.4.1945, completed as danlayer. Sold 1.59 at Malta.
VALMONT Tr 245/16, 1–6pdr. Hired as M/S 1916–19 and as M/S 11.39–11.45.
VALOROUS Dr 84/07, 1–3pdr. Hired 1915–19.
VALPA Tr 230/15. Hired 1915. Sunk 19.3.16 by mine off Spurn Head.
VALSE A/S 530 tons, 150 x 27½ ft, 1–4in, 3–20mm. Smiths Dk 12.3.1941. To War Dept 5.46, same name. BU 9.51.
VAMBERY Tr 316/17, 1–6pdr. Hired 1917–19.
VANADIS Yt 333/80, 2–6pdr. Hired as A/P Yt 12.6.1915–18.
VANDUARA Yt 337/86. Hired (free) 21.9.1914–12.2.15.
VAN DYCK 13,241/21. Hired as ABV 1939. Sunk 10.6.40 by air attack off Narvik.
VAN DYCK Tr 352/26. Belgian, hired as A/S Tr 2.1941–11.45.
VANELLUS 1,797/12. Hired as store carrier (RFA) 7.11.1914–8.10.15.
VANESSA Yt 445/99, 2–6pdr. Hired as A/P Yt 15.10.1914–5.3.19.
VANGUARD III Dr 83/04. Hired 1915–19.
VAN ISLE MFV 83/36. Hired (RCN) 1940–45.
VAN OOST Tr 352/26. Belgian, hired as A/P Tr 7.1940–11.45.
VAN ORLEY Tr 352/27. Belgian, hired as A/P Tr 7.6.1940. Sunk 4.5.41 by air attack at Liverpool. Raised 11.41 and BU.
VANQUISHER Tug 179/99. Hired 7.1914–19.
VANSITTART Cutter 10. Hired 1821–27.
VAPOUR Admiralty wood Dr, 95gr. Smith, Rye 1920. Sold 1920, same name (Served as XMAS EVE in WW.II.)

VARANGA Tr 361/29. Hired as M/S 8.1939—11.45.
VARANIS Tr 258/10, 1—6pdr. Hired as M/D 1914—19 and as A/P Tr 12.39. M/D 7.40; BBV 10.44—11.45.
VARDO (see KOS XVIII)
VASCO da GAMA Tr 265/10, 1—6pdr. Hired 1915—19.
VASCAMA Tr 447/35, 1—4in. Purchased as A/S Tr 9.1939. On sale list 7.45. (On loan Portuguese navy 10.43—8.44 as 'P.6'.)
VATERSAY Tr, 'Isles' class. Cochrane 13.11.1943. Sold 3.46, renamed *Vouri*
VELDA Yt 571gr/26. American, purchased as ABV 1942? Sale list 1946.
VELETA A/S Tr 530 tons, 150 x 27½ ft, 1—4in, 3—20mm. Smiths Dk 28.3.1941. Sold 3.46.
VELHO Tug. Hired 1939—3.42.
VELIA Tr 289/14, 1—12pdr. Hired as A/P Tr 12.1939. Sunk 19.10.40 by mine off Harwich.
VELMAR Tug 122/38. Hired 2.1918—12.18.
VENATOR Tr 293/13, 1—6pdr. Hired 1916—19.
VENCEDOR Yt 466/13. Hired (RCN) 1942—46.
VENETIA Yt 569/05, 1—12pdr, 1—6pdr. Hired as A/P Yt7.8.1914—22.2.19. (VENETIA II from 1917. ALTAIR in WW.II.)
VENETIA III Tr 201/99. Hired 1917—19.
VENETIA Yt 687/03. Hired as A/P Yt (RCN) 1942—46.
VENICE 1,874/14. Hired as fleet auxiliary 1.1917—19.
VENO MFV 50/41. Danish, seized 1941. Harbour service to 1944.
VENOSTA Tr 316/17, 1—6pdr. Hired 1917—19 and as M/S (RCN) 12.39. Boom gate vessel 1941—45.
VENTOSE Tr 185/36. French M/S seized 3.7.1940 at Southampton. A/P Tr 10.40; examination service 1941; air-sea rescue 1943—7.44.
VENTURE Tr 193/05, 1—6pdr. Hired 1914—19 and as A/P Tr 11.39. Renamed DASHER 1941. Returned 1941. Hired again as BUCEPHALUS 4.44 fuel carrier. REturned 11.44.
VENTURE II (see SEABORN)
VENUS Cutter 8. Hired 1793—97.
VENUS Transport 6. Hired 1794—1801.
VENUS Cutter 8. Hired 1796—1801.
VENUS Cutter 10, 51bm. Hired 7.1803. Captured 31.1.06 by the French lugger L'AMI-NATIONAL.
VENUS II Dr 87/07, 1—3pdr. Hired 1915—19.
VENUS STAR MFV 30net. Hired on harbour service 7.1940—45.
VERA Tr 333/07, 1—10pdr. Hired 1915—19.
VERACITY Dr 96/10, 1—3pdr. Hired 1916. Sunk 15.2.18 in action off Dover.
VERA CREINA Dr 80/11. Hired 1915—19.

VERA GRACE Tr 232/08, 1–6pdr. Hired 1914–19.

VERBENA II Tr 152/97, 1–6pdr. Hired 1916–18.

VERCHERES Tr 157/01. Hired (RCN). Lost 9.5.1943 by fire at Sorel.

VERDANT Dr 87/06, 1–3pdr. Hired 1915–19.

VERDUN (ex-*Paris*) Paddle 804/88, 1–6pdr. Hired as M/S 17.3.1916, later purchased. Sold 4.22. (VERDUN II from 1917.)

VERDURE Dr 97/08. Hired 1915–19.

VEREENIGING (see VESTFOLD IX)

VERESIS Tr 302/15, 2–6pdr. Hired 1915–20. (Served as WYOMING in WW.II.)

VERGEMERE Yt 496/03. Hired as A/P Yt 1.6.1915–20.12.15.

VERITY Dr 100/13, 1–3pdr. Hired 1915; VERITAS 6.18–19.

VERNAL Dr 98/18. Hired as M/S 12.1939. TRV 6.43 and purchased. BU 1.46.

VERONA Yt 437/90. Hired as A/P Yt 7.11.1914. Sunk 24.2.17 by mine off Portmahomack.

VERS le DESTIN Dr 68/37. French M/S seized 7.1940. A/P Dr 1.41–45.

VESPER II Tr 264/06, 1–6pdr. Hired 1916–19.

VESPER STAR Dr 79/04. Hired 1915–18.

VESTA Tr 240/05, 1–6pdr. Hired 1916–19.

VESTFOLD I Wh 312/29. Hired as M/S 11.1941. Renamed NEBULA 1942. Danlayer 1944–2.46.

VESTFOLD II Wh 312/29. Hired as M/S 11.1941. Renamed NIMBUS 1942. Danlayer 1944–2.46.

VESTFOLD III Wh 273/27. Hired as M/S 11.1941. Renamed PACKICE 1942. Laid up 5.44. Returned 1.46.

VESTFOLD V Wh 312/25. Hired as M/S 11.1941. Renamed SANDSTORM 1942. Returned 1945.

VESTFOLD VI Wh 312/25. Hired as M/S 11.1941. Renamed SHOOTING STAR 1942. Returned 1.46.

VESTFOLD VIII Wh 355/36. Fitting out as A/S Wh 1.1942. To SAN 8.42 as TURFFONTEIN. Returned 3.45.

VESTFOLD IX Wh 355/36. Fitting out as A/S Wh 1.1942. To SAN 1942 as VEREENIGING. Returned 1945.

VESTFOLD X Wh 299/35. Hired as M/S 11.1941. Renamed SQUALL 1942. Danlayer 1944–45.

VETERAN DY paddle tug 690 tons, 145 x 29 ft. Thornycroft 30.8.1915. Renamed ANCIENT 21.12.18. Sold 1954 at Malta.

VETERAN II Dr 73/10, 1–3pdr. Hired 1915–19.

VETO (ex-*AS.33*) DY tug. Transferred from War Dept 1919? Sold 8.22.

VICEREINE (see VICEROY)

VICEROY Cstr 62/02. Belgian, hired as TRV 11.1942. Renamed VICEREINE 4.43. Returned 1945.

VICEROY (see THE VICEROY)

VICTOR Tr 193/97. Hired as BDV 1914—19.

VICTOR II Tr 201/06, 1—6pdr. Hired 1914—19.

VICTOR Tug 153/98. Hired on examination service 11.1939. Harbour tug 1942—45.

VICTOR & MARY Dr 81/12. Hired 1915—19.

VICTORIA Tr 221/12, 1—6pdr. Hired 1915—19 and 3.40—1.45.

VICTORIA II Dr, 1—3pdr. Hired 1915—20.

VICTORIA Cstr. Hired as decoy ship 11.1914—15.

VICTORIA Paddle 229/84. Hired as ferry 12.4.1917—14.12.19 and on examination service 8.39—1.41.

VICTORIA I Hired as M/S 6.1940. Lost 25.3.42 by enemy action but listed to 7.42.

VICTORIA II Hired as M/S 6.1940. Degaussing vessel 1943 and purchased. On sale list 7.46.

VICTORIA MARIE 1,432/27. Hired as A/P vessel (RIN) 1939—43.

VICTORIAN 10,635/04, 8—4.7in. Hired as AMC 17.8.1914—1.20.

VICTORIAN II Tr 195/00, 1—6pdr. Hired 1915—19.

VICTORIAN Tr 447/35. Purchased as A/S Tr 8.1939. On sale list 1.46.

VICTORIAN PRINCE Tr 126/97. Hired as BDV 1915—19.

VICTORIA REGINA Tr 146/97, 1—6pdr. Hired as M/S 2.1915—18.

VICTORSIT Dr 82/07, 1—3pdr. Hired 1915—19.

VICTORY A.ship, 400bm. Hired 1649—53.

VICTORY DY tug 76 tons. Listed 1904—34. (Also known as C.210.)

VICTORY Tr 164/98. Hired on harbour service 1915—17.

VICTRIX Tr 472/37, 1—4in. Hired as A/S Tr 9.1939—12.45.

VIDETTE (ex—French VEDETTE ex-British privateer PENSEE) Brig-sloop 14. Hired 1800—01.

VIDETTE Tr 240/05, 1—10pdr. Hired 1916—19 and as fuel carrier 2.43. Renamed OUTPOST 3.43. Returned 1945.

VIDONIA Tr 276/07, 1—12pdr. Hired 1914—19 and as A/P Tr, 1—6pdr, 6.40. Fuel carrier 4.43. Sunk 6.10.44 in collision in the Channel.

VIENNA 1,767/94. Hired as accommodation ship 29.8.1914—12.14. Hired as ABS, 2—12pdr, 29.4.15—25.8.19. (Also operated as decoy ship ANTWERP 1.1.15—28.4.15.)

VIENNA 4,227/29, 1—12pdr, 8—20mm. Hired as depot ship 6.1941. For disposal 10.44.

VIERGE de LOURDES Dr 154/17. French M/S seized 3.7.1940 at Southampton. M/S 11.40—1.46.

VIERNOE Tr 273/14, 1—6pdr. Hired 1915—19 and as M/S (RCN) 1939. Boom gate vessel 1941—45.

VIGILANT Cutter 6. Hired 1793—1801.

VIGILANT DY tug 240 tons, 80½ x 17½ ft. Purchased 21.6.1900. Sold 22.10.19. (Also known as C.2.)

VIGILANT II Tr 279/04, 1–12pdr. Hired 1914–19.
VIGILANT III Dr 91/15, 1–6pdr. Hired 1915–19.
VIGILANT Tug 44gr. Hired on harbour service 6.8.1914, purchased
1916. Sold 1919.
VIGILANT Tr 139/02. Hired 1917–19 and as BBV 7.40–43.
VIGILANT 106/38, 1–3pdr. Hired as A/P vessel (RAN) 1940. Renamed
SLEUTH 4.44; HAWK 3.45; sold 10.46.
VIGILANT Tug. Listed as A/P vessel in the E.Indies 1941–46.
VIGILANT Tug, 1–6pdr, 2–MG. Hired as A/P vessel 1941–43.
VIGOROUS Dr 81/13, 1–3pdr. Hired 1915–19.
VIGRA Tr 184/99. Norwegian, hired as ferry 1940–46.
VIKING II Dr 62/00, 1–3pdr. Hired 1915–19.
VIKING Tug 386/04. Danish, seized 1940. Salvage vessel. Sunk 6.4.41
by air attack off Piraeus.
VIKING BANK Tr 335/27. Dutch, hired as M/S (Dutch crew) 7.1940–
45.
VIKING DEEPS Tr 226/16. Hired as A/P Tr 6.1940. Examination
service 1943–11.44.
VIKINGS Tr 1,159/35. French patrol vessel seized 3.7.1940. Free-
French crew 8.40. Sunk 17.4.42 by 'U.542' off the coast of Syria.
(French sources say 30.4.42.)
VIKNOR (ex-*Viking*) 5,386/88. Hired as AMC 19.11.1914. Wrecked
13.1.15 on the north coast of Ireland.
VILDA Tr 358/29. Hired as BDV 1.1940–9.46.
VIMY Tr, 'Castle' type (RCN). Polson IW 6.6.1917. Became lightship
No.5.
VINDELICIA Tr 248/13, 1–6pdr. Hired as M/S 1914–19 and as A/P
Tr, 1–6pdr, 6.40. Fuel carrier 4.43; towing duty 1944–12.45.
VINDEX (ex-*Viking*) 1,764/05, 2,950 tons, 4–12pdr, 1–6pdr, 7–A/C.
Hired as seaplane carrier 15.3.1915, purchased 9.15. Sold 12.2.20.
VINE Dr 95/07, 1–3pdr. Hired 1915–19.
VINE Dr 77/04. Hired as tender 8.1915–19 and as BBV 5.40–42.
VINELEAF (see PATRICIAN)
VINEYARD A.ship, 140bm. Hired for the Armada campaign.
VINTAGE Dr 80/07, 1–3pdr. Hired 1915–19.
VIOLA Tr 228/05, 1–6pdr. Hired as M/S 1914–19. (VIOLA II from
1916.) Hired as A/P Tr 11.39. Renamed ELENA 1940, M/S. Returned
1.45.
VIOLA III Dr 86/07. Hired 1916–19.
VIOLET Dr 88/06. Hired in WW.I.
VIOLET Dr 80/04. Hired as boom accommodation ship 5.1915–19.
VIOLET Dr 82/07. Hired as coal boat 5.1915–19.
VIOLET II Dr 84/07, 1–3pdr. Hired 1916–19.

VIOLET III Dr 86/04. Hired 1916–19.
VIOLET Tug 141/-. Hired on harbour service 7.1917–2.19.
VIOLET FLOWER Dr 87/14, 1–3pdr. Hired 1915–19 and as M/S 10.39–45.
VIOLET MAY Dr 74/06. Hired 1916–19.
VIREO Tr 192/12, 1–6pdr. Hired 1914–19 and as A/P Tr 12.39–11.43.
VIRGINIA Yt 712/30. Hired as A/S Yt 9.1939. Examination service 1942–45.
VIRGINIAN 10,757/05. Hired as AMC 13.11.1914–31.1.20.
VIRGINIAN II Tr 211/06, 1–3pdr. Hired as M/S 1915–19.
VIRGINIE Tug. Hired as M/S 1941–46.
VISCOL Oiler (RFA) 1,920 tons, 210 x 34½ ft. Craig Taylor, Stockton on Tees 21.2.1916. Sold 1947 renamed *Frecciamare.*
VISENDA Tr 455/37, 1–4in. Hired as A/S Tr 8.1939–2.46.
VISION Tug. Purchased 10.1941. Sunk 18.6.42 at Mersa Matruh.
VISON (ex-*Avalon*) Yt 422gr/31. Commissioned as A/S Yt (RCN) 5.10.1940. Training ship 1955–11.45.
VISTA Yt 95/91. Hired on harbour service 3.1918–14.4.19.
VITALITY Tr 262/14. Hired 1915. Sunk 20.10.17 by mine off Orfordness.
VITI Fiji Govt ship 700/40. Hired (RNZN) 1941–46.
VITOL Oiler (RFA) 4,900 tons, 335 x 41½ ft. Greenock & Grangemouth Co 24.5.1917. Sunk 7.3.18 by U-boat in the Irish Sea.
VITTORIA (see PARGUST)
VIVA II Yt 502/29. Hired as A/S Yt 9.1939. Sunk 8.5.41 by air attack off north Cornwall.
VIVACITY Tug 68/10, 1–6pdr. Hired as A/P vessel 12.1940–6.45.
VIVANTI Tr 226/15. Hired 1915. Foundered 7.3.17 off Hastings.
VIVIANA Tr 452/36. Hired as A/S Tr 10.1939–5.46.
VIXEN Tug. Purchased 1941 in the Mediterranean. Lost 17.6.42 at Tobruk.
VIZAGAPATAM Tr, 'Basset' class (RIN). Burn, Calcutta. Ordered 7.1942. Cancelled 10.44.
VIZALMA Tr 672/40. Purchased as A/S Tr 6.1940. Sold 12.45.
VOLANTE Tr 255/07, 1–6pdr. Hired as M/S 1914–19.
VOLATILE (see VOLCANO)
VOLCANO DY paddle tug 700 tons, 145 x 27½ ft. Barclay Curle 21.9.1899. Renamed VOLATILE 1919. Arrived 18.4.57 Ward, Grays to BU.
VOLENS (see VOLUNTEER)
VOLESUS Tr 293/13, 1–6pdr. Hired 1915–19.
VOLONTAIRE (see INGENIEUR CACHIN)
VOLTA Tr 159/90. Hired 1918–19.

VOLTAIRE 13,301/23, 8–6in, 2–3in. Hired as AMC 9.1939. Sunk
4.4.41 by the German THOR in mid-Atlantic.
VOLTURNUS Cstr 615/13. Hired as store carrier (RFA) 1.9.1914. Sunk
11.19 by mine off the Scottish coast.
VOLUNTEER DY mooring vessel 750 tons, 135 x 28 ft. Rennoldson,
S.Shields 17.3.1916. Renamed VOLENS 1.3.18. Sold 1947 Tees
Conservancy.
VOLUNTEER Tr 112/91. Hired 1917–19.
VONOLEL Tr 264/11, 1–6pdr. Hired as M/S 1915–19.
VP.19 (see JEUNE HELENE)
VRYSSIE (see LADY VAGRANT)
VULCAIN Tug 200/03. Hired 8.9.1917–18.1.19.
VULCAN II Tug 288/93. Hired 30.7.1914, later purchased. Listed to
1923.
VULCAN (ex-*Mascot*) Tr, 623 tons, 153 x 26½ ft. Purchased as depot
ship 11.7.1936. Sold 5.2.47, renamed *Fotherby*.
VULTURE II Tr 190/99, 1–6pdr. Hired 1914. Sunk 16.3.18 in collision
in Loch Eriboll.
VYNER BROOKE 1,670/28. Hired 1941? Sunk 14.2.42 by Japanese
air attack in the Banka Strait.

WAFT Admiralty steel Dr, 96gr. Scott, Bowling 1919. Sold 1921, re-
named *Genius*. (GENIUS in WW.II.)
WAHINE 4,436/13. Hired as fleet messenger 17.4.1915. Purchased as
minelayer, 2–14pdr, 2–6pdr, 200 mines, 1916. Sold 1919.
WAIAU Tr, 'Castle' type (RNZN). Mason, Auckland. Cancelled and BU
1946 on stocks.
WAIHO Tr, 'Castle' type (RNZN). Stevenson & Cook 19.2.1944. Sold
1946, renamed *Matong*. (Ordered for the RN.)
WAIITI Tr, 'Castle' type (RNZN). Stevenson & Cook, Port Chalmers.
Cancelled 10.1943. (Ordered for the RN.)
WAIKAKA Tr, 'Castle' type (RNZN). Stevenson & Cook. Cancelled
10.1943. (Ordered for the RN.)
WAIKANAE Tr, 'Castle' type (RNZN). Stevenson & Cook. Cancelled
10.1943. (Ordered for the RN.)
WAIKATO Tr, 'Castle' type (RNZN). Mason 16.10.1943, not completed.
Sold 1946, renamed *Taiaora*.
WAIMA Tr, 'Castle' type (RNZN). Stevenson & Cook 11.12.1943. Sold
1946, renamed *Moona*.
WAIMANA 8,129/11. Purchased 9.1939 as dummy battleship
RESOLUTION. Returned 2.42, renamed *Empire Waimana*.

WAINSCOT Armament tug. Listed 1920. Sold 1948.

WAIPU Tr, 'Castle' type (RNZN). Stevenson & Cook 31.7.1943. Sold 1946?

WAIRUA Cstr 352/13. Purchased as M/S (RNZN). Sold 3.45.

WAKAKURA Tr, 'Castle' type (RNZN). Commissioned as M/S 9.4.1926. Danlayer 1944. Sold 1947. (In WW.I as TR.1.)

WALDEMAR Yt 29/30. Hired on examination service 9.1939. M/S tender 10.40–44.

WALDORF Tr 293/13, 1–6pdr. Hired as M/S 1915–19. (Served as ALFREDIAN in WW.II.)

WALFISCH Tug. Belgian, hired as boom gate vessel 12.1914–2.19.

WALKERDALE Dr 99/11. Hired as BDV 12.1914–19 and on harbour service 1.40–9.45.

WALLACE Tr 100/83. Hired 1918–19.

WALLASEA Tr, 'Isles' class. Robb 22.4.1943. Sunk 6.1.44 by E-boat torpedo in Mounts Bay.

WALLASEY Tug 149/03. Hired 10.1914–12.14.

WALLENA Tr 225/14, 1–6pdr. Hired as M/S 1914–19 and as A/P Tr 11.39. M/S 6.40; boom gate vessel 4.45–9.45.

WALLINGTON Tr 259/11. Hired as BDV 1915–19.

WALLINGTON (see ST GEORGE)

WALNUT M/S Tr 520 tons, 150 x 27½ ft, 1–12pdr. Smiths Dk 12.8.1939. Danlayer 1946. Sold 1948.

WALPOLE Tr 302/14, 1–6pdr. Hired 1914–19.

WALTER BURKE Tr, 'Castle' type, 275gr. Smiths Dk 3.9.1917. Sold 1922, renamed *Gonerby*.

WALTER CAVE Tr, 'Castle' type. Greenock. Cancelled 1919.

WALTER S. BAILEY Tr 244/02, 1–4in, 1–12pdr. Hired 1916–19.

WALTON BELLE Paddle 385/97, 2–6pdr. Hired as M/S 22.12.1915–6.5.19 then as hospital carrier HC.3, to 5.20.

WALWYNS CASTLE Tr 255/13, 1–6pdr. Hired 1915–19 and as M/S 3.40–3.46.

WANDERER (see LIBERTY)

WANDERER Paddle 2–6pdr. Listed as M/S 1917. Renamed WARDEN 1918. Sold 28.11.21 Hall, Rochester to BU.

WAPPING Tug 180/94. Hired 8.1914–19.

'War' class oilers (RFA), average 5,560 gr, 11,660 tons, 400 x 52 ft:

WAR AFRIDI Duncan, Port Glasgow 11.11.1919. Oil hulk 1.49. Sold 1958.

WAR BAHADUR Armstrong 4.11.18. Arrived 9.46 Hughes Bolckow, Blyth to BU.

WAR BHARATA Palmer 6.19. To sale list 3.48.

WAR BRAHMIN Lithgow 28.11.19. Laid up 7.49. Arrived 5.2.60 at
Spezia to BU.
WAR DIWAN Lithgow 28.6.19. Sunk 16.12.44 by mine in the Schelde.
WAR GAEKWAR Lithgow 28.8.19. Sold circa 1921.
WAR GHURKA Irvine, W.Hartlepool 1919. Sold 1921, renamed
Caprella.
WAR HINDOO Hamilton, Port Glasgow 4.19. Hulk 1955. Arrived
9.5.58 Hughes Bolckow to BU.
WAR JEMADAR Laing, Sunderland 29.8.18. Sold 1921, renamed
Cliona.
WAR KRISHNA Swan Hunter 5.19. Sold 1946 as oil hulk.
WAR MEHTAR Armstrong 4.19. Sunk 20.11.41 by E-boat torpedo
off Yarmouth.
WAR NAWAB Palmer 13.6.19. Oil hulk 11.46. Arrived 26.7.58 at Troon
to BU.
WAR NIZAM Palmer 8.1918. Sold 1947, renamed *Basinghall.*
WAR PATHAN Laing 19.3.19. Sold 1947, renamed *Basingbank.*
WAR PINDARI Lithgow 29.12.19. Sold 1947, renamed *Deepdale.*
WAR RAJAH Swan Hunter 1918. Sold circa 1921, renamed *British
Sailor.*
WAR RANEE Swan Hunter 1918. Sold 1920, renamed *Corbis.*
WAR SEPOY Gray, W.Hartlepool 5.12.18. Wrecked 19.7.40 by air
attack off Dover and sunk as blockship.
WAR SHIKARI Lithgow 29.1.19. Sold 1921, renamed *Chiton.*
WAR SIRDAR Laing 6.12.19. Stranded 28.2.42 near Batavia and
became Japanese *Honan Maru.* Sunk 28.3.45 by US S/M CUBMARTIN.
WAR SUBADAR Gray 26.6.18. Sold 1921, renamed *Crenatula.*
WAR SUDRA Palmer 5.19. On sale list 1946. Sold, renamed *Germaine.*

WARBLER Tr 192/12, 1–6pdr. Hired as M/S 1914–19.
WARDEN (see WANDERER)
WARDEN Rescue tug 1,118 tons, 190 x 38½ ft, 1–3in, 2–20mm.
Robb 28.6.1945. On charter 12.46–51 as *Twyford.*
WARDEN (ex-*Empire Spitfire*) DY tug 232/43. Transferred from
MOT 3.1947. Renamed PROMPT 1951.
WARDOUR Tr 335/11. Hired as M/S 8.1939–4.46.
WARDS Wood paddle tug, 76bm. Purchased 1860. BU 1889 at Malta.
WAR DUKE Tr 246/17, 1–6pdr. Hired 1917–19 and as A/P Tr 11.39.
M/S 6.40; A/P 1944–6.45.
WAREE Tug 233/39. Hired (RAN) 9.1942–46.
WAR GREY Tr 246/17, 1–12pdr. Hired 1917–19.
WARLAND Tr 214/13, 1–6pdr. Hired 1916–19 and purchased as A/S
Tr, 1–12pdr, 24.5.40. Sunk 18.2.42 by air attack in the North Sea.

WAR LORD Tr 226/14, 1–6pdr. Hired 1915–19.

WARNER 1,273/11. Hired as decoy ship (Q.27) 17.1.1917. Sunk 13.3.17 by 'U.61' west of Ireland.

WARRAWEE Cstr 423/09. Hired as M/S (RAN) 12.1939–3.46.

WARRIOR Tug 192/95. Hired on harbour service 7.8.1914–19.

WARRIOR II Tr 236/98, 1–6pdr. Hired 1914–19.

WARRIOR Yt 1,266/04, 2–12pdr. Hired on special service 1917–12.18 and as S/M tender WARRIOR II, 9.39. Sunk 11.7.40 by air attack off Portland.

WARRIOR Yt 46/39. Hired on air-sea rescue 6.1940. Training tender 7.42–45.

WAR STAR Tr 225/14, 1–6pdr. Hired 1915–19 and as A/P Tr 5.40. M/S 7.42; fuel carrier 5.44–1.46.

WARTER PRIORY Tr 299/05, 2–6pdr. Hired 10.1914–19.

WARWICK DEEPING Tr 445/34. Purchased as A/S Tr 8.1939. Sunk 12.10.40 by gunfire in the Channel.

WARWICKSHIRE Tr 466/36. Hired as A/S Tr 8.1939. Sunk 30.4.40 by air attack off Trondheim. Salved and commissioned 2.42 as German ALANE. Finally sunk 19.7.43 by Russian S/M 'S.51'.

WAR WING Tr 226/15, 1–6pdr. Hired 1916–19 and as A/P Tr 12.39. M/S 6.40; M/S store carrier 4.44–1.46.

WASHINGTON Tug 167/-. Belgian, hired 12.1914–4.15 and 1.18–2.19.

WASHINGTON Tr 209/09, 1–6pdr. Hired as M/S 1916–19 and as M/S 11.39. Sunk 6.12.39 on passage to Yarmouth to fit out.

WASTWATER (ex-GRASSMERE renamed 1939, ex-*Kos XXVIII*) A/S Wh 560 tons, 138½ x 26½ ft, 1–12pdr, 1–20mm. Smiths Dk 31.8.1939, purchased 26.8.39. Sold 5.46. (On loan USN 3.42–10.42.)

WATCHER (ex-PLA *hopper 15*) 583/11. Hired 1.1916–19.

WATCHER (see LOOKOUT)

WATCHFUL Dr 88/03. Hired as BDV 7.1915–19.

WATER BIRD III Dr 79/10. Hired on harbour service 12.1914–19.

WATERFALL Admiralty steel Dr, 98gr. A.Hall 1919. Sold 1919, renamed *Homocea*.

WATERFALL DY tank vessel. Honk Kong & Whampoa DY 17.11.1941. Listed as completing until the fall of Hong Kong.

WATERFALL DY tank vessel, 300gr. Drypool E & DD, Hull 30.3.1966.

WATERFLY (ex-*Walpole*) Tr 387/31. Hired as M/S 9.1939. Sunk 17.9.42 by air attack off Dungeness.

WATERGATE Boom gate vessel 290 tons, 93 x·26 ft, 1–3in (dumb). Hong Kong & Whampoa 5.4.1934. Scuttled 19.12.41 at Hong Kong.

WATERMAN (see SIR CHARLES FORBES)

WATERMEYER (ex-*T.H.Watermeyer*) Tug 620/39, 1–12pdr. Hired as rescue tug 9.1939–11.40 then returned S.African Govt.

WATER RAIL Tank vessel. Purchased 1.1856 at Constantinople. Renamed HUMBER 7.1859. Sold 1866.
WATERSHED Admiralty steel Dr, 96gr. A.Hall 1919. Sold 1921, renamed *Salvian.* (Served as CONVALLARIA in WW.II.)
WATERSHED DY tank vessel, 300gr. Drypool, Hull 3.8.1966.
WATERSIDE DY tank vessel, 300gr. Drypool, Hull 20.6.1967.
WATERSMEET Admiralty steel Dr. A. Hall 1919. Sold 1919.
WATERSPOUT DY tank vessel, 300gr. Hepworth, Hull (ex-Drypool) 29.12.1966.
WATERWAY Admiralty steel Dr. Scott, Bowling. Cancelled 1919.
WATO Tug 292/04. Hired 11.1917–21 and as rescue tug (RAN), 2–MG, 1941–46.
WAVE DY tug 300 tons, 120 x 24½ ft. Taikoo DY Co 18.1.1939. Renamed WAVELET 1947.

'Wave' class oilers (RFA) 16,480 tons, 465 x 64 ft. 'Empire' names changed 1946 on transfer from MOT.
WAVE BARON (ex-*Empire Flodden)* Furness SB 19.2.1946.
WAVE CHIEF (ex-*Empire Edgehill*) Harland & Wolff, Govan 30.8.46.
WAVE COMMANDER (ex-*Empire Paladin*) Furness SB 21.4.44. Arrived 9.5.59 Ward, Inverkeithing to BU.
WAVE CONQUEROR (ex-*Empire Law*) Furness SB 27.11.43. Arrived 23.4.60 at Spezia to BU.
WAVE DUKE (ex-*Empire Mars*) Laing 16.11.44.
WAVE EMPEROR Furness SB 16.10.44. Arrived 19.6.60 Ward, Barrow to BU.
WAVE GOVERNOR Furness SB 30.11.44. Arrived 9.8.60 at Rosyth to BU.
WAVE KING Harland & Wolff, Govan 21.7.44. Arrived 16.4.60 Ward, Barrow to BU.
WAVE KNIGHT (ex-*Empire Naseby*) Laing 22.10.45. Arrived 19.10.64 at Antwerp to BU.
WAVE LAIRD (ex-*Empire Dunbar*) Laing 3.4.46.
WAVE LIBERATOR (ex-*Empire Milner*) Furness SB 9.2.44. Arrived 4.5.59 at Hong Kong to BU.
WAVE MASTER (ex-*Empire Salisbury*) Laing 20.5.44. BU 1963 at Singapore.
WAVE MONARCH Harland & Wolff, Govan 6.7.44. Sold 1960 as oil hulk *Noema.*
WAVE PREMIER Furness SB 27.6.46. Arrived 11.6.60 at Rosyth to BU.
WAVE PRINCE (ex-*Empire Herald*) Laing 27.7.45.
WAVE PROTECTOR (ex-*Empire Protector*) Furness 20.7.44. Oil hulk 3.58. Sold 1963 to BU in Italy.

WAVE REGENT Furness SB 29.3.45. Arrived 29.6.60 at Faslane to BU.
WAVE RULER (ex-*Empire Evesham*) Furness SB 17.1.46.
WAVE SOVEREIGN Furness 20.11.45. BU 1967 at Singapore.
WAVE VICTOR (ex-*Empire Bounty*) Furness 30.9.43. To Air Ministry
8.60.

WAVECREST Admiralty steel Dr. Scott, Bowling. Cancelled 1919.
WAVEFLOWER Tr 368/29. Purchased as M/S 1939. Sunk 21.10.40 by
mine off Aldeburgh.
WAVELET Admiralty steel Dr, 96gr. A.Hall 1919. Sold 1919, renamed
Ocean Dawn.
WAVELET (see WAVE)
WAVENEY II Dr 58/-. Hired 1915. Sank 27.10.16 after damage in
action with German destroyers off Dover.
WAVENEY (see JAMES CONNOR)
WAVERLEY Paddle 449/99, 2–6pdr. Hired as M/S 15.9.1915–9.7.20 and
as M/S, 537gr, 10.39. Sunk 29.5.40 by air attack off Dunkirk.
WAY (ex-*Waverley*) Paddle 240/85. Hired as M/S 11.5.1917–20.5.19.
WAYFARER Yt 77/21? Hired as A/P Yt 8.1940. Convoy service 3.42,
not listed after.
WAYFOONG 40/30. Hired as boom tender 8.1939. Listed at Hong
Kong until the Japanese invasion.
WAYSIDE FLOWER MFV 22net. Hired as boom tender 4.1941–45.
WEAL Dr 93/08. Hired on harbour service 1.1915–19.
WEALTH of the OCEAN Dr 35net/11. Hired on harbour service
12.1939–8.45.
WEAR II Dr 82/07, 1–3pdr. Hired 1914–19.
WEAR 1,164/12. Hired as fleet auxiliary 11.1914–2.19.
WEAR (see JOHN BOMKWORTH)
WEAZEL (ex-*Nubia*) Tr 196/03. Hired as A/P Tr 11.1939–6.2.40.
WEAZEL Rescue tug, 'B.A.T' class. Gulfport Co, Port Arthur 21.2.1943
on lend-lease. Returned 3.46 to the USN.
WEAZEL (ex-*Empire Madge*) DY tug 258/45. Transferred from MOT
and renamed 5.1947.
WEAZLE Schooner, 70bm. Hired 7.1808–3.1811.
WEIDA Yt 26/39. Hired on harbour service 3.1941–42.
WEIGELIA Tr 262/11. Hired 1914. Sunk 28.2.16 by mine off Dover.
WELBECK Tr 302/15, 1–6pdr, 24 mines. Hired as M/L 5.1915–19.
(Served as OHM in WW.II.)
WELBECK Tr 324/17. Hired as A/P Tr 6.1940. M/S 1941–1.46.
WELCOME Aux.schooner 119/85. Hired as BBV 8.1940–44.
WELCOME BOYS Dr 92/08. Hired 1914–19.
WELCOME FRIEND Dr 94/14. Hired 1914; SAREPTA 6.18–20.

WELCOME HOME Dr 77/06, 1–3pdr. Hired 1915–19.
WELCOME HOME Dr 104/25. Hired as M/S 11.1939–45.
WELCOME STAR Dr 81/07. Hired 1915–19.
WELFARE Dr 79/03. Hired as BDV 6.1915–19.
WELLAND II Dr 72/06, 1–3pdr. Hired 1915–19.
WELLARD Tr 514/37. Purchased as A/S Tr 8.1939. Sold 1945. (On loan USN 2.42–10.42.)
WELLHOLME Aux.ketch 113/16. Hired as decoy ship 4.9.1917. Sunk 30.1.18 by U-boat in the Channel. (Also operated as THORNHILL and WERRIBEE.)
W.ELLIOT Dr 60/-. Hired 1915. Sunk 15.2.18 in action off Dover.
WELLSBACH Tr 369/30. Hired as M/S 8.1939–9.45.
WELSHMAN DY tug 92 tons, 80 x 18½ ft. Purchased 1901. Listed to 1947. (Also known as C.320.)
WELTONDALE 1,700/13. Hired as fleet auxiliary 28.12.1914–20.5.16.
WELWYN Dr 78/14, 1–6pdr. Hired 1915–19 and as TRV 6.40–45.
WEMYSS Tr 167/05, 1–12pdr. Hired 1914–19.
WENDY (ex-*HS.85*) DY tug, 151gr, 85 x 21 ft. Transferred from War Dept 1919. Renamed EARLY 1920. Sold 4.20.
WENGEN MFV 35/28. Hired as BBV 11.1939. Harbour service 1944–45.
WENLOCH Dr 74/10. Hired 1915–19.
WENNING Cstr 787/87. Hired as store carrier (RFA) 8.10.1914. Ammo.carrier 2.2.15–1.12.18.
WENSUM Dr 58/02. Hired on harbour service 1918–19.
WERRIBEE (see WELLHOLME)

'West' type DY tugs, average 135gr, 88½ x 21 ft.
WEST ACRE Yarwood, Northwich 1919. Listed 1960. Sold, renamed *Laverock*.
WEST BAY 131gr. Yarwood 1919. Sold 7.53, renamed *Larkspur*.
WEST COAST 76/29. Hired as M/S (RCN) 1940–44.
WEST COCKER Philip, Dartmouth 1919. Wrecked 9.4.42 by air attack at Malta. BU 7.43. (Spelt WEST COKER until 1923.)
WEST CREEK 131gr. Yarwood 1918. Sold 1949, renamed *Margaret Lamey*.
WEST DEAN Philip 1919. Sunk 28.4.42 by air attack at Malta.
WEST HEATH 161gr. Crabtree, Yarmouth 1918. Sold 6.21, renamed *Astrid*.
WEST HILL 133gr. Crabtree 1919. Sold 6.21, renamed *Director Jack Letzer*.
WEST HOPE 154gr. Crabtree 1919. Sold 1921, renamed *Ocean Gull*.
WEST HYDE 154gr. Crabtree 1919. On sale list 1947. Sold, renamed *Seasider*.

WEST LING Philip 1919, not completed. Sold 19.12.19 to her builder.
WEST MILL Philip 1919. Sold 1919.
WEST PORT Cancelled 1919.
WEST VALE Cancelled 1919.
WEST WELL 1919. Sold 10.19.
WEST WINCH 134gr. Payne, Bristol 1920. Sold 24.11.20, same name.

WEST ANGLIA Dr 75/10, 1–3pdr. Hired 1915–19.
WEST COVE 2,755/12. Purchased 1940. Sunk 3.6.40 as blockship at
Dunkirk.
WESTELLA Tr 413/34. Purchased as A/S Tr 8.1939. Sunk 2.6.40 at
Dunkirk.
WESTERN EXPLORER Tr 113/38. Hired on examination service
10.1940–45.
WESTERN ISLES Yt 1,420/91. Hired as A/S training ship 4.1940.
Renamed EASTERN ISLES, accommodation ship, 17.10.41. Laid up
1945.
WESTERN ISLES (ex-*Batavier IV*) 1,569/02. Dutch, hired as A/S training
ship 1941–2.46.
WESTERN MAID MFV 26/36. Hired for M/S training (RCN) 1941–45.
WESTERN QUEEN (see WESTWARD HO)
WESTGARTH 1,553/09. Hired as fleet auxiliary 1917–19.
WESTGATE (see BV.17 under 'BD' vessels)
WESTHAVEN Dr 90/10. Hired as A/S Dr 12.1939–45.
WESTHOLME Tr 152/18. Hired on harbour service 9.1939. In 7.46
to return.
WEST HOPE (see WESTWARD HO)
WESTLAAN Cstr 199/31. Dutch, hired as BBV 5.1940–42.
WESTLYN Tr 284/¹   Purchased as BDV 2.1940. Sold 2.5.47.
WEST MEON (ex-*Hω.102*) DY tug, 130gr. Transferred from War Dept
1919. Sold 24.11.19.
WEST NEUK Dr 78/10. Hired as BBV 4.1940. Harbour service 11.40–
27.2.43.
WESPHALIA 1,467/14. Hired as store carrier (RFA) 21.10.1914–6.16
and as decoy ship 7.3.17. Sunk 11.2.18 by U-boat in the Irish Sea.
WESTRALIA 8,108/29, 7–6in, 2–3in. Hired as AMC (RAN) 2.11.1939.
Landing ship 6.43–46. Returned 27.3.51.
WESTRAY Tr 207/12, 1–6pdr. Hired as M/S 1916–19.
WESTRAY Tr, 'Isles' class. Lewis 4.11.1941. Sold 10.46, same name.
WESTS Dr 78/11. Hired 1916–19.
WESTWARD HO Paddle 438/94, 1–12pdr, 1–6pdr. Hired as M/S
4.11.1914. Renamed WEST HOPE 7.18; WESTERN QUEEN 8.18.
Returned 20.5.19. Hired again as M/S, 460gr, 1–12pdr, 2–MG, 13.9.39.
A/A ship 7.42; accommodation ship 1.44–3.46.

WESTWARD HO II Tr 146/97, 1–6pdr. Hired as M/S 1916–18.

WEST WIND Yt 33/34. Hired as A/P Yt 1940–44.

WEXFORD COAST Cstr 423/15. Hired as fleet messenger 25.8.1915. Decoy ship 2.18–10.18.

WEYMOUTH II Tr 178/03, 1–6pdr. Hired 1915–19.

WHALSAY Tr, 'Isles' class. Cook Welton & Gemmell 4.4.1942. Sold 11.6.46 Portuguese navy as SANTA MARIA. (On loan Portuguese navy 10.43–6.45 as 'P.4'.)

WHANGPU 3,204/20. Hired as S/M depot ship 1941. To the RAN 20.4.42. Repair ship 1944–46. Returned 4.46.

WHEATBERRY Cstr 405/15. Hired as fleet messenger 6.8.1915–14.9.16.

WHEATEAR (ex-*Convallaria*) MFV 23net/34. Hired as A/P vessel 6.1940–12.45.

WHEAT STALK Dr 72/10. Hired 1914–19 and on harbour service 5.1940–41.

W.H.HASTIE Tr, 1–12pdr. Hired 1916–19.

WHIMBREL 1,655/07. Hired as store carrier (RFA) 14.11.1914–5.5.15.

WHIMBREL (ex-LCT.1012) Repair craft 200 tons, 171 x 39 ft. Listed from 1956.

WHINCHAT (ex-*Daffodil*) MFV 25net. Hired on harbour service 6.1940–45.

WHIPPET (see KOS XXI)

WHIPPINGHAM Paddle 825/30, 1–12pdr. Hired as M/S 3.1942. A/A ship, 1–12pdr, 4–20mm, 1942–4.45.

WHIRLBLAST Admiralty steel Dr, 96gr. Lea SB, Thames 1919. Sold 1920 renamed *Stella Aurorae*. (Served as JACK EVE in WW.II.)

WHIRLPOOL Admiralty steel Dr, 95gr. A.Hall 10.10.1919. Sold 1947, same name.

WHISK Admiralty steel Dr. Scott, Bowling. Cancelled 1919.

WHITBURN Paddle tug 119/05. Hired on harbour service 7.1914–4.19 and 2.42–5.46.

WHITBY Tr 164/98. Hired 1918–19.

WHITBY ABBEY 1,188/08, 3–12pdr. Hired as M/S 10.2.1915–23.12.19.

WHITE BEAR (ex-*Iolanda*) Yt 1,822/08. Hired as S/M tender 1939, later purchased. Survey ship 1943. Sold 1947, renamed *Lexamine*.

WHITECLOUD Admiralty steel Dr 96gr. Lea SB 1919. Sold 1920, renamed *Admiral Startin*. (Served as FISHER LAD in WW.II.)

WHITE CROSS Dr 101/96. Hired 1915–19.

WHITE DAISY Dr 79/10. Hired 1915–19 and 4.40. Lost 25.9.40, cause and place not stated; probably near Lerwick.

WHITE EAR Tr 191/14, 1–6pdr. Hired 1914–19.

WHITE FOX II Yt 21/33. Hired 7.1940. Lost 27.8.40 by fire.

WHITE FRIARS Tr 286/06, 1–6pdr. Hired as M/S 1916–19.

WHITE FROST Admiralty steel Dr. Scott, Bowling. Cancelled 1919.
WHITE HEAD 1,172/80. Hired as store carrier (RFA) 31.8.1914. Sunk
15.10.17 by U-boat in the Mediterranean.
WHITE HILL Dr 90/15. Hired 1915–19.
WHITE HORSES Admiralty steel Dr, 96gr. A.Hall 1919. Sold 1920, re-
named *Benachie*. (BENACHIE in WW.II.)
WHITE LADY Yt 57/27. Listed as A/S Yt 11.1940 and on harbour
service 1941–43.
WHITE LILAC Dr 83/08. Hired 1915–19.
WHITE LILY Dr 87/04. Hired on harbour service 6.1915–19.
WHITE OAK Dr 75/13, 1–3pdr. Hired 1914–19.
WHITE QUEEN Tr 108/97. Hired on harbour service 7.1915–4.16.
WHITE ROSE Dr 79/-. Hired 1915. Sunk 26.7.16 in collision off Dover.
WHITE ROSE II Dr 67/92. Hired 1915–18.
WHITE SWAN 2,173/03. Hired as mine carrier (RFA) 8.8.1914–23.10.14.
WHITETHORN M/S Tr 515 tons, 150 x 27½ ft, 1–12pdr. Smiths Dk
10.11.1939. Sold 3.46.
WHITETHROAT Tr, 'Isles' class. Cook Welton & Gemmell 6.9.1944,
completed as M/L, 580 tons, 1–20mm. RCN 1944. Survey vessel 1960.
W.H.LEASK Dr 86/03. Hired on harbour service 7.1915–19.
WHOOPER Tr 302/14. Hired 1914. Sunk 30.6.16 by mine off Lowestoft.
WHYTOCK (ex-*Charles Wytock*) Wh 166/24. Hired as M/S (SAN) 1941–
6.46.
WIAY Tr, 'Isles' class. Cook Welton & Gemmell 26.4.1945, completed
as danlayer. Sold 15.12.60.
WICKSTEAD (see WYVERN)
WIDGEON of FEARN Yt 44/37. Hired as A/S Yt 4.1940, purchased
11.41. Laid up 8.45. Sold 1946?
WIGAN Tr 275/16, 1–6pdr. Hired 1916–19 and as M/S 2.40–45.
WIGHT DY store carrier, 70bm, White, Cowes 1835. BU completed
23.9.1864 at Devonport.
WIGHT (ex-*Vectis*) 1,152/13. Hired as store carrier (RFA) 21.11.1914–
7.18.
WILCANNIA (see WYRALLAH)
WILDRAKE (ex-*Drake*) 2,267/08. Hired as store carrier (RFA) 8.10.1914–
20.5.15.
WILD ROSE Tr 156/02, 1–6pdr. Hired as M/S 1914–18.
WILLA Dr. Hired as danlayer 2.1940. Harbour service 1942–45.
WILLAMETTE VALLEY 4,702/28, 1–12pdr. Hired as decoy ship
9.193. Sunk 29.6.40 by U-boat in the Atlantic. (Operated as EDGEHILL.)
WILLET Tr 199/08, 1–6pdr. Hired as M/S 1914–19.
WILLIAM A.ship, 700bm. Hired 1649–54.
WILLIAM A.ship 20. Hired 1782–83.

WILLIAM DY craft, 41bm, 44½ x 16 ft. Purchased 1804. Fate unknown.

WILLIAM ABRAHAMS Tr, non-standard 'Mersey' type, 248gr. Cochrane 24.2.1917. Sold 1921, renamed *Santini*.

WILLIAM ALLEN Tr 203/14. Hired 1915–19.

WILLIAM ASHTON Tr, non-standard 'Strath' type, 235gr. Duthie Torry 1.11.1917. Sold 1922, renamed *Star of Victory*.

WILLIAM BARLOW Tr, non-standard 'Strath' type, 226gr. Hall Russell 25.4.1917. Sold 7.20, renamed *Ben Ardna*. (Served as DORILEEN in WW.II.)

WILLIAM BARNETT Tr, non-standard 'Strath' type, 216gr. Hall Russell 8.12.1917. Sold 1919, renamed *Valerie W.*

WILLIAM BARROW Tr, 'Strath' type, 204gr. Hall Russell 30.4.1918. Sold 1921, renamed *Claribelle*. (CLARIBELLE in WW.II.)

WILLIAM BEATTY Tr, 'Castle' type, 275gr. Smiths Dk 17.9.1917. Sold 1920, renamed *Cresswell*.

WILLIAM BEAUMONT Tr, 'Strath' type, 203gr. Hall Russell 9.7.1918. Sold 1920, same name.

WILLIAM BEETON Tr, 'Castle' type, 275gr. C.Rennoldson 20.7.1917. Sold 1921, renamed *Girolamo Cassar*.

WILLIAM BELL Tr, 'Castle' type, 290gr. Cook Welton & Gemmell 17.1.1918. Sold 1919, same name. Hired as A/P Tr, 1–6pdr, 6.40. M/S 1941–2.46.

WILLIAM BENNETT Tr, 'Castle' type. Cook Welton & Gemmell. Cancelled 1919.

WILLIAM BENTLEY Tr, 'Strath' type, 203gr. Hall Russell 30.1.1919. Sold 1919, renamed *Braconhill*. (BRACONHILL in WW.II.)

WILLIAM BIGGS Tr, 'Strath' type, 203gr. Hall Russell 16.8.1917. Sold 1921, same name. (Served as KINGSCOURT in WW.II.)

WILLIAM BOND Tr, 'Strath' type, 203gr. Hall Russell 10.1.1918. Sold 1919, renamed *River Esk*. (RIVER ESK in WW.II.)

WILLIAM BORHAM Tr, 'Strath' type. Hall Russell. Cancelled 1919.

WILLIAM BRADY Tr, 'Castle' type, 290gr. Cook Welton & Gemmell 17.12.1917. Sold 1919, same name. Hired as A/P Tr, 1–12pdr, 6.40–2.46.

WILLIAM BROWIS Tr, 'Castle' type, 290gr. Cook Welton & Gemmell 18.10.1917. Sold 1921, renamed *Gonerley*. (Served as MILFORD QUEEN, 280gr, in WW.II.)

WILLIAM BROWNING Tr, non-standard 'Strath' type, 237gr. Hall Russell 17.5.1917. Sold 1919, renamed *Madden*. (MADDEN in WW.II.)

WILLIAM BUNCE Tr, 'Castle' type, 275gr. Smiths Dk 3.10.1917. Sold 1922, same name. Hired as M/S 8.39. Not listed 1940.

WILLIAM BURTE Tr, 'Castle' type. Cook Welton & Gemmell. Cancelled 1919.

WILLIAM BUTLER Tr, 'Strath' type, 203gr. Hall Russell 18.10.1917.
Sold 1920, same name.

WILLIAM CABLE Tr, 'Castle' type. Greenock. Cancelled 1919.

WILLIAM CALDWELL Tr, 'Castle' type, 290gr. Cook Welton &
Gemmell 12.6.1918. Sold 1919, same name. Purchased as BDV 1.40.
Sold 12.46.

WILLIAM CALE Tr, 'Castle' type, 276gr. Bow McLachlan 19.9.1917.
Sold 1921, same name. Hired as M/S 8.39–7.45.

WILLIAM CARBERRY Tr, 'Castle' type, 276gr. Hepple 1919. Sold
1919, renamed *Micaela de C.*

WILLIAM CARR Tr, 'Castle' type, 291gr. Bow McLachlan 1918. Sold
1921, same name. (Served as NAZARETH in WW.II.)

WILLIAM CARRICK Tr, 'Castle' type, 276gr. Bow McLachlan
18.9.1917. Sold 1919, same name.

WILLIAM CASTLE Tr, non-standard 'Strath' type, 223gr. A.Hall
18.10.1917. Sold 1921, same name.

WILLIAM CHALMERS Tr, 'Strath' type, 204gr. Hawthorns 1919. Sold
1919, renamed *Cradock*?

WILLIAM CHAMBERS In navy lists, believed to be error for WILLIAM
CHALMERS.

WILLIAM CHASEMAN Tr, 'Castle' type, 275gr. Smiths Dk 3.8.1917.
Sold 1920, renamed *Radnor Castle*. (RADNOR CASTLE in WW.II.)

WILLIAM CHATWOOD Tr, 'Mersey' type, 323gr. Goole SB 1919. Sold
1921, renamed *Blanc Nez*.

WILLIAM COBURNE Tr, 'Castle' type, 276gr. Bow McLachlan 24.7.1917.
Sold 1920, renamed *Carnarvon Castle*.

WILLIAM COGSWELL Tr, non-standard 'Strath' type, 213gr. A.Hall
10.1.1918. Sold 1921, renamed *Struan*.

WILLIAM CORAN Tr, 'Castle' type. Greenock. Cancelled 1919.

WILLIAM COURTNEY Tr, 'Mersey' type, 323gr. Goole SB 1920. Sold
1921, renamed *Ternoise*.

WILLIAM COWLING Tr, 'Castle' type, 286gr. Bow McLachlan 23.7.1917.
Sold 1922, renamed *Asterby*.

WILLIAM CUMMINS Tr, 'Castle' type, 255gr. Bow McLachlan 17.11.1917.
Sold 1922, renamed *Ernest Solvay*. (Served as NIBLICK in WW.II.)

WILLIAM DARNOLD Tr, 'Castle' type, 290gr. Cook Welton & Gemmell
11.7.1918. Sold 9.20, renamed *Cape Hatteras*.

WILLIAM DOAK Tr, 'Mersey' type, 326gr. Goole SB 1918. Sold 1922
Spanish navy as ARCILA.

WILLIAM DOGHERTY (see GEORGE BROWN)

WILLIAM DONALDS Tr, 'Mersey' type. Goole SB. Cancelled 1919.

WILLIAM DOWNES Tr, 'Castle' type, 275gr. C.Rennoldson 5.11.1917.
Sold 1921, same name.

WILLIAM DRAKE Tr, 'Castle' type. J.P.Rennoldson 1919. Sold 1919.
WILLIAM FALL Tr, 'Strath' type, 202gr. Rennie Forrest 1918. Sold
1920, renamed *Avondale.*
WILLIAM FERRINS Tr, non-standard 'Strath' type, 235gr. Duthie
Torry 1918. Sold 1921, same name.
WILLIAM FINDLAY Tug 87/84. Hired as A/P vessel 1.4.1918–20.
WILLIAM FLEMMING Tr, 'Castle' type, 275gr. Hepple 1918. Sold
1920, renamed *Trawler Prince.*
WILLIAM FORBES Tr, 'Mersey' type, 326gr. Goole SB 1919. Sold
1920, same name.
WILLIAM FORD Tr, 'Mersey' type. Cochrane. Cancelled 1919.
WILLIAM GIBBONS Tr, 'Strath' type, 202gr. Fullerton 1918. Sold
1921, renamed *Nordzee I.*
WILLIAM GILLETT Tr, 'Strath' type, 201gr. Ritchie Graham 1919.
Sold 1921, same name.
WILLIAM GRAY Tug 178/11. Hired 10.1914–20.
WILLIAM GRIFFIN Tr, 'Strath' type, 203gr. Scott, Bowling 1918.
Sold 1921, same name.
WILLIAM GRIFFITHS Tr, 'Castle' type. G.Brown 1918. Sold 1919.
WILLIAM HALLETT Tr, 'Strath' type, 202gr. Rennie Forrest 1918.
Sold 1921, same name. Hired as A/P Tr 11.39. Sunk 13.12.39 by mine
off the Tyne.
WILLIAM HANBURY Tr, 'Strath' type, 204gr. Hawthorns 1918. Sold
1921, same name. Hired as A/P Tr 11.39–40.
WILLIAM HANNAM Tr, 'Castle' type, 276gr. Duthie Torry 1918. Sold
1920, same name. Hired as BDV 10.39–4.46.
WILLIAM HARRISON Tr, 'Strath' type, 202gr. Rennie Forrest 1919.
Sold 1921, renamed *Flavia.*
WILLIAM HARVEY Tr, 'Strath' type, 201gr. Fleming & Ferguson
10.11.1919. Sold 1920, renamed *River Orchy.* (Served as FLIXTON in
WW.II.)
WILLIAM H.HASTIE Tr 229/16. Hired 1916–19 and on examination
service 8.40. Salvage vessel 1941–43.
WILLIAM HONNOR Tr, 'Mersey' type, 330gr. Ferguson 26.8.1918.
Sold 1922, renamed *Grimurkamban.*
WILLIAM HUMPHREYS Tr, 'Castle' type, 276gr. Duthie Torry 1918.
Sold 1921, same name.
WILLIAM HUTCHINSON Tr, 'Strath' type, 208gr. Hawthorns 1918.
Sold 1922, renamed *Roche Velen.* (ROCHE VELEN in WW.II.)
WILLIAM INWOOD Tr, 'Mersey' type, 324gr. Cochrane 1918. Renamed
BLACKWATER 1920. Sold 1946, renamed *Spleis.*
WILLIAM IVEY Tr, 'Strath' type, 202gr. Rennie Forrest 1918. Sold
1921, same name.

WILLIAM JACKSON Tr, 'Mersey' type, 327gr. Cochrane 1918. Sold 1921, renamed *Lord Byng.* (Served as EVELYN ROSE in WW.II.)

WILLIAM JOHNSON Tr, 'Mersey' type, 326gr. Cochrane 1918. Sold 1921, renamed *Lord Birkenhead.*

WILLIAM JONES Tr, 'Mersey' type, 324gr. Cochrane 1918. Renamed BOYNE 1920. Sold 1946, renamed *Nypuberg.*

WILLIAM KING Tr, 'Strath' type, 204gr. Williamson 1918. Sold 1921, same name.

WILLIAM KNIGHT Tr, 'Castle' type, 275gr. Duthie Torry 1919. Sold 1920, renamed *Henricus.* (Served as COBBERS in WW.II.)

WILLIAM LAMBKIN Tr, 'Castle' type, 276gr. Duthie Torry 1919. Sold 1920, renamed *Nellie Crawford.*

WILLIAM LEECH Tr, 'Mersey' type, 324gr. Cochrane 1919. Renamed EXCELLENT 1920. Sold 1922, reverted to *William Leech.*

WILLIAM LEEK Tr, 'Castle' type, 276gr. J.P. Rennoldson 1918. Sold 1919, renamed *Cavendish.* (Served as HILDINA in WW.II.)

WILLIAM LOFT Tr, 'Castle' type, 275gr. C.Rennoldson 30.8.1919. Sold 1922, renamed *Tamora.* (TAMORA in WW.II.)

WILLIAM MAINLAND Tr, 'Mersey' type. Cochrane. Cancelled 1919.

WILLIAM MANNELL Tr, 'Castle' type, 276gr. Smiths Dk 23.3.1917. Sold 1920, same name. Hired as M/S 6.40–11.45.

WILLIAM MARSHALL Tr, 'Mersey' type. Cochrane. Cancelled 1919.

WILLIAM MESSINA Tug 120/25. Hired as M/S (SAN) 1942–46.

WILLIAM MOIRIS Tr, 'Mersey' type. Cochrane. Cancelled 1919. *

WILLIAM MORTON Tr, 'Mersey' type. Cochrane. Cancelled 1919.

WILLIAM MUCK Tr, 'Mersey' type. Cochrane. Cancelled 1919.

WILLIAM MUIR Paddle 412/79, 1–MG. Hired as M/S 7.6.1917–21.5.19.

WILLIAM PITT Cutter 14. Hired 1796. Captured 6.6.1799 by the Spanish in the Mediterranean.

WILLIAM POULSOM Tug 219/17. Hired 1.4.1917–20.

WILLIAM PURDY Tr 194/14, 1–3pdr. Hired as M/S 1914–19 and as BBV 2.40–10.45.

WILLIAM RAM Tr, 'Mersey' type, 324gr. Cochrane 7.6.1917. Sold 1921, renamed *Lord Carson.* (Served as WELBECK in WW.II.)

WILLIAM RIVERS Tr, 'Mersey' type, 324gr. Cochrane 9.6.1917. Sold 1921, renamed *Mont Cassel.*

WILLIAM RYAN Tug 102/28, 1–MG. Hired as A/P Tug 11.1939–45.

WILLIAM SCORESBY Falklands Govt ship, 326/26. Hired as M/S 10.1939–1.47.

WILLIAM SPENCER Tr, 'Castle' type, 275gr. Smiths Dk 19.6.1917. Sold 1922, renamed *Normanby.* (Served as ASTROS in WW.II.)

WILLIAM STEPHEN Tr 235/17. Hired as A/P Tr 11.1939. M/S 7.40. Sunk 25.10.43 by E-boat torpedo off Cromer.

WILLIAM STROUD Tr 214/14. Hired as boom gate vessel 1914–19 and as fuel carrier 3.44–3.45.

WILLIAM SYMONS Tr, 'Castle' type, 275gr. Smiths Dk 1.10.1917. Sold 1922, renamed *Rayvernol*. (Served as LEPHRETO in WW.II.)

WILLIAM TENNANT Dr 93/93, 1–6pdr. Hired 1916. Sunk 5.3.18 in collision off the Humber.

WILLIAM WESNEY Tr 364/30, 1–12pdr. Hired as M/S 9.1939. Sunk 7.11.40 by mine off Orfordness.

WILLIAM WESTENBURGH Tr, non-standard 'Mersey' type, 325gr. Cochrane 25.1.1917. Sold 1921, renamed *Lord Talbot*. (Served as STAR of the REALM in WW.II.)

WILLIAM WILLMOT Tr, 'Castle' type, 275gr. Smiths Dk 1.10.1917. Sunk 9.20 in collision with *Meissonier* in the Irish Sea. (Listed to 1921.)

WILLIAM WILSON Dr 118/29. Hired as hospital Dr 9.1939–45.

WILLING BOYS Dr 138/30. Hired as M/S 11.1939–8.46.

WILLIWAW Admiralty steel Dr, 96gr. Brooke, Lowestoft 1919. Sold 1920, same name. (Served as MORAY ROSE in WW.II.)

WILLONYX Tr 327/15, 1–6pdr. Hired 1915–19.

WILL o'the WISP Admiralty wood Dr, 96gr. Kitto, Porthleven 1919. Sold 1920, renamed *Waterway*.

WILLOW (ex-*Cape Spartivento*) Tr 347/30. Purchased as M/S 23.11.1935. Danlayer 1945. Sold 6.46, renamed *Tronduri Gotu*.

WILLOW BANK Dr 80/09. Hired 1914–19.

WILLOW BRANCH 3,314/92. Hired as decoy ship 1.1917. Sunk 25.4.18 by U-boat in the Atlantic.

WILLOW LAKE Motor M/S (RCN), 255 tons, 126 x 26 ft. Newcastle SB, Canada 27.7.1945. To Russian navy 11.3.46.

WILLOW TIT Hired as M/L tender 10.1940–45. (Perhaps ex-Dutch De DRIE GEZUSTERS [qv].)

WILNA Yt 461/39, 1–4in, 2–MG. Hired as A/S Yt 8.1939. Sunk 24.3.41 by air attack off Portsmouth.

WILSON LINE Dr 116/32. Hired as hospital Dr 9.1939–45.

WIMPOLE Tr 320/16, 1–6pdr. Hired 1916–19.

WINCHESTER Dr 94/07, 1–3pdr. Hired as BDV 1915–19.

WINDERMERE (ex-*Kos XXVII*) A/S Wh 560 tons, 138½ x 26½ft, 1–12pdr, 1–20mm. Smiths Dk 21.7.1939, purchased 26.8.39. Sold 1947, renamed *Kos XXVII*.

WINDFALL Admiralty steel Dr, 96gr. A.Hall 1919. Sold 1920, same name.

WINDRISE Admiralty steel Dr, 97gr. Warren, New Holland 1920. Sold 1920, same name. (Served as CASSIOPEIA in WW.II.)

WINDSHIFT Admiralty steel Dr, 97gr. Warren 1920. Sold 1920, same name.

WINDSOR Tr 222/16, 1–6pdr. Hired 1916–19.

WINDSOR CASTLE A.merchant, 4–4in. Russian, seized 1918. Transferred 6.8.19 to 'White' Russians at Petrovsk.

WINDSOR LAD MFV 33net. Hired as M/S 6.1940–45.

WINDWARD Admiralty steel Dr. A.Hall 1919. Sold 1921, same name.

WINDWARD HO Tr 263/20. Hired as M/S 8.1939–45.

WINIFRED Dr 53/97. Hired as BBV tender 7.1940–45.

WINNER Dr 75/05, 1–3pdr. Hired 1915–19.

WINSOME Dr 80/07. Hired on harbour service 2.1915–19.

WINSOME Dr 46/02. Hired on harbour service 1.1941. Sunk 18.11.42 at Fairlie.

WINTONIA Yt 233/94. Hired on harbour service 3.11.1914–4.15.

WISHFUL Dr 83/10, 1–3pdr. Hired 1914–19.

WISTARIA Tr 143/91, 1–6pdr. Hired as M/S 1915–19. (WISTARIA II from 1916.)

WISTARIA M/S Tr 515 tons, 150 x 27½ ft, 1–12pdr. Smiths Dk 10.11.1939. Sold 3.46.

WITHAM Dr 76/06, 1–3pdr. Hired 1915–19.

WITHAM Tr 205/19. Hired as M/S 11.1939. Fuel carrier 4.44–11.44.

WITHERNSEA (ex-German *Lawica*) Tr 257/18. A/P Tr 12.1939. M/S 7.40. Sold 3.46.

WITTE ZEE Tug 465/14. In service as rescue tug (Dutch crew) 8.1940–11.40.

WIVENHOE Dr 100/13, 1–6pdr. Hired 1915–19.

W.J.R Dr 78/01. Hired on harbour service 1916–18.

WO KWANG Tug 350/27. Hired as M/S 3.1940. Lost at the fall of Singapore.

WOLBOROUGH Tr 459/37. Purchased as A/S Tr 9.1939. Sold 8.45.

WOLF (ex-*Blue Water*) Yt 300/15. Commissioned as A/S Yt (RCN) 2.10.1940. Paid off 22.12.45.

WOLSELEY Tr 159/03. Hired 1917–19.

WOLVES Tr 422/34. Purchased as A/S Tr 8.1939. Sold 10.45.

WONGALA 403/19. In service (RAN) 1940; WYATT EARP 8.47.

WOODAXE M/S Tr, 292gr, 130 x 23½ ft, 1–12pdr. Smiths Dk 3.8.1916. Russian T.20 seized 8.1918 in the White Sea and renamed. Listed to 1920.

WOODBRIDGE Pilot 102/26. Hired on harbour service 2.1940. Examination service 1943–44.

WOODCOCK Iron S.tug 750 tons, 148 x 26 ft. Purchased 4.1885. Renamed JACKAL 19.4.86. Sold 10.7.06.

WOODNUT (ex-*Woodcock*) 1,470/06, 3–12pdr. Hired as ABS 15.11.1914–31.5.20.

WOODS Tr 203/18. Hired as A/P Tr 11.1939–31.1.40.

WOONDA Tug 309/15. Purchased 1915. Sold 11.21.

WORCESTERSHIRE 11,402/31, 6–6in, 2–3in, 4–20mm. Hired as AMC 9.1939–43.

WORSLEY Tr 309/13. Hired as M/S 1914. Sunk 14.8.15 by mine off Aldeburgh.

WRANGLER (see TRITON)

WREN Tr 166/97, 1–6pdr. Hired as M/S 1914; WHITETHROAT 6.18–19.

WRENTHORPE Tr 225/06. Hired 1915–19.

WRESTLER Tug 346/76. Hired on harbour service 1915. Lost 10.10.15.

WRESTLER Tug 192/14. Hired as DY tug 1.1916. Renamed HOTSPUR 1918, purchased. Sold 6.20, renamed *Muria*. (Served as MURIA in WW.II.)

WREXHAM 1,414/02. Hired as fleet auxiliary 11.1916–18.

W.S. BURTON Tr 234/17. Hired 1917–19.

WUCHANG 3,204/14. Hired as S/M depot ship 1941–4.46.

WV.1–42 Moored coastguard watch-vessels, in use 1863–1905.

WV.1 ex-Revenue cutter *Victorine*, 26bm. Ransome, Hastings 1831. Renamed 7.1863. Sold 26.11.77 at Orford Haven.

WV.2 ex-RC *Fairy*, 24bm. Listed from 1842. Renamed 7.63. Sold 1866.

WV.3 ex-RC *Dolphin*, 90bm. Ransome, Hastings 1832. Renamed 7.63. BU completed 10.10.74 at Chatham.

WV.9 ex-RC *Harpy*, 145bm. White, Cowes 10.10.1837. Renamed 1863. Sold 3.69 as light vessel.

WV.14 ex-RC *Prince of Wales*, 170bm. Ransome, Hastings 1830. Renamed 1863. Sold 6.68 at Southend.

WV.15 ex-RC *Active*, 101bm. White, Cowes 1806. Renamed 1863. Sold 1868.

WV.17 ex-RC *Royal George*, 149bm. Renamed 1863. Sold 10.1866.

WV.22 ex-RC *Frances*, 46bm. Renamed 1863. Sold 1866.

WV.34 ex-RC *Stag*, 130bm. White, Cowes 20.2.1827. Renamed 7.1863. On sale list 9.66.

WV.35 ex-RC *Gertrude*, 35bm. White, Cowes 26.10.1836. Renamed 1863. Sold 1866.

WV.39 ex-RC *Victoria*, 114bm. Renamed 1869. Sold 1872 at Moville.

WV.40 ex-RC *Princess Charlotte*, 70bm. Renamed 1870. BU completed 17.2.77 at Portsmouth.

(For others, see MV 28,29,31,38,39,41–46,49–52,55,56 and mortar float 107. Also ARAB, BEAGLE, BRITOMART, CADMUS, CHANTICLEER, CLINKER, CYGNET, DART, DESPATCH, ECLIPSE, ELK, EMULOUS, FROLIC, HAVOCK, KANGAROO, LINNET, LUCIFER, MASTIFF, PARTRIDGE, PELICAN, PENGUIN, PHILOMEL, SHAMROCK, SHELDRAKE and STAR in Volume I.)

WYANDOTTE DY tug, 65gr. Rowhedge IW 1920. Sold 1948.
WYANDRA (see BARALONG)
WYDALE Dr 102/17. Hired 1917–19 and on examination service 3.40.
Harbour service 6.42–3.46.
WYEBURN Dr 94/14, 1–2½pdr. Hired 1915–19.
WYNDHAM Tr 303/16, 1–6pdr. Hired 1916–19.
WYOLA Tug 306/12. Hired as rescue tug 3.1918–20.
WYOMING Tr 302/15, 1–12pdr. Hired as A/P Tr 11.1939. M/S 1941.
Sunk 20.5.44 by mine off Harwich.
WYRALLAH 1,049/34, 1–4in. Commissioned as A/S vessel (RAN)
2.9.1940. Renamed WILCANNIA 2.42. In 1.47 to return.
WYRE Tr 295/11, 1–6pdr. Hired 1915–19 and as BDV 6.40–8.45.
WYVERN Tug 215/05. Hired 15.3.1915. Renamed WICKSTEAD 1918.
Returned 1919.

X.1–200 Landing craft 160 tons, 105 x 21 ft, 1–MG. Ordered 2.1915,
launched between 4.15 and 7.15 in the UK.
X.201–225 As above, 137 tons, 99 x 20 ft. Launched between 6.1916
and 9.16 in the UK.
DX.1–25 as X.201 but dumb. Launched between 5.1916 and 8.16 in
the UK.
About 60 of these became DY craft in 1919–21; X.3,8,42,75,77,78,
93,100,199,124 and 128 being renamed OYSTER, TANKARD,
LOBSTER, MOILER, WINKLE, COCKLE, BEAKER, TOILER, PRAWN,
PITCHER and FLAGON respectively.
The following survived to WW.II: X.21,36,40,45,64,MOILER,76,
WINKLE, COCKLE, 95,120,127,FLAGON,131,134,140,149,162,182,
201,206,207,209,213,216–19,223,224 and 225; X.134,180,216,224
were commissioned as cable-layers.

XARIFA Yt 756/30. Purchased as air target 26.6.1940. Renamed
BLACK BEAR 8.40. On sale list 12.45.
XANIA Tr 161/97, 1–16pdr. Hired 1914–19.
XERANTHENUM Dr 79/02. Hired 1915–19.
XERXES Tr 243/08. Hired as M/S 1914. Sunk 16.11.15 in collision
off Girdleness.
XMAS MA/SB. Italian MAS.452 captured 1941 in the Mediterranean.
Listed to 1945.
XMAS DAISY Dr 88/11. Hired 1915–19.
XMAS EVE Dr 95/20. Hired on harbour service 10.1939. To War Dept
8.43.

XMAS MORN Dr 89/14. Hired 3.1915–19 and on harbour service 8.39–45.

XMAS ROSE Dr 96/18, 2–MG. Hired as M/S 11.1939. A/P Dr 8.40. Sunk 21.11.40 by mine in the Thames estuary.

XYLOPIA Tr 262/11, 1–6pdr. Purchased as M/S 7.1914. Sold 1919, same name.

YANDRA 990/28, 1–4in. Commissioned as A/S vessel (RAN) 22.9.1940. Paid off 1946.

YARMOUTH II Tr 235/07, 1–3pdr. Hired as M/S 1914–19.

YARMOUTH BELLE Paddle 522/98, 2–6pdr. Hired as M/S 16.8.1915–31.1.20. (Served as THAMES QUEEN, 517gr, in WW.II.)

YARTA Yt 357/98, 2–3pdr. Hired as A/P Yt 3.7.1915–3.4.19 and as danlayer 11.39, purchased 6.41. A/S Yt 1942. On sale list 6.45.

YASHIMA Tr 303/29. Hired as M/S 8.1939–4.46.

YEHONALA Yt 48/13. Hired 1914–19 and as BBV 6.40. Renamed HILDEGARD 8.40. Foundered 11.4.41. Raised 10.43 and laid up. Returned 12.43.

YEHONALA II Yt 74/33. Hired as HDPC 10.1939–45.

YELLOW HAMMER Cstr 217/28. Hired as TRV 4.1941. Target carrier 1941; repair vessel 1942–4.46.

YESSO Tr 229/11. Hired as M/S 1914. Sunk 9.2.17 by mine off Aberdeen.

YESSO Tr 209/18. Hired as A/P Tr 11.1939. BBV 6.40. Renamed ARABESQUE 1941. Fuel carrier 4.44–11.44.

YESTOR A/S Tr 750 tons, 166 x 28 ft, 1–12pdr, 3–20mm. Cook Welton & Gemmell 21.10.1941. Sold 4.46, renamed *Cape Cleveland.*

YEZO Tr 301/24, 1–12pdr. Hired as M/S 11.1939. Wreck dispersal 2.44–46.

YINGCHOW 1,992/05. Hired as training ship 1942. Depot ship (RIN) 1.45–46.

YIN PING Tug 191/14. Hired 9.1941. Sunk 15.2.42 by Japanese gunfire.

YMUIDEN (see ZWARTE ZEE)

YOKOHAMA Tr 291/09, 1–12pdr. Hired 1915–19.

YOLANDE Yt 77/94. Hired as BBV tender 7.1941. Accommodation ship in 1945.

YORICK Tr. Hired 1918–19.

YORK 1,132/07, 1–4in, 2–12pdr. Hired as ABS 3.1.1915–4.4.19.

YORK CITY Tr 398/33. Purchased as A/S Tr 9.1939. Sold 11.45.

YORK SALVOR Salvage vessel 800 tons, 170 x 37 ft. American Car & Fndry, Wilmington 6.5.1943 for lend-lease but retained by the USN as SWIVEL.

YORKSHIRE BELLE Yt 56/38. Hired as HDPC 11.1939. Boom tender 1941. Sunk 11.4.41 by mine at the Humber entrance.

YORKSHIRE LASS Dr 111/20, 1–3pdr. Hired as flare Dr 11.1939. Radar training tender 1941–5.46.

YOUNG ALFRED Dr 85/11. Hired as BBV 12.1939–9.46.

YOUNG ARCHIE Dr 60/08. Hired 1915–17.

YOUNG CLIFF Dr 96/25. Hired as M/S 11.1939–6.46.

YOUNG CROW Dr 85/15. Hired 1915–19.

YOUNG DAWN Dr 86/16. Hired 1916–19.

YOUNG ERNIE Dr 88/24. Hired as A/P Dr 12.1939. Sunk 18.4.41 in collision off the Tyne.

YOUNG FISHERMAN Dr 95/14. Hired 1915–19 and 6.40. Grounded 29.11.40 at Oban.

YOUNG FRED Dr 83/10, 1–3pdr. Hired 1915–19.

YOUNG HENRY Dr 91/10. Hired 1914–19.

YOUNG JACOB Dr 99/14. Hired as M/S 11.1939–1.46.

YOUNG JOHN Dr 100/14, 1–6pdr. Hired 1914–19 and as degaussing vessel 5.40–46.

YOUNG KENNETH Dr 67/10. Hired 1914–19.

YOUNG LINNET Dr 93/-. Hired 1917. Sunk 15.5.17 in action in the Adriatic.

YOUNG MUN Dr 87/11, 1–3pdr. Hired 1915–19 and as flare Dr 2.40. Harbour service 1941–46. (Bore the name BRONTOSAURUS 1943–7.46 as nominal depot ship.)

YOUNG ROLAND Dr 57/08. Hired 1915–19.

YOUNG SID Dr 100/12, 1–3pdr. Hired 1915–19 and 5.40. Sunk 10.8.40 in collision in the Moray Firth.

YOUVILLE DY tug (RCN). Owen Sound 1944. Listed 1958.

YPRES Tr, 'Castle' type (RCN). Polson IW 6.6.1917. Boom gate vessel 9.39. Rammed and sunk 12.4.40 by the battleship REVENGE at Halifax.

YTHAN BRAES Tr 268/17. Hired as fuel carrier 8.1942. Water boat 11.42–2.46.

YUCCA Tr 198/12, 1–6pdr. Hired as M/S 1914. Sunk 24.5.18 by mine off Lowestoft.

YULAN Tr 144/91. Hired 1917–19.

YUNNAN 2,812/34. Hired as store carrier (RAN) 9.1944–1.46.

Z.1–60 Landing craft 216 tons, 134(oa) x 30 ft. All built in India 1943 for the RN and for disposal 1946–47. 8 built by Alcock Ashdown, Bombay; 8 by Burn, Calcutta; 14 by Garden Reach, Calcutta; 4 by Hooghly Dk & Eng Co; 11 by India Gen Nav Co, Calcutta; 4 by Mohatta,

Karachi; 2 by Port Eng Wks, Calcutta; 6 by Richardson Cruddas, Bombay and 3 by Shalimar, Calcutta.

ZAIDA Yt 350/00. Hired as A/P Yt 26.5.1916. Sunk 17.8.16 by 'U.35' gunfire in the eastern Mediterannean.

ZARA Yt 516/95, 2–3in. Hired as A/P Yt 6.3.1915–27.3.19.

ZAREBA (ex-*Ellena*) Tr 257/21. Hired as M/S 8.1940. BBV 1944–45.

ZAREE (ex-*Mars*) Tug 218gr. Purchased 1917. Sold 14.7.20.

ZAREFAH Yt 279/05. Hired 8.1914, purchased 26.5.16. Sunk 8.5.17 by mine off Mull Head.

ZARIA 4,816/04. Hired as store carrier (RFA) 26.11.1914. A/P depot ship 4.15–19.

ZAZA Yt 455/05, 1–12pdr, 2–6pdr. Hired as A/P Yt 28.9.1914–30.3.19 and purchased as A/S Yt 9.39. Accommodation ship 1941. Laid up 1945, sold 1948.

ZEAL (see ZEALOUS)

ZEALOT Dr 60/07. Hired 1918–19.

ZEALOUS DY tank vessel 415 tons, 110 x 24 ft. Hall Russell 29.8.1913. Renamed ZEST 1.12.18; ZEAL 1944. Arrived 7.2.49 at Rosyth to BU.

ZEBULON Dr 94/14, 1–3pdr. Hired 1914–19.

ZEDWHALE (Z.1) (ex-MEG renamed 1915) Admiralty Wh, 'Z' class. Smiths Dk 29.5.1915. Sold 12.2.20.

ZEE MEEUW (P.7) Dr 100/30, 1–6pdr. Belgian, hired as A/P Dr 6.1940–11.44. (Polish crew 8.40–41. Foundered 20.5.41 off Dartmouth and raised 17.11.41; sank 21.9.43 in collision off Gravesend and raised 1943. Also listed as De ZEE MEEUW.)

ZENA DARE Tr 242/09, 1–3pdr. Hired as M/S 1914–19.

ZENITH Admiralty Dr. Kitto, Porthleven. Cancelled 1919.

ZENNOR Tr 166/97. Hired 1918–19.

ZERANG Tug 361/38. Hired as M/S 9.1939–7.44.

ZEST (see ZEALOUS)

ZETLAND Tr 165/98. Hired 1917–19.

ZINAIDA 62/82. Hired (free) as A/C tender 1915–2.2.16.

ZITA Yt 283/94. Hired as accommodation ship 1941. Mooring hulk 1944–7.46.

ZOARCES Canadian coastguard vessel. On examination service (RCN) 3.1940–46.

ZODIAC Dr 80/07, 1–3pdr. Hired 1915–18.

ZODIAC II Tr 149/90. Hired 1918–19.

ZONIA Tr 150/98, 1–6pdr. Hired as M/S 1914–19.

ZOODOCHOS PIGHI Store carrier, 170gr. Commissioned 5.1941. Sunk 13.3.42 by enemy action, eastern Mediterranean.

ZORAIDE Yt 549/94, 1–12pdr, 1–6pdr. Hired as A/P Yt 12.9.1914–1.3.19.

ZULU Ferry 51/79. Hired on harbour service 8.1916–3.18.

ZWARTE ZEE Tr 194/99. Dutch, hired as M/S (Dutch crew) 7.1940. Renamed YMUIDEN 1941. RN crew 1.10.42–4.46.

ZWARTE ZEE Tug 793/33, 1–12pdr, 2–MG. Hired as rescue tug (Dutch crew) 1940–46.

ZYLPHA 2,917/94. Hired as decoy vessel (Q.6) 19.9.1915. Sunk 15.6.17 by U-boat southwest of Ireland.

ZZ.1–30 Motor M/S in service from 1944. ZZ.3,6 and 14 transferred Dutch navy 1946; ZZ.12 capsized 5.5.46 in the Forth area. All others for disposal 7.46 at Trieste or Port Said.